The Dialogues of
Plato

Volume Two

Translated by Benjamin Jowett

Copyright © 2014
**Good Time
Classic Book Collection**
All rights reserved.
ISBN-13: 978-1500713126
ISBN-10: 1500713120

Contents

Euthydemus 4

Cratylus 62

Phaedrus 184

Symposium 251

Theætetus 328

Parmenides....................... 524

EUTHYDEMUS

by Plato

Translated by Benjamin Jowett

INTRODUCTION

THE *EUTHYDEMUS*, THOUGH APT to be regarded by us only as an elaborate jest, has also a very serious purpose. It may fairly claim to be the oldest treatise on logic; for that science originates in the misunderstandings which necessarily accompany the first efforts of speculation. Several of the fallacies which are satirized in it reappear in the Sophistici Elenchi of Aristotle and are retained at the end of our manuals of logic. But if the order of history were followed, they should be placed not at the end but at the beginning of them; for they belong to the age in which the human mind was first making the attempt to distinguish thought from sense, and to separate the universal from the particular or individual. How to put together words or ideas, how to escape ambiguities in the meaning of terms or in the structure of propositions, how to resist the fixed impression of an 'eternal being' or 'perpetual flux,' how to distinguish between words and things—these were problems not easy of solution in the infancy of philosophy. They presented the same kind of difficulty to the half-educated man which spelling or arithmetic do to the mind of a child. It was long before the new world of ideas which had been sought after with such passionate yearning was set in order and made ready for use. To us the fallacies which arise in the pre-Socratic philosophy are trivial and obsolete because we are no longer liable to fall into the errors which are expressed by them. The intellectual world has become better assured to us, and we are less likely to be imposed upon by illusions of words.

The logic of Aristotle is for the most part latent in the dialogues of Plato. The nature of definition is explained not by rules but by examples in the Charmides, Lysis, Laches, Protagoras, Meno, Euthyphro, Theaetetus, Gorgias, Republic; the nature of division is likewise illustrated by examples in the Sophist and Statesman; a scheme of categories is found in the Philebus; the true doctrine of contradiction is taught, and the fallacy of arguing in a circle is exposed in the Republic; the nature of synthesis and analysis is graphically described in the Phaedrus; the nature of words is analysed in the Cratylus; the form of the syllogism is indicated in the genealogical trees of the Sophist and Statesman; a true doctrine of predication and an analysis of the sentence are given in the Sophist; the different meanings of one and being are worked out in the Parmenides. Here we have most of the important elements of logic, not yet systematized or reduced to an art or science, but scattered up and down as they would naturally occur in ordinary discourse. They are of little or no use or significance to us; but because we have grown out of the need of them we should not therefore despise them. They are still interesting and instructive for the light which they shed on the history of the human mind.

There are indeed many old fallacies which linger among us, and new ones are constantly springing up. But they are not of the kind to which ancient logic can be usefully applied. The weapons of common sense, not the analytics of Aristotle, are needed for their overthrow. Nor is the use of the Aristotelian logic any longer natural to us. We no longer put arguments into the form of syllogisms like the schoolmen; the simple use of language has been, happily, restored to us. Neither do we discuss the nature of the proposition, nor extract hidden truths from the copula, nor dispute any longer about nominalism and realism. We do not confuse the form with the matter of knowledge, or invent laws of thought, or imagine that any single science furnishes a principle of reasoning to all the rest. Neither do we require categories or heads of argument to be invented for our use. Those who have no knowledge of logic, like some of our great physical philosophers, seem to be quite as good reasoners as those who have. Most of the ancient puzzles have been settled on the basis of usage and common sense; there is no need to reopen them. No science should raise problems or invent forms of thought which add nothing to knowledge and are of no use in assisting the acquisition of it. This seems to be the natural limit of logic and metaphysics; if they give us a more comprehensive or a more definite view of the different spheres of knowledge they are to be studied; if not, not. The better part of ancient logic appears hardly in our own day to have a separate existence; it is absorbed in two other sciences: (1) rhetoric, if indeed this ancient art be not also fading away into literary criticism; (2) the science of language, under which all questions relating to words and propositions and the combinations of them may properly be included.

To continue dead or imaginary sciences, which make no signs of progress and have no definite sphere, tends to interfere with the prosecution of living ones. The study of them is apt to blind the judgment and to render men incapable of seeing the value of evidence, and even of appreciating the nature of truth. Nor should we allow the living science to become confused with the dead by an ambiguity of language. The term logic has two different meanings, an ancient and a modern one, and we vainly try to bridge the gulf between them. Many perplexities are avoided by keeping them apart. There might certainly be a new science of logic; it would not however be built up out of the fragments of the old, but would be distinct from them—relative to the state of knowledge which exists at the present time, and based chiefly on the methods of Modern Inductive philosophy. Such a science might have two legitimate fields: first, the refutation and explanation of false philosophies still hovering in the air as they appear from the point of view of later experience or are comprehended in the history of the human mind, as in a larger horizon: secondly, it might furnish new forms of thought more adequate to the expression of all the diversities and oppositions of knowledge which have grown up in these latter days; it might also suggest new methods of enquiry derived from the comparison of the sciences. Few will deny that the introduction of the words 'subject' and 'object' and the Hegelian reconciliation of opposites have been 'most gracious aids' to psychology, or that the methods of Bacon and Mill have shed a light far and wide on the realms of knowledge. These two great studies, the one destructive and corrective of error, the other conservative and constructive of truth, might be a first and second part of logic. Ancient logic would be the propaedeutic or gate of approach to logical science,—nothing more. But to pursue such speculations further, though not irrelevant, might lead us too far away from the argument of the dialogue.

The Euthydemus is, of all the Dialogues of Plato, that in which he approaches most nearly to the comic poet. The mirth is broader, the irony more sustained, the contrast between Socrates and the two Sophists, although veiled, penetrates deeper than in any other of his writings. Even Thrasymachus, in the Republic, is at last pacified, and becomes a friendly and interested auditor of the great discourse. But in the Euthydemus the mask is never dropped; the accustomed irony of Socrates continues to the end...

Socrates narrates to Crito a remarkable scene in which he has himself taken part, and in which the two brothers, Dionysodorus and Euthydemus, are the chief performers. They are natives of Chios, who had settled at Thurii, but were driven out, and in former days had been known at Athens as professors of rhetoric and of the art of fighting in armour. To this they have now added a new accomplishment—the art of Eristic, or fighting with words, which they are likewise willing to teach 'for a consideration.' But
they can also teach virtue in a very short time and in the very best manner. Socrates, who is always on the look-out for teachers of virtue, is interested in the youth Cleinias, the grandson of the great Alcibiades, andis desirous that he should have the benefit of their instructions. He is ready to fall down and worship them; although the greatness of their professions does arouse in his mind a temporary incredulity.

A circle gathers round them, in the midst of which are Socrates, the two brothers, the youth Cleinias, who is watched by the eager eyes of his lover Ctesippus, and others. The performance begins; and such a performance as might well seem to require an invocation of Memory and the Muses. It is agreed that the brothers shall question Cleinias. 'Cleinias,' says Euthydemus, 'who learn, the wise or the unwise?' 'The wise,' is the reply; given with blushing and hesitation. 'And yet when you learned you did not know and were not wise.' Then Dionysodorus takes up the ball: 'Who are they who learn dictation of the grammar-master; the wise or the foolish boys?' 'The wise.' 'Then, after all, the wise learn.' 'And do they learn,' said Euthydemus, 'what they know or what they do not know?' 'The latter.' 'And dictation is a dictation of letters?' 'Yes.' 'And you know letters?' 'Yes.' 'Then you learn what you know.' 'But,' retorts Dionysodorus, 'is not learning acquiring knowledge?' 'Yes.' 'And you acquire that which you have not got already?' 'Yes.' 'Then you learn that which you do not know.'

Socrates is afraid that the youth Cleinias may be discouraged at these repeated overthrows. He therefore explains to him the nature of the process to which he is being subjected. The two strangers are not serious; there are jests at the mysteries which precede the enthronement, and he is being initiated into the mysteries of the sophistical ritual. This is all a sort of horse-play, which is now ended. The exhortation to virtue will follow, and Socrates himself (if the wise men will not laugh at him) is desirous of showing the way in which such an exhortation should be carried on, according to his own poor notion. He proceeds to question Cleinias. The result of the investigation may be summed up as follows:—

All men desire good; and good means the possession of goods, such as wealth, health, beauty, birth, power, honour; not forgetting the virtues and wisdom. And yet in this enumeration the greatest good of all is omitted. What is that? Good fortune. But what need is there of good fortune when we have wisdom already:—in every art and business are not the wise also the fortunate? This is admitted. And again, the possession of goods is not enough; there must also be a right use of them which can only be given by knowledge: in themselves they are neither good nor evil—knowledge and wisdom are the only good, and ignorance and folly the only evil. The conclusion is that we must get 'wisdom.' But can wisdom be taught? 'Yes,' says Cleinias. The ingenuousness of the youth delights Socrates, who is at once relieved from the necessity of discussing one of his great puzzles. 'Since wisdom is the only good, he must become a philosopher, or lover of wisdom.' 'That I will,' says Cleinias.

After Socrates has given this specimen of his own mode of instruction, the two brothers recommence their exhortation to virtue, which is of quite another sort.

'You want Cleinias to be wise?' 'Yes.' 'And he is not wise yet?' 'No.' 'Then you want him to be what he is not, and not to be what he is?—not to be—that is, to perish. Pretty lovers and friends you must all be!'

Here Ctesippus, the lover of Cleinias, interposes in great excitement, thinking that he will teach the two Sophists a lesson of good manners. But he is quickly entangled in the meshes of their sophistry; and as a storm seems to be gathering Socrates pacifies him with a joke, and Ctesippus then
says that he is not reviling the two Sophists, he is only contradicting them. 'But,' says Dionysodorus, 'there is no such thing as contradiction. When you and I describe the same thing, or you describe one thing and I describe another, how can there be a contradiction?' Ctesippus is unable to reply.

Socrates has already heard of the denial of contradiction, and would like to be informed by the great master of the art, 'What is the meaning of this paradox? Is there no such thing as error, ignorance, falsehood? Then what are they professing to teach?' The two Sophists complain that Socrates is ready to answer what they said a year ago, but is 'non-plussed' at what they are saying now. 'What does the word "non-plussed" mean?' Socrates is informed, in reply, that words are lifeless things, and lifeless things have no sense or meaning. Ctesippus again breaks out, and again has to be pacified by Socrates, who renews the conversation with Cleinias. The two Sophists are like Proteus in the variety of their transformations, and he, like Menelaus in the Odyssey, hopes to restore them to their natural form.

He had arrived at the conclusion that Cleinias must become a philosopher. And philosophy is the possession of knowledge; and knowledge must be of a kind which is profitable and may be used. What knowledge is there which has such a nature? Not the knowledge which is required in any particular art; nor again the art of the composer of speeches, who knows how to write them, but cannot speak them, although he too must be admitted to be a kind of enchanter of wild animals. Neither is the knowledge which we are seeking the knowledge of the general. For the general makes over his prey to the statesman, as the huntsman does to the cook, or the

Euthydemus

taker of quails to the keeper of quails; he has not the use of that which he acquires. The two enquirers, Cleinias and Socrates, are described as wandering about in a wilderness, vainly searching after the art of life and happiness. At last they fix upon the kingly art, as having the desired sort of knowledge. But the kingly art only gives men those goods which are neither good nor evil: and if we say further that it makes us wise, in what does it make us wise? Not in special arts, such as cobbling or carpentering, but only in itself: or say again that it makes us good, there is no answer to the question, 'good in what?' At length in despair Cleinias and Socrates turn to the 'Dioscuri' and request their aid.

Euthydemus argues that Socrates knows something; and as he cannot know and not know, he cannot know some things and not know others, and therefore he knows all things: he and Dionysodorus and all other men know all things. 'Do they know shoemaking, etc?' 'Yes.' The sceptical Ctesippus would like to have some evidence of this extraordinary statement: he will believe if Euthydemus will tell him how many teeth Dionysodorus has, and if Dionysodorus will give him a like piece of information about Euthydemus. Even Socrates is incredulous, and indulges in a little raillery at the expense of the brothers. But he restrains himself, remembering that if the men who are to be his teachers think him stupid they will take no pains with him. Another fallacy is produced which turns on the absoluteness of the verb 'to know.' And here Dionysodorus is caught 'napping,' and is induced by Socrates to confess that 'he does not know the good to be unjust.' Socrates appeals to his brother Euthydemus; at the same time he acknowledges that he cannot, like Heracles, fight against a Hydra, and even Heracles, on the approach of a second monster, called upon his nephew Iolaus to help. Dionysodorus rejoins that Iolaus was no more the nephew of Heracles than of Socrates. For a nephew is a nephew, and a brother is a brother, and a father is a father, not of one man only, but of all; nor of men only, but of dogs and sea-monsters. Ctesippus makes merry with the consequences which follow: 'Much good has your father got out of the wisdom of his puppies.'

'But,' says Euthydemus, unabashed, 'nobody wants much good.' Medicine is a good, arms are a good, money is a good, and yet there may be too much of them in wrong places. 'No,' says Ctesippus, 'there cannot be too much gold.' And would you be happy if you had three talents of gold in your belly, a talent in your pate, and a stater in either eye?' Ctesippus, imitating the new wisdom, replies, 'And do not the Scythians reckon those to be the happiest of men who have their skulls gilded and see the inside of them?' 'Do you see,' retorts Euthydemus, 'what has the quality of vision or what has not the quality of vision?' 'What has the quality of vision.' 'And you see our garments?' 'Yes.' 'Then our garments have the quality of vision.' A similar play of words follows, which is successfully retorted by Ctesippus, to the great delight of Cleinias, who is rebuked by Socrates for laughing at such solemn and beautiful things.

'But are there any beautiful things? And if there are such, are they the same or not the same as absolute beauty?' Socrates replies that they are not the same, but each of them has some beauty present with it. 'And are you an ox because you have an ox present with you?' After a few more amphiboliae, in which Socrates, like Ctesippus, in self-defence borrows the weapons of the brothers, they both confess that the two heroes are invincible; and the scene concludes with a grand chorus of shouting and laughing, and a panegyrical oration from Socrates:—

First, he praises the indifference of Dionysodorus and Euthydemus to public opinion; for most persons would rather be refuted by such arguments than use them in the refutation of others. Secondly, he remarks upon their impartiality; for they stop their own mouths, as well as those of other people. Thirdly, he notes their liberality, which makes them give away their secret to all the world: they should be more reserved, and let no one be present at this exhibition who does not pay them a handsome fee; or better still they might practise on one another only. He concludes with a respectful request that they will receive him and Cleinias among their disciples.

Crito tells Socrates that he has heard one of the audience criticise severely this wisdom,—not sparing Socrates himself for countenancing such an exhibition. Socrates asks what manner of man was this censorious critic. 'Not an orator, but a great composer of speeches.' Socrates understands that he is an amphibious animal, half philosopher, half politician; one of a class who have the highest opinion of themselves and a spite against philosophers, whom they imagine to be their rivals. They are a class who are very likely to get mauled by Euthydemus and his friends, and have a great notion of their own wisdom; for they imagine themselves to have all the advantages and none of the drawbacks both of politics and of philosophy. They do not understand the principles of combination, and hence are ignorant that the union of two good things which have different ends produces a compound inferior to either of them taken separately.

Crito is anxious about the education of his children, one of whom is growing up. The description of Dionysodorus and Euthydemus suggests to him the reflection that the professors of education are strange beings. Socrates consoles him with the remark that the good in all professions are few, and recommends that 'he and his house' should continue to serve philosophy, and not mind about its professors.

* * *

THERE IS A STAGE in the history of philosophy in which the old is dying out, and the new has not yet come into full life. Great philosophies like the Eleatic or Heraclitean, which have enlarged the boundaries of the human mind, begin to pass away in words. They subsist only as forms which have rooted themselves in language—as troublesome elements of thought which cannot be either used or explained away. The same absoluteness which was once attributed to abstractions is now attached to the words which are the signs of them. The philosophy which in the first and second generation was a great and inspiring effort of reflection, in the third becomes sophistical, verbal, eristic.

It is this stage of philosophy which Plato satirises in the Euthydemus. The fallacies which are noted by him appear trifling to us now, but they were not trifling in the age before logic, in the decline of the earlier Greek philosophies, at a time when language was first beginning to perplex human thought. Besides he is caricaturing them; they probably received more subtle forms at the hands of those who seriously maintained them. They are patent to us in Plato, and we are inclined to wonder how any one could ever have been deceived by them; but we must remember also that there was a time when the human mind was only with great difficulty disentangled from such fallacies.

Plato

To appreciate fully the drift of the Euthydemus, we should imagine a mental state in which not individuals only, but whole schools during more than one generation, were animated by the desire to exclude the conception of rest, and therefore the very word 'this' (Theaet.) from language; in which the ideas of space, time, matter, motion, were proved to be contradictory and imaginary; in which the nature of qualitative change was a puzzle, and even differences of degree, when applied to abstract notions, were not understood; in which there was no analysis of grammar, and mere puns or plays of words received serious attention; in which contradiction itself was denied, and, on the one hand, every predicate was affirmed to be true of every subject, and on the other, it was held that no predicate was true of any subject, and that nothing was, or was known, or could be spoken. Let us imagine disputes carried on with religious earnestness and more than scholastic subtlety, in which the catchwords of philosophy are completely detached from their context. (Compare Theaet.) To such disputes the humour, whether of Plato in the ancient, or of Pope and Swift in the modern world, is the natural enemy. Nor must we forget that in modern times also there is no fallacy so gross, no trick of language so transparent, no abstraction so barren and unmeaning, no form of thought so contradictory to experience, which has not been found to satisfy the minds of philosophical enquirers at a certain stage, or when regarded from a certain point of view only. The peculiarity of the fallacies of our own age is that we live within them, and are therefore generally unconscious of them.

Aristotle has analysed several of the same fallacies in his book '*De Sophisticis Elenchis*,' which Plato, with equal command of their true nature, has preferred to bring to the test of ridicule. At first we are only struck with the broad humour of this 'reductio ad absurdum:' gradually we perceive that some important questions begin to emerge. Here, as everywhere else, Plato is making war against the philosophers who put words in the place of things, who tear arguments to tatters, who deny predication, and thus make knowledge impossible, to whom ideas and objects of sense have no fixedness, but are in a state of perpetual oscillation and transition. Two great truths seem to be indirectly taught through these fallacies: (1) The uncer-

Euthydemus

tainty of language, which allows the same words to be used in different meanings, or with different degrees of meaning: (2) The necessary limitation or relative nature of all phenomena. Plato is aware that his own doctrine of ideas, as well as the Eleatic Being and Notbeing, alike admit of being regarded as verbal fallacies. The sophism advanced in the Meno, 'that you cannot enquire either into what you know or do not know,' is lightly touched upon at the commencement of the Dialogue; the thesis of Protagoras, that everything is true to him to whom it seems to be true, is satirized. In contrast with these fallacies is maintained the Socratic doctrine that happiness is gained by knowledge. The grammatical puzzles with which the Dialogue concludes probably contain allusions to tricks of language which may have been practised by the disciples of Prodicus or Antisthenes. They would have had more point, if we were acquainted with the writings against which Plato's humour is directed. Most of the jests appear to have a serious meaning; but we have lost the clue to some of them, and cannot determine whether, as in the Cratylus, Plato has or has not mixed up purely unmeaning fun with his satire.

The two discourses of Socrates may be contrasted in several respects with the exhibition of the Sophists: (1) In their perfect relevancy to the subject of discussion, whereas the Sophistical discourses are wholly irrelevant: (2) In their enquiring sympathetic tone, which encourages the youth, instead of 'knocking him down,' after the manner of the two Sophists: (3) In the absence of any definite conclusion—for while Socrates and the youth are agreed that philosophy is to be studied, they are not able to arrive at any certain result about the art which is to teach it. This is a question which will hereafter be answered in the Republic; as the conception of the kingly art is more fully developed in the Politicus, and the caricature of rhetoric in the Gorgias.

The characters of the Dialogue are easily intelligible. There is Socrates once more in the character of an old man; and his equal in years, Crito, the father of Critobulus, like Lysimachus in the Laches, his fellow demesman (Apol.), to whom the scene is narrated, and who once or twice interrupts with a remark after the manner of the interlocutor in the Phaedo, and adds his commentary at the end;

Plato

Socrates makes a playful allusion to his money-getting habits. There is the youth Cleinias, the grandson of Alcibiades, who may be compared with Lysis, Charmides, Menexenus, and other ingenuous youths out of whose mouths Socrates draws his own lessons, and to whom he always seems to stand in a kindly and sympathetic relation. Crito will not believe that Socrates has not improved or perhaps invented the answers of Cleinias (compare Phaedrus). The name of the grandson of Alcibiades, who is described as long dead, (Greek), and who died at the age of forty-four, in the year 404 B.C., suggests not only that the intended scene of the Euthydemus could not have been earlier than 404, but that as a fact this Dialogue could not have been composed before 390 at the soonest. Ctesippus, who is the lover of Cleinias, has been already introduced to us in the Lysis, and seems there too to deserve the character which is here given him, of a somewhat uproarious young man. But the chief study of all is the picture of the two brothers, who are unapproachable in their effrontery, equally careless of what they say to others and of what is said to them, and never at a loss. They are '*Arcades ambo et cantare pares et respondere parati.*' Some superior degree of wit or subtlety is attributed to Euthydemus, who sees the trap in which Socrates catches Dionysodorus.

The epilogue or conclusion of the Dialogue has been criticised as inconsistent with the general scheme. Such a criticism is like similar criticisms on Shakespeare, and proceeds upon a narrow notion of the variety which the Dialogue, like the drama, seems to admit. Plato in the abundance of his dramatic power has chosen to write a play upon a play, just as he often gives us an argument within an argument. At the sa me time he takes the opportunity of assailing another class of persons who are as alien from the spirit of philosophy as Euthydemus and Dionysodorus. The Eclectic, the Syncretist, the Doctrinaire, have been apt to have a bad name both in ancient and modern times. The persons whom Plato ridicules in the epilogue to the Euthydemus are of this class. They occupy a borderground between philosophy and politics; they keep out of the dangers of politics, and at the same time use philosophy as a means of serving their own interests. Plato quaintly describes them as making two good things, philosophy and politics, a little worse by pervert-

15

Euthydemus

ing the objects of both. Men like Antiphon or Lysias would be types of the class. Out of a regard to the respectabilities of life, they are disposed to censure the interest which Socrates takes in the exhibition of the two brothers. They do not understand, any more than Crito, that he is pursuing his vocation of detecting the follies of mankind, which he finds 'not unpleasant.' (Compare Apol.)

Education is the common subject of all Plato's earlier Dialogues. The concluding remark of Crito, that he has a difficulty in educating his two sons, and the advice of Socrates to him that he should not give up philosophy because he has no faith in philosophers, seems to be a preparation for the more peremptory declaration of the Meno that 'Virtue cannot be taught because there are no teachers.'

The reasons for placing the Euthydemus early in the series are: (1) the similarity in plan and style to the Protagoras, Charmides, and Lysis;—the relation of Socrates to the Sophists is still that of humorous antagonism, not, as in the later Dialogues of Plato, of embittered hatred; and the places and persons have a considerable family likeness; (2) the Euthydemus belongs to the Socratic period in which Socrates is represented as willing to learn, but unable to teach; and in the spirit of Xenophon's Memorabilia, philosophy is defined as 'the knowledge which will make us happy;' (3) we seem to have passed the stage arrived at in the Protagoras, for Socrates is no longer discussing whether virtue can be taught—from this question he is relieved by the ingenuous declaration of the youth Cleinias; and (4) not yet to have reached the point at which he asserts 'that there are no teachers.' Such grounds are precarious, as arguments from style and plan are apt to be (Greek). But no arguments equally strong can be urged in favour of assigning to the Euthydemus any other position in the series.

EUTHYDEMUS

by

Plato

Translated by Benjamin Jowett

PERSONS OF THE DIALOGUE:
Socrates, who is the narrator of the Dialogue.
Crito, Cleinias, Euthydemus, Dionysodorus, Ctesippus.

SCENE: The Lyceum.

CRITO: Who was the person, Socrates, with whom you were talking yesterday at the Lyceum? There was such a crowd around you that I could not get within hearing, but I caught a sight of him over their heads, and I made out, as I thought, that he was a stranger with whom you were talking: who was he?

SOCRATES: There were two, Crito; which of them do you mean?

CRITO: The one whom I mean was seated second from you on the right-hand side. In the middle was Cleinias the young son of Axiochus, who has wonderfully grown; he is only about the age of my own Critobulus, but he is much forwarder and very good-looking: the other is thin and looks younger than he is.

SOCRATES: He whom you mean, Crito, is Euthydemus; and on my left hand there was his brother Dionysodorus, who also took part in the conversation.

CRITO: Neither of them are known to me, Socrates; they are a new importation of Sophists, as I should imagine. Of what country are

Euthydemus

they, and what is their line of wisdom?

SOCRATES: As to their origin, I believe that they are natives of this part of the world, and have migrated from Chios to Thurii; they were driven out of Thurii, and have been living for many years past in these regions. As to their wisdom, about which you ask, Crito, they are wonderful—consummate! I never knew what the true pancratiast was before; they are simply made up of fighting, not like the two Acarnanian brothers who fight with their bodies only, but this pair of heroes, besides being perfect in the use of their bodies, are invincible in every sort of warfare; for they are capital at fighting in armour, and will teach the art to any one who pays them; and also they are most skilful in legal warfare; they will plead themselves and teach others to speak and to compose speeches which will have an effect upon the courts. And this was only the beginning of their wisdom, but they have at last carried out the pancratiastic art to the very end, and have mastered the only mode of fighting which had been hitherto neglected by them; and now no one dares even to stand up against them: such is their skill in the war of words, that they can refute any proposition whether true or false. Now I am thinking, Crito, of placing myself in their hands; for they say that in a short time they can impart their skill to any one.

CRITO: But, Socrates, are you not too old? there may be reason to fear that.

SOCRATES: Certainly not, Crito; as I will prove to you, for I have the consolation of knowing that they began this art of disputation which I covet, quite, as I may say, in old age; last year, or the year before, they had none of their new wisdom. I am only apprehensive that I may bring the two strangers into disrepute, as I have done Connus the son of Metrobius, the harp-player, who is still my music-master; for when the boys who go to him see me going with them, they laugh at me and call him grandpapa's master. Now I should not like the strangers to experience similar treatment; the fear of ridicule may make them unwilling to receive me; and therefore, Crito, I shall try and persuade some old men to accompany me to them, as I persuaded them to go with me to Connus, and I hope that you will make one: and perhaps we had better take your sons as a bait; they will want to have them as pupils, and for the sake of them willing to receive us.

CRITO: I see no objection, Socrates, if you like; but first I wish that you would give me a description of their wisdom, that I may know beforehand what we are going to learn.

SOCRATES: In less than no time you shall hear; for I cannot say that I did not attend—I paid great attention to them, and I remember and will endeavour to repeat the whole story. Providentially I was sitting alone in the dressing-room of the Lyceum where you saw me, and was about to depart; when I was getting up I recognized the familiar divine sign: so I sat down again, and in a little while the two brothers Euthydemus and Dionysodorus came in, and several others with them, whom I believe to be their disciples, and they walked about in the covered court; they had not taken more than two or three turns when Cleinias entered, who, as you truly say, is very much improved: he was followed by a host of lovers, one of whom was Ctesippus the Paeanian, a well-bred youth, but also having the wildness of youth. Cleinias saw me from the entrance as I was sitting alone, and at once came and sat down on the right hand of me, as you describe; and Dionysodorus and Euthydemus, when they saw him, at first stopped and talked with one another, now and then glancing at us, for I particularly watched them; and then Euthydemus came and sat down by the youth, and the other by me on the left hand; the rest anywhere. I saluted the brothers, whom I had not seen for a long time; and then I said to Cleinias: Here are two wise men, Euthydemus and Dionysodorus, Cleinias, wise not in a small but in a large way of wisdom, for they know all about war,—all that a good general ought to know about the array and command of an army, and the whole art of fighting in armour: and they know about law too, and can teach a man how to use the weapons of the courts when he is injured.

They heard me say this, but only despised me. I observed that they looked at one another, and both of them laughed; and then

Euthydemus

Euthydemus said: Those, Socrates, are matters which we no longer pursue seriously; to us they are secondary occupations.

Indeed, I said, if such occupations are regarded by you as secondary, what must the principal one be; tell me, I beseech you, what that noble study is?

The teaching of virtue, Socrates, he replied, is our principal occupation; and we believe that we can impart it better and quicker than any man.

My God! I said, and where did you learn that? I always thought, as I was saying just now, that your chief accomplishment was the art of fighting in armour; and I used to say as much of you, for I remember that you professed this when you were here before. But now if you really have the other knowledge, O forgive me: I address you as I would superior beings, and ask you to pardon the impiety of my former expressions. But are you quite sure about this, Dionysodorus and Euthydemus? the promise is so vast, that a feeling of incredulity steals over me.

You may take our word, Socrates, for the fact.

Then I think you happier in having such a treasure than the great king is in the possession of his kingdom. And please to tell me whether you intend to exhibit your wisdom; or what will you do?

That is why we have come hither, Socrates; and our purpose is not only to exhibit, but also to teach any one who likes to learn.

But I can promise you, I said, that every unvirtuous person will want to learn. I shall be the first; and there is the youth Cleinias, and Ctesippus: and here are several others, I said, pointing to the lovers of Cleinias, who were beginning to gather round us. Now Ctesippus was sitting at some distance from Cleinias; and when Euthydemus leaned forward in talking with me, he was prevented from seeing Cleinias, who was between us; and so, partly because he wanted to look at his love, and also because he was interested, he jumped up and stood opposite to us: and all the other admirers of Cleinias, as well as the disciples of Euthydemus and Dionysodorus, followed his example. And these were the persons whom I showed to Euthydemus, telling him that they were all eager to learn: to which Ctesippus and all of them with one voice vehemently assented, and bid him exhibit the power of his wisdom. Then I said: O Euthydemus and Dionysodorus, I earnestly request you to do myself and the company the favour to exhibit. There may be some trouble in giving the whole exhibition; but tell me one thing,—can you make a good man of him only who is already convinced that he ought to learn of you, or of him also who is not convinced, either because he imagines that virtue is a thing which cannot be taught at all, or that you are not the teachers of it? Has your art power to persuade him, who is of the latter temper of mind, that virtue can be taught; and that you are the men from whom he will best learn it?

Certainly, Socrates, said Dionysodorus; our art will do both.

And you and your brother, Dionysodorus, I said, of all men who are now living are the most likely to stimulate him to philosophy and to the study of virtue?

Yes, Socrates, I rather think that we are.

Then I wish that you would be so good as to defer the other part of the exhibition, and only try to persuade the youth whom you see here that he ought to be a philosopher and study virtue. Exhibit that, and you will confer a great favour on me and on every one present; for the fact is I and all of us are extremely anxious that he should become truly good. His name is Cleinias, and he is the son of Axiochus, and grandson of the old Alcibiades, cousin of the Alcibiades that now is. He is quite young, and we are naturally afraid that some one may get the start of us, and turn his mind in a wrong direction, and he may be ruined. Your visit, therefore, is most happily timed; and I hope that you will make a trial of the young man, and converse with him in our presence, if you have no objection.

These were pretty nearly the expressions which I used; and Euthydemus, in a manly and at the same time encouraging tone, replied: There can be no objection, Socrates, if the young man is only willing to answer questions.

He is quite accustomed to do so, I replied; for his friends often come and ask him questions and argue with him; and therefore he is quite at home in answering.

What followed, Crito, how can I rightly narrate? For not slight is the task of rehearsing infinite wisdom, and therefore, like the poets, I ought to commence my relation with an invocation to Memory and the Muses. Now Euthydemus, if I remember rightly, began nearly as follows: O Cleinias, are those who learn the wise or the ignorant?

The youth, overpowered by the question blushed, and in his per-

Euthydemus

plexity looked at me for help; and I, knowing that he was disconcerted, said: Take courage, Cleinias, and answer like a man whichever you think; for my belief is that you will derive the greatest benefit from their questions.

Whichever he answers, said Dionysodorus, leaning forward so as to catch my ear, his face beaming with laughter, I prophesy that he will be refuted, Socrates.

While he was speaking to me, Cleinias gave his answer: and therefore I had no time to warn him of the predicament in which he was placed, and he answered that those who learned were the wise.

Euthydemus proceeded: There are some whom you would call teachers, are there not?

The boy assented.

And they are the teachers of those who learn—the grammar-master and the lyre-master used to teach you and other boys; and you were the learners?

Yes.

And when you were learners you did not as yet know the things which you were learning?

No, he said.

And were you wise then?

No, indeed, he said.

But if you were not wise you were unlearned?

Certainly.

You then, learning what you did not know, were unlearned when you were learning?

The youth nodded assent.

Then the unlearned learn, and not the wise, Cleinias, as you imagine.

At these words the followers of Euthydemus, of whom I spoke, like a chorus at the bidding of their director, laughed and cheered. Then, before the youth had time to recover his breath, Dionysodorus cleverly took him in hand, and said: Yes, Cleinias; and when the grammar-master dictated
anything to you, were they the wise boys or the unlearned who learned the dictation?

The wise, replied Cleinias.

Then after all the wise are the learners and not the unlearned; and your last answer to Euthydemus was wrong.

Then once more the admirers of the two heroes, in an ecstasy at their wisdom, gave vent to another peal of laughter, while the rest of us were silent and amazed. Euthydemus, observing this, determined to persevere with the youth; and in order to heighten the effect went on asking another similar question, which might be compared to the double turn of an expert dancer. Do those, said he, who learn, learn what they know, or what they do not know?

Again Dionysodorus whispered to me: That, Socrates, is just another of the same sort.

Good heavens, I said; and your last question was so good!

Like all our other questions, Socrates, he replied—inevitable.

I see the reason, I said, why you are in such reputation among your disciples.

Meanwhile Cleinias had answered Euthydemus that those who learned learn what they do not know; and he put him through a series of questions the same as before.

Do you not know letters?

He assented.

All letters?

Yes.

But when the teacher dictates to you, does he not dictate letters? To this also he assented.

Then if you know all letters, he dictates that which you know?

This again was admitted by him.

Then, said the other, you do not learn that which he dictates; but he only who does not know letters learns?

Nay, said Cleinias; but I do learn.

Then, said he, you learn what you know, if you know all the letters?

He admitted that.

Then, he said, you were wrong in your answer.

The word was hardly out of his mouth when Dionysodorus took up the argument, like a ball which he caught, and had another throw at the youth. Cleinias, he said, Euthydemus is deceiving you. For tell me now, is not learning acquiring knowledge of that which one learns?

Euthydemus

Cleinias assented.
And knowing is having knowledge at the time?
He agreed.
And not knowing is not having knowledge at the time?
He admitted that.
And are those who acquire those who have or have not a thing?
Those who have not.
And have you not admitted that those who do not know are of the number of those who have not?
He nodded assent.
Then those who learn are of the class of those who acquire, and not of those who have?
He agreed.
Then, Cleinias, he said, those who do not know learn, and not those who know.

Euthydemus was proceeding to give the youth a third fall; but I knew that he was in deep water, and therefore, as I wanted to give him a respite lest he should be disheartened, I said to him consolingly: You must not be surprised, Cleinias, at the singularity of their mode of speech: this I say because you may not understand what the two strangers are doing with you; they are only initiating you after the manner of the Corybantes in the mysteries; and this answers to the enthronement, which, if you have ever been initiated, is, as you will know, accompanied by dancing and sport; and now they are just prancing and dancing about you, and will next proceed to initiate you; imagine then that you have gone through the first part of the sophistical ritual, which, as Prodicus says, begins with initiation into the correct use of terms. The two foreign gentlemen, perceiving that you did not know, wanted to explain to you that the word 'to learn' has two meanings, and is used, first, in the sense of acquiring knowledge of some matter of which you previously have no knowledge, and also, when you have the knowledge, in the sense of reviewing this matter, whether something done or spoken by the light of this newly-acquired knowledge; the latter is generally called 'knowing' rather than 'learning,' but the word 'learning' is also used; and you did not see, as they explained to you, that the term is employed of two opposite sorts of men, of those who know, and of those who do not know. There was a similar trick in the second question, when they asked you whether men learn what they know or what they do not know. These parts of learning are not serious, and therefore I say that the gentlemen are not serious, but are only playing with you. For if a man had all that sort of knowledge that ever was, he would not be at all the wiser; he would only be able to play with men, tripping them up and oversetting them with distinctions of words. He would be like a person who pulls away a stool from some one when he is about to sit down, and then laughs and makes merry at the sight of his friend overturned and laid on his back. And you must regard all that has hitherto passed between you and them as merely play. But in what is to follow I am certain that they will exhibit to you their serious purpose, and keep their promise (I will show them how); for they promised to give me a sample of the hortatory philosophy, but I suppose that they wanted to have a game with you first. And now, Euthydemus and Dionysodorus, I think that we have had enough of this. Will you let me see you explaining to the young man how he is to apply himself to the study of virtue and wisdom? And I will first show you what I conceive to be the nature of the task, and what sort of a discourse I desire to hear; and if I do this in a very inartistic and ridiculous manner, do not laugh at me, for I only venture to improvise before you because I am eager to hear your wisdom: and I must therefore ask you and your disciples to refrain from laughing. And now, O son of Axiochus, let me put a question to you: Do not all men desire happiness? And yet, perhaps, this is one of those ridiculous questions which I am afraid to ask, and which ought not to be asked by a sensible man: for what human being is there who does not desire happiness?

There is no one, said Cleinias, who does not.

Well, then, I said, since we all of us desire happiness, how can we be happy?—that is the next question. Shall we not be happy if we have many good things? And this, perhaps, is even a more simple question than the first, for there can be no doubt of the answer.

He assented.

And what things do we esteem good? No solemn sage is required to tell us this, which may be easily answered; for every one will say that wealth is a good.

Certainly, he said.

And are not health and beauty goods, and other personal gifts?

He agreed.

Can there be any doubt that good birth, and power, and honours in one's own land, are goods?

He assented.

And what other goods are there? I said. What do you say of temperance, justice, courage: do you not verily and indeed think, Cleinias, that we shall be more right in ranking them as goods than in not ranking them as goods? For a dispute might possibly arise about this. What then do you say?

They are goods, said Cleinias.

Very well, I said; and where in the company shall we find a place for wisdom—among the goods or not?

Among the goods.

And now, I said, think whether we have left out any considerable goods.

I do not think that we have, said Cleinias.

Upon recollection, I said, indeed I am afraid that we have left out the greatest of them all.

What is that? he asked.

Fortune, Cleinias, I replied; which all, even the most foolish, admit to be the greatest of goods.

True, he said.

On second thoughts, I added, how narrowly, O son of Axiochus, have you and I escaped making a laughing-stock of ourselves to the strangers.

Why do you say so?

Why, because we have already spoken of good-fortune, and are but repeating ourselves.

What do you mean?

I mean that there is something ridiculous in again putting forward good-fortune, which has a place in the list already, and saying the same thing twice over.

He asked what was the meaning of this, and I replied: Surely wisdom is good-fortune; even a child may know that.

The simple-minded youth was amazed; and, observing his surprise, I said to him: Do you not know, Cleinias, that flute-players are most fortunate and successful in performing on the flute?

He assented.

And are not the scribes most fortunate in writing and reading letters?

Certainly.

Amid the dangers of the sea, again, are any more fortunate on the whole than wise pilots?

None, certainly.

And if you were engaged in war, in whose company would you rather take the risk—in company with a wise general, or with a foolish one?

With a wise one.

And if you were ill, whom would you rather have as a companion in a dangerous illness—a wise physician, or an ignorant one?

A wise one.

You think, I said, that to act with a wise man is more fortunate than to act with an ignorant one?

He assented.

Then wisdom always makes men fortunate: for by wisdom no man would ever err, and therefore he must act rightly and succeed, or his wisdom would be wisdom no longer.

We contrived at last, somehow or other, to agree in a general conclusion, that he who had wisdom had no need of fortune. I then recalled to his mind the previous state of the question. You remember, I said, our making the admission that we should be happy and fortunate if many good things were present with us?

He assented.

And should we be happy by reason of the presence of good things, if they profited us not, or if they profited us?

If they profited us, he said.

And would they profit us, if we only had them and did not use them? For example, if we had a great deal of food and did not eat, or a great deal of drink and did not drink, should we be profited?

Certainly not, he said.

Or would an artisan, who had all the implements necessary for his work, and did not use them, be any the better for the possession of them? For example, would a carpenter be any the better for having all his tools and plenty of wood, if he never worked?

Certainly not, he said.

And if a person had wealth and all the goods of which we were just now speaking, and did not use them, would he be happy because he possessed them?

No indeed, Socrates.

Then, I said, a man who would be happy must not only have the good things, but he must also use them; there is no advantage in merely having them?

True.

Well, Cleinias, but if you have the use as well as the possession of good things, is that sufficient to confer happiness?

Yes, in my opinion.

And may a person use them either rightly or wrongly?

He must use them rightly.

That is quite true, I said. And the wrong use of a thing is far worse than the non-use; for the one is an evil, and the other is neither a good nor an evil. You admit that?

He assented.

Now in the working and use of wood, is not that which gives the right use simply the knowledge of the carpenter?

Nothing else, he said.

And surely, in the manufacture of vessels, knowledge is that which gives the right way of making them?

He agreed.

And in the use of the goods of which we spoke at first—wealth and health and beauty, is not knowledge that which directs us to the right use of them, and regulates our practice about them?

He assented.

Then in every possession and every use of a thing, knowledge is that which gives a man not only good-fortune but success?

He again assented.

And tell me, I said, O tell me, what do possessions profit a man, if he have neither good sense nor wisdom? Would a man be better off, having and doing many things without wisdom, or a few things with wisdom? Look at the matter thus: If he did fewer things would he not make fewer mistakes? if he made fewer mistakes would he not have fewer misfortunes? and if he had fewer misfortunes would he not be less miserable?

Certainly, he said.

And who would do least—a poor man or a rich man?

A poor man.

A weak man or a strong man?

A weak man.

A noble man or a mean man?

A mean man.

And a coward would do less than a courageous and temperate man?

Yes.

And an indolent man less than an active man?

He assented.

And a slow man less than a quick; and one who had dull perceptions of seeing and hearing less than one who had keen ones?

All this was mutually allowed by us.

Then, I said, Cleinias, the sum of the matter appears to be that the goods of which we spoke before are not to be regarded as goods in themselves, but the degree of good and evil in them depends on whether they are or are not under the guidance of knowledge: under the guidance of ignorance, they are greater evils than their opposites, inasmuch as they are more able to minister to the evil principle which rules them; and when under the guidance of wisdom and prudence, they are greater goods: but in themselves they are nothing?

That, he replied, is obvious.

What then is the result of what has been said? Is not this the result—that other things are indifferent, and that wisdom is the only good, and ignorance the only evil?

He assented.

Let us consider a further point, I said: Seeing that all men desire happiness, and happiness, as has been shown, is gained by a use, and a right use, of the things of life, and the right use of them, and good-fortune in the use of them, is given by knowledge,—the inference is that everybody ought by all means to try and make himself as wise as he can?

Yes, he said.

And when a man thinks that he ought to obtain this treasure, far more than money, from a father or a guardian or a friend or a suitor, whether citizen or stranger—the eager desire and prayer to them that they would impart wisdom to you, is not at all dishonourable, Cleinias; nor is any one to be blamed for doing any honourable service or ministration to any man, whether a lover or not, if his aim is to get wisdom. Do you agree? I said.

Yes, he said, I quite agree, and think that you are right.

Yes, I said, Cleinias, if only wisdom can be taught, and does not come to man spontaneously; for this is a point which has still to be considered, and is not yet agreed upon by you and me—

But I think, Socrates, that wisdom can be taught, he said.

Best of men, I said, I am delighted to hear you say so; and I am also grateful to you for having saved me from a long and tiresome investigation as to whether wisdom can be taught or not. But now, as you think that wisdom can be taught, and that wisdom only can make a man happy and fortunate, will you not acknowledge that all of us ought to love wisdom, and you individually will try to love her?

Certainly, Socrates, he said; I will do my best.

I was pleased at hearing this; and I turned to Dionysodorus and Euthydemus and said: That is an example, clumsy and tedious I admit, of the sort of exhortations which I would have you give; and I hope that one of you will set forth what I have been saying in a more artistic style: or at least take up the enquiry where I left off, and proceed to show the youth whether he should have all knowledge; or whether there is one sort of knowledge only which will make him good and happy, and what that is. For, as I was saying at first, the improvement of this young man in virtue and wisdom is a matter which we have very much at heart.

Thus I spoke, Crito, and was all attention to what was coming. I wanted to see how they would approach the question, and where they would start in their exhortation to the young man that he should practise wisdom and virtue. Dionysodorus, who was the elder, spoke first. Everybody's eyes were directed towards him, perceiving that something wonderful might shortly be expected. And certainly they were not far wrong; for the man, Crito, began a remarkable discourse well worth hearing, and wonderfully persuasive regarded as an exhortation to virtue.

Tell me, he said, Socrates and the rest of you who say that you want this young man to become wise, are you in jest or in real earnest?

I was led by this to imagine that they fancied us to have been jesting when we asked them to converse with the youth, and that this made them jest and play, and being under this impression, I was the more decided in saying that we were in profound earnest. Dionysodorus said:

Reflect, Socrates; you may have to deny your words.

I have reflected, I said; and I shall never deny my words.

Well, said he, and so you say that you wish Cleinias to become wise?

Undoubtedly.

And he is not wise as yet?

At least his modesty will not allow him to say that he is.

You wish him, he said, to become wise and not, to be ignorant?

That we do.

You wish him to be what he is not, and no longer to be what he is?

I was thrown into consternation at this.

Taking advantage of my consternation he added: You wish him no longer to be what he is, which can only mean that you wish him to perish. Pretty lovers and friends they must be who want their favourite not to be, or to perish!

When Ctesippus heard this he got very angry (as a lover well might) and said: Stranger of Thurii—if politeness would allow me I should say, A plague upon you! What can make you tell such a lie about me and the others, which I hardly like to repeat, as that I wish Cleinias to perish?

Euthydemus replied: And do you think, Ctesippus, that it is possible to tell a lie?

Yes, said Ctesippus; I should be mad to say anything else.

And in telling a lie, do you tell the thing of which you speak or not?

You tell the thing of which you speak.

And he who tells, tells that thing which he tells, and no other?
Yes, said Ctesippus.
And that is a distinct thing apart from other things?
Certainly.
And he who says that thing says that which is?
Yes.
And he who says that which is, says the truth. And therefore Dionysodorus, if he says that which is, says the truth of you and no lie.
Yes, Euthydemus, said Ctesippus; but in saying this, he says what is not.
Euthydemus answered: And that which is not is not?
True.
And that which is not is nowhere?
Nowhere.
And can any one do anything about that which has no existence, or do to Cleinias that which is not and is nowhere?
I think not, said Ctesippus.
Well, but do rhetoricians, when they speak in the assembly, do nothing?
Nay, he said, they do something.
And doing is making?
Yes.
And speaking is doing and making?
He agreed.
Then no one says that which is not, for in saying what is not he would be doing something; and you have already acknowledged that no one can do what is not. And therefore, upon your own showing, no one says what is false; but if Dionysodorus says anything, he says what is true and what is.
Yes, Euthydemus, said Ctesippus; but he speaks of things in a certain way and manner, and not as they really are.
Why, Ctesippus, said Dionysodorus, do you mean to say that any one speaks of things as they are?
Yes, he said—all gentlemen and truth-speaking persons.
And are not good things good, and evil things evil?
He assented.

Plato

And you say that gentlemen speak of things as they are?

Yes.

Then the good speak evil of evil things, if they speak of them as they are?

Yes, indeed, he said; and they speak evil of evil men. And if I may give you a piece of advice, you had better take care that they do not speak evil of you, since I can tell you that the good speak evil of the evil.

And do they speak great things of the great, rejoined Euthydemus, and warm things of the warm?

To be sure they do, said Ctesippus; and they speak coldly of the insipid and cold dialectician.

You are abusive, Ctesippus, said Dionysodorus, you are abusive!

Indeed, I am not, Dionysodorus, he replied; for I love you and am giving you friendly advice, and, if I could, would persuade you not like a boor to say in my presence that I desire my beloved, whom I value above all men, to perish.

I saw that they were getting exasperated with one another, so I made a joke with him and said: O Ctesippus, I think that we must allow the strangers to use language in their own way, and not quarrel with them about words, but be thankful for what they give us. If they know how to destroy men in such a way as to make good and sensible men out of bad and foolish ones—whether this is a discovery of their own, or whether they have learned from some one else this new sort of death and destruction which enables them to get rid of a bad man and turn him into a good one—if they know this (and they do know this—at any rate they said just now that this was the secret of their newly-discovered art)—let them, in their phraseology, destroy the youth and make him wise, and all of us with him. But if you young men do not like to trust yourselves with them, then fiat experimentum in corpore senis; I will be the Carian on whom they shall operate. And here I offer my old person to Dionysodorus; he may put me into the pot, like Medea the Colchian, kill me, boil me, if he will only make me good.

Ctesippus said: And I, Socrates, am ready to commit myself to the strangers; they may skin me alive, if they please (and I am pretty well skinned by them already), if only my skin is made at last, not like that of Marsyas, into a leathern bottle, but into a piece of virtue. And here is Dionysodorus fancying that I am angry with him, when really I am not angry at all; I do but contradict him when I think that he is speaking improperly to me: and you must not confound abuse and contradiction, O illustrious Dionysodorus; for they are quite different things.

Contradiction! said Dionysodorus; why, there never was such a thing.

Certainly there is, he replied; there can be no question of that. Do you, Dionysodorus, maintain that there is not?

You will never prove to me, he said, that you have heard any one contradicting any one else.

Indeed, said Ctesippus; then now you may hear me contradicting Dionysodorus.

Are you prepared to make that good?

Certainly, he said.

Well, have not all things words expressive of them?

Yes.

Of their existence or of their non-existence?

Of their existence.

Yes, Ctesippus, and we just now proved, as you may remember, that no man could affirm a negative; for no one could affirm that which is not.

And what does that signify? said Ctesippus; you and I may contradict all the same for that.

But can we contradict one another, said Dionysodorus, when both of us are describing the same thing? Then we must surely be speaking the same thing?

He assented.

Or when neither of us is speaking of the same thing? For then neither of us says a word about the thing at all?

He granted that proposition also.

But when I describe something and you describe another thing, or I say something and you say nothing—is there any contradiction? How can he who speaks contradict him who speaks not?

Here Ctesippus was silent; and I in my astonishment said: What do you mean, Dionysodorus? I have often heard, and have been amazed to hear, this thesis of yours, which is maintained and employed by the disciples of Protagoras, and others before them, and which to me appears to be quite wonderful, and suicidal as well as destructive, and I think that I am most likely to hear the truth about it from you. The dictum is that there is no such thing as falsehood; a man must either say what is true or say nothing. Is not that your position?

He assented.

But if he cannot speak falsely, may he not think falsely?

No, he cannot, he said.

Then there is no such thing as false opinion?

No, he said.

Then there is no such thing as ignorance, or men who are ignorant; for is not ignorance, if there be such a thing, a mistake of fact?

Certainly, he said.

And that is impossible?

Impossible, he replied.

Are you saying this as a paradox, Dionysodorus; or do you seriously maintain no man to be ignorant?

Refute me, he said.

But how can I refute you, if, as you say, to tell a falsehood is impossible?

Very true, said Euthydemus.

Neither did I tell you just now to refute me, said Dionysodorus; for howb can I tell you to do that which is not?

O Euthydemus, I said, I have but a dull conception of these subtleties and excellent devices of wisdom; I am afraid that I hardly understand them, and you must forgive me therefore if I ask a very stupid question: if there be no falsehood or false opinion or ignorance, there can be no such thing as erroneous action, for a man cannot fail of acting as he is acting—that is what you mean?

Yes, he replied.

And now, I said, I will ask my stupid question: If there is no such thing as error in deed, word, or thought, then what, in the name of goodness, do you come hither to teach? And were you not just now saying that you could teach virtue best of all men, to any one who was willing to learn?

Euthydemus

And are you such an old fool, Socrates, rejoined Dionysodorus, that you bring up now what I said at first—and if I had said anything last year, I suppose that you would bring that up too—but are non-plussed at the words which I have just uttered?

Why, I said, they are not easy to answer; for they are the words of wise men: and indeed I know not what to make of this word 'non-plussed,' which you used last: what do you mean by it, Dionysodorus? You must mean that I cannot refute your argument. Tell me if the words have any other sense.

No, he replied, they mean what you say. And now answer.

What, before you, Dionysodorus? I said.

Answer, said he.

And is that fair?

Yes, quite fair, he said.

Upon what principle? I said. I can only suppose that you are a very wise man who comes to us in the character of a great logician, and who knows when to answer and when not to answer—and now you will not open your mouth at all, because you know that you ought not.

You prate, he said, instead of answering. But if, my good sir, you admit that I am wise, answer as I tell you.

I suppose that I must obey, for you are master. Put the question.

Are the things which have sense alive or lifeless?

They are alive.

And do you know of any word which is alive?

I cannot say that I do.

Then why did you ask me what sense my words had?

Why, because I was stupid and made a mistake. And yet, perhaps, I was right after all in saying that words have a sense;—what do you say, wise man? If I was not in error, even you will not refute me, and all your wisdom will be non-plussed; but if I did fall into error, then again you are wrong in saying that there is no error,—and this remark was made by you not quite a year ago. I am inclined to think, however, Dionysodorus and Euthydemus, that this argument lies where it was and is not very likely to advance: even your skill in the subtleties of logic, which is really amazing, has not found out the way of throwing another and not falling yourself, now any more than of old.

Ctesippus said: Men of Chios, Thurii, or however and whatever you call yourselves, I wonder at you, for you seem to have no objection to talking nonsense.

Fearing that there would be high words, I again endeavoured to soothe Ctesippus, and said to him: To you, Ctesippus, I must repeat what I said before to Cleinias—that you do not understand the ways of these philosophers from abroad. They are not serious, but, like the Egyptian wizard, Proteus, they take different forms and deceive us by their enchantments: and let us, like Menelaus, refuse to let them go until they show themselves to us in earnest. When they begin to be in earnest their full beauty will appear: let us then beg and entreat and beseech them to shine forth. And I think that I had better once more exhibit the form in which I pray to behold them; it might be a guide to them. I will go on therefore where I left off, as well as I can, in the hope that I may touch their hearts and move them to pity, and that when they see me deeply serious and interested, they also may be serious. You, Cleinias, I said, shall remind me at what point we left off. Did we not agree that philosophy should be studied? and was not that our conclusion?

Yes, he replied.

And philosophy is the acquisition of knowledge?

Yes, he said.

And what knowledge ought we to acquire? May we not answer with absolute truth—A knowledge which will do us good?

Certainly, he said.

And should we be any the better if we went about having a knowledge of the places where most gold was hidden in the earth?

Perhaps we should, he said.

But have we not already proved, I said, that we should be none the better off, even if without trouble and digging all the gold which there is in the earth were ours? And if we knew how to convert stones into gold, the knowledge would be of no value to us, unless we also knew how to use the gold? Do you not remember? I said.

I quite remember, he said.

Nor would any other knowledge, whether of money-making, or of medicine, or of any other art which knows only how to make a thing, and not to use it when made, be of any good to us. Am I not right?

He agreed.

And if there were a knowledge which was able to make men immortal, without giving them the knowledge of the way to use the immortality, neither would there be any use in that, if we may argue from the analogy of the previous instances?

To all this he agreed.

Then, my dear boy, I said, the knowledge which we want is one that uses as well as makes?

True, he said.

And our desire is not to be skilful lyre-makers, or artists of that sort—far otherwise; for with them the art which makes is one, and the art which uses is another. Although they have to do with the same, they are divided: for the art which makes and the art which plays on the lyre differ widely from one another. Am I not right?

He agreed.

And clearly we do not want the art of the flute-maker; this is only another of the same sort?

He assented.

But suppose, I said, that we were to learn the art of making speeches—would that be the art which would make us happy?

I should say, no, rejoined Cleinias.

And why should you say so? I asked.

I see, he replied, that there are some composers of speeches who do not know how to use the speeches which they make, just as the makers of lyres do not know how to use the lyres; and also some who are of themselves unable to compose speeches, but are able to use the speeches which the others make for them; and this proves that the art of making speeches is not the same as the art of using them.

Yes, I said; and I take your words to be a sufficient proof that the art of making speeches is not one which will make a man happy. And yet I did think that the art which we have so long been seeking might be discovered in that direction; for the composers of speeches, whenever I meet them, always appear to me to be very extraordinary men, Cleinias, and their art is lofty and divine, and no wonder. For their art is a part of the great art of enchantment, and hardly, if at all, inferior to it: and whereas the art of the enchanter is a mode of charming snakes and spiders and scorpions, and other monsters and pests, this art of their's acts upon dicasts and ecclesiasts and bodies of men, for the charming and pacifying of them. Do you agree with me?

Yes, he said, I think that you are quite right.

Whither then shall we go, I said, and to what art shall we have recourse?

I do not see my way, he said.

But I think that I do, I replied.

And what is your notion? asked Cleinias.

I think that the art of the general is above all others the one of which the possession is most likely to make a man happy.

I do not think so, he said.

Why not? I said.

The art of the general is surely an art of hunting mankind.

What of that? I said.

Why, he said, no art of hunting extends beyond hunting and capturing; and when the prey is taken the huntsman or fisherman cannot use it; but they hand it over to the cook, and the geometricians and astronomers and calculators (who all belong to the hunting class, for they do not make their diagrams, but only find out that which was previously contained in them)—they, I say, not being able to use but only to catch their prey, hand over their inventions to the dialectician to be applied by him, if they have any sense in them.

Good, I said, fairest and wisest Cleinias. And is this true?

Certainly, he said; just as a general when he takes a city or a camp hands over his new acquisition to the statesman, for he does not know how to use them himself; or as the quail-taker transfers the quails to the keeper of them. If we are looking for the art which is to make us blessed, and which is able to use that which it makes or takes, the art of the general is not the one, and some other must be found.

CRITO: And do you mean, Socrates, that the youngster said all this?

Euthydemus

SOCRATES: Are you incredulous, Crito?

CRITO: Indeed, I am; for if he did say so, then in my opinion he needs neither Euthydemus nor any one else to be his instructor.

SOCRATES: Perhaps I may have forgotten, and Ctesippus was the real answerer.

CRITO: Ctesippus! nonsense.

SOCRATES: All I know is that I heard these words, and that they were not spoken either by Euthydemus or Dionysodorus. I dare say, my good Crito, that they may have been spoken by some superior person: that I heard them I am certain.

CRITO: Yes, indeed, Socrates, by some one a good deal superior, as I should be disposed to think. But did you carry the search any further, and did you find the art which you were seeking?

SOCRATES: Find! my dear sir, no indeed. And we cut a poor figure; we were like children after larks, always on the point of catching the art, which was always getting away from us. But why should I repeat the whole story? At last we came to the kingly art, and enquired whether that gave and caused happiness, and then we got into a labyrinth, and when we thought we were at the end, came out again at the beginning, having still to seek as much as ever.

CRITO: How did that happen, Socrates?

SOCRATES: I will tell you; the kingly art was identified by us with the political.

CRITO: Well, and what came of that?

SOCRATES: To this royal or political art all the arts, including the art of the general, seemed to render up the supremacy, that being the only one which knew how to use what they produce. Here obviously was the very art which we were seeking—the art which is the source of good government, and which may be described, in the language of Aeschylus, as alone sitting at the helm of the vessel of state, piloting and governing all things, and utilizing them.

CRITO: And were you not right, Socrates?

SOCRATES: You shall judge, Crito, if you are willing to hear what followed; for we resumed the enquiry, and a question of this sort was asked: Does the kingly art, having this supreme authority, do anything for us? To be sure, was the answer. And would not you, Crito, say the same?

CRITO: Yes, I should.

SOCRATES: And what would you say that the kingly art does? If medicine were supposed to have supreme authority over the subordinate arts, and I were to ask you a similar question about that, you would say—it produces health?

CRITO: I should.

SOCRATES: And what of your own art of husbandry, supposing that to have supreme authority over the subject arts—what does that do? Does it not supply us with the fruits of the earth?

CRITO: Yes.

SOCRATES: And what does the kingly art do when invested with supreme power? Perhaps you may not be ready with an answer?

CRITO: Indeed I am not, Socrates.

SOCRATES: No more were we, Crito. But at any rate you know that if this is the art which we were seeking, it ought to be useful.

CRITO: Certainly.

Euthydemus

SOCRATES: And surely it ought to do us some good?

CRITO: Certainly, Socrates.

SOCRATES: And Cleinias and I had arrived at the conclusion that knowledge of some kind is the only good.

CRITO: Yes, that was what you were saying.

SOCRATES: All the other results of politics, and they are many, as for example, wealth, freedom, tranquillity, were neither good nor evil in themselves; but the political science ought to make us wise, and impart knowledge to us, if that is the science which is likely to do us good, and make us happy.

CRITO: Yes; that was the conclusion at which you had arrived, according to your report of the conversation.

SOCRATES: And does the kingly art make men wise and good?

CRITO: Why not, Socrates?

SOCRATES: What, all men, and in every respect? and teach them all the arts,—carpentering, and cobbling, and the rest of them?

CRITO: I think not, Socrates.

SOCRATES: But then what is this knowledge, and what are we to do with it? For it is not the source of any works which are neither good nor evil, and gives no knowledge, but the knowledge of itself; what then can it be, and what are we to do with it? Shall we say, Crito, that it is the knowledge by which we are to make other men good?

CRITO: By all means.

SOCRATES: And in what will they be good and useful? Shall we repeat that they will make others good, and that these others will make others again, without ever determining in what they are to be good; for we have put aside the results of politics, as they are called. This is the old, old song over again; and we are just as far as ever, if not farther, from the knowledge of the art or science of happiness.

CRITO: Indeed, Socrates, you do appear to have got into a great perplexity.

SOCRATES: Thereupon, Crito, seeing that I was on the point of shipwreck, I lifted up my voice, and earnestly entreated and called upon the strangers to save me and the youth from the whirlpool of the argument; they were our Castor and Pollux, I said, and they should be serious, and show us in sober earnest what that knowledge was which would enable us to pass the rest of our lives in happiness.

CRITO: And did Euthydemus show you this knowledge?

SOCRATES: Yes, indeed; he proceeded in a lofty strain to the following effect: Would you rather, Socrates, said he, that I should show you this knowledge about which you have been doubting, or shall I prove that you already have it?
  What, I said, are you blessed with such a power as this?
  Indeed I am.
  Then I would much rather that you should prove me to have such a knowledge; at my time of life that will be more agreeable than having to learn.
  Then tell me, he said, do you know anything?
  Yes, I said, I know many things, but not anything of much importance.
  That will do, he said: And would you admit that anything is what it is, and at the same time is not what it is?
  Certainly not.
  And did you not say that you knew something?
  I did.
  If you know, you are knowing.

Euthydemus

Certainly, of the knowledge which I have.

That makes no difference;—and must you not, if you are knowing, know all things?

Certainly not, I said, for there are many other things which I do not know.

And if you do not know, you are not knowing.

Yes, friend, of that which I do not know.

Still you are not knowing, and you said just now that you were knowing; and therefore you are and are not at the same time, and in reference to the same things.

A pretty clatter, as men say, Euthydemus, this of yours! and will you explain how I possess that knowledge for which we were seeking? Do you mean to say that the same thing cannot be and also not be; and therefore, since I know one thing, that I know all, for I cannot be knowing and not knowing at the same time, and if I know all things, then I must have the knowledge for which we are seeking—May I assume this to be your ingenious notion?

Out of your own mouth, Socrates, you are convicted, he said.

Well, but, Euthydemus, I said, has that never happened to you? for if I am only in the same case with you and our beloved Dionysodorus, I cannot complain. Tell me, then, you two, do you not know some things, and not know others?

Certainly not, Socrates, said Dionysodorus.

What do you mean, I said; do you know nothing?

Nay, he replied, we do know something.

Then, I said, you know all things, if you know anything?

Yes, all things, he said; and that is as true of you as of us.

O, indeed, I said, what a wonderful thing, and what a great blessing! And do all other men know all things or nothing?

Certainly, he replied; they cannot know some things, and not know others, and be at the same time knowing and not knowing.

Then what is the inference? I said.

They all know all things, he replied, if they know one thing.

O heavens, Dionysodorus, I said, I see now that you are in earnest; hardly have I got you to that point. And do you really and truly know all things, including carpentering and leather-cutting?

Certainly, he said.

And do you know stitching?

Yes, by the gods, we do, and cobbling, too.

And do you know things such as the numbers of the stars and of the sand?

Certainly; did you think we should say No to that?

By Zeus, said Ctesippus, interrupting, I only wish that you would give me some proof which would enable me to know whether you speak truly.

What proof shall I give you? he said.

Will you tell me how many teeth Euthydemus has? and Euthydemus shall tell how many teeth you have.

Will you not take our word that we know all things?

Certainly not, said Ctesippus: you must further tell us this one thing, and then we shall know that you are speak the truth; if you tell us the number, and we count them, and you are found to be right, we will believe the rest. They fancied that Ctesippus was making game of them, and they refused, and they would only say in answer to each of his questions, that they knew all things. For at last Ctesippus began to throw off all restraint; no question in fact was too bad for him; he would ask them if they knew the foulest things, and they, like wild boars, came rushing on his blows, and fearlessly replied that they did. At last, Crito, I too was carried away by my incredulity, and asked Euthydemus whether Dionysodorus could dance.

Certainly, he replied.

And can he vault among swords, and turn upon a wheel, at his age? has he got to such a height of skill as that?

He can do anything, he said.

And did you always know this?

Always, he said.

When you were children, and at your birth?

They both said that they did.

This we could not believe. And Euthydemus said: You are incredulous, Socrates.

Yes, I said, and I might well be incredulous, if I did not know you to be wise men.

But if you will answer, he said, I will make you confess to similar marvels.

Euthydemus

Well, I said, there is nothing that I should like better than to be self-convicted of this, for if I am really a wise man, which I never knew before, and you will prove to me that I know and have always known all things, nothing in life would be a greater gain to me.

Answer then, he said.

Ask, I said, and I will answer.

Do you know something, Socrates, or nothing?

Something, I said.

And do you know with what you know, or with something else?

With what I know; and I suppose that you mean with my soul?

Are you not ashamed, Socrates, of asking a question when you are asked one?

Well, I said; but then what am I to do? for I will do whatever you bid; when I do not know what you are asking, you tell me to answer nevertheless, and not to ask again.

Why, you surely have some notion of my meaning, he said.

Yes, I replied.

Well, then, answer according to your notion of my meaning.

Yes, I said; but if the question which you ask in one sense is understood and answered by me in another, will that please you—if I answer what is not to the point?

That will please me very well; but will not please you equally well, as I imagine.

I certainly will not answer unless I understand you, I said.

You will not answer, he said, according to your view of the meaning, because you will be prating, and are an ancient.

Now I saw that he was getting angry with me for drawing distinctions, when he wanted to catch me in his springes of words. And I remembered that Connus was always angry with me when I opposed him, and then he neglected me, because he thought that I was stupid; and as I was intending to go to Euthydemus as a pupil, I reflected that I had better let him have his way, as he might think me a blockhead, and refuse to take me. So I said: You are a far better dialectician than myself, Euthydemus, for I have never made a profession of the art, and therefore do as you say; ask your questions once more, and I will answer.

Answer then, he said, again, whether you know what you know with something, or with nothing.

Yes, I said; I know with my soul.

The man will answer more than the question; for I did not ask you, he said, with what you know, but whether you know with something.

Again I replied, Through ignorance I have answered too much, but I hope that you will forgive me. And now I will answer simply that I always know what I know with something.

And is that something, he rejoined, always the same, or sometimes one thing, and sometimes another thing?

Always, I replied, when I know, I know with this.

Will you not cease adding to your answers?

My fear is that this word 'always' may get us into trouble.

You, perhaps, but certainly not us. And now answer: Do you always know with this?

Always; since I am required to withdraw the words 'when I know.'

You always know with this, or, always knowing, do you know some things with this, and some things with something else, or do you know all things with this?

All that I know, I replied, I know with this.

There again, Socrates, he said, the addition is superfluous.

Well, then, I said, I will take away the words 'that I know.'

Nay, take nothing away; I desire no favours of you; but let me ask: Would you be able to know all things, if you did not know all things?

Quite impossible.

And now, he said, you may add on whatever you like, for you confess that you know all things.

I suppose that is true, I said, if my qualification implied in the words 'that I know' is not allowed to stand; and so I do know all things.

And have you not admitted that you always know all things with that which you know, whether you make the addition of 'when you know them' or not? for you have acknowledged that you have always and at once known all things, that is to say, when you were a child, and at your birth, and when you were growing up, and before you were born, and before the heaven and earth existed, you knew all things, if you always know them; and I swear that you shall always continue to know all things, if I am of the mind to make you.

Euthydemus

But I hope that you will be of that mind, reverend Euthydemus, I said, if you are really speaking the truth, and yet I a little doubt your power to make good your words unless you have the help of your brother Dionysodorus; then you may do it. Tell me now, both of you, for although in the main I cannot doubt that I really do know all things, when I am told so by men of your prodigious wisdom—how can I say that I know such things, Euthydemus, as that the good are unjust; come, do I know that or not?

Certainly, you know that.

What do I know?

That the good are not unjust.

Quite true, I said; and that I have always known; but the question is, where did I learn that the good are unjust?

Nowhere, said Dionysodorus.

Then, I said, I do not know this.

You are ruining the argument, said Euthydemus to Dionysodorus; he will be proved not to know, and then after all he will be knowing and not knowing at the same time.

Dionysodorus blushed.

I turned to the other, and said, What do you think, Euthydemus? Does not your omniscient brother appear to you to have made a mistake?

What, replied Dionysodorus in a moment; am I the brother of Euthydemus?

Thereupon I said, Please not to interrupt, my good friend, or prevent Euthydemus from proving to me that I know the good to be unjust; such a lesson you might at least allow me to learn.

You are running away, Socrates, said Dionysodorus, and refusing to answer.

No wonder, I said, for I am not a match for one of you, and a fortiori I must run away from two. I am no Heracles; and even Heracles could not fight against the Hydra, who was a she-Sophist, and had the wit to shoot up many new heads when one of them was cut off; especially when he saw a second monster of a sea-crab, who was also a Sophist, and appeared to have newly arrived from a sea-voyage, bearing down upon him from the left, opening his mouth and biting. When the monster was growing troublesome he called

Iolaus, his nephew, to his help, who ably succoured him; but if my Iolaus, who is my brother Patrocles (the statuary), were to come, he would only make a bad business worse.

And now that you have delivered yourself of this strain, said Dionysodorus, will you inform me whether Iolaus was the nephew of Heracles any more than he is yours?

I suppose that I had best answer you, Dionysodorus, I said, for you will insist on asking—that I pretty well know—out of envy, in order to prevent me from learning the wisdom of Euthydemus.

Then answer me, he said.

Well then, I said, I can only reply that Iolaus was not my nephew at all, but the nephew of Heracles; and his father was not my brother Patrocles, but Iphicles, who has a name rather like his, and was the brother of Heracles.

And is Patrocles, he said, your brother?

Yes, I said, he is my half-brother, the son of my mother, but not of my father.

Then he is and is not your brother.

Not by the same father, my good man, I said, for Chaeredemus was his father, and mine was Sophroniscus.

And was Sophroniscus a father, and Chaeredemus also?

Yes, I said; the former was my father, and the latter his.

Then, he said, Chaeredemus is not a father.

He is not my father, I said.

But can a father be other than a father? or are you the same as a stone?

I certainly do not think that I am a stone, I said, though I am afraid that you may prove me to be one.

Are you not other than a stone?

I am.

And being other than a stone, you are not a stone; and being other than gold, you are not gold?

Very true.

And so Chaeredemus, he said, being other than a father, is not a father?

I suppose that he is not a father, I replied.

For if, said Euthydemus, taking up the argument, Chaeredemus

Euthydemus

is a father, then Sophroniscus, being other than a father, is not a father; and you, Socrates, are without a father.

Ctesippus, here taking up the argument, said: And is not your father in the same case, for he is other than my father?

Assuredly not, said Euthydemus.

Then he is the same?

He is the same.

I cannot say that I like the connection; but is he only my father, Euthydemus, or is he the father of all other men?

Of all other men, he replied. Do you suppose the same person to be a father and not a father?

Certainly, I did so imagine, said Ctesippus.

And do you suppose that gold is not gold, or that a man is not a man?

They are not 'in pari materia,' Euthydemus, said Ctesippus, and you had better take care, for it is monstrous to suppose that your father is the father of all.

But he is, he replied.

What, of men only, said Ctesippus, or of horses and of all other animals?

Of all, he said.

And your mother, too, is the mother of all?

Yes, our mother too.

Yes; and your mother has a progeny of sea-urchins then?

Yes; and yours, he said.

And gudgeons and puppies and pigs are your brothers?

And yours too.

And your papa is a dog?

And so is yours, he said.

If you will answer my questions, said Dionysodorus, I will soon extract the same admissions from you, Ctesippus. You say that you have a dog.

Yes, a villain of a one, said Ctesippus.

And he has puppies?

Yes, and they are very like himself.

And the dog is the father of them?

Yes, he said, I certainly saw him and the mother of the puppies come together.

And is he not yours?

To be sure he is.

Then he is a father, and he is yours; ergo, he is your father, and the puppies are your brothers.

Let me ask you one little question more, said Dionysodorus, quickly interposing, in order that Ctesippus might not get in his word: You beat this dog?

Ctesippus said, laughing, Indeed I do; and I only wish that I could beat you instead of him.

Then you beat your father, he said.

I should have far more reason to beat yours, said Ctesippus; what could he have been thinking of when he begat such wise sons? much good has this father of you and your brethren the puppies got out of this wisdom of yours.

But neither he nor you, Ctesippus, have any need of much good.

And have you no need, Euthydemus? he said.

Neither I nor any other man; for tell me now, Ctesippus, if you think it good or evil for a man who is sick to drink medicine when he wants it; or to go to war armed rather than unarmed.

Good, I say. And yet I know that I am going to be caught in one of your charming puzzles.

That, he replied, you will discover, if you answer; since you admit medicine to be good for a man to drink, when wanted, must it not be good for him to drink as much as possible; when he takes his medicine, a cartload of hellebore will not be too much for him?

Ctesippus said: Quite so, Euthydemus, that is to say, if he who drinks is as big as the statue of Delphi.

And seeing that in war to have arms is a good thing, he ought to have as many spears and shields as possible?

Very true, said Ctesippus; and do you think, Euthydemus, that he ought to have one shield only, and one spear?

I do.

And would you arm Geryon and Briareus in that way? Considering that you and your companion fight in armour, I thought that you would have known better...Here Euthydemus held his peace, but Dionysodorus returned to the previous answer of Ctesippus and said:—

Euthydemus

Do you not think that the possession of gold is a good thing?
Yes, said Ctesippus, and the more the better.
And to have money everywhere and always is a good?
Certainly, a great good, he said.
And you admit gold to be a good?
Certainly, he replied.

And ought not a man then to have gold everywhere and always, and as much as possible in himself, and may he not be deemed the happiest of men who has three talents of gold in his belly, and a talent in his pate, and a stater of gold in either eye?

Yes, Euthydemus, said Ctesippus; and the Scythians reckon those who have gold in their own skulls to be the happiest and bravest of men (that is only another instance of your manner of speaking about the dog and father), and what is still more extraordinary, they drink out of their own skulls gilt, and see the inside of them, and hold their own head in their hands.

And do the Scythians and others see that which has the quality of vision, or that which has not? said Euthydemus.

That which has the quality of vision clearly.

And you also see that which has the quality of vision? he said. (Note: the ambiguity of (Greek), 'things visible and able to see,' (Greek), 'the speaking of the silent,' the silent denoting either the speaker or the subject of the speech, cannot be perfectly rendered in English. Compare
Aristot. Soph. Elenchi (Poste's translation):—

'Of ambiguous propositions the following are instances:—

'I hope that you the enemy may slay.

'Whom one knows, he knows. Either the person knowing or the person known is here affirmed to know.

'What one sees, that one sees: one sees a pillar: ergo, that one pillar sees.

'What you *are* holding, that you are: you are holding a stone: ergo, a stone you are.

'Is a speaking of the silent possible? "The silent" denotes either the speaker are the subject of speech.

'There are three kinds of ambiguity of term or proposition. The first is when there is an equal linguistic propriety in several interpretations; the second when one is improper but customary; the third when the ambiguity arises in the combination of elements that are in themselves unambiguous, as in "knowing letters." "Knowing" and "letters" are perhaps separately unambiguous, but in combination may imply either that the letters are known, or that they themselves have knowledge. Such are the modes in which propositions and terms may be ambiguous.'

Yes, I do.

Then do you see our garments?

Yes.

Then our garments have the quality of vision.

They can see to any extent, said Ctesippus.

What can they see?

Nothing; but you, my sweet man, may perhaps imagine that they do not see; and certainly, Euthydemus, you do seem to me to have been caught napping when you were not asleep, and that if it be possible to speak and say nothing—you are doing so.

And may there not be a silence of the speaker? said Dionysodorus.

Impossible, said Ctesippus.

Or a speaking of the silent?

That is still more impossible, he said.

But when you speak of stones, wood, iron bars, do you not speak of the silent?

Not when I pass a smithy; for then the iron bars make a tremendous noise and outcry if they are touched: so that here your wisdom is strangely mistaken; please, however, to tell me how you can be silent when speaking (I thought that Ctesippus was put upon his mettle because Cleinias was present).

When you are silent, said Euthydemus, is there not a silence of all things?

Yes, he said.

But if speaking things are included in all things, then the speaking are silent.

What, said Ctesippus; then all things are not silent?

Certainly not, said Euthydemus.

Then, my good friend, do they all speak?

Yes; those which speak.

Euthydemus

Nay, said Ctesippus, but the question which I ask is whether all things are silent or speak?

Neither and both, said Dionysodorus, quickly interposing; I am sure that you will be 'non-plussed' at that answer.

Here Ctesippus, as his manner was, burst into a roar of laughter; he said, That brother of yours, Euthydemus, has got into a dilemma; all is over with him. This delighted Cleinias, whose laughter made Ctesippus ten times as uproarious; but I cannot help thinking that the rogue must have picked up this answer from them; for there has been no wisdom like theirs in our time. Why do you laugh, Cleinias, I said, at such solemn and beautiful things?

Why, Socrates, said Dionysodorus, did you ever see a beautiful thing?

Yes, Dionysodorus, I replied, I have seen many.

Were they other than the beautiful, or the same as the beautiful?

Now I was in a great quandary at having to answer this question, and I thought that I was rightly served for having opened my mouth at all: I said however, They are not the same as absolute beauty, but they have beauty present with each of them.

And are you an ox because an ox is present with you, or are you Dionysodorus, because Dionysodorus is present with you?

God forbid, I replied.

But how, he said, by reason of one thing being present with another, will one thing be another?

Is that your difficulty? I said. For I was beginning to imitate their skill, on which my heart was set.

Of course, he replied, I and all the world are in a difficulty about the non-existent.

What do you mean, Dionysodorus? I said. Is not the honourable honourable and the base base?

That, he said, is as I please.

And do you please?

Yes, he said.

And you will admit that the same is the same, and the other other; for surely the other is not the same; I should imagine that even a child will hardly deny the other to be other. But I think, Dionysodorus, that you must have intentionally missed the last question; for in general you and your brother seem to me to be good workmen in your own department, and to do the dialectician's business excellently well.

What, said he, is the business of a good workman? tell me, in the first place, whose business is hammering?

The smith's.

And whose the making of pots?

The potter's.

And who has to kill and skin and mince and boil and roast?

The cook, I said.

And if a man does his business he does rightly?

Certainly.

And the business of the cook is to cut up and skin; you have admitted that?

Yes, I have admitted that, but you must not be too hard upon me.

Then if some one were to kill, mince, boil, roast the cook, he would do his business, and if he were to hammer the smith, and make a pot of the potter, he would do their business.

Poseidon, I said, this is the crown of wisdom; can I ever hope to have such wisdom of my own?

And would you be able, Socrates, to recognize this wisdom when it has become your own?

Certainly, I said, if you will allow me.

What, he said, do you think that you know what is your own?

Yes, I do, subject to your correction; for you are the bottom, and Euthydemus is the top, of all my wisdom.

Is not that which you would deem your own, he said, that which you have in your own power, and which you are able to use as you would desire, for example, an ox or a sheep—would you not think that which you could sell and give and sacrifice to any god whom you pleased, to be your own, and that which you could not give or sell or sacrifice you would think not to be in your own power?

Yes, I said (for I was certain that something good would come out of the questions, which I was impatient to hear); yes, such things, and such things only are mine.

Yes, he said, and you would mean by animals living beings?

Yes, I said.

Euthydemus

You agree then, that those animals only are yours with which you have the power to do all these things which I was just naming?

I agree.

Then, after a pause, in which he seemed to be lost in the contemplation of something great, he said: Tell me, Socrates, have you an ancestral Zeus? Here, anticipating the final move, like a person caught in a net, who gives a desperate twist that he may get away, I said: No, Dionysodorus, I have not.

What a miserable man you must be then, he said; you are not an Athenian at all if you have no ancestral gods or temples, or any other mark of gentility.

Nay, Dionysodorus, I said, do not be rough; good words, if you please; in the way of religion I have altars and temples, domestic and ancestral, and all that other Athenians have.

And have not other Athenians, he said, an ancestral Zeus?

That name, I said, is not to be found among the Ionians, whether colonists or citizens of Athens; an ancestral Apollo there is, who is the father of Ion, and a family Zeus, and a Zeus guardian of the phratry, and an Athene guardian of the phratry. But the name of ancestral Zeus is unknown to us.

No matter, said Dionysodorus, for you admit that you have Apollo, Zeus, and Athene.

Certainly, I said.

And they are your gods, he said.

Yes, I said, my lords and ancestors.

At any rate they are yours, he said, did you not admit that?

I did, I said; what is going to happen to me?

And are not these gods animals? for you admit that all things which have life are animals; and have not these gods life?

They have life, I said.

Then are they not animals?

They are animals, I said.

And you admitted that of animals those are yours which you could give away or sell or offer in sacrifice, as you pleased?

I did admit that, Euthydemus, and I have no way of escape.

Well then, said he, if you admit that Zeus and the other gods are yours, can you sell them or give them away or do what you will with them, as you would with other animals?

At this I was quite struck dumb, Crito, and lay prostrate. Ctesippus came to the rescue.

Bravo, Heracles, brave words, said he.

Bravo Heracles, or is Heracles a Bravo? said Dionysodorus.

Poseidon, said Ctesippus, what awful distinctions. I will have no more of them; the pair are invincible.

Then, my dear Crito, there was universal applause of the speakers and their words, and what with laughing and clapping of hands and rejoicings the two men were quite overpowered; for hitherto their partisans only had cheered at each successive hit, but now the whole company shouted with delight until the columns of the Lyceum returned the sound, seeming to sympathize in their joy. To such a pitch was I affected myself, that I made a speech, in which I acknowledged that I had never seen the like of their wisdom; I was their devoted servant, and fell to praising and admiring of them. What marvellous dexterity of wit, I said, enabled you to acquire this great perfection in such a short time? There is much, indeed, to admire in your words, Euthydemus and Dionysodorus, but there is nothing that I admire more than your magnanimous disregard of any opinion—whether of the many, or of the grave and reverend seigniors—you regard only those who are like yourselves. And I do verily believe that there are few who are like you, and who would approve of such arguments; the majority of mankind are so ignorant of their value, that they would be more ashamed of employing them in the refutation of others than of being refuted by them. I must further express my approval of your kind and public-spirited denial of all differences, whether of good and evil, white or black, or any other; the result of which is that, as you say, every mouth is sewn up, not excepting your own, which graciously follows the example of others; and thus all ground of offence is taken away. But what appears to me to be more than all is, that this art and invention of yours has been so admirably contrived by you, that in a very short time it can be imparted to any one. I observed that Ctesippus learned to imitate you in no time. Now this quickness of attainment is an excellent thing; but at the same time I would advise you not to have any more public entertainments; there is a danger that men may undervalue an art which they have so easy an opportunity of acquiring; the exhibition would be best of all, if the discussion were confined to your two selves; but if there must be an audience, let him only be present who is willing to pay a handsome fee;—you should be careful of this;—and if you are wise, you will also bid your disciples discourse with no man but you and themselves. For only what is rare is valuable; and 'water,' which, as Pindar says, is the 'best of all things,' is also the cheapest. And now I have only to request that you will receive Cleinias and me among your pupils.

Such was the discussion, Crito; and after a few more words had passed between us we went away. I hope that you will come to them with me, since they say that they are able to teach any one who will give them money; no age or want of capacity is an impediment. And I must repeat one thing which they said, for your especial benefit,—that the learning of their art did not at all interfere with the business of money-making.

CRITO: Truly, Socrates, though I am curious and ready to learn, yet I fear that I am not like-minded with Euthydemus, but one of the other sort, who, as you were saying, would rather be refuted by such arguments than use them in refutation of others. And though I may appear ridiculous in venturing to advise you, I think that you may as well hear what was said to me by a man of very considerable pretensions—he was a professor of legal oratory—who came away from you while I was walking up and down. 'Crito,' said he to me, 'are you giving no attention to these wise men?' 'No, indeed,' I said to him; 'I could not get within hearing of them—there was such a crowd.' 'You would have heard something worth hearing if you had.' 'What was that?' I said. 'You would have heard the greatest masters of the art of rhetoric discoursing.' 'And what did you think of them?' I said. 'What did I think of them?' he said:—'theirs was the sort of discourse which anybody might hear from men who were playing the fool, and making much ado about nothing.' That was the expression which he used. 'Surely,' I said, 'philosophy is a charming thing.' 'Charming!' he said; 'what simplicity! philosophy is nought; and I think that if you had been present you would have been ashamed of your friend—his conduct was so very strange in placing himself at the mercy of men who care not what they say, and fasten upon every word. And these, as I was telling you, are supposed to be the most eminent professors of their time. But the truth is, Crito, that the study itself and the men themselves are utterly mean and ridiculous.' Now censure of the pursuit, Socrates, whether coming from him or from others, appears to me to be undeserved; but as to the impropriety of holding a public discussion with such men, there, I confess that, in my opinion, he was in the right.

SOCRATES: O Crito, they are marvellous men; but what was I going to say? First of all let me know;—What manner of man was he who came up to you and censured philosophy; was he an orator who himself practises in the courts, or an instructor of orators, who makes the speeches with which they do battle?

CRITO: He was certainly not an orator, and I doubt whether he had ever been into court; but they say that he knows the business, and is a clever man, and composes wonderful speeches.

SOCRATES: Now I understand, Crito; he is one of an amphibious class, whom I was on the point of mentioning—one of those whom Prodicus describes as on the border-ground between philosophers and statesmen—they think that they are the wisest of all men, and that they are generally esteemed the wisest; nothing but the rivalry of the philosophers stands in their way; and they are of the opinion that if they can prove the philosophers to be good for nothing, no one will dispute their title to the palm of wisdom, for that they are themselves really the wisest, although they are apt to be mauled by Euthydemus and his friends, when they get hold of them in conversation. This opinion which they entertain of their own wisdom is very natural; for they have a certain amount of philosophy, and a certain amount of political wisdom; there is reason in what they say, for they argue that they have just enough of both, and so they keep out of the way of all risks and conflicts and reap the fruits of their wisdom.

CRITO: What do you say of them, Socrates? There is certainly something specious in that notion of theirs.

Euthydemus

SOCRATES: Yes, Crito, there is more speciousness than truth; they cannot be made to understand the nature of intermediates. For all persons or things, which are intermediate between two other things, and participate in both of them—if one of these two things is good and the other evil, are better than the one and worse than the other; but if they are in a mean between two good things which do not tend to the same end, they fall short of either of their component elements in the attainment of their ends. Only in the case when the two component elements which do not tend to the same end are evil is the participant better than either. Now, if philosophy and political action are both good, but tend to different ends, and they participate in both, and are in a mean between them, then they are talking nonsense, for they are worse than either; or, if the one be good and the other evil, they are better than the one and worse than the other; only on the supposition that they are both evil could there be any truth in what they say. I do not think that they will admit that their two pursuits are either wholly or partly evil; but the truth is, that these philosopher-politicians who aim at both fall short of both in the attainment of their respective ends, and are really third, although they would like to stand first. There is no need, however, to be angry at this ambition of theirs—which may be forgiven; for every man ought to be loved who says and manfully pursues and works out anything which is at all like wisdom: at the same time we shall do well to see them as they really are.

CRITO: I have often told you, Socrates, that I am in a constant difficulty about my two sons. What am I to do with them? There is no hurry about the younger one, who is only a child; but the other, Critobulus, is getting on, and needs some one who will improve him. I cannot help thinking, when I hear you talk, that there is a sort of madness in many of our anxieties about our children:—in the first place, about marrying a wife of good family to be the mother of them, and then about heaping up money for them—and yet taking no care about their education. But then again, when I contemplate any of those who pretend to educate others, I am amazed. To me, if I am to confess the truth, they all seem to be such outrageous beings: so that I do not know how I can advise the youth to study philosophy.

SOCRATES: Dear Crito, do you not know that in every profession the inferior sort are numerous and good for nothing, and the good are few and beyond all price: for example, are not gymnastic and rhetoric and money-making and the art of the general, noble arts?

CRITO: Certainly they are, in my judgment.

SOCRATES: Well, and do you not see that in each of these arts the many are ridiculous performers?

CRITO: Yes, indeed, that is very true.

SOCRATES: And will you on this account shun all these pursuits yourself and refuse to allow them to your son?

CRITO: That would not be reasonable, Socrates.

SOCRATES: Do you then be reasonable, Crito, and do not mind whether the teachers of philosophy are good or bad, but think only of philosophy herself. Try and examine her well and truly, and if she be evil seek to turn away all men from her, and not your sons only; but if she be what I believe that she is, then follow her and serve her, you and your house, as the saying is, and be of good cheer.

CRATYLUS

by

Plato

Translated by Benjamin Jowett

PERSONS OF THE DIALOGUE: Socrates, Hermogenes, Cratylus.

HERMOGENES: Suppose that we make Socrates a party to the argument?

CRATYLUS: If you please.

HERMOGENES: I should explain to you, Socrates, that our friend Cratylus has been arguing about names; he says that they are natural and not conventional; not a portion of the human voice which men agree to use; but that there is a truth or correctness in them, which is the same for Hellenes as for barbarians. Whereupon I ask him, whether his own name of Cratylus is a true name or not, and he answers 'Yes.' And Socrates? 'Yes.' Then every man's name, as I tell him, is that which he is called. To this he replies—'If all the world were to call you Hermogenes, that would not be your name.' And when I am anxious to have a further explanation he is ironical and mysterious, and seems to imply that he has a notion of his own about the matter, if he would only tell, and could entirely convince me, if he chose to be intelligible. Tell me, Socrates, what this oracle means; or rather tell me, if you will be so good, what is your own view of the truth or correctness of names, which I would far sooner hear.

SOCRATES: Son of Hipponicus, there is an ancient saying, that 'hard is the knowledge of the good.' And the knowledge of names is a great part of knowledge. If I had not been poor, I might have heard the fifty-drachma course of the great Prodicus, which is a complete education in grammar and language—these are his own words—and then I should have been at once able to answer your question about the correctness of names. But, indeed, I have only heard the single-drachma course, and therefore, I do not know the truth about such matters; I will, however, gladly assist you and Cratylus in the investigation of them. When he declares that your name is not really Hermogenes, I suspect that he is only making fun of you;—he means to say that you are no true son of Hermes, because you are always looking after a fortune and never in luck. But, as I was saying, there is a good deal of difficulty in this sort of knowledge, and therefore we had better leave the question open until we have heard both sides.

HERMOGENES: I have often talked over this matter, both with Cratylus and others, and cannot convince myself that there is any principle of correctness in names other than convention and agreement; any name which you give, in my opinion, is the right one, and if you change that and give another, the new name is as correct as the old—we frequently change the names of our slaves, and the newly-imposed name is as good as the old: for there is no name given to anything by nature; all is convention and habit of the users;—such is my view. But if I am mistaken I shall be happy to hear and learn of Cratylus, or of any one else.

SOCRATES: I dare say that you may be right, Hermogenes: let us see;—Your meaning is, that the name of each thing is only that which anybody agrees to call it?

HERMOGENES: That is my notion.

SOCRATES: Whether the giver of the name be an individual or a city?

HERMOGENES: Yes.

SOCRATES: Well, now, let me take an instance;—suppose that I call a man a horse or a horse a man, you mean to say that a man will be rightly called a horse by me individually, and rightly called a man by the rest of the world; and a horse again would be rightly called a man by me and a horse by the world:—that is your meaning?

HERMOGENES: He would, according to my view.

SOCRATES: But how about truth, then? you would acknowledge that there is in words a true and a false?

HERMOGENES: Certainly.

SOCRATES: And there are true and false propositions?

HERMOGENES: To be sure.

SOCRATES: And a true proposition says that which is, and a false proposition says that which is not?

HERMOGENES: Yes; what other answer is possible?

SOCRATES: Then in a proposition there is a true and false?

HERMOGENES: Certainly.

SOCRATES: But is a proposition true as a whole only, and are the parts untrue?

HERMOGENES: No; the parts are true as well as the whole.

SOCRATES: Would you say the large parts and not the smaller ones, or every part?

HERMOGENES: I should say that every part is true.

SOCRATES: Is a proposition resolvable into any part smaller than a name?

HERMOGENES: No; that is the smallest.

SOCRATES: Then the name is a part of the true proposition?

HERMOGENES: Yes.

SOCRATES: Yes, and a true part, as you say.

HERMOGENES: Yes.

SOCRATES: And is not the part of a falsehood also a falsehood?

HERMOGENES: Yes.

SOCRATES: Then, if propositions may be true and false, names may be true and false?

HERMOGENES: So we must infer.

SOCRATES: And the name of anything is that which any one affirms to be the name?

HERMOGENES: Yes.

SOCRATES: And will there be so many names of each thing as everybody says that there are? and will they be true names at the time of uttering them?

HERMOGENES: Yes, Socrates, I can conceive no correctness of names other than this; you give one name, and I another; and in different cities and countries there are different names for the same things; Hellenes differ from barbarians in their use of names, and the several Hellenic tribes from one another.

Cratylus

SOCRATES: But would you say, Hermogenes, that the things differ as the names differ? and are they relative to individuals, as Protagoras tells us? For he says that man is the measure of all things, and that things are to me as they appear to me, and that they are to you as they appear to you. Do you agree with him, or would you say that things have a permanent essence of their own?

HERMOGENES: There have been times, Socrates, when I have been driven in my perplexity to take refuge with Protagoras; not that I agree with him at all.

SOCRATES: What! have you ever been driven to admit that there was no such thing as a bad man?

HERMOGENES: No, indeed; but I have often had reason to think that there are very bad men, and a good many of them.

SOCRATES: Well, and have you ever found any very good ones?

HERMOGENES: Not many.

SOCRATES: Still you have found them?

HERMOGENES: Yes.

SOCRATES: And would you hold that the very good were the very wise, and the very evil very foolish? Would that be your view?

HERMOGENES: It would.

SOCRATES: But if Protagoras is right, and the truth is that things are as they appear to any one, how can some of us be wise and some of us foolish?

HERMOGENES: Impossible.

SOCRATES: And if, on the other hand, wisdom and folly are really distinguishable, you will allow, I think, that the assertion of Protagoras can hardly be correct. For if what appears to each man is true to him, one man cannot in reality be wiser than another.

HERMOGENES: He cannot.

SOCRATES: Nor will you be disposed to say with Euthydemus, that all things equally belong to all men at the same moment and always; for neither on his view can there be some good and others bad, if virtue and vice are always equally to be attributed to all.

HERMOGENES: There cannot.

SOCRATES: But if neither is right, and things are not relative to individuals, and all things do not equally belong to all at the same moment and always, they must be supposed to have their own proper and permanent essence: they are not in relation to us, or influenced by us, fluctuating according to our fancy, but they are independent, and maintain to their own essence the relation prescribed by nature.

HERMOGENES: I think, Socrates, that you have said the truth.

SOCRATES: Does what I am saying apply only to the things themselves, or equally to the actions which proceed from them? Are not actions also a class of being?

HERMOGENES: Yes, the actions are real as well as the things.

SOCRATES: Then the actions also are done according to their proper nature, and not according to our opinion of them? In cutting, for example, we do not cut as we please, and with any chance instrument; but we cut with the proper instrument only, and according to the natural process of cutting; and the natural process is right and will succeed, but any other will fail and be of no use at all.

HERMOGENES: I should say that the natural way is the right way.

Cratylus

SOCRATES: Again, in burning, not every way is the right way; but the right way is the natural way, and the right instrument the natural instrument.

HERMOGENES: True.

SOCRATES: And this holds good of all actions?

HERMOGENES: Yes.

SOCRATES: And speech is a kind of action?

HERMOGENES: True.

SOCRATES: And will a man speak correctly who speaks as he pleases? Will not the successful speaker rather be he who speaks in the natural way of speaking, and as things ought to be spoken, and with the natural instrument? Any other mode of speaking will result in error and failure.

HERMOGENES: I quite agree with you.

SOCRATES: And is not naming a part of speaking? for in giving names men speak.

HERMOGENES: That is true.

SOCRATES: And if speaking is a sort of action and has a relation to acts, is not naming also a sort of action?

HERMOGENES: True.

SOCRATES: And we saw that actions were not relative to ourselves, but had a special nature of their own?

HERMOGENES: Precisely.

SOCRATES: Then the argument would lead us to infer that names ought to be given according to a natural process, and with a proper instrument, and not at our pleasure: in this and no other way shall we name with success.

HERMOGENES: I agree.

SOCRATES: But again, that which has to be cut has to be cut with something?

HERMOGENES: Yes.

SOCRATES: And that which has to be woven or pierced has to be woven or pierced with something?

HERMOGENES: Certainly.

SOCRATES: And that which has to be named has to be named with something?

HERMOGENES: True.

SOCRATES: What is that with which we pierce?

HERMOGENES: An awl.

SOCRATES: And with which we weave?

HERMOGENES: A shuttle.

SOCRATES: And with which we name?

HERMOGENES: A name.

SOCRATES: Very good: then a name is an instrument?

HERMOGENES: Certainly.

Cratylus

SOCRATES: Suppose that I ask, 'What sort of instrument is a shuttle?' And you answer, 'A weaving instrument.'

HERMOGENES: Well.

SOCRATES: And I ask again, 'What do we do when we weave?'— The answer is, that we separate or disengage the warp from the woof.

HERMOGENES: Very true.

SOCRATES: And may not a similar description be given of an awl, and of instruments in general?

HERMOGENES: To be sure.

SOCRATES: And now suppose that I ask a similar question about names: will you answer me? Regarding the name as an instrument, what do we do when we name?

HERMOGENES: I cannot say.

SOCRATES: Do we not give information to one another, and distinguish things according to their natures?

HERMOGENES: Certainly we do.

SOCRATES: Then a name is an instrument of teaching and of distinguishing natures, as the shuttle is of distinguishing the threads of the web.

HERMOGENES: Yes.

SOCRATES: And the shuttle is the instrument of the weaver?

HERMOGENES: Assuredly.

SOCRATES: Then the weaver will use the shuttle well—and well means like a weaver? and the teacher will use the name well—and well means like a teacher?

HERMOGENES: Yes.

SOCRATES: And when the weaver uses the shuttle, whose work will he be using well?

HERMOGENES: That of the carpenter.

SOCRATES: And is every man a carpenter, or the skilled only?

HERMOGENES: Only the skilled.

SOCRATES: And when the piercer uses the awl, whose work will he be using well?

HERMOGENES: That of the smith.

SOCRATES: And is every man a smith, or only the skilled?

HERMOGENES: The skilled only.

SOCRATES: And when the teacher uses the name, whose work will he be using?

HERMOGENES: There again I am puzzled.

SOCRATES: Cannot you at least say who gives us the names which we use?

HERMOGENES: Indeed I cannot.

SOCRATES: Does not the law seem to you to give us them?

HERMOGENES: Yes, I suppose so.

Cratylus

SOCRATES: Then the teacher, when he gives us a name, uses the work of the legislator?

HERMOGENES: I agree.

SOCRATES: And is every man a legislator, or the skilled only?

HERMOGENES: The skilled only.

SOCRATES: Then, Hermogenes, not every man is able to give a name, but only a maker of names; and this is the legislator, who of all skilled artisans in the world is the rarest.

HERMOGENES: True.

SOCRATES: And how does the legislator make names? and to what does he look? Consider this in the light of the previous instances: to what does the carpenter look in making the shuttle? Does he not look to that which is naturally fitted to act as a shuttle?

HERMOGENES: Certainly.

SOCRATES: And suppose the shuttle to be broken in making, will he make another, looking to the broken one? or will he look to the form according to which he made the other?

HERMOGENES: To the latter, I should imagine.

SOCRATES: Might not that be justly called the true or ideal shuttle?

HERMOGENES: I think so.

SOCRATES: And whatever shuttles are wanted, for the manufacture of garments, thin or thick, of flaxen, woollen, or other material, ought all of them to have the true form of the shuttle; and whatever is the shuttle best adapted to each kind of work, that ought to be the form which the maker produces in each case.

HERMOGENES: Yes.

SOCRATES: And the same holds of other instruments: when a man has discovered the instrument which is naturally adapted to each work, he must express this natural form, and not others which he fancies, in the material, whatever it may be, which he employs; for example, he ought to know how to put into iron the forms of awls adapted by nature to their several uses?

HERMOGENES: Certainly.

SOCRATES: And how to put into wood forms of shuttles adapted by nature to their uses?

HERMOGENES: True.

SOCRATES: For the several forms of shuttles naturally answer to the several kinds of webs; and this is true of instruments in general.

HERMOGENES: Yes.

SOCRATES: Then, as to names: ought not our legislator also to know how to put the true natural name of each thing into sounds and syllables, and to make and give all names with a view to the ideal name, if he is to be a namer in any true sense? And we must remember that different legislators will not use the same syllables. For neither does every smith, although he may be making the same instrument for the same purpose, make them all of the same iron. The form must be the same, but the material may vary, and still the instrument may be equally good of whatever iron made, whether in Hellas or in a foreign country;—there is no difference.

HERMOGENES: Very true.

SOCRATES: And the legislator, whether he be Hellene or barbarian, is not therefore to be deemed by you a worse legislator, provided he gives the true and proper form of the name in whatever

Cratylus

syllables; this or that country makes no matter.

HERMOGENES: Quite true.

SOCRATES: But who then is to determine whether the proper form is given to the shuttle, whatever sort of wood may be used? the carpenter who makes, or the weaver who is to use them?

HERMOGENES: I should say, he who is to use them, Socrates.

SOCRATES: And who uses the work of the lyre-maker? Will not he be the man who knows how to direct what is being done, and who will know also whether the work is being well done or not?

HERMOGENES: Certainly.

SOCRATES: And who is he?

HERMOGENES: The player of the lyre.

SOCRATES: And who will direct the shipwright?

HERMOGENES: The pilot.

SOCRATES: And who will be best able to direct the legislator in his work, and will know whether the work is well done, in this or any other country? Will not the user be the man?

HERMOGENES: Yes.

SOCRATES: And this is he who knows how to ask questions?

HERMOGENES: Yes.

SOCRATES: And how to answer them?

HERMOGENES: Yes.

SOCRATES: And him who knows how to ask and answer you would call a dialectician?

HERMOGENES: Yes; that would be his name.

SOCRATES: Then the work of the carpenter is to make a rudder, and the pilot has to direct him, if the rudder is to be well made.

HERMOGENES: True.

SOCRATES: And the work of the legislator is to give names, and the dialectician must be his director if the names are to be rightly given?

HERMOGENES: That is true.

SOCRATES: Then, Hermogenes, I should say that this giving of names can be no such light matter as you fancy, or the work of light or chance persons; and Cratylus is right in saying that things have names by nature, and that not every man is an artificer of names, but he only who looks to the name which each thing by nature has, and is able to express the true forms of things in letters and syllables.

HERMOGENES: I cannot answer you, Socrates; but I find a difficulty in changing my opinion all in a moment, and I think that I should be more readily persuaded, if you would show me what this is which you term the natural fitness of names.

SOCRATES: My good Hermogenes, I have none to show. Was I not telling you just now (but you have forgotten), that I knew nothing, and proposing to share the enquiry with you? But now that you and I have talked over the matter, a step has been gained; for we have discovered that names have by nature a truth, and that not every man knows how to give a thing a name.

HERMOGENES: Very good.

Cratylus

SOCRATES: And what is the nature of this truth or correctness of names? That, if you care to know, is the next question.

HERMOGENES: Certainly, I care to know.

SOCRATES: Then reflect.

HERMOGENES: How shall I reflect?

SOCRATES: The true way is to have the assistance of those who know, and you must pay them well both in money and in thanks; these are the Sophists, of whom your brother, Callias, has—rather dearly—bought the reputation of wisdom. But you have not yet come into your inheritance, and therefore you had better go to him, and beg and entreat him to tell you what he has learnt from Protagoras about the fitness of names.

HERMOGENES: But how inconsistent should I be, if, whilst repudiating Protagoras and his truth ('Truth' was the title of the book of Protagoras; compare Theaet.), I were to attach any value to what he and his book affirm!

SOCRATES: Then if you despise him, you must learn of Homer and the poets.

HERMOGENES: And where does Homer say anything about names, and what does he say?

SOCRATES: He often speaks of them; notably and nobly in the places where he distinguishes the different names which Gods and men give to the same things. Does he not in these passages make a remarkable statement about
the correctness of names? For the Gods must clearly be supposed to call things by their right and natural names; do you not think so?

HERMOGENES: Why, of course they call them rightly, if they call them at all. But to what are you referring?

SOCRATES: Do you not know what he says about the river in Troy who had a single combat with Hephaestus?

'Whom,' as he says, 'the Gods call Xanthus, and men call Scamander.'

HERMOGENES: I remember.

SOCRATES: Well, and about this river—to know that he ought to be called Xanthus and not Scamander—is not that a solemn lesson? Or about the bird which, as he says,

'The Gods call Chalcis, and men Cymindis:'

to be taught how much more correct the name Chalcis is than the name Cymindis—do you deem that a light matter? Or about Batieia and Myrina? (Compare Il. 'The hill which men call Batieia and the immortals the tomb of the sportive Myrina.') And there are many other observations of the same kind in Homer and other poets. Now, I think that this is beyond the understanding of you and me; but the names of Scamandrius and Astyanax, which he affirms to have been the names of Hector's son, are more within the range of human faculties, as I am disposed to think; and what the poet means by correctness may be more readily apprehended in that instance: you will remember I dare say the lines to which I refer? (Il.)

HERMOGENES: I do.

SOCRATES: Let me ask you, then, which did Homer think the more correct of the names given to Hector's son—Astyanax or Scamandrius?

HERMOGENES: I do not know.

SOCRATES: How would you answer, if you were asked whether the wise or the unwise are more likely to give correct names?

HERMOGENES: I should say the wise, of course.

Cratylus

SOCRATES: And are the men or the women of a city, taken as a class, the wiser?

HERMOGENES: I should say, the men.

SOCRATES: And Homer, as you know, says that the Trojan men called him Astyanax (king of the city); but if the men called him Astyanax, the other name of Scamandrius could only have been given to him by the women.

HERMOGENES: That may be inferred.

SOCRATES: And must not Homer have imagined the Trojans to be wiser than their wives?

HERMOGENES: To be sure.

SOCRATES: Then he must have thought Astyanax to be a more correct name for the boy than Scamandrius?

HERMOGENES: Clearly.

SOCRATES: And what is the reason of this? Let us consider:— does he not himself suggest a very good reason, when he says,

'For he alone defended their city and long walls'?

This appears to be a good reason for calling the son of the saviour king of the city which his father was saving, as Homer observes.

HERMOGENES: I see.

SOCRATES: Why, Hermogenes, I do not as yet see myself; and do you?

HERMOGENES: No, indeed; not I.

SOCRATES: But tell me, friend, did not Homer himself also give Hector his name?

HERMOGENES: What of that?

SOCRATES: The name appears to me to be very nearly the same as the name of Astyanax—both are Hellenic; and a king (anax) and a holder (ektor) have nearly the same meaning, and are both descriptive of a king; for a man is clearly the holder of that of which he is king; he rules, and owns, and holds it. But, perhaps, you may think that I am talking nonsense; and indeed I believe that I myself did not know what I meant when I imagined that I had found some indication of the opinion of Homer about the correctness of names.

HERMOGENES: I assure you that I think otherwise, and I believe you to be on the right track.

SOCRATES: There is reason, I think, in calling the lion's whelp a lion, and the foal of a horse a horse; I am speaking only of the ordinary course of nature, when an animal produces after his kind, and not of extraordinary births;—if contrary to nature a horse have a calf, then I should not call that a foal but a calf; nor do I call any inhuman birth a man, but only a natural birth. And the same may be said of trees and other things. Do you agree with me?

HERMOGENES: Yes, I agree.

SOCRATES: Very good. But you had better watch me and see that I do not play tricks with you. For on the same principle the son of a king is to be called a king. And whether the syllables of the name are the same or not the same, makes no difference, provided the meaning is retained; nor does the addition or subtraction of a letter make any difference so long as the essence of the thing remains in possession of the name and appears in it.

HERMOGENES: What do you mean?

Cratylus

SOCRATES: A very simple matter. I may illustrate my meaning by the names of letters, which you know are not the same as the letters themselves with the exception of the four epsilon, upsilon, omicron, omega; the names of the rest, whether vowels or consonants, are made up of other letters which we add to them; but so long as we introduce the meaning, and there can be no mistake, the name of the letter is quite correct. Take, for example, the letter beta—the addition of eta, tau, alpha, gives no offence, and does not prevent the whole name from having the value which the legislator intended—so well did he know how to give the letters names.

HERMOGENES: I believe you are right.

SOCRATES: And may not the same be said of a king? a king will often be the son of a king, the good son or the noble son of a good or noble sire; and similarly the offspring of every kind, in the regular course of nature, is like the parent, and therefore has the same name. Yet the syllables may be disguised until they appear different to the ignorant person, and he may not recognize them, although they are the same, just as any one of us would not recognize the same drugs under different disguises of colour and smell, although to the physician, who regards the power of them, they are the same, and he is not put out by the addition; and in like manner the etymologist is not put out by the addition or transposition or subtraction of a letter or two, or indeed by the change of all the letters, for this need not interfere with the meaning. As was just now said, the names of Hector and Astyanax have only one letter alike, which is *tau*, and yet they have the same meaning. And how little in common with the letters of their names has Archepolis (ruler of the city)—and yet the meaning is the same. And there are many other names which just mean 'king.' Again, there are several names for a general, as, for example, Agis (leader) and Polemarchus (chief in war) and Eupolemus (good warrior); and others which denote a physician, as Iatrocles (famous healer) and Acesimbrotus (curer of mortals); and there are many others which might be cited, differing in their syllables and letters, but having the same meaning. Would you not say so?

HERMOGENES: Yes.

SOCRATES: The same names, then, ought to be assigned to those who follow in the course of nature?

HERMOGENES: Yes.

SOCRATES: And what of those who follow out of the course of nature, and are prodigies? for example, when a good and religious man has an irreligious son, he ought to bear the name not of his father, but of the class to which he belongs, just as in the case which was before supposed of a horse foaling a calf.

HERMOGENES: Quite true.

SOCRATES: Then the irreligious son of a religious father should be called irreligious?

HERMOGENES: Certainly.

SOCRATES: He should not be called Theophilus (beloved of God) or Mnesitheus (mindful of God), or any of these names: if names are correctly given, his should have an opposite meaning.

HERMOGENES: Certainly, Socrates.

SOCRATES: Again, Hermogenes, there is Orestes (the man of the mountains) who appears to be rightly called; whether chance gave the name, or perhaps some poet who meant to express the brutality and fierceness and mountain wildness of his hero's nature.

HERMOGENES: That is very likely, Socrates.

SOCRATES: And his father's name is also according to nature.

HERMOGENES: Clearly.

Cratylus

SOCRATES: Yes, for as his name, so also is his nature; Agamemnon (admirable for remaining) is one who is patient and persevering in the accomplishment of his resolves, and by his virtue crowns them; and his continuance at Troy with all the vast army is a proof of that admirable endurance in him which is signified by the name Agamemnon. I also think that Atreus is rightly called; for his murder of Chrysippus and his exceeding cruelty to Thyestes are damaging and destructive to his reputation—the name is a little altered and disguised so as not to be intelligible to every one, but to the etymologist there is no difficulty in seeing the meaning, for whether you think of him as *ateires* the stubborn, or as *atrestos* the fearless, or as *ateros* the destructive one, the name is perfectly correct in every point of view. And I think that Pelops is also named appropriately; for, as the name implies, he is rightly called Pelops who sees what is near only (*o ta pelas oron*).

HERMOGENES: How so?

SOCRATES: Because, according to the tradition, he had no forethought or foresight of all the evil which the murder of Myrtilus would entail upon his whole race in remote ages; he saw only what was at hand and immediate, —or in other words, *pelas* (near), in his eagerness to win Hippodamia by all means for his bride. Every one would agree that the name of Tantalus is rightly given and in accordance with nature, if the traditions about him are true.

HERMOGENES: And what are the traditions?

SOCRATES: Many terrible misfortunes are said to have happened to him in his life—last of all, came the utter ruin of his country; and after his death he had the stone suspended (*talanteia*) over his head in the world below—all this agrees wonderfully well with his name. You might imagine that some person who wanted to call him Talantatos (the most weighted down by misfortune), disguised the name by altering it into Tantalus; and into this form, by some accident of tradition, it has actually been transmuted. The name of Zeus, who is his alleged father, has also an excellent meaning, although hard to be understood, because really like a sentence, which is divided into two parts, for some call him Zena, and use the one half, and others who use the other half call him Dia; the two together signify the nature of the God, and the business of a name, as we were saying, is to express the nature. For there is none who is more the author of life to us and to all, than the lord and king of all. Wherefore we are right in calling him Zena and Dia, which are one name, although divided, meaning the God through whom all creatures always have life (*di on zen aei pasi tois zosin uparchei*). There is an irreverence, at first sight, in calling him son of Cronos (who is a proverb for stupidity), and we might rather expect Zeus to be the child of a mighty intellect. Which is the fact; for this is the meaning of his father's name: Kronos quasi Koros (Choreo, to sweep), not in the sense of a youth, but signifying to *chatharon chai acheraton tou nou*, the pure and garnished mind (sc. *apo tou chorein*). He, as we are informed by tradition, was begotten of Uranus, rightly so called (*apo tou oran ta ano*) from looking upwards; which, as philosophers tell us, is the way to have a pure mind, and the name Uranus is therefore correct. If I could remember the genealogy of Hesiod, I would have gone on and tried more conclusions of the same sort on the remoter ancestors of the Gods,—then I might have seen whether this wisdom, which has come to me all in an instant, I know not whence, will or will not hold good to the end.

HERMOGENES: You seem to me, Socrates, to be quite like a prophet newly inspired, and to be uttering oracles.

SOCRATES: Yes, Hermogenes, and I believe that I caught the inspiration from the great Euthyphro of the *Prospaltian deme*, who gave me a long lecture which commenced at dawn: he talked and I listened, and his wisdom and enchanting ravishment has not only filled my ears but taken possession of my soul, and to-day I shall let his superhuman power work and finish the investigation of names—that will be the way; but to-morrow, if you are so disposed, we will conjure him away, and make a purgation of him, if we can only find some priest or sophist who is skilled in purifications of this sort.

Cratylus

HERMOGENES: With all my heart; for am very curious to hear the rest of the enquiry about names.

SOCRATES: Then let us proceed; and where would you have us begin, now that we have got a sort of outline of the enquiry? Are there any names which witness of themselves that they are not given arbitrarily, but have a natural fitness? The names of heroes and of men in general are apt to be deceptive because they are often called after ancestors with whose names, as we were saying, they may have no business; or they are the expression of a wish like Eutychides (the son of good fortune), or Sosias (the Saviour), or Theophilus (the beloved of God), and others. But I think that we had better leave these, for there will be more chance of finding correctness in the names of immutable essences;—there ought to have been more care taken about them when they were named, and perhaps there may have been some more than human power at work occasionally in giving them names.

HERMOGENES: I think so, Socrates.

SOCRATES: Ought we not to begin with the consideration of the Gods, and show that they are rightly named Gods?

HERMOGENES: Yes, that will be well.

SOCRATES: My notion would be something of this sort:—I suspect that the sun, moon, earth, stars, and heaven, which are still the Gods of many barbarians, were the only Gods known to the aboriginal Hellenes. Seeing that they were always moving and running, from their running nature they were called Gods or runners (Theous, Theontas); and when men became acquainted with the other Gods, they proceeded to apply the same name to them all. Do you think that likely?

HERMOGENES: I think it very likely indeed.

SOCRATES: What shall follow the Gods?

HERMOGENES: Must not demons and heroes and men come next?

SOCRATES: Demons! And what do you consider to be the meaning of this word? Tell me if my view is right.

HERMOGENES: Let me hear.

SOCRATES: You know how Hesiod uses the word?

HERMOGENES: I do not.

SOCRATES: Do you not remember that he speaks of a golden race of men who came first?

HERMOGENES: Yes, I do.

SOCRATES: He says of them—

> 'But now that fate has closed over this race
> They are holy demons upon the earth,
> Beneficent, averters of ills, guardians of mortal men.'
> (Hesiod, Works and Days.)

HERMOGENES: What is the inference?

SOCRATES: What is the inference! Why, I suppose that he means by the golden men, not men literally made of gold, but good and noble; and I am convinced of this, because he further says that we are the iron race.

HERMOGENES: That is true.

SOCRATES: And do you not suppose that good men of our own day would by him be said to be of golden race?

HERMOGENES: Very likely.

Cratylus

SOCRATES: And are not the good wise?

HERMOGENES: Yes, they are wise.

SOCRATES: And therefore I have the most entire conviction that he called them demons, because they were *daemones* (knowing or wise), and in our older Attic dialect the word itself occurs. Now he and other poets say truly, that when a good man dies he has honour and a mighty portion among the dead, and becomes a demon; which is a name given to him signifying wisdom. And I say too, that every wise man who happens to be a good man is more than human (*daimonion*) both in life and death, and is rightly called a demon.

HERMOGENES: Then I rather think that I am of one mind with you; but what is the meaning of the word 'hero'? (Eros with an *eta*, in the old writing eros with an epsilon.)

SOCRATES: I think that there is no difficulty in explaining, for the name is not much altered, and signifies that they were born of love.

HERMOGENES: What do you mean?

SOCRATES: Do you not know that the heroes are demigods?

HERMOGENES: What then?

SOCRATES: All of them sprang either from the love of a God for a mortal woman, or of a mortal man for a Goddess; think of the word in the old Attic, and you will see better that the name *heros* is only a slight alteration of Eros, from whom the heroes sprang: either this is the meaning, or, if not this, then they must have been skilful as rhetoricians and dialecticians, and able to put the question (*erotan*), for eirein is equivalent to legein. And therefore, as I was saying, in the Attic dialect the heroes turn out to be rhetoricians and questioners. All this is easy enough; the noble breed of heroes are a tribe of sophists and rhetors. But can you tell me why men are called *anthropoi*?— that is more difficult.

Plato

HERMOGENES: No, I cannot; and I would not try even if I could, because I think that you are the more likely to succeed.

SOCRATES: That is to say, you trust to the inspiration of Euthyphro.

HERMOGENES: Of course.

SOCRATES: Your faith is not vain; for at this very moment a new and ingenious thought strikes me, and, if I am not careful, before to-morrow's dawn I shall be wiser than I ought to be. Now, attend to me; and first, remember that we often put in and pull out letters in words, and give names as we please and change the accents. Take, for example, the word *Dii* Philos; in order to convert this from a sentence into a noun, we omit one of the *iotas* and sound the middle syllable grave instead of acute; as, on the other hand, letters are sometimes inserted in words instead of being omitted, and the acute takes the place of the grave.

HERMOGENES: That is true.

SOCRATES: The name *anthropos*, which was once a sentence, and is now a noun, appears to be a case just of this sort, for one letter, which is the alpha, has been omitted, and the acute on the last syllable has been changed to a grave.

HERMOGENES: What do you mean?

SOCRATES: I mean to say that the word 'man' implies that other animals never examine, or consider, or look up at what they see, but that man not only sees (*opope*) but considers and looks up at that which he sees, and hence he alone of all animals is rightly *anthropos*, meaning *anathron* a *opopen*.

HERMOGENES: May I ask you to examine another word about which I am curious?

SOCRATES: Certainly.

Cratylus

HERMOGENES: I will take that which appears to me to follow next in order. You know the distinction of soul and body?

SOCRATES: Of course.

HERMOGENES: Let us endeavour to analyze them like the previous words.

SOCRATES: You want me first of all to examine the natural fitness of the word *psuche* (soul), and then of the word soma (body)?

HERMOGENES: Yes.

SOCRATES: If I am to say what occurs to me at the moment, I should imagine that those who first used the name *psuche* meant to express that the soul when in the body is the source of life, and gives the power of breath and revival (*anapsuchon*), and when this reviving power fails then the body perishes and dies, and this, if I am not mistaken, they called psyche. But please stay a moment; I fancy that I can discover something which will be more acceptable to the disciples of Euthyphro, for I am afraid that they will scorn this explanation. What do you say to another?

HERMOGENES: Let me hear.

SOCRATES: What is that which holds and carries and gives life and motion to the entire nature of the body? What else but the soul?

HERMOGENES: Just that.

SOCRATES: And do you not believe with Anaxagoras, that mind or soul is the ordering and containing principle of all things?

HERMOGENES: Yes; I do.

SOCRATES: Then you may well call that power *phuseche* which

Plato

carries and holds nature (*e phusin okei, kai ekei*), and this may be refined away into *psuche*.

HERMOGENES: Certainly; and this derivation is, I think, more scientific than the other.

SOCRATES: It is so; but I cannot help laughing, if I am to suppose that this was the true meaning of the name.

HERMOGENES: But what shall we say of the next word?

SOCRATES: You mean soma (the body).

HERMOGENES: Yes.

SOCRATES: That may be variously interpreted; and yet more variously if a little permutation is allowed. For some say that the body is the grave (*sema*) of the soul which may be thought to be buried in our present life; or again the index of the soul, because the soul gives indications to (*semainei*) the body; probably the Orphic poets were the inventors of the name, and they were under the impression that the soul is suffering the punishment of sin, and that the body is an enclosure or prison in which the soul is incarcerated, kept safe (soma, *sozetai*), as the name soma implies, until the penalty is paid; according to this view, not even a letter of the word need be changed.

HERMOGENES: I think, Socrates, that we have said enough of this class of words. But have we any more explanations of the names of the Gods, like that which you were giving of Zeus? I should like to know whether any similar principle of correctness is to be applied to them.

SOCRATES: Yes, indeed, Hermogenes; and there is one excellent principle which, as men of sense, we must acknowledge,—that of the Gods we know nothing, either of their natures or of the names which they give themselves; but we are sure that the names by which they call themselves, whatever they may be, are true. And this is the

Cratylus

best of all principles; and the next best is to say, as in prayers, that we will call them by any sort or kind of names or patronymics which they like, because we do not know of any other. That also, I think, is a very good custom, and one which I should much wish to observe. Let us, then, if you please, in the first place announce to them that we are not enquiring about them; we do not presume that we are able to do so; but we are enquiring about the meaning of men in giving them these names,—in this there can be small blame.

HERMOGENES: I think, Socrates, that you are quite right, and I would like to do as you say.

SOCRATES: Shall we begin, then, with Hestia, according to custom?

HERMOGENES: Yes, that will be very proper.

SOCRATES: What may we suppose him to have meant who gave the name Hestia?

HERMOGENES: That is another and certainly a most difficult question.

SOCRATES: My dear Hermogenes, the first imposers of names must surely have been considerable persons; they were philosophers, and had a good deal to say.

HERMOGENES: Well, and what of them?

SOCRATES: They are the men to whom I should attribute the imposition of names. Even in foreign names, if you analyze them, a meaning is still discernible. For example, that which we term *ousia* is by some called *esia*, and by others again *osia*. Now that the essence of things should be called *estia*, which is akin to the first of these (*esia* = *estia*), is rational enough. And there is reason in the Athenians calling that estia which participates in *ousia*. For in ancient times we too seem to have said *esia* for *ousia*, and this you may note to have been the idea of those who appointed that sacrifices should be first offered to *estia*, which was natural enough if they meant that *estia* was the essence of things. Those again who read *osia* seem to have inclined to the opinion of Heracleitus, that all things flow and nothing stands; with them the pushing principle (*othoun*) is the cause and ruling power of all things, and is therefore rightly called *osia*. Enough of this, which is all that we who know nothing can affirm. Next in order after Hestia we ought to consider Rhea and Cronos, although the name of Cronos has been already discussed. But I dare say that I am talking great nonsense.

HERMOGENES: Why, Socrates?

SOCRATES: My good friend, I have discovered a hive of wisdom.

HERMOGENES: Of what nature?

SOCRATES: Well, rather ridiculous, and yet plausible.

HERMOGENES: How plausible?

SOCRATES: I fancy to myself Heracleitus repeating wise traditions of antiquity as old as the days of Cronos and Rhea, and of which Homer also spoke.

HERMOGENES: How do you mean?

SOCRATES: Heracleitus is supposed to say that all things are in motion and nothing at rest; he compares them to the stream of a river, and says that you cannot go into the same water twice.

HERMOGENES: That is true.

SOCRATES: Well, then, how can we avoid inferring that he who gave the names of Cronos and Rhea to the ancestors of the Gods, agreed pretty much in the doctrine of Heracleitus? Is the giving of the names of streams to both of them purely accidental? Compare

Cratylus

the line in which Homer, and, as I believe, Hesiod also, tells of

> 'Ocean, the origin of Gods, and mother Tethys
> (Il.—the line is not found in the extant works of Hesiod.).'

And again, Orpheus says, that

> 'The fair river of Ocean was the first to marry, and he espoused his sister Tethys, who was his mother's daughter.'

You see that this is a remarkable coincidence, and all in the direction of Heracleitus.

HERMOGENES: I think that there is something in what you say, Socrates; but I do not understand the meaning of the name Tethys.

SOCRATES: Well, that is almost self-explained, being only the name of a spring, a little disguised; for that which is strained and filtered (*diattomenon, ethoumenon*) may be likened to a spring, and the name Tethys is made up of these two words.

HERMOGENES: The idea is ingenious, Socrates.

SOCRATES: To be sure. But what comes next?—of Zeus we have spoken.

HERMOGENES: Yes.

SOCRATES: Then let us next take his two brothers, Poseidon and Pluto, whether the latter is called by that or by his other name.

HERMOGENES: By all means.

SOCRATES: Poseidon is Posidesmos, the chain of the feet; the original inventor of the name had been stopped by the watery element in his walks, and not allowed to go on, and therefore he called the ruler of this element Poseidon; the epsilon was probably inserted as an ornament. Yet, perhaps, not so; but the name may have been originally written with a double *lamda* and not with a sigma, meaning that the God knew many things (*Polla eidos*). And perhaps also he being the shaker of the earth, has been named from shaking (*seiein*), and then pi and delta have been added. Pluto gives wealth (Ploutos), and his name means the giver of wealth, which comes out of the earth beneath. People in general appear to imagine that the term Hades is connected with the invisible (*aeides*) and so they are led by their fears to call the God Pluto instead.

HERMOGENES: And what is the true derivation?

SOCRATES: In spite of the mistakes which are made about the power of this deity, and the foolish fears which people have of him, such as the fear of always being with him after death, and of the soul denuded of the body going to him (compare Rep.), my belief is that all is quite consistent, and that the office and name of the God really correspond.

HERMOGENES: Why, how is that?

SOCRATES: I will tell you my own opinion; but first, I should like to ask you which chain does any animal feel to be the stronger? and which confines him more to the same spot,—desire or necessity?

HERMOGENES: Desire, Socrates, is stronger far.

SOCRATES: And do you not think that many a one would escape from Hades, if he did not bind those who depart to him by the strongest of chains?

HERMOGENES: Assuredly they would.

SOCRATES: And if by the greatest of chains, then by some desire, as I should certainly infer, and not by necessity?

HERMOGENES: That is clear.

Cratylus

SOCRATES: And there are many desires?

HERMOGENES: Yes.

SOCRATES: And therefore by the greatest desire, if the chain is to be the greatest?

HERMOGENES: Yes.

SOCRATES: And is any desire stronger than the thought that you will be made better by associating with another?

HERMOGENES: Certainly not.

SOCRATES: And is not that the reason, Hermogenes, why no one, who has been to him, is willing to come back to us? Even the Sirens, like all the rest of the world, have been laid under his spells. Such a charm, as I imagine, is the God able to infuse into his words. And, according to this view, he is the perfect and accomplished Sophist, and the great benefactor of the inhabitants of the other world; and even to us who are upon earth he sends from below exceeding blessings. For he has much more than he wants down there; wherefore he is called Pluto (or the rich). Note also, that he will have nothing to do with men while they are in the body, but only when the soul is liberated from the desires and evils of the body. Now there is a great deal of philosophy and reflection in that; for in their liberated state he can bind them with the desire of virtue, but while they are flustered and maddened by the body, not even father Cronos himself would suffice to keep them with him in his own far-famed chains.

HERMOGENES: There is a deal of truth in what you say.

SOCRATES: Yes, Hermogenes, and the legislator called him Hades, not from the unseen (*aeides*)—far otherwise, but from his knowledge (*eidenai*) of all noble things.

HERMOGENES: Very good; and what do we say of Demeter, and

Here, and Apollo, and Athene, and Hephaestus, and Ares, and the other deities?

SOCRATES: Demeter is e didousa meter, who gives food like a mother; Here is the lovely one (*erate*)—for Zeus, according to tradition, loved and married her; possibly also the name may have been given when the legislator was thinking of the heavens, and may be only a disguise of the air (*aer*), putting the end in the place of the beginning. You will recognize the truth of this if you repeat the letters of Here several times over. People dread the name of Pherephatta as they dread the name of Apollo,—and with as little reason; the fear, if I am not mistaken, only arises from their ignorance of the nature of names. But they go changing the name into Phersephone, and they are terrified at this; whereas the new name means only that the Goddess is wise (*sophe*); for seeing that all things in the world are in motion (*pheromenon*), that principle which embraces and touches and is able to follow them, is wisdom. And therefore the Goddess may be truly called Pherepaphe (Pherepapha), or some name like it, because she touches that which is in motion (*tou pheromenon ephaptomene*), herein showing her wisdom. And Hades, who is wise, consorts with her, because she is wise. They alter her name into Pherephatta now-a-days, because the present generation care for euphony more than truth. There is the other name, Apollo, which, as I was saying, is generally supposed to have some terrible signification. Have you remarked this fact?

HERMOGENES: To be sure I have, and what you say is true.

SOCRATES: But the name, in my opinion, is really most expressive of the power of the God.

HERMOGENES: How so?

SOCRATES: I will endeavour to explain, for I do not believe that any single name could have been better adapted to express the attributes of the God, embracing and in a manner signifying all four of them,—music, and prophecy, and medicine, and archery.

HERMOGENES: That must be a strange name, and I should like to hear the explanation.

SOCRATES: Say rather an harmonious name, as beseems the God of Harmony. In the first place, the purgations and purifications which doctors and diviners use, and their fumigations with drugs magical or medicinal, as well as their washings and lustral sprinklings, have all one and the same object, which is to make a man pure both in body and soul.

HERMOGENES: Very true.

SOCRATES: And is not Apollo the purifier, and the washer, and the absolver from all impurities?

HERMOGENES: Very true.

SOCRATES: Then in reference to his ablutions and absolutions, as being the physician who orders them, he may be rightly called Apolouon (purifier); or in respect of his powers of divination, and his truth and sincerity, which is the same as truth, he may be most fitly called Aplos, from *aplous* (sincere), as in the Thessalian dialect, for all the Thessalians call him Aplos; also he is aei Ballon (always shooting), because he is a master archer who never misses; or again, the name may refer to his musical attributes, and then, as in *akolouthos*, and *akoitis*, and in many other words the alpha is supposed to mean 'together,' so the meaning of the name Apollo will be 'moving together,' whether in the poles of heaven as they are called, or in the harmony of song, which is termed concord, because he moves all together by an harmonious power, as astronomers and musicians ingeniously declare. And he is the God who presides over harmony, and makes all things move together, both among Gods and among men. And as in the words *akolouthos* and *akoitis* the alpha is substituted for an omicron, so the name Apollon is equivalent to *omopolon*; only the second lambda is added in order to avoid the ill-omened sound of destruction (*apolon*). Now the suspicion of this destructive power still haunts the minds of some who do not consider the true value of the name, which, as I was saying just now, has reference to all the powers of the God, who is the single one, the everdarting, the purifier, the mover together (*aplous, aei Ballon, apolouon, omopolon*). The name of the Muses and of music would seem to be derived from their making philosophical enquiries (*mosthai*); and Leto is called by this name, because she is such a gentle Goddess, and so willing (*ethelemon*) to grant our requests; or her name may be Letho, as she is often called by strangers—they seem to imply by it her amiability, and her smooth and easy-going way of behaving. Artemis is named from her healthy (artemes), well-ordered nature, and because of her love of virginity, perhaps because she is a proficient in virtue (arete), and perhaps also as hating intercourse of the sexes (*ton aroton misesasa*). He who gave the Goddess her name may have had any or all of these reasons.

HERMOGENES: What is the meaning of Dionysus and Aphrodite?

SOCRATES: Son of Hipponicus, you ask a solemn question; there is a serious and also a facetious explanation of both these names; the serious explanation is not to be had from me, but there is no objection to your hearing the facetious one; for the Gods too love a joke. Dionusos is simply *didous* oinon (giver of wine), Didoinusos, as he might be called in fun,—and oinos is properly *oionous*, because wine makes those who drink, think (*oiesthai*) that they have a mind (noun) when they have none. The derivation of Aphrodite, born of the foam (*aphros*), may be fairly accepted on the authority of Hesiod.

HERMOGENES: Still there remains Athene, whom you, Socrates, as an Athenian, will surely not forget; there are also Hephaestus and Ares.

SOCRATES: I am not likely to forget them.

HERMOGENES: No, indeed.

SOCRATES: There is no difficulty in explaining the other appellation of Athene.

Cratylus

HERMOGENES: What other appellation?

SOCRATES: We call her Pallas.

HERMOGENES: To be sure.

SOCRATES: And we cannot be wrong in supposing that this is derived from armed dances. For the elevation of oneself or anything else above the earth, or by the use of the hands, we call shaking (*pallein*), or dancing.

HERMOGENES: That is quite true.

SOCRATES: Then that is the explanation of the name Pallas?

HERMOGENES: Yes; but what do you say of the other name?

SOCRATES: Athene?

HERMOGENES: Yes.

SOCRATES: That is a graver matter, and there, my friend, the modern interpreters of Homer may, I think, assist in explaining the view of the ancients. For most of these in their explanations of the poet, assert that he meant by Athene 'mind' (*nous*) and 'intelligence' (*dianoia*), and the maker of names appears to have had a singular notion about her; and indeed calls her by a still higher title, 'divine intelligence' (Thou *noesis*), as though he would say: This is she who has the mind of God (Theonoa);—using alpha as a dialectical variety for eta, and taking away iota and sigma (There seems to be some error in the MSS. The meaning is that the word *theonoa* = *theounoa* is a curtailed form of *theou noesis*, but the omitted letters do not agree.). Perhaps, however, the name Theonoe may mean 'she who knows divine things' (*Theia noousa*) better than others. Nor shall we be far wrong in supposing that the author of it wished to identify this Goddess with moral intelligence (*en ethei noesin*), and therefore gave her the name *ethonoe*; which, however, either he or his successors have altered into what they thought a nicer form, and called her Athene.

HERMOGENES: But what do you say of Hephaestus?

SOCRATES: Speak you of the princely lord of light (*Phaeos istora*)?

HERMOGENES: Surely.

SOCRATES: Ephaistos is Phaistos, and has added the *eta* by attraction; that is obvious to anybody.

HERMOGENES: That is very probable, until some more probable notion gets into your head.

SOCRATES: To prevent that, you had better ask what is the derivation of Ares.

HERMOGENES: What is Ares?

SOCRATES: Ares may be called, if you will, from his manhood (*arren*) and manliness, or if you please, from his hard and unchangeable nature, which is the meaning of *arratos*: the latter is a derivation in every way appropriate to the God of war.

HERMOGENES: Very true.

SOCRATES: And now, by the Gods, let us have no more of the Gods, for I am afraid of them; ask about anything but them, and thou shalt see how the steeds of Euthyphro can prance.

HERMOGENES: Only one more God! I should like to know about Hermes, of whom I am said not to be a true son. Let us make him out, and then I shall know whether there is any meaning in what Cratylus says.

SOCRATES: I should imagine that the name Hermes has to do

Cratylus

with speech, and signifies that he is the interpreter (*ermeneus*), or messenger, or thief, or liar, or bargainer; all that sort of thing has a great deal to do with language; as I was telling you, the word *eirein* is expressive of the use of speech, and there is an often-recurring Homeric word *emesato*, which means 'he contrived'—out of these two words, *eirein* and *mesasthai*, the legislator formed the name of the God who invented language and speech; and we may imagine him dictating to us the use of this name: 'O my friends,' says he to us, 'seeing that he is the contriver of tales or speeches, you may rightly call him Eirhemes.' And this has been improved by us, as we think, into Hermes. Iris also appears to have been called from the verb 'to tell' (*eirein*), because she was a messenger.

HERMOGENES: Then I am very sure that Cratylus was quite right in saying that I was no true son of Hermes (Ermogenes), for I am not a good hand at speeches.

SOCRATES: There is also reason, my friend, in Pan being the double-formed son of Hermes.

HERMOGENES: How do you make that out?

SOCRATES: You are aware that speech signifies all things (pan), and is always turning them round and round, and has two forms, true and false?

HERMOGENES: Certainly.

SOCRATES: Is not the truth that is in him the smooth or sacred form which dwells above among the Gods, whereas falsehood dwells among men below, and is rough like the goat of tragedy; for tales and falsehoods have generally to do with the tragic or goatish life, and tragedy is the place of them?

HERMOGENES: Very true.

SOCRATES: Then surely Pan, who is the declarer of all things (*pan*) and the perpetual mover (*aei polon*) of all things, is rightly called *aipolos* (goat-herd), he being the two-formed son of Hermes, smooth in his upper part, and rough and goatlike in his lower regions. And, as the son of Hermes, he is speech or the brother of speech, and that brother should be like brother is no marvel. But, as I was saying, my dear Hermogenes, let us get away from the Gods.

HERMOGENES: From these sort of Gods, by all means, Socrates. But why should we not discuss another kind of Gods—the sun, moon, stars, earth, aether, air, fire, water, the seasons, and the year?

SOCRATES: You impose a great many tasks upon me. Still, if you wish, I will not refuse.

HERMOGENES: You will oblige me.

SOCRATES: How would you have me begin? Shall I take first of all him whom you mentioned first—the sun?

HERMOGENES: Very good.

SOCRATES: The origin of the sun will probably be clearer in the Doric form, for the Dorians call him *alios*, and this name is given to him because when he rises he gathers (*alizoi*) men together or because he is always rolling in his course (*aei eilein* ion) about the earth; or from *aiolein*, of which the meaning is the same as *poikillein* (to variegate), because he variegates the productions of the earth.

HERMOGENES: But what is *selene* (the moon)?

SOCRATES: That name is rather unfortunate for Anaxagoras.

HERMOGENES: How so?

SOCRATES: The word seems to forestall his recent discovery, that the moon receives her light from the sun.

HERMOGENES: Why do you say so?

Cratylus

SOCRATES: The two words *selas* (brightness) and *phos* (light) have much the same meaning?

HERMOGENES: Yes.

SOCRATES: This light about the moon is always new (*neon*) and always old (*enon*), if the disciples of Anaxagoras say truly. For the sun in his revolution always adds new light, and there is the old light of the previous month.

HERMOGENES: Very true.

SOCRATES: The moon is not unfrequently called *selanaia*.

HERMOGENES: True.

SOCRATES: And as she has a light which is always old and always new (*enon neon aei*) she may very properly have the name *selaenoneoaeia*; and this when hammered into shape becomes *selanaia*.

HERMOGENES: A real dithyrambic sort of name that, Socrates. But what do you say of the month and the stars?

SOCRATES: *Meis* (month) is called from *meiousthai* (to lessen), because suffering diminution; the name of *astra* (stars) seems to be derived from *astrape*, which is an improvement on *anastrope*, signifying the upsetting of the eyes (*anastrephein opa*).

HERMOGENES: What do you say of *pur* (fire) and *udor* (water)?

SOCRATES: I am at a loss how to explain *pur*; either the muse of Euthyphro has deserted me, or there is some very great difficulty in the word. Please, however, to note the contrivance which I adopt whenever I am in a difficulty of this sort.

HERMOGENES: What is it?

Plato

SOCRATES: I will tell you; but I should like to know first whether you can tell me what is the meaning of the *pur*?

HERMOGENES: Indeed I cannot.

SOCRATES: Shall I tell you what I suspect to be the true explanation of this and several other words?—My belief is that they are of foreign origin. For the Hellenes, especially those who were under the dominion of the barbarians, often borrowed from them.

HERMOGENES: What is the inference?

SOCRATES: Why, you know that any one who seeks to demonstrate the fitness of these names according to the Hellenic language, and not according to the language from which the words are derived, is rather likely to be at fault.

HERMOGENES: Yes, certainly.

SOCRATES: Well then, consider whether this *pur* is not foreign; for the word is not easily brought into relation with the Hellenic tongue, and the Phrygians may be observed to have the same word slightly changed, just as they have *udor* (water) and *kunes* (dogs), and many other words.

HERMOGENES: That is true.

SOCRATES: Any violent interpretations of the words should be avoided; for something to say about them may easily be found. And thus I get rid of *pur* and *udor*. *Aer* (air), Hermogenes, may be explained as the element which raises (airei) things from the earth, or as ever flowing (*aei rei*), or because the flux of the air is wind, and the poets call the winds 'air-blasts,' (*aetai*); he who uses the term may mean, so to speak, air-flux (*aetorroun*), in the sense of wind-flux (*pneumatorroun*); and because this moving wind may be expressed by either term he employs the word air (*aer* = *aetes rheo*). Aither (*aether*) I should interpret as aeitheer; this may be correctly

Cratylus

said, because this element is always running in a flux about the air (*aei thei peri tou aera reon*). The meaning of the word *ge* (earth) comes out better when in the form of *gaia*, for the earth may be truly called 'mother' (*gaia, genneteira*), as in the language of Homer (Od.) *gegaasi* means *gegennesthai*.

HERMOGENES: Good.

SOCRATES: What shall we take next?

HERMOGENES: There are *orai* (the seasons), and the two names of the year, *eniautos* and *etos*.

SOCRATES: The *orai* should be spelt in the old Attic way, if you desire to know the probable truth about them; they are rightly called the orai because they divide (*orizousin*) the summers and winters and winds and the fruits of the earth. The words *eniautos* and *etos* appear to be the same,— 'that which brings to light the plants and growths of the earth in their turn, and passes them in review within itself (*en eauto exetazei*)': this is broken up into two words, *eniautos* from *en eauto*, and *etos* from *etazei*, just as the original name of Zeus was divided into Zena and Dia; and the whole proposition means that his power of reviewing from within is one, but has two names, two words *etos* and *eniautos* being thus formed out of a single proposition.

HERMOGENES: Indeed, Socrates, you make surprising progress.

SOCRATES: I am run away with.

HERMOGENES: Very true.

SOCRATES: But am not yet at my utmost speed.

HERMOGENES: I should like very much to know, in the next place, how you would explain the virtues. What principle of correctness is there in those charming words—wisdom, understanding, justice, and the rest of them?

SOCRATES: That is a tremendous class of names which you are disinterring; still, as I have put on the lion's skin, I must not be faint of heart; and I suppose that I must consider the meaning of wisdom (*phronesis*) and understanding (*sunesis*), and judgment (*gnome*), and knowledge (*episteme*), and all those other charming words, as you call them?

HERMOGENES: Surely, we must not leave off until we find out their meaning.

SOCRATES: By the dog of Egypt I have a not bad notion which came into my head only this moment: I believe that the primeval givers of names were undoubtedly like too many of our modern philosophers, who, in their search after the nature of things, are always getting dizzy from constantly going round and round, and then they imagine that the world is going round and round and moving in all directions; and this appearance, which arises out of their own internal condition, they suppose to be a reality of nature; they think that there is nothing stable or permanent, but only flux and motion, and that the world is always full of every sort of motion and change. The consideration of the names which I mentioned has led me into making this reflection.

HERMOGENES: How is that, Socrates?

SOCRATES: Perhaps you did not observe that in the names which have been just cited, the motion or flux or generation of things is most surely indicated.

HERMOGENES: No, indeed, I never thought of it.

SOCRATES: Take the first of those which you mentioned; clearly that is a name indicative of motion.

HERMOGENES: What was the name?

SOCRATES: *Phronesis* (wisdom), which may signify *phoras kai rhou noesis* (perception of motion and flux), or perhaps *phoras onesis* (the blessing of motion), but is at any rate connected with *pheresthai* (motion); gnome (judgment), again, certainly implies the ponderation or consideration (*nomesis*) of generation, for to ponder is the same as to consider; or, if you would rather, here is *noesis*, the very word just now mentioned, which is *neou esis* (the desire of the new); the word neos implies that the world is always in process of creation. The giver of the name wanted to express this longing of the soul, for the original name was *neoesis*, and not *noesis*; but eta took the place of a double epsilon. The word *sophrosune* is the salvation (*soteria*) of that wisdom (*phronesis*) which we were just now considering. *Epioteme* (knowledge) is akin to this, and indicates that the soul which is good for anything follows (*epetai*) the motion of things, neither anticipating them nor falling behind them; wherefore the word should rather be read as *epistemene*, inserting epsilon nu. *Sunesis* (understanding) may be regarded in like manner as a kind of conclusion; the word is derived from *sunienai* (to go along with), and, like *epistasthai* (to know), implies the progression of the soul in company with the nature of things. Sophia (wisdom) is very dark, and appears not to be of native growth; the meaning is, touching the motion or stream of things. You must remember that the poets, when they speak of the commencement of any rapid motion, often use the word *esuthe* (he rushed); and there was a famous Lacedaemonian who was named *Sous* (Rush), for by this word the Lacedaemonians signify rapid motion, and the touching (*epaphe*) of motion is expressed by *sophia*, for all things are supposed to be in motion. Good (*agathon*) is the name which is given to the admirable (*agasto*) in nature; for, although all things move, still there are degrees of motion; some are swifter, some slower; but there are some things which are admirable for their swiftness, and this admirable part of nature is called *agathon*. *Dikaiosune* (justice) is clearly *dikaiou sunesis* (understanding of the just); but the actual word dikaion is more difficult: men are only agreed to a certain extent about justice, and then they begin to disagree. For those who suppose all things to be in motion conceive the greater part of nature to be a mere receptacle; and they say that there is a penetrating power which passes through all this, and is the instrument of creation in all, and is the subtlest and swiftest element; for if it were not the subtlest, and a power which none can keep out, and also the swiftest, passing by other things as if they were standing still, it could not penetrate through the moving universe. And this element, which superintends all things and pierces (*diaion*) all, is rightly called dikaion; the letter k is only added for the sake of euphony. Thus far, as I was saying, there is a general agreement about the nature of justice; but I, Hermogenes, being an enthusiastic disciple, have been told in a mystery that the justice of which I am speaking is also the cause of the world: now a cause is that because of which anything is created; and some one comes and whispers in my ear that justice is rightly so called because partaking of the nature of the cause, and I begin, after hearing what he has said, to interrogate him gently: 'Well, my excellent friend,' say I, 'but if all this be true, I still want to know what is justice.' Thereupon they think that I ask tiresome questions, and am leaping over the barriers, and have been already sufficiently answered, and they try to satisfy me with one derivation after another, and at length they quarrel. For one of them says that justice is the sun, and that he only is the piercing (*diaionta*) and burning (*kaonta*) element which is the guardian of nature. And when I joyfully repeat this beautiful notion, I am answered by the satirical remark, 'What, is there no justice in the world when the sun is down?' And when I earnestly beg my questioner to tell me his own honest opinion, he says, 'Fire in the abstract'; but this is not very intelligible. Another says, 'No, not fire in the abstract, but the abstraction of heat in the fire.' Another man professes to laugh at all this, and says, as Anaxagoras says, that justice is mind, for mind, as they say, has absolute power, and mixes with nothing, and orders all things, and passes through all things. At last, my friend, I find myself in far greater perplexity about the nature of justice than I was before I began to learn. But still I am of opinion that the name, which has led me into this digression, was given to justice for the reasons which I have mentioned.

HERMOGENES: I think, Socrates, that you are not improvising now; you must have heard this from some one else.

Cratylus

SOCRATES: And not the rest?

HERMOGENES: Hardly.

SOCRATES: Well, then, let me go on in the hope of making you believe in the originality of the rest. What remains after justice? I do not think that we have as yet discussed courage (*andreia*),—injustice (*adikia*), which is obviously nothing more than a hindrance to the penetrating principle (diaiontos), need not be considered. Well, then, the name of *andreia* seems to imply a battle;—this battle is in the world of existence, and according to the doctrine of flux is only the *counterflux* (*enantia rhon*): if you extract the delta from *andreia*, the name at once signifies the thing, and you may clearly understand that andreia is not the stream opposed to every stream, but only to that which is contrary to justice, for otherwise courage would not have been praised. The words *arren* (male) and *aner* (man) also contain a similar allusion to the same principle of the upward flux (*te ano rhon*). *Gune* (woman) I suspect to be the same word as *goun* (birth): *thelu* (female) appears to be partly derived from *thele* (the teat), because the teat is like rain, and makes things flourish (*tethelenai*).

HERMOGENES: That is surely probable.

SOCRATES: Yes; and the very word *thallein* (to flourish) seems to figure the growth of youth, which is swift and sudden ever. And this is expressed by the legislator in the name, which is a compound of *thein* (running), and *allesthai* (leaping). Pray observe how I gallop away when I get on smooth ground. There are a good many names generally thought to be of importance, which have still to be explained.

HERMOGENES: True.

SOCRATES: There is the meaning of the word *techne* (art), for example.

HERMOGENES: Very true.

SOCRATES: That may be identified with *echonoe*, and expresses the possession of mind: you have only to take away the *tau* and insert two *omichrons*, one between the chi and nu, and another between the *nu* and eta.

HERMOGENES: That is a very shabby etymology.

SOCRATES: Yes, my dear friend; but then you know that the original names have been long ago buried and disguised by people sticking on and stripping off letters for the sake of euphony, and twisting and bedizening them in all sorts of ways: and time too may have had a share in the change. Take, for example, the word *katoptron*; why is the letter *rho* inserted? This must surely be the addition of some one who cares nothing about the truth, but thinks only of putting the mouth into shape. And the additions are often such that at last no human being can possibly make out the original meaning of the word. Another example is the word *sphigx*, *sphiggos*, which ought properly to be *phigx*, *phiggos*, and there are other examples.

HERMOGENES: That is quite true, Socrates.

SOCRATES: And yet, if you are permitted to put in and pull out any letters which you please, names will be too easily made, and any name may be adapted to any object.

HERMOGENES: True.

SOCRATES: Yes, that is true. And therefore a wise dictator, like yourself, should observe the laws of moderation and probability.

HERMOGENES: Such is my desire.

SOCRATES: And mine, too, Hermogenes. But do not be too much of a precisian, or 'you will unnerve me of my strength (Iliad.).' When you have allowed me to add *mechane* (contrivance) to *techne* (art) I shall be

Cratylus

at the top of my bent, for I conceive *mechane* to be a sign of great accomplishment—*anein*; for *mekos* has the meaning of greatness, and these two, *mekos* and *anein*, make up the word *mechane*. But, as I was saying, being now at the top of my bent, I should like to consider the meaning of the two words *arete* (virtue) and *kakia* (vice); *arete* I do not as yet understand, but *kakia* is transparent, and agrees with the principles which preceded, for all things being in a flux (*ionton*), *kakia* is *kakos* ion (going badly); and this evil motion when existing in the soul has the general name of *kakia*, or vice, specially appropriated to it. The meaning of *kakos ienai* may be further illustrated by the use of *deilia* (cowardice), which ought to have come after *andreia*, but was forgotten, and, as I fear, is not the only word which has been passed over. *Deilia* signifies that the soul is bound with a strong chain (*desmos*), for *lian* means strength, and therefore *deilia* expresses the greatest and strongest bond of the soul; and *aporia* (difficulty) is an evil of the same nature (from a (*alpha*) not, and *poreuesthai* to go), like anything else which is an impediment to motion and movement. Then the word *kakia* appears to mean *kakos ienai*, or going badly, or limping and halting; of which the consequence is, that the soul becomes filled with vice. And if *kakia* is the name of this sort of thing, *arete* will be the opposite of it, signifying in the first place ease of motion, then that the stream of the good soul is unimpeded, and has therefore the attribute of ever flowing without let or hindrance, and is therefore called *arete*, or, more correctly, *aeireite* (ever-flowing), and may perhaps have had another form, *airete* (eligible), indicating that nothing is more eligible than virtue, and this has been hammered into *arete*. I daresay that you will deem this to be another invention of mine, but I think that if the previous word *kakia* was right, then *arete* is also right.

HERMOGENES: But what is the meaning of *kakon*, which has played so great a part in your previous discourse?

SOCRATES: That is a very singular word about which I can hardly form an opinion, and therefore I must have recourse to my ingenious device.

HERMOGENES: What device?

SOCRATES: The device of a foreign origin, which I shall give to this word also.

HERMOGENES: Very likely you are right; but suppose that we leave these words and endeavour to see the rationale of *kalon* and *aischron*.

SOCRATES: The meaning of *aischron* is evident, being only *aei ischon roes* (always preventing from flowing), and this is in accordance with our former derivations. For the name-giver was a great enemy to stagnation of all sorts, and hence he gave the name *aeischoroun* to that which hindered the flux (*aei ischon roun*), and that is now beaten together into *aischron*.

HERMOGENES: But what do you say of *kalon*?

SOCRATES: That is more obscure; yet the form is only due to the quantity, and has been changed by altering omicron upsilon into omicron.

HERMOGENES: What do you mean?

SOCRATES: This name appears to denote mind.

HERMOGENES: How so?

SOCRATES: Let me ask you what is the cause why anything has a name; is not the principle which imposes the name the cause?

HERMOGENES: Certainly.

SOCRATES: And must not this be the mind of Gods, or of men, or of both?

HERMOGENES: Yes.

SOCRATES: Is not mind that which called (*kalesan*) things by their names, and is not mind the beautiful (*kalon*)?

HERMOGENES: That is evident.

SOCRATES: And are not the works of intelligence and mind worthy of praise, and are not other works worthy of blame?

HERMOGENES: Certainly.

SOCRATES: Physic does the work of a physician, and carpentering does the works of a carpenter?

HERMOGENES: Exactly.

SOCRATES: And the principle of beauty does the works of beauty?

HERMOGENES: Of course.

SOCRATES: And that principle we affirm to be mind?

HERMOGENES: Very true.

SOCRATES: Then mind is rightly called beauty because she does the works which we recognize and speak of as the beautiful?

HERMOGENES: That is evident.

SOCRATES: What more names remain to us?

HERMOGENES: There are the words which are connected with *agathon* and *kalon*, such as *sumpheron* and *lusiteloun*, *ophelimon*, *kerdaleon*, and their opposites.

SOCRATES: The meaning of *sumpheron* (expedient) I think that you may discover for yourself by the light of the previous examples,— for it is a sister word to *episteme*, meaning just the motion (*pora*) of the soul accompanying the world, and things which are done upon this principle are called *sumphora* or *sumpheronta*, because they are carried round with the world.

HERMOGENES: That is probable.

SOCRATES: Again, *cherdaleon* (gainful) is called from *cherdos* (gain), but you must alter the delta into *nu* if you want to get at the meaning; for this word also signifies good, but in another way; he who gave the name intended to express the power of admixture (*kerannumenon*) and universal penetration in the good; in forming the word, however, he inserted a delta instead of a *nu*, and so made *kerdos*.

HERMOGENES: Well, but what is *lusiteloun* (profitable)?

SOCRATES: I suppose, Hermogenes, that people do not mean by the profitable the gainful or that which pays (*luei*) the retailer, but they use the word in the sense of swift. You regard the profitable (*lusiteloun*), as that which being the swiftest thing in existence, allows of no stay in things and no pause or end of motion, but always, if there begins to be any end, lets things go again (*luei*), and makes motion immortal and unceasing: and in this point of view, as appears to me, the good is happily denominated lusiteloun—being that which looses (*luon*) the end (*telos*) of motion. *Ophelimon* (the advantageous) is derived from *ophellein*, meaning that which creates and increases; this latter is a common Homeric word, and has a foreign character.

HERMOGENES: And what do you say of their opposites?

SOCRATES: Of such as are mere negatives I hardly think that I need speak.

HERMOGENES: Which are they?

SOCRATES: The words *axumphoron* (inexpedient), *anopheles* (unprofitable), *alusiteles* (unadvantageous), *akerdes* (ungainful).

HERMOGENES: True.

SOCRATES: I would rather take the words *blaberon* (harmful), *zemiodes* (hurtful).

Cratylus

HERMOGENES: Good.

SOCRATES: The word *blaberon* is that which is said to hinder or harm (blaptein) the stream (roun); *blapton* is *boulomenon aptein* (seeking to hold or bind); for aptein is the same as *dein*, and *dein* is always a term of censure; *boulomenon aptein roun* (wanting to bind the stream) would properly be *boulapteroun*, and this, as I imagine, is improved into *blaberon*.

HERMOGENES: You bring out curious results, Socrates, in the use of names; and when I hear the word boulapteroun I cannot help imagining that you are making your mouth into a flute, and puffing away at some prelude to Athene.

SOCRATES: That is the fault of the makers of the name, Hermogenes; not mine.

HERMOGENES: Very true; but what is the derivation of zemiodes?

SOCRATES: What is the meaning of *zemiodes?*—let me remark, Hermogenes, how right I was in saying that great changes are made in the meaning of words by putting in and pulling out letters; even a very slight permutation will sometimes give an entirely opposite sense; I may instance the word *deon*, which occurs to me at the moment, and reminds me of what I was going to say to you, that the fine fashionable language of modern times has twisted and disguised and entirely altered the original meaning both of deon, and also of *zemiodes*, which in the old language is clearly indicated.

HERMOGENES: What do you mean?

SOCRATES: I will try to explain. You are aware that our forefathers loved the sounds iota and delta, especially the women, who are most conservative of the ancient language, but now they change *iota* into *eta* or epsilon, and delta into *zeta*; this is supposed to increase the grandeur of the sound.

HERMOGENES: How do you mean?

SOCRATES: For example, in very ancient times they called the day either *imera* or *emera* (short e), which is called by us *emera* (long *e*).

HERMOGENES: That is true.

SOCRATES: Do you observe that only the ancient form shows the intention of the giver of the name? of which the reason is, that men long for (*imeirousi*) and love the light which comes after the darkness, and is therefore called *imera*, from *imeros*, desire.

HERMOGENES: Clearly.

SOCRATES: But now the name is so travestied that you cannot tell the meaning, although there are some who imagine the day to be called *emera* because it makes things gentle (*emera* different accents).

HERMOGENES: Such is my view.

SOCRATES: And do you know that the ancients said *duogon* and not *zugon*?

HERMOGENES: They did so.

SOCRATES: And *zugon* (yoke) has no meaning,—it ought to be *duogon*, which word expresses the binding of two together (*duein agoge*) for the purpose of drawing;—this has been changed into *zugon*, and there are many other examples of similar changes.

HERMOGENES: There are.

SOCRATES: Proceeding in the same train of thought I may remark that the word *deon* (obligation) has a meaning which is the opposite of all the other appellations of good; for deon is here a species of good, and is, nevertheless, the chain (*desmos*) or hinderer of motion, and therefore own brother of *blaberon*.

Cratylus

HERMOGENES: Yes, Socrates; that is quite plain.

SOCRATES: Not if you restore the ancient form, which is more likely to be the correct one, and read *dion* instead of *deon*; if you convert the epsilon into an iota after the old fashion, this word will then agree with other words meaning good; for *dion*, not deon, signifies the good, and is a term of praise; and the author of names has not contradicted himself, but in all these various appellations, *deon* (obligatory), *ophelimon* (advantageous), *lusiteloun* (profitable), *kerdaleon* (gainful), *agathon* (good), *sumpheron* (expedient), *euporon* (plenteous), the same conception is implied of the ordering or all-pervading principle which is praised, and the restraining and binding principle which is censured. And this is further illustrated by the word *zemiodes* (hurtful), which if the *zeta* is only changed into delta as in the ancient language, becomes *demiodes*; and this name, as you will perceive, is given to that which binds motion (*dounti ion*).

HERMOGENES: What do you say of *edone* (pleasure), *lupe* (pain), *epithumia* (desire), and the like, Socrates?

SOCRATES: I do not think, Hermogenes, that there is any great difficulty about them—*edone* is e (*eta*) *onesis*, the action which tends to advantage; and the original form may be supposed to have been *eone*, but this has been altered by the insertion of the delta. *Lupe* appears to be derived from the relaxation (*luein*) which the body feels when in sorrow; ania (trouble) is the hindrance of motion (*alpha* and *ienai*); *algedon* (distress), if I am not mistaken, is a foreign word, which is derived from *aleinos* (grievous); *odune* (grief) is called from the putting on (*endusis*) sorrow; in *achthedon* (vexation) 'the word too labours,' as any one may see; *chara* (joy) *is* the very expression of the fluency and diffusion of the soul (*cheo*); terpsis (delight) is so called from the pleasure creeping (*erpon*) through the soul, which may be likened to a breath (*pnoe*) and is properly *erpnoun*, but has been altered by time into *terpnon*; *eupherosune* (cheerfulness) and *epithumia* explain themselves; the former, which ought to be eupherosune and has been changed *euphrosune*, is named, as every one may see, from the soul moving (*pheresthai*) in harmony with nature; epithumia is really e epi ton thumon *iousa dunamis*, the power which enters into the soul; thumos (passion) is called from the rushing (*thuseos*) and boiling of the soul; *imeros* (desire) denotes the stream (*rous*) which most draws the soul dia ten esin tes roes—because flowing with desire (*iemenos*), and expresses a longing after things and violent attraction of the soul to them, and is termed imeros from possessing this power; *pothos* (longing) is expressive of the desire of that which is not present but absent, and in another place (*pou*); this is the reason why the name *pothos* is applied to things absent, as *imeros* is to things present; *eros* (love) is so called because flowing in (*esron*) from without; the stream is not inherent, but is an influence introduced through the eyes, and from flowing in was called *esros* (influx) in the old time when they used *omicron* for *omega*, and is called *eros*, now that omega is substituted for *omicron*. But why do you not give me another word?

HERMOGENES: What do you think of *doxa* (opinion), and that class of words?

SOCRATES: Doxa is either derived from *dioxis* (pursuit), and expresses the march of the soul in the pursuit of knowledge, or from the shooting of a bow (*toxon*); the latter is more likely, and is confirmed by *oiesis* (thinking), which is only *oisis* (moving), and implies the movement of the soul to the essential nature of each thing—just as boule (counsel) has to do with shooting (*bole*); and *boulesthai* (to wish) combines the notion of aiming and deliberating—all these words seem to follow *doxa*, and all involve the idea of shooting, just as *aboulia*, absence of counsel, on the other hand, is a mishap, or missing, or mistaking of the mark, or aim, or proposal, or object.

HERMOGENES: You are quickening your pace now, Socrates.

SOCRATES: Why yes, the end I now dedicate to God, not, however, until I have explained *anagke* (necessity), which ought to come next, and *ekousion* (the voluntary). *Ekousion* is certainly the yielding (*eikon*) and unresisting—the notion implied is yielding and not

Cratylus

opposing, yielding, as I was just now saying, to that motion which is in accordance with our will; but the necessary and resistant being contrary to our will, implies error and ignorance; the idea is taken from walking through a ravine which is impassable, and rugged, and overgrown, and impedes motion—and this is the derivation of the word *anagkaion* (necessary) an *agke* ion, going through a ravine. But while my strength lasts let us persevere, and I hope that you will persevere with your questions.

HERMOGENES: Well, then, let me ask about the greatest and noblest, such as *aletheia* (truth) and *pseudos* (falsehood) and on (being), not forgetting to enquire why the word *onoma* (name), which is the theme of our discussion, has this name of onoma.

SOCRATES: You know the word *maiesthai* (to seek)?

HERMOGENES: Yes;—meaning the same as *zetein* (to enquire).

SOCRATES: The word onoma seems to be a compressed sentence, signifying on *ou zetema* (being for which there is a search); as is still more obvious in *onomaston* (notable), which states in so many words that real existence is that for which there is a seeking (*on ou masma*); *aletheia* is also an agglomeration of *theia ale* (divine wandering), implying the divine motion of existence; *pseudos* (falsehood) is the opposite of motion; here is another ill name given by the legislator to stagnation and forced inaction, which he compares to sleep (*eudein*); but the original meaning of the word is disguised by the addition of *psi*; on and *ousia* are ion with an iota broken off; this agrees with the true principle, for being (*on*) is also moving (*ion*), and the same may be said of not being, which is likewise called not going (*oukion* or *ouki on* = *ouk ion*).

HERMOGENES: You have hammered away at them manfully; but suppose that some one were to say to you, what is the word ion, and what are reon and doun?—show me their fitness.

SOCRATES: You mean to say, how should I answer him?

HERMOGENES: Yes.

SOCRATES: One way of giving the appearance of an answer has been already suggested.

HERMOGENES: What way?

SOCRATES: To say that names which we do not understand are of foreign origin; and this is very likely the right answer, and something of this kind may be true of them; but also the original forms of words may have been lost in the lapse of ages; names have been so twisted in all manner of ways, that I should not be surprised if the old language when compared with that now in use would appear to us to be a barbarous tongue.

HERMOGENES: Very likely.

SOCRATES: Yes, very likely. But still the enquiry demands our earnest attention and we must not flinch. For we should remember, that if a person go on analysing names into words, and enquiring also into the elements out of which the words are formed, and keeps on always repeating this process, he who has to answer him must at last give up the enquiry in despair.

HERMOGENES: Very true.

SOCRATES: And at what point ought he to lose heart and give up the enquiry? Must he not stop when he comes to the names which are the elements of all other names and sentences; for these cannot be supposed to be made up of other names? The word *agathon* (good), for example, is, as we were saying, a compound of *agastos* (admirable) and *thoos* (swift). And probably *thoos* is made up of other elements, and these again of others. But if we take a word which is incapable of further resolution, then we shall be right in saying that we have at last reached a primary element, which need not be resolved any further.

Cratylus

HERMOGENES: I believe you to be in the right.

SOCRATES: And suppose the names about which you are now asking should turn out to be primary elements, must not their truth or law be examined according to some new method?

HERMOGENES: Very likely.

SOCRATES: Quite so, Hermogenes; all that has preceded would lead to this conclusion. And if, as I think, the conclusion is true, then I shall again say to you, come and help me, that I may not fall into some absurdity in stating the principle of primary names.

HERMOGENES: Let me hear, and I will do my best to assist you.

SOCRATES: I think that you will acknowledge with me, that one principle is applicable to all names, primary as well as secondary—when they are regarded simply as names, there is no difference in them.

HERMOGENES: Certainly not.

SOCRATES: All the names that we have been explaining were intended to indicate the nature of things.

HERMOGENES: Of course.

SOCRATES: And that this is true of the primary quite as much as of the secondary names, is implied in their being names.

HERMOGENES: Surely.

SOCRATES: But the secondary, as I conceive, derive their significance from the primary.

HERMOGENES: That is evident.

SOCRATES: Very good; but then how do the primary names which precede analysis show the natures of things, as far as they can be shown; which they must do, if they are to be real names? And here I will ask you a question: Suppose that we had no voice or tongue, and wanted to communicate with one another, should we not, like the deaf and dumb, make signs with the hands and head and the rest of the body?

HERMOGENES: There would be no choice, Socrates.

SOCRATES: We should imitate the nature of the thing; the elevation of our hands to heaven would mean lightness and upwardness; heaviness and downwardness would be expressed by letting them drop to the ground; if we were describing the running of a horse, or any other animal, we should make our bodies and their gestures as like as we could to them.

HERMOGENES: I do not see that we could do anything else.

SOCRATES: We could not; for by bodily imitation only can the body ever express anything.

HERMOGENES: Very true.

SOCRATES: And when we want to express ourselves, either with the voice, or tongue, or mouth, the expression is simply their imitation of that which we want to express.

HERMOGENES: It must be so, I think.

SOCRATES: Then a name is a vocal imitation of that which the vocal imitator names or imitates?

HERMOGENES: I think so.

SOCRATES: Nay, my friend, I am disposed to think that we have not reached the truth as yet.

HERMOGENES: Why not?

SOCRATES: Because if we have we shall be obliged to admit that the people who imitate sheep, or cocks, or other animals, name that which they imitate.

HERMOGENES: Quite true.

SOCRATES: Then could I have been right in what I was saying?

HERMOGENES: In my opinion, no. But I wish that you would tell me, Socrates, what sort of an imitation is a name?

SOCRATES: In the first place, I should reply, not a musical imitation, although that is also vocal; nor, again, an imitation of what music imitates; these, in my judgment, would not be naming. Let me put the matter as follows: All objects have sound and figure, and many have colour?

HERMOGENES: Certainly.

SOCRATES: But the art of naming appears not to be concerned with imitations of this kind; the arts which have to do with them are music and drawing?

HERMOGENES: True.

SOCRATES: Again, is there not an essence of each thing, just as there is a colour, or sound? And is there not an essence of colour and sound as well as of anything else which may be said to have an essence?

HERMOGENES: I should think so.

SOCRATES: Well, and if any one could express the essence of each thing in letters and syllables, would he not express the nature of each thing?

HERMOGENES: Quite so.

SOCRATES: The musician and the painter were the two names which you gave to the two other imitators. What will this imitator be called?

HERMOGENES: I imagine, Socrates, that he must be the namer, or name-giver, of whom we are in search.

SOCRATES: If this is true, then I think that we are in a condition to consider the names ron (stream), ienai (to go), schesis (retention), about which you were asking; and we may see whether the namer has grasped the nature of them in letters and syllables in such a manner as to imitate the essence or not.

HERMOGENES: Very good.

SOCRATES: But are these the only primary names, or are there others?

HERMOGENES: There must be others.

SOCRATES: So I should expect. But how shall we further analyse them, and where does the imitator begin? Imitation of the essence is made by syllables and letters; ought we not, therefore, first to separate the letters, just as those who are beginning rhythm first distinguish the powers of elementary, and then of compound sounds, and when they have done so, but not before, they proceed to the consideration of rhythms?

HERMOGENES: Yes.

SOCRATES: Must we not begin in the same way with letters; first separating the vowels, and then the consonants and mutes (letters which are neither vowels nor semivowels), into classes, according to the received distinctions of the learned; also the semivowels, which are neither vowels, nor yet mutes; and distinguishing into classes the vowels themselves? And when we have perfected the classification of things, we shall give them names, and see whether, as in the case of letters, there are any classes to which they may be all referred (cf. Phaedrus); and hence we shall see their natures, and see, too, whether they have in them classes as there are in the letters; and when we have well considered all this, we shall know how to apply them to what they resemble—whether one letter is used to denote one thing, or whether there is to be an admixture of several of them; just, as in painting, the painter who wants to depict anything sometimes uses purple only, or any other colour, and sometimes mixes up several colours, as his method is when he has to paint flesh colour or anything of that kind—he uses his colours as his figures appear to require them; and so, too, we shall apply letters to the expression of objects, either single letters when required, or several letters; and so we shall form syllables, as they are called, and from syllables make nouns and verbs; and thus, at last, from the combinations of nouns and verbs arrive at language, large and fair and whole; and as the painter made a figure, even so shall we make speech by the art of the namer or the rhetorician, or by some other art. Not that I am literally speaking of ourselves, but I was carried away—meaning to say that this was the way in which (not we but) the ancients formed language, and what they put together we must take to pieces in like manner, if we are to attain a scientific view of the whole subject, and we must see whether the primary, and also whether the secondary elements are rightly given or not, for if they are not, the composition of them, my dear Hermogenes, will be a sorry piece of work, and in the wrong direction.

HERMOGENES: That, Socrates, I can quite believe.

SOCRATES: Well, but do you suppose that you will be able to analyse them in this way? for I am certain that I should not.

HERMOGENES: Much less am I likely to be able.

SOCRATES: Shall we leave them, then? or shall we seek to discover, if we can, something about them, according to the measure of our ability, saying by way of preface, as I said before of the Gods, that of the truth about them we know nothing, and do but entertain human notions of them. And in this present enquiry, let us say to ourselves, before we proceed, that the higher method is the one which we or others who would analyse language to any good purpose must follow; but under the circumstances, as men say, we must do as well as we can. What do you think?

HERMOGENES: I very much approve.

SOCRATES: That objects should be imitated in letters and syllables, and so find expression, may appear ridiculous, Hermogenes, but it cannot be avoided—there is no better principle to which we can look for the truth of first names. Deprived of this, we must have recourse to divine help, like the tragic poets, who in any perplexity have their gods waiting in the air; and must get out of our difficulty in like fashion, by saying that 'the Gods gave the first names, and therefore they are right.' This will be the best contrivance, or perhaps that other notion may be even better still, of deriving them from some barbarous people, for the barbarians are older than we are; or we may say that antiquity has cast a veil over them, which is the same sort of excuse as the last; for all these are not reasons but only ingenious excuses for having no reasons concerning the truth of words. And yet any sort of ignorance of first or primitive names involves an ignorance of secondary words; for they can only be explained by the primary. Clearly then the professor of languages should be able to give a very lucid explanation of first names, or let him be assured he will only talk nonsense about the rest. Do you not suppose this to be true?

HERMOGENES: Certainly, Socrates.

SOCRATES: My first notions of original names are truly wild and ridiculous, though I have no objection to impart them to you if you desire, and I hope that you will communicate to me in return anything better which you may have.

HERMOGENES: Fear not; I will do my best.

Cratylus

SOCRATES: In the first place, the letter *rho* appears to me to be the general instrument expressing all motion (*kinesis*). But I have not yet explained the meaning of this latter word, which is just *iesis* (going); for the letter *eta* was not in use among the ancients, who only employed epsilon; and the root is *kiein*, which is a foreign form, the same as ienai. And the old word *kinesis* will be correctly given as iesis in corresponding modern letters. Assuming this foreign root *kiein*, and allowing for the change of the *eta* and the insertion of the nu, we have *kinesis*, which should have been *kieinsis* or *eisis*; and stasis is the negative of *ienai* (or *eisis*), and has been improved into stasis. Now the letter *rho*, as I was saying, appeared to the imposer of names an excellent instrument for the expression of motion; and he frequently uses the letter for this purpose: for example, in the actual words rein and roe he represents motion by rho; also in the words *tromos* (trembling), *trachus* (rugged); and again, in words such as *krouein* (strike), *thrauein* (crush), *ereikein* (bruise), *thruptein* (break), *kermatixein* (crumble), *rumbein* (whirl): of all these sorts of movements he generally finds an expression in the letter R, because, as I imagine, he had observed that the tongue was most agitated and least at rest in the pronunciation of this letter, which he therefore used in order to express motion, just as by the letter iota he expresses the subtle elements which pass through all things. This is why he uses the letter iota as imitative of motion, *ienai*, *iesthai*. And there is another class of letters, *phi*, *psi*, sigma, and *xi*, of which the pronunciation is accompanied by great expenditure of breath; these are used in the imitation of such notions as *psuchron* (shivering), *xeon* (seething), *seiesthai*, (to be shaken), *seismos* (shock), and are always introduced by the giver of names when he wants to imitate what is *phusodes* (windy). He seems to have thought that the closing and pressure of the tongue in the utterance of *delta* and tau was expressive of binding and rest in a place: he further observed the liquid movement of *lambda*, in the pronunciation of which the tongue slips, and in this he found the expression of smoothness, as in leios (level), and in the word *oliothanein* (to slip) itself, *liparon* (sleek), in the word *kollodes* (gluey), and the like: the heavier sound of gamma detained the slipping tongue, and the union of the two gave the notion of a glutinous clammy nature, as in *glischros*, *glukus*, *gloiodes*. The nu he observed to be sounded from within, and therefore to have a notion of inwardness; hence he introduced the sound in *endos* and *entos*: *alpha* he assigned to the expression of size, and *nu* of length, because they are great letters: *omicron* was the sign of roundness, and therefore there is plenty of omicron mixed up in the word *goggulon* (round). Thus did the legislator, reducing all things into letters and syllables, and impressing on them names and signs, and out of them by imitation compounding other signs. That is my view, Hermogenes, of the truth of names; but I should like to hear what Cratylus has more to say.

HERMOGENES: But, Socrates, as I was telling you before, Cratylus mystifies me; he says that there is a fitness of names, but he never explains what is this fitness, so that I cannot tell whether his obscurity is intended or not. Tell me now, Cratylus, here in the presence of Socrates, do you agree in what Socrates has been saying about names, or have you something better of your own? and if you have, tell me what your view is, and then you will either learn of Socrates, or Socrates and I will learn of you.

CRATYLUS: Well, but surely, Hermogenes, you do not suppose that you can learn, or I explain, any subject of importance all in a moment; at any rate, not such a subject as language, which is, perhaps, the very greatest of all.

HERMOGENES: No, indeed; but, as Hesiod says, and I agree with him, 'to add little to little' is worth while. And, therefore, if you think that you can add anything at all, however small, to our knowledge, take a little trouble and oblige Socrates, and me too, who certainly have a claim upon you.

SOCRATES: I am by no means positive, Cratylus, in the view which Hermogenes and myself have worked out; and therefore do not hesitate to say what you think, which if it be better than my own view I shall gladly accept. And I should not be at all surprized to find that you have found some better notion. For you have evidently reflected on these matters and have had teachers, and if you have really a better theory of the truth of names, you may count me in the number of your disciples.

CRATYLUS: You are right, Socrates, in saying that I have made a study of these matters, and I might possibly convert you into a disciple. But I fear that the opposite is more probable, and I already find myself moved to say to you what Achilles in the 'Prayers' says to Ajax,—

> 'Illustrious Ajax, son of Telamon, lord of the people,
> You appear to have spoken in all things much to my mind.'

And you, Socrates, appear to me to be an oracle, and to give answers much to my mind, whether you are inspired by Euthyphro, or whether some Muse may have long been an inhabitant of your breast, unconsciously to yourself.

SOCRATES: Excellent Cratylus, I have long been wondering at my own wisdom; I cannot trust myself. And I think that I ought to stop and ask myself What am I saying? for there is nothing worse than self-deception—when the deceiver is always at home and always with you—it is quite terrible, and therefore I ought often to retrace my steps and endeavour to 'look fore and aft,' in the words of the aforesaid Homer. And now let me see; where are we? Have we not been saying that the correct name indicates the nature of the thing:—has this proposition been sufficiently proven?

CRATYLUS: Yes, Socrates, what you say, as I am disposed to think, is quite true.

SOCRATES: Names, then, are given in order to instruct?

CRATYLUS: Certainly.

SOCRATES: And naming is an art, and has artificers?

CRATYLUS: Yes.

SOCRATES: And who are they?

CRATYLUS: The legislators, of whom you spoke at first.

SOCRATES: And does this art grow up among men like other arts? Let me explain what I mean: of painters, some are better and some worse?

CRATYLUS: Yes.

SOCRATES: The better painters execute their works, I mean their figures, better, and the worse execute them worse; and of builders also, the better sort build fairer houses, and the worse build them worse.

CRATYLUS: True.

SOCRATES: And among legislators, there are some who do their work better and some worse?

CRATYLUS: No; there I do not agree with you.

SOCRATES: Then you do not think that some laws are better and others worse?

CRATYLUS: No, indeed.

SOCRATES: Or that one name is better than another?

CRATYLUS: Certainly not.

SOCRATES: Then all names are rightly imposed?

CRATYLUS: Yes, if they are names at all.

SOCRATES: Well, what do you say to the name of our friend Hermogenes, which was mentioned before:—assuming that he has

Cratylus

nothing of the nature of Hermes in him, shall we say that this is a wrong name, or not his name at all?

CRATYLUS: I should reply that Hermogenes is not his name at all, but only appears to be his, and is really the name of somebody else, who has the nature which corresponds to it.

SOCRATES: And if a man were to call him Hermogenes, would he not be even speaking falsely? For there may be a doubt whether you can call him Hermogenes, if he is not.

CRATYLUS: What do you mean?

SOCRATES: Are you maintaining that falsehood is impossible? For if this is your meaning I should answer, that there have been plenty of liars in all ages.

CRATYLUS: Why, Socrates, how can a man say that which is not?—say something and yet say nothing? For is not falsehood saying the thing which is not?

SOCRATES: Your argument, friend, is too subtle for a man of my age. But I should like to know whether you are one of those philosophers who think that falsehood may be spoken but not said?

CRATYLUS: Neither spoken nor said.

SOCRATES: Nor uttered nor addressed? For example: If a person, saluting you in a foreign country, were to take your hand and say: 'Hail, Athenian stranger, Hermogenes, son of Smicrion'—these words, whether spoken, said, uttered, or addressed, would have no application to you but only to our friend Hermogenes, or perhaps to nobody at all?

CRATYLUS: In my opinion, Socrates, the speaker would only be talking nonsense.

SOCRATES: Well, but that will be quite enough for me, if you will tell me whether the nonsense would be true or false, or partly true and partly false:—which is all that I want to know.

CRATYLUS: I should say that he would be putting himself in motion to no purpose; and that his words would be an unmeaning sound like the noise of hammering at a brazen pot.

SOCRATES: But let us see, Cratylus, whether we cannot find a meeting-point, for you would admit that the name is not the same with the thing named?

CRATYLUS: I should.

SOCRATES: And would you further acknowledge that the name is an imitation of the thing?

CRATYLUS: Certainly.

SOCRATES: And you would say that pictures are also imitations of things, but in another way?

CRATYLUS: Yes.

SOCRATES: I believe you may be right, but I do not rightly understand you. Please to say, then, whether both sorts of imitation (I mean both pictures or words) are not equally attributable and applicable to the things of which they are the imitation.

CRATYLUS: They are.

SOCRATES: First look at the matter thus: you may attribute the likeness of the man to the man, and of the woman to the woman; and so on?

CRATYLUS: Certainly.

Cratylus

SOCRATES: And conversely you may attribute the likeness of the man to the woman, and of the woman to the man?

CRATYLUS: Very true.

SOCRATES: And are both modes of assigning them right, or only the first?

CRATYLUS: Only the first.

SOCRATES: That is to say, the mode of assignment which attributes to each that which belongs to them and is like them?

CRATYLUS: That is my view.

SOCRATES: Now then, as I am desirous that we being friends should have a good understanding about the argument, let me state my view to you: the first mode of assignment, whether applied to figures or to names, I call right, and when applied to names only, true as well as right; and the other mode of giving and assigning the name which is unlike, I call wrong, and in the case of names, false as well as wrong.

CRATYLUS: That may be true, Socrates, in the case of pictures; they may be wrongly assigned; but not in the case of names—they must be always right.

SOCRATES: Why, what is the difference? May I not go to a man and say to him, 'This is your picture,' showing him his own likeness, or perhaps the likeness of a woman; and when I say 'show,' I mean bring before the sense of sight.

CRATYLUS: Certainly.

SOCRATES: And may I not go to him again, and say, 'This is your name'?—for the name, like the picture, is an imitation. May I not say to him—'This is your name'? and may I not then bring to his sense of hearing the imitation of himself, when I say, 'This is a man'; or of a female of the human species, when I say, 'This is a woman,' as the case may be? Is not all that quite possible?

CRATYLUS: I would fain agree with you, Socrates; and therefore I say, Granted.

SOCRATES: That is very good of you, if I am right, which need hardly be disputed at present. But if I can assign names as well as pictures to objects, the right assignment of them we may call truth, and the wrong assignment of them falsehood. Now if there be such a wrong assignment of names, there may also be a wrong or inappropriate assignment of verbs; and if of names and verbs then of the sentences, which are made up of them. What do you say, Cratylus?

CRATYLUS: I agree; and think that what you say is very true.

SOCRATES: And further, primitive nouns may be compared to pictures, and in pictures you may either give all the appropriate colours and figures, or you may not give them all—some may be wanting; or there may be too many or too much of them—may there not?

CRATYLUS: Very true.

SOCRATES: And he who gives all gives a perfect picture or figure; and he who takes away or adds also gives a picture or figure, but not a good one.

CRATYLUS: Yes.

SOCRATES: In like manner, he who by syllables and letters imitates the nature of things, if he gives all that is appropriate will produce a good image, or in other words a name; but if he subtracts or perhaps adds a little, he will make an image but not a good one; whence I infer that some names are well and others ill made.

Cratylus

CRATYLUS: That is true.

SOCRATES: Then the artist of names may be sometimes good, or he may be bad?

CRATYLUS: Yes.

SOCRATES: And this artist of names is called the legislator?

CRATYLUS: Yes.

SOCRATES: Then like other artists the legislator may be good or he may be bad; it must surely be so if our former admissions hold good?

CRATYLUS: Very true, Socrates; but the case of language, you see, is different; for when by the help of grammar we assign the letters alpha or beta, or any other letters to a certain name, then, if we add, or subtract, or misplace a letter, the name which is written is not only written wrongly, but not written at all; and in any of these cases becomes other than a name.

SOCRATES: But I doubt whether your view is altogether correct, Cratylus.

CRATYLUS: How so?

SOCRATES: I believe that what you say may be true about numbers, which must be just what they are, or not be at all; for example, the number ten at once becomes other than ten if a unit be added or subtracted, and so of any other number: but this does not apply to that which is qualitative or to anything which is represented under an image. I should say rather that the image, if expressing in every point the entire reality, would no longer be an image. Let us suppose the existence of two objects: one of them shall be Cratylus, and the other the image of Cratylus; and we will suppose, further, that some God makes not only a representation such as a painter would make of your outward form and colour, but also creates an inward organization like yours, having the same warmth and softness; and into this infuses motion, and soul, and mind, such as you have, and in a word copies all your qualities, and places them by you in another form; would you say that this was Cratylus and the image of Cratylus, or that there were two Cratyluses?

CRATYLUS: I should say that there were two Cratyluses.

SOCRATES: Then you see, my friend, that we must find some other principle of truth in images, and also in names; and not insist that an image is no longer an image when something is added or subtracted. Do you not perceive that images are very far from having qualities which are the exact counterpart of the realities which they represent?

CRATYLUS: Yes, I see.

SOCRATES: But then how ridiculous would be the effect of names on things, if they were exactly the same with them! For they would be the doubles of them, and no one would be able to determine which were the names and which were the realities.

CRATYLUS: Quite true.

SOCRATES: Then fear not, but have the courage to admit that one name may be correctly and another incorrectly given; and do not insist that the name shall be exactly the same with the thing; but allow the occasional substitution of a wrong letter, and if of a letter also of a noun in a sentence, and if of a noun in a sentence also of a sentence which is not appropriate to the matter, and acknowledge that the thing may be named, and described, so long as the general character of the thing which you are describing is retained; and this, as you will remember, was remarked by Hermogenes and myself in the particular instance of the names of the letters.

CRATYLUS: Yes, I remember.

SOCRATES: Good; and when the general character is preserved, even if some of the proper letters are wanting, still the thing is signified;—well, if all the letters are given; not well, when only a few of them are given. I think that we had better admit this, lest we be punished like travellers in Aegina who wander about the street late at night: and be likewise told by truth herself that we have arrived too late; or if not, you must find out some new notion of correctness of names, and no longer maintain that a name is the expression of a thing in letters or syllables; for if you say both, you will be inconsistent with yourself.

CRATYLUS: I quite acknowledge, Socrates, what you say to be very reasonable.

SOCRATES: Then as we are agreed thus far, let us ask ourselves whether a name rightly imposed ought not to have the proper letters.

CRATYLUS: Yes.

SOCRATES: And the proper letters are those which are like the things?

CRATYLUS: Yes.

SOCRATES: Enough then of names which are rightly given. And in names which are incorrectly given, the greater part may be supposed to be made up of proper and similar letters, or there would be no likeness; but there will be likewise a part which is improper and spoils the beauty and formation of the word: you would admit that?

CRATYLUS: There would be no use, Socrates, in my quarrelling with you, since I cannot be satisfied that a name which is incorrectly given is a name at all.

SOCRATES: Do you admit a name to be the representation of a thing?

CRATYLUS: Yes, I do.

SOCRATES: But do you not allow that some nouns are primitive, and some derived?

CRATYLUS: Yes, I do.

SOCRATES: Then if you admit that primitive or first nouns are representations of things, is there any better way of framing representations than by assimilating them to the objects as much as you can; or do you prefer the notion of Hermogenes and of many others, who say that names are conventional, and have a meaning to those who have agreed about them, and who have previous knowledge of the things intended by them, and that convention is the only principle; and whether you abide by our present convention, or make a new and opposite one, according to which you call small great and great small—that, they would say, makes no difference, if you are only agreed. Which of these two notions do you prefer?

CRATYLUS: Representation by likeness, Socrates, is infinitely better than representation by any chance sign.

SOCRATES: Very good: but if the name is to be like the thing, the letters out of which the first names are composed must also be like things. Returning to the image of the picture, I would ask, How could any one ever compose a picture which would be like anything at all, if there were not pigments in nature which resembled the things imitated, and out of which the picture is composed?

CRATYLUS: Impossible.

SOCRATES: No more could names ever resemble any actually existing thing, unless the original elements of which they are compounded bore some degree of resemblance to the objects of which the names are the imitation: And the original elements are letters?

CRATYLUS: Yes.

Cratylus

SOCRATES: Let me now invite you to consider what Hermogenes and I were saying about sounds. Do you agree with me that the letter rho is expressive of rapidity, motion, and hardness? Were we right or wrong in saying so?

CRATYLUS: I should say that you were right.

SOCRATES: And that lamda was expressive of smoothness, and softness, and the like?

CRATYLUS: There again you were right.

SOCRATES: And yet, as you are aware, that which is called by us sklerotes, is by the Eretrians called skleroter.

CRATYLUS: Very true.

SOCRATES: But are the letters rho and sigma equivalents; and is there the same significance to them in the termination rho, which there is to us in sigma, or is there no significance to one of us?

CRATYLUS: Nay, surely there is a significance to both of us.

SOCRATES: In as far as they are like, or in as far as they are unlike?

CRATYLUS: In as far as they are like.

SOCRATES: Are they altogether alike?

CRATYLUS: Yes; for the purpose of expressing motion.

SOCRATES: And what do you say of the insertion of the lamda? for that is expressive not of hardness but of softness.

CRATYLUS: Why, perhaps the letter lamda is wrongly inserted, Socrates, and should be altered into rho, as you were saying to Hermogenes and in my opinion rightly, when you spoke of adding and subtracting letters upon occasion.

SOCRATES: Good. But still the word is intelligible to both of us; when I say skleros (hard), you know what I mean.

CRATYLUS: Yes, my dear friend, and the explanation of that is custom.

SOCRATES: And what is custom but convention? I utter a sound which I understand, and you know that I understand the meaning of the sound: this is what you are saying?

CRATYLUS: Yes.

SOCRATES: And if when I speak you know my meaning, there is an indication given by me to you?

CRATYLUS: Yes.

SOCRATES: This indication of my meaning may proceed from unlike as well as from like, for example in the lamda of sklerotes. But if this is true, then you have made a convention with yourself, and the correctness of a name turns out to be convention, since letters which are unlike are indicative equally with those which are like, if they are sanctioned by custom and convention. And even supposing that you distinguish custom from convention ever so much, still you must say that the signification of words is given by custom and not by likeness, for custom may indicate by the unlike as well as by the like. But as we are agreed thus far, Cratylus (for I shall assume that your silence gives consent), then custom and convention must be supposed to contribute to the indication of our thoughts; for suppose we take the instance of number, how can you ever imagine, my good friend, that you will find names resembling every individual number, unless you allow that which you term convention and agreement to have authority in determining the correctness of names? I quite agree with you that words should as far as possible resemble things; but I fear that this dragging in of resem-

Cratylus

blance, as Hermogenes says, is a shabby thing, which has to be supplemented by the mechanical aid of convention with a view to correctness; for I believe that if we could always, or almost always, use likenesses, which are perfectly appropriate, this would be the most perfect state of language; as the opposite is the most imperfect. But let me ask you, what is the force of names, and what is the use of them?

CRATYLUS: The use of names, Socrates, as I should imagine, is to inform: the simple truth is, that he who knows names knows also the things which are expressed by them.

SOCRATES: I suppose you mean to say, Cratylus, that as the name is, so also is the thing; and that he who knows the one will also know the other, because they are similars, and all similars fall under the same art or science; and therefore you would say that he who knows names will also know things.

CRATYLUS: That is precisely what I mean.

SOCRATES: But let us consider what is the nature of this information about things which, according to you, is given us by names. Is it the best sort of information? or is there any other? What do you say?

CRATYLUS: I believe that to be both the only and the best sort of information about them; there can be no other.

SOCRATES: But do you believe that in the discovery of them, he who discovers the names discovers also the things; or is this only the method of instruction, and is there some other method of enquiry and discovery.
CRATYLUS: I certainly believe that the methods of enquiry and discovery are of the same nature as instruction.

SOCRATES: Well, but do you not see, Cratylus, that he who follows names in the search after things, and analyses their meaning, is in great danger of being deceived?

CRATYLUS: How so?

SOCRATES: Why clearly he who first gave names gave them according to his conception of the things which they signified—did he not?

CRATYLUS: True.

SOCRATES: And if his conception was erroneous, and he gave names according to his conception, in what position shall we who are his followers find ourselves? Shall we not be deceived by him?

CRATYLUS: But, Socrates, am I not right in thinking that he must surely have known; or else, as I was saying, his names would not be names at all? And you have a clear proof that he has not missed the truth, and the proof is—that he is perfectly consistent. Did you ever observe in speaking that all the words which you utter have a common character and purpose?

SOCRATES: But that, friend Cratylus, is no answer. For if he did begin in error, he may have forced the remainder into agreement with the original error and with himself; there would be nothing strange in this, any more than in geometrical diagrams, which have often a slight and invisible flaw in the first part of the process, and are consistently mistaken in the long deductions which follow. And this is the reason why every man should expend his chief thought and attention on the consideration of his first principles:—are they or are they not rightly laid down? and when he has duly sifted them, all the rest will follow. Now I should be astonished to find that names are really consistent. And here let us revert to our former discussion: Were we not saying that all things are in motion and progress and flux, and that this idea of motion is expressed by names? Do you not conceive that to be the meaning of them?

CRATYLUS: Yes; that is assuredly their meaning, and the true meaning.

Cratylus

SOCRATES: Let us revert to *episteme* (knowledge) and observe how ambiguous this word is, seeming rather to signify stopping the soul at things than going round with them; and therefore we should leave the beginning as at present, and not reject the *epsilon*, but make an insertion of an iota instead of an epsilon (not *pioteme*, but *epiisteme*). Take another example: bebaion (sure) is clearly the expression of station and position, and not of motion. Again, the word *istoria* (enquiry) bears upon the face of it the stopping (*istanai*) of the stream; and the word *piston* (faithful) certainly indicates cessation of motion; then, again, *mneme* (memory), as any one may see, expresses rest in the soul, and not motion. Moreover, words such as *amartia* and *sumphora*, which have a bad sense, viewed in the light of their etymologies will be the same as *sunesis* and *episteme* and other words which have a good sense (compare *omartein, sunienai, epesthai, sumpheresthai*); and much the same may be said of *amathia* and *akolasia*, for *amathia* may be explained as *e ama theo iontos poreia*, and akolasia as e *akolouthia tois pragmasin*. Thus the names which in these instances we find to have the worst sense, will turn out to be framed on the same principle as those which have the best. And any one I believe who would take the trouble might find many other examples in which the giver of names indicates, not that things are in motion or progress, but that they are at rest; which is the opposite of motion.

CRATYLUS: Yes, Socrates, but observe; the greater number express motion.

SOCRATES: What of that, Cratylus? Are we to count them like votes? and is correctness of names the voice of the majority? Are we to say of whichever sort there are most, those are the true ones?

CRATYLUS: No; that is not reasonable.

SOCRATES: Certainly not. But let us have done with this question and proceed to another, about which I should like to know whether you think with me. Were we not lately acknowledging that the first givers of names in states, both Hellenic and barbarous, were the legislators, and that the art which gave names was the art of the legislator?

CRATYLUS: Quite true.

SOCRATES: Tell me, then, did the first legislators, who were the givers of the first names, know or not know the things which they named?

CRATYLUS: They must have known, Socrates.

SOCRATES: Why, yes, friend Cratylus, they could hardly have been ignorant.

CRATYLUS: I should say not.

SOCRATES: Let us return to the point from which we digressed. You were saying, if you remember, that he who gave names must have known the things which he named; are you still of that opinion?

CRATYLUS: I am.

SOCRATES: And would you say that the giver of the first names had also a knowledge of the things which he named?

CRATYLUS: I should.

SOCRATES: But how could he have learned or discovered things from names if the primitive names were not yet given? For, if we are correct in our view, the only way of learning and discovering things, is either to discover names for ourselves or to learn them from others.

CRATYLUS: I think that there is a good deal in what you say, Socrates.

SOCRATES: But if things are only to be known through names, how can we suppose that the givers of names had knowledge, or were legislators before there were names at all, and therefore before they could have known them?

Cratylus

CRATYLUS: I believe, Socrates, the true account of the matter to be, that a power more than human gave things their first names, and that the names which are thus given are necessarily their true names.

SOCRATES: Then how came the giver of the names, if he was an inspired being or God, to contradict himself? For were we not saying just now that he made some names expressive of rest and others of motion? Were we mistaken?

CRATYLUS: But I suppose one of the two not to be names at all.

SOCRATES: And which, then, did he make, my good friend; those which are expressive of rest, or those which are expressive of motion? This is a point which, as I said before, cannot be determined by counting them.

CRATYLUS: No; not in that way, Socrates.

SOCRATES: But if this is a battle of names, some of them asserting that they are like the truth, others contending that *they* are, how or by what criterion are we to decide between them? For there are no other names to which appeal can be made, but obviously recourse must be had to another standard which, without employing names, will make clear which of the two are right; and this must be a standard which shows the truth of things.

CRATYLUS: I agree.

SOCRATES: But if that is true, Cratylus, then I suppose that things may be known without names?

CRATYLUS: Clearly.

SOCRATES: But how would you expect to know them? What other way can there be of knowing them, except the true and natural way, through their affinities, when they are akin to each other, and through themselves? For that which is other and different from them must signify something other and different from them.

CRATYLUS: What you are saying is, I think, true.

SOCRATES: Well, but reflect; have we not several times acknowledged that names rightly given are the likenesses and images of the things which they name?

CRATYLUS: Yes.

SOCRATES: Let us suppose that to any extent you please you can learn things through the medium of names, and suppose also that you can learn them from the things themselves—which is likely to be the nobler and clearer way; to learn of the image, whether the image and the truth of which the image is the expression have been rightly conceived, or to learn of the truth whether the truth and the image of it have been duly executed?

CRATYLUS: I should say that we must learn of the truth.

SOCRATES: How real existence is to be studied or discovered is, I suspect, beyond you and me. But we may admit so much, that the knowledge of things is not to be derived from names. No; they must be studied and investigated in themselves.

CRATYLUS: Clearly, Socrates.

SOCRATES: There is another point. I should not like us to be imposed upon by the appearance of such a multitude of names, all tending in the same direction. I myself do not deny that the givers of names did really give them under the idea that all things were in motion and flux; which was their sincere but, I think, mistaken opinion. And having fallen into a kind of whirlpool themselves, they are carried round, and want to drag us in after them. There is a matter, master Cratylus, about which I often dream, and should like to ask your opinion: Tell me, whether there is or is not any absolute beauty or good, or any other absolute existence?

CRATYLUS: Certainly, Socrates, I think so.

SOCRATES: Then let us seek the true beauty: not asking whether a face is fair, or anything of that sort, for all such things appear to be in a flux; but let us ask whether the true beauty is not always beautiful.

CRATYLUS: Certainly.

SOCRATES: And can we rightly speak of a beauty which is always passing away, and is first this and then that; must not the same thing be born and retire and vanish while the word is in our mouths?

CRATYLUS: Undoubtedly.

SOCRATES: Then how can that be a real thing which is never in the same state? for obviously things which are the same cannot change while they remain the same; and if they are always the same and in the same state, and never depart from their original form, they can never change or be moved.

CRATYLUS: Certainly they cannot.

SOCRATES: Nor yet can they be known by any one; for at the moment that the observer approaches, then they become other and of another nature, so that you cannot get any further in knowing their nature or state, for you cannot know that which has no state.

CRATYLUS: True.

SOCRATES: Nor can we reasonably say, Cratylus, that there is knowledge at all, if everything is in a state of transition and there is nothing abiding; for knowledge too cannot continue to be knowledge unless continuing always to abide and exist. But if the very nature of knowledge changes, at the time when the change occurs there will be no knowledge; and if the transition is always going on, there will always be no knowledge, and, according to this view, there will be no one to know and nothing to be known: but if that which knows and that which is known exists ever, and the beautiful and the good and every other thing also exist, then I do not think that they can resemble a process or flux, as we were just now supposing. Whether there is this eternal nature in things, or whether the truth is what Heracleitus and his followers and many others say, is a question hard to determine; and no man of sense will like to put himself or the education of his mind in the power of names: neither will he so far trust names or the givers of names as to be confident in any knowledge which condemns himself and other existences to an unhealthy state of unreality; he will not believe that all things leak like a pot, or imagine that the world is a man who has a running at the nose. This may be true, Cratylus, but is also very likely to be untrue; and therefore I would not have you be too easily persuaded of it. Reflect well and like a man, and do not easily accept such a doctrine; for you are young and of an age to learn. And when you have found the truth, come and tell me.

CRATYLUS: I will do as you say, though I can assure you, Socrates, that I have been considering the matter already, and the result of a great deal of trouble and consideration is that I incline to Heracleitus.

SOCRATES: Then, another day, my friend, when you come back, you shall give me a lesson; but at present, go into the country, as you are intending, and Hermogenes shall set you on your way.

CRATYLUS: Very good, Socrates; I hope, however, that you will continue to think about these things yourself.

PHAEDRUS

by

Plato

Translated by Benjamin Jowett

INTRODUCTION

THE *PHAEDRUS* IS closely connected with the Symposium, and may be regarded either as introducing or following it. The two Dialogues together contain the whole philosophy of Plato on the nature of love, which in the Republic and in the later writings of Plato is only introduced playfully or as a figure of speech. But in the Phaedrus and Symposium love and philosophy join hands, and one is an aspect of the other. The spiritual and emotional part is elevated into the ideal, to which in the Symposium mankind are described as looking forward, and which in the Phaedrus, as well as in the Phaedo, they are seeking to recover from a former state of existence. Whether the subject of the Dialogue is love or rhetoric, or the union of the two, or the relation of philosophy to love and to art in general, and to the human soul, will be hereafter considered. And perhaps we may arrive at some conclusion such as the following—that the dialogue is not strictly confined to a single subject, but passes from one to another with the natural freedom of conversation.

Phaedrus has been spending the morning with Lysias, the celebrated rhetorician, and is going to refresh himself by taking a walk outside the wall, when he is met by Socrates, who professes that he will not leave him until he has delivered up the speech with which Lysias has regaled him, and which he is carrying about in his mind, or more probably in a book hidden under his cloak, and is intending to study as he walks. The imputation is not denied, and the two agree to direct their steps out of the public way along the stream of the Ilissus towards a plane-tree which is seen in the distance. There, lying down amidst pleasant sounds and scents, they will read the speech of Lysias. The country is a novelty to Socrates, who never goes out of the town; and hence he is full of admiration for the beauties of nature, which he seems to be drinking in for the first time.

As they are on their way, Phaedrus asks the opinion of Socrates respecting the local tradition of Boreas and Oreithyia. Socrates, after a satirical allusion to the 'rationalizers' of his day, replies that he has no time for these 'nice' interpretations of mythology, and he pities anyone who has. When you once begin there is no end of them, and they spring from an uncritical philosophy after all. 'The proper study of mankind is man;' and he is a far more complex and wonderful being than the serpent Typho. Socrates as yet does not know himself; and why should he care to know about unearthly monsters? Engaged in such conversation, they arrive at the plane-tree; when they have found a convenient resting-place, Phaedrus pulls out the speech and reads:—

The speech consists of a foolish paradox which is to the effect that the non-lover ought to be accepted rather than the lover—because he is more rational, more agreeable, more enduring, less suspicious, less hurtful, less boastful, less engrossing, and because there are more of them, and for a great many other reasons which are equally unmeaning. Phaedrus is captivated with the beauty of the periods, and wants to make Socrates say that nothing was or ever could be written better. Socrates does not think much of the matter, but then he has only attended to the form, and in that he has detected several repetitions and other marks of haste. He cannot agree with Phaedrus in the extreme value which he sets upon this performance, because he is afraid of doing injustice to Anacreon and Sappho and other great writers, and is almost inclined to think that he himself, or rather some power residing within him, could make a speech better than that of Lysias on the same theme, and also different from his, if he may be allowed the use of a few commonplaces which all speakers must equally employ.

Phaedrus is delighted at the prospect of having another speech, and promises that he will set up a golden statue of Socrates at Delphi, if he keeps his word. Some raillery ensues, and at length Socrates, conquered by the threat that he shall never again hear a speech of Lysias unless he fulfils his promise, veils his face and begins.

First, invoking the Muses and assuming ironically the person of the non-lover (who is a lover all the same), he will enquire into the nature and power of love. For this is a necessary preliminary to the other question—How is the non-lover to be distinguished from the lover? In all of us there are two principles—a better and a worse—reason and desire, which are generally at war with one another; and the victory of the rational is called temperance, and the victory of the irrational intemperance or excess. The latter takes many forms and has many bad names—gluttony, drunkenness, and the like. But of all the irrational desires or excesses the greatest is that which is led away by desires of a kindred nature to the enjoyment of personal beauty. And this is the master power of love.

Here Socrates fancies that he detects in himself an unusual flow of eloquence—this newly-found gift he can only attribute to the inspiration of the place, which appears to be dedicated to the nymphs. Starting again from the philosophical basis which has been laid down, he proceeds to show how many advantages the non-lover has over the lover. The one encourages softness and effeminacy and exclusiveness; he cannot endure any superiority in his beloved; he will train him in luxury, he will keep him out of society, he will deprive him of parents, friends, money, knowledge, and of every other good, that he may have him all to himself. Then again his ways are not ways of pleasantness; he is mighty disagreeable; 'crabbed age and youth cannot live together.' At every hour of the night and day he is intruding upon him; there is the same old withered face and the remainder to match—and he is always repeating, in season or out of season, the praises or dispraises of his beloved, which are bad enough when he is sober, and published all over the world when he is drunk. At length his love ceases; he is converted into an enemy, and the spectacle may be seen of the lover running away from the beloved, who pursues him with vain reproaches, and demands his reward which the other refuses to pay. Too late the beloved learns, after all his pains and disagreeables, that 'As wolves love lambs so lovers love their loves.' (Compare Char.) Here is the end; the 'other' or 'non-lover' part of the speech had better be understood, for if in the censure of the lover Socrates has broken out in verse, what will he not do in his praise of the non-lover? He has said his say and is preparing to go away.

Phaedrus begs him to remain, at any rate until the heat of noon has passed; he would like to have a little more conversation before they go. Socrates, who has risen, recognizes the oracular sign which forbids him to depart until he has done penance. His conscious has been awakened, and like Stesichorus when he had reviled the lovely Helen he will sing a palinode for having blasphemed the majesty of love. His palinode takes the form of a myth.

Socrates begins his tale with a glorification of madness, which he divides into four kinds: first, there is the art of divination or prophecy—this, in a vein similar to that pervading the Cratylus and Io, he connects with madness by an etymological explanation (mantike, manike—compare oionoistike, oionistike, ''tis all one reckoning, save the phrase is a little variations'); secondly, there is the art of purification by mysteries; thirdly, poetry or the inspiration of the Muses (compare Ion), without which no man can enter their temple. All this shows that madness is one of heaven's blessings, and may sometimes be a great deal better than sense. There is also a fourth kind of madness—that of love—which cannot be explained without enquiring into the nature of the soul.

All soul is immortal, for she is the source of all motion both in herself and in others. Her form may be described in a figure as a composite nature made up of a charioteer and a pair of winged steeds. The steeds of the gods are immortal, but ours are one mortal and the other immortal. The immortal soul soars upwards into the heavens, but the mortal drops her plumes and settles upon the earth.

Now the use of the wing is to rise and carry the downward element into the upper world—there to behold beauty, wisdom, goodness, and the other things of God by which the soul is nourished. On a certain day Zeus the lord of heaven goes forth in a winged chariot; and an array of gods and demi-gods and of human souls in their train, follows him. There are glorious and blessed sights in the interior of heaven, and he who will may freely behold them. The

Phaedrus

great vision of all is seen at the feast of the gods, when they ascend the heights of the empyrean—all but Hestia, who is left at home to keep house. The chariots of the gods glide readily upwards and stand upon the outside; the revolution of the spheres carries them round, and they have a vision of the world beyond. But the others labour in vain; for the mortal steed, if he has not been properly trained, keeps them down and sinks them towards the earth. Of the world which is beyond the heavens, who can tell? There is an essence formless, colourless, intangible, perceived by the mind only, dwelling in the region of true knowledge. The divine mind in her revolution enjoys this fair prospect, and beholds justice, temperance, and knowledge in their everlasting essence. When fulfilled with the sight of them she returns home, and the charioteer puts up the horses in their stable, and gives them ambrosia to eat and nectar to drink. This is the life of the gods; the human soul tries to reach the same heights, but hardly succeeds; and sometimes the head of the charioteer rises above, and sometimes sinks below, the fair vision, and he is at last obliged, after much contention, to turn away and leave the plain of truth. But if the soul has followed in the train of her god and once beheld truth she is preserved from harm, and is carried round in the next revolution of the spheres; and if always following, and always seeing the truth, is then for ever unharmed. If, however, she drops her wings and falls to the earth, then she takes the form of man, and the soul which has seen most of the truth passes into a philosopher or lover; that which has seen truth in the second degree, into a king or warrior; the third, into a householder or money-maker; the fourth, into a gymnast; the fifth, into a prophet or mystic; the sixth, into a poet or imitator; the seventh, into a husbandman or craftsman; the eighth, into a sophist or demagogue; the ninth, into a tyrant. All these are states of probation, wherein he who lives righteously is improved, and he who lives unrighteously deteriorates. After death comes the judgment; the bad depart to houses of correction under the earth, the good to places of joy in heaven. When a thousand years have elapsed the souls meet together and choose the lives which they will lead for another period of existence. The soul which three times in succession has chosen the life of a philosopher or of a lover who is not without philosophy receives her wings at the close of the third millennium; the remainder have to complete a cycle of ten thousand years before their wings are restored to them. Each time there is full liberty of choice. The soul of a man may descend into a beast, and return again into the form of man. But the form of man will only be taken by the soul which has once seen truth and acquired some conception of the universal:—this is the recollection of the knowledge which she attained when in the company of the Gods. And men in general recall only with difficulty the things of another world, but the mind of the philosopher has a better remembrance of them. For when he beholds the visible beauty of earth his enraptured soul passes in thought to those glorious sights of justice and wisdom and temperance and truth which she once gazed upon in heaven. Then she celebrated holy mysteries and beheld blessed apparitions shining in pure light, herself pure, and not as yet entombed in the body. And still, like a bird eager to quit its cage, she flutters and looks upwards, and is therefore deemed mad. Such a recollection of past days she receives through sight, the keenest of our senses, because beauty, alone of the ideas, has any representation on earth: wisdom is invisible to mortal eyes. But the corrupted nature, blindly excited by this vision of beauty, rushes on to enjoy, and would fain wallow like a brute beast in sensual pleasures. Whereas the true mystic, who has seen the many sights of bliss, when he beholds a god-like form or face is amazed with delight, and if he were not afraid of being thought mad he would fall down and worship. Then the stiffened wing begins to relax and grow again; desire which has been imprisoned pours over the soul of the lover; the germ of the wing unfolds, and stings, and pangs of birth, like the cutting of teeth, are everywhere felt. (Compare *Symp.*) Father and mother, and goods and laws and proprieties are nothing to him; his beloved is his physician, who can alone cure his pain. An apocryphal sacred writer says that the power which thus works in him is by mortals called love, but the immortals call him dove, or the winged one, in order to represent the force of his wings—such at any rate is his nature. Now the characters of lovers depend upon the god whom they followed in the other world; and they choose their loves in this world accordingly. The followers of Ares are fierce and violent; those of Zeus seek out some philosophical and imperial nature; the attendants of Here find a royal love; and in like manner the followers of every god seek a love who is like their god; and to him they communicate the nature which they have received from their god. The manner in which they take their love is as follows:—

I told you about the charioteer and his two steeds, the one a noble animal who is guided by word and admonition only, the other an ill-looking villain who will hardly yield to blow or spur. Together all three, who are a figure of the soul, approach the vision of love. And now a fierce conflict begins. The ill-conditioned steed rushes on to enjoy, but the charioteer, who beholds the beloved with awe, falls back in adoration, and forces both the steeds on their haunches; again the evil steed rushes forwards and pulls shamelessly. The conflict grows more and more severe; and at last the charioteer, throwing himself backwards, forces the bit out of the clenched teeth of the brute, and pulling harder than ever at the reins, covers his tongue and jaws with blood, and forces him to rest his legs and haunches with pain upon the ground. When this has happened several times, the villain is tamed and humbled, and from that time forward the soul of the lover follows the beloved in modesty and holy fear. And now their bliss is consummated; the same image of love dwells in the breast of either, and if they have self-control, they pass their lives in the greatest happiness which is attainable by man—they continue masters of themselves, and conquer in one of the three heavenly victories. But if they choose the lower life of ambition they may still have a happy destiny, though inferior, because they have not the approval of the whole soul. At last they leave the body and proceed on their pilgrim's progress, and those who have once begun can never go back. When the time comes they receive their wings and fly away, and the lovers have the same wings.

Socrates concludes:—

These are the blessings of love, and thus have I made my recantation in finer language than before: I did so in order to please Phaedrus. If I said what was wrong at first, please to attribute my error to Lysias, who ought to study philosophy instead of rhetoric, and then he will not mislead his disciple Phaedrus.

Phaedrus is afraid that he will lose conceit of Lysias, and that Lysias will be out of conceit with himself, and leave off making speeches, for the politicians have been deriding him. Socrates is of opinion that there is small danger of this; the politicians are themselves the great rhetoricians of the age, who desire to attain immortality by the authorship of laws. And therefore there is nothing with which they can reproach Lysias in being a writer; but there may be disgrace in being a bad one.

And what is good or bad writing or speaking? While the sun is hot in the sky above us, let us ask that question: since by rational conversation man lives, and not by the indulgence of bodily pleasures. And the grasshoppers who are chirruping around may carry our words to the Muses, who are their patronesses; for the grasshoppers were human beings themselves in a world before the Muses, and when the Muses came they died of hunger for the love of song. And they carry to them in heaven the report of those who honour them on earth.

The first rule of good speaking is to know and speak the truth; as a Spartan proverb says, 'true art is truth'; whereas rhetoric is an art of enchantment, which makes things appear good and evil, like and unlike, as the speaker pleases. Its use is not confined, as people commonly suppose, to arguments in the law courts and speeches in the assembly; it is rather a part of the art of disputation, under which are included both the rules of Gorgias and the eristic of Zeno. But it is not wholly devoid of truth. Superior knowledge enables us to deceive another by the help of resemblances, and to escape from such a deception when employed against ourselves. We see therefore that even in rhetoric an element of truth is required. For if we do not know the truth, we can neither make the gradual departures from truth by which men are most easily deceived, nor guard ourselves against deception.

Socrates then proposes that they shall use the two speeches as illustrations of the art of rhetoric; first distinguishing between the debatable and undisputed class of subjects. In the debatable class there ought to be a definition of all disputed matters. But there was no such definition in the speech of Lysias; nor is there any order or connection in his words any more than in a nursery rhyme. With this he compares the regular divisions of the other speech, which was his own (and yet not his own, for the local deities must have inspired him). Although only a playful composition, it will be found to embody two principles: first, that of synthesis or the comprehension of parts in a whole; secondly, analysis, or the resolution of the whole into parts. These are the processes of division and generalization which are so dear to the dialectician, that king of men. They are effected by dialectic, and not by rhetoric, of which the remains are but scanty after order and arrangement have been subtracted. There is nothing left but a heap of 'ologies' and other technical terms invented by Polus, Theodorus, Evenus, Tisias, Gorgias, and others, who have rules for everything, and who teach how to be short or long at pleasure. Prodicus showed his good sense when he said that there was a better thing than either to be short or long, which was to be of convenient length.

Still, notwithstanding the absurdities of Polus and others, rhetoric has great power in public assemblies. This power, however, is not given by any technical rules, but is the gift of genius. The real art is always being confused by rhetoricians with the preliminaries of the art. The perfection of oratory is like the perfection of anything else; natural power must be aided by art. But the art is not that which is taught in the schools of rhetoric; it is nearer akin to philosophy. Pericles, for instance, who was the most accomplished of all speakers, derived his eloquence not from rhetoric but from the philosophy of nature which he learnt of Anaxagoras. True rhetoric is like medicine, and the rhetorician has to consider the natures of men's souls as the physician considers the natures of their bodies. Such and such persons are to be affected in this way, such and such others in that; and he must know the times and the seasons for saying this or that. This is not an easy task, and this, if there be such an art, is the art of rhetoric.

I know that there are some professors of the art who maintain probability to be stronger than truth. But we maintain that probability is engendered by likeness of the truth which can only be attained by the knowledge of it, and that the aim of the good man should not be to please or persuade his fellow-servants, but to please his good masters who are the gods. Rhetoric has a fair beginning in this.

Enough of the art of speaking; let us now proceed to consider the true use of writing. There is an old Egyptian tale of Theuth, the inventor of writing, showing his invention to the god Thamus, who told him that he would only spoil men's memories and take away their understandings. From this tale, of which young Athens will probably make fun, may be gathered the lesson that writing is inferior to speech. For it is like a picture, which can give no answer to a question, and has only a deceitful likeness of a living creature. It has no power of adaptation, but uses the same words for all. It is not a legitimate son of knowledge, but a bastard, and when an attack is made upon this bastard neither parent nor anyone else is there to defend it. The husbandman will not seriously incline to sow his seed in such a hotbed or garden of Adonis; he will rather sow in the natural soil of the human soul which has depth of earth; and he will anticipate the inner growth of the mind, by writing only, if at all, as a remedy against old age. The natural process will be far nobler, and will bring forth fruit in the minds of others as well as in his own.

The conclusion of the whole matter is just this,—that until a man knows the truth, and the manner of adapting the truth to the natures of other men, he cannot be a good orator; also, that the living is better than the written word, and that the principles of justice and truth when delivered by word of mouth are the legitimate offspring of a man's own bosom, and their lawful descendants take up their abode in others. Such an orator as he is who is possessed of them, you and I would fain become. And to all composers in the world, poets, orators, legislators, we hereby announce that if their compositions are based upon these principles, then they are not only poets, orators, legislators, but philosophers. All others are mere flatterers and putters together of words. This is the message which Phaedrus undertakes to carry to Lysias from the local deities, and Socrates himself will carry a similar message to his favourite Isocrates, whose future distinction as a great rhetorician he prophesies. The heat of the day has passed, and after offering up a prayer to Pan and the nymphs, Socrates and Phaedrus depart.

There are two principal controversies which have been raised about the Phaedrus; the first relates to the subject, the second to the date of the Dialogue.

There seems to be a notion that the work of a great artist like Plato cannot fail in unity, and that the unity of a dialogue requires a single subject. But the conception of unity really applies in very different degrees and ways to different kinds of art; to a statue, for example, far more than to any kind of literary composition, and to some species of literature far more than to others. Nor does the dialogue appear to be a style of composition in which the requirement of unity is most stringent; nor should the idea of unity derived from one sort of art be hastily transferred to another. The double titles of several of the Platonic Dialogues are a further proof that the severer rule was not observed by Plato. The Republic is divided between the search after justice and the construction of the ideal state; the Parmenides between the criticism of the Platonic ideas and of the Eleatic one or being; the Gorgias between the art of speaking and the nature of the good; the Sophist between the detection of the Sophist and the correlation of ideas. The Theaetetus, the Politicus, and the Philebus have also digressions which are but remotely connected with the main subject.

Thus the comparison of Plato's other writings, as well as the reason of the thing, lead us to the conclusion that we must not expect to find one idea pervading a whole work, but one, two, or more, as the invention of the writer may suggest, or his fancy wander. If each dialogue were confined to the development of a single idea, this would appear on the face of the dialogue, nor could any controversy be raised as to whether the Phaedrus treated of love or rhetoric. But the truth is that Plato subjects himself to no rule of this sort. Like every great artist he gives unity of form to the different and apparently distracting topics which he brings together. He works freely and is not to be supposed to have arranged every part of the dialogue before he begins to write. He fastens or weaves together the frame of his discourse loosely and imperfectly, and which is the warp and which is the woof cannot always be determined.

The subjects of the Phaedrus (exclusive of the short introductory passage about mythology which is suggested by the local tradition) are first the false or conventional art of rhetoric; secondly, love or the inspiration of beauty and knowledge, which is described as madness; thirdly, dialectic or the art of composition and division; fourthly, the true rhetoric, which is based upon dialectic, and is neither the art of persuasion nor knowledge of the truth alone, but the art of persuasion founded on knowledge of truth and knowledge of character; fifthly, the superiority of the spoken over the written word. The continuous thread which appears and reappears throughout is rhetoric; this is the ground into which the rest of the Dialogue is worked, in parts embroidered with fine words which are not in Socrates' manner, as he says, 'in order to please Phaedrus.' The speech of Lysias which has thrown Phaedrus into an ecstacy is adduced as an example of the false rhetoric; the first speech of Socrates, though an improvement, partakes of the same character; his second speech, which is full of that higher element said to have been learned of Anaxagoras by Pericles, and which in the midst of poetry does not forget order, is an illustration of the higher or true rhetoric. This higher rhetoric is based upon dialectic, and dialectic is a sort of inspiration akin to love (compare Symp.); in these two aspects of philosophy the technicalities of rhetoric are absorbed. And so the example becomes also the deeper theme of discourse. The true knowledge of things in heaven and earth is based upon enthusiasm or love of the ideas going before us and ever present to us in this world and in another; and the true order of speech or writing proceeds accordingly. Love, again, has three degrees: first, of interested love corresponding to the conventionalities of rhetoric; secondly, of disinterested or mad love, fixed on objects of sense, and answering, perhaps, to poetry; thirdly, of disinterested love directed towards the unseen, answering to dialectic or the science of the ideas. Lastly, the art of rhetoric in the lower sense is found to rest on a knowledge of the natures and characters of men, which Socrates at the commencement of the Dialogue has described as his own peculiar study.

Thus amid discord a harmony begins to appear; there are many links of connection which are not visible at first sight. At the same time the Phaedrus, although one of the most beautiful of the Platonic Dialogues, is also more irregular than any other. For insight into the world, for sustained irony, for depth of thought, there is no Dialogue superior, or perhaps equal to it. Nevertheless the form of the work has tended to obscure some of Plato's higher aims.

The first speech is composed 'in that balanced style in which the wise love to talk' (*Symp.*). The characteristics of rhetoric are insipidity, mannerism, and monotonous parallelism of clauses. There is more rhythm than reason; the creative power of imagination is wanting.

"'Tis Greece, but living Greece no more.'

Plato has seized by anticipation the spirit which hung over Greek literature for a thousand years afterwards. Yet doubtless there were some who, like Phaedrus, felt a delight in the harmonious cadence and the pedantic reasoning of the rhetoricians newly imported from Sicily, which had ceased to be awakened in them by really great works, such as the odes of Anacreon or Sappho or the orations of Pericles. That the first speech was really written by Lysias is improbable. Like the poem of Solon, or the story of Thamus and Theuth, or the funeral oration of Aspasia (if genuine), or the pretence of Socrates in the Cratylus that his knowledge of philology is derived from Euthyphro, the invention is really due to the imagination of Plato, and may be compared to the parodies of the Sophists in the Protagoras. Numerous fictions of this sort occur in the Dialogues, and the gravity of Plato has sometimes imposed upon his commentators. The introduction of a considerable writing of another would seem not to be in keeping with a great work of art, and has no parallel elsewhere.

In the second speech Socrates is exhibited as beating the rhetoricians at their own weapons; he 'an unpractised man and they masters of the art.' True to his character, he must, however, profess that the speech which he makes is not his own, for he knows nothing of himself. (Compare *Symp.*) Regarded as a rhetorical exercise, the superiority of his speech seems to consist chiefly in a better arrangement of the topics; he begins with a definition of love, and he gives weight to his words by going back to general maxims; a lesser merit is the greater liveliness of Socrates, which hurries him into verse and relieves the monotony of the style.

But Plato had doubtless a higher purpose than to exhibit Socrates as the rival or superior of the Athenian rhetoricians. Even in the speech of Lysias there is a germ of truth, and this is further developed in the parallel oration of Socrates. First, passionate love is overthrown by the sophistical or interested, and then both yield to that higher view of love which is afterwards revealed to us. The extreme of commonplace is contrasted with the most ideal and imaginative of speculations. Socrates, half in jest and to satisfy his own wild humour, takes the disguise of Lysias, but he is also in profound earnest and in a deeper vein of irony than usual. Having improvised his own speech, which is based upon the model of the preceding, he condemns them both. Yet the condemnation is not to be taken seriously, for he is evidently trying to express an aspect of the truth. To understand him, we must make abstraction of morality and of the Greek manner of regarding the relation of the sexes. In this, as in his other discussions about love, what Plato says of the loves of men must be transferred to the loves of women before we can attach any serious meaning to his words. Had he lived in our times he would have made the transposition himself. But seeing in his own age the impossibility of woman being the intellectual helpmate or friend of man (except in the rare instances of a Diotima or an Aspasia), seeing that, even as to personal beauty, her place was taken by young mankind instead of womankind, he tries to work out the problem of love without regard to the distinctions of nature. And full of the evils which he recognized as flowing from the spurious form of love, he proceeds with a deep meaning, though partly in joke, to show that the 'non-lover's' love is better than the 'lover's.'

We may raise the same question in another form: Is marriage preferable with or without love? 'Among ourselves,' as we may say, a little parodying the words of Pausanias in the Symposium, 'there would be one answer to this question: the practice and feeling of some foreign countries appears to be more doubtful.' Suppose a modern Socrates, in defiance of the received notions of society and the sentimental literature of the day, alone against all the writers and readers of novels, to suggest this enquiry, would not the younger 'part of the world be ready to take off its coat and run at him might and main?' (Republic.) Yet, if like Peisthetaerus in Aristophanes, he could persuade the 'birds' to hear him, retiring a little behind a rampart, not of pots and dishes, but of unreadable books, he might have something to say for himself. Might he not argue, 'that a rational being should not follow the dictates of passion in the most important act of his or her life'? Who would willingly enter into a contract at first sight, almost without thought, against the advice and opinion of his friends, at a time when he acknowledges that he is not in his right mind? And yet they are praised by the authors of romances, who reject the warnings of their friends or parents, rather than those who listen to them in such matters. Two inexperienced persons, ignorant of the world and of one another, how can they be said to choose?—they draw lots, whence also the saying, 'marriage is a lottery.' Then he would describe their way of life after marriage; how they monopolize one another's affections to the exclusion of friends and relations: how they pass their days in unmeaning fondness or trivial conversation; how the inferior of the two drags the other down to his or her level; how the cares of a family 'breed meanness in their souls.' In the fulfilment of military or public duties, they are not helpers but hinderers of one another: they cannot undertake any noble enterprise, such as makes the names of men and women famous, from domestic considerations. Too late their eyes are opened; they were taken unawares and desire to part company. Better, he would say, a 'little love at the beginning,' for heaven might have increased it; but now their foolish fondness has changed into mutual dislike. In the days of their honeymoon they never understood that they must provide against offences, that they must have interests, that they must learn the art of living as well as loving. Our misogamist will not appeal to Anacreon or Sappho for a confirmation of his view, but to the universal experience of mankind. How much nobler, in conclusion, he will say, is friendship, which does not receive unmeaning praises from novelists and poets, is not exacting or exclusive, is not impaired by familiarity, is much less expensive, is not so likely to take offence, seldom changes, and may be dissolved from time to time without the assistance of the courts. Besides, he will remark that there is a much greater choice of friends than of wives—you may have more of them and they will be far more improving to your mind. They will not keep you dawdling at home, or dancing attendance upon them; or withdraw you from the great world and stirring scenes of life and action which would make a man of you.

In such a manner, turning the seamy side outwards, a modern Socrates might describe the evils of married and domestic life. They are evils which mankind in general have agreed to conceal, partly because they are compensated by greater goods. Socrates or Archilochus would soon have to sing a palinode for the injustice done to lovely Helen, or some misfortune worse than blindness might befall them. Then they would take up their parable again and say:—that there were two loves, a higher and a lower, holy and unholy, a love of the mind and a love of the body.

> 'Let me not to the marriage of true minds
> Admit impediments. Love is not love
> Which alters when it alteration finds.
>
> ...
>
> Love's not time's fool, though rosy lips and cheeks
> Within his bending sickle's compass come;
> Love alters not with his brief hours and weeks,
> But bears it out even to the edge of doom.'

But this true love of the mind cannot exist between two souls, until they are purified from the grossness of earthly passion: they must pass through a time of trial and conflict first; in the language of religion they must be converted or born again. Then they would see the world transformed into a scene of heavenly beauty; a divine idea would accompany them in all their thoughts and actions. Something too of the recollections of childhood might float about them still; they might regain that old simplicity which had been theirs in other days at their first entrance on life. And although their love of one another was ever present to them, they would acknowledge also a higher love of duty and of God, which united them. And their happiness would depend upon their preserving in them this principle—not losing the ideals of justice and holiness and truth, but renewing them at the fountain of light. When they have attained to this exalted state, let them marry (something too may be conceded to the animal nature of man): or live together in holy and innocent friendship. The poet might describe in eloquent words the nature of such a union; how after many struggles the true love was found:

how the two passed their lives together in the service of God and man; how their characters were reflected upon one another, and seemed to grow more like year by year; how they read in one another's eyes the thoughts, wishes, actions of the other; how they saw each other in God; how in a figure they grew wings like doves, and were 'ready to fly away together and be at rest.' And lastly, he might tell how, after a time at no long intervals, first one and then the other fell asleep, and 'appeared to the unwise' to die, but were reunited in another state of being, in which they saw justice and holiness and truth, not according to the imperfect copies of them which are found in this world, but justice absolute in existence absolute, and so of the rest. And they would hold converse not only with each other, but with blessed souls everywhere; and would be employed in the service of God, every soul fulfilling his own nature and character, and would see into the wonders of earth and heaven, and trace the works of creation to their author.

So, partly in jest but also 'with a certain degree of seriousness,' we may appropriate to ourselves the words of Plato. The use of such a parody, though very imperfect, is to transfer his thoughts to our sphere of religion and feeling, to bring him nearer to us and us to him. Like the Scriptures, Plato admits of endless applications, if we allow for the difference of times and manners; and we lose the better half of him when we regard his Dialogues merely as literary compositions. Any ancient work which is worth reading has a practical and speculative as well as a literary interest. And in Plato, more than in any other Greek writer, the local and transitory is inextricably blended with what is spiritual and eternal. Socrates is necessarily ironical; for he has to withdraw from the received opinions and beliefs of mankind. We cannot separate the transitory from the permanent; nor can we translate the language of irony into that of plain reflection and common sense. But we can imagine the mind of Socrates in another age and country; and we can interpret him by analogy with reference to the errors and prejudices which prevail among ourselves. To return to the Phaedrus:—

Both speeches are strongly condemned by Socrates as sinful and blasphemous towards the god Love, and as worthy only of some haunt of sailors to which good manners were unknown. The meaning of this and other wild language to the same effect, which is introduced by way of contrast to the formality of the two speeches (Socrates has a sense of relief when he has escaped from the trammels of rhetoric), seems to be that the two speeches proceed upon the supposition that love is and ought to be interested, and that no such thing as a real or disinterested passion, which would be at the same time lasting, could be conceived. 'But did I call this "love"? O God, forgive my blasphemy. This is not love. Rather it is the love of the world. But there is another kingdom of love, a kingdom not of this world, divine, eternal. And this other love I will now show you in a mystery.'

Then follows the famous myth, which is a sort of parable, and like other parables ought not to receive too minute an interpretation. In all such allegories there is a great deal which is merely ornamental, and the interpreter has to separate the important from the unimportant. Socrates himself has given the right clue when, in using his own discourse afterwards as the text for his examination of rhetoric, he characterizes it as a 'partly true and tolerably credible mythus,' in which amid poetical figures, order and arrangement were not forgotten.

The soul is described in magnificent language as the self-moved and the source of motion in all other things. This is the philosophical theme or proem of the whole. But ideas must be given through something, and under the pretext that to realize the true nature of the soul would be not only tedious but impossible, we at once pass on to describe the souls of gods as well as men under the figure of two winged steeds and a charioteer. No connection is traced between the soul as the great motive power and the triple soul which is thus imaged. There is no difficulty in seeing that the charioteer represents the reason, or that the black horse is the symbol of the sensual or concupiscent element of human nature. The white horse also represents rational impulse, but the description, 'a lover of honour and modesty and temperance, and a follower of true glory,' though similar, does not at once recall the 'spirit' (thumos) of the Republic. The two steeds really correspond in a figure more nearly to the appetitive and moral or semi-rational soul of Aristotle. And thus, for the first time perhaps in the history of philosophy, we have represented to us the threefold division of psychology. The image of the charioteer and the steeds has been compared with a similar image which occurs in the verses of Parmenides; but it is important to remark that the horses of Parmenides have no allegorical meaning, and that the poet is only describing his own approach in a chariot to the regions of light and the house of the goddess of truth.

The triple soul has had a previous existence, in which following in the train of some god, from whom she derived her character, she beheld partially and imperfectly the vision of absolute truth. All her after existence, passed in many forms of men and animals, is spent in regaining this. The stages of the conflict are many and various; and she is sorely let and hindered by the animal desires of the inferior or concupiscent steed. Again and again she beholds the flashing beauty of the beloved. But before that vision can be finally enjoyed the animal desires must be subjected.

The moral or spiritual element in man is represented by the immortal steed which, like thumos in the Republic, always sides with the reason. Both are dragged out of their course by the furious impulses of desire. In the end something is conceded to the desires, after they have been finally humbled and overpowered. And yet the way of philosophy, or perfect love of the unseen, is total abstinence from bodily delights. 'But all men cannot receive this saying': in the lower life of ambition they may be taken off their guard and stoop to folly unawares, and then, although they do not attain to the highest bliss, yet if they have once conquered they may be happy enough.

The language of the Meno and the Phaedo as well as of the Phaedrus seems to show that at one time of his life Plato was quite serious in maintaining a former state of existence. His mission was to realize the abstract; in that, all good and truth, all the hopes of this and another life seemed to centre. To him abstractions, as we call them, were another kind of knowledge—an inner and unseen world, which seemed to exist far more truly than the fleeting objects of sense which were without him. When we are once able to imagine the intense power which abstract ideas exercised over the mind of Plato, we see that there was no more difficulty to him in realizing the eternal existence of them and of the human minds which were associated with them, in the past and future than in the present. The difficulty was not how they could exist, but how they could fail to exist. In the attempt to regain this 'saving' knowledge of the ideas, the sense was found to be as great an enemy as the desires; and hence two things which to us seem quite distinct are inextricably blended in the representation of Plato.

Thus far we may believe that Plato was serious in his conception of the soul as a motive power, in his reminiscence of a former state of being, in his elevation of the reason over sense and passion, and perhaps in his doctrine of transmigration. Was he equally serious in the rest? For example, are we to attribute his tripartite division of the soul to the gods? Or is this merely assigned to them by way of parallelism with men? The latter is the more probable; for the horses of the gods are both white, i.e. their every impulse is in harmony with reason; their dualism, on the other hand, only carries out the figure of the chariot. Is he serious, again, in regarding love as 'a madness'? That seems to arise out of the antithesis to the former conception of love. At the same time he appears to intimate here, as in the Ion, Apology, Meno, and elsewhere, that there is a faculty in man, whether to be termed in modern language genius, or inspiration, or imagination, or idealism, or communion with God, which cannot be reduced to rule and measure. Perhaps, too, he is ironically repeating the common language of mankind about philosophy, and is turning their jest into a sort of earnest. (Compare *Phaedo*, *Symp*.) Or is he serious in holding that each soul bears the character of a god? He may have had no other account to give of the differences of human characters to which he afterwards refers. Or, again, in his absurd derivation of mantike and oionistike and imeros (compare *Cratylus*)? It is characteristic of the irony of Socrates to mix up sense and nonsense in such a way that no exact line can be drawn between them. And allegory helps to increase this sort of confusion.

As is often the case in the parables and prophecies of Scripture, the meaning is allowed to break through the figure, and the details are not always consistent. When the charioteers and their steeds stand upon the dome of heaven they behold the intangible invisible essences which are not objects of sight. This is because the force of language can no further go. Nor can we dwell much on the circumstance, that at the completion of ten thousand years all are to return to the place from whence they came; because he represents their return as dependent on their own good conduct in the successive stages of existence. Nor again can we attribute anything to the accidental inference which would also follow, that even a tyrant may live righteously in the condition of life to which fate has called him ('he aiblins might, I dinna ken'). But to suppose this would be at variance with Plato himself and with Greek notions generally. He is much more serious in distinguishing men from animals by their recognition of the universal which they have known in a former state, and in denying that this gift of reason can ever be obliterated or lost. In the language of some modern theologians he might be said to maintain the 'final perseverance' of those who have entered on their pilgrim's progress. Other intimations of a 'metaphysic' or 'theology' of the future may also be discerned in him: (1) The moderate predestinarianism which here, as in the Republic, acknowledges the element of chance in human life, and yet asserts the freedom and responsibility of man; (2) The recognition of a moral as well as an intellectual principle in man under the image of an immortal steed; (3) The notion that the divine nature exists by the contemplation of ideas of virtue and justice—or, in other words, the assertion of the essentially moral nature of God; (4) Again, there is the hint that human life is a life of aspiration only, and that the true ideal is not to be found in art; (5) There occurs the first trace of the distinction between necessary and contingent matter; (6) The conception of the soul itself as the motive power and reason of the universe.

The conception of the philosopher, or the philosopher and lover in one, as a sort of madman, may be compared with the Republic and Theaetetus, in both of which the philosopher is regarded as a stranger and monster upon the earth. The whole myth, like the other myths of Plato, describes in a figure things which are beyond the range of human faculties, or inaccessible to the knowledge of the age. That philosophy should be represented as the inspiration of love is a conception that has already become familiar to us in the Symposium, and is the expression partly of Plato's enthusiasm for the idea, and is also an indication of the real power exercised by the passion of friendship over the mind of the Greek. The master in the art of love knew that there was a mystery in these feelings and their associations, and especially in the contrast of the sensible and permanent which is afforded by them; and he sought to explain this, as he explained universal ideas, by a reference to a former state of existence. The capriciousness of love is also derived by him from an attachment to some god in a former world. The singular remark that the beloved is more affected than the lover at the final consummation of their love, seems likewise to hint at a psychological truth.

It is difficult to exhaust the meanings of a work like the Phaedrus, which indicates so much more than it expresses; and is full of inconsistencies and ambiguities which were not perceived by Plato himself. For example, when he is speaking of the soul does he mean the human or the divine soul? and are they both equally self-moving and constructed on the same threefold principle? We should certainly be disposed to reply that the self-motive is to be attributed to God only; and on the other hand that the appetitive and passionate elements have no place in His nature. So we should infer from the reason of the thing, but there is no indication in Plato's own writings that this was his meaning. Or, again, when he explains the different characters of men by referring them back to the nature of the God whom they served in a former state of existence, we are inclined to ask whether he is serious: Is he not rather using a mythological figure, here as elsewhere, to draw a veil over things which are beyond the limits of mortal knowledge? Once more, in speaking of beauty is he really thinking of some external form such as might have been expressed in the works of Phidias or Praxiteles; and not rather of an imaginary beauty, of a sort which extinguishes rather than stimulates vulgar love,—a heavenly beauty like that which flashed from time to time before the eyes of Dante or Bunyan? Surely the latter. But it would be idle to reconcile all the details of the passage: it is a picture, not a system, and a picture which is for the greater part an allegory, and an allegory which allows the meaning to come through. The image of the charioteer and his steeds is placed side by side with the absolute forms of justice, temperance, and the like, which are abstract ideas only, and which are seen with the eye of the soul in her heavenly journey. The first impression of such a passage, in which no attempt is made to separate the substance from the form, is far truer than an elaborate philosophical analysis.

Phaedrus

It is too often forgotten that the whole of the second discourse of Socrates is only an allegory, or figure of speech. For this reason, it is unnecessary to enquire whether the love of which Plato speaks is the love of men or of women. It is really a general idea which includes both, and in which the sensual element, though not wholly eradicated, is reduced to order and measure. We must not attribute a meaning to every fanciful detail. Nor is there any need to call up revolting associations, which as a matter of good taste should be banished, and which were far enough away from the mind of Plato. These and similar passages should be interpreted by the Laws. Nor is there anything in the Symposium, or in the Charmides, in reality inconsistent with the sterner rule which Plato lays down in the Laws. At the same time it is not to be denied that love and philosophy are described by Socrates in figures of speech which would not be used in Christian times; or that nameless vices were prevalent at Athens and in other Greek cities; or that friendships between men were a more sacred tie, and had a more important social and educational influence than among ourselves. (See note on *Symposium*.)

In the Phaedrus, as well as in the Symposium, there are two kinds of love, a lower and a higher, the one answering to the natural wants of the animal, the other rising above them and contemplating with religious awe the forms of justice, temperance, holiness, yet finding them also 'too dazzling bright for mortal eye,' and shrinking from them in amazement. The opposition between these two kinds of love may be compared to the opposition between the flesh and the spirit in the Epistles of St. Paul. It would be unmeaning to suppose that Plato, in describing the spiritual combat, in which the rational soul is finally victor and master of both the steeds, condescends to allow any indulgence of unnatural lusts.

Two other thoughts about love are suggested by this passage. First of all, love is represented here, as in the Symposium, as one of the great powers of nature, which takes many forms and two principal ones, having a predominant influence over the lives of men. And these two, though opposed, are not absolutely separated the one from the other. Plato, with his great knowledge of human nature, was well aware how easily one is transformed into the other, or how soon the noble but fleeting aspiration may return into the nature of the animal, while the lower instinct which is latent always remains. The intermediate sentimentalism, which has exercised so great an influence on the literature of modern Europe, had no place in the classical times of Hellas; the higher love, of which Plato speaks, is the subject, not of poetry or fiction, but of philosophy.

Secondly, there seems to be indicated a natural yearning of the human mind that the great ideas of justice, temperance, wisdom, should be expressed in some form of visible beauty, like the absolute purity and goodness which Christian art has sought to realize in the person of the Madonna. But although human nature has often attempted to represent outwardly what can be only 'spiritually discerned,' men feel that in pictures and images, whether painted or carved, or described in words only, we have not the substance but the shadow of the truth which is in heaven. There is no reason to suppose that in the fairest works of Greek art, Plato ever conceived himself to behold an image, however faint, of ideal truths. 'Not in that way was wisdom seen.'

We may now pass on to the second part of the Dialogue, which is a criticism on the first. Rhetoric is assailed on various grounds: first, as desiring to persuade, without a knowledge of the truth; and secondly, as ignoring the distinction between certain and probable matter. The three speeches are then passed in review: the first of them has no definition of the nature of love, and no order in the topics (being in these respects far inferior to the second); while the third of them is found (though a fancy of the hour) to be framed upon real dialectical principles. But dialectic is not rhetoric; nothing on that subject is to be found in the endless treatises of rhetoric, however prolific in hard names. When Plato has sufficiently put them to the test of ridicule he touches, as with the point of a needle, the real error, which is the confusion of preliminary knowledge with creative power. No attainments will provide the speaker with genius; and the sort of attainments which can alone be of any value are the higher philosophy and the power of psychological analysis, which is given by dialectic, but not by the rules of the rhetoricians.

In this latter portion of the Dialogue there are many texts which may help us to speak and to think. The names dialectic and rhetoric are passing out of use; we hardly examine seriously into their nature and limits, and probably the arts both of speaking and of conversation have been unduly neglected by us. But the mind of Socrates pierces through the differences of times and countries into the essential nature of man; and his words apply equally to the modern world and to the Athenians of old. Would he not have asked of us, or rather is he not asking of us, Whether we have ceased to prefer appearances to reality? Let us take a survey of the professions to which he refers and try them by his standard. Is not all literature passing into criticism, just as Athenian literature in the age of Plato was degenerating into sophistry and rhetoric? We can discourse and write about poems and paintings, but we seem to have lost the gift of creating them. Can we wonder that few of them 'come sweetly from nature,' while ten thousand reviewers (*mala murioi*) are engaged in dissecting them? Young men, like Phaedrus, are enamoured of their own literary clique and have but a feeble sympathy with the master-minds of former ages. They recognize 'a *poetical* necessity in the writings of their favourite author, even when he boldly wrote off just what came in his head.' They are beginning to think that Art is enough, just at the time when Art is about to disappear from the world. And would not a great painter, such as Michael Angelo, or a great poet, such as Shakespeare, returning to earth, 'courteously rebuke' us—would he not say that we are putting 'in the place of Art the preliminaries of Art,' confusing Art the expression of mind and truth with Art the composition of colours and forms; and perhaps he might more severely chastise some of us for trying to invent 'a new shudder' instead of bringing to the birth living and healthy creations? These he would regard as the signs of an age wanting in original power.

Turning from literature and the arts to law and politics, again we fall under the lash of Socrates. For do we not often make 'the worse appear the better cause;' and do not 'both parties sometimes agree to tell lies'? Is not pleading 'an art of speaking unconnected with the truth'? There is another text of Socrates which must not be forgotten in relation to this subject. In the endless maze of English law is there any 'dividing the whole into parts or reuniting the parts into a whole'—any semblance of an organized being 'having hands and feet and other members'? Instead of a system there is the Chaos of

Anaxagoras (omou panta chremata) and no Mind or Order. Then again in the noble art of politics, who thinks of first principles and of true ideas? We avowedly follow not the truth but the will of the many (compare Republic). Is not legislation too a sort of literary effort, and might not statesmanship be described as the 'art of enchanting' the house? While there are some politicians who have no knowledge of the truth, but only of what is likely to be approved by 'the many who sit in judgment,' there are others who can give no form to their ideal, neither having learned 'the art of persuasion,' nor having any insight into the 'characters of men.' Once more, has not medical science become a professional routine, which many 'practise without being able to say who were their instructors'—the application of a few drugs taken from a book instead of a life-long study of the natures and constitutions of human beings? Do we see as clearly as Hippocrates 'that the nature of the body can only be understood as a whole'? (Compare *Charm.*) And are not they held to be the wisest physicians who have the greatest distrust of their art? What would Socrates think of our newspapers, of our theology? Perhaps he would be afraid to speak of them;—the one *vox populi*, the other *vox Dei*, he might hesitate to attack them; or he might trace a fanciful connexion between them, and ask doubtfully, whether they are not equally inspired? He would remark that we are always searching for a belief and deploring our unbelief, seeming to prefer popular opinions unverified and contradictory to unpopular truths which are assured to us by the most certain proofs: that our preachers are in the habit of praising God 'without regard to truth and falsehood, attributing to Him every species of greatness and glory, saying that He is all this and the cause of all that, in order that we may exhibit Him as the fairest and best of all' (*Symp.*) without any consideration of His real nature and character or of the laws by which He governs the world—seeking for a 'private judgment' and not for the truth or 'God's judgment.' What would he say of the Church, which we praise in like manner, 'meaning ourselves,' without regard to history or experience? Might he not ask, whether we 'care more for the truth of religion, or for the speaker and the country from which the truth comes'? or, whether the 'select wise' are not 'the many' after all? (*Symp.*) So we may fill up the sketch of Socrates, lest, as Phaedrus says, the argument should be too 'abstract and barren of illustrations.' (Compare *Symp.*, *Apol.*, *Euthyphro*.)

He next proceeds with enthusiasm to define the royal art of dialectic as the power of dividing a whole into parts, and of uniting the parts in a whole, and which may also be regarded (compare *Soph.*) as the process of the mind talking with herself. The latter view has probably led Plato to the paradox that speech is superior to writing, in which he may seem also to be doing an injustice to himself. For the two cannot be fairly compared in the manner which Plato suggests. The contrast of the living and dead word, and the example of Socrates, which he has represented in the form of the Dialogue, seem to have misled him. For speech and writing have really different functions; the one is more transitory, more diffuse, more elastic and capable of adaptation to moods and times; the other is more permanent, more concentrated, and is uttered not to this or that person or audience, but to all the world. In the Politicus the paradox is carried further; the mind or will of the king is preferred to the written law; he is supposed to be the Law personified, the ideal made Life.

Yet in both these statements there is also contained a truth; they may be compared with one another, and also with the other famous paradox, that 'knowledge cannot be taught.' Socrates means to say, that what is truly written is written in the soul, just as what is truly taught grows up in the soul from within and is not forced upon it from without. When planted in a congenial soil the little seed becomes a tree, and 'the birds of the air build their nests in the branches.' There is an echo of this in the prayer at the end of the Dialogue, 'Give me beauty in the inward soul, and may the inward and outward man be at one.' We may further compare the words of St. Paul, 'Written not on tables of stone, but on fleshly tables of the heart;' and again, 'Ye are my epistles known and read of all men.' There may be a use in writing as a preservative against the forgetfulness of old age, but to live is higher far, to be ourselves the book, or the epistle, the truth embodied in a person, the Word made flesh. Something like this we may believe to have passed before Plato's mind when he affirmed that speech was superior to writing. So in other ages, weary of literature and criticism, of making many books,

Plato

of writing articles in reviews, some have desired to live more closely in communion with their fellow-men, to speak heart to heart, to speak and act only, and not to write, following the example of Socrates and of Christ...

Some other touches of inimitable grace and art and of the deepest wisdom may be also noted; such as the prayer or 'collect' which has just been cited, 'Give me beauty,' etc.; or 'the great name which belongs to God alone;' or 'the saying of wiser men than ourselves that a man of sense should try to please not his fellow-servants, but his good and noble masters,' like St. Paul again; or the description of the 'heavenly originals'...

The chief criteria for determining the date of the Dialogue are (1) the ages of Lysias and Isocrates; (2) the character of the work.

Lysias was born in the year 458; Isocrates in the year 436, about seven years before the birth of Plato. The first of the two great rhetoricians is described as in the zenith of his fame; the second is still young and full of promise. Now it is argued that this must have been written in the youth of Isocrates, when the promise was not yet fulfilled. And thus we should have to assign the Dialogue to a year not later than 406, when Isocrates was thirty and Plato twenty-three years of age, and while Socrates himself was still alive.

Those who argue in this way seem not to reflect how easily Plato can 'invent Egyptians or anything else,' and how careless he is of historical truth or probability. Who would suspect that the wise Critias, the virtuous Charmides, had ended their lives among the thirty tyrants? Who would imagine that Lysias, who is here assailed by Socrates, is the son of his old friend Cephalus? Or that Isocrates himself is the enemy of Plato and his school? No arguments can be drawn from the appropriateness or inappropriateness of the characters of Plato. (Else, perhaps, it might be further argued that, judging from their extant remains, insipid rhetoric is far more characteristic of Isocrates than of Lysias.) But Plato makes use of names which have often hardly any connection with the historical characters to whom they belong. In this instance the comparative favour shown to Isocrates may possibly be accounted for by the circumstance of his belonging to the aristocratical, as Lysias to the democratical party.

Few persons will be inclined to suppose, in the superficial manner of some ancient critics, that a dialogue which treats of love must necessarily have been written in youth. As little weight can be attached to the argument that Plato must have visited Egypt before he wrote the story of Theuth and Thamus. For there is no real proof that he ever went to Egypt; and even if he did, he might have known or invented Egyptian traditions before he went there. The late date of the Phaedrus will have to be established by other arguments than these: the maturity of the thought, the perfection of the style, the insight, the relation to the other Platonic Dialogues, seem to contradict the notion that it could have been the work of a youth of twenty or twenty-three years of age. The cosmological notion of the mind as the primum mobile, and the admission of impulse into the immortal nature, also afford grounds for assigning a later date. (Compare *Tim.*, *Soph.*, *Laws*.) Add to this that the picture of Socrates, though in some lesser particulars,—e.g. his going without sandals, his habit of remaining within the walls, his emphatic declaration that his study is human nature,—an exact resemblance, is in the main the Platonic and not the real Socrates. Can we suppose 'the young man to have told such lies' about his master while he was still alive? Moreover, when two Dialogues are so closely connected as the Phaedrus and Symposium, there is great improbability in supposing that one of them was written at least twenty years after the other. The conclusion seems to be, that the Dialogue was written at some comparatively late but unknown period of Plato's life, after he had deserted the purely Socratic point of view, but before he had entered on the more abstract speculations of the Sophist or the Philebus. Taking into account the divisions of the soul, the doctrine of transmigration, the contemplative nature of the philosophic life, and the character of the style, we shall not be far wrong in placing the Phaedrus in the neighbourhood of the Republic; remarking only that allowance must be made for the poetical element in the Phaedrus, which, while falling short of the Republic in definite philosophic results, seems to have glimpses of a truth beyond.

Two short passages, which are unconnected with the main subject of the Dialogue, may seem to merit a more particular notice: (1) the locus classicus about mythology; (2) the tale of the grasshoppers.

The first passage is remarkable as showing that Plato was entirely free from what may be termed the Euhemerism of his age. For there were Euhemerists in Hellas long before Euhemerus. Early philosophers, like Anaxagoras and Metrodorus, had found in Homer and mythology hidden meanings. Plato, with a truer instinct, rejects these attractive interpretations; he regards the inventor of them as 'unfortunate;' and they draw a man off from the knowledge of himself. There is a latent criticism, and also a poetical sense in Plato, which enable him to discard them, and yet in another way to make use of poetry and mythology as a vehicle of thought and feeling. What would he have said of the discovery of Christian doctrines in these old Greek legends? While acknowledging that such interpretations are 'very nice,' would he not have remarked that they are found in all sacred literatures? They cannot be tested by any criterion of truth, or used to establish any truth; they add nothing to the sum of human knowledge; they are—what we please, and if employed as 'peacemakers' between the new and old are liable to serious misconstruction, as he elsewhere remarks (*Republic*). And therefore he would have 'bid Farewell to them; the study of them would take up too much of his time; and he has not as yet learned the true nature of religion.' The 'sophistical' interest of Phaedrus, the little touch about the two versions of the story, the ironical manner in which these explanations are set aside—'the common opinion about them is enough for me'—the allusion to the serpent Typho may be noted in passing; also the general agreement between the tone of this speech and the remark of Socrates which follows afterwards, 'I am a diviner, but a poor one.'

The tale of the grasshoppers is naturally suggested by the surrounding scene. They are also the representatives of the Athenians as children of the soil. Under the image of the lively chirruping grasshoppers who inform the Muses in heaven about those who honour them on earth, Plato intends to represent an Athenian audience (*tettigessin eoikotes*). The story is introduced, apparently, to mark a change of subject, and also, like several other allusions which occur in the course of the Dialogue, in order to preserve the scene in the recollection of the reader.

* * *

Phaedrus

No one can duly appreciate the dialogues of Plato, especially the Phaedrus, Symposium, and portions of the Republic, who has not a sympathy with mysticism. To the uninitiated, as he would himself have acknowledged, they will appear to be the dreams of a poet who is disguised as a philosopher. There is a twofold difficulty in apprehending this aspect of the Platonic writings. First, we do not immediately realize that under the marble exterior of Greek literature was concealed a soul thrilling with spiritual emotion. Secondly, the forms or figures which the Platonic philosophy assumes, are not like the images of the prophet Isaiah, or of the Apocalypse, familiar to us in the days of our youth. By mysticism we mean, not the extravagance of an erring fancy, but the concentration of reason in feeling, the enthusiastic love of the good, the true, the one, the sense of the infinity of knowledge and of the marvel of the human faculties. When feeding upon such thoughts the 'wing of the soul' is renewed and gains strength; she is raised above 'the manikins of earth' and their opinions, waiting in wonder to know, and working with reverence to find out what God in this or in another life may reveal to her.

ON THE DECLINE OF GREEK LITERATURE

One of the main purposes of Plato in the *Phaedrus* is to satirize Rhetoric, or rather the Professors of Rhetoric who swarmed at Athens in the fourth century before Christ. As in the opening of the Dialogue he ridicules the interpreters of mythology; as in the Protagoras he mocks at the Sophists; as in the Euthydemus he makes fun of the word-splitting Eristics; as in the *Cratylus* he ridicules the fancies of Etymologers; as in the Meno and Gorgias and some other dialogues he makes reflections and casts sly imputation upon the higher classes at Athens; so in the Phaedrus, chiefly in the latter part, he aims his shafts at the rhetoricians. The profession of rhetoric was the greatest and most popular in Athens, necessary 'to a man's salvation,' or at any rate to his attainment of wealth or power; but Plato finds nothing wholesome or genuine in the purpose of it. It is a veritable 'sham,' having no relation to fact, or to truth of any kind. It is antipathetic to him not only as a philosopher, but also as a great writer. He cannot abide the tricks of the rhetoricians, or the pedantries and mannerisms which they introduce into speech and writing. He sees clearly how far removed they are from the ways of simplicity and truth, and how ignorant of the very elements of the art which they are professing to teach. The thing which is most necessary of all, the knowledge of human nature, is hardly if at all considered by them. The true rules of composition, which are very few, are not to be found in their voluminous systems. Their pretentiousness, their omniscience, their large fortunes, their impatience of argument, their indifference to first principles, their stupidity, their progresses through Hellas accompanied by a troop of their disciples—these things were very distasteful to Plato, who esteemed genius far above art, and was quite sensible of the interval which separated them (*Phaedrus*). It is the interval which separates Sophists and rhetoricians from ancient famous men and women such as Homer and Hesiod, Anacreon and Sappho, Aeschylus and Sophocles; and the Platonic Socrates is afraid that, if he approves the former, he will be disowned by the latter. The spirit of rhetoric was soon to overspread all Hellas; and Plato with prophetic insight may have seen, from afar, the great literary waste or dead level, or interminable marsh, in which Greek literature was soon to disappear. A similar vision of the decline of the Greek drama and of the contrast of the old literature and the new was present to the mind of Aristophanes after the death of the three great tragedians (*Frogs*). After about a hundred, or at most two hundred years if we exclude Homer, the genius of Hellas had ceased to flower or blossom. The dreary waste which follows, beginning with the Alexandrian writers and even before them in the platitudes of Isocrates and his school, spreads over much more than a thousand years. And from this decline the Greek language and literature, unlike the Latin, which has come to life in new forms and been developed into the great European languages, never recovered.

This monotony of literature, without merit, without genius and without character, is a phenomenon which deserves more attention than it has hitherto received; it is a phenomenon unique in the literary history of the world. How could there have been so much cultivation, so much diligence in writing, and so little mind or real creative power? Why did a thousand years invent nothing better than Sibylline books, Orphic poems, Byzantine imitations of classical histories, Christian reproductions of Greek plays, novels like the silly and obscene romances of Longus and Heliodorus, innumerable forged epistles, a great many epigrams, biographies of the meanest and most meagre description, a sham philosophy which was the bastard progeny of the union between Hellas and the East? Only in Plutarch, in Lucian, in Longinus, in the Roman emperors Marcus Aurelius and Julian, in some of the Christian fathers are there any traces of good sense or originality, or any power of arousing the interest of later ages. And when new books ceased to be written, why did hosts of grammarians and interpreters flock in, who never attain to any sound notion either of grammar or interpretation? Why did the physical sciences never arrive at any true knowledge or make any real progress? Why did poetry droop and languish? Why did history degenerate into fable? Why did words lose their power of expression? Why were ages of external greatness and magnificence attended by all the signs of decay in the human mind which are possible?

To these questions many answers may be given, which if not the true causes, are at least to be reckoned among the symptoms of the decline. There is the want of method in physical science, the want of criticism in history, the want of simplicity or delicacy in poetry, the want of political freedom, which is the true atmosphere of public speaking, in oratory. The ways of life were luxurious and commonplace. Philosophy had become extravagant, eclectic, abstract, devoid of any real content. At length it ceased to exist. It had spread words like plaster over the whole field of knowledge. It had grown ascetic on one side, mystical on the other. Neither of these tendencies was favourable to literature. There was no sense of beauty either in language or in art. The Greek world became vacant, barbaric, oriental. No one had anything new to say, or any conviction of truth. The age had no remembrance of the past, no power of understanding what other ages thought and felt. The Catholic faith had degenerated into dogma and controversy. For more than a thousand years not a single writer of first-rate, or even of second-rate, reputation has a place in the innumerable rolls of Greek literature.

If we seek to go deeper, we can still only describe the outward nature of the clouds or darkness which were spread over the heavens during so many ages without relief or light. We may say that this, like several other long periods in the history of the human race, was destitute, or deprived of the moral qualities which are the root of literary excellence. It had no life or aspiration, no national or political force, no desire for consistency, no love of knowledge for its own sake. It did not attempt to pierce the mists which surrounded it. It did not propose to itself to go forward and scale the heights of knowledge, but to go backwards and seek at the beginning what can only be found towards the end. It was lost in doubt and ignorance. It rested upon tradition and authority. It had none of the higher play of fancy which creates poetry; and where there is no true poetry, neither can there be any good prose. It had no great characters, and therefore it had no great writers. It was incapable of distinguishing between words and things. It was so hopelessly below the ancient standard of classical Greek art and literature that it had no power of understanding or of valuing them. It is doubtful whether any Greek author was justly appreciated in antiquity except by his own contemporaries; and this neglect of the great authors of the past led to the disappearance of the larger part of them, while the Greek fathers were mostly preserved. There is no reason to suppose that, in the century before the taking of Constantinople, much more was in existence than the scholars of the Renaissance carried away with them to Italy.

The character of Greek literature sank lower as time went on. It consisted more and more of compilations, of scholia, of extracts, of commentaries, forgeries, imitations. The commentator or interpreter had no conception of his author as a whole, and very little of the context of any passage which he was explaining. The least things were preferred by him to the greatest. The question of a reading, or a grammatical form, or an accent, or the uses of a word, took the place of the aim or subject of the book. He had no sense of the beauties of an author, and very little light is thrown by him on real difficulties. He interprets past ages by his own. The greatest classical writers are the least appreciated by him. This seems to be the reason why so many of them have perished, why the lyric poets have almost wholly disappeared; why, out of the eighty or ninety tragedies of Aeschylus and Sophocles, only seven of each had been preserved.

Such an age of sciolism and scholasticism may possibly once more get the better of the literary world. There are those who prophesy that the signs of such a day are again appearing among us, and that at the end of the present century no writer of the first class will be still alive. They think that the Muse of Literature may transfer herself to other countries less dried up or worn out than our own. They seem to see the withering effect of criticism on original genius. No one can doubt that such a decay or decline of literature and of art seriously affects the manners and character of a nation. It takes away half the joys and refinements of life; it increases its dulness and grossness. Hence it becomes a matter of great interest to consider how, if at all, such a degeneracy may be averted. Is there any elixir which can restore life and youth to the literature of a nation, or at any rate which can prevent it becoming unmanned and enfeebled?

First there is the progress of education. It is possible, and even probable, that the extension of the means of knowledge over a wider area and to persons living under new conditions may lead to many new combinations of thought and language. But, as yet, experience does not favour the realization of such a hope or promise. It may be truly answered that at present the training of teachers and the methods of education are very imperfect, and therefore that we cannot judge of the future by the present. When more of our youth are trained in the best literatures, and in the best parts of them, their minds may be expected to have a larger growth. They will have more interests, more thoughts, more material for conversation; they will have a higher standard and begin to think for themselves. The number of persons who will have the opportunity of receiving the highest education through the cheap press, and by the help of high schools and colleges, may increase tenfold. It is likely that in every thousand persons there is at least one who is far above the average in natural capacity, but the seed which is in him dies for want of cultivation. It has never had any stimulus to grow, or any field in which to blossom and produce fruit. Here is a great reservoir or treasure-house of human intelligence out of which new waters may flow and cover the earth. If at any time the great men of the world should die out, and originality or genius appear to suffer a partial eclipse, there is a boundless hope in the multitude of intelligences for future generations. They may bring gifts to men such as the world has never received before. They may begin at a higher point and yet take with them all the results of the past. The co-operation of many may have effects not less striking, though different in character from those which the creative genius of a single man, such as Bacon or Newton, formerly produced. There is also great hope to be derived, not merely from the extension of education over a wider area, but from the continuance of it during many generations. Educated parents will have children fit to receive education; and these again will grow up under circumstances far more favourable to the growth of intelligence than any which have hitherto existed in our own or in former ages.

Even if we were to suppose no more men of genius to be produced, the great writers of ancient or of modern times will remain to furnish abundant materials of education to the coming generation. Now that every nation holds communication with every other, we may truly say in a fuller sense than formerly that 'the thoughts of men are widened with the process of the suns.' They will not be 'cribbed, cabined, and confined' within a province or an island. The East will provide elements of culture to the West as well as the West to the East. The religions and literatures of the world will be open books, which he who wills may read. The human race may not be always ground down by bodily toil, but may have greater leisure for the improvement of the mind. The increasing sense of the greatness and infinity of nature will tend to awaken in men larger and more liberal thoughts. The love of mankind may be the source of a greater development of literature than nationality has ever been. There may be a greater freedom from prejudice and party; we may better understand the whereabouts of truth, and therefore there may be more success and fewer failures in the search for it. Lastly, in the coming ages we shall carry with us the recollection of the past, in which are necessarily contained many seeds of revival and renaissance in the future. So far is the world from becoming exhausted, so groundless is the fear that literature will ever die out.

PHAEDRUS

by

Plato

Translated by Benjamin Jowett

PERSONS OF THE DIALOGUE: Socrates, Phaedrus.

SCENE: Under a plane-tree, by the banks of the Ilissus.

SOCRATES: My dear Phaedrus, whence come you, and whither are you going?

PHAEDRUS: I come from Lysias the son of Cephalus, and I am going to take a walk outside the wall, for I have been sitting with him the whole morning; and our common friend Acumenus tells me that it is much more refreshing to walk in the open air than to be shut up in a cloister.

SOCRATES: There he is right. Lysias then, I suppose, was in the town?

PHAEDRUS: Yes, he was staying with Epicrates, here at the house of Morychus; that house which is near the temple of Olympian Zeus.

SOCRATES: And how did he entertain you? Can I be wrong in supposing that Lysias gave you a feast of discourse?

PHAEDRUS: You shall hear, if you can spare time to accompany me.

SOCRATES: And should I not deem the conversation of you and Lysias 'a thing of higher import,' as I may say in the words of Pindar, 'than any business'?

PHAEDRUS: Will you go on?

SOCRATES: And will you go on with the narration?

PHAEDRUS: My tale, Socrates, is one of your sort, for love was the theme which occupied us—love after a fashion: Lysias has been writing about a
fair youth who was being tempted, but not by a lover; and this was the point: he ingeniously proved that the non-lover should be accepted rather than the lover.

SOCRATES: O that is noble of him! I wish that he would say the poor man rather than the rich, and the old man rather than the young one;—then he would meet the case of me and of many a man; his words would be quite refreshing, and he would be a public benefactor. For my part, I do so long to hear his speech, that if you walk all the way to Megara, and when you have reached the wall come back, as Herodicus recommends, without going in, I will keep you company.

PHAEDRUS: What do you mean, my good Socrates? How can you imagine that my unpractised memory can do justice to an elaborate work, which the greatest rhetorician of the age spent a long time in composing. Indeed, I cannot; I would give a great deal if I could.

SOCRATES: I believe that I know Phaedrus about as well as I know myself, and I am very sure that the speech of Lysias was repeated to him, not once only, but again and again;—he insisted on hearing it many times over and Lysias was very willing to gratify him; at last, when nothing else would do, he got hold of the book, and looked at what he most wanted to see,—this occupied him during the whole morning;—and then when he was tired with sitting, he went out to

Phaedrus

take a walk, not until, by the dog, as I believe, he had simply learned by heart the entire discourse, unless it was unusually long, and he went to a place outside the wall that he might practise his lesson. There he saw a certain lover of discourse who had a similar weakness;—he saw and rejoiced; now thought he, 'I shall have a partner in my revels.' And he invited him to come and walk with him. But when the lover of discourse begged that he would repeat the tale, he gave himself airs and said, 'No I cannot,' as if he were indisposed; although, if the hearer had refused, he would sooner or later have been compelled by him to listen whether he would or no. Therefore, Phaedrus, bid him do at once what he will soon do whether bidden or not.

PHAEDRUS: I see that you will not let me off until I speak in some fashion or other; verily therefore my best plan is to speak as I best can.

SOCRATES: A very true remark, that of yours.

PHAEDRUS: I will do as I say; but believe me, Socrates, I did not learn the very words—O no; nevertheless I have a general notion of what he said, and will give you a summary of the points in which the lover differed from the non-lover. Let me begin at the beginning.

SOCRATES: Yes, my sweet one; but you must first of all show what you have in your left hand under your cloak, for that roll, as I suspect, is the actual discourse. Now, much as I love you, I would not have you suppose that I am going to have your memory exercised at my expense, if you have Lysias himself here.

PHAEDRUS: Enough; I see that I have no hope of practising my art upon you. But if I am to read, where would you please to sit?

SOCRATES: Let us turn aside and go by the Ilissus; we will sit down at some quiet spot.

PHAEDRUS: I am fortunate in not having my sandals, and as you never have any, I think that we may go along the brook and cool our feet in the water; this will be the easiest way, and at midday and in the summer is far from being unpleasant.

SOCRATES: Lead on, and look out for a place in which we can sit down.

PHAEDRUS: Do you see the tallest plane-tree in the distance?

SOCRATES: Yes.

PHAEDRUS: There are shade and gentle breezes, and grass on which we may either sit or lie down.

SOCRATES: Move forward.

PHAEDRUS: I should like to know, Socrates, whether the place is not somewhere here at which Boreas is said to have carried off Orithyia from the banks of the Ilissus?

SOCRATES: Such is the tradition.

PHAEDRUS: And is this the exact spot? The little stream is delightfully clear and bright; I can fancy that there might be maidens playing near.

SOCRATES: I believe that the spot is not exactly here, but about a quarter of a mile lower down, where you cross to the temple of Artemis, and there is, I think, some sort of an altar of Boreas at the place.

PHAEDRUS: I have never noticed it; but I beseech you to tell me, Socrates, do you believe this tale?

SOCRATES: The wise are doubtful, and I should not be singular if, like them, I too doubted. I might have a rational explanation that

Orithyia was playing with Pharmacia, when a northern gust carried her over the neighbouring rocks; and this being the manner of her death, she was said to have been carried away by Boreas. There is a discrepancy, however, about the locality; according to another version of the story she was taken from Areopagus, and not from this place. Now I quite acknowledge that these allegories are very nice, but he is not to be envied who has to invent them; much labour and ingenuity will be required of him; and when he has once begun, he must go on and rehabilitate Hippocentaurs and chimeras dire. Gorgons and winged steeds flow in apace, and numberless other inconceivable and portentous natures. And if he is sceptical about them, and would fain reduce them one after another to the rules of probability, this sort of crude philosophy will take up a great deal of time. Now I have no leisure for such enquiries; shall I tell you why? I must first know myself, as the Delphian inscription says; to be curious about that which is not my concern, while I am still in ignorance of my own self, would be ridiculous. And therefore I bid farewell to all this; the common opinion is enough for me. For, as I was saying, I want to know not about this, but about myself: am I a monster more complicated and swollen with passion than the serpent Typho, or a creature of a gentler and simpler sort, to whom Nature has given a diviner and lowlier destiny? But let me ask you, friend: have we not reached the plane-tree to which you were conducting us?

PHAEDRUS: Yes, this is the tree.

SOCRATES: By Here, a fair resting-place, full of summer sounds and scents. Here is this lofty and spreading plane-tree, and the agnus castus high and clustering, in the fullest blossom and the greatest fragrance; and the stream which flows beneath the plane-tree is deliciously cold to the feet. Judging from the ornaments and images, this must be a spot sacred to Achelous and the Nymphs. How delightful is the breeze:—so very sweet; and there is a sound in the air shrill and summerlike which makes answer to the chorus of the cicadae. But the greatest charm of all is the grass, like a pillow gently sloping to the head. My dear Phaedrus, you have been an admirable guide.

PHAEDRUS: What an incomprehensible being you are, Socrates: when you are in the country, as you say, you really are like some stranger who is led about by a guide. Do you ever cross the border? I rather think that you never venture even outside the gates.

SOCRATES: Very true, my good friend; and I hope that you will excuse me when you hear the reason, which is, that I am a lover of knowledge, and the men who dwell in the city are my teachers, and not the trees or the country. Though I do indeed believe that you have found a spell with which to draw me out of the city into the country, like a hungry cow before whom a bough or a bunch of fruit is waved. For only hold up before me in like manner a book, and you may lead me all round Attica, and over the wide world. And now having arrived, I intend to lie down, and do you choose any posture in which you can read best. Begin.

PHAEDRUS: Listen. You know how matters stand with me; and how, as I conceive, this affair may be arranged for the advantage of both of us. And I maintain that I ought not to fail in my suit, because I am not your lover: for lovers repent of the kindnesses which they have shown when their passion ceases, but to the non-lovers who are free and not under any compulsion, no time of repentance ever comes; for they confer their benefits according to the measure of their ability, in the way which is most conducive to their own interest. Then again, lovers consider how by reason of their love they have neglected their own concerns and rendered service to others: and when to these benefits conferred they add on the troubles which they have endured, they think that they have long ago made to the beloved a very ample return. But the non-lover has no such tormenting recollections; he has never neglected his affairs or quarrelled with his relations; he has no troubles to add up or excuses to invent; and being well rid of all these evils, why should he not freely do what will gratify the beloved? If you say that the lover is more to be esteemed, because his love is thought to be greater; for he is willing to say and do what is hateful to other men, in order to please his beloved;—that, if true, is only a proof that he will prefer any future love to his present, and will injure his old love at the pleasure of the new. And how, in a matter of such infinite importance, can a man be right in trusting himself to one who is afflicted with a malady which no experienced person would attempt to cure, for the patient himself admits that he is not in his right mind, and acknowledges that he is wrong in his mind, but says that he is unable to control himself? And if he came to his right mind, would he ever imagine that the desires were good which he conceived when in his wrong mind? Once more, there are many more non-lovers than lovers; and if you choose the best of the lovers, you will not have many to choose from; but if from the non-lovers, the choice will be larger, and you will be far more likely to find among them a person who is worthy of your friendship. If public opinion be your dread, and you would avoid reproach, in all probability the lover, who is always thinking that other men are as emulous of him as he is of them, will boast to some one of his successes, and make a show of them openly in the pride of his heart;—he wants others to know that his labour has not been lost; but the non-lover is more his own master, and is desirous of solid good, and not of the opinion of mankind. Again, the lover may be generally noted or seen following the beloved (this is his regular occupation), and whenever they are observed to exchange two words they are supposed to meet about some affair of love either past or in contemplation; but when non-lovers meet, no one asks the reason why, because people know that talking to another is natural, whether friendship or mere pleasure be the motive. Once more, if you fear the fickleness of friendship, consider that in any other case a quarrel might be a mutual calamity; but now, when you have given up what is most precious to you, you will be the greater loser, and therefore, you will have more reason in being afraid of the lover, for his vexations are many, and he is always fancying that every one is leagued against him. Wherefore also he debars his beloved from society; he will not have you intimate with the wealthy, lest they should exceed him in wealth, or with men of education, lest they should be his superiors in understanding; and he is equally afraid of anybody's influence who has any other advantage over himself. If he can persuade you to break with them, you are left without a friend in the world; or if, out of a regard to your own interest, you have more sense than to comply with his desire, you will have to quarrel with him. But those who are non-lovers, and whose success in love is the reward of their merit, will not be jealous of the companions of their beloved, and will rather hate those who refuse to be his associates, thinking that their favourite is slighted by the latter and benefited by the former; for more love than hatred may be expected to come to him out of his friendship with others. Many lovers too have loved the person of a youth before they knew his character or his belongings; so that when their passion has passed away, there is no knowing whether they will continue to be his friends; whereas, in the case of non-lovers who were always friends, the friendship is not lessened by the favours granted; but the recollection of these remains with them, and is an earnest of good things to come.

Further, I say that you are likely to be improved by me, whereas the lover will spoil you. For they praise your words and actions in a wrong way; partly, because they are afraid of offending you, and also, their judgment is weakened by passion. Such are the feats which love exhibits; he makes things painful to the disappointed which give no pain to others; he compels the successful lover to praise what ought not to give him pleasure, and therefore the beloved is to be pitied rather than envied. But if you listen to me, in the first place, I, in my intercourse with you, shall not merely regard present enjoyment, but also future advantage, being not mastered by love, but my own master; nor for small causes taking violent dislikes, but even when the cause is great, slowly laying up little wrath—unintentional offences I shall forgive, and intentional ones I shall try to prevent; and these are the marks of a friendship which will last.

Do you think that a lover only can be a firm friend? reflect:—if this were true, we should set small value on sons, or fathers, or mothers; nor should we ever have loyal friends, for our love of them arises not from passion, but from other associations. Further, if we ought to shower favours on those who are the most eager suitors,—on that principle, we ought always to do good, not to the most virtuous, but to the most needy; for they are the persons who will be most relieved, and will therefore be the most grateful; and when you make a feast you should invite not your friend, but the beggar and the empty soul; for they will love you, and attend you, and come about your doors, and will be the best pleased, and the most grateful, and will invoke many a blessing on your head. Yet surely you ought not to be granting favours to those who besiege you with prayer, but to those who are best able to reward you; nor to the lover only, but to those who are worthy of love; nor to those who will enjoy the bloom of your youth, but to those who will share their possessions with you in age; nor to those who, having succeeded, will glory in their success to others, but to those who will be modest and tell no tales; nor to those who care about you for a moment only, but to those who will continue your friends through life; nor to those who, when their passion is over, will pick a quarrel with you, but rather to those who, when the charm of youth has left you, will show their own virtue. Remember what I have said; and consider yet this further point: friends admonish the lover under the idea that his way of life is bad, but no one of his kindred ever yet censured the non-lover, or thought that he was ill-advised about his own interests.

'Perhaps you will ask me whether I propose that you should indulge every non-lover. To which I reply that not even the lover would advise you to indulge all lovers, for the indiscriminate favour is less esteemed by the rational recipient, and less easily hidden by him who would escape the censure of the world. Now love ought to be for the advantage of both parties, and for the injury of neither.

'I believe that I have said enough; but if there is anything more which you desire or which in your opinion needs to be supplied, ask and I will answer.'

Now, Socrates, what do you think? Is not the discourse excellent, more especially in the matter of the language?

SOCRATES: Yes, quite admirable; the effect on me was ravishing. And this I owe to you, Phaedrus, for I observed you while reading to be in an ecstasy, and thinking that you are more experienced in these matters than I am, I followed your example, and, like you, my divine darling, I became inspired with a phrenzy.

PHAEDRUS: Indeed, you are pleased to be merry.

SOCRATES: Do you mean that I am not in earnest?

PHAEDRUS: Now don't talk in that way, Socrates, but let me have your real opinion; I adjure you, by Zeus, the god of friendship, to tell me whether you think that any Hellene could have said more or spoken better on the same subject.

SOCRATES: Well, but are you and I expected to praise the sentiments of the author, or only the clearness, and roundness, and finish, and tournure of the language? As to the first I willingly submit to your better judgment, for I am not worthy to form an opinion, having only attended to the rhetorical manner; and I was doubting whether this could have been defended even by Lysias himself; I thought, though I speak under correction, that he repeated himself two or three times, either from want of words or from want of pains; and also, he appeared to me ostentatiously to exult in showing how well he could say the same thing in two or three ways.

PHAEDRUS: Nonsense, Socrates; what you call repetition was the especial merit of the speech; for he omitted no topic of which the subject rightly allowed, and I do not think that any one could have spoken better or more exhaustively.

SOCRATES: There I cannot go along with you. Ancient sages, men and women, who have spoken and written of these things, would rise up in judgment against me, if out of complaisance I assented to you.

PHAEDRUS: Who are they, and where did you hear anything better than this?

SOCRATES: I am sure that I must have heard; but at this moment I do not remember from whom; perhaps from Sappho the fair, or Anacreon the wise; or, possibly, from a prose writer. Why do I say so? Why, because I perceive that my bosom is full, and that I could make another speech as good as that of Lysias, and different. Now I am certain that this is not an invention of my own, who am well aware that I know nothing, and therefore I can only infer that I have been filled through the ears, like a pitcher, from the waters of another, though I have actually forgotten in my stupidity who was my informant.

PHAEDRUS: That is grand:—but never mind where you heard the discourse or from whom; let that be a mystery not to be divulged even at my earnest desire. Only, as you say, promise to make another and better oration, equal in length and entirely new, on the same subject; and I, like the nine Archons, will promise to set up a golden image at Delphi, not only of myself, but of you, and as large as life.

SOCRATES: You are a dear golden ass if you suppose me to mean that Lysias has altogether missed the mark, and that I can make a speech from which all his arguments are to be excluded. The worst of authors will say something which is to the point. Who, for example, could speak on this thesis of yours without praising the discretion of the non-lover and blaming the indiscretion of the lover? These are the commonplaces of the subject which must come in (for what else is there to be said?) and must be allowed and excused; the only merit is in the arrangement of them, for there can be none in the invention; but when you leave the commonplaces, then there may be some originality.

PHAEDRUS: I admit that there is reason in what you say, and I too will be reasonable, and will allow you to start with the premiss that the lover is more disordered in his wits than the non-lover; if in what remains you make a longer and better speech than Lysias, and use other arguments, then I say again, that a statue you shall have of beaten gold, and take your place by the colossal offerings of the Cypselids at Olympia.

SOCRATES: How profoundly in earnest is the lover, because to tease him I lay a finger upon his love! And so, Phaedrus, you really imagine that I am going to improve upon the ingenuity of Lysias?

PHAEDRUS: There I have you as you had me, and you must just speak 'as you best can.' Do not let us exchange 'tu quoque' as in a farce, or compel me to say to you as you said to me, 'I know Socrates as well as I know myself, and he was wanting to speak, but he gave himself airs.' Rather I would have you consider that from this place we stir not until you have unbosomed yourself of the speech; for here are we all alone, and I am stronger, remember, and younger than you:—Wherefore perpend, and do not compel me to use violence.

SOCRATES: But, my sweet Phaedrus, how ridiculous it would be of me to compete with Lysias in an extempore speech! He is a master in his art and I am an untaught man.

PHAEDRUS: You see how matters stand; and therefore let there be no more pretences; for, indeed, I know the word that is irresistible.

SOCRATES: Then don't say it.

PHAEDRUS: Yes, but I will; and my word shall be an oath. 'I say, or rather swear'—but what god will be witness of my oath?—'By this plane-tree I swear, that unless you repeat the discourse here in the face of this very plane-tree, I will never tell you another; never let you have word of another!'

SOCRATES: Villain! I am conquered; the poor lover of discourse has no more to say.

PHAEDRUS: Then why are you still at your tricks?

SOCRATES: I am not going to play tricks now that you have taken the oath, for I cannot allow myself to be starved.

PHAEDRUS: Proceed.

SOCRATES: Shall I tell you what I will do?

PHAEDRUS: What?

SOCRATES: I will veil my face and gallop through the discourse as fast as I can, for if I see you I shall feel ashamed and not know what to say.

PHAEDRUS: Only go on and you may do anything else which you please.

SOCRATES: Come, O ye Muses, melodious, as ye are called, whether you have received this name from the character of your strains, or because the Melians are a musical race, help, O help me in the tale which my good friend here desires me to rehearse, in order that his friend whom he always deemed wise may seem to him to be wiser than ever.

Once upon a time there was a fair boy, or, more properly speaking, a youth; he was very fair and had a great many lovers; and there was one special cunning one, who had persuaded the youth that he did not love him, but he really loved him all the same; and one day when he was paying his addresses to him, he used this very argument—that he ought to accept the non-lover rather than the lover; his words were as follows:—

'All good counsel begins in the same way; a man should know what he is advising about, or his counsel will all come to nought. But people imagine that they know about the nature of things, when they don't know about them, and, not having come to an understanding at first because they think that they know, they end, as might be expected, in contradicting one another and themselves. Now you and I must not be guilty of this fundamental error which we condemn in others; but as our question is whether the lover or non-lover is to be preferred, let us first of all agree in defining the nature and power of love, and then, keeping our eyes upon the definition and to this appealing, let us further enquire whether love brings advantage or disadvantage.

'Every one sees that love is a desire, and we know also that non-lovers desire the beautiful and good. Now in what way is the lover to be distinguished from the non-lover? Let us note that in every one of us there are two guiding and ruling principles which lead us whither they will; one is the natural desire of pleasure, the other is an acquired opinion which aspires after the best; and these two are sometimes in harmony and then again at war, and sometimes the one, sometimes the other conquers. When opinion by the help of reason leads us to the best, the conquering principle is called temperance; but when desire, which is devoid of reason, rules in us and drags us to pleasure, that power of misrule is called excess. Now excess has many names, and many members, and many forms, and any of these forms when very marked gives a name, neither honourable nor creditable, to the bearer of the name. The desire of eating, for example, which gets the better of the higher reason and the other desires, is called gluttony, and he who is possessed by it is called a glutton; the tyrannical desire of drink, which inclines the possessor of the desire to drink, has a name which is only too obvious, and there can be as little doubt by what name any other appetite of the same family would be called;—it will be the name of that which happens to be dominant. And now I think that you will perceive the drift of my discourse; but as every spoken word is in a manner plainer than the unspoken, I had better say further that the irrational desire which overcomes the tendency of opinion towards right, and is led away to the enjoyment of beauty, and especially of personal beauty, by the desires which are her own kindred—that supreme desire, I say, which by leading conquers and by the force of passion is reinforced, from this very force, receiving a name, is called love (erromenos eros).'

And now, dear Phaedrus, I shall pause for an instant to ask whether you do not think me, as I appear to myself, inspired?

PHAEDRUS: Yes, Socrates, you seem to have a very unusual flow of words.

SOCRATES: Listen to me, then, in silence; for surely the place is holy; so that you must not wonder, if, as I proceed, I appear to be in a divine fury, for already I am getting into dithyrambics.

PHAEDRUS: Nothing can be truer.

Phaedrus

SOCRATES: The responsibility rests with you. But hear what follows, and perhaps the fit may be averted; all is in their hands above. I will go on talking to my youth. Listen:—

Thus, my friend, we have declared and defined the nature of the subject. Keeping the definition in view, let us now enquire what advantage or disadvantage is likely to ensue from the lover or the non-lover to him who accepts their advances.

He who is the victim of his passions and the slave of pleasure will of course desire to make his beloved as agreeable to himself as possible. Now to him who has a mind diseased anything is agreeable which is not opposed to him, but that which is equal or superior is hateful to him, and therefore the lover will not brook any superiority or equality on the part of his beloved; he is always employed in reducing him to inferiority. And the ignorant is the inferior of the wise, the coward of the brave, the slow of speech of the speaker, the dull of the clever. These, and not these only, are the mental defects of the beloved;—defects which, when implanted by nature, are necessarily a delight to the lover, and when not implanted, he must contrive to implant them in him, if he would not be deprived of his fleeting joy. And therefore he cannot help being jealous, and will debar his beloved from the advantages of society which would make a man of him, and especially from that society which would have given him wisdom, and thereby he cannot fail to do him great harm. That is to say, in his excessive fear lest he should come to be despised in his eyes he will be compelled to banish from him divine philosophy; and there is no greater injury which he can inflict upon him than this. He will contrive that his beloved shall be wholly ignorant, and in everything shall look to him; he is to be the delight of the lover's heart, and a curse to himself. Verily, a lover is a profitable guardian and associate for him in all that relates to his mind.

Let us next see how his master, whose law of life is pleasure and not good, will keep and train the body of his servant. Will he not choose a beloved who is delicate rather than sturdy and strong? One brought up in shady bowers and not in the bright sun, a stranger to manly exercises and the sweat of toil, accustomed only to a soft and luxurious diet, instead of the hues of health having the colours of paint and ornament, and the rest of a piece?—such a life as any one can imagine and which I need not detail at length. But I may sum up all that I have to say in a word, and pass on. Such a person in war, or in any of the great crises of life, will be the anxiety of his friends and also of his lover, and certainly not the terror of his enemies; which nobody can deny.

And now let us tell what advantage or disadvantage the beloved will receive from the guardianship and society of his lover in the matter of his property; this is the next point to be considered. The lover will be the first to see what, indeed, will be sufficiently evident to all men, that he desires above all things to deprive his beloved of his dearest and best and holiest possessions, father, mother, kindred, friends, of all whom he thinks may be hinderers or reprovers of their most sweet converse; he will even cast a jealous eye upon his gold and silver or other property, because these make him a less easy prey, and when caught less manageable; hence he is of necessity displeased at his possession of them and rejoices at their loss; and he would like him to be wifeless, childless, homeless, as well; and the longer the better, for the longer he is all this, the longer he will enjoy him.

There are some sort of animals, such as flatterers, who are dangerous and mischievous enough, and yet nature has mingled a temporary pleasure and grace in their composition. You may say that a courtesan is hurtful, and disapprove of such creatures and their practices, and yet for the time they are very pleasant. But the lover is not only hurtful to his love; he is also an extremely disagreeable companion. The old proverb says that 'birds of a feather flock together'; I suppose that equality of years inclines them to the same pleasures, and similarity begets friendship; yet you may have more than enough even of this; and verily constraint is always said to be grievous. Now the lover is not only unlike his beloved, but he forces himself upon him. For he is old and his love is young, and neither day nor night will he leave him if he can help; necessity and the sting of desire drive him on, and allure him with the pleasure which he receives from seeing, hearing, touching, perceiving him in every way. And therefore he is delighted to fasten upon him and to minister to him. But what pleasure or consolation can the beloved be receiving all this time? Must he not feel the extremity of disgust when he looks at

Phaedrus

an old shrivelled face and the remainder to match, which even in a description is disagreeable, and quite detestable when he is forced into daily contact with his lover; moreover he is jealously watched and guarded against everything and everybody, and has to hear misplaced and exaggerated praises of himself, and censures equally inappropriate, which are intolerable when the man is sober, and, besides being intolerable, are published all over the world in all their indelicacy and wearisomeness when he is drunk.

And not only while his love continues is he mischievous and unpleasant, but when his love ceases he becomes a perfidious enemy of him on whom he showered his oaths and prayers and promises, and yet could hardly prevail upon him to tolerate the tedium of his company even from motives of interest. The hour of payment arrives, and now he is the servant of another master; instead of love and infatuation, wisdom and temperance are his bosom's lords; but the beloved has not discovered the change which has taken place in him, when he asks for a return and recalls to his recollection former sayings and doings; he believes himself to be speaking to the same person, and the other, not having the courage to confess the truth, and not knowing how to fulfil the oaths and promises which he made when under the dominion of folly, and having now grown wise and temperate, does not want to do as he did or to be as he was before. And so he runs away and is constrained to be a defaulter; the oyster-shell (In allusion to a game in which two parties fled or pursued according as an oyster-shell which was thrown into the air fell with the dark or light side uppermost.) has fallen with the other side uppermost—he changes pursuit into flight, while the other is compelled to follow him with passion and imprecation, not knowing that he ought never from the first to have accepted a demented lover instead of a sensible non-lover; and that in making such a choice he was giving himself up to a faithless, morose, envious, disagreeable being, hurtful to his estate, hurtful to his bodily health, and still more hurtful to the cultivation of his mind, than which there neither is nor ever will be anything more honoured in the eyes both of gods and men. Consider this, fair youth, and know that in the friendship of the lover there is no real kindness; he has an appetite and wants to feed upon you:

'As wolves love lambs so lovers love their loves.'

But I told you so, I am speaking in verse, and therefore I had better make an end; enough.

PHAEDRUS: I thought that you were only half-way and were going to make a similar speech about all the advantages of accepting the non-lover. Why do you not proceed?

SOCRATES: Does not your simplicity observe that I have got out of dithyrambics into heroics, when only uttering a censure on the lover? And if I am to add the praises of the non-lover what will become of me? Do you not perceive that I am already overtaken by the Nymphs to whom you have mischievously exposed me? And therefore I will only add that the non-lover has all the advantages in which the lover is accused of being deficient. And now I will say no more; there has been enough of both of them. Leaving the tale to its fate, I will cross the river and make the best of my way home, lest a worse thing be inflicted upon me by you.

PHAEDRUS: Not yet, Socrates; not until the heat of the day has passed; do you not see that the hour is almost noon? there is the midday sun standing still, as people say, in the meridian. Let us rather stay and talk over what has been said, and then return in the cool.

SOCRATES: Your love of discourse, Phaedrus, is superhuman, simply marvellous, and I do not believe that there is any one of your contemporaries who has either made or in one way or another has compelled others to make an equal number of speeches. I would except Simmias the Theban, but all the rest are far behind you. And now I do verily believe that you have been the cause of another.

PHAEDRUS: That is good news. But what do you mean?

SOCRATES: I mean to say that as I was about to cross the stream

Phaedrus

the usual sign was given to me,—that sign which always forbids, but never bids, me to do anything which I am going to do; and I thought that I heard a voice saying in my ear that I had been guilty of impiety, and that I must not go away until I had made an atonement. Now I am a diviner, though not a very good one, but I have enough religion for my own use, as you might say of a bad writer—his writing is good enough for him; and I am beginning to see that I was in error. O my friend, how prophetic is the human soul! At the time I had a sort of misgiving, and, like Ibycus, 'I was troubled; I feared that I might be buying honour from men at the price of sinning against the gods.' Now I recognize my error.

PHAEDRUS: What error?

SOCRATES: That was a dreadful speech which you brought with you, and you made me utter one as bad.

PHAEDRUS: How so?

SOCRATES: It was foolish, I say,—to a certain extent, impious; can anything be more dreadful?

PHAEDRUS: Nothing, if the speech was really such as you describe.

SOCRATES: Well, and is not Eros the son of Aphrodite, and a god?

PHAEDRUS: So men say.

SOCRATES: But that was not acknowledged by Lysias in his speech, nor by you in that other speech which you by a charm drew from my lips. For if love be, as he surely is, a divinity, he cannot be evil. Yet this was the error of both the speeches. There was also a simplicity about them which was refreshing; having no truth or honesty in them, nevertheless they pretended to be something, hoping to succeed in deceiving the manikins of earth and gain celebrity among them. Wherefore I must have a purgation. And I bethink me of an ancient purgation of mythological error which was devised, not by Homer, for he never had the wit to discover why he was blind, but by Stesichorus, who was a philosopher and knew the reason why; and therefore, when he lost his eyes, for that was the penalty which was inflicted upon him for reviling the lovely Helen, he at once purged himself. And the purgation was a recantation, which began thus,—

> 'False is that word of mine—the truth is that thou didst not embark in ships, nor ever go to the walls of Troy;'

and when he had completed his poem, which is called 'the recantation,' immediately his sight returned to him. Now I will be wiser than either Stesichorus or Homer, in that I am going to make my recantation for reviling love before I suffer; and this I will attempt, not as before, veiled and ashamed, but with forehead bold and bare.

PHAEDRUS: Nothing could be more agreeable to me than to hear you say so.

SOCRATES: Only think, my good Phaedrus, what an utter want of delicacy was shown in the two discourses; I mean, in my own and in that which you recited out of the book. Would not any one who was himself of a noble and gentle nature, and who loved or ever had loved a nature like his own, when we tell of the petty causes of lovers' jealousies, and of their exceeding animosities, and of the injuries which they do to their beloved, have imagined that our ideas of love were taken from some haunt of sailors to which good manners were unknown—he would certainly never have admitted the justice of our censure?

PHAEDRUS: I dare say not, Socrates.

SOCRATES: Therefore, because I blush at the thought of this person, and also because I am afraid of Love himself, I desire to wash

Phaedrus

the brine out of my ears with water from the spring; and I would counsel Lysias not to delay, but to write another discourse, which shall prove that 'ceteris paribus' the lover ought to be accepted rather than the non-lover.

PHAEDRUS: Be assured that he shall. You shall speak the praises of the lover, and Lysias shall be compelled by me to write another discourse on the same theme.

SOCRATES: You will be true to your nature in that, and therefore I believe you.

PHAEDRUS: Speak, and fear not.

SOCRATES: But where is the fair youth whom I was addressing before, and who ought to listen now; lest, if he hear me not, he should accept a non-lover before he knows what he is doing?

PHAEDRUS: He is close at hand, and always at your service.

SOCRATES: Know then, fair youth, that the former discourse was the word of Phaedrus, the son of Vain Man, who dwells in the city of Myrrhina (Myrrhinusius). And this which I am about to utter is the recantation of Stesichorus the son of Godly Man (Euphemus), who comes from the town of Desire (Himera), and is to the following effect: 'I told a lie when I said' that the beloved ought to accept the non-lover when he might have the lover, because the one is sane, and the other mad. It might be so if madness were simply an evil; but there is also a madness which is a divine gift, and the source of the chiefest blessings granted to men. For prophecy is a madness, and the prophetess at Delphi and the priestesses at Dodona when out of their senses have conferred great benefits on Hellas, both in public and private life, but when in their senses few or none. And I might also tell you how the Sibyl and other inspired persons have given to many an one many an intimation of the future which has saved them from falling. But it would be tedious to speak of what every one knows.

There will be more reason in appealing to the ancient inventors of names (compare *Cratylus*), who would never have connected prophecy (*mantike*) which foretells the future and is the noblest of arts, with madness (*manike*), or called them both by the same name, if they had deemed madness to be a disgrace or dishonour;—they must have thought that there was an inspired madness which was a noble thing; for the two words, mantike and manike, are really the same, and the letter tau is only a modern and tasteless insertion. And this is confirmed by the name which was given by them to the rational investigation of futurity, whether made by the help of birds or of other signs—this, for as much as it is an art which supplies from the reasoning faculty mind (*nous*) and information (*istoria*) to human thought (*oiesis*) they originally termed oionoistike, but the word has been lately altered and made sonorous by the modern introduction of the letter Omega (*oionoistike* and *oionistike*), and in proportion as prophecy (*mantike*) is more perfect and august than augury, both in name and fact, in the same proportion, as the ancients testify, is madness superior to a sane mind (*sophrosune*) for the one is only of human, but the other of divine origin. Again, where plagues and mightiest woes have bred in certain families, owing to some ancient blood-guiltiness, there madness has entered with holy prayers and rites, and by inspired utterances found a way of deliverance for those who are in need; and he who has part in this gift, and is truly possessed and duly out of his mind, is by the use of purifications and mysteries made whole and exempt from evil, future as well as present, and has a release from the calamity which was afflicting him. The third kind is the madness of those who are possessed by the Muses; which taking hold of a delicate and virgin soul, and there inspiring frenzy, awakens lyrical and all other numbers; with these adorning the myriad actions of ancient heroes for the instruction of posterity. But he who, having no touch of the Muses' madness in his soul, comes to the door and thinks that he will get into the temple by the help of art—he, I say, and his poetry are not admitted; the sane man disappears and is nowhere when he enters into rivalry with the madman.

I might tell of many other noble deeds which have sprung from inspired madness. And therefore, let no one frighten or flutter us by saying that the temperate friend is to be chosen rather than the inspired, but let him further show that love is not sent by the gods for any good to lover or beloved; if he can do so we will allow him to carry off the palm. And we, on our part, will prove in answer to him that the madness of love is the greatest of heaven's blessings, and the proof shall be one which the wise will receive, and the witling disbelieve. But first of all, let us view the affections and actions of the soul divine and human, and try to ascertain the truth about them. The beginning of our proof is as follows:—

(Translated by Cic. Tus. Quaest.) The soul through all her being is immortal, for that which is ever in motion is immortal; but that which moves another and is moved by another, in ceasing to move ceases also to live. Only the self-moving, never leaving self, never ceases to move, and is the fountain and beginning of motion to all that moves besides. Now, the beginning is unbegotten, for that which is begotten has a beginning; but the beginning is begotten of nothing, for if it were begotten of something, then the begotten would not come from a beginning. But if unbegotten, it must also be indestructible; for if beginning were destroyed, there could be no beginning out of anything, nor anything out of a beginning; and all things must have a beginning. And therefore the self-moving is the beginning of motion; and this can neither be destroyed nor begotten, else the whole heavens and all creation would collapse and stand still, and never again have motion or birth. But if the self-moving is proved to be immortal, he who affirms that self-motion is the very idea and essence of the soul will not be put to confusion. For the body which is moved from without is soulless; but that which is moved from within has a soul, for such is the nature of the soul. But if this be true, must not the soul be the self-moving, and therefore of necessity unbegotten and immortal? Enough of the soul's immortality.

Of the nature of the soul, though her true form be ever a theme of large and more than mortal discourse, let me speak briefly, and in a figure. And let the figure be composite—a pair of winged horses and a charioteer. Now the winged horses and the charioteers of the gods are all of them noble and of noble descent, but those of other races are mixed; the human charioteer drives his in a pair; and one of them is noble and of noble breed, and the other is ignoble and of ignoble breed; and the driving of them of necessity gives a great deal of trouble to him. I will endeavour to explain to you in what way the mortal differs from the immortal creature. The soul in her totality has the care of inanimate being everywhere, and traverses the whole heaven in divers forms appearing—when perfect and fully winged she soars upward, and orders the whole world; whereas the imperfect soul, losing her wings and drooping in her flight at last settles on the solid ground—there, finding a home, she receives an earthly frame which appears to be self-moved, but is really moved by her power; and this composition of soul and body is called a living and mortal creature. For immortal no such union can be reasonably believed to be; although fancy, not having seen nor surely known the nature of God, may imagine an immortal creature having both a body and also a soul which are united throughout all time. Let that, however, be as God wills, and be spoken of acceptably to him. And now let us ask the reason why the soul loses her wings!

The wing is the corporeal element which is most akin to the divine, and which by nature tends to soar aloft and carry that which gravitates downwards into the upper region, which is the habitation of the gods. The divine is beauty, wisdom, goodness, and the like; and by these the wing of the soul is nourished, and grows apace; but when fed upon evil and foulness and the opposite of good, wastes and falls away. Zeus, the mighty lord, holding the reins of a winged chariot, leads the way in heaven, ordering all and taking care of all; and there follows him the array of gods and demi-gods, marshalled in eleven bands; Hestia alone abides at home in the house of heaven; of the rest they who are reckoned among the princely twelve march in their appointed order. They see many blessed sights in the inner heaven, and there are many ways to and fro, along which the blessed gods are passing, every one doing his own work; he may follow who will and can, for jealousy has no place in the celestial choir. But when they go to banquet and festival, then they move up the steep to the top of the vault of heaven. The chariots of the gods in even poise, obeying the rein, glide rapidly; but the others labour, for the vicious steed goes heavily, weighing down the charioteer to the earth when his steed has not been thoroughly trained:—and this is the hour of agony and extremest conflict for the soul. For the immortals, when they are at the end of their course, go forth and stand upon the outside of heaven, and the revolution of the spheres carries them round, and they behold the things beyond. But of the heaven which is above the heavens, what earthly poet ever did or ever will sing worthily? It is such as I will describe; for I must dare to speak the truth, when truth is my theme. There abides the very being with which true knowledge is concerned; the colourless, formless, intangible essence, visible only to mind, the pilot of the soul. The divine intelligence, being nurtured upon mind and pure knowledge, and the intelligence of every soul which is capable of receiving the food proper to it, rejoices at beholding reality, and once more gazing upon truth, is replenished and made glad, until the revolution of the worlds brings her round again to the same place. In the revolution she beholds justice, and temperance, and knowledge absolute, not in the form of generation or of relation, which men call existence, but knowledge absolute in existence absolute; and beholding the other true existences in like manner, and feasting upon them, she passes down into the interior of the heavens and returns home; and there the charioteer putting up his horses at the stall, gives them ambrosia to eat and nectar to drink.

Such is the life of the gods; but of other souls, that which follows God best and is likest to him lifts the head of the charioteer into the outer world, and is carried round in the revolution, troubled indeed by the steeds, and with difficulty beholding true being; while another only rises and falls, and sees, and again fails to see by reason of the unruliness of the steeds. The rest of the souls are also longing after the upper world and they all follow, but not being strong enough they are carried round below the surface, plunging, treading on one another, each striving to be first; and there is confusion and perspiration and the extremity of effort; and many of them are lamed or have their wings broken through the ill-driving of the charioteers; and all of them after a fruitless toil, not having attained to the mysteries of true being, go away, and feed upon opinion. The reason why the souls exhibit this exceeding eagerness to behold the plain of truth is that pasturage is found there, which is suited to the highest part of the soul; and the wing on which the soul soars is nourished with this. And there is a law of Destiny, that the soul which attains any vision of truth in company with a god is preserved from harm until the next period, and if attaining always is always unharmed. But when she is unable to follow, and fails to behold the truth, and through some ill-hap sinks beneath the double load of forgetfulness and vice, and her wings fall from her and she drops to the ground, then the law ordains that this soul shall at her first birth pass, not into any other animal, but only into man; and the soul which has seen most of truth shall come to the birth as a philosopher, or artist, or some musical and loving nature; that which has seen truth in the second degree shall be some righteous king or warrior chief; the soul which is of the third class shall be a politician, or economist, or trader; the fourth shall be a lover of gymnastic toils, or a physician; the fifth shall lead the life of a prophet or hierophant; to the sixth the character of poet or some other imitative artist will be assigned; to the seventh the life of an artisan or husbandman; to the eighth that of a sophist or demagogue; to the ninth that of a tyrant—all these are states of probation, in which he who does righteously improves, and he who does unrighteously, deteriorates his lot.

Ten thousand years must elapse before the soul of each one can return to the place from whence she came, for she cannot grow her wings in less; only the soul of a philosopher, guileless and true, or the soul of a lover, who is not devoid of philosophy, may acquire wings in the third of the recurring periods of a thousand years; he is distinguished from the ordinary good man who gains wings in three thousand years:—and they who choose this life three times in succession have wings given them, and go away at the end of three thousand years. But the others (The philosopher alone is not subject to judgment (krisis), for he has never lost the vision of truth.) receive judgment when they have completed their first life, and after the judgment they go, some of them to the houses of correction which are under the earth, and are punished; others to some place in heaven whither they are lightly borne by justice, and there they live in a manner worthy of the life which they led here when in the form of men. And at the end of the first thousand years the good souls and also the evil souls both come to draw lots and choose their second life, and they may take any which they please. The soul of a man may pass into the life of a beast, or from the beast return again into the man. But the soul which has never seen the truth will not pass into the human form. For a man must have intelligence of universals, and be able to proceed from the many particulars of sense to one conception of reason;—this is the recollection of those things which our soul once saw while following God—when regardless of that which we now call being she raised her head up towards the true being. And therefore the mind of the philosopher alone has wings; and this is just, for he is always, according to the measure of his abilities, clinging in recollection to those things in which God abides, and in beholding which He is what He is. And he who employs aright these memories is ever being initiated into perfect mysteries and alone becomes truly perfect. But, as he forgets earthly interests and is rapt in the divine, the vulgar deem him mad, and rebuke him; they do not see that he is inspired.

Thus far I have been speaking of the fourth and last kind of madness, which is imputed to him who, when he sees the beauty of earth, is transported with the recollection of the true beauty; he would like to fly away, but he cannot; he is like a bird fluttering and looking upward and careless of the world below; and he is therefore thought to be mad. And I have shown this of all inspirations to be the noblest and highest and the offspring of the highest to him who has or shares in it, and that he who loves the beautiful is called a lover because he partakes of it. For, as has been already said, every soul of man has in the way of nature beheld true being; this was the condition of her passing into the form of man. But all souls do not easily recall the things of the other world; they may have seen them for a short time only, or they may have been unfortunate in their earthly lot, and, having had their hearts turned to unrighteousness through some corrupting influence, they may have lost the memory of the holy things which once they saw. Few only retain an adequate remembrance of them; and they, when they behold here any image of that other world, are rapt in amazement; but they are ignorant of what this rapture means, because they do not clearly perceive. For there is no light of justice or temperance or any of the higher ideas which are precious to souls in the earthly copies of them: they are seen through a glass dimly; and there are few who, going to the images, behold in them the realities, and these only with difficulty. There was a time when with the rest of the happy band they saw beauty shining in brightness,—we philosophers following in the train of Zeus, others in company with other gods; and then we beheld the beatific vision and were initiated into a mystery which may be truly called most blessed, celebrated by us in our state of innocence, before we had any experience of evils to come, when we were admitted to the sight of apparitions innocent and simple and calm and happy, which we beheld shining in pure light, pure ourselves and not yet enshrined in that living tomb which we carry about, now that we are imprisoned in the body, like an oyster in his shell. Let me linger over the memory of scenes which have passed away.

But of beauty, I repeat again that we saw her there shining in company with the celestial forms; and coming to earth we find her here too, shining in clearness through the clearest aperture of sense. For sight is the most piercing of our bodily senses; though not by that is wisdom seen; her loveliness would have been transporting if there had been a visible image of her, and the other ideas, if they had visible counterparts, would be equally lovely. But this is the privilege of beauty, that being the loveliest she is also the most palpable to sight. Now he who is not newly initiated or who has become corrupted, does not easily rise out of this world to the sight of true beauty in the other; he looks only at her earthly namesake, and instead of being awed at the sight of her, he is given over to pleasure, and like a brutish beast he rushes on to enjoy and beget; he consorts with wantonness, and is not afraid or ashamed of pursuing pleasure in violation of nature. But he whose initiation is recent, and who has been the spectator of many glories in the other world, is amazed when he sees any one having a godlike face or form, which is the expression of divine beauty; and at first a shudder runs through him, and again the old awe steals over him; then looking upon the face of his beloved as of a god he reverences him, and if he were not afraid of being thought a downright madman, he would sacrifice to his beloved as to the image of a god; then while he gazes on him there is a sort of reaction, and the shudder passes into an unusual heat and perspiration; for, as he receives the effluence of beauty through the eyes, the wing moistens and he warms. And as he warms, the parts out of which the wing grew, and which had been hitherto closed and rigid, and had prevented the wing from shooting forth, are melted, and as nourishment streams upon him, the lower end of the wing begins to swell and grow from the root upwards; and the growth extends under the whole soul—for once the whole was winged. During this process the whole soul is all in a state of ebullition and effervescence,—which may be compared to the irritation and uneasiness in the gums at the time of cutting teeth,—bubbles up, and has a feeling of uneasiness and tickling; but when in like manner the soul is beginning to grow wings, the beauty of the beloved meets her eye and she receives the sensible warm motion of particles which flow towards her, therefore called emotion (imeros), and is refreshed and warmed by them, and then she ceases from her pain with joy. But when she is parted from her beloved and her moisture fails, then the orifices of the passage out of which the wing shoots dry up and close, and intercept the germ of the wing; which, being shut up with the emotion, throbbing as with the pulsations of an artery, pricks the aperture which is nearest, until at length the entire soul is pierced and maddened and pained, and at the recollection of beauty is again delighted. And from both of them together the soul is oppressed at the strangeness of her condition, and is in a great strait and excitement, and in her madness can neither sleep by night nor abide in her place by day. And wherever she thinks that she will behold the beautiful one, thither in her desire she runs. And when she has seen him, and bathed herself in the waters of beauty, her constraint is loosened, and she is refreshed, and has no more pangs and pains; and this is the sweetest of all pleasures at the time, and is the reason why the soul of the lover will never forsake his beautiful one, whom he esteems above all; he has forgotten mother and brethren and companions, and he thinks nothing of the neglect and loss of his property; the rules and proprieties of life, on which he formerly prided himself, he now despises, and is ready to sleep like a servant, wherever he is allowed, as near as he can to his desired one, who is the object of his worship, and the physician who can alone assuage the greatness of his pain. And this state, my dear imaginary youth to whom I am talking, is by men called love, and among the gods has a name at which you, in your simplicity, may be inclined to mock; there are two lines in the apocryphal writings of Homer in which the name occurs. One of them is rather outrageous, and not altogether metrical. They are as follows:

> 'Mortals call him fluttering love,
> But the immortals call him winged one,

Because the growing of wings (Or, reading pterothoiton, 'the movement of wings.') is a necessity to him.'

You may believe this, but not unless you like. At any rate the loves of lovers and their causes are such as I have described.

Now the lover who is taken to be the attendant of Zeus is better able to bear the winged god, and can endure a heavier burden; but the attendants and companions of Ares, when under the influence of love, if they fancy that they have been at all wronged, are ready to kill and put an end to themselves and their beloved. And he who follows in the train of any other god, while he is unspoiled and the impression lasts, honours and imitates him, as far as he is able; and after the manner of his God he behaves in his intercourse with his beloved and with the rest of the world during the first period of his earthly existence. Every one chooses his love from the ranks of beauty according to his character, and this he makes his god, and fashions and adorns as a sort of image which he is to fall down and worship. The followers of Zeus desire that their beloved should have a soul like him; and therefore they seek out some one of a philosophical and imperial nature, and when they have found him and loved him, they do all they can to confirm such a nature in him, and if they have no experience of such a disposition hitherto, they learn of any one who can teach them, and themselves follow in the same way. And they have the less difficulty in finding the nature of their own god in themselves, because they have been compelled to gaze intensely on him; their recollection clings to him, and they become possessed of him, and receive from him their character and disposition, so far as man can participate in God. The qualities of their god they attribute to the beloved, wherefore they love him all the more, and if, like the Bacchic Nymphs, they draw inspiration from Zeus, they pour out their own fountain upon him, wanting to make him as like as possible to their own god. But those who are the followers of Here seek a royal love, and when they have found him they do just the same with him; and in like manner the followers of Apollo, and of every other god walking in the ways of their god, seek a love who is to be made like him whom they serve, and when they have found him, they themselves imitate their god, and persuade their love to do the same, and educate him into the manner and nature of the god as far as they each can; for no feelings of envy or jealousy are entertained by them towards their beloved, but they do their utmost to create in him the greatest likeness of themselves and of the god whom they honour. Thus fair and blissful to the beloved is the desire of the inspired lover, and the initiation of which I speak into the mysteries of true love, if he be captured by the lover and their purpose is effected. Now the beloved is taken captive in the following manner:—

As I said at the beginning of this tale, I divided each soul into three—two horses and a charioteer; and one of the horses was good and the other bad: the division may remain, but I have not yet explained in what the goodness or badness of either consists, and to that I will now proceed. The right-hand horse is upright and cleanly made; he has a lofty neck and an aquiline nose; his colour is white, and his eyes dark; he is a lover of honour and modesty and temperance, and the follower of true glory; he needs no touch of the whip, but is guided by word and admonition only. The other is a crooked lumbering animal, put together anyhow; he has a short thick neck; he is flat-faced and of a dark colour, with grey eyes and blood-red complexion (Or with grey and blood-shot eyes.); the mate of insolence and pride, shag-eared and deaf, hardly yielding to whip and spur. Now when the charioteer beholds the vision of love, and has his whole soul warmed through sense, and is full of the prickings and ticklings of desire, the obedient steed, then as always under the government of shame, refrains from leaping on the beloved; but the other, heedless of the pricks and of the blows of the whip, plunges and runs away, giving all manner of trouble to his companion and the charioteer, whom he forces to approach the beloved and to remember the joys of love. They at first indignantly oppose him and will not be urged on to do terrible and unlawful deeds; but at last, when he persists in plaguing them, they yield and agree to do as he bids them. And now they are at the spot and behold the flashing beauty of the beloved; which when the charioteer sees, his memory is carried to the true beauty, whom he beholds in company with Modesty like an image placed upon a holy pedestal. He sees her, but he is afraid and falls backwards in adoration, and by his fall is compelled to pull back the reins with such violence as to bring both the steeds on their haunches, the one willing and unresisting, the unruly one very unwilling; and when they have gone back a little, the one is overcome with shame and wonder, and his whole soul is bathed in perspiration; the other, when the pain is over which the bridle and the fall had given him, having with difficulty taken breath, is full of wrath and reproaches, which he heaps upon the charioteer and his fellow-steed, for want of courage and manhood, declaring that they have been false to their agreement and guilty of desertion. Again they refuse, and again he urges them on, and will scarce yield to their prayer that he would wait until another time. When the appointed hour comes, they make as if they had forgotten, and he reminds them, fighting and neighing and dragging them on, until at length he on the same thoughts intent, forces them to draw near again. And when they are near he stoops his head and puts up his tail, and takes the bit in his teeth and pulls shamelessly. Then the charioteer is worse off than ever; he falls back like a racer at the barrier, and with a still more violent wrench drags the bit out of the teeth of the wild steed and covers his abusive tongue and jaws with blood, and forces his legs and haunches to the ground and punishes him sorely. And when this has happened several times and the villain has ceased from his wanton way, he is tamed and humbled, and follows the will of the charioteer, and when he sees the beautiful one he is ready to die of fear. And from that time forward the soul of the lover follows the beloved in modesty and holy fear.

And so the beloved who, like a god, has received every true and loyal service from his lover, not in pretence but in reality, being also himself of a nature friendly to his admirer, if in former days he has blushed to own his passion and turned away his lover, because his youthful companions or others slanderously told him that he would be disgraced, now as years advance, at the appointed age and time, is led to receive him into communion. For fate which has ordained that there shall be no friendship among the evil has also ordained that there shall ever be friendship among the good. And the beloved when he has received him into communion and intimacy, is quite amazed at the good-will of the lover; he recognises that the inspired friend is worth all other friends or kinsmen; they have nothing of friendship in them worthy to be compared with his. And when this feeling continues and he is nearer to him and embraces him, in gymnastic exercises and at other times of meeting, then the fountain of that stream, which Zeus when he was in love with Ganymede named Desire, overflows upon the lover, and some enters into his soul, and some when he is filled flows out again; and as a breeze or an echo rebounds from the smooth rocks and returns whence it came, so does the stream of beauty, passing through the eyes which are the windows of the soul, come back to the beautiful one; there arriving and quickening the passages of the wings, watering them and inclining them to grow, and filling the soul of the beloved also with love. And thus he loves, but he knows not what; he does not understand and cannot explain his own state; he appears to have caught the infection of blindness from another; the lover is his mirror in whom he is beholding himself, but he is not aware of this. When he is with the lover, both cease from their pain, but when he is away then he longs as he is longed for, and has love's image, love for love (Anteros) lodging in his breast, which he calls and believes to be not love but friendship only, and his desire is as the desire of the other, but weaker; he wants to see him, touch him, kiss him, embrace him, and probably not long afterwards his desire is accomplished. When they meet, the wanton steed of the lover has a word to say to the charioteer; he would like to have a little pleasure in return for many pains, but the wanton steed of the beloved says not a word, for he is bursting with passion which he understands not;— he throws his arms round the lover and embraces him as his dearest friend; and, when they are side by side, he is not in a state in which he can refuse the lover anything, if he ask him; although his fellow-steed and the charioteer oppose him with the arguments of shame and reason. After this their happiness depends upon their self-control; if the better elements of the mind which lead to order and philosophy prevail, then they pass their life here in happiness and harmony—masters of themselves and orderly—enslaving the vicious and emancipating the virtuous elements of the soul; and when the end comes, they are light and winged for flight, having conquered in one of the three heavenly or truly Olympian victories; nor can human discipline or divine inspiration confer any greater blessing on man than this. If, on the other hand, they leave philosophy and lead the lower life of ambition, then probably, after wine or in some other careless hour, the two wanton animals take the two souls when off their guard and bring them together, and they accomplish that desire of their hearts which to the many is bliss; and this having once enjoyed they continue to enjoy, yet rarely because they have not the approval of the whole soul. They too are dear, but not so dear to one another as the others, either at the time of their love or afterwards. They consider that they have given and taken from each other the most sacred pledges, and they may not break them and fall into enmity. At last they pass out of the body, unwinged, but eager to soar, and thus obtain no mean reward of love and madness. For those who have once begun the heavenward pilgrimage may not go down again to darkness and the journey beneath the earth, but they live in light always; happy companions in their pilgrimage, and when the time comes at which they receive their wings they have the same plumage because of their love.

Thus great are the heavenly blessings which the friendship of a lover will confer upon you, my youth. Whereas the attachment of the non-lover, which is alloyed with a worldly prudence and has worldly and niggardly ways of doling out benefits, will breed in your soul those vulgar qualities which the populace applaud, will send you bowling round the earth during a period of nine thousand years, and leave you a fool in the world below.

And thus, dear Eros, I have made and paid my recantation, as well and as fairly as I could; more especially in the matter of the poetical figures which I was compelled to use, because Phaedrus would have them. And now forgive the past and accept the present, and be gracious and merciful to me, and do not in thine anger deprive me of sight, or take from me the art of love which thou hast

Phaedrus

given me, but grant that I may be yet more esteemed in the eyes of the fair. And if Phaedrus or I myself said anything rude in our first speeches, blame Lysias, who is the father of the brat, and let us have no more of his progeny; bid him study philosophy, like his brother Polemarchus; and then his lover Phaedrus will no longer halt between two opinions, but will dedicate himself wholly to love and to philosophical discourses.

PHAEDRUS: I join in the prayer, Socrates, and say with you, if this be for my good, may your words come to pass. But why did you make your second oration so much finer than the first? I wonder why. And I begin to be afraid that I shall lose conceit of Lysias, and that he will appear tame in comparison, even if he be willing to put another as fine and as long as yours into the field, which I doubt. For quite lately one of your politicians was abusing him on this very account; and called him a 'speech writer' again and again. So that a feeling of pride may probably induce him to give up writing speeches.

SOCRATES: What a very amusing notion! But I think, my young man, that you are much mistaken in your friend if you imagine that he is frightened at a little noise; and, possibly, you think that his assailant was in earnest?

PHAEDRUS: I thought, Socrates, that he was. And you are aware that the greatest and most influential statesmen are ashamed of writing speeches and leaving them in a written form, lest they should be called Sophists by posterity.

SOCRATES: You seem to be unconscious, Phaedrus, that the 'sweet elbow' (A proverb, like 'the grapes are sour,' applied to pleasures which cannot be had, meaning sweet things which, like the elbow, are out of the reach of the mouth. The promised pleasure turns out to be a long and tedious affair.) of the proverb is really the long arm of the Nile. And you appear to be equally unaware of the fact that this sweet elbow of theirs is also a long arm. For there is nothing of which our great politicians are so fond as of writing speeches and bequeathing them to posterity. And they add their admirers' names at the top of the writing, out of gratitude to them.

PHAEDRUS: What do you mean? I do not understand.

SOCRATES: Why, do you not know that when a politician writes, he begins with the names of his approvers?

PHAEDRUS: How so?

SOCRATES: Why, he begins in this manner: 'Be it enacted by the senate, the people, or both, on the motion of a certain person,' who is our author; and so putting on a serious face, he proceeds to display his own wisdom to his admirers in what is often a long and tedious composition. Now what is that sort of thing but a regular piece of authorship?

PHAEDRUS: True.

SOCRATES: And if the law is finally approved, then the author leaves the theatre in high delight; but if the law is rejected and he is done out of his speech-making, and not thought good enough to write, then he and his party are in mourning.

PHAEDRUS: Very true.

SOCRATES: So far are they from despising, or rather so highly do they value the practice of writing.

PHAEDRUS: No doubt.

SOCRATES: And when the king or orator has the power, as Lycurgus or Solon or Darius had, of attaining an immortality or authorship in a state, is he not thought by posterity, when they see his compositions, and does he not think himself, while he is yet alive, to be a god?

PHAEDRUS: Very true.

SOCRATES: Then do you think that any one of this class, however ill-disposed, would reproach Lysias with being an author?

PHAEDRUS: Not upon your view; for according to you he would be casting a slur upon his own favourite pursuit.

SOCRATES: Any one may see that there is no disgrace in the mere fact of writing.

PHAEDRUS: Certainly not.

SOCRATES: The disgrace begins when a man writes not well, but badly.

PHAEDRUS: Clearly.

SOCRATES: And what is well and what is badly—need we ask Lysias, or any other poet or orator, who ever wrote or will write either a political or any other work, in metre or out of metre, poet or prose writer, to teach us this?

PHAEDRUS: Need we? For what should a man live if not for the pleasures of discourse? Surely not for the sake of bodily pleasures, which almost always have previous pain as a condition of them, and therefore are rightly called slavish.

SOCRATES: There is time enough. And I believe that the grasshoppers chirruping after their manner in the heat of the sun over our heads are talking to one another and looking down at us. What would they say if they saw that we, like the many, are not conversing, but slumbering at mid-day, lulled by their voices, too indolent to think? Would they not have a right to laugh at us? They might imagine that we were slaves, who, coming to rest at a place of resort of theirs, like sheep lie asleep at noon around the well. But if they see us discoursing, and like Odysseus sailing past them, deaf to their siren voices, they may perhaps, out of respect, give us of the gifts which they receive from the gods that they may impart them to men.

PHAEDRUS: What gifts do you mean? I never heard of any.

SOCRATES: A lover of music like yourself ought surely to have heard the story of the grasshoppers, who are said to have been human beings in an age before the Muses. And when the Muses came and song appeared they were ravished with delight; and singing always, never thought of eating and drinking, until at last in their forgetfulness they died. And now they live again in the grasshoppers; and this is the return which the Muses make to them—they neither hunger, nor thirst, but from the hour of their birth are always singing, and never eating or drinking; and when they die they go and inform the Muses in heaven who honours them on earth. They win the love of Terpsichore for the dancers by their report of them; of Erato for the lovers, and of the other Muses for those who do them honour, according to the several ways of honouring them;—of Calliope the eldest Muse and of Urania who is next to her, for the philosophers, of whose music the grasshoppers make report to them; for these are the Muses who are chiefly concerned with heaven and thought, divine as well as human, and they have the sweetest utterance. For many reasons, then, we ought always to talk and not to sleep at mid-day.

PHAEDRUS: Let us talk.

SOCRATES: Shall we discuss the rules of writing and speech as we were proposing?

PHAEDRUS: Very good.

SOCRATES: In good speaking should not the mind of the speaker know the truth of the matter about which he is going to speak?

PHAEDRUS: And yet, Socrates, I have heard that he who would be an orator has nothing to do with true justice, but only with that which is likely to be approved by the many who sit in judgment; nor with the truly good or honourable, but only with opinion about them, and that from opinion comes persuasion, and not from the truth.

SOCRATES: The words of the wise are not to be set aside; for there is probably something in them; and therefore the meaning of this saying is not hastily to be dismissed.

PHAEDRUS: Very true.

SOCRATES: Let us put the matter thus:—Suppose that I persuaded you to buy a horse and go to the wars. Neither of us knew what a horse was like, but I knew that you believed a horse to be of tame animals the one which has the longest ears.

PHAEDRUS: That would be ridiculous.

SOCRATES: There is something more ridiculous coming:—Suppose, further, that in sober earnest I, having persuaded you of this, went and composed a speech in honour of an ass, whom I entitled a horse beginning: 'A noble animal and a most useful possession, especially in war, and you may get on his back and fight, and he will carry baggage or anything.'

PHAEDRUS: How ridiculous!

SOCRATES: Ridiculous! Yes; but is not even a ridiculous friend better than a cunning enemy?

PHAEDRUS: Certainly.

SOCRATES: And when the orator instead of putting an ass in the place of a horse, puts good for evil, being himself as ignorant of their true nature as the city on which he imposes is ignorant; and having studied the notions of the multitude, falsely persuades them not about 'the shadow of an ass,' which he confounds with a horse, but about good which he confounds with evil,—what will be the harvest which rhetoric will be likely to gather after the sowing of that seed?

PHAEDRUS: The reverse of good.

SOCRATES: But perhaps rhetoric has been getting too roughly handled by us, and she might answer: What amazing nonsense you are talking! As if I forced any man to learn to speak in ignorance of the truth! Whatever my advice may be worth, I should have told him to arrive at the truth first, and then come to me. At the same time I boldly assert that mere knowledge of the truth will not give you the art of persuasion.

PHAEDRUS: There is reason in the lady's defence of herself.

SOCRATES: Quite true; if only the other arguments which remain to be brought up bear her witness that she is an art at all. But I seem to hear them arraying themselves on the opposite side, declaring that she speaks falsely, and that rhetoric is a mere routine and trick, not an art. Lo! a Spartan appears, and says that there never is nor ever will be a real art of speaking which is divorced from the truth.

PHAEDRUS: And what are these arguments, Socrates? Bring them out that we may examine them.

SOCRATES: Come out, fair children, and convince Phaedrus, who is the father of similar beauties, that he will never be able to speak about anything as he ought to speak unless he have a knowledge of philosophy. And let Phaedrus answer you.

PHAEDRUS: Put the question.

SOCRATES: Is not rhetoric, taken generally, a universal art of enchanting the mind by arguments; which is practised not only in courts and public assemblies, but in private houses also, having to do with all matters, great as well as small, good and bad alike, and is in all equally right, and equally to be esteemed—that is what you have heard?

PHAEDRUS: Nay, not exactly that; I should say rather that I have heard the art confined to speaking and writing in lawsuits, and to speaking in public assemblies—not extended farther.

SOCRATES: Then I suppose that you have only heard of the rhetoric of Nestor and Odysseus, which they composed in their leisure hours when at Troy, and never of the rhetoric of Palamedes?

PHAEDRUS: No more than of Nestor and Odysseus, unless Gorgias is your Nestor, and Thrasymachus or Theodorus your Odysseus.

SOCRATES: Perhaps that is my meaning. But let us leave them. And do you tell me, instead, what are plaintiff and defendant doing in a law court—are they not contending?

PHAEDRUS: Exactly so.

SOCRATES: About the just and unjust—that is the matter in dispute?

PHAEDRUS: Yes.

SOCRATES: And a professor of the art will make the same thing appear to the same persons to be at one time just, at another time, if he is so inclined, to be unjust?

PHAEDRUS: Exactly.

SOCRATES: And when he speaks in the assembly, he will make the same things seem good to the city at one time, and at another time the reverse of good?

PHAEDRUS: That is true.

SOCRATES: Have we not heard of the Eleatic Palamedes (Zeno), who has an art of speaking by which he makes the same things appear to his hearers like and unlike, one and many, at rest and in motion?

PHAEDRUS: Very true.

SOCRATES: The art of disputation, then, is not confined to the courts and the assembly, but is one and the same in every use of language; this is the art, if there be such an art, which is able to find a likeness of everything to which a likeness can be found, and draws into the light of day the likenesses and disguises which are used by others?

PHAEDRUS: How do you mean?

SOCRATES: Let me put the matter thus: When will there be more chance of deception—when the difference is large or small?

PHAEDRUS: When the difference is small.

SOCRATES: And you will be less likely to be discovered in passing by degrees into the other extreme than when you go all at once?

PHAEDRUS: Of course.

SOCRATES: He, then, who would deceive others, and not be deceived, must exactly know the real likenesses and differences of things?

PHAEDRUS: He must.

SOCRATES: And if he is ignorant of the true nature of any subject, how can he detect the greater or less degree of likeness in other things to that of which by the hypothesis he is ignorant?

PHAEDRUS: He cannot.

SOCRATES: And when men are deceived and their notions are at variance with realities, it is clear that the error slips in through resemblances?

PHAEDRUS: Yes, that is the way.

SOCRATES: Then he who would be a master of the art must understand the real nature of everything; or he will never know either how to make the gradual departure from truth into the opposite of truth which is effected by the help of resemblances, or how to avoid it?

PHAEDRUS: He will not.

SOCRATES: He then, who being ignorant of the truth aims at appearances, will only attain an art of rhetoric which is ridiculous and is not an art at all?

PHAEDRUS: That may be expected.

SOCRATES: Shall I propose that we look for examples of art and want of art, according to our notion of them, in the speech of Lysias which you have in your hand, and in my own speech?

PHAEDRUS: Nothing could be better; and indeed I think that our previous argument has been too abstract and wanting in illustrations.

SOCRATES: Yes; and the two speeches happen to afford a very good example of the way in which the speaker who knows the truth may, without any serious purpose, steal away the hearts of his hearers. This piece of good-fortune I attribute to the local deities; and, perhaps, the prophets of the Muses who are singing over our heads may have imparted their inspiration to me. For I do not imagine that I have any rhetorical art of my own.

PHAEDRUS: Granted; if you will only please to get on.

SOCRATES: Suppose that you read me the first words of Lysias' speech.

PHAEDRUS: 'You know how matters stand with me, and how, as I conceive, they might be arranged for our common interest; and I maintain that I ought not to fail in my suit, because I am not your lover. For lovers repent—'

SOCRATES: Enough:—Now, shall I point out the rhetorical error of those words?

PHAEDRUS: Yes.

SOCRATES: Every one is aware that about some things we are agreed, whereas about other things we differ.

PHAEDRUS: I think that I understand you; but will you explain yourself?

SOCRATES: When any one speaks of iron and silver, is not the same thing present in the minds of all?

PHAEDRUS: Certainly.

SOCRATES: But when any one speaks of justice and goodness we part company and are at odds with one another and with ourselves?

PHAEDRUS: Precisely.

SOCRATES: Then in some things we agree, but not in others?

PHAEDRUS: That is true.

SOCRATES: In which are we more likely to be deceived, and in which has rhetoric the greater power?

PHAEDRUS: Clearly, in the uncertain class.

SOCRATES: Then the rhetorician ought to make a regular division, and acquire a distinct notion of both classes, as well of that in which the many err, as of that in which they do not err?

Phaedrus

PHAEDRUS: He who made such a distinction would have an excellent principle.

SOCRATES: Yes; and in the next place he must have a keen eye for the observation of particulars in speaking, and not make a mistake about the class to which they are to be referred.

PHAEDRUS: Certainly.

SOCRATES: Now to which class does love belong—to the debatable or to the undisputed class?

PHAEDRUS: To the debatable, clearly; for if not, do you think that love would have allowed you to say as you did, that he is an evil both to the lover and the beloved, and also the greatest possible good?

SOCRATES: Capital. But will you tell me whether I defined love at the beginning of my speech? for, having been in an ecstasy, I cannot well remember.

PHAEDRUS: Yes, indeed; that you did, and no mistake.

SOCRATES: Then I perceive that the Nymphs of Achelous and Pan the son of Hermes, who inspired me, were far better rhetoricians than Lysias the son of Cephalus. Alas! how inferior to them he is! But perhaps I am mistaken; and Lysias at the commencement of his lover's speech did insist on our supposing love to be something or other which he fancied him to be, and according to this model he fashioned and framed the remainder of his discourse. Suppose we read his beginning over again:

PHAEDRUS: If you please; but you will not find what you want.

SOCRATES: Read, that I may have his exact words.

PHAEDRUS: 'You know how matters stand with me, and how, as I conceive, they might be arranged for our common interest; and I maintain I ought not to fail in my suit because I am not your lover, for lovers repent of the kindnesses which they have shown, when their love is over.'

SOCRATES: Here he appears to have done just the reverse of what he ought; for he has begun at the end, and is swimming on his back through the flood to the place of starting. His address to the fair youth begins where the lover would have ended. Am I not right, sweet Phaedrus?

PHAEDRUS: Yes, indeed, Socrates; he does begin at the end.

SOCRATES: Then as to the other topics—are they not thrown down anyhow? Is there any principle in them? Why should the next topic follow next in order, or any other topic? I cannot help fancying in my ignorance that he wrote off boldly just what came into his head, but I dare say that you would recognize a rhetorical necessity in the succession of the several parts of the composition?

PHAEDRUS: You have too good an opinion of me if you think that I have any such insight into his principles of composition.

SOCRATES: At any rate, you will allow that every discourse ought to be a living creature, having a body of its own and a head and feet; there should be a middle, beginning, and end, adapted to one another and to the whole?

PHAEDRUS: Certainly.

SOCRATES: Can this be said of the discourse of Lysias? See whether you can find any more connexion in his words than in the epitaph which is said by some to have been inscribed on the grave of Midas the Phrygian.

PHAEDRUS: What is there remarkable in the epitaph?

Phaedrus

SOCRATES: It is as follows:—

> 'I am a maiden of bronze and lie on the tomb of Midas;
> So long as water flows and tall trees grow,
> So long here on this spot by his sad tomb abiding,
> I shall declare to passers-by that Midas sleeps below.'

Now in this rhyme whether a line comes first or comes last, as you will perceive, makes no difference.

PHAEDRUS: You are making fun of that oration of ours.

SOCRATES: Well, I will say no more about your friend's speech lest I should give offence to you; although I think that it might furnish many other examples of what a man ought rather to avoid. But I will proceed to the other speech, which, as I think, is also suggestive to students of rhetoric.

PHAEDRUS: In what way?

SOCRATES: The two speeches, as you may remember, were unlike; the one argued that the lover and the other that the non-lover ought to be accepted.

PHAEDRUS: And right manfully.

SOCRATES: You should rather say 'madly;' and madness was the argument of them, for, as I said, 'love is a madness.'

PHAEDRUS: Yes.

SOCRATES: And of madness there were two kinds; one produced by human infirmity, the other was a divine release of the soul from the yoke of custom and convention.

PHAEDRUS: True.

SOCRATES: The divine madness was subdivided into four kinds, prophetic, initiatory, poetic, erotic, having four gods presiding over them; the first was the inspiration of Apollo, the second that of Dionysus, the third that of the Muses, the fourth that of Aphrodite and Eros. In the description of the last kind of madness, which was also said to be the best, we spoke of the affection of love in a figure, into which we introduced a tolerably credible and possibly true though partly erring myth, which was also a hymn in honour of Love, who is your lord and also mine, Phaedrus, and the guardian of fair children, and to him we sung the hymn in measured and solemn strain.

PHAEDRUS: I know that I had great pleasure in listening to you.

SOCRATES: Let us take this instance and note how the transition was made from blame to praise.

PHAEDRUS: What do you mean?

SOCRATES: I mean to say that the composition was mostly playful. Yet in these chance fancies of the hour were involved two principles of which we should be too glad to have a clearer description if art could give us one.

PHAEDRUS: What are they?

SOCRATES: First, the comprehension of scattered particulars in one idea; as in our definition of love, which whether true or false certainly gave clearness and consistency to the discourse, the speaker should define his several notions and so make his meaning clear.

PHAEDRUS: What is the other principle, Socrates?

SOCRATES: The second principle is that of division into species according to the natural formation, where the joint is, not breaking any part as a bad carver might. Just as our two discourses, alike assumed, first of all, a single form of unreason; and then, as the body which from being one becomes double and may be divided into a left side and right side, each having parts right and left of the same name—after this manner the speaker proceeded to divide the parts of the left side and did not desist until he found in them an evil or left-handed love which he justly reviled; and the other discourse leading us to the madness which lay on the right side, found another love, also having the same name, but divine, which the speaker held up before us and applauded and affirmed to be the author of the greatest benefits.

PHAEDRUS: Most true.

SOCRATES: I am myself a great lover of these processes of division and generalization; they help me to speak and to think. And if I find any man who is able to see 'a One and Many' in nature, him I follow, and 'walk in his footsteps as if he were a god.' And those who have this art, I have hitherto been in the habit of calling dialecticians; but God knows whether the name is right or not. And I should like to know what name you would give to your or to Lysias' disciples, and whether this may not be that famous art of rhetoric which Thrasymachus and others teach and practise? Skilful speakers they are, and impart their skill to any who is willing to make kings of them and to bring gifts to them.

PHAEDRUS: Yes, they are royal men; but their art is not the same with the art of those whom you call, and rightly, in my opinion, dialecticians:—Still we are in the dark about rhetoric.

SOCRATES: What do you mean? The remains of it, if there be anything remaining which can be brought under rules of art, must be a fine thing; and, at any rate, is not to be despised by you and me. But how much is left?

PHAEDRUS: There is a great deal surely to be found in books of rhetoric?

SOCRATES: Yes; thank you for reminding me:—There is the

exordium, showing how the speech should begin, if I remember rightly; that is what you mean—the niceties of the art?

PHAEDRUS: Yes.

SOCRATES: Then follows the statement of facts, and upon that witnesses; thirdly, proofs; fourthly, probabilities are to come; the great Byzantian word-maker also speaks, if I am not mistaken, of confirmation and further confirmation.

PHAEDRUS: You mean the excellent Theodorus.

SOCRATES: Yes; and he tells how refutation or further refutation is to be managed, whether in accusation or defence. I ought also to mention the illustrious Parian, Evenus, who first invented insinuations and indirect praises; and also indirect censures, which according to some he put into verse to help the memory. But shall I 'to dumb forgetfulness consign' Tisias and Gorgias, who are not ignorant that probability is superior to truth, and who by force of argument make the little appear great and the great little, disguise the new in old fashions and the old in new fashions, and have discovered forms for everything, either short or going on to infinity. I remember Prodicus laughing when I told him of this; he said that he had himself discovered the true rule of art, which was to be neither long nor short, but of a convenient length.

PHAEDRUS: Well done, Prodicus!

SOCRATES: Then there is Hippias the Elean stranger, who probably agrees with him.

PHAEDRUS: Yes.

SOCRATES: And there is also Polus, who has treasuries of diplasiology, and gnomology, and eikonology, and who teaches in them the names of which Licymnius made him a present; they were to give a polish.

PHAEDRUS: Had not Protagoras something of the same sort?

SOCRATES: Yes, rules of correct diction and many other fine precepts; for the 'sorrows of a poor old man,' or any other pathetic case, no one is better than the Chalcedonian giant; he can put a whole company of people into a passion and out of one again by his mighty magic, and is first-rate at inventing or disposing of any sort of calumny on any grounds or none. All of them agree in asserting that a speech should end in a recapitulation, though they do not all agree to use the same word.

PHAEDRUS: You mean that there should be a summing up of the arguments in order to remind the hearers of them.

SOCRATES: I have now said all that I have to say of the art of rhetoric: have you anything to add?

PHAEDRUS: Not much; nothing very important.

SOCRATES: Leave the unimportant and let us bring the really important question into the light of day, which is: What power has this art of rhetoric, and when?

PHAEDRUS: A very great power in public meetings.

SOCRATES: It has. But I should like to know whether you have the same feeling as I have about the rhetoricians? To me there seem to be a great many holes in their web.

PHAEDRUS: Give an example.

SOCRATES: I will. Suppose a person to come to your friend Eryximachus, or to his father Acumenus, and to say to him: 'I know how to apply drugs which shall have either a heating or a cooling effect, and I can give a vomit and also a purge, and all that sort of thing; and knowing all this, as I do, I claim to be a physician and to make physicians by imparting this knowledge to others,'—what do you suppose that they would say?

PHAEDRUS: They would be sure to ask him whether he knew 'to whom' he would give his medicines, and 'when,' and 'how much.'

SOCRATES: And suppose that he were to reply: 'No; I know nothing of all that; I expect the patient who consults me to be able to do these things for himself'?

PHAEDRUS: They would say in reply that he is a madman or a pedant who fancies that he is a physician because he has read something in a book, or has stumbled on a prescription or two, although he has no real understanding of the art of medicine.

SOCRATES: And suppose a person were to come to Sophocles or Euripides and say that he knows how to make a very long speech about a small matter, and a short speech about a great matter, and also a sorrowful speech, or a terrible, or threatening speech, or any other kind of speech, and in teaching this fancies that he is teaching the art of tragedy—?

PHAEDRUS: They too would surely laugh at him if he fancies that tragedy is anything but the arranging of these elements in a manner which will be suitable to one another and to the whole.

SOCRATES: But I do not suppose that they would be rude or abusive to him: Would they not treat him as a musician a man who thinks that he is a harmonist because he knows how to pitch the highest and lowest note; happening to meet such an one he would not say to him savagely, 'Fool, you are mad!' But like a musician, in a gentle and harmonious tone of voice, he would answer: 'My good friend, he who would be a harmonist must certainly know this, and yet he may understand nothing of harmony if he has not got beyond your stage of knowledge, for you only know the preliminaries of harmony and not harmony itself.'

PHAEDRUS: Very true.

SOCRATES: And will not Sophocles say to the display of the would-

Phaedrus

be tragedian, that this is not tragedy but the preliminaries of tragedy? and will not Acumenus say the same of medicine to the would-be physician?

PHAEDRUS: Quite true.

SOCRATES: And if Adrastus the mellifluous or Pericles heard of these wonderful arts, brachylogies and eikonologies and all the hard names which we have been endeavouring to draw into the light of day, what would they say? Instead of losing temper and applying uncomplimentary epithets, as you and I have been doing, to the authors of such an imaginary art, their superior wisdom would rather censure us, as well as them. 'Have a little patience, Phaedrus and Socrates, they would say; you should not be in such a passion with those who from some want of dialectical skill are unable to define the nature of rhetoric, and consequently suppose that they have found the art in the preliminary conditions of it, and when these have been taught by them to others, fancy that the whole art of rhetoric has been taught by them; but as to using the several instruments of the art effectively, or making the composition a whole,—an application of it such as this is they regard as an easy thing which their disciples may make for themselves.'

PHAEDRUS: I quite admit, Socrates, that the art of rhetoric which these men teach and of which they write is such as you describe—there I agree with you. But I still want to know where and how the true art of rhetoric and persuasion is to be acquired.

SOCRATES: The perfection which is required of the finished orator is, or rather must be, like the perfection of anything else; partly given by nature, but may also be assisted by art. If you have the natural power and add to it knowledge and practice, you will be a distinguished speaker; if you fall short in either of these, you will be to that extent defective. But the art, as far as there is an art, of rhetoric does not lie in the direction of Lysias or Thrasymachus.

PHAEDRUS: In what direction then?

SOCRATES: I conceive Pericles to have been the most accomplished of rhetoricians.

PHAEDRUS: What of that?

SOCRATES: All the great arts require discussion and high speculation about the truths of nature; hence come loftiness of thought and completeness of execution. And this, as I conceive, was the quality which, in addition to his natural gifts, Pericles acquired from his intercourse with Anaxagoras whom he happened to know. He was thus imbued with the higher philosophy, and attained the knowledge of Mind and the negative of Mind, which were favourite themes of Anaxagoras, and applied what suited his purpose to the art of speaking.

PHAEDRUS: Explain.

SOCRATES: Rhetoric is like medicine.

PHAEDRUS: How so?

SOCRATES: Why, because medicine has to define the nature of the body and rhetoric of the soul—if we would proceed, not empirically but scientifically, in the one case to impart health and strength by giving medicine and food, in the other to implant the conviction or virtue which you desire, by the right application of words and training.

PHAEDRUS: There, Socrates, I suspect that you are right.

SOCRATES: And do you think that you can know the nature of the soul intelligently without knowing the nature of the whole?

PHAEDRUS: Hippocrates the Asclepiad says that the nature even of the body can only be understood as a whole. (Compare *Charmides*.)

SOCRATES: Yes, friend, and he was right:—still, we ought not to be content with the name of Hippocrates, but to examine and see whether his argument agrees with his conception of nature.

PHAEDRUS: I agree.

SOCRATES: Then consider what truth as well as Hippocrates says about this or about any other nature. Ought we not to consider first whether that which we wish to learn and to teach is a simple or multiform thing, and if simple, then to enquire what power it has of acting or being acted upon in relation to other things, and if multiform, then to number the forms; and see first in the case of one of them, and then in the case of all of them, what is that power of acting or being acted upon which makes each and all of them to be what they are?

PHAEDRUS: You may very likely be right, Socrates.

SOCRATES: The method which proceeds without analysis is like the groping of a blind man. Yet, surely, he who is an artist ought not to admit of a comparison with the blind, or deaf. The rhetorician, who teaches his pupil to speak scientifically, will particularly set forth the nature of that being to which he addresses his speeches; and this, I conceive, to be the soul.

PHAEDRUS: Certainly.

SOCRATES: His whole effort is directed to the soul; for in that he seeks to produce conviction.

PHAEDRUS: Yes.

SOCRATES: Then clearly, Thrasymachus or any one else who teaches rhetoric in earnest will give an exact description of the nature of the soul; which will enable us to see whether she be single and same, or, like the body, multiform. That is what we should call showing the nature of the soul.

PHAEDRUS: Exactly.

SOCRATES: He will explain, secondly, the mode in which she acts or is acted upon.

PHAEDRUS: True.

SOCRATES: Thirdly, having classified men and speeches, and their kinds and affections, and adapted them to one another, he will tell the reasons of his arrangement, and show why one soul is persuaded by a particular form of argument, and another not.

PHAEDRUS: You have hit upon a very good way.

SOCRATES: Yes, that is the true and only way in which any subject can be set forth or treated by rules of art, whether in speaking or writing. But the writers of the present day, at whose feet you have sat, craftily conceal the nature of the soul which they know quite well. Nor, until they adopt our method of reading and writing, can we admit that they write by rules of art?

PHAEDRUS: What is our method?

SOCRATES: I cannot give you the exact details; but I should like to tell you generally, as far as is in my power, how a man ought to proceed according to rules of art.

PHAEDRUS: Let me hear.

SOCRATES: Oratory is the art of enchanting the soul, and therefore he who would be an orator has to learn the differences of human souls—they are so many and of such a nature, and from them come the differences between man and man. Having proceeded thus far in his analysis, he will next divide speeches into their different classes:—'Such and such persons,' he will say, are affected by this or that kind of speech in this or that way,' and he will tell you why. The pupil must have a good theoretical notion of them first, and then he must have experience of them in actual life, and be able to follow them with all his senses about him, or he will never get beyond the precepts of his masters. But when he understands what persons are persuaded by what arguments, and sees the person about whom he was speaking in the abstract actually before him, and knows that it is he, and can say to himself, 'This is the man or this is the character who ought to have a certain argument applied to him in order to convince him of a certain opinion;'—he who knows all this, and knows also when he should speak and when he should refrain, and when he should use pithy sayings, pathetic appeals, sensational effects, and all the other modes of speech which he has learned;—when, I say, he knows the times and seasons of all these things, then, and not till then, he is a perfect master of his art; but if he fail in any of these points, whether in speaking or teaching or writing them, and yet declares that he speaks by rules of art, he who says 'I don't believe you' has the better of him. Well, the teacher will say, is this, Phaedrus and Socrates, your account of the so-called art of rhetoric, or am I to look for another?

PHAEDRUS: He must take this, Socrates, for there is no possibility of another, and yet the creation of such an art is not easy.

SOCRATES: Very true; and therefore let us consider this matter in every light, and see whether we cannot find a shorter and easier road; there is no use in taking a long rough roundabout way if there be a shorter and easier one. And I wish that you would try and remember whether you have heard from Lysias or any one else anything which might be of service to us.

PHAEDRUS: If trying would avail, then I might; but at the moment I can think of nothing.

SOCRATES: Suppose I tell you something which somebody who knows told me.

PHAEDRUS: Certainly.

SOCRATES: May not 'the wolf,' as the proverb says, 'claim a hearing'?

PHAEDRUS: Do you say what can be said for him.

SOCRATES: He will argue that there is no use in putting a solemn face on these matters, or in going round and round, until you arrive at first principles; for, as I said at first, when the question is of justice and good, or is a question in which men are concerned who are just and good, either by nature or habit, he who would be a skilful rhetorician has no need of truth—for that in courts of law men literally care nothing about truth, but only about conviction: and this is based on probability, to which he who would be a skilful orator should therefore give his whole attention. And they say also that there are cases in which the actual facts, if they are improbable, ought to be withheld, and only the probabilities should be told either in accusation or defence, and that always in speaking, the orator should keep probability in view, and say good-bye to the truth. And the observance of this principle throughout a speech furnishes the whole art.

PHAEDRUS: That is what the professors of rhetoric do actually say, Socrates. I have not forgotten that we have quite briefly touched upon this matter already; with them the point is all-important.

SOCRATES: I dare say that you are familiar with Tisias. Does he not define probability to be that which the many think?

PHAEDRUS: Certainly, he does.

SOCRATES: I believe that he has a clever and ingenious case of this sort: —He supposes a feeble and valiant man to have assaulted a strong and cowardly one, and to have robbed him of his coat or of something or other; he is brought into court, and then Tisias says that both parties should tell lies: the coward should say that he was assaulted by more men than one; the other should prove that they were alone, and should argue thus: 'How could a weak man like me

Phaedrus

have assaulted a strong man like him?' The complainant will not like to confess his own cowardice, and will therefore invent some other lie which his adversary will thus gain an opportunity of refuting. And there are other devices of the same kind which have a place in the system. Am I not right, Phaedrus?

PHAEDRUS: Certainly.

SOCRATES: Bless me, what a wonderfully mysterious art is this which Tisias or some other gentleman, in whatever name or country he rejoices, has discovered. Shall we say a word to him or not?

PHAEDRUS: What shall we say to him?

SOCRATES: Let us tell him that, before he appeared, you and I were saying that the probability of which he speaks was engendered in the minds of the many by the likeness of the truth, and we had just been affirming that he who knew the truth would always know best how to discover the resemblances of the truth. If he has anything else to say about the art of speaking we should like to hear him; but if not, we are satisfied with our own view, that unless a man estimates the various characters of his hearers and is able to divide all things into classes and to comprehend them under single ideas, he will never be a skilful rhetorician even within the limits of human power. And this skill he will not attain without a great deal of trouble, which a good man ought to undergo, not for the sake of speaking and acting before men, but in order that he may be able to say what is acceptable to God and always to act acceptably to Him as far as in him lies; for there is a saying of wiser men than ourselves, that a man of sense should not try to please his fellow-servants (at least this should not be his first object) but his good and noble masters; and therefore if the way is long and circuitous, marvel not at this, for, where the end is great, there we may take the longer road, but not for lesser ends such as yours. Truly, the argument may say, Tisias, that if you do not mind going so far, rhetoric has a fair beginning here.

PHAEDRUS: I think, Socrates, that this is admirable, if only practicable.

SOCRATES: But even to fail in an honourable object is honourable.

PHAEDRUS: True.

SOCRATES: Enough appears to have been said by us of a true and false art of speaking.

PHAEDRUS: Certainly.

SOCRATES: But there is something yet to be said of propriety and impropriety of writing.

PHAEDRUS: Yes.

SOCRATES: Do you know how you can speak or act about rhetoric in a manner which will be acceptable to God?

PHAEDRUS: No, indeed. Do you?

SOCRATES: I have heard a tradition of the ancients, whether true or not they only know; although if we had found the truth ourselves, do you think that we should care much about the opinions of men?

PHAEDRUS: Your question needs no answer; but I wish that you would tell me what you say that you have heard.

SOCRATES: At the Egyptian city of Naucratis, there was a famous old god, whose name was Theuth; the bird which is called the Ibis is sacred to him, and he was the inventor of many arts, such as arithmetic and calculation and geometry and astronomy and draughts and dice, but his great discovery was the use of letters. Now in those days the god Thamus was the king of the whole country of Egypt; and he dwelt in that great city of Upper Egypt which the Hellenes call Egyptian Thebes, and the god himself is called by them Ammon. To him came Theuth and showed his inventions, desiring that the other Egyptians might be allowed to have the benefit of them; he enumerated them, and Thamus enquired about their several uses, and praised some of them and censured others, as he approved or disapproved of them. It would take a long time to repeat all that Thamus said to Theuth in praise or blame of the various arts. But when they came to letters, This, said Theuth, will make the Egyptians wiser and give them better memories; it is a specific both for the memory and for the wit. Thamus replied: O most ingenious Theuth, the parent or inventor of an art is not always the best judge of the utility or inutility of his own inventions to the users of them. And in this instance, you who are the father of letters, from a paternal love of your own children have been led to attribute to them a quality which they cannot have; for this discovery of yours will create forgetfulness in the learners' souls, because they will not use their memories; they will trust to the external written characters and not remember of themselves. The specific which you have discovered is an aid not to memory, but to reminiscence, and you give your disciples not truth, but only the semblance of truth; they will be hearers of many things and will have learned nothing; they will appear to be omniscient and will generally know nothing; they will be tiresome company, having the show of wisdom without the reality.

PHAEDRUS: Yes, Socrates, you can easily invent tales of Egypt, or of any other country.

SOCRATES: There was a tradition in the temple of Dodona that oaks first gave prophetic utterances. The men of old, unlike in their simplicity to young philosophy, deemed that if they heard the truth even from 'oak or rock,' it was enough for them; whereas you seem to consider not whether a thing is or is not true, but who the speaker is and from what country the tale comes.

PHAEDRUS: I acknowledge the justice of your rebuke; and I think that the Theban is right in his view about letters.

SOCRATES: He would be a very simple person, and quite a stranger to the oracles of Thamus or Ammon, who should leave in writing or receive in writing any art under the idea that the written word would be intelligible or certain; or who deemed that writing was at all better than knowledge and recollection of the same matters?

PHAEDRUS: That is most true.

SOCRATES: I cannot help feeling, Phaedrus, that writing is unfortunately like painting; for the creations of the painter have the attitude of life, and yet if you ask them a question they preserve a solemn silence. And the same may be said of speeches. You would imagine that they had intelligence, but if you want to know anything and put a question to one of them, the speaker always gives one unvarying answer. And when they have been once written down they are tumbled about anywhere among those who may or may not understand them, and know not to whom they should reply, to whom not: and, if they are maltreated or abused, they have no parent to protect them; and they cannot protect or defend themselves.

PHAEDRUS: That again is most true.

SOCRATES: Is there not another kind of word or speech far better than this, and having far greater power—a son of the same family, but lawfully begotten?

PHAEDRUS: Whom do you mean, and what is his origin?

SOCRATES: I mean an intelligent word graven in the soul of the learner, which can defend itself, and knows when to speak and when to be silent.

PHAEDRUS: You mean the living word of knowledge which has a soul, and of which the written word is properly no more than an image?

SOCRATES: Yes, of course that is what I mean. And now may I be allowed to ask you a question: Would a husbandman, who is a man of sense, take the seeds, which he values and which he wishes to bear fruit, and in sober seriousness plant them during the heat of summer, in some garden of Adonis, that he may rejoice when he sees them in eight days appearing in beauty? at least he would do so, if at all, only for the sake of amusement and pastime. But when he is in earnest he sows in fitting soil, and practises husbandry, and is satisfied if in eight months the seeds which he has sown arrive at perfection?

PHAEDRUS: Yes, Socrates, that will be his way when he is in earnest; he will do the other, as you say, only in play.

SOCRATES: And can we suppose that he who knows the just and good and honourable has less understanding, than the husbandman, about his own seeds?

PHAEDRUS: Certainly not.

SOCRATES: Then he will not seriously incline to 'write' his thoughts 'in water' with pen and ink, sowing words which can neither speak for themselves nor teach the truth adequately to others?

PHAEDRUS: No, that is not likely.

SOCRATES: No, that is not likely—in the garden of letters he will sow and plant, but only for the sake of recreation and amusement; he will write them down as memorials to be treasured against the forgetfulness of old age, by himself, or by any other old man who is treading the same path. He will rejoice in beholding their tender growth; and while others are refreshing their souls with banqueting and the like, this will be the pastime in which his days are spent.

PHAEDRUS: A pastime, Socrates, as noble as the other is ignoble, the pastime of a man who can be amused by serious talk, and can discourse merrily about justice and the like.

SOCRATES: True, Phaedrus. But nobler far is the serious pursuit of the dialectician, who, finding a congenial soul, by the help of science sows and plants therein words which are able to help themselves and him who planted them, and are not unfruitful, but have in them a seed which others brought up in different soils render immortal, making the possessors of it happy to the utmost extent of human happiness.

PHAEDRUS: Far nobler, certainly.

SOCRATES: And now, Phaedrus, having agreed upon the premises we may decide about the conclusion.

PHAEDRUS: About what conclusion?

SOCRATES: About Lysias, whom we censured, and his art of writing, and his discourses, and the rhetorical skill or want of skill which was shown in them—these are the questions which we sought to determine, and they brought us to this point. And I think that we are now pretty well informed about the nature of art and its opposite.

PHAEDRUS: Yes, I think with you; but I wish that you would repeat what was said.

SOCRATES: Until a man knows the truth of the several particulars of which he is writing or speaking, and is able to define them as they are, and having defined them again to divide them until they can be no longer divided, and until in like manner he is able to discern the nature of the soul, and discover the different modes of discourse which are adapted to different natures, and to arrange and dispose them in such a way that the simple form of speech may be addressed to the simpler nature, and the complex and composite to the more complex nature—until he has accomplished all this, he will be unable to handle arguments according to rules of art, as far as their nature allows them to be subjected to art, either for the purpose of teaching or persuading;—such is the view which is implied in the whole preceding argument.

PHAEDRUS: Yes, that was our view, certainly.

SOCRATES: Secondly, as to the censure which was passed on the speaking or writing of discourses, and how they might be rightly or wrongly censured—did not our previous argument show—?

PHAEDRUS: Show what?

SOCRATES: That whether Lysias or any other writer that ever was or will be, whether private man or statesman, proposes laws and so becomes the author of a political treatise, fancying that there is any great certainty and clearness in his performance, the fact of his so writing is only a disgrace to him, whatever men may say. For not to know the nature of justice and injustice, and good and evil, and not to be able to distinguish the dream from the reality, cannot in truth be otherwise than disgraceful to him, even though he have the applause of the whole world.

PHAEDRUS: Certainly.

SOCRATES: But he who thinks that in the written word there is necessarily much which is not serious, and that neither poetry nor prose, spoken or written, is of any great value, if, like the compositions of the rhapsodes, they are only recited in order to be believed, and not with any view to criticism or instruction; and who thinks that even the best of writings are but a reminiscence of what we know, and that only in principles of justice and goodness and nobility taught and communicated orally for the sake of instruction and graven in the soul, which is the true way of writing, is there clearness and perfection and seriousness, and that such principles are a man's own and his legitimate offspring;—being, in the first place, the word which he finds in his own bosom; secondly, the brethren and descendants and relations of his idea which have been duly implanted by him in the souls of others;—and who cares for them and no others—this is the right sort of man; and you and I, Phaedrus, would pray that we may become like him.

PHAEDRUS: That is most assuredly my desire and prayer.

SOCRATES: And now the play is played out; and of rhetoric enough. Go and tell Lysias that to the fountain and school of the Nymphs we went down, and were bidden by them to convey a message to him and to other composers of speeches—to Homer and other writers of poems, whether set to music or not; and to Solon and others who have composed writings in the form of political discourses which they would term laws—to all of them we are to say that if their compositions are based on knowledge of the truth, and they can defend or prove them, when they are put to the test, by spoken arguments, which leave their writings poor in comparison of them, then they are to be called, not only poets, orators, legislators, but are worthy of a higher name, befitting the serious pursuit of their life.

PHAEDRUS: What name would you assign to them?

SOCRATES: Wise, I may not call them; for that is a great name which belongs to God alone,—lovers of wisdom or philosophers is their modest and befitting title.

PHAEDRUS: Very suitable.

SOCRATES: And he who cannot rise above his own compilations and compositions, which he has been long patching and piecing, adding some and taking away some, may be justly called poet or speech-maker or law-maker.

PHAEDRUS: Certainly.

SOCRATES: Now go and tell this to your companion.

PHAEDRUS: But there is also a friend of yours who ought not to be forgotten.

SOCRATES: Who is he?

Phaedrus

PHAEDRUS: Isocrates the fair:—What message will you send to him, and how shall we describe him?

SOCRATES: Isocrates is still young, Phaedrus; but I am willing to hazard a prophecy concerning him.

PHAEDRUS: What would you prophesy?

SOCRATES: I think that he has a genius which soars above the orations of Lysias, and that his character is cast in a finer mould. My impression of him is that he will marvellously improve as he grows older, and that all former rhetoricians will be as children in comparison of him. And I believe that he will not be satisfied with rhetoric, but that there is in him a divine inspiration which will lead him to things higher still. For he has an element of philosophy in his nature. This is the message of the gods dwelling in this place, and which I will myself deliver to Isocrates, who is my delight; and do you give the other to Lysias, who is yours.

PHAEDRUS: I will; and now as the heat is abated let us depart.

SOCRATES: Should we not offer up a prayer first of all to the local deities?

PHAEDRUS: By all means.

SOCRATES: Beloved Pan, and all ye other gods who haunt this place, give me beauty in the inward soul; and may the outward and inward man be at one. May I reckon the wise to be the wealthy, and may I have such a quantity of gold as a temperate man and he only can bear and carry.—Anything more? The prayer, I think, is enough for me.

PHAEDRUS: Ask the same for me, for friends should have all things in common.

SOCRATES: Let us go.

SYMPOSIUM

by Plato

Translated by Benjamin Jowett

INTRODUCTION

OF ALL THE WORKS OF PLATO the Symposium is the most perfect in form, and may be truly thought to contain more than any commentator has ever dreamed of; or, as Goethe said of one of his own writings, more than the author himself knew. For in philosophy as in prophecy glimpses of the future may often be conveyed in words which could hardly have been understood or interpreted at the time when they were uttered (compare Symp.)—which were wiser than the writer of them meant, and could not have been expressed by him if he had been interrogated about them. Yet Plato was not a mystic, nor in any degree affected by the Eastern influences which afterwards overspread the Alexandrian world. He was not an enthusiast or a sentimentalist, but one who aspired only to see reasoned truth, and whose thoughts are clearly explained in his language. There is no foreign element either of Egypt or of Asia to be found in his writings. And more than any other Platonic work the Symposium is Greek both in style and subject, having a beauty 'as of a statue,' while the companion Dialogue of the Phaedrus is marked by a sort of Gothic irregularity. More too than in any other of his Dialogues, Plato is emancipated from former philosophies. The genius of Greek art seems to triumph over the traditions of Pythagorean, Eleatic, or Megarian systems, and the old quarrel of poetry and philosophy 'has at least a superficial reconcilement. (Rep.)

An unknown person who had heard of the discourses in praise of love spoken by Socrates and others at the banquet of Agathon is desirous of having an authentic account of them, which he thinks that he can obtain from Apollodorus, the same excitable, or rather

Symposium

'mad' friend of Socrates, who is afterwards introduced in the Phaedo. He had imagined that the discourses were recent. There he is mistaken: but they are still fresh in the memory of his informant, who had just been repeating them to Glaucon, and is quite prepared to have another rehearsal of them in a walk from the Piraeus to Athens. Although he had not been present himself, he had heard them from the best authority. Aristodemus, who is described as having been in past times a humble but inseparable attendant of Socrates, had reported them to him (compare Xen. Mem.).

The narrative which he had heard was as follows:—

Aristodemus meeting Socrates in holiday attire, is invited by him to a banquet at the house of Agathon, who had been sacrificing in thanksgiving for his tragic victory on the day previous. But no sooner has he entered the house than he finds that he is alone; Socrates has stayed behind in a fit of abstraction, and does not appear until the banquet is half over. On his appearing he and the host jest a little; the question is then asked by Pausanias, one of the guests, 'What shall they do about drinking? as they had been all well drunk on the day before, and drinking on two successive days is such a bad thing.' This is confirmed by the authority of Eryximachus the physician, who further proposes that instead of listening to the flute-girl and her 'noise' they shall make speeches in honour of love, one after another, going from left to right in the order in which they are reclining at the table. All of them agree to this proposal, and Phaedrus, who is the 'father' of the idea, which he has previously communicated to Eryximachus, begins as follows:—

He descants first of all upon the antiquity of love, which is proved by the authority of the poets; secondly upon the benefits which love gives to man. The greatest of these is the sense of honour and dishonour. The lover is ashamed to be seen by the beloved doing or suffering any cowardly or mean act. And a state or army which was made up only of lovers and their loves would be invincible. For love will convert the veriest coward into an inspired hero.

And there have been true loves not only of men but of women also. Such was the love of Alcestis, who dared to die for her husband, and in recompense of her virtue was allowed to come again from the dead. But Orpheus, the miserable harper, who went down to Hades alive, that he might bring back his wife, was mocked with an apparition only, and the gods afterwards contrived his death as the punishment of his cowardliness. The love of Achilles, like that of Alcestis, was courageous and true; for he was willing to avenge his lover Patroclus, although he knew that his own death would immediately follow: and the gods, who honour the love of the beloved above that of the lover, rewarded him, and sent him to the islands of the blest.

Pausanias, who was sitting next, then takes up the tale:—He says that Phaedrus should have distinguished the heavenly love from the earthly, before he praised either. For there are two loves, as there are two Aphrodites—one the daughter of Uranus, who has no mother and is the elder and wiser goddess, and the other, the daughter of Zeus and Dione, who is popular and common. The first of the two loves has a noble purpose, and delights only in the intelligent nature of man, and is faithful to the end, and has no shadow of wantonness or lust. The second is the coarser kind of love, which is a love of the body rather than of the soul, and is of women and boys as well as of men. Now the actions of lovers vary, like every other sort of action, according to the manner of their performance. And in different countries there is a difference of opinion about male loves. Some, like the Boeotians, approve of them; others, like the Ionians, and most of the barbarians, disapprove of them; partly because they are aware of the political dangers which ensue from them, as may be seen in the instance of Harmodius and Aristogeiton. At Athens and Sparta there is an apparent contradiction about them. For at times they are encouraged, and then the lover is allowed to play all sorts of fantastic tricks; he may swear and forswear himself (and 'at lovers' perjuries they say Jove laughs'); he may be a servant, and lie on a mat at the door of his love, without any loss of character; but there are also times when elders look grave and guard their young relations, and personal remarks are made. The truth is that some of these loves are disgraceful and others honourable. The vulgar love of the body which takes wing and flies away when the bloom of youth is over, is disgraceful, and so is the interested love of power or wealth; but the love of the noble mind is lasting. The lover should be tested, and the beloved should not be too ready to yield. The rule in our country is that the beloved may do the same service to the lover in the way of virtue which the lover may do to him.

A voluntary service to be rendered for the sake of virtue and wisdom is permitted among us; and when these two customs—one the love of youth, the other the practice of virtue and philosophy—meet in one, then the lovers may lawfully unite. Nor is there any disgrace to a disinterested lover in being deceived: but the interested lover is doubly disgraced, for if he loses his love he loses his character; whereas the noble love of the other remains the same, although the object of his love is unworthy: for nothing can be nobler than love for the sake of virtue. This is that love of the heavenly goddess which is of great price to individuals and cities, making them work together for their improvement.

The turn of Aristophanes comes next; but he has the hiccough, and therefore proposes that Eryximachus the physician shall cure him or speak in his turn. Eryximachus is ready to do both, and after prescribing for the hiccough, speaks as follows:—

He agrees with Pausanias in maintaining that there are two kinds of love; but his art has led him to the further conclusion that the empire of this double love extends over all things, and is to be found in animals and plants as well as in man. In the human body also there are two loves; and the art of medicine shows which is the good and which is the bad love, and persuades the body to accept the good and reject the bad, and reconciles conflicting elements and makes them friends. Every art, gymnastic and husbandry as well as medicine, is the reconciliation of opposites; and this is what Heracleitus meant, when he spoke of a harmony of opposites: but in strictness he should rather have spoken of a harmony which succeeds opposites, for an agreement of disagreements there cannot be. Music too is concerned with the principles of love in their application to harmony and rhythm. In the abstract, all is simple, and we are not troubled with the twofold love; but when they are applied in education with their accompaniments of song and metre, then the discord begins. Then the old tale has to be repeated of fair Urania and the coarse Polyhymnia, who must be indulged sparingly, just as in my own art of medicine care must be taken that the taste of the epicure be gratified without inflicting upon him the attendant penalty of disease.

There is a similar harmony or disagreement in the course of the seasons and in the relations of moist and dry, hot and cold, hoar frost and blight; and diseases of all sorts spring from the excesses or disorders of the element of love. The knowledge of these elements of love and discord in the heavenly bodies is termed astronomy, in the relations of men towards gods and parents is called divination. For divination is the peacemaker of gods and men, and works by a knowledge of the tendencies of merely human loves to piety and impiety. Such is the power of love; and that love which is just and temperate has the greatest power, and is the source of all our happiness and friendship with the gods and with one another. I dare say that I have omitted to mention many things which you, Aristophanes, may supply, as I perceive that you are cured of the hiccough.

Aristophanes is the next speaker:—

He professes to open a new vein of discourse, in which he begins by treating of the origin of human nature. The sexes were originally three, men, women, and the union of the two; and they were made round—having four hands, four feet, two faces on a round neck, and the rest to correspond. Terrible was their strength and swiftness; and they were essaying to scale heaven and attack the gods. Doubt reigned in the celestial councils; the gods were divided between the desire of quelling the pride of man and the fear of losing the sacrifices. At last Zeus hit upon an expedient. Let us cut them in two, he said; then they will only have half their strength, and we shall have twice as many sacrifices. He spake, and split them as you might split an egg with an hair; and when this was done, he told Apollo to give their faces a twist and re-arrange their persons, taking out the wrinkles and tying the skin in a knot about the navel. The two halves went about looking for one another, and were ready to die of hunger in one another's arms. Then Zeus invented an adjustment of the sexes, which enabled them to marry and go their way to the business of life. Now the characters of men differ accordingly as they are derived from the original man or the original woman, or the original man-woman. Those who come from the man-woman are lascivious and adulterous; those who come from the woman form female attachments; those who are a section of the male follow

Symposium

the male and embrace him, and in him all their desires centre. The pair are inseparable and live together in pure and manly affection; yet they cannot tell what they want of one another. But if Hephaestus were to come to them with his instruments and propose that they should be melted into one and remain one here and hereafter, they would acknowledge that this was the very expression of their want. For love is the desire of the whole, and the pursuit of the whole is called love. There was a time when the two sexes were only one, but now God has halved them,—much as the Lacedaemonians have cut up the Arcadians,—and if they do not behave themselves he will divide them again, and they will hop about with half a nose and face in basso relievo. Wherefore let us exhort all men to piety, that we may obtain the goods of which love is the author, and be reconciled to God, and find our own true loves, which rarely happens in this world. And now I must beg you not to suppose that I am alluding to Pausanias and Agathon (compare Protag.), for my words refer to all mankind everywhere.

Some raillery ensues first between Aristophanes and Eryximachus, and then between Agathon, who fears a few select friends more than any number of spectators at the theatre, and Socrates, who is disposed to begin an argument. This is speedily repressed by Phaedrus, who reminds the disputants of their tribute to the god. Agathon's speech follows:—

He will speak of the god first and then of his gifts: He is the fairest and blessedest and best of the gods, and also the youngest, having had no existence in the old days of Iapetus and Cronos when the gods were at war. The things that were done then were done of necessity and not of love. For love is young and dwells in soft places,—not like Ate in Homer, walking on the skulls of men, but in their hearts and souls, which are soft enough. He is all flexibility and grace, and his habitation is among the flowers, and he cannot do or suffer wrong; for all men serve and obey him of their own free will, and where there is love there is obedience, and where obedience, there is justice; for none can be wronged of his own free will. And he is temperate as well as just, for he is the ruler of the desires, and if he rules them he must be temperate. Also he is courageous, for he is the conqueror of the lord of war. And he is wise too; for he is a poet, and the author of poesy in others. He created the animals; he is the inventor of the arts; all the gods are his subjects; he is the fairest and best himself, and the cause of what is fairest and best in others; he makes men to be of one mind at a banquet, filling them with affection and emptying them of disaffection; the pilot, helper, defender, saviour of men, in whose footsteps let every man follow, chanting a strain of love. Such is the discourse, half playful, half serious, which I dedicate to the god.

The turn of Socrates comes next. He begins by remarking satirically that he has not understood the terms of the original agreement, for he fancied that they meant to speak the true praises of love, but now he finds that they only say what is good of him, whether true or false. He begs to be absolved from speaking falsely, but he is willing to speak the truth, and proposes to begin by questioning Agathon. The result of his questions may be summed up as follows:—

Love is of something, and that which love desires is not that which love is or has; for no man desires that which he is or has. And love is of the beautiful, and therefore has not the beautiful. And the beautiful is the good, and therefore, in wanting and desiring the beautiful, love also wants and desires the good. Socrates professes to have asked the same questions and to have obtained the same answers from Diotima, a wise woman of Mantinea, who, like Agathon, had spoken first of love and then of his works. Socrates, like Agathon, had told her that Love is a mighty god and also fair, and she had shown him in return that Love was neither, but in a mean between fair and foul, good and evil, and not a god at all, but only a great demon or intermediate power (compare the speech of Eryximachus) who conveys to the gods the prayers of men, and to men the commands of the gods.

Socrates asks: Who are his father and mother? To this Diotima replies that he is the son of Plenty and Poverty, and partakes of the nature of both, and is full and starved by turns. Like his mother he is poor and squalid, lying on mats at doors (compare the speech of Pausanias); like his father he is bold and strong, and full of arts and resources. Further, he is in a mean between ignorance and knowledge:—in this he resembles the philosopher who is also in a mean

Symposium

between the wise and the ignorant. Such is the nature of Love, who is not to be confused with the beloved.

But Love desires the beautiful; and then arises the question, What does he desire of the beautiful? He desires, of course, the possession of the beautiful;—but what is given by that? For the beautiful let us substitute the good, and we have no difficulty in seeing the possession of the good to be happiness, and Love to be the desire of happiness, although the meaning of the word has been too often confined to one kind of love. And Love desires not only the good, but the everlasting possession of the good. Why then is there all this flutter and excitement about love? Because all men and women at a certain age are desirous of bringing to the birth. And love is not of beauty only, but of birth in beauty; this is the principle of immortality in a mortal creature. When beauty approaches, then the conceiving power is benign and diffuse; when foulness, she is averted and morose.

But why again does this extend not only to men but also to animals? Because they too have an instinct of immortality. Even in the same individual there is a perpetual succession as well of the parts of the material body as of the thoughts and desires of the mind; nay, even knowledge comes and goes. There is no sameness of existence, but the new mortality is always taking the place of the old. This is the reason why parents love their children—for the sake of immortality; and this is why men love the immortality of fame. For the creative soul creates not children, but conceptions of wisdom and virtue, such as poets and other creators have invented. And the noblest creations of all are those of legislators, in honour of whom temples have been raised. Who would not sooner have these children of the mind than the ordinary human ones? (Compare Bacon's Essays, 8:—'Certainly the best works and of greatest merit for the public have proceeded from the unmarried or childless men; which both in affection and means have married and endowed the public.')

I will now initiate you, she said, into the greater mysteries; for he who would proceed in due course should love first one fair form, and then many, and learn the connexion of them; and from beautiful bodies he should proceed to beautiful minds, and the beauty of laws and institutions, until he perceives that all beauty is of one kindred; and from institutions he should go on to the sciences, until at last the vision is revealed to him of a single science of universal beauty, and then he will behold the everlasting nature which is the cause of all, and will be near the end. In the contemplation of that supreme being of love he will be purified of earthly leaven, and will behold beauty, not with the bodily eye, but with the eye of the mind, and will bring forth true creations of virtue and wisdom, and be the friend of God and heir of immortality.

Such, Phaedrus, is the tale which I heard from the stranger of Mantinea, and which you may call the encomium of love, or what you please.

The company applaud the speech of Socrates, and Aristophanes is about to say something, when suddenly a band of revellers breaks into the court, and the voice of Alcibiades is heard asking for Agathon. He is led in drunk, and welcomed by Agathon, whom he has come to crown with a garland. He is placed on a couch at his side, but suddenly, on recognizing Socrates, he starts up, and a sort of conflict is carried on between them, which Agathon is requested to appease. Alcibiades then insists that they shall drink, and has a large wine-cooler filled, which he first empties himself, and then fills again and passes on to Socrates. He is informed of the nature of the entertainment; and is ready to join, if only in the character of a drunken and disappointed lover he may be allowed to sing the praises of Socrates:—

He begins by comparing Socrates first to the busts of Silenus, which have images of the gods inside them; and, secondly, to Marsyas the flute-player. For Socrates produces the same effect with the voice which Marsyas did with the flute. He is the great speaker and enchanter who ravishes the souls of men; the convincer of hearts too, as he has convinced Alcibiades, and made him ashamed of his mean and miserable life. Socrates at one time seemed about to fall in love with him; and he thought that he would thereby gain a wonderful opportunity of receiving lessons of wisdom. He narrates the failure of his design. He has suffered agonies from him, and is at his wit's end. He then proceeds to mention some other particulars of the life of Socrates; how they were at Potidaea together, where Socrates

Symposium

showed his superior powers of enduring cold and fatigue; how on one occasion he had stood for an entire day and night absorbed in reflection amid the wonder of the spectators; how on another occasion he had saved Alcibiades' life; how at the battle of Delium, after the defeat, he might be seen stalking about like a pelican, rolling his eyes as Aristophanes had described him in the Clouds. He is the most wonderful of human beings, and absolutely unlike anyone but a satyr. Like the satyr in his language too; for he uses the commonest words as the outward mask of the divinest truths.

When Alcibiades has done speaking, a dispute begins between him and Agathon and Socrates. Socrates piques Alcibiades by a pretended affection for Agathon. Presently a band of revellers appears, who introduce disorder into the feast; the sober part of the company, Eryximachus, Phaedrus, and others, withdraw; and Aristodemus, the follower of Socrates, sleeps during the whole of a long winter's night. When he wakes at cockcrow the revellers are nearly all asleep. Only Socrates, Aristophanes, and Agathon hold out; they are drinking from a large goblet, which they pass round, and Socrates is explaining to the two others, who are half-asleep, that the genius of tragedy is the same as that of comedy, and that the writer of tragedy ought to be a writer of comedy also. And first Aristophanes drops, and then, as the day is dawning, Agathon. Socrates, having laid them to rest, takes a bath and goes to his daily avocations until the evening. Aristodemus follows.

IF IT BE TRUE that there are more things in the Symposium of Plato than any commentator has dreamed of, it is also true that many things have been imagined which are not really to be found there. Some writings hardly admit of a more distinct interpretation than a musical composition; and every reader may form his own accompaniment of thought or feeling to the strain which he hears. The Symposium of Plato is a work of this character, and can with difficulty be rendered in any words but the writer's own. There are so many half-lights and cross-lights, so much of the colour of mythology, and of the manner of sophistry adhering—rhetoric and poetry, the playful and the serious, are so subtly intermingled in it, and vestiges of old philosophy so curiously blend with germs of future knowledge, that agreement among interpreters is not to be expected. The expression '*poema magis putandum quam comicorum poetarum,*' which has been applied to all the writings of Plato, is especially applicable to the Symposium.

The power of love is represented in the Symposium as running through all nature and all being: at one end descending to animals and plants, and attaining to the highest vision of truth at the other. In an age when man was seeking for an expression of the world around him, the conception of love greatly affected him. One of the first distinctions of language and of mythology was that of gender; and at a later period the ancient physicist, anticipating modern science, saw, or thought that he saw, a sex in plants; there were elective affinities among the elements, marriages of earth and heaven. (Aesch. Frag. Dan.) Love became a mythic personage whom philosophy, borrowing from poetry, converted into an efficient cause of creation. The traces of the existence of love, as of number and figure, were everywhere discerned; and in the Pythagorean list of opposites male and female were ranged side by side with odd and even, finite and infinite.

But Plato seems also to be aware that there is a mystery of love in man as well as in nature, extending beyond the mere immediate relation of the sexes. He is conscious that the highest and noblest things in the world are not easily severed from the sensual desires, or may even be regarded as a spiritualized form of them. We may observe that Socrates himself is not represented as originally unimpassioned, but as one who has overcome his passions; the secret of his power over others partly lies in his passionate but self-controlled nature. In the Phaedrus and Symposium love is not merely the feeling usually so called, but the mystical contemplation of the beautiful and the good. The same passion which may wallow in the mire is capable of rising to the loftiest heights—of penetrating the inmost secret of philosophy. The highest love is the love not of a person, but of the highest and purest abstraction. This abstraction is the far-off heaven on which the eye of the mind is fixed in fond amazement. The unity of truth, the consistency of the warring elements of the world, the enthusiasm for knowledge when first beaming upon mankind, the relativity of ideas to the human mind, and of the human mind to ideas, the faith in the invisible, the adoration of the eternal nature, are all included, consciously or unconsciously, in Plato's doctrine of love.

The successive speeches in praise of love are characteristic of the speakers, and contribute in various degrees to the final result; they are all designed to prepare the way for Socrates, who gathers up the threads anew, and skims the highest points of each of them. But they are not to be regarded as the stages of an idea, rising above one another to a climax. They are fanciful, partly facetious performances, 'yet also having a certain measure of seriousness,' which the successive speakers dedicate to the god. All of them are rhetorical and poetical rather than dialectical, but glimpses of truth appear in them. When Eryximachus says that the principles of music are simple in themselves, but confused in their application, he touches lightly upon a difficulty which has troubled the moderns as well as the ancients in music, and may be extended to the other applied sciences. That confusion begins in the concrete, was the natural feeling of a mind dwelling in the world of ideas. When Pausanias remarks that personal attachments are inimical to despots. The experience of Greek history confirms the truth of his remark. When Aristophanes declares that love is the desire of the whole, he expresses a feeling not unlike that of the German philosopher, who says that 'philosophy is home sickness.' When Agathon says that no man 'can be wronged of his own free will,' he is alluding playfully to a serious problem of Greek philosophy (compare Arist. Nic. Ethics). So naturally does Plato mingle jest and earnest, truth and opinion in the same work.

The characters—of Phaedrus, who has been the cause of more philosophical discussions than any other man, with the exception of Simmias the Theban (Phaedrus); of Aristophanes, who disguises under comic imagery a serious purpose; of Agathon, who in later life is satirized by Aristophanes in the Thesmophoriazusae, for his effeminate manners and the feeble rhythms of his verse; of Alcibiades, who is the same strange contrast of great powers and great vices, which meets us in history—are drawn to the life; and we may suppose the less-known characters of Pausanias and Eryximachus to be also true to the traditional recollection of them (compare Phaedr., Protag.; and compare Sympos. with Phaedr.). We may also remark that Aristodemus is called 'the little' in Xenophon's Memorabilia (compare Symp.).

The speeches have been said to follow each other in pairs: Phaedrus and Pausanias being the ethical, Eryximachus and Aristophanes the physical speakers, while in Agathon and Socrates poetry and philosophy blend together. The speech of Phaedrus is also described as the mythological, that of Pausanias as the political, that of Eryximachus as the scientific, that of Aristophanes as the artistic (!), that of Socrates as the philosophical. But these and similar distinctions are not found in Plato; —they are the points of view of his critics, and seem to impede rather than to assist us in understanding him.

When the turn of Socrates comes round he cannot be allowed to disturb the arrangement made at first. With the leave of Phaedrus he asks a few questions, and then he throws his argument into the form of a speech (compare Gorg., Protag.). But his speech is really the narrative of a dialogue between himself and Diotima. And as at a banquet good manners would not allow him to win a victory either over his host or any of the guests, the superiority which he gains over Agathon is ingeniously represented as having been already gained over himself by her. The artifice has the further advantage of maintaining his accustomed profession of ignorance (compare Menex.). Even his knowledge of the mysteries of love, to which he lays claim here and elsewhere (Lys.), is given by Diotima.

The speeches are attested to us by the very best authority. The madman Apollodorus, who for three years past has made a daily study of the actions of Socrates—to whom the world is summed up in the words 'Great is Socrates'—he has heard them from another 'madman,' Aristodemus, who was the 'shadow' of Socrates in days of old, like him going about barefooted, and who had been present at the time. 'Would you desire better witness?' The extraordinary narrative of Alcibiades is ingeniously represented as admitted by Socrates, whose silence when he is invited to contradict gives consent to the narrator. We may observe, by the way, (1) how the very appearance of Aristodemus by himself is a sufficient indication to Agathon that Socrates has been left behind; also, (2) how the courtesy of Agathon anticipates the excuse which Socrates was to have made on Aristodemus' behalf for coming uninvited; (3) how the story of the fit or trance of Socrates is confirmed by the mention which Alcibiades makes of a similar fit of abstraction occurring when he was serving with the army at Potidaea; like (4) the drinking powers of Socrates and his love of the fair, which receive a similar attestation in the concluding scene; or the attachment of Aristodemus, who is not forgotten when Socrates takes his departure. (5) We may notice the manner in which Socrates himself regards the first five speeches, not as true, but as fanciful and exaggerated encomiums of the god Love; (6) the satirical character of them, shown especially in the appeals to mythology, in the reasons which are given by Zeus for reconstructing the frame of man, or by the Boeotians and Eleans for encouraging male loves; (7) the ruling passion of Socrates for dialectics, who will argue with Agathon instead of making a speech, and will only speak at all upon the condition that he is allowed to speak the truth. We may note also the touch of Socratic irony, (8) which admits of a wide application and reveals a deep insight into the world:—that in speaking of holy things and persons there is a general understanding that you should praise them, not that you should speak the truth about them—this is the sort of praise which Socrates is unable to give. Lastly, (9) we may remark that the banquet is a real banquet after all, at which love is the theme of discourse, and huge quantities of wine are drunk.

The discourse of Phaedrus is half-mythical, half-ethical; and he himself, true to the character which is given him in the Dialogue bearing his name, is half-sophist, half-enthusiast. He is the critic of poetry also, who compares Homer and Aeschylus in the insipid and irrational manner of the schools of the day, characteristically reasoning about the probability of matters which do not admit of reasoning. He starts from a noble text: 'That without the sense of honour and dishonour neither states nor individuals ever do any good or great work.' But he soon passes on to more common-place topics. The antiquity of love, the blessing of having a lover, the incentive which love offers to daring deeds, the examples of Alcestis and Achilles, are the chief themes of his discourse. The love of women is regarded by him as almost on an equality with that of men; and he makes the singular remark that the gods favour the return of love which is made by the beloved more than the original sentiment, because the lover is of a nobler and diviner nature.

There is something of a sophistical ring in the speech of Phaedrus, which recalls the first speech in imitation of Lysias, occurring in the Dialogue called the Phaedrus. This is still more marked in the speech of Pausanias which follows; and which is at once hyperlogical in form and also extremely confused and pedantic. Plato is attacking the logical feebleness of the sophists and rhetoricians, through their pupils, not forgetting by the way to satirize the monotonous and unmeaning rhythms which Prodicus and others were introducing into Attic prose (compare Protag.). Of course, he is 'playing both sides of the game,' as in the Gorgias and Phaedrus; but it is not necessary in order to understand him that we should discuss the fairness of his mode of proceeding. The love of Pausanias for Agathon has already been touched upon in the Protagoras, and is alluded to by Aristophanes. Hence he is naturally the upholder of male loves, which, like all the other affections or actions of men, he regards as varying according to the manner of their performance. Like the sophists and like Plato himself, though in a different sense, he begins his discussion by an appeal to mythology, and distinguishes between the elder and younger love. The value which he attributes to such loves as motives to virtue and philosophy is at variance with modern and Christian notions, but is in accordance with Hellenic sentiment. The opinion of Christendom has not altogether condemned passionate friendships between persons of the same sex, but has certainly not encouraged them, because though innocent in themselves in a few temperaments they are liable to degenerate into fearful evil. Pausanias is very earnest in the defence of such loves; and he speaks of them as generally approved among Hellenes and disapproved by barbarians. His speech is 'more words than matter,' and might have been composed by a pupil of Lysias or of Prodicus, although there is no hint given that Plato is specially referring to them. As Eryximachus says, 'he makes a fair beginning, but a lame ending.'

Plato transposes the two next speeches, as in the Republic he would transpose the virtues and the mathematical sciences. This is done partly to avoid monotony, partly for the sake of making Aristophanes

Symposium

'the cause of wit in others,' and also in order to bring the comic and tragic poet into juxtaposition, as if by accident. A suitable 'expectation' of Aristophanes is raised by the ludicrous circumstance of his having the hiccough, which is appropriately cured by his substitute, the physician Eryximachus. To Eryximachus Love is the good physician; he sees everything as an intelligent physicist, and, like many professors of his art in modern times, attempts to reduce the moral to the physical; or recognises one law of love which pervades them both. There are loves and strifes of the body as well as of the mind. Like Hippocrates the Asclepiad, he is a disciple of Heracleitus, whose conception of the harmony of opposites he explains in a new way as the harmony after discord; to his common sense, as to that of many moderns as well as ancients, the identity of contradictories is an absurdity. His notion of love may be summed up as the harmony of man with himself in soul as well as body, and of all things in heaven and earth with one another.

Aristophanes is ready to laugh and make laugh before he opens his mouth, just as Socrates, true to his character, is ready to argue before he begins to speak. He expresses the very genius of the old comedy, its coarse and forcible imagery, and the licence of its language in speaking about the gods. He has no sophistical notions about love, which is brought back by him to its common-sense meaning of love between intelligent beings. His account of the origin of the sexes has the greatest (comic) probability and verisimilitude. Nothing in Aristophanes is more truly Aristophanic than the description of the human monster whirling round on four arms and four legs, eight in all, with incredible rapidity. Yet there is a mixture of earnestness in this jest; three serious principles seem to be insinuated:—

first, that man cannot exist in isolation; he must be reunited if he is to be perfected: secondly, that love is the mediator and reconciler of poor, divided human nature: thirdly, that the loves of this world are an indistinct anticipation of an ideal union which is not yet realized.

The speech of Agathon is conceived in a higher strain, and receives the real, if half-ironical, approval of Socrates. It is the speech of the tragic poet and a sort of poem, like tragedy, moving among the gods of Olympus, and not among the elder or Orphic deities. In the idea of the antiquity of love he cannot agree; love is not of the olden time, but present and youthful ever. The speech may be compared with that speech of Socrates in the Phaedrus in which he describes himself as talking dithyrambs. It is at once a preparation for Socrates and a foil to him. The rhetoric of Agathon elevates the soul to 'sunlit heights,' but at the same time contrasts with the natural and necessary eloquence of Socrates. Agathon contributes the distinction between love and the works of love, and also hints incidentally that love is always of beauty, which Socrates afterwards raises into a principle. While the consciousness of discord is stronger in the comic poet Aristophanes, Agathon, the tragic poet, has a deeper sense of harmony and reconciliation, and speaks of Love as the creator and artist.

All the earlier speeches embody common opinions coloured with a tinge of philosophy. They furnish the material out of which Socrates proceeds to form his discourse, starting, as in other places, from mythology and the opinions of men. From Phaedrus he takes the thought that love is stronger than death; from Pausanias, that the true love is akin to intellect and political activity; from Eryximachus, that love is a universal phenomenon and the great power of nature; from Aristophanes, that love is the child of want, and is not merely the love of the congenial or of the whole, but (as he adds) of the good; from Agathon, that love is of beauty, not however of beauty only, but of birth in beauty. As it would be out of character for Socrates to make a lengthened harangue, the speech takes the form of a dialogue between Socrates and a mysterious woman of foreign extraction. She elicits the final truth from one who knows nothing, and who, speaking by the lips of another, and himself a despiser of rhetoric, is proved also to be the most consummate of rhetoricians (compare Menexenus).

The last of the six discourses begins with a short argument which overthrows not only Agathon but all the preceding speakers by the help of a distinction which has escaped them. Extravagant praises have been ascribed to Love as the author of every good; no sort of encomium was too high for him, whether deserved and true or not. But Socrates has no talent for speaking anything but the truth, and if he is to speak the truth of Love he must honestly confess that he is not a good at all: for love is of the good, and no man can desire that which he has. This piece of dialectics is ascribed to Diotima, who has already urged upon Socrates the argument which he urges against Agathon. That the distinction is a fallacy is obvious; it is almost acknowledged to be so by Socrates himself. For he who has beauty or good may desire more of them; and he who has beauty or good in himself may desire beauty and good in others. The fallacy seems to arise out of a confusion between the abstract ideas of good and beauty, which do not admit of degrees, and their partial realization in individuals.

But Diotima, the prophetess of Mantineia, whose sacred and superhuman character raises her above the ordinary proprieties of women, has taught Socrates far more than this about the art and mystery of love. She has taught him that love is another aspect of philosophy. The same want in the human soul which is satisfied in the vulgar by the procreation of children, may become the highest aspiration of intellectual desire. As the Christian might speak of hungering and thirsting after righteousness; or of divine loves under the figure of human (compare Eph. 'This is a great mystery, but I speak concerning Christ and the church'); as the mediaeval saint might speak of the 'fruitio Dei;' as Dante saw all things contained in his love of Beatrice, so Plato would have us absorb all other loves and desires in the love of knowledge. Here is the beginning of Neoplatonism, or rather, perhaps, a proof (of which there are many) that the so-called mysticism of the East was not strange to the Greek of the fifth century before Christ. The first tumult of the affections was not wholly subdued; there were longings of a creature

Moving about in worlds not realized, which no art could satisfy. To most men reason and passion appear to be antagonistic both in idea and fact. The union of the greatest comprehension of knowledge and the burning intensity of love is a contradiction in nature, which may have existed in a far-off primeval age in the mind of some Hebrew prophet or other Eastern sage, but has now become an imagination only. Yet this 'passion of the reason' is the theme of the Symposium of Plato. And as there is no impossibility in supposing that 'one king, or son of a king, may be a philosopher,' so also there is a probability that there may be some few—perhaps one or two in a whole generation—in whom the light of truth may not lack the warmth of desire. And if there be such natures, no one will be disposed to deny that 'from them flow most of the benefits of individuals and states;' and even from imperfect combinations of the two elements in teachers or statesmen great good may often arise.

Yet there is a higher region in which love is not only felt, but satisfied, in the perfect beauty of eternal knowledge, beginning with the beauty of earthly things, and at last reaching a beauty in which all existence is seen to be harmonious and one. The limited affection is enlarged, and enabled to behold the ideal of all things. And here the highest summit which is reached in the Symposium is seen also to be the highest summit which is attained in the Republic, but approached from another side; and there is 'a way upwards and downwards,' which is the same and not the same in both. The ideal beauty of the one is the ideal good of the other; regarded not with the eye of knowledge, but of faith and desire; and they are respectively the source of beauty and the source of good in all other things. And by the steps of a 'ladder reaching to heaven' we pass from images of visible beauty (Greek), and from the hypotheses of the Mathematical sciences, which are not yet based upon the idea of good, through the concrete to the abstract, and, by different paths arriving, behold the vision of the eternal (compare Symp. Republic also Phaedrus). Under one aspect 'the idea is love'; under another, 'truth.' In both the lover of wisdom is the 'spectator of all time and of all existence.' This is a 'mystery' in which Plato also obscurely intimates the union of the spiritual and fleshly, the interpenetration of the moral and intellectual faculties.

The divine image of beauty which resides within Socrates has been revealed; the Silenus, or outward man, has now to be exhibited. The description of Socrates follows immediately after the speech of Socrates; one is the complement of the other. At the height of divine inspiration, when the force of nature can no further go, by way of contrast to this extreme idealism, Alcibiades, accompanied by a troop of revellers and a flute-girl, staggers in, and being drunk is able to tell of things which he would have been ashamed to make known if he had been sober. The state of his affections towards Socrates, unintelligible to us and perverted as they appear, affords an illustration of the power ascribed to the loves of man in the speech of Pausanias. He does not suppose his feelings to be peculiar to himself: there are several other persons in the company who have been equally in love with Socrates, and like himself have been deceived by him. The singular part of this confession is the combination of the most degrading passion with the desire of virtue and improvement. Such an union is not wholly untrue to human nature, which is capable of combining good and evil in a degree beyond what we can easily conceive. In imaginative persons, especially, the God and beast in man seem to part asunder more than is natural in a well-regulated mind. The Platonic Socrates (for of the real Socrates this may be doubted: compare his public rebuke of Critias for his shameful love of Euthydemus in Xenophon, Memorabilia) does not regard the greatest evil of Greek life as a thing not to be spoken of; but it has a ridiculous element (Plato's Symp.), and is a subject for irony, no less than for moral reprobation (compare Plato's Symp.). It is also used as a figure of speech which no one interpreted literally (compare Xen. Symp.). Nor does Plato feel any repugnance, such as would be felt in modern times, at bringing his great master and hero into connexion with nameless crimes. He is contented with representing him as a saint, who has won 'the Olympian victory' over the temptations of human nature. The fault of taste, which to us is so glaring and which was recognized by the Greeks of a later age (Athenaeus), was not perceived by Plato himself. We are still more surprised to find that the philosopher is incited to take the first step in his upward progress (Symp.) by the beauty of young men and boys, which was alone capable of inspiring the modern feeling of romance in the Greek mind. The passion of love took the spurious form of an enthusiasm for the ideal of beauty—a worship as of some godlike image of an Apollo or Antinous. But the love of youth when not depraved was a love of virtue and modesty as well as of beauty, the one being the expression of the other; and in certain Greek states, especially at Sparta and Thebes, the honourable attachment of a youth to an elder man was a part of his education. The 'army of lovers and their beloved who would be invincible if they could be united by such a tie' Symp.), is not a mere fiction of Plato's, but seems actually to have existed at Thebes in the days of Epaminondas and Pelopidas, if we may believe writers cited anonymously by Plutarch, Pelop. Vit. It is observable that Plato never in the least degree excuses the depraved love of the body (compare Charm.; Rep.; Laws; Symp.; and once more Xenophon, Mem.), nor is there any Greek writer of mark who condones or approves such connexions. But owing partly to the puzzling nature of the subject these friendships are spoken of by Plato in a manner different from that customary among ourselves. To most of them we should hesitate to ascribe, any more than to the attachment of Achilles and Patroclus in Homer, an immoral or licentious character. There were many, doubtless, to whom the love of the fair mind was the noblest form of friendship (Rep.), and who deemed the friendship of man with man to be higher than the love of woman, because altogether separated from the bodily appetites. The existence of such attachments may be reasonably attributed to the inferiority and seclusion of woman, and the want of a real family or social life and parental influence in Hellenic cities; and they were encouraged by the practice of gymnastic exercises, by the meetings of political clubs, and by the tie of military companionship. They were also an educational institution: a young person was specially entrusted by his parents to some elder friend who was expected by them to train their son in manly exercises and in virtue. It is not likely that a Greek parent committed him to a lover, any more than we should to a schoolmaster, in the expectation that he would be corrupted by him, but rather in the hope that his morals would be better cared for than was possible in a great household of slaves.

It is difficult to adduce the authority of Plato either for or against such practices or customs, because it is not always easy to determine whether he is speaking of 'the heavenly and philosophical love, or of the coarse Polyhymnia:' and he often refers to this (e.g. in the Symposium) half in jest, yet 'with a certain degree of seriousness.' We observe that they entered into one part of Greek literature, but not into another, and that the larger part is free from such associations. Indecency was an element of the ludicrous in the old Greek Comedy, as it has been in other ages and countries. But effeminate love was always condemned as well as ridiculed by the Comic poets; and in the New Comedy the allusions to such topics have disappeared. They seem to have been no longer tolerated by the greater refinement of the age. False sentiment is found in the Lyric and Elegiac poets; and in mythology 'the greatest of the Gods' (Rep.) is not exempt from evil imputations. But the morals of a nation are not to be judged of wholly by its literature. Hellas was not necessarily more corrupted in the days of the Persian and Peloponnesian wars, or of Plato and the Orators, than England in the time of Fielding and Smollett, or France in the nineteenth century. No one supposes certain French novels to be a representation of ordinary French life. And the greater part of Greek literature, beginning with Homer and including the tragedians, philosophers, and, with the exception of the Comic poets (whose business was to raise a laugh by whatever means), all the greater writers of Hellas who have been preserved to us, are free from the taint of indecency.

Some general considerations occur to our mind when we begin to reflect on this subject. (1) That good and evil are linked together in human nature, and have often existed side by side in the world and in man to an extent hardly credible. We cannot distinguish them, and are therefore unable to part them; as in the parable 'they grow together unto the harvest:' it is only a rule of external decency by which society can divide them. Nor should we be right in inferring from the prevalence of any one vice or corruption that a state or individual was demoralized in their whole character. Not only has the corruption of the best been sometimes thought to be the worst, but it may be remarked that this very excess of evil has been the stimulus to good (compare Plato, Laws, where he says that in the most corrupt cities individuals are to be found beyond all praise). (2) It may be observed that evils which admit of degrees can seldom be rightly estimated, because under the same name actions of the most different degrees of culpability may be included. No charge is more easily set going than the imputation of secret wickedness (which cannot be either proved or disproved and often cannot be defined) when directed against a person of whom the world, or a section of it, is predisposed to think evil. And it is quite possible that the malignity of Greek scandal, aroused by some personal jealousy or party enmity, may have converted the innocent friendship of a great man for a noble youth into a connexion of another kind. Such accusations were brought against several of the leading men of Hellas, e.g. Cimon, Alcibiades, Critias, Demosthenes, Epaminondas: several of the Roman emperors were assailed by similar weapons which have been used even in our own day against statesmen of the highest character. (3) While we know that in this matter there is a great gulf fixed between Greek and Christian Ethics, yet, if we would do justice to the Greeks, we must also acknowledge that there was a greater outspokenness among them than among ourselves about the things which nature hides, and that the more frequent mention of such topics is not to be taken as the measure of the prevalence of offences, or as a proof of the general corruption of society. It is likely that every religion in the world has used words or practised rites in one age, which have become distasteful or repugnant to another. We cannot, though for different reasons, trust the representations either of Comedy or Satire; and still less of Christian Apologists. (4) We observe that at Thebes and Lacedemon the attachment of an elder friend to a beloved youth was often deemed to be a part of his education; and was encouraged by his parents—it was only shameful if it degenerated into licentiousness. Such we may believe to have been the tie which united Asophychus and Cephisodorus with the great Epaminondas in whose companionship they fell (Plutarch, Amat.; Athenaeus on the authority of Theopompus). (5) A small matter: there appears to be a difference of custom among the Greeks and among ourselves, as between ourselves and continental nations at the present time, in modes of salutation. We must not suspect evil in the hearty kiss or embrace of a male friend 'returning from the army at Potidaea' any more than in a similar salutation when practised by members of the same family. But those who make these admissions, and who regard, not without pity, the victims of such illusions in our own day, whose life has been blasted by them, may be none the less resolved that the natural and healthy instincts of mankind shall alone be tolerated (Greek); and that the lesson of manliness which we have inherited from our fathers shall not degenerate into sentimentalism or effeminacy. The possibility of an honourable connexion of this kind seems to have died out with Greek civilization. Among the Romans, and also among barbarians, such as the Celts and Persians, there is no trace of such attachments existing in any noble or virtuous form.

(Compare Hoeck's Creta and the admirable and exhaustive article of Meier in Ersch and Grueber's Cyclopedia on this subject; Plutarch, Amatores; Athenaeus; Lysias contra Simonem; Aesch. c. Timarchum.)

The character of Alcibiades in the Symposium is hardly less remarkable than that of Socrates, and agrees with the picture given of him in the first of the two Dialogues which are called by his name, and also with the slight sketch of him in the Protagoras. He is the impersonation of lawlessness—'the lion's whelp, who ought not to be reared in the city,' yet not without a certain generosity which gained the hearts of men,—strangely fascinated by Socrates, and possessed of a genius which might have been either the destruction or salvation of Athens. The dramatic interest of the character is heightened by the recollection of his after history. He seems to have been present to the mind of Plato in the description of the democratic man of the Republic (compare also Alcibiades 1).

There is no criterion of the date of the Symposium, except that which is furnished by the allusion to the division of Arcadia after the destruction of Mantinea. This took place in the year B.C. 384, which is the forty-fourth year of Plato's life. The Symposium cannot therefore be regarded as a youthful work. As Mantinea was restored in the year 369, the composition of the Dialogue will probably fall between 384 and 369. Whether the recollection of the event is more likely to have been renewed at the destruction or restoration of the city, rather than at some intermediate period, is a consideration not worth raising.

The Symposium is connected with the Phaedrus both in style and subject; they are the only Dialogues of Plato in which the theme of love is discussed at length. In both of them philosophy is regarded as a sort of enthusiasm or madness; Socrates is himself 'a prophet new inspired' with Bacchanalian revelry, which, like his philosophy, he characteristically pretends to have derived not from himself but from others. The Phaedo also presents some points of comparison with the Symposium. For there, too, philosophy might be described as 'dying for love;' and there are not wanting many touches of humour and fancy, which remind us of the Symposium. But while the Phaedo and Phaedrus look backwards and forwards to past and future states of existence, in the Symposium there is no break between this world and another; and we rise from one to the other by a regular series of steps or stages, proceeding from the particulars of sense to the universal of reason, and from one universal to many, which are finally reunited in a single science (compare Rep.). At first immortality means only the succession of existences; even knowledge comes and goes. Then follows, in the language of the mysteries, a higher and a higher degree of initiation; at last we arrive at the perfect vision of beauty, not relative or changing, but eternal and absolute; not bounded by this world, or in or out of this world, but an aspect of the divine, extending over all things, and having no limit of space or time: this is the highest knowledge of which the human mind is capable. Plato does not go on to ask whether the individual is absorbed in the sea of light and beauty or retains his personality. Enough for him to have attained the true beauty or good, without enquiring precisely into the relation in which human beings stood to it. That the soul has such a reach of thought, and is capable of partaking of the eternal nature, seems to imply that she too is eternal (compare Phaedrus). But Plato does not distinguish the eternal in man from the eternal in the world or in God. He is willing to rest in the contemplation of the idea, which to him is the cause of all things (Rep.), and has no strength to go further.

The Symposium of Xenophon, in which Socrates describes himself as a pander, and also discourses of the difference between sensual and sentimental love, likewise offers several interesting points of comparison. But the suspicion which hangs over other writings of Xenophon, and the numerous minute references to the Phaedrus and Symposium, as well as to some of the other writings of Plato, throw a doubt on the genuineness of the work. The Symposium of Xenophon, if written by him at all, would certainly show that he wrote against Plato, and was acquainted with his works. Of this hostility there is no trace in the Memorabilia. Such a rivalry is more

Symposium

characteristic of an imitator than of an original writer. The (so-called) Symposium of Xenophon may therefore have no more title to be regarded as genuine than the confessedly spurious Apology.

There are no means of determining the relative order in time of the Phaedrus, Symposium, Phaedo. The order which has been adopted in this translation rests on no other principle than the desire to bring together in a series the memorials of the life of Socrates.

Plato

SYMPOSIUM

by

Plato

Translated by Benjamin Jowett

PERSONS OF THE DIALOGUE:

Apollodorus, who repeats to his companion the dialogue which he had heard from Aristodemus, and had already once narrated to Glaucon.

Phaedrus, Pausanias, Eryximachus, Aristophanes, Agathon, Socrates,

Alcibiades, A Troop of Revellers.

SCENE: The House of Agathon.

Concerning the things about which you ask to be informed I believe that I am not ill-prepared with an answer. For the day before yesterday I was coming from my own home at Phalerum to the city, and one of my acquaintance, who had caught a sight of me from behind, calling out playfully in the distance, said: Apollodorus, O thou Phalerian (Probably a play of words on (Greek), 'bald-headed.') man, halt! So I did as I was bid; and then he said, I was looking for you, Apollodorus, only just now, that I might ask you about the speeches in praise of love, which were delivered by Socrates, Alcibiades, and others, at Agathon's supper. Phoenix, the son of Philip, told another person who told me of them; his narrative was very indistinct, but he said that you knew, and I wish that you would give me an account of them. Who, if not you, should be the reporter of the words of your friend? And first tell me, he said, were you present at this meeting?

Your informant, Glaucon, I said, must have been very indistinct indeed, if you imagine that the occasion was recent; or that I could have been of the party.

Why, yes, he replied, I thought so.

Impossible: I said. Are you ignorant that for many years Agathon has not resided at Athens; and not three have elapsed since I became acquainted with Socrates, and have made it my daily business to know all that he says and does. There was a time when I was running about the world, fancying myself to be well employed, but I was really a most wretched being, no better than you are now. I thought that I ought to do anything rather than be a philosopher.

Well, he said, jesting apart, tell me when the meeting occurred.

In our boyhood, I replied, when Agathon won the prize with his first tragedy, on the day after that on which he and his chorus offered the sacrifice of victory.

Then it must have been a long while ago, he said; and who told you—did Socrates?

No indeed, I replied, but the same person who told Phoenix;— he was a little fellow, who never wore any shoes, Aristodemus, of the deme of Cydathenaeum. He had been at Agathon's feast; and I think that in those days there was no one who was a more devoted admirer of Socrates. Moreover, I have asked Socrates about the truth of some parts of his narrative, and he confirmed them. Then, said Glaucon, let us have the tale over again; is not the road to Athens just made for conversation? And so we walked, and talked of the discourses on love; and therefore, as I said at first, I am not ill-prepared to comply with your request, and will have another rehearsal of them if you like. For to speak or to hear others speak of philosophy always gives me the greatest pleasure, to say nothing of the profit. But when I hear another strain, especially that of you rich men and traders, such conversation displeases me; and I pity you who are my companions, because you think that you are doing something when in reality you are doing nothing. And I dare say that you pity me in return, whom you regard as an unhappy creature, and very probably you are right. But I certainly know of you what you only think of me—there is the difference.

COMPANION: I see, Apollodorus, that you are just the same—always speaking evil of yourself, and of others; and I do believe that you pity all mankind, with the exception of Socrates, yourself first of all, true in this to your old name, which, however deserved, I know not how you acquired, of Apollodorus the madman; for you are always raging against yourself and everybody but Socrates.

APOLLODORUS: Yes, friend, and the reason why I am said to be mad, and out of my wits, is just because I have these notions of myself and you; no other evidence is required.

COMPANION: No more of that, Apollodorus; but let me renew my request that you would repeat the conversation.

APOLLODORUS: Well, the tale of love was on this wise:—But perhaps I had better begin at the beginning, and endeavour to give you the exact words of Aristodemus:

He said that he met Socrates fresh from the bath and sandalled; and as the sight of the sandals was unusual, he asked him whither he was going that he had been converted into such a beau:—

To a banquet at Agathon's, he replied, whose invitation to his sacrifice of victory I refused yesterday, fearing a crowd, but promising that I would come to-day instead; and so I have put on my finery, because he is such a fine man. What say you to going with me unasked?

I will do as you bid me, I replied.

Follow then, he said, and let us demolish the proverb:—

'To the feasts of inferior men the good unbidden go;' instead of which our proverb will run:— 'To the feasts of the good the good unbidden go;' and this alteration may be supported by the authority of Homer himself, who not only demolishes but literally outrages the proverb. For, after picturing Agamemnon as the most valiant of men, he makes Menelaus, who is but a fainthearted warrior, come unbidden (*Iliad*) to the banquet of Agamemnon, who is feasting and offering sacrifices, not the better to the worse, but the worse to the better.

I rather fear, Socrates, said Aristodemus, lest this may still be my case; and that, like Menelaus in Homer, I shall be the inferior person, who

'To the feasts of the wise unbidden goes.'

But I shall say that I was bidden of you, and then you will have to make an excuse.

'Two going together,' he replied, in Homeric fashion, one or other of them may invent an excuse by the way (*Iliad*).

This was the style of their conversation as they went along. Socrates dropped behind in a fit of abstraction, and desired Aristodemus, who was waiting, to go on before him. When he reached the house of Agathon he found the doors wide open, and a comical thing happened. A servant coming out met him, and led him at once into the banqueting-hall in which the guests were reclining, for the banquet was about to begin. Welcome, Aristodemus, said Agathon, as soon as he appeared—you are just in time to sup with us; if you come on any other matter put it off, and make one of us, as I was looking for you yesterday and meant to have asked you, if I could have found you. But what have you done with Socrates?

I turned round, but Socrates was nowhere to be seen; and I had to explain that he had been with me a moment before, and that I came by his invitation to the supper.

You were quite right in coming, said Agathon; but where is he himself?

He was behind me just now, as I entered, he said, and I cannot think what has become of him.

Go and look for him, boy, said Agathon, and bring him in; and do you, Aristodemus, meanwhile take the place by Eryximachus.

The servant then assisted him to wash, and he lay down, and presently another servant came in and reported that our friend Socrates had retired into the portico of the neighbouring house. 'There he is fixed,' said he, 'and when I call to him he will not stir.'

How strange, said Agathon; then you must call him again, and keep calling him.

Let him alone, said my informant; he has a way of stopping anywhere and losing himself without any reason. I believe that he will soon appear; do not therefore disturb him.

Well, if you think so, I will leave him, said Agathon. And then, turning to the servants, he added, 'Let us have supper without waiting for him. Serve up whatever you please, for there is no one to give you orders; hitherto I have never left you to yourselves. But on this occasion imagine that you are our hosts, and that I and the company are your guests; treat us well, and then we shall commend you.' After this, supper was served, but still no Socrates; and during the meal Agathon several times expressed a wish to send for him, but Aristodemus objected; and at last when the feast was about half over—for the fit, as usual, was not of long duration—Socrates entered. Agathon, who was reclining alone at the end of the table, begged that he would take the place next to him; that 'I may touch you,' he said, 'and have the benefit of that wise thought which came into your mind in the portico, and is now in your possession; for I am certain that you would not have come away until you had found what you sought.'

How I wish, said Socrates, taking his place as he was desired, that wisdom could be infused by touch, out of the fuller into the emptier man, as water runs through wool out of a fuller cup into an emptier one; if that were so, how greatly should I value the privilege of reclining at your side! For you would have filled me full with a stream of wisdom plenteous and fair; whereas my own is of a very mean and questionable sort, no better than a dream. But yours is bright and full of promise, and was manifested forth in all the splendour of youth the day before yesterday, in the presence of more than thirty thousand Hellenes.

You are mocking, Socrates, said Agathon, and ere long you and I will have to determine who bears off the palm of wisdom—of this Dionysus shall be the judge; but at present you are better occupied with supper.

Socrates took his place on the couch, and supped with the rest; and then libations were offered, and after a hymn had been sung to the god, and there had been the usual ceremonies, they were about to commence drinking, when Pausanias said, And now, my friends, how can we drink with least injury to ourselves? I can assure you that I feel severely the effect of yesterday's potations, and must have time to recover; and I suspect that most of you are in the same predicament, for you were of the party yesterday. Consider then: How can the drinking be made easiest?

I entirely agree, said Aristophanes, that we should, by all means, avoid hard drinking, for I was myself one of those who were yesterday drowned in drink.

I think that you are right, said Eryximachus, the son of Acumenus; but I should still like to hear one other person speak: Is Agathon able to drink hard?

I am not equal to it, said Agathon.

Then, said Eryximachus, the weak heads like myself, Aristodemus, Phaedrus, and others who never can drink, are fortunate in finding that the stronger ones are not in a drinking mood. (I do not include Socrates, who is able either to drink or to abstain, and will not mind, whichever we do.) Well, as of none of the company seem disposed to drink much, I may be forgiven for saying, as a physician, that drinking deep is a bad practice, which I never follow, if I can help, and certainly do not recommend to another, least of all to any one who still feels the effects of yesterday's carouse.

I always do what you advise, and especially what you prescribe as a physician, rejoined Phaedrus the Myrrhinusian, and the rest of the company, if they are wise, will do the same.

It was agreed that drinking was not to be the order of the day, but that they were all to drink only so much as they pleased.

Then, said Eryximachus, as you are all agreed that drinking is to be voluntary, and that there is to be no compulsion, I move, in the next place, that the flute-girl, who has just made her appearance, be told to go away and play to herself, or, if she likes, to the women who are within (compare Prot.). To-day let us have conversation instead; and, if you will allow me, I will tell you what sort of conversation. This proposal having been accepted, Eryximachus proceeded as follows:—

I will begin, he said, after the manner of Melanippe in Euripides, 'Not mine the word' which I am about to speak, but that of Phaedrus. For often he says to me in an indignant tone:—'What a strange thing it is, Eryximachus, that, whereas other gods have poems and hymns made in their honour, the great and glorious god, Love, has no encomiast among all the poets who are so many. There are the worthy sophists too—the excellent Prodicus for example, who have descanted in prose on the virtues of Heracles and other heroes; and, what is still more extraordinary, I have met with a philosophical work in which the utility of salt has been made the theme of an eloquent discourse; and many other like things have had a like honour bestowed upon them. And only to think that there should have been an eager interest created about them, and yet that to this day no one has ever dared worthily to hymn Love's praises! So entirely has this great deity been neglected.' Now in this Phaedrus seems to me to be quite right, and therefore I want to offer him a contribution; also I think that at the present moment we who are here assembled cannot do better than honour the god Love. If you agree with me, there will be no lack of conversation; for I mean to propose that each of us in turn, going from left to right, shall make a speech in honour of Love. Let him give us the best which he can; and Phaedrus, because he is sitting first on the left hand, and because he is the father of the thought, shall begin.

No one will vote against you, Eryximachus, said Socrates. How can I oppose your motion, who profess to understand nothing but matters of love; nor, I presume, will Agathon and Pausanias; and there can be no doubt of Aristophanes, whose whole concern is with Dionysus and Aphrodite; nor will any one disagree of those whom I see around me. The proposal, as I am aware, may seem rather hard upon us whose place is last; but we shall be contented if we hear some good speeches first. Let Phaedrus begin the praise of Love, and good luck to him. All the company expressed their assent, and desired him to do as Socrates bade him.

Aristodemus did not recollect all that was said, nor do I recollect all that he related to me; but I will tell you what I thought most worthy of remembrance, and what the chief speakers said.

Phaedrus began by affirming that Love is a mighty god, and wonderful among gods and men, but especially wonderful in his birth. For he is the eldest of the gods, which is an honour to him; and a proof of his claim to this honour is, that of his parents there is no memorial; neither poet nor prose-writer has ever affirmed that he had any. As Hesiod says:—

'First Chaos came, and then broad-bosomed Earth, The everlasting seat of all that is, And Love.'

In other words, after Chaos, the Earth and Love, these two, came into being. Also Parmenides sings of Generation:

'First in the train of gods, he fashioned Love.'

And Acusilaus agrees with Hesiod. Thus numerous are the witnesses who acknowledge Love to be the eldest of the gods. And not only is he the eldest, he is also the source of the greatest benefits to us. For I know not any greater blessing to a young man who is beginning life than a virtuous lover, or to the lover than a beloved youth. For the principle which ought to be the guide of men who would nobly live—that principle, I say, neither kindred, nor honour, nor wealth, nor any other motive is able to implant so well as love. Of what am I speaking? Of the sense of honour and dishonour, without which neither states nor individuals ever do any good or great work. And I say that a lover who is detected in doing any dishonourable act, or submitting through cowardice when any dishonour is done to him by another, will be more pained at being detected by his beloved than at being seen by his father, or by his companions, or by any one else. The beloved too, when he is found in any disgraceful situation, has the same feeling about his lover. And if there were only some way of contriving that a state or an army should be made up of lovers and their loves (compare Rep.), they would be the very best governors of their own city, abstaining from all dishonour, and emulating one another in honour; and when fighting at each other's side, although a mere handful, they would overcome the world. For what lover would not choose rather to be seen by all mankind than by his beloved, either when abandoning his post or throwing away his arms? He would be ready to die a thousand deaths rather than endure this. Or who would desert his beloved or fail him in the hour of danger? The veriest coward would become an inspired hero, equal to the bravest, at such a time; Love would inspire him. That courage which, as Homer says, the god breathes into the souls of some heroes, Love of his own nature infuses into the lover.

Love will make men dare to die for their beloved—love alone; and women as well as men. Of this, Alcestis, the daughter of Pelias, is a monument to all Hellas; for she was willing to lay down her life on behalf of her husband, when no one else would, although he had a father and mother; but the tenderness of her love so far exceeded theirs, that she made them seem to be strangers in blood to their own son, and in name only related to him; and so noble did this action of hers appear to the gods, as well as to men, that among the many who have done virtuously she is one of the very few to whom, in admiration of her noble action, they have granted the privilege of returning alive to earth; such exceeding honour is paid by the gods to the devotion and virtue of love. But Orpheus, the son of Oeagrus, the harper, they sent empty away, and presented to him an apparition only of her whom he sought, but herself they would not give up, because he showed no spirit; he was only a harp-player, and did not dare like Alcestis to die for love, but was contriving how he might enter Hades alive; moreover, they afterwards caused him to suffer death at the hands of women, as the punishment of his cowardliness. Very different was the reward of the true love of Achilles towards his lover Patroclus—his lover and not his love (the notion that Patroclus was the beloved one is a foolish error into which Aeschylus has fallen, for Achilles was surely the fairer of the two, fairer also than all the other heroes; and, as Homer informs us, he was still beardless, and younger far). And greatly as the gods honour the virtue of love, still the return of love on the part of the beloved to the lover is more admired and valued and rewarded by them, for the lover is more divine; because he is inspired by God. Now Achilles was quite aware, for he had been told by his mother, that he might avoid death and return home, and live to a good old age, if he abstained from slaying Hector. Nevertheless he gave his life to revenge his friend, and dared to die, not only in his defence, but after he was dead. Wherefore the gods honoured him even above Alcestis, and sent him to the Islands of the Blest. These are my reasons for affirming that Love is the eldest and noblest and mightiest of the gods; and the chiefest author and giver of virtue in life, and of happiness after death.

This, or something like this, was the speech of Phaedrus; and some other speeches followed which Aristodemus did not remember; the next which he repeated was that of Pausanias. Phaedrus, he said, the argument has not been set before us, I think, quite in the right form;—we should not be called upon to praise Love in such an indiscriminate manner. If there were only one Love, then what you said would be well enough; but since there are more Loves than one,—should have begun by determining which of them was to be the theme of our praises. I will amend this defect; and first of all I will tell you which Love is deserving of praise, and then try to hymn the praiseworthy one in a manner worthy of him. For we all know that Love is inseparable from Aphrodite, and if there were only one Aphrodite there would be only one Love; but as there are two goddesses there must be two Loves. And am I not right in asserting that there are two goddesses? The elder one, having no mother, who is called the heavenly Aphrodite—she is the daughter of Uranus; the younger, who is the daughter of Zeus and Dione —her we call common; and the Love who is her fellow-worker is rightly named common, as the other love is called heavenly. All the gods ought to have praise given to them, but not without distinction of their natures; and therefore I must try to distinguish the characters of the two Loves. Now actions vary according to the manner of their performance. Take, for example, that which we are now doing, drinking, singing and talking—these actions are not in themselves either good or evil, but they turn out in this or that way according to the mode of performing them; and when well done they are good, and when wrongly done they are evil; and in like manner not every love, but only that which has a noble purpose, is noble and worthy of praise. The Love who is the offspring of the common Aphrodite is essentially common, and has no discrimination, being such as the meaner sort of men feel, and is apt to be of women as well as of youths, and is of the body rather than of the soul—the most foolish beings are the objects of this love which desires only to gain an end, but never thinks of accomplishing the end nobly, and therefore does good and evil quite indiscriminately. The goddess who is his mother is far younger than the other, and she was born of the union of the male and female, and partakes of both. But the offspring of the heavenly Aphrodite is derived from a mother in whose birth the female has no part,—she is from the male only; this is that love which is of youths, and the goddess being older, there is nothing of wantonness in her. Those who are inspired by this love turn to the male, and delight in him who is the more valiant and intelligent nature; any one may recognise the pure enthusiasts in the very character of their attachments. For they love not boys, but intelligent beings whose reason is beginning to be developed, much about the time at which their beards begin to grow. And in choosing young men to be their companions, they mean to be faithful to them, and pass their whole life in company with them, not to take them in their inexperience, and deceive them, and play the fool with them, or run away from one to another of them. But the love of young boys should be forbidden by law, because their future is uncertain; they may turn out good or bad, either in body or soul, and much noble enthusiasm may be thrown away upon them; in this matter the good are a law to themselves, and the coarser sort of lovers ought to be restrained by force; as we restrain or attempt to restrain them from fixing their affections on women of free birth. These are the persons who bring a reproach on love; and some have been led to deny the lawfulness of such attachments because they see the impropriety and evil of them; for surely nothing that is decorously and lawfully done can justly be censured. Now here and in Lacedaemon the rules about love are perplexing, but in most cities they are simple and easily intelligible; in Elis and Boeotia, and in countries having no gifts of eloquence, they are very straightforward; the law is simply in favour of these connexions, and no one, whether young or old, has anything to say to their discredit; the reason being, as I suppose, that they are men of few words in those parts, and therefore the lovers do not like the trouble of pleading their suit. In Ionia and other places, and generally in countries which are subject to the barbarians, the custom is held to be dishonourable; loves of youths share the evil repute in which philosophy and gymnastics are held, because they are inimical to tyranny; for the interests of rulers require that their subjects should be poor in spirit (compare Arist. Politics), and that there should be no strong bond of friendship or society among them, which love, above all other motives, is likely to inspire, as our Athenian tyrants learned by experience; for the love of

Aristogeiton and the constancy of Harmodius had a strength which undid their power. And, therefore, the ill-repute into which these attachments have fallen is to be ascribed to the evil condition of those who make them to be ill-reputed; that is to say, to the self-seeking of the governors and the cowardice of the governed; on the other hand, the indiscriminate honour which is given to them in some countries is attributable to the laziness of those who hold this opinion of them. In our own country a far better principle prevails, but, as I was saying, the explanation of it is rather perplexing. For, observe that open loves are held to be more honourable than secret ones, and that the love of the noblest and highest, even if their persons are less beautiful than others, is especially honourable. Consider, too, how great is the encouragement which all the world gives to the lover; neither is he supposed to be doing anything dishonourable; but if he succeeds he is praised, and if he fail he is blamed. And in the pursuit of his love the custom of mankind allows him to do many strange things, which philosophy would bitterly censure if they were done from any motive of interest, or wish for office or power. He may pray, and entreat, and supplicate, and swear, and lie on a mat at the door, and endure a slavery worse than that of any slave—in any other case friends and enemies would be equally ready to prevent him, but now there is no friend who will be ashamed of him and admonish him, and no enemy will charge him with meanness or flattery; the actions of a lover have a grace which ennobles them; and custom has decided that they are highly commendable and that there no loss of character in them; and, what is strangest of all, he only may swear and forswear himself (so men say), and the gods will forgive his transgression, for there is no such thing as a lover's oath. Such is the entire liberty which gods and men have allowed the lover, according to the custom which prevails in our part of the world. From this point of view a man fairly argues that in Athens to love and to be loved is held to be a very honourable thing. But when parents forbid their sons to talk with their lovers, and place them under a tutor's care, who is appointed to see to these things, and their companions and equals cast in their teeth anything of the sort which they may observe, and their elders refuse to silence the reprovers and do not rebuke them—any one who reflects on all this will, on the contrary, think that we hold these practices to be most disgraceful. But, as I was saying at first, the truth as I imagine is, that whether such practices are honourable or whether they are dishonourable is not a simple question; they are honourable to him who follows them honourably, dishonourable to him who follows them dishonourably. There is dishonour in yielding to the evil, or in an evil manner; but there is honour in yielding to the good, or in an honourable manner. Evil is the vulgar lover who loves the body rather than the soul, inasmuch as he is not even stable, because he loves a thing which is in itself unstable, and therefore when the bloom of youth which he was desiring is over, he takes wing and flies away, in spite of all his words and promises; whereas the love of the noble disposition is life-long, for it becomes one with the everlasting. The custom of our country would have both of them proven well and truly, and would have us yield to the one sort of lover and avoid the other, and therefore encourages some to pursue, and others to fly; testing both the lover and beloved in contests and trials, until they show to which of the two classes they respectively belong. And this is the reason why, in the first place, a hasty attachment is held to be dishonourable, because time is the true test of this as of most other things; and secondly there is a dishonour in being overcome by the love of money, or of wealth, or of political power, whether a man is frightened into surrender by the loss of them, or, having experienced the benefits of money and political corruption, is unable to rise above the seductions of them. For none of these things are of a permanent or lasting nature; not to mention that no generous friendship ever sprang from them. There remains, then, only one way of honourable attachment which custom allows in the beloved, and this is the way of virtue; for as we admitted that any service which the lover does to him is not to be accounted flattery or a dishonour to himself, so the beloved has one way only of voluntary service which is not dishonourable, and this is virtuous service.

For we have a custom, and according to our custom any one who does service to another under the idea that he will be improved by him either in wisdom, or in some other particular of virtue—such a voluntary service, I say, is not to be regarded as a dishonour, and is not open to the charge of flattery. And these two customs, one the love of youth, and the other the practice of philosophy and virtue in general, ought to meet in one, and then the beloved may honourably indulge the lover. For when the lover and beloved come together, having each of them a law, and the lover thinks that he is right in doing any service which he can to his gracious loving one; and the other that he is right in showing any kindness which he can to him who is making him wise and good; the one capable of communicating wisdom and virtue, the other seeking to acquire them with a view to education and wisdom, when the two laws of love are fulfilled and meet in one—then, and then only, may the beloved yield with honour to the lover. Nor when love is of this disinterested sort is there any disgrace in being deceived, but in every other case there is equal disgrace in being or not being deceived. For he who is gracious to his lover under the impression that he is rich, and is disappointed of his gains because he turns out to be poor, is disgraced all the same: for he has done his best to show that he would give himself up to any one's 'uses base' for the sake of money; but this is not honourable. And on the same principle he who gives himself to a lover because he is a good man, and in the hope that he will be improved by his company, shows himself to be virtuous, even though the object of his affection turn out to be a villain, and to have no virtue; and if he is deceived he has committed a noble error. For he has proved that for his part he will do anything for anybody with a view to virtue and improvement, than which there can be nothing nobler. Thus noble in every case is the acceptance of another for the sake of virtue. This is that love which is the love of the heavenly godess, and is heavenly, and of great price to individuals and cities, making the lover and the beloved alike eager in the work of their own improvement. But all other loves are the offspring of the other, who is the common goddess. To you, Phaedrus, I offer this my contribution in praise of love, which is as good as I could make extempore.

Pausanias came to a pause—this is the balanced way in which I have been taught by the wise to speak; and Aristodemus said that the turn of Aristophanes was next, but either he had eaten too much, or from some other cause he had the hiccough, and was obliged to change turns with Eryximachus the physician, who was reclining on the couch below him. Eryximachus, he said, you ought either to stop my hiccough, or to speak in my turn until I have left off.

I will do both, said Eryximachus: I will speak in your turn, and do you speak in mine; and while I am speaking let me recommend you to hold your breath, and if after you have done so for some time the hiccough is no better, then gargle with a little water; and if it still continues, tickle your nose with something and sneeze; and if you sneeze once or twice, even the most violent hiccough is sure to go. I will do as you prescribe, said Aristophanes, and now get on.

Eryximachus spoke as follows: Seeing that Pausanias made a fair beginning, and but a lame ending, I must endeavour to supply his deficiency. I think that he has rightly distinguished two kinds of love. But my art further informs me that the double love is not merely an affection of the soul of man towards the fair, or towards anything, but is to be found in the bodies of all animals and in productions of the earth, and I may say in all that is; such is the conclusion which I seem to have gathered from my own art of medicine, whence I learn how great and wonderful and universal is the deity of love, whose empire extends over all things, divine as well as human. And from medicine I will begin that I may do honour to my art. There are in the human body these two kinds of love, which are confessedly different and unlike, and being unlike, they have loves and desires which are unlike; and the desire of the healthy is one, and the desire of the diseased is another; and as Pausanias was just now saying that to indulge good men is honourable, and bad men dishonourable:—so too in the body the good and healthy elements are to be indulged, and the bad elements and the elements of disease are not to be indulged, but discouraged. And this is what the physician has to do, and in this the art of medicine consists: for medicine may be regarded generally as the knowledge of the loves and desires of the body, and how to satisfy them or not; and the best physician is he who is able to separate fair love from foul, or to convert one into the other; and he who knows how to eradicate and how to implant love, whichever is required, and can reconcile the most hostile elements in the constitution and make them loving friends, is a skilful practitioner. Now the most hostile are the most opposite, such as hot and cold, bitter and sweet, moist and dry, and the like. And my ancestor, Asclepius, knowing how to implant friendship and accord in these elements, was the creator of our art, as our friends the poets here tell us, and I believe them; and not only medicine in every branch but the arts of gymnastic and husbandry are under his dominion. Any one who pays the least attention to the subject will also perceive that in music there is the same reconciliation of opposites; and I suppose that this must have been the meaning of Heracleitus, although his words are not accurate; for he says that The One is united by disunion, like the harmony of the bow and the lyre. Now there is an absurdity saying that harmony is discord or is composed of elements which are still in a state of discord. But what he probably meant was, that harmony is composed of differing notes of higher or lower pitch which disagreed once, but are now reconciled by the art of music; for if the higher and lower notes still disagreed, there could be no harmony,—clearly not. For harmony is a symphony, and symphony is an agreement; but an agreement of disagreements while they disagree there cannot be; you cannot harmonize that which disagrees. In like manner rhythm is compounded of elements short and long, once differing and now in accord; which accordance, as in the former instance, medicine, so in all these other cases, music implants, making love and unison to grow up among them; and thus music, too, is concerned with the principles of love in their application to harmony and rhythm. Again, in the essential nature of harmony and rhythm there is no difficulty in discerning love which has not yet become double. But when you want to use them in actual life, either in the composition of songs or in the correct performance of airs or metres composed already, which latter is called education, then the difficulty begins, and the good artist is needed. Then the old tale has to be repeated of fair and heavenly love—the love of Urania the fair and heavenly muse, and of the duty of accepting the temperate, and those who are as yet intemperate only that they may become temperate, and of preserving their love; and again, of the vulgar Polyhymnia, who must be used with circumspection that the pleasure be enjoyed, but may not generate licentiousness; just as in my own art it is a great matter so to regulate the desires of the epicure that he may gratify his tastes without the attendant evil of disease. Whence I infer that in music, in medicine, in all other things human as well as divine, both loves ought to be noted as far as may be, for they are both present.

The course of the seasons is also full of both these principles; and when, as I was saying, the elements of hot and cold, moist and dry, attain the harmonious love of one another and blend in temperance and harmony, they bring to men, animals, and plants health and plenty, and do them no harm; whereas the wanton love, getting the upper hand and affecting the seasons of the year, is very destructive and injurious, being the source of pestilence, and bringing many other kinds of diseases on animals and plants; for hoar-frost and hail and blight spring from the excesses and disorders of these elements of love, which to know in relation to the revolutions of the heavenly bodies and the seasons of the year is termed astronomy. Furthermore all sacrifices and the whole province of divination, which is the art of communion between gods and men—these, I say, are concerned only with the preservation of the good and the cure of the evil love. For all manner of impiety is likely to ensue if, instead of accepting and honouring and reverencing the harmonious love in all his actions, a man honours the other love, whether in his feelings towards gods or parents, towards the living or the dead. Wherefore the business of divination is to see to these loves and to heal them, and divination is the peacemaker of gods and men, working by a knowledge of the religious or irreligious tendencies which exist in human loves. Such is the great and mighty, or rather omnipotent force of love in general. And the love, more especially, which is concerned with the good, and which is perfected in company with temperance and justice, whether among gods or men, has the greatest power, and is the source of all our happiness and harmony, and makes us friends with the gods who are above us, and with one another. I dare say that I too have omitted several things which might be said in praise of Love, but this was not intentional, and you, Aristophanes, may now supply the omission or take some other line of commendation; for I perceive that you are rid of the hiccough.

Yes, said Aristophanes, who followed, the hiccough is gone; not, however, until I applied the sneezing; and I wonder whether the harmony of the body has a love of such noises and ticklings, for I no sooner applied the sneezing than I was cured.

Eryximachus said: Beware, friend Aristophanes, although you are going to speak, you are making fun of me; and I shall have to watch and see whether I cannot have a laugh at your expense, when you might speak in peace.

You are right, said Aristophanes, laughing. I will unsay my words; but do you please not to watch me, as I fear that in the speech which I am about to make, instead of others laughing with me, which is to the manner born of our muse and would be all the better, I shall only be laughed at by them.

Do you expect to shoot your bolt and escape, Aristophanes? Well, perhaps if you are very careful and bear in mind that you will be called to account, I may be induced to let you off.

Aristophanes professed to open another vein of discourse; he had a mind to praise Love in another way, unlike that either of Pausanias or Eryximachus. Mankind, he said, judging by their neglect of him, have never, as I think, at all understood the power of Love. For if they had understood him they would surely have built noble temples and altars, and offered solemn sacrifices in his honour; but this is not done, and most certainly ought to be done: since of all the gods he is the best friend of men, the helper and the healer of the ills which are the great impediment to the happiness of the race. I will try to describe his power to you, and you shall teach the rest of the world what I am teaching you. In the first place, let me treat of the nature of man and what has happened to it; for the original human nature was not like the present, but different. The sexes were not two as they are now, but originally three in number; there was man, woman, and the union of the two, having a name corresponding to this double nature, which had once a real existence, but is now lost, and the word 'Androgynous' is only preserved as a term of reproach. In the second place, the primeval man was round, his back and sides forming a circle; and he had four hands and four feet, one head with two faces, looking opposite ways, set on a round neck and precisely alike; also four ears, two privy members, and the remainder to correspond. He could walk upright as men now do, backwards or forwards as he pleased, and he could also roll over and over at a great pace, turning on his four hands and four feet, eight in all, like tumblers going over and over with their legs in the air; this was when he wanted to run fast. Now the sexes were three, and such as I have described them; because the sun, moon, and earth are three; and the man was originally the child of the sun, the woman of the earth, and the man-woman of the moon, which is made up of sun and earth, and they were all round and moved round and round like their parents. Terrible was their might and strength, and the thoughts of their hearts were great, and they made an attack upon the gods; of them is told the tale of Otys and Ephialtes who, as Homer says, dared to scale heaven, and would have laid hands upon the gods. Doubt reigned in the celestial councils. Should they kill them and annihilate the race with thunderbolts, as they had done the giants, then there would be an end of the sacrifices and worship which men offered to them; but, on the other hand, the gods could not suffer their insolence to be unrestrained. At last, after a good deal of reflection, Zeus discovered a way. He said: 'Methinks I have a plan which will humble their pride and improve their manners; men shall continue to exist, but I will cut them in two and then they will be diminished in strength and increased in numbers; this will have the advantage of making them more profitable to us. They shall walk upright on two legs, and if they continue insolent and will not be quiet, I will split them again and they shall hop about on a single leg.' He spoke and cut men in two, like a sorb-apple which is halved for pickling, or as you might divide an egg with a hair; and as he cut them one after another, he bade Apollo give the face and the half of the neck a turn in order that the man might contemplate the section of himself: he would thus learn a lesson of humility. Apollo was also bidden to heal their wounds and compose their forms. So he gave a turn to the face and pulled the skin from the sides all over that which in our language is called the belly, like the purses which draw in, and he made one mouth at the centre, which he fastened in a knot (the same which is called the navel); he also moulded the breast and took out most of the wrinkles, much as a shoemaker might smooth leather upon a last; he left a few, however, in the region of the belly and navel, as a memorial of the primeval state. After the division the two parts of man, each desiring his other half, came together, and throwing their arms about one another, entwined in mutual embraces, longing to grow into one, they were on the point of dying from hunger and self-neglect, because they did not like to do anything apart; and when one of the halves died and the other survived, the survivor sought another mate, man or woman as we call them,—being the sections of entire men or women,—and clung to that. They were being destroyed, when Zeus in pity of them invented a new plan: he turned the parts of generation round to the front, for this had not been always their position, and they sowed the seed no longer as hitherto like grasshoppers in the ground, but in one another; and after the transposition the male generated in the female in order that by the mutual embraces of man and woman they might breed, and the race might continue; or if man came to man they might be satisfied, and rest, and go their ways to the business of life: so ancient is the desire of one another which is implanted in us, reuniting our original nature, making one of two, and healing the state of man. Each of us when separated, having one side only, like a flat fish, is but the indenture of a man, and he is always looking for his other half. Men who are a section of that double nature which was once called Androgynous are lovers of women; adulterers are generally of this breed, and also adulterous women who lust after men: the women who are a section of the woman do not care for men, but have female attachments; the female companions are of this sort. But they who are a section of the male follow the male, and while they are young, being slices of the original man, they hang about men and embrace them, and they are themselves the best of boys and youths, because they have the most manly nature. Some indeed assert that they are shameless, but this is not true; for they do not act thus from any want of shame, but because they are valiant and manly, and have a manly countenance, and they embrace that which is like them. And these when they grow up become our statesmen, and these only, which is a great proof of the truth of what I am saying. When they reach manhood they are lovers of youth, and are not naturally inclined to marry or beget children,—if at all, they do so only in obedience to the law; but they are satisfied if they may be allowed to live with one another unwedded; and such a nature is prone to love and ready to return love, always embracing that which is akin to him. And when one of them meets with his other half, the actual half of himself, whether he be a lover of youth or a lover of another sort, the pair are lost in an amazement of love and friendship and intimacy, and one will not be out of the other's sight, as I may say, even for a moment: these are the people who pass their whole lives together; yet they could not explain what they desire of one another. For the intense yearning which each of them has towards the other does not appear to be the desire of lover's intercourse, but of something else which the soul of either evidently desires and cannot tell, and of which she has only a dark and doubtful presentiment. Suppose Hephaestus, with his instruments, to come to the pair who are lying side by side and to say to them, 'What do you people want of one another?' they would be unable to explain. And suppose further, that when he saw their perplexity he said: 'Do you desire to be wholly one; always day and night to be in one another's company? for if this is what you desire, I am ready to melt you into one and let you grow together, so that being two you shall become one, and while you live live a common life as if you were a single man, and after your death in the world below still be one departed soul instead of two—I ask whether this is what you lovingly desire, and whether you are satisfied to attain this?'—there is not a man of them who when he heard the proposal would deny or would not acknowledge that this meeting and melting into one another, this becoming one instead of two, was the very expression of his ancient need (compare Arist. Pol.). And the reason is that human nature was originally one and we were a whole, and the desire and pursuit of the whole is called love. There was a time, I say, when we were one, but now because of the wickedness of mankind God has dispersed us, as the Arcadians were dispersed into villages by the Lacedaemonians (compare Arist. Pol.). And if we are not obedient to the gods, there is a danger that we shall be split up again and go about in basso-relievo, like the profile figures having only half a nose which are sculptured on monuments, and that we shall be like tallies. Wherefore let us exhort all men to piety, that we may avoid evil, and obtain the good, of which Love is to us the lord and minister; and let no one oppose him—he is the enemy of the gods who opposes him. For if we are friends of the

God and at peace with him we shall find our own true loves, which rarely happens in this world at present. I am serious, and therefore I must beg Eryximachus not to make fun or to find any allusion in what I am saying to Pausanias and Agathon, who, as I suspect, are both of the manly nature, and belong to the class which I have been describing. But my words have a wider application —they include men and women everywhere; and I believe that if our loves were perfectly accomplished, and each one returning to his primeval nature had his original true love, then our race would be happy. And if this would be best of all, the best in the next degree and under present circumstances must be the nearest approach to such an union; and that will be the attainment of a congenial love. Wherefore, if we would praise him who has given to us the benefit, we must praise the god Love, who is our greatest benefactor, both leading us in this life back to our own nature, and giving us high hopes for the future, for he promises that if we are pious, he will restore us to our original state, and heal us and make us happy and blessed. This, Eryximachus, is my discourse of love, which, although different to yours, I must beg you to leave unassailed by the shafts of your ridicule, in order that each may have his turn; each, or rather either, for Agathon and Socrates are the only ones left.

Indeed, I am not going to attack you, said Eryximachus, for I thought your speech charming, and did I not know that Agathon and Socrates are masters in the art of love, I should be really afraid that they would have nothing to say, after the world of things which have been said already. But, for all that, I am not without hopes.

Socrates said: You played your part well, Eryximachus; but if you were as I am now, or rather as I shall be when Agathon has spoken, you would, indeed, be in a great strait.

You want to cast a spell over me, Socrates, said Agathon, in the hope that I may be disconcerted at the expectation raised among the audience that I shall speak well.

I should be strangely forgetful, Agathon replied Socrates, of the courage and magnanimity which you showed when your own compositions were about to be exhibited, and you came upon the stage with the actors and faced the vast theatre altogether undismayed, if I thought that your nerves could be fluttered at a small party of friends.

Do you think, Socrates, said Agathon, that my head is so full of the theatre as not to know how much more formidable to a man of sense a few good judges are than many fools?

Nay, replied Socrates, I should be very wrong in attributing to you, Agathon, that or any other want of refinement. And I am quite aware that if you happened to meet with any whom you thought wise, you would care for their opinion much more than for that of the many. But then we, having been a part of the foolish many in the theatre, cannot be regarded as the select wise; though I know that if you chanced to be in the presence, not of one of ourselves, but of some really wise man, you would be ashamed of disgracing yourself before him—would you not?

Yes, said Agathon.

But before the many you would not be ashamed, if you thought that you were doing something disgraceful in their presence?

Here Phaedrus interrupted them, saying: not answer him, my dear Agathon; for if he can only get a partner with whom he can talk, especially a good-looking one, he will no longer care about the completion of our plan. Now I love to hear him talk; but just at present I must not forget the encomium on Love which I ought to receive from him and from every one. When you and he have paid your tribute to the god, then you may talk.

Very good, Phaedrus, said Agathon; I see no reason why I should not proceed with my speech, as I shall have many other opportunities of conversing with Socrates. Let me say first how I ought to speak, and then speak:—

The previous speakers, instead of praising the god Love, or unfolding his nature, appear to have congratulated mankind on the benefits which he confers upon them. But I would rather praise the god first, and then speak of his gifts; this is always the right way of praising everything. May I say without impiety or offence, that of all the blessed gods he is the most blessed because he is the fairest and best? And he is the fairest: for, in the first place, he is the youngest, and of his youth he is himself the witness, fleeing out of the way of age, who is swift enough, swifter truly than most of us like:— Love hates him and will not come near him; but youth and love live and move together—like to like, as the proverb says. Many things

Symposium

were said by Phaedrus about Love in which I agree with him; but I cannot agree that he is older than Iapetus and Kronos:—not so; I maintain him to be the youngest of the gods, and youthful ever. The ancient doings among the gods of which Hesiod and Parmenides spoke, if the tradition of them be true, were done of Necessity and not of Love; had Love been in those days, there would have been no chaining or mutilation of the gods, or other violence, but peace and sweetness, as there is now in heaven, since the rule of Love began. Love is young and also tender; he ought to have a poet like Homer to describe his tenderness, as Homer says of Ate, that she is a goddess and tender:—

'Her feet are tender, for she sets her steps,
Not on the ground but on the heads of men:'

herein is an excellent proof of her tenderness,—that she walks not upon the hard but upon the soft. Let us adduce a similar proof of the tenderness of Love; for he walks not upon the earth, nor yet upon the skulls of men, which are not so very soft, but in the hearts and souls of both gods and men, which are of all things the softest: in them he walks and dwells and makes his home. Not in every soul without exception, for where there is hardness he departs, where there is softness there he dwells; and nestling always with his feet and in all manner of ways in the softest of soft places, how can he be other than the softest of all things? Of a truth he is the tenderest as well as the youngest, and also he is of flexile form; for if he were hard and without flexure he could not enfold all things, or wind his way into and out of every soul of man undiscovered. And a proof of his flexibility and symmetry of form is his grace, which is universally admitted to be in an especial manner the attribute of Love; ungrace and love are always at war with one another. The fairness of his complexion is revealed by his habitation among the flowers; for he dwells not amid bloomless or fading beauties, whether of body or soul or aught else, but in the place of flowers and scents, there he sits and abides. Concerning the beauty of the god I have said enough; and yet there remains much more which I might say. Of his virtue I have now to speak: his greatest glory is that he can neither do nor suffer wrong to or from any god or any man; for he suffers not by force if he suffers; force comes not near him, neither when he acts does he act by force. For all men in all things serve him of their own free will, and where there is voluntary agreement, there, as the laws which are the lords of the city say, is justice. And not only is he just but exceedingly temperate, for Temperance is the acknowledged ruler of the pleasures and desires, and no pleasure ever masters Love; he is their master and they are his servants; and if he conquers them he must be temperate indeed. As to courage, even the God of War is no match for him; he is the captive and Love is the lord, for love, the love of Aphrodite, masters him, as the tale runs; and the master is stronger than the servant. And if he conquers the bravest of all others, he must be himself the bravest. Of his courage and justice and temperance I have spoken, but I have yet to speak of his wisdom; and according to the measure of my ability I must try to do my best. In the first place he is a poet (and here, like Eryximachus, I magnify my art), and he is also the source of poesy in others, which he could not be if he were not himself a poet. And at the touch of him every one becomes a poet, even though he had no music in him before (A fragment of the Sthenoaoea of Euripides.); this also is a proof that Love is a good poet and accomplished in all the fine arts; for no one can give to another that which he has not himself, or teach that of which he has no knowledge. Who will deny that the creation of the animals is his doing? Are they not all the works of his wisdom, born and begotten of him? And as to the artists, do we not know that he only of them whom love inspires has the light of fame?—he whom Love touches not walks in darkness. The arts of medicine and archery and divination were discovered by Apollo, under the guidance of love and desire; so that he too is a disciple of Love. Also the melody of the Muses, the metallurgy of Hephaestus, the weaving of Athene, the empire of Zeus over gods and men, are all due to Love, who was the inventor of them. And so Love set in order the empire of the gods—the love of beauty, as is evident, for with deformity Love has no concern. In the days of old, as I began by saying, dreadful deeds were done among the gods, for they were ruled by Necessity; but now since the birth of Love, and from the Love of the beautiful, has sprung every good in heaven and earth. Therefore, Phaedrus, I say of Love that he is the fairest and best in himself, and the cause of what is fairest and best in all other things. And there comes into my mind a line of poetry in which he is said to be the god who

> 'Gives peace on earth and calms the stormy deep,
> Who stills the winds and bids the sufferer sleep.'

This is he who empties men of disaffection and fills them with affection, who makes them to meet together at banquets such as these: in sacrifices, feasts, dances, he is our lord—who sends courtesy and sends away discourtesy, who gives kindness ever and never gives unkindness; the friend of the good, the wonder of the wise, the amazement of the gods; desired by those who have no part in him, and precious to those who have the better part in him; parent of delicacy, luxury, desire, fondness, softness, grace; regardful of the good, regardless of the evil: in every word, work, wish, fear—saviour, pilot, comrade, helper; glory of gods and men, leader best and brightest: in whose footsteps let every man follow, sweetly singing in his honour and joining in that sweet strain with which love charms the souls of gods and men. Such is the speech, Phaedrus, half-playful, yet having a certain measure of seriousness, which, according to my ability, I dedicate to the god.

When Agathon had done speaking, Aristodemus said that there was a general cheer; the young man was thought to have spoken in a manner worthy of himself, and of the god. And Socrates, looking at Eryximachus, said: Tell me, son of Acumenus, was there not reason in my fears? and was I not a true prophet when I said that Agathon would make a wonderful oration, and that I should be in a strait?

The part of the prophecy which concerns Agathon, replied Eryximachus, appears to me to be true; but not the other part—that you will be in a strait.

Why, my dear friend, said Socrates, must not I or any one be in a strait who has to speak after he has heard such a rich and varied discourse? I am especially struck with the beauty of the concluding words—who could listen to them without amazement? When I reflected on the immeasurable inferiority of my own powers, I was ready to run away for shame, if there had been a possibility of escape. For I was reminded of Gorgias, and at the end of his speech I fancied that Agathon was shaking at me the Gorginian or Gorgonian head of the great master of rhetoric, which was simply to turn me and my speech into stone, as Homer says (Odyssey), and strike me dumb. And then I perceived how foolish I had been in consenting to take my turn with you in praising love, and saying that I too was a master of the art, when I really had no conception how anything ought to be praised. For in my simplicity I imagined that the topics of praise should be true, and that this being presupposed, out of the true the speaker was to choose the best and set them forth in the best manner. And I felt quite proud, thinking that I knew the nature of true praise, and should speak well. Whereas I now see that the intention was to attribute to Love every species of greatness and glory, whether really belonging to him or not, without regard to truth or falsehood—that was no matter; for the original proposal seems to have been not that each of you should really praise Love, but only that you should appear to praise him. And so you attribute to Love every imaginable form of praise which can be gathered anywhere; and you say that 'he is all this,' and 'the cause of all that,' making him appear the fairest and best of all to those who know him not, for you cannot impose upon those who know him. And a noble and solemn hymn of praise have you rehearsed. But as I misunderstood the nature of the praise when I said that I would take my turn, I must beg to be absolved from the promise which I made in ignorance, and which (as Euripides would say (Eurip. Hyppolytus)) was a promise of the lips and not of the mind. Farewell then to such a strain: for I do not praise in that way; no, indeed, I cannot. But if you like to hear the truth about love, I am ready to speak in my own manner, though I will not make myself ridiculous by entering into any rivalry with you. Say then, Phaedrus, whether you would like to have the truth about love, spoken in any words and in any order which may happen to come into my mind at the time. Will that be agreeable to you?

Aristodemus said that Phaedrus and the company bid him speak in any manner which he thought best. Then, he added, let me have your permission first to ask Agathon a few more questions, in order that I may take his admissions as the premises of my discourse.

I grant the permission, said Phaedrus: put your questions. Socrates then proceeded as follows:—

In the magnificent oration which you have just uttered, I think that you were right, my dear Agathon, in proposing to speak of the nature of Love first and afterwards of his works—that is a way of beginning which I very much approve. And as you have spoken so eloquently of his nature, may I ask you further, Whether love is the love of something or of nothing? And here I must explain myself: I do not want you to say that love is the love of a father or the love of a mother—that would be ridiculous; but to answer as you would, if I asked is a father a father of something? to which you would find no difficulty in replying, of a son or daughter: and the answer would be right.

Very true, said Agathon.

And you would say the same of a mother?

He assented.

Yet let me ask you one more question in order to illustrate my meaning: Is not a brother to be regarded essentially as a brother of something?

Certainly, he replied.

That is, of a brother or sister?

Yes, he said.

And now, said Socrates, I will ask about Love:—Is Love of something or of nothing?

Of something, surely, he replied.

Keep in mind what this is, and tell me what I want to know—whether Love desires that of which love is.

Yes, surely.

And does he possess, or does he not possess, that which he loves and desires?

Probably not, I should say.

Nay, replied Socrates, I would have you consider whether 'necessarily' is not rather the word. The inference that he who desires something is in want of something, and that he who desires nothing is in want of nothing, is in my judgment, Agathon, absolutely and necessarily true. What do you think?

I agree with you, said Agathon.

Very good. Would he who is great, desire to be great, or he who is strong, desire to be strong?

That would be inconsistent with our previous admissions.

True. For he who is anything cannot want to be that which he is?

Very true.

And yet, added Socrates, if a man being strong desired to be strong, or being swift desired to be swift, or being healthy desired to be healthy, in that case he might be thought to desire something which he already has or is. I give the example in order that we may avoid misconception. For the possessors of these qualities, Agathon, must be supposed to have their respective advantages at the time, whether they choose or not; and who can desire that which he has? Therefore, when a person says, I am well and wish to be well, or I am rich and wish to be rich, and I desire simply to have what I have—to him we shall reply: 'You, my friend, having wealth and health and strength, want to have the continuance of them; for at this moment, whether you choose or no, you have them. And when you say, I desire that which I have and nothing else, is not your meaning that you want to have what you now have in the future?' He must agree with us—must he not?

He must, replied Agathon.

Then, said Socrates, he desires that what he has at present may be preserved to him in the future, which is equivalent to saying that he desires something which is non-existent to him, and which as yet he has not got:

Very true, he said.

Then he and every one who desires, desires that which he has not already, and which is future and not present, and which he has not, and is not, and of which he is in want;—these are the sort of things which love and desire seek?

Very true, he said.

Then now, said Socrates, let us recapitulate the argument. First, is not love of something, and of something too which is wanting to a man?

Yes, he replied.

Remember further what you said in your speech, or if you do not remember I will remind you: you said that the love of the beautiful set in order the empire of the gods, for that of deformed things there is no love—did you not say something of that kind?

Yes, said Agathon.

Yes, my friend, and the remark was a just one. And if this is true, Love is the love of beauty and not of deformity?

He assented.

And the admission has been already made that Love is of something which a man wants and has not?

True, he said.

Then Love wants and has not beauty?

Certainly, he replied.

And would you call that beautiful which wants and does not possess beauty?

Certainly not.

Then would you still say that love is beautiful?

Agathon replied: I fear that I did not understand what I was saying.

You made a very good speech, Agathon, replied Socrates; but there is yet one small question which I would fain ask:—Is not the good also the

beautiful?

Yes.

Then in wanting the beautiful, love wants also the good?

I cannot refute you, Socrates, said Agathon:—Let us assume that what you say is true.

Say rather, beloved Agathon, that you cannot refute the truth; for Socrates is easily refuted.

And now, taking my leave of you, I would rehearse a tale of love which I heard from Diotima of Mantineia (compare 1 Alcibiades), a woman wise in this and in many other kinds of knowledge, who in the days of old, when the Athenians offered sacrifice before the coming of the plague, delayed the disease ten years. She was my instructress in the art of love, and I shall repeat to you what she said to me, beginning with the admissions made by Agathon, which are nearly if not quite the same which I made to the wise woman when she questioned me: I think that this will be the easiest way, and I shall take both parts myself as well as I can (compare Gorgias). As you, Agathon, suggested (supra), I must speak first of the being and nature of Love, and then of his works. First I said to her in nearly the same words which he used to me, that Love was a mighty god, and likewise fair; and she proved to me as I proved to him that, by my own showing, Love was neither fair nor good. 'What do you mean, Diotima,' I said, 'is love then evil and foul?' 'Hush,' she cried; 'must that be foul which is not fair?' 'Certainly,' I said. 'And is that which is not wise, ignorant? do you not see that there is a mean between wisdom and ignorance?' 'And what may that be?' I said. 'Right opinion,' she replied; 'which, as you know, being incapable of giving a reason, is not knowledge (for how can knowledge be devoid of reason? nor again, ignorance, for neither can ignorance attain the truth), but is clearly something which is a mean between ignorance and wisdom.' 'Quite true,' I replied. 'Do not then insist,' she said, 'that what is not fair is of necessity foul, or what is not good evil; or infer that because love is not fair and good he is therefore foul and evil; for he is in a mean between them.' 'Well,' I said, 'Love is surely admitted by all to be a great god.' 'By those who know or by those who do not know?' 'By all.' 'And how, Socrates,' she said with a smile, 'can Love be acknowledged to be a great god by those who say that he is not a god at all?' 'And who are they?' I said. 'You and I are two of them,' she replied. 'How can that be?' I said. 'It is quite intelligible,' she replied; 'for you yourself would acknowledge that the gods are happy and fair—of course you would—would you dare to say that any god was not?' 'Certainly not,' I replied. 'And you mean by the happy, those who are the possessors of things good or fair?' 'Yes.' 'And you admitted that Love, because he was in want, desires those good and fair things of which he is in want?' 'Yes, I did.' 'But how can he be a god who has no portion in what is either good or fair?' 'Impossible.' 'Then you see that you also deny the divinity of Love.'

'What then is Love?' I asked; 'Is he mortal?' 'No.' 'What then?' 'As in the former instance, he is neither mortal nor immortal, but in a mean between the two.' 'What is he, Diotima?' 'He is a great spirit (daimon), and like all spirits he is intermediate between the divine and the mortal.' 'And what,' I said, 'is his power?' 'He interprets,' she replied, 'between gods and men, conveying and taking across to the gods the prayers and sacrifices of men, and to men the commands and replies of the gods; he is the mediator who spans the chasm which divides them, and therefore in him all is bound together, and through him the arts of the prophet and the priest, their sacrifices and mysteries and charms, and all prophecy and incantation, find their way. For God mingles not with man; but through Love all the intercourse and converse of God with man, whether awake or asleep, is carried on. The wisdom which understands this is spiritual; all other wisdom, such as that of arts and handicrafts, is mean and vulgar. Now these spirits or intermediate powers are many and diverse, and one of them is Love.' 'And who,' I said, 'was his father, and who his mother?' 'The tale,' she said, 'will take time; nevertheless I will tell you. On the birthday of Aphrodite there was a feast of the gods, at which the god Poros or Plenty, who is the son of Metis or Discretion, was one of the guests. When the feast was over, Penia or Poverty, as the manner is on such occasions, came about the doors to beg. Now Plenty who was the worse for nectar (there was no wine in those days), went into the garden of Zeus and fell into a heavy sleep, and Poverty considering her own straitened circumstances, plotted to have a child by him, and accordingly she lay down at his side and conceived Love, who partly because he is naturally a lover of the beautiful, and because Aphrodite is herself beautiful, and also because he was born on her birthday, is her follower and attendant. And as his parentage is, so also are his fortunes. In the first place he is always poor, and anything but tender and fair, as the many imagine him; and he is rough and squalid, and has no shoes, nor a house to dwell in; on the bare earth exposed he lies under the open heaven, in the streets, or at the doors of houses, taking his rest; and like his mother he is always in distress. Like his father too, whom he also partly resembles, he is always plotting against the fair and good; he is bold, enterprising, strong, a mighty hunter, always weaving some intrigue or other, keen in the pursuit of wisdom, fertile in resources; a philosopher at all times, terrible as an enchanter, sorcerer, sophist. He is by nature neither mortal nor immortal, but alive and flourishing at one moment when he is in plenty, and dead at another moment, and again alive by reason of his father's nature. But that which is always flowing in is always flowing out, and so he is never in want and never in wealth; and, further, he is in a mean between ignorance and knowledge. The truth of the matter is this: No god is a philosopher or seeker after wisdom, for he is wise already; nor does any man who is wise seek after wisdom. Neither do the ignorant seek after wisdom. For herein is the evil of ignorance, that he who is neither good nor wise is nevertheless satisfied with himself: he has no desire for that of which he feels no want.' 'But who then, Diotima,' I said, 'are the lovers of wisdom, if they are neither the wise nor the foolish?' 'A child may answer that question,' she replied; 'they are those who are in a mean between the two; Love is one of them. For wisdom is a most beautiful thing, and Love is of the beautiful; and therefore Love is also a philosopher or lover of wisdom, and being a lover of wisdom is in a mean between the wise and the ignorant. And of this too his birth is the cause; for his father is wealthy and wise, and his mother poor and foolish. Such, my dear Socrates, is the nature of the spirit Love. The error in your conception of him was very natural, and as I imagine from what you say, has arisen out of a confusion of love and the beloved, which made you think that love was all beautiful. For the beloved is the truly beautiful, and delicate, and perfect, and blessed; but the principle of love is of another nature, and is such as I have described.'

I said, 'O thou stranger woman, thou sayest well; but, assuming Love to be such as you say, what is the use of him to men?' 'That, Socrates,' she replied, 'I will attempt to unfold: of his nature and birth I have already spoken; and you acknowledge that love is of the beautiful. But some one will say: Of the beautiful in what, Socrates and Diotima?—or rather let me put the question more clearly, and ask: When a man loves the beautiful, what does he desire?' I answered her 'That the beautiful may be his.' 'Still,' she said, 'the answer suggests a further question: What is given by the possession of beauty?' 'To what you have asked,' I replied, 'I have no answer ready.' 'Then,' she said, 'let me put the word "good" in the place of the beautiful, and repeat the question once more: If he who loves loves the good, what is it then that he loves?' 'The possession of the good,' I said. 'And what does he gain who possesses the good?' 'Happiness,' I replied; 'there is less difficulty in answering that question.' 'Yes,' she said, 'the happy are made happy by the acquisition of good things. Nor is there any need to ask why a man desires happiness; the answer is already final.' 'You are right.' I said. 'And is this wish and this desire common to all? and do all men always desire their own good, or only some men?—what say you?' 'All men,' I replied; 'the desire is common to all.' 'Why, then,' she rejoined, 'are not all men, Socrates, said to love, but only some of them? whereas you say that all men are always loving the same things.' 'I myself wonder,' I said, 'why this is.' 'There is nothing to wonder at,' she replied; 'the reason is that one part of love is separated off and receives the name of the whole, but the other parts have other names.' 'Give an illustration,' I said. She answered me as follows: 'There is poetry, which, as you know, is complex and manifold. All creation or passage of non-being into being is poetry or making, and the processes of all art are creative; and the masters of arts are all poets or makers.' 'Very true.' 'Still,' she said, 'you know that they are not called poets, but have other names; only that portion of the art which is separated off from the rest, and is concerned with music and metre, is termed poetry, and they who possess poetry in this sense of the word are called poets.' 'Very true,' I said. 'And the same holds of love. For you may say generally that all desire of good and happiness is only the great and subtle power of love; but they who are drawn towards him by any other path, whether the path of money-making or gymnastics or philosophy, are not called lovers—the name of the whole is appropriated to those whose affection takes one form only—they alone are said to love, or to be lovers.' 'I dare say,' I replied, 'that you are right.' 'Yes,' she added, 'and you hear people say that lovers are seeking for their other half; but I say that they are seeking neither for the half of themselves, nor for the whole, unless the half or the whole be also a good. And they will cut off their own hands and feet and cast them away, if they are evil; for they love not what is their own, unless perchance there be some one who calls what belongs to him the good, and what belongs to another the evil. For there is nothing which men love but the good. Is there anything?' 'Certainly, I should say, that there is nothing.' 'Then,' she said, 'the simple truth is, that men love the good.' 'Yes,'

I said. 'To which must be added that they love the possession of the good?' 'Yes, that must be added.' 'And not only the possession, but the everlasting possession of the good?' 'That must be added too.' 'Then love,' she said, 'may be described generally as the love of the everlasting possession of the good?' 'That is most true.'

'Then if this be the nature of love, can you tell me further,' she said, 'what is the manner of the pursuit? what are they doing who show all this eagerness and heat which is called love? and what is the object which they have in view? Answer me.' 'Nay, Diotima,' I replied, 'if I had known, I should not have wondered at your wisdom, neither should I have come to learn from you about this very matter.' 'Well,' she said, 'I will teach you:—The object which they have in view is birth in beauty, whether of body or soul.' 'I do not understand you,' I said; 'the oracle requires an explanation.' 'I will make my meaning clearer,' she replied. 'I mean to say, that all men are bringing to the birth in their bodies and in their souls. There is a certain age at which human nature is desirous of procreation—procreation which must be in beauty and not in deformity; and this procreation is the union of man and woman, and is a divine thing; for conception and generation are an immortal principle in the mortal creature, and in the inharmonious they can never be. But the deformed is always inharmonious with the divine, and the beautiful harmonious. Beauty, then, is the destiny or goddess of parturition who presides at birth, and therefore, when approaching beauty, the conceiving power is propitious, and diffusive, and benign, and begets and bears fruit: at the sight of ugliness she frowns and contracts and has a sense of pain, and turns away, and shrivels up, and not without a pang refrains from conception. And this is the reason why, when the hour of conception arrives, and the teeming nature is full, there is such a flutter and ecstasy about beauty whose approach is the alleviation of the pain of travail. For love, Socrates, is not, as you imagine, the love of the beautiful only.' 'What then?' 'The love of generation and of birth in beauty.' 'Yes,' I said. 'Yes, indeed,' she replied. 'But why of generation?' 'Because to the mortal creature, generation is a sort of eternity and immortality,' she replied; 'and if, as has been already admitted, love is of the everlasting possession of the good, all men will necessarily desire immortality together with good: Wherefore love is of immortality.'

All this she taught me at various times when she spoke of love. And I remember her once saying to me, 'What is the cause, Socrates, of love, and the attendant desire? See you not how all animals, birds, as well as beasts, in their desire of procreation, are in agony when they take the infection of love, which begins with the desire of union; whereto is added the care of offspring, on whose behalf the weakest are ready to battle against the strongest even to the uttermost, and to die for them, and will let themselves be tormented with hunger or suffer anything in order to maintain their young. Man may be supposed to act thus from reason; but why should animals have these passionate feelings? Can you tell me why?' Again I replied that I did not know. She said to me: 'And do you expect ever to become a master in the art of love, if you do not know this?' 'But I have told you already, Diotima, that my ignorance is the reason why I come to you; for I am conscious that I want a teacher; tell me then the cause of this and of the other mysteries of love.' 'Marvel not,' she said, 'if you believe that love is of the immortal, as we have several times acknowledged; for here again, and on the same principle too, the mortal nature is seeking as far as is possible to be everlasting and immortal: and this is only to be attained by generation, because generation always leaves behind a new existence in the place of the old. Nay even in the life of the same individual there is succession and not absolute unity: a man is called the same, and yet in the short interval which elapses between youth and age, and in which every animal is said to have life and identity, he is undergoing a perpetual process of loss and reparation—hair, flesh, bones, blood, and the whole body are always changing. Which is true not only of the body, but also of the soul, whose habits, tempers, opinions, desires, pleasures, pains, fears, never remain the same in any one of us, but are always coming and going; and equally true of knowledge, and what is still more surprising to us mortals, not only do the sciences in general spring up and decay, so that in respect of them we are never the same; but each of them individually experiences a like change. For what is implied in the word "recollection," but the departure of knowledge, which is ever being forgotten, and is renewed and preserved by recollection, and appears to be the same although in reality new, according to that law of succession by which all mortal things are preserved, not absolutely the same, but by substitution, the old worn-out mortality leaving another new and similar existence behind—unlike the divine, which is always the same and not another? And in this way, Socrates, the mortal body, or mortal anything, partakes of immortality; but the immortal in another way. Marvel not then at the love which all men have of their offspring; for that universal love and interest is for the sake of immortality.'

I was astonished at her words, and said: 'Is this really true, O thou wise Diotima?' And she answered with all the authority of an accomplished sophist: 'Of that, Socrates, you may be assured;—think only of the ambition of men, and you will wonder at the senselessness of their ways, unless you consider how they are stirred by the love of an immortality of fame. They are ready to run all risks greater far than they would have run for their children, and to spend money and undergo any sort of toil, and even to die, for the sake of leaving behind them a name which shall be eternal. Do you imagine that Alcestis would have died to save Admetus, or Achilles to avenge Patroclus, or your own Codrus in order to preserve the kingdom for his sons, if they had not imagined that the memory of their virtues, which still survives among us, would be immortal? Nay,' she said, 'I am persuaded that all men do all things, and the better they are the more they do them, in hope of the glorious fame of immortal virtue; for they desire the immortal.

'Those who are pregnant in the body only, betake themselves to women and beget children—this is the character of their love; their offspring, as they hope, will preserve their memory and giving them the blessedness and immortality which they desire in the future. But souls which are pregnant—for there certainly are men who are more creative in their souls than in their bodies—conceive that which is proper for the soul to conceive or contain. And what are these conceptions?—wisdom and virtue in general. And such creators are poets and all artists who are deserving of the name inventor. But the greatest and fairest sort of wisdom by far is that which is concerned with the ordering of states and families, and which is called temperance and justice. And he who in youth has the seed of these implanted in him and is himself inspired, when he comes to maturity desires to beget and generate. He wanders about seeking beauty that he may beget offspring—for in deformity he will beget nothing—and naturally embraces the beautiful rather than the deformed body; above all when he finds a fair and noble and well-nurtured soul, he embraces the two in one person, and to such an one he is full of speech about virtue and the nature and pursuits of a good man; and he tries to educate him; and at the touch of the beautiful which is ever present to his memory, even when absent, he brings forth that which he had conceived long before, and in company with him tends that which he brings forth; and they are married by a far nearer tie and have a closer friendship than those who beget mortal children, for the children who are their common offspring are fairer and more immortal. Who, when he thinks of Homer and Hesiod and other great poets, would not rather have their children than ordinary human ones? Who would not emulate them in the creation of children such as theirs, which have preserved their memory and given them everlasting glory? Or who would not have such children as Lycurgus left behind him to be the saviours, not only of Lacedaemon, but of Hellas, as one may say? There is Solon, too, who is the revered father of Athenian laws; and many others there are in many other places, both among Hellenes and barbarians, who have given to the world many noble works, and have been the parents of virtue of every kind; and many temples have been raised in their honour for the sake of children such as theirs; which were never raised in honour of any one, for the sake of his mortal children.

'These are the lesser mysteries of love, into which even you, Socrates, may enter; to the greater and more hidden ones which are the crown of these, and to which, if you pursue them in a right spirit, they will lead, I know not whether you will be able to attain. But I will do my utmost to inform you, and do you follow if you can. For he who would proceed aright in this matter should begin in youth to visit beautiful forms; and first, if he be guided by his instructor aright, to love one such form only—out of that he should create fair thoughts; and soon he will of himself perceive that the beauty of one form is akin to the beauty of another; and then if beauty of form in general is his pursuit, how foolish would he be not to recognize that the beauty in every form is and the same!

And when he perceives this he will abate his violent love of the one, which he will despise and deem a small thing, and will become a lover of all beautiful forms; in the next stage he will consider that the beauty of the mind is more honourable than the beauty of the outward form. So that if a virtuous soul have but a little comeliness, he will be content to love and tend him, and will search out and bring to the birth thoughts which may improve the young, until he is compelled to contemplate and see the beauty of institutions and laws, and to understand that the beauty of them all is of one family, and that personal beauty is a trifle; and after laws and institutions he will go on to the sciences, that he may see their beauty, being not like a servant in love with the beauty of one youth or man or institution, himself a slave mean and narrow-minded, but drawing towards and contemplating the vast sea of beauty, he will create many fair and noble thoughts and notions in boundless love of wisdom; until on that shore he grows and waxes strong, and at last the vision is revealed to him of a single science, which is the science of beauty everywhere. To this I will proceed; please to give me your very best attention:

'He who has been instructed thus far in the things of love, and who has learned to see the beautiful in due order and succession, when he comes toward the end will suddenly perceive a nature of wondrous beauty (and this, Socrates, is the final cause of all our former toils)—a nature which in the first place is everlasting, not growing and decaying, or waxing and waning; secondly, not fair in one point of view and foul in another, or at one time or in one relation or at one place fair, at another time or in another relation or at another place foul, as if fair to some and foul to others, or in the likeness of a face or hands or any other part of the bodily frame, or in any form of speech or knowledge, or existing in any other being, as for example, in an animal, or in heaven, or in earth, or in any other place; but beauty absolute, separate, simple, and everlasting, which without diminution and without increase, or any change, is imparted to the ever-growing and perishing beauties of all other things. He who from these ascending under the influence of true love, begins to perceive that beauty, is not far from the end. And the true order of going, or being led by another, to the things of love, is to begin from the beauties of earth and mount upwards for the sake of that other beauty, using these as steps only, and from one going on to two, and from two to all fair forms, and from fair forms to fair practices, and from fair practices to fair notions, until from fair notions he arrives at the notion of absolute beauty, and at last knows what the essence of beauty is. This, my dear Socrates,' said the stranger of Mantineia, 'is that life above all others which man should live, in the contemplation of beauty absolute; a beauty which if you once beheld, you would see not to be after the measure of gold, and garments, and fair boys and youths, whose presence now entrances you; and you and many a one would be content to live seeing them only and conversing with them without meat or drink, if that were possible—you only want to look at them and to be with them. But what if man had eyes to see the true beauty—the divine beauty, I mean, pure and clear and unalloyed, not clogged with the pollutions of mortality and all the colours and vanities of human life—thither looking, and holding converse with the true beauty simple and divine? Remember how in that communion only, beholding beauty with the eye of the mind, he will be enabled to bring forth, not images of beauty, but realities (for he has hold not of an image but of a reality), and bringing forth and nourishing true virtue to become the friend of God and be immortal, if mortal man may. Would that be an ignoble life?'

Such, Phaedrus—and I speak not only to you, but to all of you—were the words of Diotima; and I am persuaded of their truth. And being persuaded of them, I try to persuade others, that in the attainment of this end human nature will not easily find a helper better than love: And therefore, also, I say that every man ought to honour him as I myself honour him, and walk in his ways, and exhort others to do the same, and praise the power and spirit of love according to the measure of my ability now and ever.

The words which I have spoken, you, Phaedrus, may call an encomium of love, or anything else which you please.

When Socrates had done speaking, the company applauded, and Aristophanes was beginning to say something in answer to the allusion which Socrates had made to his own speech, when suddenly there was a great knocking at the door of the house, as of revellers, and the sound of a flute-girl was heard. Agathon told the attendants to go and see who were the intruders. 'If they are friends of ours,' he said, 'invite them in, but if not, say that the drinking is over.' A little while afterwards they heard the voice of Alcibiades resounding in the court; he was in a great state of intoxication, and kept roaring and shouting 'Where is Agathon? Lead me to Agathon,' and at length, supported by the flute-girl and some of his attendants, he found his way to them. 'Hail, friends,' he said, appearing at the door crowned with a massive garland of ivy and violets, his head flowing with ribands. 'Will you have a very drunken man as a companion of your revels? Or shall I crown Agathon, which was my intention in coming, and go away? For I was unable to come yesterday, and therefore I am here to-day, carrying on my head these ribands, that taking them from my own head, I may crown the head of this fairest and wisest of men, as I may be allowed to call him. Will you laugh at me because I am drunk? Yet I know very well that I am speaking the truth, although you may laugh. But first tell me; if I come in shall we have the understanding of which I spoke (supra Will you have a very drunken man? etc.)? Will you drink with me or not?'

The company were vociferous in begging that he would take his place among them, and Agathon specially invited him. Thereupon he was led in by the people who were with him; and as he was being led, intending to crown Agathon, he took the ribands from his own head and held them in front of his eyes; he was thus prevented from seeing Socrates, who made way for him, and Alcibiades took the vacant place between Agathon and Socrates, and in taking the place he embraced Agathon and crowned him. Take off his sandals, said Agathon, and let him make a third on the same couch.

By all means; but who makes the third partner in our revels? said Alcibiades, turning round and starting up as he caught sight of Socrates. By Heracles, he said, what is this? here is Socrates always lying in wait for me, and always, as his way is, coming out at all sorts of unsuspected places: and now, what have you to say for yourself, and why are you lying here, where I perceive that you have contrived to find a place, not by a joker or lover of jokes, like Aristophanes, but by the fairest of the company?

Socrates turned to Agathon and said: I must ask you to protect me, Agathon; for the passion of this man has grown quite a serious matter to me. Since I became his admirer I have never been allowed to speak to any other fair one, or so much as to look at them. If I do, he goes wild with envy and jealousy, and not only abuses me but can hardly keep his hands off me, and at this moment he may do me some harm. Please to see to this, and either reconcile me to him, or, if he attempts violence, protect me, as I am in bodily fear of his mad and passionate attempts.

There can never be reconciliation between you and me, said Alcibiades; but for the present I will defer your chastisement. And I must beg you, Agathon, to give me back some of the ribands that I may crown the marvellous head of this universal despot—I would not have him complain of me for crowning you, and neglecting him, who in conversation is the conqueror of all mankind; and this not only once, as you were the day before yesterday, but always. Whereupon, taking some of the ribands, he crowned Socrates, and again reclined.

Then he said: You seem, my friends, to be sober, which is a thing not to be endured; you must drink—for that was the agreement under which I was admitted—and I elect myself master of the feast until you are well drunk. Let us have a large goblet, Agathon, or rather, he said, addressing the attendant, bring me that wine-cooler. The wine-cooler which had caught his eye was a vessel holding more than two quarts—this he filled and emptied, and bade the attendant fill it again for Socrates. Observe, my friends, said Alcibiades, that this ingenious trick of mine will have no effect on Socrates, for he can drink any quantity of wine and not be at all nearer being drunk. Socrates drank the cup which the attendant filled for him.

Eryximachus said: What is this, Alcibiades? Are we to have neither conversation nor singing over our cups; but simply to drink as if we were thirsty?

Alcibiades replied: Hail, worthy son of a most wise and worthy sire!

The same to you, said Eryximachus; but what shall we do?

That I leave to you, said Alcibiades.

'The wise physician skilled our wounds to heal (from Pope's Homer, Il.)'shall prescribe and we will obey. What do you want?

Well, said Eryximachus, before you appeared we had passed a

resolution that each one of us in turn should make a speech in praise of love, and as good a one as he could: the turn was passed round from left to right; and as all of us have spoken, and you have not spoken but have well drunken, you ought to speak, and then impose upon Socrates any task which you please, and he on his right hand neighbour, and so on.

That is good, Eryximachus, said Alcibiades; and yet the comparison of a drunken man's speech with those of sober men is hardly fair; and I should like to know, sweet friend, whether you really believe what Socrates was just now saying; for I can assure you that the very reverse is the fact, and that if I praise any one but himself in his presence, whether God or man, he will hardly keep his hands off me.

For shame, said Socrates.

Hold your tongue, said Alcibiades, for by Poseidon, there is no one else whom I will praise when you are of the company.

Well then, said Eryximachus, if you like praise Socrates.

What do you think, Eryximachus? said Alcibiades: shall I attack him and inflict the punishment before you all?

What are you about? said Socrates; are you going to raise a laugh at my expense? Is that the meaning of your praise?

I am going to speak the truth, if you will permit me.

I not only permit, but exhort you to speak the truth.

Then I will begin at once, said Alcibiades, and if I say anything which is not true, you may interrupt me if you will, and say 'that is a lie,' though my intention is to speak the truth. But you must not wonder if I speak any how as things come into my mind; for the fluent and orderly enumeration of all your singularities is not a task which is easy to a man in my condition.

And now, my boys, I shall praise Socrates in a figure which will appear to him to be a caricature, and yet I speak, not to make fun of him, but only for the truth's sake. I say, that he is exactly like the busts of Silenus, which are set up in the statuaries' shops, holding pipes and flutes in their mouths; and they are made to open in the middle, and have images of gods inside them. I say also that he is like Marsyas the satyr. You yourself will not deny, Socrates, that your face is like that of a satyr. Aye, and there is a resemblance in other points too. For example, you are a bully, as I can prove by witnesses, if you will not confess. And are you not a flute-player? That you are, and a performer far more wonderful than Marsyas. He indeed with instruments used to charm the souls of men by the power of his breath, and the players of his music do so still: for the melodies of Olympus (compare Arist. Pol.) are derived from Marsyas who taught them, and these, whether they are played by a great master or by a miserable flute-girl, have a power which no others have; they alone possess the soul and reveal the wants of those who have need of gods and mysteries, because they are divine. But you produce the same effect with your words only, and do not require the flute: that is the difference between you and him. When we hear any other speaker, even a very good one, he produces absolutely no effect upon us, or not much, whereas the mere fragments of you and your words, even at second-hand, and however imperfectly repeated, amaze and possess the souls of every man, woman, and child who comes within hearing of them. And if I were not afraid that you would think me hopelessly drunk, I would have sworn as well as spoken to the influence which they have always had and still have over me. For my heart leaps within me more than that of any Corybantian reveller, and my eyes rain tears when I hear them. And I observe that many others are affected in the same manner. I have heard Pericles and other great orators, and I thought that they spoke well, but I never had any similar feeling; my soul was not stirred by them, nor was I angry at the thought of my own slavish state. But this Marsyas has often brought me to such a pass, that I have felt as if I could hardly endure the life which I am leading (this, Socrates, you will admit); and I am conscious that if I did not shut my ears against him, and fly as from the voice of the siren, my fate would be like that of others,—he would transfix me, and I should grow old sitting at his feet. For he makes me confess that I ought not to live as I do, neglecting the wants of my own soul, and busying myself with the concerns of the Athenians; therefore I hold my ears and tear myself away from him. And he is the only person who ever made me ashamed, which you might think not to be in my nature, and there is no one else who does the same. For I know that I cannot answer him or say that I ought not to do as he bids, but when I leave his presence the love of popularity gets the better of me. And therefore I run away and fly from him, and when I see him I am ashamed of what I have confessed to him. Many a time have I wished that he were dead, and yet I know that I should be much more sorry than glad, if he were to die: so that I am at my wit's end.

And this is what I and many others have suffered from the flute-playing of this satyr. Yet hear me once more while I show you how exact the image is, and how marvellous his power. For let me tell you; none of you know him; but I will reveal him to you; having begun, I must go on. See you how fond he is of the fair? He is always with them and is always being smitten by them, and then again he knows nothing and is ignorant of all things—such is the appearance which he puts on. Is he not like a Silenus in this? To be sure he is: his outer mask is the carved head of the Silenus; but, O my companions in drink, when he is opened, what temperance there is residing within! Know you that beauty and wealth and honour, at which the many wonder, are of no account with him, and are utterly despised by him: he regards not at all the persons who are gifted with them; mankind are nothing to him; all his life is spent in mocking and flouting at them. But when I opened him, and looked within at his serious purpose, I saw in him divine and golden images of such fascinating beauty that I was ready to do in a moment whatever Socrates commanded: they may have escaped the observation of others, but I saw them. Now I fancied that he was seriously enamoured of my beauty, and I thought that I should therefore have a grand opportunity of hearing him tell what he knew, for I had a wonderful opinion of the attractions of my youth. In the prosecution of this design, when I next went to him, I sent away the attendant who usually accompanied me (I will confess the whole truth, and beg you to listen; and if I speak falsely, do you, Socrates, expose the falsehood). Well, he and I were alone together, and I thought that when there was nobody with us, I should hear him speak the language which lovers use to their loves when they are by themselves, and I was delighted. Nothing of the sort; he conversed as usual, and spent the day with me and then went away. Afterwards I challenged him to the palaestra; and he wrestled and closed with me several times when there was no one present; I fancied that I might succeed in this manner. Not a bit; I made no way with him. Lastly, as I had failed hitherto, I thought that I must take stronger measures and attack him boldly, and, as I had begun, not give him up, but see how matters stood between him and me. So I invited him to sup with me, just as if he were a fair youth, and I a designing lover. He was not easily persuaded to come; he did, however, after a while accept the invitation, and when he came the first time, he wanted to go away at once as soon as supper was over, and I had not the face to detain him. The second time, still in pursuance of my design, after we had supped, I went on conversing far into the night, and when he wanted to go away, I pretended that the hour was late and that he had much better remain. So he lay down on the couch next to me, the same on which he had supped, and there was no one but ourselves sleeping in the apartment. All this may be told without shame to any one. But what follows I could hardly tell you if I were sober. Yet as the proverb says, 'In vino veritas,' whether with boys, or without them (In allusion to two proverbs.); and therefore I must speak. Nor, again, should I be justified in concealing the lofty actions of Socrates when I come to praise him. Moreover I have felt the serpent's sting; and he who has suffered, as they say, is willing to tell his fellow-sufferers only, as they alone will be likely to understand him, and will not be extreme in judging of the sayings or doings which have been wrung from his agony. For I have been bitten by a more than viper's tooth; I have known in my soul, or in my heart, or in some other part, that worst of pangs, more violent in ingenuous youth than any serpent's tooth, the pang of philosophy, which will make a man say or do anything. And you whom I see around me, Phaedrus and Agathon and Eryximachus and Pausanias and Aristodemus and Aristophanes, all of you, and I need not say Socrates himself, have had experience of the same madness and passion in your longing after wisdom. Therefore listen and excuse my doings then and my sayings now. But let the attendants and other profane and unmannered persons close up the doors of their ears.

When the lamp was put out and the servants had gone away, I thought that I must be plain with him and have no more ambiguity. So I gave him a shake, and I said: 'Socrates, are you asleep?' 'No,' he said. 'Do you know what I am meditating?' 'What are you meditating?' he said. 'I think,' I replied, 'that of all the lovers whom I have ever had you are the only one who is worthy of me, and you appear to be too modest to speak. Now I feel that I should be a fool to refuse you this or any other favour, and therefore I come to lay at your feet all that I have and all that my friends have, in the hope that you will assist me in the way of virtue, which I desire above all things, and in which I believe that you can help me better than any one else. And I should certainly have more reason to be ashamed of what wise men would say if I were to refuse a favour to such as you, than of what the world, who are mostly fools, would say of me if I granted it.' To these words he replied in the ironical manner which is so characteristic of him:—'Alcibiades, my friend, you have indeed an elevated aim if what you say is true, and if there really is in me any power by which you may become better; truly you must see in me some rare beauty of a kind infinitely higher than any which I see in you. And therefore, if you mean to share with me and to exchange beauty for beauty, you will have greatly the advantage of me; you will gain true beauty in return for appearance—like Diomede, gold in exchange for brass. But look again, sweet friend, and see whether you are not deceived in me. The mind begins to grow critical when the bodily eye fails, and it will be a long time before you get old.' Hearing this, I said: 'I have told you my purpose, which is quite serious, and do you consider what you think best for you and me.' 'That is good,' he said; 'at some other time then we will consider and act as seems best about this and about other matters.' Whereupon, I fancied that he was smitten, and that the words which I had uttered like arrows had wounded him, and so without waiting to hear more I got up, and throwing my coat about him crept under his threadbare cloak, as the time of year was winter, and there I lay during the whole night having this wonderful monster in my arms. This again, Socrates, will not be denied by you. And yet, notwithstanding all, he was so superior to my solicitations, so contemptuous and derisive and disdainful of my beauty—which really, as I fancied, had some attractions—hear, O judges; for judges you shall be of the haughty virtue of Socrates—nothing more happened, but in the morning when I awoke (let all the gods and goddesses be my witnesses) I arose as from the couch of a father or an elder brother.

What do you suppose must have been my feelings, after this rejection, at the thought of my own dishonour? And yet I could not help wondering at his natural temperance and self-restraint and manliness. I never imagined that I could have met with a man such as he is in wisdom and endurance. And therefore I could not be angry with him or renounce his company, any more than I could hope to win him. For I well knew that if Ajax could not be wounded by steel, much less he by money; and my only chance of captivating him by my personal attractions had failed. So I was at my wit's end; no one was ever more hopelessly enslaved by another. All this happened before he and I went on the expedition to Potidaea; there we messed together, and I had the opportunity of observing his extraordinary power of sustaining fatigue. His endurance was simply marvellous when, being cut off from our supplies, we were compelled to go without food—on such occasions, which often happen in time of war, he was superior not only to me but to everybody; there was no one to be compared to him. Yet at a festival he was the only person who had any real powers of enjoyment; though not willing to drink, he could if compelled beat us all at that,—wonderful to relate! no human being had ever seen Socrates drunk; and his powers, if I am not mistaken, will be tested before long. His fortitude in enduring cold was also surprising. There was a severe frost, for the winter in that region is really tremendous, and everybody else either remained indoors, or if they went out had on an amazing quantity of clothes, and were well shod, and had their feet swathed in felt and fleeces: in the midst of this, Socrates with his bare feet on the ice and in his ordinary dress marched better than the other soldiers who had shoes, and they looked daggers at him because he seemed to despise them.

I have told you one tale, and now I must tell you another, which is worth hearing, 'Of the doings and sufferings of the enduring man'while he was on the expedition. One morning he was thinking about something which he could not resolve; he would not give it up, but continued thinking from early dawn until noon—there he stood fixed in thought; and at noon attention was drawn to him, and the rumour ran through the wondering crowd that Socrates had been standing and thinking about something ever since the break of day. At last, in the evening after supper, some Ionians out of curiosity (I should explain that this was not in winter but in summer), brought out their mats and slept in the open air that they might watch him and see whether he would stand all night. There he stood until the following morning; and with the return of light he offered up a prayer to the sun, and went his way (compare supra). I will also tell, if you please—and indeed I am bound to tell—of his courage in battle; for who but he saved my life? Now this was the engagement in which I received the prize of valour: for I was wounded and he would not leave me, but he rescued me and my arms; and he ought to have received the prize of valour which the generals wanted to confer on me partly on account of my rank, and I told them so, (this, again, Socrates will not impeach or deny), but he was more eager than the generals that I and not he should have the prize. There was another occasion on which his behaviour was very remarkable—in the flight of the army after the battle of Delium, where he served among the heavy-armed,—I had a better opportunity of seeing him than at Potidaea, for I was myself on horseback, and therefore comparatively out of danger. He and Laches were retreating, for the troops were in flight, and I met them and told them not to be discouraged, and promised to remain with them; and there you might see him, Aristophanes, as you describe (Aristoph. Clouds), just as he is in the streets of Athens, stalking like a pelican, and rolling his eyes, calmly contemplating enemies as well as friends, and making very intelligible to anybody, even from a distance, that whoever attacked him would be likely to meet with a stout resistance; and in this way he and his companion escaped—for this is the sort of man who is never touched in war; those only are pursued who are running away headlong. I particularly observed how superior he was to Laches in presence of mind. Many are the marvels which I might narrate in praise of Socrates; most of his ways might perhaps be paralleled in another man, but his absolute unlikeness to any human being that is or ever has been is perfectly astonishing. You may imagine Brasidas and others to have been like Achilles; or you may imagine Nestor and Antenor to have been like Pericles; and the same may be said of other famous men, but of this strange being you will never be able to find any likeness, however remote, either among men who now are or who ever have been—other than

Symposium

that which I have already suggested of Silenus and the satyrs; and they represent in a figure not only himself, but his words. For, although I forgot to mention this to you before, his words are like the images of Silenus which open; they are ridiculous when you first hear them; he clothes himself in language that is like the skin of the wanton satyr—for his talk is of pack-asses and smiths and cobblers and curriers, and he is always repeating the same things in the same words (compare Gorg.), so that any ignorant or inexperienced person might feel disposed to laugh at him; but he who opens the bust and sees what is within will find that they are the only words which have a meaning in them, and also the most divine, abounding in fair images of virtue, and of the widest comprehension, or rather extending to the whole duty of a good and honourable man.

This, friends, is my praise of Socrates. I have added my blame of him for his ill-treatment of me; and he has ill-treated not only me, but Charmides the son of Glaucon, and Euthydemus the son of Diocles, and many others in the same way—beginning as their lover he has ended by making them pay their addresses to him. Wherefore I say to you, Agathon, 'Be not deceived by him; learn from me and take warning, and do not be a fool and learn by experience, as the proverb says.'

When Alcibiades had finished, there was a laugh at his outspokenness; for he seemed to be still in love with Socrates. You are sober, Alcibiades, said Socrates, or you would never have gone so far about to hide the purpose of your satyr's praises, for all this long story is only an ingenious circumlocution, of which the point comes in by the way at the end; you want to get up a quarrel between me and Agathon, and your notion is that I ought to love you and nobody else, and that you and you only ought to love Agathon. But the plot of this Satyric or Silenic drama has been detected, and you must not allow him, Agathon, to set us at variance.

I believe you are right, said Agathon, and I am disposed to think that his intention in placing himself between you and me was only to divide us; but he shall gain nothing by that move; for I will go and lie on the couch next to you.

Yes, yes, replied Socrates, by all means come here and lie on the couch below me.

Alas, said Alcibiades, how I am fooled by this man; he is determined to get the better of me at every turn. I do beseech you, allow Agathon to lie between us.

Certainly not, said Socrates, as you praised me, and I in turn ought to praise my neighbour on the right, he will be out of order in praising me again when he ought rather to be praised by me, and I must entreat you to consent to this, and not be jealous, for I have a great desire to praise the youth.

Hurrah! cried Agathon, I will rise instantly, that I may be praised by Socrates.

The usual way, said Alcibiades; where Socrates is, no one else has any chance with the fair; and now how readily has he invented a specious reason for attracting Agathon to himself.

Agathon arose in order that he might take his place on the couch by Socrates, when suddenly a band of revellers entered, and spoiled the order of the banquet. Some one who was going out having left the door open, they had found their way in, and made themselves at home; great confusion ensued, and every one was compelled to drink large quantities of wine. Aristodemus said that Eryximachus, Phaedrus, and others went away—he himself fell asleep, and as the nights were long took a good rest: he was awakened towards daybreak by a crowing of cocks, and when he awoke, the others were either asleep, or had gone away; there remained only Socrates, Aristophanes, and Agathon, who were drinking out of a large goblet which they passed round, and Socrates was discoursing to them. Aristodemus was only half awake, and he did not hear the beginning of the discourse; the chief thing which he remembered was Socrates compelling the other two to acknowledge that the genius of comedy was the same with that of tragedy, and that the true artist in tragedy was an artist in comedy also. To this they were constrained to assent, being drowsy, and not quite following the argument. And first of all Aristophanes dropped off, then, when the day was already dawning, Agathon. Socrates, having laid them to sleep, rose to depart; Aristodemus, as his manner was, following him. At the Lyceum he took a bath, and passed the day as usual. In the evening he retired to rest at his own home.

Theætetus

by

Plato

Translated by Benjamin Jowett

INTRODUCTION AND ANALYSIS.

Some dialogues of Plato are of so various a character that their relation to the other dialogues cannot be determined with any degree of certainty. The Theætetus, like the Parmenides, has points of similarity both with his earlier and his later writings. The perfection of style, the humour, the dramatic interest, the complexity of structure, the fertility of illustration, the shifting of the points of view, are characteristic of his best period of authorship. The vain search, the negative conclusion, the figure of the midwives, the constant profession of ignorance on the part of Socrates, also bear the stamp of the early dialogues, in which the original Socrates is not yet Platonized. Had we no other indications, we should be disposed to range the Theætetus with the Apology and the Phaedrus, and perhaps even with the Protagoras and the Laches.

But when we pass from the style to an examination of the subject, we trace a connection with the later rather than with the earlier dialogues. In the first place there is the connexion, indicated by Plato himself at the end of the dialogue, with the Sophist, to which in many respects the Theætetus is so little akin. (1) The same persons reappear, including the younger Socrates, whose name is just mentioned in the Theætetus; (2) the theory of rest, which Socrates has declined to consider, is resumed by the Eleatic Stranger; (3) there is a similar allusion in both dialogues to the meeting of Parmenides and Socrates (Theaet., Soph.); and (4) the inquiry into not-being in the Sophist supplements the question of false opinion which is raised in the Theætetus. (Compare also Theaet. and Soph. for parallel turns of thought.) Secondly, the later date of the dialogue is confirmed by the absence of the doctrine of recollection and of any doctrine of ideas except that which derives them from generalization and from reflection of the mind upon itself. The general character of the Theætetus is dialectical, and there are traces of the same Megarian influences which appear in the Parmenides, and which later writers, in their matter of fact way, have explained by the residence of Plato at Megara. Socrates disclaims the character of a professional eristic, and also, with a sort of ironical admiration, expresses his inability to attain the Megarian precision in the use of terms. Yet he too employs a similar sophistical skill in overturning every conceivable theory of knowledge.

The direct indications of a date amount to no more than this: the conversation is said to have taken place when Theætetus was a youth, and shortly before the death of Socrates. At the time of his own death he is supposed to be a full-grown man. Allowing nine or ten years for the interval between youth and manhood, the dialogue could not have been written earlier than 390, when Plato was about thirty-nine years of age. No more definite date is indicated by the engagement in which Theætetus is said to have fallen or to have been wounded, and which may have taken place any time during the Corinthian war, between the years 390-387. The later date which has been suggested, 369, when the Athenians and Lacedaemonians disputed the Isthmus with Epaminondas, would make the age of Theætetus at his death forty-five or forty-six. This a little impairs the beauty of Socrates' remark, that 'he would be a great man if he lived.'

In this uncertainty about the place of the Theætetus, it seemed better, as in the case of the Republic, Timaeus, Critias, to retain the order in which Plato himself has arranged this and the two companion dialogues. We cannot exclude the possibility which has been already noticed in reference to other works of Plato, that the Theætetus may not have been all written continuously; or the probability that the Sophist and Politicus, which differ greatly in style, were only appended after a long interval of time. The allusion to

Parmenides compared with the Sophist, would probably imply that the dialogue which is called by his name was already in existence; unless, indeed, we suppose the passage in which the allusion occurs to have been inserted afterwards. Again, the Theætetus may be connected with the Gorgias, either dialogue from different points of view containing an analysis of the real and apparent (Schleiermacher); and both may be brought into relation with the Apology as illustrating the personal life of Socrates. The Philebus, too, may with equal reason be placed either after or before what, in the language of Thrasyllus, may be called the Second Platonic Trilogy. Both the Parmenides and the Sophist, and still more the Theætetus, have points of affinity with the Cratylus, in which the principles of rest and motion are again contrasted, and the Sophistical or Protagorean theory of language is opposed to that which is attributed to the disciple of Heracleitus, not to speak of lesser resemblances in thought and language. The Parmenides, again, has been thought by some to hold an intermediate position between the Theætetus and the Sophist; upon this view, the Sophist may be regarded as the answer to the problems about One and Being which have been raised in the Parmenides. Any of these arrangements may suggest new views to the student of Plato; none of them can lay claim to an exclusive probability in its favour.

The Theætetus is one of the narrated dialogues of Plato, and is the only one which is supposed to have been written down. In a short introductory scene, Euclides and Terpsion are described as meeting before the door of Euclides' house in Megara. This may have been a spot familiar to Plato (for Megara was within a walk of Athens), but no importance can be attached to the accidental introduction of the founder of the Megarian philosophy. The real intention of the preface is to create an interest about the person of Theætetus, who has just been carried up from the army at Corinth in a dying state. The expectation of his death recalls the promise of his youth, and especially the famous conversation which Socrates had with him when he was quite young, a few days before his own trial and death, as we are once more reminded at the end of the dialogue. Yet we may observe that Plato has himself forgotten this, when he represents Euclides as from time to time coming to Athens and correcting the copy from Socrates' own mouth. The narrative, having introduced Theætetus, and having guaranteed the authenticity of the dialogue (compare Symposium, Phaedo, Parmenides), is then dropped. No further use is made of the device. As Plato himself remarks, who in this as in some other minute points is imitated by Cicero (De Amicitia), the interlocutory words are omitted.

Theætetus, the hero of the battle of Corinth and of the dialogue, is a disciple of Theodorus, the great geometrician, whose science is thus indicated to be the propaedeutic to philosophy. An interest has been already excited about him by his approaching death, and now he is introduced to us anew by the praises of his master Theodorus. He is a youthful Socrates, and exhibits the same contrast of the fair soul and the ungainly face and frame, the Silenus mask and the god within, which are described in the Symposium. The picture which Theodorus gives of his courage and patience and intelligence and modesty is verified in the course of the dialogue. His courage is shown by his behaviour in the battle, and his other qualities shine forth as the argument proceeds. Socrates takes an evident delight in 'the wise Theætetus,' who has more in him than 'many bearded men'; he is quite inspired by his answers. At first the youth is lost in wonder, and is almost too modest to speak, but, encouraged by Socrates, he rises to the occasion, and grows full of interest and enthusiasm about the great question. Like a youth, he has not finally made up his mind, and is very ready to follow the lead of Socrates, and to enter into each successive phase of the discussion which turns up. His great dialectical talent is shown in his power of drawing distinctions, and of foreseeing the consequences of his own answers. The enquiry about the nature of knowledge is not new to him; long ago he has felt the 'pang of philosophy,' and has experienced the youthful intoxication which is depicted in the Philebus. But he has hitherto been unable to make the transition from mathematics to metaphysics. He can form a general conception of square and oblong numbers, but he is unable to attain a similar expression of knowledge in the abstract. Yet at length he begins to recognize that there are universal conceptions of being, likeness, sameness, number, which the mind contemplates in herself, and with the help of Socrates is conducted from a theory of sense to a theory of ideas.

There is no reason to doubt that Theætetus was a real person, whose name survived in the next generation. But neither can any importance be attached to the notices of him in Suidas and Proclus, which are probably based on the mention of him in Plato. According to a confused statement in Suidas, who mentions him twice over, first, as a pupil of Socrates, and then of Plato, he is said to have written the first work on the Five Solids. But no early authority cites the work, the invention of which may have been easily suggested by the division of roots, which Plato attributes to him, and the allusion to the backward state of solid geometry in the Republic. At any rate, there is no occasion to recall him to life again after the battle of Corinth, in order that we may allow time for the completion of such a work (Muller). We may also remark that such a supposition entirely destroys the pathetic interest of the introduction.

Theodorus, the geometrician, had once been the friend and disciple of Protagoras, but he is very reluctant to leave his retirement and defend his old master. He is too old to learn Socrates' game of question and answer, and prefers the digressions to the main argument, because he finds them easier to follow. The mathematician, as Socrates says in the Republic, is not capable of giving a reason in the same manner as the dialectician, and Theodorus could not therefore have been appropriately introduced as the chief respondent. But he may be fairly appealed to, when the honour of his master is at stake. He is the 'guardian of his orphans,' although this is a responsibility which he wishes to throw upon Callias, the friend and patron of all Sophists, declaring that he himself had early 'run away' from philosophy, and was absorbed in mathematics. His extreme dislike to the Heraclitean fanatics, which may be compared with the dislike of Theætetus to the materialists, and his ready acceptance of the noble words of Socrates, are noticeable traits of character.

The Socrates of the Theætetus is the same as the Socrates of the earlier dialogues. He is the invincible disputant, now advanced in years, of the Protagoras and Symposium; he is still pursuing his divine mission, his 'Herculean labours,' of which he has described the origin in the Apology; and he still hears the voice of his oracle, bidding him receive or not receive the truant souls. There he is supposed to have a mission to convict men of self-conceit; in the Theætetus he has assigned to him by God the functions of a man-midwife, who delivers men of their thoughts, and under this character he is present throughout the dialogue. He is the true prophet who has an insight into the natures of men, and can divine their future; and he knows that sympathy is the secret power which unlocks their thoughts. The hit at Aristides, the son of Lysimachus, who was specially committed to his charge in the Laches, may be remarked by the way. The attempt to discover the definition of knowledge is in accordance with the character of Socrates as he is described in the Memorabilia, asking What is justice? what is temperance? and the like. But there is no reason to suppose that he would have analyzed the nature of perception, or traced the connexion of Protagoras and Heracleitus, or have raised the difficulty respecting false opinion. The humorous illustrations, as well as the serious thoughts, run through the dialogue. The snubnosedness of Theætetus, a characteristic which he shares with Socrates, and the man-midwifery of Socrates, are not forgotten in the closing words. At the end of the dialogue, as in the Euthyphro, he is expecting to meet Meletus at the porch of the king Archon; but with the same indifference to the result which is everywhere displayed by him, he proposes that they shall reassemble on the following day at the same spot. The day comes, and in the Sophist the three friends again meet, but no further allusion is made to the trial, and the principal share in the argument is assigned, not to Socrates, but to an Eleatic stranger; the youthful Theætetus also plays a different and less independent part. And there is no allusion in the Introduction to the second and third dialogues, which are afterwards appended. There seems, therefore, reason to think that there is a real change, both in the characters and in the design.

The dialogue is an enquiry into the nature of knowledge, which is interrupted by two digressions. The first is the digression about the midwives, which is also a leading thought or continuous image, like the wave in the Republic, appearing and reappearing at intervals. Again and again we are reminded that the successive conceptions of knowledge are extracted from Theætetus, who in his turn truly declares that Socrates has got a great deal more out of him than ever was in him. Socrates is never weary of working out the image in humorous details,—discerning the symptoms of labour, carrying the child round the hearth, fearing that Theætetus will bite him, comparing his conceptions to wind-eggs, asserting an hereditary right to the occupation. There is also a serious side to the image, which is an apt similitude of the Socratic theory of education (compare Republic, Sophist), and accords with the ironical spirit in which the wisest of men delights to speak of himself.

The other digression is the famous contrast of the lawyer and philosopher. This is a sort of landing-place or break in the middle of the dialogue. At the commencement of a great discussion, the reflection naturally arises, How happy are they who, like the philosopher, have time for such discussions (compare Republic)! There is no reason for the introduction of such a digression; nor is a reason always needed, any more than for the introduction of an episode in a poem, or of a topic in conversation. That which is given by Socrates is quite sufficient, viz. that the philosopher may talk and write as he pleases. But though not very closely connected, neither is the digression out of keeping with the rest of the dialogue. The philosopher naturally desires to pour forth the thoughts which are always present to him, and to discourse of the higher life. The idea of knowledge, although hard to be defined, is realised in the life of philosophy. And the contrast is the favourite antithesis between the world, in the various characters of sophist, lawyer, statesman, speaker, and the philosopher,—between opinion and knowledge,—between the conventional and the true.

The greater part of the dialogue is devoted to setting up and throwing down definitions of science and knowledge. Proceeding from the lower to the higher by three stages, in which perception, opinion, reasoning are successively examined, we first get rid of the confusion of the idea of knowledge and specific kinds of knowledge,— a confusion which has been already noticed in the Lysis, Laches, Meno, and other dialogues. In the infancy of logic, a form of thought has to be invented before the content can be filled up. We cannot define knowledge until the nature of definition has been ascertained. Having succeeded in making his meaning plain, Socrates proceeds to analyze (1) the first definition which Theætetus proposes: 'Knowledge is sensible perception.' This is speedily identified with the Protagorean saying, 'Man is the measure of all things;' and of this again the foundation is discovered in the perpetual flux of Heracleitus. The relativeness of sensation is then developed at length, and for a moment the definition appears to be accepted. But soon the Protagorean thesis is pronounced to be suicidal; for the adversaries of Protagoras are as good a measure as he is, and they deny his doctrine. He is then supposed to reply that the perception may be true at any given instant. But the reply is in the end shown to be inconsistent with the Heraclitean foundation, on which the doctrine has been affirmed to rest. For if the Heraclitean flux is extended to every sort of change in every instant of time, how can any thought or word be detained even for an instant? Sensible perception, like everything else, is tumbling to pieces. Nor can Protagoras himself maintain that one man is as good as another in his knowledge of the future; and 'the expedient,' if not 'the just and true,' belongs to the sphere of the future.

And so we must ask again, What is knowledge? The comparison of sensations with one another implies a principle which is above sensation, and which resides in the mind itself. We are thus led to look for knowledge in a higher sphere, and accordingly Theætetus, when again interrogated, replies (2) that 'knowledge is true opinion.' But how is false opinion possible? The Megarian or Eristic spirit within us revives the question, which has been already asked and indirectly answered in the Meno: 'How can a man be ignorant of that which he knows?' No answer is given to this not unanswerable question. The comparison of the mind to a block of wax, or to a decoy of birds, is found wanting.

But are we not inverting the natural order in looking for opinion before we have found knowledge? And knowledge is not true opinion; for the Athenian dicasts have true opinion but not knowledge. What then is knowledge? We answer (3), 'True opinion, with definition or explanation.' But all the different ways in which this statement may be understood are set aside, like the definitions of courage in the Laches, or of friendship in the Lysis, or of temperance in the Charmides. At length we arrive at the conclusion, in which nothing is concluded.

Theætetus

There are two special difficulties which beset the student of the Theætetus: (1) he is uncertain how far he can trust Plato's account of the theory of Protagoras; and he is also uncertain (2) how far, and in what parts of the dialogue, Plato is expressing his own opinion. The dramatic character of the work renders the answer to both these questions difficult.

1. In reply to the first, we have only probabilities to offer. Three main points have to be decided: (a) Would Protagoras have identified his own thesis, 'Man is the measure of all things,' with the other, 'All knowledge is sensible perception'? (b) Would he have based the relativity of knowledge on the Heraclitean flux? (c) Would he have asserted the absoluteness of sensation at each instant? Of the work of Protagoras on 'Truth' we know nothing, with the exception of the two famous fragments, which are cited in this dialogue, 'Man is the measure of all things,' and, 'Whether there are gods or not, I cannot tell.' Nor have we any other trustworthy evidence of the tenets of Protagoras, or of the sense in which his words are used. For later writers, including Aristotle in his Metaphysics, have mixed up the Protagoras of Plato, as they have the Socrates of Plato, with the real person.

Returning then to the Theætetus, as the only possible source from which an answer to these questions can be obtained, we may remark, that Plato had 'The Truth' of Protagoras before him, and frequently refers to the book. He seems to say expressly, that in this work the doctrine of the Heraclitean flux was not to be found; 'he told the real truth' (not in the book, which is so entitled, but) 'privately to his disciples,'—words which imply that the connexion between the doctrines of Protagoras and Heracleitus was not generally recognized in Greece, but was really discovered or invented by Plato. On the other hand, the doctrine that 'Man is the measure of all things,' is expressly identified by Socrates with the other statement, that 'What appears to each man is to him;' and a reference is made to the books in which the statement occurs;—this Theætetus, who has 'often read the books,' is supposed to acknowledge (so Cratylus). And Protagoras, in the speech attributed to him, never says that he has been misunderstood: he rather seems to imply that the absoluteness of sensation at each instant was to be found in his

Plato

words. He is only indignant at the 'reductio ad absurdum' devised by Socrates for his 'homo mensura,' which Theodorus also considers to be 'really too bad.'

The question may be raised, how far Plato in the Theætetus could have misrepresented Protagoras without violating the laws of dramatic probability. Could he have pretended to cite from a well-known writing what was not to be found there? But such a shadowy enquiry is not worth pursuing further. We need only remember that in the criticism which follows of the thesis of Protagoras, we are criticizing the Protagoras of Plato, and not attempting to draw a precise line between his real sentiments and those which Plato has attributed to him.

2. The other difficulty is a more subtle, and also a more important one, because bearing on the general character of the Platonic dialogues. On a first reading of them, we are apt to imagine that the truth is only spoken by Socrates, who is never guilty of a fallacy himself, and is the great detector of the errors and fallacies of others. But this natural presumption is disturbed by the discovery that the Sophists are sometimes in the right and Socrates in the wrong. Like the hero of a novel, he is not to be supposed always to represent the sentiments of the author. There are few modern readers who do not side with Protagoras, rather than with Socrates, in the dialogue which is called by his name. The Cratylus presents a similar difficulty: in his etymologies, as in the number of the State, we cannot tell how far Socrates is serious; for the Socratic irony will not allow him to distinguish between his real and his assumed wisdom. No one is the superior of the invincible Socrates in argument (except in the first part of the Parmenides, where he is introduced as a youth); but he is by no means supposed to be in possession of the whole truth. Arguments are often put into his mouth (compare Introduction to the Gorgias) which must have seemed quite as untenable to Plato as to a modern writer. In this dialogue a great part of the answer of Protagoras is just and sound; remarks are made by him on verbal criticism, and on the importance of understanding an opponent's meaning, which are conceived in the true spirit of philosophy. And the distinction which he is supposed to draw between Eristic and Dialectic, is really a criticism of Plato on himself and his own criticism of Protagoras.

The difficulty seems to arise from not attending to the dramatic character of the writings of Plato. There are two, or more, sides to questions; and these are parted among the different speakers. Sometimes one view or aspect of a question is made to predominate over the rest, as in the Gorgias or Sophist; but in other dialogues truth is divided, as in the Laches and Protagoras, and the interest of the piece consists in the contrast of opinions. The confusion caused by the irony of Socrates, who, if he is true to his character, cannot say anything of his own knowledge, is increased by the circumstance that in the Theætetus and some other dialogues he is occasionally playing both parts himself, and even charging his own arguments with unfairness. In the Theætetus he is designedly held back from arriving at a conclusion. For we cannot suppose that Plato conceived a definition of knowledge to be impossible. But this is his manner of approaching and surrounding a question. The lights which he throws on his subject are indirect, but they are not the less real for that. He has no intention of proving a thesis by a cut-and-dried argument; nor does he imagine that a great philosophical problem can be tied up within the limits of a definition. If he has analyzed a proposition or notion, even with the severity of an impossible logic, if half-truths have been compared by him with other half-truths, if he has cleared up or advanced popular ideas, or illustrated a new method, his aim has been sufficiently accomplished.

The writings of Plato belong to an age in which the power of analysis had outrun the means of knowledge; and through a spurious use of dialectic, the distinctions which had been already 'won from the void and formless infinite,' seemed to be rapidly returning to their original chaos. The two great speculative philosophies, which a century earlier had so deeply impressed the mind of Hellas, were now degenerating into Eristic. The contemporaries of Plato and Socrates were vainly trying to find new combinations of them, or to transfer them from the object to the subject. The Megarians, in their first attempts to attain a severer logic, were making knowledge impossible (compare Theaet.). They were asserting 'the one good under many names,' and, like the Cynics, seem to have denied predication, while the Cynics themselves were depriving virtue of all which made virtue desirable in the eyes of Socrates and Plato. And besides these, we find mention in the later writings of Plato, especially in the Theætetus, Sophist, and Laws, of certain impenetrable godless persons, who will not believe what they 'cannot hold in their hands'; and cannot be approached in argument, because they cannot argue (Theat; Soph.). No school of Greek philosophers exactly answers to these persons, in whom Plato may perhaps have blended some features of the Atomists with the vulgar materialistic tendencies of mankind in general (compare Introduction to the Sophist).

And not only was there a conflict of opinions, but the stage which the mind had reached presented other difficulties hardly intelligible to us, who live in a different cycle of human thought. All times of mental progress are times of confusion; we only see, or rather seem to see things clearly, when they have been long fixed and defined. In the age of Plato, the limits of the world of imagination and of pure abstraction, of the old world and the new, were not yet fixed. The Greeks, in the fourth century before Christ, had no words for 'subject' and 'object,' and no distinct conception of them; yet they were always hovering about the question involved in them. The analysis of sense, and the analysis of thought, were equally difficult to them; and hopelessly confused by the attempt to solve them, not through an appeal to facts, but by the help of general theories respecting the nature of the universe.

Plato, in his Theætetus, gathers up the sceptical tendencies of his age, and compares them. But he does not seek to reconstruct out of them a theory of knowledge. The time at which such a theory could be framed had not yet arrived. For there was no measure of experience with which the ideas swarming in men's minds could be compared; the meaning of the word 'science' could scarcely be explained to them, except from the mathematical sciences, which alone offered the type of universality and certainty. Philosophy was becoming more and more vacant and abstract, and not only the Platonic Ideas and the Eleatic Being, but all abstractions seemed to be at variance with sense and at war with one another.

The want of the Greek mind in the fourth century before Christ was not another theory of rest or motion, or Being or atoms, but rather a philosophy which could free the mind from the power of abstractions and alternatives, and show how far rest and how far

Theætetus

motion, how far the universal principle of Being and the multitudinous principle of atoms, entered into the composition of the world; which could distinguish between the true and false analogy, and allow the negative as well as the positive a place in human thought. To such a philosophy Plato, in the Theætetus, offers many contributions. He has followed philosophy into the region of mythology, and pointed out the similarities of opposing phases of thought. He has also shown that extreme abstractions are self-destructive, and, indeed, hardly distinguishable from one another. But his intention is not to unravel the whole subject of knowledge, if this had been possible; and several times in the course of the dialogue he rejects explanations of knowledge which have germs of truth in them; as, for example, 'the resolution of the compound into the simple;' or 'right opinion with a mark of difference.'

* * *

Terpsion, who has come to Megara from the country, is described as having looked in vain for Euclides in the Agora; the latter explains that he has been down to the harbour, and on his way thither had met Theætetus, who was being carried up from the army to Athens. He was scarcely alive, for he had been badly wounded at the battle of Corinth, and had taken the dysentery which prevailed in the camp. The mention of his condition suggests the reflection, 'What a loss he will be!' 'Yes, indeed,' replies Euclid; 'only just now I was hearing of his noble conduct in the battle.' 'That I should expect; but why did he not remain at Megara?' 'I wanted him to remain, but he would not; so I went with him as far as Erineum; and as I parted from him, I remembered that Socrates had seen him when he was a youth, and had a remarkable conversation with him, not long before his own death; and he then prophesied of him that he would be a great man if he lived.' 'How true that has been; how like all that Socrates said! And could you repeat the conversation?' 'Not from memory; but I took notes when I returned home, which I afterwards filled up at leisure, and got Socrates to correct them from time to time, when I came to Athens'...Terpsion had long intended to ask for a sight of this writing, of which he had already heard. They are both tired, and agree to rest and have the conversation read to them by a servant...'Here is the roll, Terpsion; I need only observe that I have omitted, for the sake of convenience, the interlocutory words, "said I," "said he"; and that Theætetus, and Theodorus, the geometrician of Cyrene, are the persons with whom Socrates is conversing.'

Socrates begins by asking Theodorus whether, in his visit to Athens, he has found any Athenian youth likely to attain distinction in science. 'Yes, Socrates, there is one very remarkable youth, with whom I have become acquainted. He is no beauty, and therefore you need not imagine that I am in love with him; and, to say the truth, he is very like you, for he has a snub nose, and projecting eyes, although these features are not so marked in him as in you. He combines the most various qualities, quickness, patience, courage; and he is gentle as well as wise, always silently flowing on, like a river of oil. Look! he is the middle one of those who are entering the palaestra.'

Socrates, who does not know his name, recognizes him as the son of Euphronius, who was himself a good man and a rich. He is informed by Theodorus that the youth is named Theætetus, but the property of his father has disappeared in the hands of trustees; this does not, however, prevent him from adding liberality to his other virtues. At the desire of Socrates he invites Theætetus to sit by them.

'Yes,' says Socrates, 'that I may see in you, Theætetus, the image of my ugly self, as Theodorus declares. Not that his remark is of any importance; for though he is a philosopher, he is not a painter, and therefore he is no judge of our faces; but, as he is a man of science, he may be a judge of our intellects. And if he were to praise the mental endowments of either of us, in that case the hearer of the eulogy ought to examine into what he says, and the subject should not refuse to be examined.' Theætetus consents, and is caught in a trap (compare the similar trap which is laid for Theodorus). 'Then, Theætetus, you will have to be examined, for Theodorus has been praising you in a style of which I never heard the like.' 'He was only jesting.' 'Nay, that is not his way; and I cannot allow you, on that pretence, to retract the assent which you have already given, or I shall make Theodorus repeat your praises, and swear to them.' Theætetus, in reply, professes that he is willing to be examined, and Socrates begins by asking him what he learns of Theodorus. He is himself anxious to learn anything of anybody; and now he has a little question to which he wants Theætetus or Theodorus (or whichever of the company would not be 'donkey' to the rest) to find an answer. Without further preface, but at the same time apologizing for his eagerness, he asks, 'What is knowledge?' Theodorus is too old to answer questions, and begs him to interrogate Theætetus, who has the advantage of youth.

Theætetus replies, that knowledge is what he learns of Theodorus, i.e. geometry and arithmetic; and that there are other kinds of knowledge—shoemaking, carpentering, and the like. But Socrates rejoins, that this answer contains too much and also too little. For although Theætetus has enumerated several kinds of knowledge, he has not explained the common nature of them; as if he had been asked, 'What is clay?' and instead of saying 'Clay is moistened earth,' he had answered, 'There is one clay of image-makers, another of potters, another of oven-makers.' Theætetus at once divines that Socrates means him to extend to all kinds of knowledge the same process of generalization which he has already learned to apply to arithmetic. For he has discovered a division of numbers into square numbers, 4, 9, 16, etc., which are composed of equal factors, and represent figures which have equal sides, and oblong numbers, 3, 5, 6, 7, etc., which are composed of unequal factors, and represent figures which have unequal sides. But he has never succeeded in attaining a similar conception of knowledge, though he has often tried; and, when this and similar questions were brought to him from Socrates, has been sorely distressed by them. Socrates explains to him that he is in labour. For men as well as women have pangs of labour; and both at times require the assistance of midwives. And he, Socrates, is a midwife, although this is a secret; he has inherited the art from his mother bold and bluff, and he ushers into light, not children, but the thoughts of men. Like the midwives, who are 'past bearing children,' he too can have no offspring—the God will not allow him to bring anything into the world of his own. He also reminds Theætetus that the midwives are or ought to be the only matchmakers (this is the preparation for a biting jest); for those who reap the fruit are most likely to know on what soil the plants will grow. But respectable midwives avoid this department of practice—they do not want to be called procuresses. There are some other differences between the two sorts of pregnancy. For women do not bring into the world at one time real children and at another time idols which are with difficulty distinguished from them. 'At first,' says Socrates in his character of the man-midwife, 'my patients are barren and stolid, but after a while they "round apace," if the gods are propitious to them; and this is due not to me but to themselves; I and the god only assist in bringing their ideas to the birth. Many of them have left me too soon, and the result has been that they have produced abortions; or when I have delivered them of children they have lost them by an ill bringing up, and have ended by seeing themselves, as others see them, to be great fools. Aristides, the son of Lysimachus, is one of these, and there have been others. The truants often return to me and beg to be taken back; and then, if my familiar allows me, which is not always the case, I receive them, and they begin to grow again. There come to me also those who have nothing in them, and have no need of my art; and I am their matchmaker (see above), and marry them to Prodicus or some other inspired sage who is likely to suit them. I tell you this long story because I suspect that you are in labour. Come then to me, who am a midwife, and the son of a midwife, and I will deliver you. And do not bite me, as the women do, if I abstract your first-born; for I am acting out of goodwill towards you; the God who is within me is the friend of man, though he will not allow me to dissemble the truth. Once more then, Theætetus, I repeat my old question—"What is knowledge?" Take courage, and by the help of God you will discover an answer.' 'My answer is, that knowledge is perception.' 'That is the theory of Protagoras, who has another way of expressing the same thing when he says, "Man is the measure of all things." He was a very wise man, and we should try to understand him. In order to illustrate his meaning let me suppose that there is the same wind blowing in our faces, and one of us may be hot and the other cold. How is this? Protagoras will reply that the wind is hot to him who is cold, cold to him who is hot. And "is" means "appears," and when you say "appears to him," that means "he feels." Thus feeling, appearance, perception, coincide with being. I suspect, however, that this was only a "façon de parler," by which he imposed on the common herd like you and me; he told "the truth" (in allusion to the title of his book, which was called "The Truth") in secret to his disciples. For he was really a votary of that famous philosophy in which all things are said to be relative; nothing is great or small, or heavy or light, or one, but all is in motion and mixture and transition and flux and generation, not "being," as we ignorantly affirm, but "becoming." This has been the doctrine, not of Protagoras only, but of all philosophers, with the single exception of Parmenides; Empedocles, Heracleitus, and others, and all the poets, with Epicharmus, the king of Comedy, and Homer, the king of Tragedy, at their head, have said the same; the latter has these words—

"Ocean, whence the gods sprang, and mother Tethys."

And many arguments are used to show, that motion is the source of life, and rest of death: fire and warmth are produced by friction, and living creatures owe their origin to a similar cause; the bodily frame is preserved by exercise and destroyed by indolence; and if the sun ceased to move, "chaos would come again." Now apply this doctrine of "All is motion" to the senses, and first of all to the sense of sight. The colour of white, or any other colour, is neither in the eyes nor out of them, but ever in motion between the object and the eye, and varying in the case of every percipient. All is relative, and, as the followers of Protagoras remark, endless contradictions arise when we deny this; e.g. here are six dice; they are more than four and less than twelve; "more and also less," would you not say?' 'Yes.' 'But Protagoras will retort: "Can anything be more or less without addition or subtraction?"'

'I should say "No" if I were not afraid of contradicting my former answer.'

'And if you say "Yes," the tongue will escape conviction but not the mind, as Euripides would say?' 'True.' 'The thoroughbred Sophists, who know all that can be known, would have a sparring match over this, but you and I, who have no professional pride, want only to discover whether our ideas are clear and consistent. And we cannot be wrong in saying, first, that nothing can be greater or less while remaining equal; secondly, that there can be no becoming greater or less without addition or subtraction; thirdly, that what is and was not, cannot be without having become. But then how is this reconcilable with the case of the dice, and with similar examples?—that is the question.' 'I am often perplexed and amazed, Socrates, by these difficulties.' 'That is because you are a philosopher, for philosophy begins in wonder, and Iris is the child of Thaumas. Do you know the original principle on which the doctrine of Protagoras is based?' 'No.' 'Then I will tell you; but we must not let the uninitiated hear, and by the uninitiated I mean the obstinate people who believe in nothing which they cannot hold in their hands. The brethren whose mysteries I am about to unfold to you are far more ingenious. They maintain that all is motion; and that motion has two forms, action and passion, out of which endless phenomena are created, also in two forms—sense and the object of sense—which come to the birth together. There are two kinds of motions, a slow and a fast; the motions of the agent and the patient are slower, because they move and create in and about themselves, but the things which are born of them have a swifter motion, and pass rapidly from place to place. The eye and the appropriate object come together, and give birth to whiteness and the sensation of whiteness; the eye is filled with seeing, and becomes not sight but a seeing eye, and the object is filled with whiteness, and becomes not whiteness but white; and no other compound of either with another would have produced the same effect. All sensation is to be resolved into a similar combination of an agent and patient. Of either, taken separately, no idea can be formed; and the agent may become a patient, and the patient an agent. Hence there arises a general reflection that nothing is, but all things become; no name can detain or fix them. Are not these speculations charming, Theætetus, and very good for a person in your interesting situation? I am offering you specimens of other men's wisdom, because I have no wisdom of my own, and I want to deliver you of something; and presently we will see whether you have brought forth wind or not. Tell me, then, what do you think of the notion that "All things are becoming"?'

'When I hear your arguments, I am marvellously ready to assent.'

'But I ought not to conceal from you that there is a serious objec-

Theætetus

tion which may be urged against this doctrine of Protagoras. For there are states, such as madness and dreaming, in which perception is false; and half our life is spent in dreaming; and who can say that at this instant we are not dreaming? Even the fancies of madmen are real at the time. But if knowledge is perception, how can we distinguish between the true and the false in such cases? Having stated the objection, I will now state the answer. Protagoras would deny the continuity of phenomena; he would say that what is different is entirely different, and whether active or passive has a different power. There are infinite agents and patients in the world, and these produce in every combination of them a different perception. Take myself as an instance:—Socrates may be ill or he may be well,—and remember that Socrates, with all his accidents, is spoken of. The wine which I drink when I am well is pleasant to me, but the same wine is unpleasant to me when I am ill. And there is nothing else from which I can receive the same impression, nor can another receive the same impression from the wine. Neither can I and the object of sense become separately what we become together. For the one in becoming is relative to the other, but they have no other relation; and the combination of them is absolute at each moment. (In modern language, the act of sensation is really indivisible, though capable of a mental analysis into subject and object.) My sensation alone is true, and true to me only. And therefore, as Protagoras says, "To myself I am the judge of what is and what is not." Thus the flux of Homer and Heracleitus, the great Protagorean saying that "Man is the measure of all things," the doctrine of Theætetus that "Knowledge is perception," have all the same meaning. And this is thy new-born child, which by my art I have brought to light; and you must not be angry if instead of rearing your infant we expose him.'

' Theætetus will not be angry,' says Theodorus; 'he is very good-natured. But I should like to know, Socrates, whether you mean to say that all this is untrue?'

'First reminding you that I am not the bag which contains the arguments, but that I extract them from Theætetus, shall I tell you what amazes me in your friend Protagoras?'

'What may that be?'

'I like his doctrine that what appears is; but I wonder that he did not begin his great work on Truth with a declaration that a pig, or a dog-faced baboon, or any other monster which has sensation, is a measure of all things; then, while we were reverencing him as a god, he might have produced a magnificent effect by expounding to us that he was no wiser than a tadpole. For if sensations are always true, and one man's discernment is as good as another's, and every man is his own judge, and everything that he judges is right and true, then what need of Protagoras to be our instructor at a high figure; and why should we be less knowing than he is, or have to go to him, if every man is the measure of all things? My own art of midwifery, and all dialectic, is an enormous folly, if Protagoras' "Truth" be indeed truth, and the philosopher is not merely amusing himself by giving oracles out of his book.'

Theodorus thinks that Socrates is unjust to his master, Protagoras; but he is too old and stiff to try a fall with him, and therefore refers him to Theætetus, who is already driven out of his former opinion by the arguments of Socrates.

Socrates then takes up the defence of Protagoras, who is supposed to reply in his own person—'Good people, you sit and declaim about the gods, of whose existence or non-existence I have nothing to say, or you discourse about man being reduced to the level of the brutes; but what proof have you of your statements? And yet surely you and Theodorus had better reflect whether probability is a safe guide. Theodorus would be a bad geometrician if he had nothing better to offer.'... Theætetus is affected by the appeal to geometry, and Socrates is induced by him to put the question in a new form. He proceeds as follows:—'Should we say that we know what we see and hear,—e.g. the sound of words or the sight of letters in a foreign tongue?'

'We should say that the figures of the letters, and the pitch of the voice in uttering them, were known to us, but not the meaning of them.'

'Excellent; I want you to grow, and therefore I will leave that answer and ask another question: Is not seeing perceiving?' 'Very true.' 'And he who sees knows?' 'Yes.' 'And he who remembers, remembers that which he sees and knows?' 'Very true.' 'But if he closes his eyes, does he not remember?' 'He does.' 'Then he may remember and not see; and if seeing is knowing, he may remember and not know. Is not this a "reductio ad absurdum" of the hypothesis that knowledge is sensible perception? Yet perhaps we are crowing too soon; and if Protagoras, "the father of the myth," had been alive, the result might have been very different. But he is dead, and Theodorus, whom he left guardian of his "orphan," has not been very zealous in defending him.'

Theodorus objects that Callias is the true guardian, but he hopes that Socrates will come to the rescue. Socrates prefaces his defence by resuming the attack. He asks whether a man can know and not know at the same time? 'Impossible.' Quite possible, if you maintain that seeing is knowing. The confident adversary, suiting the action to the word, shuts one of your eyes; and now, says he, you see and do not see, but do you know and not know? And a fresh opponent darts from his ambush, and transfers to knowledge the terms which are commonly applied to sight. He asks whether you can know near and not at a distance; whether you can have a sharp and also a dull knowledge. While you are wondering at his incomparable wisdom, he gets you into his power, and you will not escape until you have come to an understanding with him about the money which is to be paid for your release.

But Protagoras has not yet made his defence; and already he may be heard contemptuously replying that he is not responsible for the admissions which were made by a boy, who could not foresee the coming move, and therefore had answered in a manner which enabled Socrates to raise a laugh against himself. 'But I cannot be fairly charged,' he will say, 'with an answer which I should not have given; for I never maintained that the memory of a feeling is the same as a feeling, or denied that a man might know and not know the same thing at the same time. Or, if you will have extreme precision, I say that man in different relations is many or rather infinite in number. And I challenge you, either to show that his perceptions are not individual, or that if they are, what appears to him is not what is. As to your pigs and baboons, you are yourself a pig, and you make my writings a sport of other swine. But I still affirm that man is the measure of all things, although I admit that one man may be a thousand times better than another, in proportion as he has better impressions. Neither do I deny the existence of wisdom or of the wise man. But I maintain that wisdom is a practical remedial power of turning evil into good, the bitterness of disease into the sweetness of health, and does not consist in any greater truth or superior knowledge. For the impressions of the sick are as true as the impressions of the healthy; and the sick are as wise as the healthy. Nor can any man be cured of a false opinion, for there is no such thing; but he may be cured of the evil habit which generates in him an evil opinion. This is effected in the body by the drugs of the physician, and in the soul by the words of the Sophist; and the new state or opinion is not truer, but only better than the old. And philosophers are not tadpoles, but physicians and husbandmen, who till the soil and infuse health into animals and plants, and make the good take the place of the evil, both in individuals and states. Wise and good rhetoricians make the good to appear just in states (for that is just which appears just to a state), and in return, they deserve to be well paid. And you, Socrates, whether you please or not, must continue to be a measure. This is my defence, and I must request you to meet me fairly. We are professing to reason, and not merely to dispute; and there is a great difference between reasoning and disputation. For the disputer is always seeking to trip up his opponent; and this is a mode of argument which disgusts men with philosophy as they grow older. But the reasoner is trying to understand him and to point out his errors to him, whether arising from his own or from his companion's fault; he does not argue from the customary use of names, which the vulgar pervert in all manner of ways. If you are gentle to an adversary he will follow and love you; and if defeated he will lay the blame on himself, and seek to escape from his own prejudices into philosophy. I would recommend you, Socrates, to adopt this humaner method, and to avoid captious and verbal criticisms.'

Such, Theodorus, is the very slight help which I am able to afford to your friend; had he been alive, he would have helped himself in far better style.

'You have made a most valorous defence.'

Yes; but did you observe that Protagoras bade me be serious, and complained of our getting up a laugh against him with the aid of a boy? He meant to intimate that you must take the place of

Theætetus, who may be wiser than many bearded men, but not wiser than you, Theodorus.

'The rule of the Spartan Palaestra is, Strip or depart; but you are like the giant Antaeus, and will not let me depart unless I try a fall with you.'

Yes, that is the nature of my complaint. And many a Hercules, many a Theseus mighty in deeds and words has broken my head; but I am always at this rough game. Please, then, to favour me.

'On the condition of not exceeding a single fall, I consent.'

Socrates now resumes the argument. As he is very desirous of doing justice to Protagoras, he insists on citing his own words,—'What appears to each man is to him.' And how, asks Socrates, are these words reconcileable with the fact that all mankind are agreed in thinking themselves wiser than others in some respects, and inferior to them in others? In the hour of danger they are ready to fall down and worship any one who is their superior in wisdom as if he were a god. And the world is full of men who are asking to be taught and willing to be ruled, and of other men who are willing to rule and teach them. All which implies that men do judge of one another's impressions, and think some wise and others foolish. How will Protagoras answer this argument? For he cannot say that no one deems another ignorant or mistaken. If you form a judgment, thousands and tens of thousands are ready to maintain the opposite. The multitude may not and do not agree in Protagoras' own thesis that 'Man is the measure of all things;' and then who is to decide? Upon his own showing must not his 'truth' depend on the number of suffrages, and be more or less true in proportion as he has more or fewer of them? And he must acknowledge further, that they speak truly who deny him to speak truly, which is a famous jest. And if he admits that they speak truly who deny him to speak truly, he must admit that he himself does not speak truly. But his opponents will refuse to admit this of themselves, and he must allow that they are right in their refusal. The conclusion is, that all mankind, including Protagoras himself, will deny that he speaks truly; and his truth will be true neither to himself nor to anybody else.

Theodorus is inclined to think that this is going too far. Socrates ironically replies, that he is not going beyond the truth. But if the old Protagoras could only pop his head out of the world below, he would doubtless give them both a sound castigation and be off to the shades in an instant. Seeing that he is not within call, we must examine the question for ourselves. It is clear that there are great differences in the understandings of men. Admitting, with Protagoras, that immediate sensations of hot, cold, and the like, are to each one such as they appear, yet this hypothesis cannot be extended to judgments or opinions. And even if we were to admit further,—and this is the view of some who are not thorough-going followers of Protagoras,—that right and wrong, holy and unholy, are to each state or individual such as they appear, still Protagoras will not venture to maintain that every man is equally the measure of expediency, or that the thing which seems is expedient to every one. But this begins a new question. 'Well, Socrates, we have plenty of leisure. Yes, we have, and, after the manner of philosophers, we are digressing; I have often observed how ridiculous this habit of theirs makes them when they appear in court. 'What do you mean?' I mean to say that a philosopher is a gentleman, but a lawyer is a servant. The one can have his talk out, and wander at will from one subject to another, as the fancy takes him; like ourselves, he may be long or short, as he pleases. But the lawyer is always in a hurry; there is the clepsydra limiting his time, and the brief limiting his topics, and his adversary is standing over him and exacting his rights. He is a servant disputing about a fellow-servant before his master, who holds the cause in his hands; the path never diverges, and often the race is for his life. Such experiences render him keen and shrewd; he learns the arts of flattery, and is perfect in the practice of crooked ways; dangers have come upon him too soon, when the tenderness of youth was unable to meet them with truth and honesty, and he has resorted to counter-acts of dishonesty and falsehood, and become warped and distorted; without any health or freedom or sincerity in him he has grown up to manhood, and is or esteems himself to be a master of cunning. Such are the lawyers; will you have the companion picture of philosophers? or will this be too much of a digression?

'Nay, Socrates, the argument is our servant, and not our master. Who is the judge or where is the spectator, having a right to control us?'

Theætetus

I will describe the leaders, then: for the inferior sort are not worth the trouble. The lords of philosophy have not learned the way to the dicastery or ecclesia; they neither see nor hear the laws and votes of the state, written or recited; societies, whether political or festive, clubs, and singing maidens do not enter even into their dreams. And the scandals of persons or their ancestors, male and female, they know no more than they can tell the number of pints in the ocean. Neither are they conscious of their own ignorance; for they do not practise singularity in order to gain reputation, but the truth is, that the outer form of them only is residing in the city; the inner man, as Pindar says, is going on a voyage of discovery, measuring as with line and rule the things which are under and in the earth, interrogating the whole of nature, only not condescending to notice what is near them.

'What do you mean, Socrates?'

I will illustrate my meaning by the jest of the witty maid-servant, who saw Thales tumbling into a well, and said of him, that he was so eager to know what was going on in heaven, that he could not see what was before his feet. This is applicable to all philosophers. The philosopher is unacquainted with the world; he hardly knows whether his neighbour is a man or an animal. For he is always searching into the essence of man, and enquiring what such a nature ought to do or suffer different from any other. Hence, on every occasion in private life and public, as I was saying, when he appears in a law-court or anywhere, he is the joke, not only of maid-servants, but of the general herd, falling into wells and every sort of disaster; he looks such an awkward, inexperienced creature, unable to say anything personal, when he is abused, in answer to his adversaries (for he knows no evil of any one); and when he hears the praises of others, he cannot help laughing from the bottom of his soul at their pretensions; and this also gives him a ridiculous appearance. A king or tyrant appears to him to be a kind of swine-herd or cow-herd, milking away at an animal who is much more troublesome and dangerous than cows or sheep; like the cow-herd, he has no time to be educated, and the pen in which he keeps his flock in the mountains is surrounded by a wall. When he hears of large landed properties of ten thousand acres or more, he thinks of the whole earth; or if he is told of the antiquity of a family, he remembers that every one has had myriads of progenitors, rich and poor, Greeks and barbarians, kings and slaves. And he who boasts of his descent from Amphitryon in the twenty-fifth generation, may, if he pleases, add as many more, and double that again, and our philosopher only laughs at his inability to do a larger sum. Such is the man at whom the vulgar scoff; he seems to them as if he could not mind his feet. 'That is very true, Socrates.' But when he tries to draw the quick-witted lawyer out of his pleas and rejoinders to the contemplation of absolute justice or injustice in their own nature, or from the popular praises of wealthy kings to the view of happiness and misery in themselves, or to the reasons why a man should seek after the one and avoid the other, then the situation is reversed; the little wretch turns giddy, and is ready to fall over the precipice; his utterance becomes thick, and he makes himself ridiculous, not to servant-maids, but to every man of liberal education. Such are the two pictures: the one of the philosopher and gentleman, who may be excused for not having learned how to make a bed, or cook up flatteries; the other, a serviceable knave, who hardly knows how to wear his cloak,—still less can he awaken harmonious thoughts or hymn virtue's praises.

'If the world, Socrates, were as ready to receive your words as I am, there would be greater peace and less evil among mankind.'

Evil, Theodorus, must ever remain in this world to be the antagonist of good, out of the way of the gods in heaven. Wherefore also we should fly away from ourselves to them; and to fly to them is to become like them; and to become like them is to become holy, just and true. But many live in the old wives' fable of appearances; they think that you should follow virtue in order that you may seem to be good. And yet the truth is, that God is righteous; and of men, he is most like him who is most righteous. To know this is wisdom; and in comparison of this the wisdom of the arts or the seeming wisdom of politicians is mean and common. The unrighteous man is apt to pride himself on his cunning; when others call him rogue, he says to himself: 'They only mean that I am one who deserves to live, and not a mere burden of the earth.' But he should reflect that his ignorance makes his condition worse than if he knew. For the penalty of injustice is not death or stripes, but the fatal necessity of becoming more and more unjust. Two patterns of life are set before him; the one blessed and divine, the other godless and wretched; and he is growing more and more like the one and unlike the other. He does not see that if he continues in his cunning, the place of innocence will not receive him after death. And yet if such a man has the courage to hear the argument out, he often becomes dissatisfied with himself, and has no more strength in him than a child.—But we have digressed enough.

'For my part, Socrates, I like the digressions better than the argument, because I understand them better.'

To return. When we left off, the Protagoreans and Heracliteans were maintaining that the ordinances of the State were just, while they lasted. But no one would maintain that the laws of the State were always good or expedient, although this may be the intention of them. For the expedient has to do with the future, about which we are liable to mistake. Now, would Protagoras maintain that man is the measure not only of the present and past, but of the future; and that there is no difference in the judgments of men about the future? Would an untrained man, for example, be as likely to know when he is going to have a fever, as the physician who attended him? And if they differ in opinion, which of them is likely to be right; or are they both right? Is not a vine-grower a better judge of a vintage which is not yet gathered, or a cook of a dinner which is in preparation, or Protagoras of the probable effect of a speech than an ordinary person? The last example speaks 'ad hominen.' For Protagoras would never have amassed a fortune if every man could judge of the future for himself. He is, therefore, compelled to admit that he is a measure; but I, who know nothing, am not equally convinced that I am. This is one way of refuting him; and he is refuted also by the authority which he attributes to the opinions of others, who deny his opinions. I am not equally sure that we can disprove the truth of immediate states of feeling. But this leads us to the doctrine of the universal flux, about which a battle-royal is always going on in the cities of Ionia. 'Yes; the Ephesians are downright mad about the flux; they cannot stop to argue with you, but are in perpetual motion, obedient to their text-books. Their restlessness is beyond expression, and if you ask any of them a question, they will not answer, but dart at you some unintelligible saying, and another and another, making no way either with themselves or with others; for nothing is fixed in them or their ideas,—they are at war with fixed principles.' I suppose, Theodorus, that you have never seen them in time of peace, when they discourse at leisure to their disciples? 'Disciples! they have none; they are a set of uneducated fanatics, and each of them says of the other that they have no knowledge. We must trust to ourselves, and not to them for the solution of the problem.' Well, the doctrine is old, being derived from the poets, who speak in a figure of Oceanus and Tethys; the truth was once concealed, but is now revealed by the superior wisdom of a later generation, and made intelligible to the cobbler, who, on hearing that all is in motion, and not some things only, as he ignorantly fancied, may be expected to fall down and worship his teachers. And the opposite doctrine must not be forgotten:—

'Alone being remains unmoved which is the name for all,'

as Parmenides affirms. Thus we are in the midst of the fray; both parties are dragging us to their side; and we are not certain which of them are in the right; and if neither, then we shall be in a ridiculous position, having to set up our own opinion against ancient and famous men.

Let us first approach the river-gods, or patrons of the flux.

When they speak of motion, must they not include two kinds of motion, change of place and change of nature?—And all things must be supposed to have both kinds of motion; for if not, the same things would be at rest and in motion, which is contrary to their theory. And did we not say, that all sensations arise thus: they move about between the agent and patient together with a perception, and the patient ceases to be a perceiving power and becomes a percipient, and the agent a quale instead of a quality; but neither has any absolute existence? But now we make the further discovery, that neither white or whiteness, nor any sense or sensation, can be predicated of anything, for they are in a perpetual flux. And therefore we must modify the doctrine of Theætetus and Protagoras, by asserting further that knowledge is and is not sensation; and of every-

Theætetus

thing we must say equally, that this is and is not, or becomes or becomes not. And still the word 'this' is not quite correct, for language fails in the attempt to express their meaning.

At the close of the discussion, Theodorus claims to be released from the argument, according to his agreement. But Theætetus insists that they shall proceed to consider the doctrine of rest. This is declined by Socrates, who has too much reverence for the great Parmenides lightly to attack him. (We shall find that he returns to the doctrine of rest in the Sophist; but at present he does not wish to be diverted from his main purpose, which is, to deliver Theætetus of his conception of knowledge.) He proceeds to interrogate him further. When he says that 'knowledge is in perception,' with what does he perceive? The first answer is, that he perceives sights with the eye, and sounds with the ear. This leads Socrates to make the reflection that nice distinctions of words are sometimes pedantic, but sometimes necessary; and he proposes in this case to substitute the word 'through' for 'with.' For the senses are not like the Trojan warriors in the horse, but have a common centre of perception, in which they all meet. This common principle is able to compare them with one another, and must therefore be distinct from them (compare Republic). And as there are facts of sense which are perceived through the organs of the body, there are also mathematical and other abstractions, such as sameness and difference, likeness and unlikeness, which the soul perceives by herself. Being is the most universal of these abstractions. The good and the beautiful are abstractions of another kind, which exist in relation and which above all others the mind perceives in herself, comparing within her past, present, and future. For example; we know a thing to be hard or soft by the touch, of which the perception is given at birth to men and animals. But the essence of hardness or softness, or the fact that this hardness is, and is the opposite of softness, is slowly learned by reflection and experience. Mere perception does not reach being, and therefore fails of truth; and therefore has no share in knowledge. But if so, knowledge is not perception. What then is knowledge? The mind, when occupied by herself with being, is said to have opinion—shall we say that 'Knowledge is true opinion'? But still an old difficulty recurs; we ask ourselves, 'How is false opinion possible?' This difficulty may be stated as follows:—

Either we know or do not know a thing (for the intermediate processes of learning and forgetting need not at present be considered); and in thinking or having an opinion, we must either know or not know that which we think, and we cannot know and be ignorant at the same time; we cannot confuse one thing which we do not know, with another thing which we do not know; nor can we think that which we do not know to be that which we know, or that which we know to be that which we do not know. And what other case is conceivable, upon the supposition that we either know or do not know all things? Let us try another answer in the sphere of being: 'When a man thinks, and thinks that which is not.' But would this hold in any parallel case? Can a man see and see nothing? or hear and hear nothing? or touch and touch nothing? Must he not see, hear, or touch some one existing thing? For if he thinks about nothing he does not think, and not thinking he cannot think falsely. And so the path of being is closed against us, as well as the path of knowledge. But may there not be 'heterodoxy,' or transference of opinion;—I mean, may not one thing be supposed to be another? Theætetus is confident that this must be 'the true falsehood,' when a man puts good for evil or evil for good. Socrates will not discourage him by attacking the paradoxical expression 'true falsehood,' but passes on. The new notion involves a process of thinking about two things, either together or alternately. And thinking is the conversing of the mind with herself, which is carried on in question and answer, until she no longer doubts, but determines and forms an opinion. And false opinion consists in saying to yourself, that one thing is another. But did you ever say to yourself, that good is evil, or evil good? Even in sleep, did you ever imagine that odd was even? Or did any man in his senses ever fancy that an ox was a horse, or that two are one? So that we can never think one thing to be another; for you must not meet me with the verbal quibble that one—eteron—is other—eteron (both 'one' and 'other' in Greek are called 'other'—eteron). He who has both the two things in his mind, cannot misplace them; and he who has only one of them in his mind, cannot misplace them—on either supposition transplacement is inconceivable.

But perhaps there may still be a sense in which we can think that which we do not know to be that which we know: e.g. Theætetus may know Socrates, but at a distance he may mistake another person for him. This process may be conceived by the help of an image. Let us suppose that every man has in his mind a block of wax of various qualities, the gift of Memory, the mother of the Muses; and on this he receives the seal or stamp of those sensations and perceptions which he wishes to remember. That which he succeeds in stamping is remembered and known by him as long as the impression lasts; but that, of which the impression is rubbed out or imperfectly made, is forgotten, and not known. No one can think one thing to be another, when he has the memorial or seal of both of these in his soul, and a sensible impression of neither; or when he knows one and does not know the other, and has no memorial or seal of the other; or when he knows neither; or when he perceives both, or one and not the other, or neither; or when he perceives and knows both, and identifies what he perceives with what he knows (this is still more impossible); or when he does not know one, and does not know and does not perceive the other; or does not perceive one, and does not know and does not perceive the other; or has no perception or knowledge of either—all these cases must be excluded. But he may err when he confuses what he knows or perceives, or what he perceives and does not know, with what he knows, or what he knows and perceives with what he knows and perceives.

Theætetus is unable to follow these distinctions; which Socrates proceeds to illustrate by examples, first of all remarking, that knowledge may exist without perception, and perception without knowledge. I may know Theodorus and Theætetus and not see them; I may see them, and not know them. 'That I understand.' But I could not mistake one for the other if I knew you both, and had no perception of either; or if I knew one only, and perceived neither; or if I knew and perceived neither, or in any other of the excluded cases. The only possibility of error is: 1st, when knowing you and Theodorus, and having the impression of both of you on the waxen block, I, seeing you both imperfectly and at a distance, put the foot in the wrong shoe—that is to say, put the seal or stamp on the wrong object: or 2ndly, when knowing both of you I only see one;

or when, seeing and knowing you both, I fail to identify the impression and the object. But there could be no error when perception and knowledge correspond.

The waxen block in the heart of a man's soul, as I may say in the words of Homer, who played upon the words ker and keros, may be smooth and deep, and large enough, and then the signs are clearly marked and lasting, and do not get confused. But in the 'hairy heart,' as the all-wise poet sings, when the wax is muddy or hard or moist, there is a corresponding confusion and want of retentiveness; in the muddy and impure there is indistinctness, and still more in the hard, for there the impressions have no depth of wax, and in the moist they are too soon effaced. Yet greater is the indistinctness when they are all jolted together in a little soul, which is narrow and has no room. These are the sort of natures which have false opinion; from stupidity they see and hear and think amiss; and this is falsehood and ignorance. Error, then, is a confusion of thought and sense.

Theætetus is delighted with this explanation. But Socrates has no sooner found the new solution than he sinks into a fit of despondency. For an objection occurs to him:—May there not be errors where there is no confusion of mind and sense? e.g. in numbers. No one can confuse the man whom he has in his thoughts with the horse which he has in his thoughts, but he may err in the addition of five and seven. And observe that these are purely mental conceptions. Thus we are involved once more in the dilemma of saying, either that there is no such thing as false opinion, or that a man knows what he does not know.

We are at our wit's end, and may therefore be excused for making a bold diversion. All this time we have been repeating the words 'know,' 'understand,' yet we do not know what knowledge is. 'Why, Socrates, how can you argue at all without using them?' Nay, but the true hero of dialectic would have forbidden me to use them until I had explained them. And I must explain them now. The verb 'to know' has two senses, to have and to possess knowledge, and I distinguish 'having' from 'possessing.' A man may possess a garment which he does not wear; or he may have wild birds in an aviary; these in one sense he possesses, and in another he has none of them. Let this aviary be an image of the mind, as the waxen block was; when we are young, the aviary is empty; after a time the birds are put in; for under this figure we may describe different forms of knowledge;—there are some of them in groups, and some single, which are flying about everywhere; and let us suppose a hunt after the science of odd and even, or some other science. The possession of the birds is clearly not the same as the having them in the hand. And the original chase of them is not the same as taking them in the hand when they are already caged.

This distinction between use and possession saves us from the absurdity of supposing that we do not know what we know, because we may know in one sense, i.e. possess, what we do not know in another, i.e. use. But have we not escaped one difficulty only to encounter a greater? For how can the exchange of two kinds of knowledge ever become false opinion? As well might we suppose that ignorance could make a man know, or that blindness could make him see. Theætetus suggests that in the aviary there may be flying about mock birds, or forms of ignorance, and we put forth our hands and grasp ignorance, when we are intending to grasp knowledge. But how can he who knows the forms of knowledge and the forms of ignorance imagine one to be the other? Is there some other form of knowledge which distinguishes them? and another, and another? Thus we go round and round in a circle and make no progress.

All this confusion arises out of our attempt to explain false opinion without having explained knowledge. What then is knowledge? Theætetus repeats that knowledge is true opinion. But this seems to be refuted by the instance of orators and judges. For surely the orator cannot convey a true knowledge of crimes at which the judges were not present; he can only persuade them, and the judge may form a true opinion and truly judge. But if true opinion were knowledge they could not have judged without knowledge.

Once more. Theætetus offers a definition which he has heard: Knowledge is true opinion accompanied by definition or explanation. Socrates has had a similar dream, and has further heard that the first elements are names only, and that definition or explanation begins when they are combined; the letters are unknown, the syllables or combinations are known. But this new hypothesis when tested by the letters of the alphabet is found to break down. The first syllable of

Socrates' name is SO. But what is SO? Two letters, S and O, a sibilant and a vowel, of which no further explanation can be given. And how can any one be ignorant of either of them, and yet know both of them? There is, however, another alternative:—We may suppose that the syllable has a separate form or idea distinct from the letters or parts. The all of the parts may not be the whole. Theætetus is very much inclined to adopt this suggestion, but when interrogated by Socrates he is unable to draw any distinction between the whole and all the parts. And if the syllables have no parts, then they are those original elements of which there is no explanation. But how can the syllable be known if the letter remains unknown? In learning to read as children, we are first taught the letters and then the syllables. And in music, the notes, which are the letters, have a much more distinct meaning to us than the combination of them.

Once more, then, we must ask the meaning of the statement, that 'Knowledge is right opinion, accompanied by explanation or definition.' Explanation may mean, (1) the reflection or expression of a man's thoughts—but every man who is not deaf and dumb is able to express his thoughts—or (2) the enumeration of the elements of which anything is composed. A man may have a true opinion about a waggon, but then, and then only, has he knowledge of a waggon when he is able to enumerate the hundred planks of Hesiod. Or he may know the syllables of the name Theætetus, but not the letters; yet not until he knows both can he be said to have knowledge as well as opinion. But on the other hand he may know the syllable 'The' in the name Theætetus, yet he may be mistaken about the same syllable in the name Theodorus, and in learning to read we often make such mistakes. And even if he could write out all the letters and syllables of your name in order, still he would only have right opinion. Yet there may be a third meaning of the definition, besides the image or expression of the mind, and the enumeration of the elements, viz. (3) perception of difference.

For example, I may see a man who has eyes, nose, and mouth;— that will not distinguish him from any other man. Or he may have a snub-nose and prominent eyes;—that will not distinguish him from myself and you and others who are like me. But when I see a certain kind of snub-nosedness, then I recognize Theætetus. And having this sign of difference, I have knowledge. But have I knowledge or opinion of this difference; if I have only opinion I have not knowledge; if I have knowledge we assume a disputed term; for knowledge will have to be defined as right opinion with knowledge of difference.

And so, Theætetus, knowledge is neither perception nor true opinion, nor yet definition accompanying true opinion. And I have shown that the children of your brain are not worth rearing. Are you still in labour, or have you brought all you have to say about knowledge to the birth? If you have any more thoughts, you will be the better for having got rid of these; or if you have none, you will be the better for not fancying that you know what you do not know. Observe the limits of my art, which, like my mother's, is an art of midwifery; I do not pretend to compare with the good and wise of this and other ages.

And now I go to meet Meletus at the porch of the King Archon; but to-morrow I shall hope to see you again, Theodorus, at this place.

* * *

I. The saying of Theætetus, that 'Knowledge is sensible perception,' may be assumed to be a current philosophical opinion of the age. 'The ancients,' as Aristotle (De Anim.) says, citing a verse of Empedocles, 'affirmed knowledge to be the same as perception.' We may now examine these words, first, with reference to their place in the history of philosophy, and secondly, in relation to modern speculations.

(a) In the age of Socrates the mind was passing from the object to the subject. The same impulse which a century before had led men to form conceptions of the world, now led them to frame general notions of the human faculties and feelings, such as memory, opinion, and the like. The simplest of these is sensation, or sensible perception, by which Plato seems to mean the generalized notion of feelings and impressions of sense, without determining whether they are conscious or not.

The theory that 'Knowledge is sensible perception' is the antithesis of that which derives knowledge from the mind (Theaet.), or which assumes the existence of ideas independent of the mind (Parm.). Yet from their extreme abstraction these theories do not represent the opposite poles of thought in the same way that the corresponding differences would in modern philosophy. The most ideal and the most sensational have a tendency to pass into one another; Heracleitus, like his great successor Hegel, has both aspects. The Eleatic isolation of Being and the Megarian or Cynic isolation of individuals are placed in the same class by Plato (Soph.); and the same principle which is the symbol of motion to one mind is the symbol of rest to another. The Atomists, who are sometimes regarded as the Materialists of Plato, denied the reality of sensation. And in the ancient as well as the modern world there were reactions from theory to experience, from ideas to sense. This is a point of view from which the philosophy of sensation presented great attraction to the ancient thinker. Amid the conflict of ideas and the variety of opinions, the impression of sense remained certain and uniform. Hardness, softness, cold, heat, etc. are not absolutely the same to different persons, but the art of measuring could at any rate reduce them all to definite natures (Republic). Thus the doctrine that knowledge is perception supplies or seems to supply a firm standing ground. Like the other notions of the earlier Greek philosophy, it was held in a very simple way, without much basis of reasoning, and without suggesting the questions which naturally arise in our own minds on the same subject.

(b) The fixedness of impressions of sense furnishes a link of connexion between ancient and modern philosophy. The modern thinker often repeats the parallel axiom, 'All knowledge is experience.' He means to say that the outward and not the inward is both the original source and the final criterion of truth, because the outward can be observed and analyzed; the inward is only known by external results, and is dimly perceived by each man for himself. In what does this differ from the saying of Theætetus? Chiefly in this—that the modern term 'experience,' while implying a point of departure in sense and a return to sense, also includes all the processes of reasoning and imagination which have intervened. The necessary connexion between them by no means affords a measure of the relative degree of importance which is to be ascribed to either element.

For the inductive portion of any science may be small, as in mathematics or ethics, compared with that which the mind has attained by reasoning and reflection on a very few facts.

II. The saying that 'All knowledge is sensation' is identified by Plato with the Protagorean thesis that 'Man is the measure of all things.' The interpretation which Protagoras himself is supposed to give of these latter words is: 'Things are to me as they appear to me, and to you as they appear to you.' But there remains still an ambiguity both in the text and in the explanation, which has to be cleared up. Did Protagoras merely mean to assert the relativity of knowledge to the human mind? Or did he mean to deny that there is an objective standard of truth?

These two questions have not been always clearly distinguished; the relativity of knowledge has been sometimes confounded with uncertainty. The untutored mind is apt to suppose that objects exist independently of the human faculties, because they really exist independently of the faculties of any individual. In the same way, knowledge appears to be a body of truths stored up in books, which when once ascertained are independent of the discoverer. Further consideration shows us that these truths are not really independent of the mind; there is an adaptation of one to the other, of the eye to the object of sense, of the mind to the conception. There would be no world, if there neither were nor ever had been any one to perceive the world. A slight effort of reflection enables us to understand this; but no effort of reflection will enable us to pass beyond the limits of our own faculties, or to imagine the relation or adaptation of objects to the mind to be different from that of which we have experience. There are certain laws of language and logic to which we are compelled to conform, and to which our ideas naturally adapt themselves; and we can no more get rid of them than we can cease to be ourselves. The absolute and infinite, whether explained as self-existence, or as the totality of human thought, or as the Divine nature, if known to us at all, cannot escape from the category of relation.

But because knowledge is subjective or relative to the mind, we are not to suppose that we are therefore deprived of any of the tests or criteria of truth. One man still remains wiser than another, a more accurate observer and relater of facts, a truer measure of the proportions of knowledge. The nature of testimony is not altered, nor the verification of causes by prescribed methods less certain. Again, the truth must often come to a man through others, according to the measure of his capacity and education. But neither does this affect the testimony, whether written or oral, which he knows by experience to be trustworthy. He cannot escape from the laws of his own mind; and he cannot escape from the further accident of being dependent for his knowledge on others. But still this is no reason why he should always be in doubt; of many personal, of many historical and scientific facts he may be absolutely assured. And having such a mass of acknowledged truth in the mathematical and physical, not to speak of the moral sciences, the moderns have certainly no reason to acquiesce in the statement that truth is appearance only, or that there is no difference between appearance and truth.

The relativity of knowledge is a truism to us, but was a great psychological discovery in the fifth century before Christ. Of this discovery, the first distinct assertion is contained in the thesis of Protagoras. Probably he had no intention either of denying or affirming an objective standard of truth. He did not consider whether man in the higher or man in the lower sense was a 'measure of all things.' Like other great thinkers, he was absorbed with one idea, and that idea was the absoluteness of perception. Like Socrates, he seemed to see that philosophy must be brought back from 'nature' to 'truth,' from the world to man. But he did not stop to analyze whether he meant 'man' in the concrete or man in the abstract, any man or some men, 'quod semper quod ubique' or individual private judgment. Such an analysis lay beyond his sphere of thought; the age before Socrates had not arrived at these distinctions. Like the Cynics, again, he discarded knowledge in any higher sense than perception. For 'truer' or 'wiser' he substituted the word 'better,' and is not unwilling to admit that both states and individuals are capable of practical improvement. But this improvement does not arise from intellectual enlightenment, nor yet from the exertion of the will, but from a change of circumstances and impressions; and he who can effect this change in himself or others may be deemed a philosopher. In the mode of effecting it, while agreeing with Socrates and the Cynics in the importance which he attaches to practical life, he is at variance with both of them. To suppose that practice can be divorced from speculation, or that we may do good without caring about truth, is by no means singular, either in philosophy or life. The singularity of this, as of some other (so-called) sophistical doctrines, is the frankness with which they are avowed, instead of being veiled, as in modern times, under ambiguous and convenient phrases.

Plato appears to treat Protagoras much as he himself is treated by Aristotle; that is to say, he does not attempt to understand him from his own point of view. But he entangles him in the meshes of a more advanced logic. To which Protagoras is supposed to reply by Megarian quibbles, which destroy logic, 'Not only man, but each man, and each man at each moment.' In the arguments about sight and memory there is a palpable unfairness which is worthy of the great 'brainless brothers,' Euthydemus and Dionysodorus, and may be compared with the egkekalummenos ('obvelatus') of Eubulides. For he who sees with one eye only cannot be truly said both to see and not to see; nor is memory, which is liable to forget, the immediate knowledge to which Protagoras applies the term. Theodorus justly charges Socrates with going beyond the truth; and Protagoras has equally right on his side when he protests against Socrates arguing from the common use of words, which 'the vulgar pervert in all manner of ways.'

III. The theory of Protagoras is connected by Aristotle as well as Plato with the flux of Heracleitus. But Aristotle is only following Plato, and Plato, as we have already seen, did not mean to imply that such a connexion was admitted by Protagoras himself. His metaphysical genius saw or seemed to see a common tendency in them, just as the modern historian of ancient philosophy might perceive a parallelism between two thinkers of which they were probably unconscious themselves. We must remember throughout that Plato is not speaking of Heracleitus, but of the Heracliteans, who succeeded him; nor of the great original ideas of the master, but of the Eristic into which they had degenerated a hundred years later. There is nothing in the fragments of Heracleitus which at all justifies Plato's account of him. His philosophy may be resolved into two elements—first, change, secondly, law or measure pervading the change: these he saw everywhere, and often expressed in strange mythological symbols. But he has no analysis of sensible perception such as Plato attributes to him; nor is there any reason to suppose that he pushed his philosophy into that absolute negation in which Heracliteanism was sunk in the age of Plato. He never said that 'change means every sort of change;' and he expressly distinguished between 'the general and particular understanding.' Like a poet, he surveyed the elements of mythology, nature, thought, which lay before him, and sometimes by the light of genius he saw or seemed to see a mysterious principle working behind them. But as has been the case with other great philosophers, and with Plato and Aristotle themselves, what was really permanent and original could not be understood by the next generation, while a perverted logic carried out his chance expressions with an illogical consistency. His simple and noble thoughts, like those of the great Eleatic, soon degenerated into a mere strife of words. And when thus reduced to mere words, they seem to have exercised a far wider influence in the cities of Ionia (where the people 'were mad about them') than in the lifetime of Heracleitus—a phenomenon which, though at first sight singular, is not without a parallel in the history of philosophy and theology.

It is this perverted form of the Heraclitean philosophy which is supposed to effect the final overthrow of Protagorean sensationalism. For if all things are changing at every moment, in all sorts of ways, then there is nothing fixed or defined at all, and therefore no sensible perception, nor any true word by which that or anything else can be described. Of course Protagoras would not have admitted the justice of this argument any more than Heracleitus would have acknowledged the 'uneducated fanatics' who appealed to his writings. He might have said, 'The excellent Socrates has first confused me with Heracleitus, and Heracleitus with his Ephesian successors, and has then disproved the existence both of knowledge and sensation. But I am not responsible for what I never said, nor will I admit that my common-sense account of knowledge can be overthrown by unintelligible Heraclitean paradoxes.'

IV. Still at the bottom of the arguments there remains a truth, that knowledge is something more than sensible perception;—this alone would not distinguish man from a tadpole. The absoluteness of sensations at each moment destroys the very consciousness of sensations (compare Phileb.), or the power of comparing them. The senses are not mere holes in a 'Trojan horse,' but the organs of a presiding nature, in which they meet. A great advance has been made in psychology when the senses are recognized as organs of sense, and we are admitted to see or feel 'through them' and not 'by them,' a distinction of words which, as Socrates observes, is by no means pedantic. A still further step has been made when the most abstract notions, such as Being and Not-being, sameness and difference, unity and plurality, are acknowledged to be the creations of the mind herself, working upon the feelings or impressions of sense. In this manner Plato describes the process of acquiring them, in the words 'Knowledge consists not in the feelings or affections (pathemasi), but in the process of reasoning about them (sullogismo).' Here, is in the Parmenides, he means something not really different from generalization. As in the Sophist, he is laying the foundation of a rational psychology, which is to supersede the Platonic reminiscence of Ideas as well as the Eleatic Being and the individualism of Megarians and Cynics.

V. Having rejected the doctrine that 'Knowledge is perception,' we now proceed to look for a definition of knowledge in the sphere of opinion. But here we are met by a singular difficulty: How is false opinion possible? For we must either know or not know that which is presented to the mind or to sense. We of course should answer at once: 'No; the alternative is not necessary, for there may be degrees of knowledge; and we may know and have forgotten, or we may be learning, or we may have a general but not a particular knowledge, or we may know but not be able to explain;' and many other ways may be imagined in which we know and do not know at the same time. But these answers belong to a later stage of metaphysical discussion; whereas the difficulty in question naturally arises owing to the childhood of the human mind, like the parallel difficulty respecting Not-being. Men had only recently arrived at the notion of opinion; they could not at once define the true and pass beyond into the false. The very word doxa was full of ambiguity, being sometimes, as in the Eleatic philosophy, applied to the sensible world, and again used in the more ordinary sense of opinion. There is no connexion between sensible appearance and probability, and yet both of them met in the word doxa, and could hardly be disengaged from one another in the mind of the Greek living in the fifth or fourth century B.C. To this was often added, as at the end of the fifth book of the Republic, the idea of relation, which is equally distinct from either of them; also a fourth notion, the conclusion of the dialectical process, the making up of the mind after she has been 'talking to herself' (Theat.).

We are not then surprised that the sphere of opinion and of Not-being should be a dusky, half-lighted place (Republic), belonging neither to the old world of sense and imagination, nor to the new world of reflection and reason. Plato attempts to clear up this darkness. In his accustomed manner he passes from the lower to the higher, without omitting the intermediate stages. This appears to be the reason why he seeks for the definition of knowledge first in the sphere of opinion. Hereafter we shall find that something more than opinion is required.

False opinion is explained by Plato at first as a confusion of mind and sense, which arises when the impression on the mind does not correspond to the impression made on the senses. It is obvious that this explanation (supposing the distinction between impressions on the mind and impressions on the senses to be admitted) does not account for all forms of error; and Plato has excluded himself from the consideration of the greater number, by designedly omitting the intermediate processes of learning and forgetting; nor does he include fallacies in the use of language or erroneous inferences. But he is struck by one possibility of error, which is not covered by his theory, viz. errors in arithmetic. For in numbers and calculation there is no combination of thought and sense, and yet errors may often happen. Hence he is led to discard the explanation which might nevertheless have been supposed to hold good (for anything which he says to the contrary) as a rationale of error, in the case of facts derived from sense.

Another attempt is made to explain false opinion by assigning to error a sort of positive existence. But error or ignorance is essentially negative—a not-knowing; if we knew an error, we should be no longer in error. We may veil our difficulty under figures of speech, but these, although telling arguments with the multitude, can never be the real foundation of a system of psychology. Only they lead us to dwell upon mental phenomena which if expressed in an abstract form would not be realized by us at all. The figure of the mind receiving impressions is one of those images which have rooted themselves for ever in language. It may or may not be a 'gracious aid' to thought; but it cannot be got rid of. The other figure of the enclosure is also remarkable as affording the first hint of universal all-pervading ideas,—a notion further carried out in the Sophist. This is implied in the birds, some in flocks, some solitary, which fly about anywhere and everywhere. Plato discards both figures, as not really solving the question which to us appears so simple: 'How do we make mistakes?' The failure of the enquiry seems to show that we should return to knowledge, and begin with that; and we may afterwards proceed, with a better hope of success, to the examination of opinion.

But is true opinion really distinct from knowledge? The difference between these he seeks to establish by an argument, which to us appears singular and unsatisfactory. The existence of true opinion is proved by the rhetoric of the law courts, which cannot give knowledge, but may give true opinion. The rhetorician cannot put the judge or juror in possession of all the facts which prove an act of violence, but he may truly persuade them of the commission of such an act. Here the idea of true opinion seems to be a right conclusion from imperfect knowledge. But the correctness of such an opinion will be purely accidental; and is really the effect of one man, who has the means of knowing, persuading another who has not. Plato would have done better if he had said that true opinion was a contradiction in terms.

Assuming the distinction between knowledge and opinion, Theætetus, in answer to Socrates, proceeds to define knowledge as true opinion, with definite or rational explanation. This Socrates identifies with another and different theory, of those who assert that knowledge first begins with a proposition.

The elements may be perceived by sense, but they are names, and cannot be defined. When we assign to them some predicate, they first begin to have a meaning (onomaton sumploke logou ousia). This seems equivalent to saying, that the individuals of sense become the subject of knowledge when they are regarded as they are in nature in relation to other individuals.

Yet we feel a difficulty in following this new hypothesis. For must not opinion be equally expressed in a proposition? The difference between true and false opinion is not the difference between the particular and the universal, but between the true universal and the false. Thought may be as much at fault as sight. When we place individuals under a class, or assign to them attributes, this is not knowledge, but a very rudimentary process of thought; the first generalization of all, without which language would be impossible. And has Plato kept altogether clear of a confusion, which the analogous word logos tends to create, of a proposition and a definition? And is not the confusion increased by the use of the analogous term 'elements,' or 'letters'? For there is no real resemblance between the relation of letters to a syllable, and of the terms to a proposition.

Plato, in the spirit of the Megarian philosophy, soon discovers a flaw in the explanation. For how can we know a compound of which the simple elements are unknown to us? Can two unknowns make a known? Can a whole be something different from the parts? The answer of experience is that they can; for we may know a compound, which we are unable to analyze into its elements; and all the parts, when united, may be more than all the parts separated: e.g. the number four, or any other number, is more than the units which are contained in it; any chemical compound is more than and different from the simple elements. But ancient philosophy in this, as in many other instances, proceeding by the path of mental analysis, was perplexed by doubts which warred against the plainest facts.

Three attempts to explain the new definition of knowledge still remain to be considered. They all of them turn on the explanation of logos. The first account of the meaning of the word is the reflection of thought in speech—a sort of nominalism 'La science est une langue bien faite.' But anybody who is not dumb can say what he thinks; therefore mere speech cannot be knowledge. And yet we may observe, that there is in this explanation an element of truth which is not recognized by Plato; viz. that truth and thought are inseparable from language, although mere expression in words is not truth. The second explanation of logos is the enumeration of the elementary parts of the complex whole. But this is only definition accompanied with right opinion, and does not yet attain to the certainty of knowledge. Plato does not mention the greater objection, which is, that the enumeration of particulars is endless; such a definition would be based on no principle, and would not help us at all in gaining a common idea. The third is the best explanation,—the possession of a characteristic mark, which seems to answer to the logical definition by genus and difference. But this, again, is equally necessary for right opinion; and we have already determined, although not on very satisfactory grounds, that knowledge must be distinguished from opinion. A better distinction is drawn between them in the Timaeus. They might be opposed as philosophy and rhetoric, and as conversant respectively with necessary and contingent matter. But no true idea of the nature of either of them, or of their relation to one another, could be framed until science obtained a content. The ancient philosophers in the age of Plato thought of science only as pure abstraction, and to this opinion stood in no relation.

Like Theætetus, we have attained to no definite result. But an interesting phase of ancient philosophy has passed before us. And the negative result is not to be despised. For on certain subjects, and in certain states of knowledge, the work of negation or clearing the ground must go on, perhaps for a generation, before the new structure can begin to rise. Plato saw the necessity of combating the illogical logic of the Megarians and Eristics. For the completion of the edifice, he makes preparation in the Theætetus, and crowns the work in the Sophist.

Many (1) fine expressions, and (2) remarks full of wisdom, (3) also germs of a metaphysic of the future, are scattered up and down in the dialogue. Such, for example, as (1) the comparison of Theætetus' progress in learning to the 'noiseless flow of a river of oil'; the satirical touch, 'flavouring a sauce or fawning speech'; or the remarkable expression, 'full of impure dialectic'; or the lively images under which the argument is described,—'the flood of arguments pouring in,' the fresh discussions 'bursting in like a band of revellers.' (2) As illustrations of the second head, may be cited the remark of Socrates, that 'distinctions of words, although sometimes pedantic, are also necessary'; or the fine touch in the character of the lawyer, that 'dangers came upon him when the tenderness of youth was unequal to them'; or the description of the manner in which the spirit is broken in a wicked man who listens to reproof until he becomes like a child; or the punishment of the wicked, which is not physical suffering, but the perpetual companionship of evil (compare Gorgias); or the saying, often repeated by Aristotle and others, that 'philosophy begins in wonder, for Iris is the child of Thaumas'; or the superb contempt with which the philosopher takes down the pride of wealthy landed proprietors by comparison of the whole earth. (3) Important metaphysical ideas are: a. the conception of thought, as the mind talking to herself; b. the notion of a common sense, developed further by Aristotle, and the explicit declaration, that the mind gains her conceptions of Being, sameness, number, and the like, from reflection on herself; c. the excellent distinction of Theætetus (which Socrates, speaking with emphasis, 'leaves to grow') between seeing the forms or hearing the sounds of words in a foreign language, and understanding the meaning of them; and d. the distinction of Socrates himself between 'having' and 'possessing' knowledge, in which the answer to the whole discussion appears to be contained.

* * *

There is a difference between ancient and modern psychology, and we have a difficulty in explaining one in the terms of the other. To us the inward and outward sense and the inward and outward worlds of which they are the organs are parted by a wall, and appear as if they could never be confounded. The mind is endued with faculties, habits, instincts, and a personality or consciousness in which they are bound together. Over against these are placed forms, colours, external bodies coming into contact with our own body. We speak of a subject which is ourselves, of an object which is all the rest. These are separable in thought, but united in any act of sensation, reflection, or volition. As there are various degrees in which the mind may enter into or be abstracted from the operations of sense, so there are various points at which this separation or union may be supposed to occur. And within the sphere of mind the analogy of sense reappears; and we distinguish not only external objects, but objects of will and of knowledge which we contrast with them. These again are comprehended in a higher object, which reunites with the subject. A multitude of abstractions are created by the efforts of successive thinkers which become logical determinations; and they have to be arranged in order, before the scheme of thought is complete. The framework of the human intellect is not the peculium of an individual, but the joint work of many who are of all ages and countries. What we are in mind is due, not merely to our physical, but to our mental antecedents which we trace in history, and more especially in the history of philosophy. Nor can mental phenomena be truly explained either by physiology or by the observation of consciousness apart from their history. They have a growth of their own, like the growth of a flower, a tree, a human being. They may be conceived as of themselves constituting a common mind, and having a sort of personal identity in which they coexist.

So comprehensive is modern psychology, seeming to aim at constructing anew the entire world of thought. And prior to or simultaneously with this construction a negative process has to be carried on, a clearing away of useless abstractions which we have inherited from the past. Many erroneous conceptions of the mind derived from former philosophies have found their way into language, and we with difficulty disengage ourselves from them. Mere figures of speech have unconsciously influenced the minds of great thinkers. Also there are some distinctions, as, for example, that of the will and of the reason, and of the moral and intellectual faculties, which are carried further than is justified by experience. Any separation of things which we cannot see or exactly define, though it may be necessary, is a fertile source of error. The division of the mind into faculties or powers or virtues is too deeply rooted in language to be got rid of, but it gives a false impression. For if we reflect on ourselves we see that all our faculties easily pass into one another, and are bound together in a single mind or consciousness; but this mental unity is apt to be concealed from us by the distinctions of language.

A profusion of words and ideas has obscured rather than enlightened mental science. It is hard to say how many fallacies have arisen from the representation of the mind as a box, as a 'tabula rasa,' a book, a mirror, and the like. It is remarkable how Plato in the Theætetus, after having indulged in the figure of the waxen tablet and the decoy, afterwards discards them. The mind is also represented by another class of images, as the spring of a watch, a motive power, a breath, a stream, a succession of points or moments. As Plato remarks in the Cratylus, words expressive of motion as well as of rest are employed to describe the faculties and operations of the mind; and in these there is contained another store of fallacies. Some shadow or reflection of the body seems always to adhere to our thoughts about ourselves, and mental processes are hardly distinguished in language from bodily ones. To see or perceive are used indifferently of both; the words intuition, moral sense, common sense, the mind's eye, are figures of speech transferred from one to the other. And many other words used in early poetry or in sacred writings to express the works of mind have a materialistic sound; for old mythology was allied to sense, and the distinction of matter and mind had not as yet arisen. Thus materialism receives an illusive aid from language; and both in philosophy and religion the imaginary figure or association easily takes the place of real knowledge.

Again, there is the illusion of looking into our own minds as if our thoughts or feelings were written down in a book. This is another figure of speech, which might be appropriately termed 'the fallacy of the looking-glass.' We cannot look at the mind unless we have the eye which sees, and we can only look, not into, but out of the mind at the thoughts, words, actions of ourselves and others. What we dimly recognize within us is not experience, but rather the suggestion of an experience, which we may gather, if we will, from the observation of the world. The memory has but a feeble recollection of what we were saying or doing a few weeks or a few months ago, and still less of what we were thinking or feeling. This is one among many reasons why there is so little self-knowledge among mankind; they do not carry with them the thought of what they are or have been. The so-called 'facts of consciousness' are equally evanescent; they are facts which nobody ever saw, and which can neither be defined nor described. Of the three laws of thought the first (All A = A) is an identical proposition—that is to say, a mere word or symbol claiming to be a proposition: the two others (Nothing can be A and not A, and Everything is either A or not A) are untrue, because they exclude degrees and also the mixed modes and double aspects under which truth is so often presented to us. To assert that man is man is unmeaning; to say that he is free or necessary and cannot be both is a half truth only. These are a few of the entanglements which impede the natural course of human thought. Lastly, there is the fallacy which lies still deeper, of regarding the individual mind apart from the universal, or either, as a self-existent entity apart from the ideas which are contained in them.

In ancient philosophies the analysis of the mind is still rudimentary and imperfect. It naturally began with an effort to disengage the universal from sense—this was the first lifting up of the mist. It wavered between object and subject, passing imperceptibly from one or Being to mind and thought. Appearance in the outward object was for a time indistinguishable from opinion in the subject. At length mankind spoke of knowing as well as of opining or perceiving. But when the word 'knowledge' was found how was it to be explained or defined? It was not an error, it was a step in the right direction, when Protagoras said that 'Man is the measure of all things,' and that 'All knowledge is perception.' This was the subjective which corresponded to the objective 'All is flux.' But the thoughts of men deepened, and soon they began to be aware that knowledge was neither sense, nor yet opinion—with or without explanation; nor the expression of thought, nor the enumeration of parts, nor the addition of characteristic marks. Motion and rest were equally ill adapted to express its nature, although both must in some sense be attributed to it; it might be described more truly as the mind conversing with herself; the discourse of reason; the hymn of dialectic, the science of relations, of ideas, of the so-called arts and sciences, of the one, of the good, of the all:—this is the way along which Plato is leading us in his later dialogues. In its higher signification it was the knowledge, not of men, but of gods, perfect and all sufficing:—like other ideals always passing out of sight, and nevertheless present to the mind of Aristotle as well as Plato, and the reality to which they were both tending. For Aristotle as well as Plato would in modern phraseology have been termed a mystic; and like him would have defined the higher philosophy to be 'Knowledge of being or essence,'—words to which in our own day we have a difficulty in attaching a meaning.

Yet, in spite of Plato and his followers, mankind have again and again returned to a sensational philosophy. As to some of the early thinkers, amid the fleetings of sensible objects, ideas alone seemed to be fixed, so to a later generation amid the fluctuation of philosophical opinions the only fixed points appeared to be outward objects. Any pretence of knowledge which went beyond them implied logical processes, of the correctness of which they had no assurance and which at best were only probable. The mind, tired of wandering, sought to rest on firm ground; when the idols of philosophy and language were stripped off, the perception of outward objects alone remained. The ancient Epicureans never asked whether the comparison of these with one another did not involve principles of another kind which were above and beyond them. In like manner the modern inductive philosophy forgot to enquire into the meaning of experience, and did not attempt to form a conception of outward objects apart from the mind, or of the mind apart from them. Soon objects of sense were merged in sensations and feelings, but feelings and sensations were still unanalyzed. At last we return to the doctrine attributed by Plato to Protagoras, that the mind is only a succession of momentary perceptions. At this point the modern philosophy of experience forms an alliance with ancient scepticism.

The higher truths of philosophy and religion are very far removed from sense. Admitting that, like all other knowledge, they are derived from experience, and that experience is ultimately resolvable into facts which come to us through the eye and ear, still their origin is a mere accident which has nothing to do with their true nature. They are universal and unseen; they belong to all times—past, present, and future. Any worthy notion of mind or reason includes them. The proof of them is, 1st, their comprehensiveness and consistency with one another; 2ndly, their agreement with history and experience. But sensation is of the present only, is isolated, is and is not in successive moments. It takes the passing hour as it comes, following the lead of the eye or ear instead of the command of reason. It is a faculty which man has in common with the animals, and in which he is inferior to many of them. The importance of the senses in us is that they are the apertures of the mind, doors and windows through which we take in and make our own the materials of knowledge. Regarded in any other point of view sensation is of all mental acts the most trivial and superficial. Hence the term 'sensational' is rightly used to express what is shallow in thought and feeling.

We propose in what follows, first of all, like Plato in the Theætetus, to analyse sensation, and secondly to trace the connexion between theories of sensation and a sensational or Epicurean philosophy.

Paragraph I. We, as well as the ancients, speak of the five senses, and of a sense, or common sense, which is the abstraction of them. The term 'sense' is also used metaphorically, both in ancient and modern philosophy, to express the operations of the mind which are immediate or intuitive. Of the five senses, two—the sight and the hearing—are of a more subtle and complex nature, while two others—the smell and the taste—seem to be only more refined varieties of touch. All of them are passive, and by this are distinguished from the active faculty of speech: they receive impressions, but do not produce them, except in so far as they are objects of sense themselves.

Physiology speaks to us of the wonderful apparatus of nerves, muscles, tissues, by which the senses are enabled to fulfil their functions. It traces the connexion, though imperfectly, of the bodily organs with the operations of the mind. Of these latter, it seems rather to know the conditions than the causes. It can prove to us that without the brain we cannot think, and that without the eye we cannot see: and yet there is far more in thinking and seeing than is given by the brain and the eye. It observes the 'concomitant variations' of body and mind. Psychology, on the other hand, treats of the same subject regarded from another point of view. It speaks of the relation of the senses to one another; it shows how they meet the mind; it analyzes the transition from sense to thought. The one describes their nature as apparent to the outward eye; by the other they are regarded only as the instruments of the mind. It is in this latter point of view that we propose to consider them.

The simplest sensation involves an unconscious or nascent operation of the mind; it implies objects of sense, and objects of sense have differences of form, number, colour. But the conception of an object without us, or the power of discriminating numbers, forms, colours, is not given by the sense, but by the mind. A mere sensation does not attain to distinctness: it is a confused impression, sugkechumenon ti, as Plato says (Republic), until number introduces light and order into the confusion. At what point confusion becomes distinctness is a question of degree which cannot be precisely determined. The distant object, the undefined notion, come out into relief as we approach them or attend to them. Or we may assist the analysis by attempting to imagine the world first dawning upon the eye of the infant or of a person newly restored to sight. Yet even with them the mind as well as the eye opens or enlarges. For all three are inseparably bound together—the object would be nowhere and nothing, if not perceived by the sense, and the sense would have no power of distinguishing without the mind.

But prior to objects of sense there is a third nature in which they are contained—that is to say, space, which may be explained in various ways. It is the element which surrounds them; it is the vacuum or void which they leave or occupy when passing from one portion of space to another. It might be described in the language of ancient philosophy, as 'the Not-being' of objects. It is a negative idea which in the course of ages has become positive. It is originally derived from the contemplation of the world without us—the boundless earth or sea, the vacant heaven, and is therefore acquired chiefly through the sense of sight: to the blind the conception of space is feeble and inadequate, derived for the most part from touch or from the descriptions of others. At first it appears to be continuous; afterwards we perceive it to be capable of division by lines or points, real or imaginary. By the help of mathematics we form another idea of space, which is altogether independent of experience. Geometry teaches us that the innumerable lines and figures by which space is or may be intersected are absolutely true in all their combinations and consequences. New and unchangeable properties of space are thus developed, which are proved to us in a thousand ways by mathematical reasoning as well as by common experience. Through quantity and measure we are conducted to our simplest and purest notion of matter, which is to the cube or solid what space is to the square or surface. And all our applications of mathematics are applications of our ideas of space to matter. No wonder then that they seem to have a necessary existence to us. Being the simplest of our ideas, space is also the one of which we have the most difficulty in ridding ourselves. Neither can we set a limit to it, for wherever we fix a limit, space is springing up beyond. Neither can we conceive a smallest or indivisible portion of it; for within the smallest there is a smaller still; and even these inconceivable qualities of space, whether the infinite or the infinitesimal, may be made the subject of reasoning and have a certain truth to us.

Whether space exists in the mind or out of it, is a question which has no meaning. We should rather say that without it the mind is incapable of conceiving the body, and therefore of conceiving itself. The mind may be indeed imagined to contain the body, in the same way that Aristotle (partly following Plato) supposes God to be the outer heaven or circle of the universe. But how can the individual mind carry about the universe of space packed up within, or how can separate minds have either a universe of their own or a common universe? In such conceptions there seems to be a confusion of the individual and the universal. To say that we can only have a true idea of ourselves when we deny the reality of that by which we have any idea of ourselves is an absurdity. The earth which is our habitation and 'the starry heaven above' and we ourselves are equally an illusion, if space is only a quality or condition of our minds.

Again, we may compare the truths of space with other truths derived from experience, which seem to have a necessity to us in proportion to the frequency of their recurrence or the truth of the consequences which may be inferred from them. We are thus led to remark that the necessity in our ideas of space on which much stress has been laid, differs in a slight degree only from the necessity which appears to belong to other of our ideas, e.g. weight, motion, and the like. And there is another way in which this necessity may be explained. We have been taught it, and the truth which we were taught or which we inherited has never been contradicted in all our experience and is therefore confirmed by it. Who can resist an idea which is presented to him in a general form in every moment of his life and of which he finds no instance to the contrary? The greater part of what is sometimes regarded as the a priori intuition of space is really the conception of the various geometrical figures of which the properties have been revealed by mathematical analysis. And the certainty of these properties is immeasurably increased to us by our finding that they hold good not only in every instance, but in all the consequences which are supposed to flow from them.

Neither must we forget that our idea of space, like our other ideas, has a history. The Homeric poems contain no word for it; even the later Greek philosophy has not the Kantian notion of space, but only the definite 'place' or 'the infinite.' To Plato, in the Timaeus, it is known only as the 'nurse of generation.' When therefore we speak of the necessity of our ideas of space we must remember that this is a necessity which has grown up with the growth of the human mind, and has been made by ourselves. We can free ourselves from the perplexities which are involved in it by ascending to a time in which they did not as yet exist. And when space or time are described as 'a priori forms or intuitions added to the matter given in sensation,' we should consider that such expressions belong really to the 'prehistoric study' of philosophy, i.e. to the eighteenth century, when men sought to explain the human mind without regard to history or language or the social nature of man.

In every act of sense there is a latent perception of space, of which we only become conscious when objects are withdrawn from it. There are various ways in which we may trace the connexion between them. We may think of space as unresisting matter, and of matter as divided into objects; or of objects again as formed by abstraction into a collective notion of matter, and of matter as rarefied into space. And motion may be conceived as the union of there and not there in space, and force as the materializing or solidification of motion. Space again is the individual and universal in one; or, in other words, a perception and also a conception. So easily do what are sometimes called our simple ideas pass into one another, and differences of kind resolve themselves into differences of degree.

Within or behind space there is another abstraction in many respects similar to it—time, the form of the inward, as space is the form of the outward. As we cannot think of outward objects of sense or of outward sensations without space, so neither can we think of a succession of sensations without time. It is the vacancy of thoughts or sensations, as space is the void of outward objects, and we can no more imagine the mind without the one than the world without the other. It is to arithmetic what space is to geometry; or, more strictly, arithmetic may be said to be equally applicable to both. It is defined in our minds, partly by the analogy of space and partly by the recollection of events which have happened to us, or the consciousness of feelings which we are experiencing. Like space, it is without limit, for whatever beginning or end of time we fix, there is a beginning and end before them, and so on without end. We speak of a past, present, and future, and again the analogy of space assists us in conceiving of them as coexistent. When the limit of time is removed there arises in our minds the idea of eternity, which at first, like time itself, is only negative, but gradually, when connected with the world and the divine nature, like the other negative infinity of space, becomes positive. Whether time is prior to the mind and to experience, or coeval with them, is (like the parallel question about space) unmeaning. Like space it has been realized gradually: in the Homeric poems, or even in the Hesiodic cosmogony, there is no more notion of time than of space. The conception of being is more general than either, and might therefore with greater plausibility be affirmed to be a condition or quality of the mind. The a priori intuitions of Kant would have been as unintelligible to Plato as his a priori synthetical propositions to Aristotle. The philosopher of Konigsberg supposed himself to be analyzing a necessary mode of thought: he was not aware that he was dealing with a mere abstraction. But now that we are able to trace the gradual developement of ideas through religion, through language, through abstractions, why should we interpose the fiction of time between ourselves and realities? Why should we single out one of these abstractions to be the a priori condition of all the others? It comes last and not first in the order of our thoughts, and is not the condition precedent of them, but the last generalization of them. Nor can any principle be imagined more suicidal to philosophy than to assume that all the truth which we are capable of attaining is seen only through an unreal medium. If all that exists in time is illusion, we may well ask with Plato, 'What becomes of the mind?'

Leaving the a priori conditions of sensation we may proceed to consider acts of sense. These admit of various degrees of duration or intensity; they admit also of a greater or less extension from one object, which is perceived directly, to many which are perceived indirectly or in a less degree, and to the various associations of the object which are latent in the mind. In general the greater the intension the less the extension of them. The simplest sensation implies some relation of objects to one another, some position in space, some relation to a previous or subsequent sensation. The acts of seeing and hearing may be almost unconscious and may pass away unnoted; they may also leave an impression behind them or power of recalling them. If, after seeing an object we shut our eyes, the object remains dimly seen in the same or about the same place, but with form and lineaments half filled up. This is the simplest act of memory. And as we cannot see one thing without at the same time seeing another, different objects hang together in recollection, and when we call for one the other quickly follows. To think of the place in which we have last seen a thing is often the best way of recalling it to the mind. Hence memory is dependent on association. The act of recollection may be compared to the sight of an object at a great distance which we have previously seen near and seek to bring near to us in thought. Memory is to sense as dreaming is to waking; and like dreaming has a wayward and uncertain power of recalling impressions from the past.

Thus begins the passage from the outward to the inward sense. But as yet there is no conception of a universal—the mind only remembers the individual object or objects, and is always attaching to them some colour or association of sense. The power of recollection seems to depend on the intensity or largeness of the perception, or on the strength of some emotion with which it is inseparably connected. This is the natural memory which is allied to sense, such as children appear to have and barbarians and animals. It is necessarily limited in range, and its limitation is its strength. In later life, when the mind has become crowded with names, acts, feelings, images innumerable, we acquire by education another memory of system and arrangement which is both stronger and weaker than the first —weaker in the recollection of sensible impressions as they are represented to us by eye or ear—stronger by the natural connexion of ideas with objects or with one another. And many of the notions which form a part of the train of our thoughts are hardly realized by us at the time, but, like numbers or algebraical symbols, are used as signs only, thus lightening the labour of recollection.

And now we may suppose that numerous images present themselves to the mind, which begins to act upon them and to arrange them in various ways. Besides the impression of external objects present with us or just absent from us, we have a dimmer conception of other objects which have disappeared from our immediate recollection and yet continue to exist in us. The mind is full of fancies which are passing to and fro before it. Some feeling or association calls them up, and they are uttered by the lips. This is the first rudimentary imagination, which may be truly described in the language of Hobbes, as 'decaying sense,' an expression which may be applied with equal truth to memory as well. For memory and imagination, though we sometimes oppose them, are nearly allied; the difference between them seems chiefly to lie in the activity of the one compared with the passivity of the other. The sense decaying in memory receives a flash of light or life from imagination. Dreaming is a link of connexion between them; for in dreaming we feebly recollect and also feebly imagine at one and the same time. When reason is asleep the lower part of the mind wanders at will amid the images which have been received from without, the intelligent element retires, and the sensual or sensuous takes its place. And so in the first efforts of imagination reason is latent or set aside; and images, in part disorderly, but also having a unity (however imperfect) of their own, pour like a flood over the mind. And if we could penetrate into the heads of animals we should probably find that their intelligence, or the state of what in them is analogous to our intelligence, is of this nature.

Thus far we have been speaking of men, rather in the points in which they resemble animals than in the points in which they differ from them. The animal too has memory in various degrees, and the elements of imagination, if, as appears to be the case, he dreams.

How far their powers or instincts are educated by the circumstances of their lives or by intercourse with one another or with mankind, we cannot precisely tell. They, like ourselves, have the physical inheritance of form, scent, hearing, sight, and other qualities or instincts. But they have not the mental inheritance of thoughts and ideas handed down by tradition, 'the slow additions that build up the mind' of the human race. And language, which is the great educator of mankind, is wanting in them; whereas in us language is ever present—even in the infant the latent power of naming is almost immediately observable. And therefore the description which has been already given of the nascent power of the faculties is in reality an anticipation. For simultaneous with their growth in man a growth of language must be supposed. The child of two years old sees the fire once and again, and the feeble observation of the same recurring object is associated with the feeble utterance of the name by which he is taught to call it. Soon he learns to utter the name when the object is no longer there, but the desire or imagination of it is present to him. At first in every use of the word there is a colour of sense, an indistinct picture of the object which accompanies it. But in later years he sees in the name only the universal or class word, and the more abstract the notion becomes, the more vacant is the image which is presented to him. Henceforward all the operations of his mind, including the perceptions of sense, are a synthesis of sensations, words, conceptions. In seeing or hearing or looking or listening the sensible impression prevails over the conception and the word. In reflection the process is reversed—the outward object fades away into nothingness, the name or the conception or both together are everything. Language, like number, is intermediate between the two, partaking of the definiteness of the outer and of the universality of the inner world. For logic teaches us that every word is really a universal, and only condescends by the help of position or circumlocution to become the expression of individuals or particulars. And sometimes by using words as symbols we are able to give a 'local habitation and a name' to the infinite and inconceivable.

Thus we see that no line can be drawn between the powers of sense and of reflection—they pass imperceptibly into one another. We may indeed distinguish between the seeing and the closed eye—

between the sensation and the recollection of it. But this distinction carries us a very little way, for recollection is present in sight as well as sight in recollection. There is no impression of sense which does not simultaneously recall differences of form, number, colour, and the like. Neither is such a distinction applicable at all to our internal bodily sensations, which give no sign of themselves when unaccompanied with pain, and even when we are most conscious of them, have often no assignable place in the human frame. Who can divide the nerves or great nervous centres from the mind which uses them? Who can separate the pains and pleasures of the mind from the pains and pleasures of the body? The words 'inward and outward,' 'active and passive,' 'mind and body,' are best conceived by us as differences of degree passing into differences of kind, and at one time and under one aspect acting in harmony and then again opposed. They introduce a system and order into the knowledge of our being; and yet, like many other general terms, are often in advance of our actual analysis or observation.

According to some writers the inward sense is only the fading away or imperfect realization of the outward. But this leaves out of sight one half of the phenomenon. For the mind is not only withdrawn from the world of sense but introduced to a higher world of thought and reflection, in which, like the outward sense, she is trained and educated. By use the outward sense becomes keener and more intense, especially when confined within narrow limits. The savage with little or no thought has a quicker discernment of the track than the civilised man; in like manner the dog, having the help of scent as well as of sight, is superior to the savage. By use again the inward thought becomes more defined and distinct; what was at first an effort is made easy by the natural instrumentality of language, and the mind learns to grasp universals with no more exertion than is required for the sight of an outward object. There is a natural connexion and arrangement of them, like the association of objects in a landscape. Just as a note or two of music suffices to recall a whole piece to the musician's or composer's mind, so a great principle or leading thought suggests and arranges a world of particulars. The power of reflection is not feebler than the faculty of sense, but of a higher and more comprehensive nature. It not only receives the universals of sense, but gives them a new content by comparing and combining them with one another. It withdraws from the seen that it may dwell in the unseen. The sense only presents us with a flat and impenetrable surface: the mind takes the world to pieces and puts it together on a new pattern. The universals which are detached from sense are reconstructed in science. They and not the mere impressions of sense are the truth of the world in which we live; and (as an argument to those who will only believe 'what they can hold in their hands') we may further observe that they are the source of our power over it. To say that the outward sense is stronger than the inward is like saying that the arm of the workman is stronger than the constructing or directing mind.

Returning to the senses we may briefly consider two questions—first their relation to the mind, secondly, their relation to outward objects:—

1. The senses are not merely 'holes set in a wooden horse' (Theaet.), but instruments of the mind with which they are organically connected. There is no use of them without some use of words—some natural or latent logic—some previous experience or observation. Sensation, like all other mental processes, is complex and relative, though apparently simple. The senses mutually confirm and support one another; it is hard to say how much our impressions of hearing may be affected by those of sight, or how far our impressions of sight may be corrected by the touch, especially in infancy. The confirmation of them by one another cannot of course be given by any one of them. Many intuitions which are inseparable from the act of sense are really the result of complicated reasonings. The most cursory glance at objects enables the experienced eye to judge approximately of their relations and distance, although nothing is impressed upon the retina except colour, including gradations of light and shade. From these delicate and almost imperceptible differences we seem chiefly to derive our ideas of distance and position. By comparison of what is near with what is distant we learn that the tree, house, river, etc. which are a long way off are objects of a like nature with those which are seen by us in our immediate neighbourhood, although the actual impression made on the eye is very different in one case and in the other. This is a language of

Theætetus

'large and small letters' (Republic), slightly differing in form and exquisitely graduated by distance, which we are learning all our life long, and which we attain in various degrees according to our powers of sight or observation. There is nor the consideration. The greater or less strain upon the nerves of the eye or ear is communicated to the mind and silently informs the judgment. We have also the use not of one eye only, but of two, which give us a wider range, and help us to discern, by the greater or less acuteness of the angle which the rays of sight form, the distance of an object and its relation to other objects. But we are already passing beyond the limits of our actual knowledge on a subject which has given rise to many conjectures. More important than the addition of another conjecture is the observation, whether in the case of sight or of any other sense, of the great complexity of the causes and the great simplicity of the effect.

The sympathy of the mind and the ear is no less striking than the sympathy of the mind and the eye. Do we not seem to perceive instinctively and as an act of sense the differences of articulate speech and of musical notes? Yet how small a part of speech or of music is produced by the impression of the ear compared with that which is furnished by the mind!

Again: the more refined faculty of sense, as in animals so also in man, seems often to be transmitted by inheritance. Neither must we forget that in the use of the senses, as in his whole nature, man is a social being, who is always being educated by language, habit, and the teaching of other men as well as by his own observation. He knows distance because he is taught it by a more experienced judgment than his own; he distinguishes sounds because he is told to remark them by a person of a more discerning ear. And as we inherit from our parents or other ancestors peculiar powers of sense or feeling, so we improve and strengthen them, not only by regular teaching, but also by sympathy and communion with other persons.

2. The second question, namely, that concerning the relation of the mind to external objects, is really a trifling one, though it has been made the subject of a famous philosophy. We may if we like, with Berkeley, resolve objects of sense into sensations; but the change

is one of name only, and nothing is gained and something is lost by such a resolution or confusion of them. For we have not really made a single step towards idealism, and any arbitrary inversion of our ordinary modes of speech is disturbing to the mind. The youthful metaphysician is delighted at his marvellous discovery that nothing is, and that what we see or feel is our sensation only: for a day or two the world has a new interest to him; he alone knows the secret which has been communicated to him by the philosopher, that mind is all—when in fact he is going out of his mind in the first intoxication of a great thought. But he soon finds that all things remain as they were —the laws of motion, the properties of matter, the qualities of substances. After having inflicted his theories on any one who is willing to receive them 'first on his father and mother, secondly on some other patient listener, thirdly on his dog,' he finds that he only differs from the rest of mankind in the use of a word. He had once hoped that by getting rid of the solidity of matter he might open a passage to worlds beyond. He liked to think of the world as the representation of the divine nature, and delighted to imagine angels and spirits wandering through space, present in the room in which he is sitting without coming through the door, nowhere and everywhere at the same instant. At length he finds that he has been the victim of his own fancies; he has neither more nor less evidence of the supernatural than he had before. He himself has become unsettled, but the laws of the world remain fixed as at the beginning. He has discovered that his appeal to the fallibility of sense was really an illusion. For whatever uncertainty there may be in the appearances of nature, arises only out of the imperfection or variation of the human senses, or possibly from the deficiency of certain branches of knowledge; when science is able to apply her tests, the uncertainty is at an end. We are apt sometimes to think that moral and metaphysical philosophy are lowered by the influence which is exercised over them by physical science. But any interpretation of nature by physical science is far in advance of such idealism. The philosophy of Berkeley, while giving unbounded license to the imagination, is still grovelling on the level of sense.

We may, if we please, carry this scepticism a step further, and deny, not only objects of sense, but the continuity of our sensations themselves. We may say with Protagoras and Hume that what is appears, and that what appears appears only to individuals, and to the same individual only at one instant. But then, as Plato asks,—and we must repeat the question,—What becomes of the mind? Experience tells us by a thousand proofs that our sensations of colour, taste, and the like, are the same as they were an instant ago—that the act which we are performing one minute is continued by us in the next—and also supplies abundant proof that the perceptions of other men are, speaking generally, the same or nearly the same with our own. After having slowly and laboriously in the course of ages gained a conception of a whole and parts, of the constitution of the mind, of the relation of man to God and nature, imperfect indeed, but the best we can, we are asked to return again to the 'beggarly elements' of ancient scepticism, and acknowledge only atoms and sensations devoid of life or unity. Why should we not go a step further still and doubt the existence of the senses of all things? We are but 'such stuff as dreams are made of;' for we have left ourselves no instruments of thought by which we can distinguish man from the animals, or conceive of the existence even of a mollusc. And observe, this extreme scepticism has been allowed to spring up among us, not, like the ancient scepticism, in an age when nature and language really seemed to be full of illusions, but in the eighteenth and nineteenth centuries, when men walk in the daylight of inductive science.

The attractiveness of such speculations arises out of their true nature not being perceived. They are veiled in graceful language; they are not pushed to extremes; they stop where the human mind is disposed also to stop—short of a manifest absurdity. Their inconsistency is not observed by their authors or by mankind in general, who are equally inconsistent themselves. They leave on the mind a pleasing sense of wonder and novelty: in youth they seem to have a natural affinity to one class of persons as poetry has to another; but in later life either we drift back into common sense, or we make them the starting-points of a higher philosophy.

We are often told that we should enquire into all things before we accept them;—with what limitations is this true? For we cannot use our senses without admitting that we have them, or think without presupposing that there is in us a power of thought, or affirm that all knowledge is derived from experience without implying that this first principle of knowledge is prior to experience. The truth seems to be that we begin with the natural use of the mind as of the body, and we seek to describe this as well as we can. We eat before we know the nature of digestion; we think before we know the nature of reflection. As our knowledge increases, our perception of the mind enlarges also. We cannot indeed get beyond facts, but neither can we draw any line which separates facts from ideas. And the mind is not something separate from them but included in them, and they in the mind, both having a distinctness and individuality of their own. To reduce our conception of mind to a succession of feelings and sensations is like the attempt to view a wide prospect by inches through a microscope, or to calculate a period of chronology by minutes. The mind ceases to exist when it loses its continuity, which though far from being its highest determination, is yet necessary to any conception of it. Even an inanimate nature cannot be adequately represented as an endless succession of states or conditions.

Paragraph II. Another division of the subject has yet to be considered: Why should the doctrine that knowledge is sensation, in ancient times, or of sensationalism or materialism in modern times, be allied to the lower rather than to the higher view of ethical philosophy? At first sight the nature and origin of knowledge appear to be wholly disconnected from ethics and religion, nor can we deny that the ancient Stoics were materialists, or that the materialist doctrines prevalent in modern times have been associated with great virtues, or that both religious and philosophical idealism have not unfrequently parted company with practice. Still upon the whole it must be admitted that the higher standard of duty has gone hand in hand with the higher conception of knowledge. It is Protagoras who is seeking to adapt himself to the opinions of the world; it is Plato who rises above them: the one maintaining that all knowledge is sensation; the other basing the virtues on the idea of good. The reason of this phenomenon has now to be examined.

By those who rest knowledge immediately upon sense, that explanation of human action is deemed to be the truest which is nearest to sense. As knowledge is reduced to sensation, so virtue is reduced to feeling, happiness or good to pleasure. The different virtues—the various characters which exist in the world—are the disguises of self-interest. Human nature is dried up; there is no place left for imagination, or in any higher sense for religion. Ideals of a whole, or of a state, or of a law of duty, or of a divine perfection, are out of place in an Epicurean philosophy. The very terms in which they are expressed are suspected of having no meaning. Man is to bring himself back as far as he is able to the condition of a rational beast. He is to limit himself to the pursuit of pleasure, but of this he is to make a far-sighted calculation;—he is to be rationalized, secularized, animalized: or he is to be an amiable sceptic, better than his own philosophy, and not falling below the opinions of the world.

Imagination has been called that 'busy faculty' which is always intruding upon us in the search after truth. But imagination is also that higher power by which we rise above ourselves and the commonplaces of thought and life. The philosophical imagination is another name for reason finding an expression of herself in the outward world. To deprive life of ideals is to deprive it of all higher and comprehensive aims and of the power of imparting and communicating them to others. For men are taught, not by those who are on a level with them, but by those who rise above them, who see the distant hills, who soar into the empyrean. Like a bird in a cage, the mind confined to sense is always being brought back from the higher to the lower, from the wider to the narrower view of human knowledge. It seeks to fly but cannot: instead of aspiring towards perfection, 'it hovers about this lower world and the earthly nature.' It loses the religious sense which more than any other seems to take a man out of himself. Weary of asking 'What is truth?' it accepts the 'blind witness of eyes and ears;' it draws around itself the curtain of the physical world and is satisfied. The strength of a sensational philosophy lies in the ready accommodation of it to the minds of men; many who have been metaphysicians in their youth, as they advance in years are prone to acquiesce in things as they are, or rather appear to be. They are spectators, not thinkers, and the best philosophy is that which requires of them the least amount of mental effort.

As a lower philosophy is easier to apprehend than a higher, so a lower way of life is easier to follow; and therefore such a philosophy seems to derive a support from the general practice of mankind. It appeals to principles which they all know and recognize: it gives back to them in a generalized form the results of their own experience. To the man of the world they are the quintessence of his own reflections upon life. To follow custom, to have no new ideas or opinions, not to be straining after impossibilities, to enjoy to-day with just so much forethought as is necessary to provide for the morrow, this is regarded by the greater part of the world as the natural way of passing through existence. And many who have lived thus have attained to a lower kind of happiness or equanimity. They have possessed their souls in peace without ever allowing them to wander into the region of religious or political controversy, and without any care for the higher interests of man. But nearly all the good (as well as some of the evil) which has ever been done in this world has been the work of another spirit, the work of enthusiasts and idealists, of apostles and martyrs. The leaders of mankind have not been of the gentle Epicurean type; they have personified ideas; they have sometimes also been the victims of them. But they have always been seeking after a truth or ideal of which they fell short; and have died in a manner disappointed of their hopes that they might lift the human race out of the slough in which they found them. They have done little compared with their own visions and aspirations; but they have done that little, only because they sought to do, and once perhaps thought that they were doing, a great deal more.

The philosophies of Epicurus or Hume give no adequate or dignified conception of the mind. There is no organic unity in a succession of feeling or sensations; no comprehensiveness in an infinity of separate actions. The individual never reflects upon himself as a whole; he can hardly regard one act or part of his life as the cause or effect of any other act or part. Whether in practice or speculation, he is to himself only in successive instants. To such thinkers, whether in ancient or in modern times, the mind is only the poor recipient of impressions—not the heir of all the ages, or connected with all other minds. It begins again with its own modicum of experience having only such vague conceptions of the wisdom of the past as are inseparable from language and popular opinion. It seeks

Theætetus

to explain from the experience of the individual what can only be learned from the history of the world. It has no conception of obligation, duty, conscience—these are to the Epicurean or Utilitarian philosopher only names which interfere with our natural perceptions of pleasure and pain.

There seem then to be several answers to the question, Why the theory that all knowledge is sensation is allied to the lower rather than to the higher view of ethical philosophy:—1st, Because it is easier to understand and practise; 2ndly, Because it is fatal to the pursuit of ideals, moral, political, or religious; 3rdly, Because it deprives us of the means and instruments of higher thought, of any adequate conception of the mind, of knowledge, of conscience, of moral obligation.

ON THE NATURE AND LIMITS Of PSYCHOLOGY

O gar arche men o me oide, teleute de kai ta metaxu ex ou me oide sumpeplektai, tis mechane ten toiauten omologian pote epistemen genesthai; Plato Republic.

Monon gar auto legeiv, osper gumnon kai aperemomenon apo ton onton apanton, adunaton. Soph.

Since the above essay first appeared, many books on Psychology have been given to the world, partly based upon the views of Herbart and other German philosophers, partly independent of them. The subject has gained in bulk and extent; whether it has had any true growth is more doubtful. It begins to assume the language and claim the authority of a science; but it is only an hypothesis or outline, which may be filled up in many ways according to the fancy of individual thinkers. The basis of it is a precarious one,—consciousness of ourselves and a somewhat uncertain observation of the rest of mankind. Its relations to other sciences are not yet determined: they seem to be almost too complicated to be ascertained. It may be compared to an irregular building, run up hastily and not likely to last, because its foundations are weak, and in many places rest only on the surface of the ground. It has sought rather to put together scattered observations and to make them into a system than to describe or prove them. It has never severely drawn the line between facts and opinions. It has substituted a technical phraseology for the common use of language, being neither able to win acceptance for the one nor to get rid of the other.

The system which has thus arisen appears to be a kind of metaphysic narrowed to the point of view of the individual mind, through which, as through some new optical instrument limiting the sphere of vision, the interior of thought and sensation is examined. But the individual mind in the abstract, as distinct from the mind of a particular individual and separated from the environment of circumstances, is a fiction only. Yet facts which are partly true gather around this fiction and are naturally described by the help of it. There is also a common type of the mind which is derived from the comparison of many minds with one another and with our own. The phenomena of which Psychology treats are familiar to us, but they are for the most part indefinite; they relate to a something inside the body, which seems also to overleap the limits of space. The operations of this something, when isolated, cannot be analyzed by us or subjected to observation and experiment. And there is another point to be considered. The mind, when thinking, cannot survey that part of itself which is used in thought. It can only be contemplated in the past, that is to say, in the history of the individual or of the world. This is the scientific method of studying the mind. But Psychology has also some other supports, specious rather than real. It is partly sustained by the false analogy of Physical Science and has great expectations from its near relationship to Physiology. We truly remark that there is an infinite complexity of the body corresponding to the infinite subtlety of the mind; we are conscious that they are very nearly connected. But in endeavouring to trace the nature of the connexion we are baffled and disappointed. In our knowledge of them the gulf remains the same: no microscope has ever seen into thought; no reflection on ourselves has supplied the missing link between mind and matter...These are the conditions of this very inexact science, and we shall only know less of it by pretending to know more, or by assigning to it a form or style to which it has not yet attained and is not really entitled.

Experience shows that any system, however baseless and ineffectual, in our own or in any other age, may be accepted and continue to be studied, if it seeks to satisfy some unanswered question or is based upon some ancient tradition, especially if it takes the form and uses the language of inductive philosophy. The fact therefore that such a science exists and is popular, affords no evidence of its truth or value. Many who have pursued it far into detail have never examined the foundations on which it rests. The have been many imaginary subjects of knowledge of which enthusiastic persons have made a lifelong study, without ever asking themselves what is the evidence for them, what is the use of them, how long they will last? They may pass away, like the authors of them, and 'leave not a wrack behind;' or they may survive in fragments. Nor is it only in the Middle Ages, or in the literary desert of China or of India, that such systems have arisen; in our own enlightened age, growing up by the side of Physics, Ethics, and other really progressive sciences, there is a weary waste of knowledge, falsely so-called. There are sham sciences which no logic has ever put to the test, in which the desire for knowledge invents the materials of it.

And therefore it is expedient once more to review the bases of Psychology, lest we should be imposed upon by its pretensions. The study of it may have done good service by awakening us to the sense of inveterate errors familiarized by language, yet it may have fallen into still greater ones; under the pretence of new investigations it may be wasting the lives of those who are engaged in it. It may also be found that the discussion of it will throw light upon some points in the Theætetus of Plato,—the oldest work on Psychology which has come down to us. The imaginary science may be called, in the language of ancient philosophy, 'a shadow of a part of Dialectic or Metaphysic' (Gorg.).

In this postscript or appendix we propose to treat, first, of the true bases of Psychology; secondly, of the errors into which the students of it are most likely to fall; thirdly, of the principal subjects which are usually comprehended under it; fourthly, of the form which facts relating to the mind most naturally assume.

We may preface the enquiry by two or three remarks:—

(1) We do not claim for the popular Psychology the position of a science at all; it cannot, like the Physical Sciences, proceed by the Inductive Method: it has not the necessity of Mathematics: it does not, like Metaphysic, argue from abstract notions or from internal coherence. It is made up of scattered observations. A few of these, though they may sometimes appear to be truisms, are of the greatest value, and free from all doubt. We are conscious of them in ourselves; we observe them working in others; we are assured of them at all times. For example, we are absolutely certain, (a) of the influence exerted by the mind over the body or by the body over the mind: (b) of the power of association, by which the appearance of some person or the occurrence of some event recalls to mind, not always but often, other persons and events: (c) of the effect of habit, which is strongest when least disturbed by reflection, and is to the mind what the bones are to the body: (d) of the real, though not unlimited, freedom of the human will: (e) of the reference, more or

less distinct, of our sensations, feelings, thoughts, actions, to ourselves, which is called consciousness, or, when in excess, self-consciousness: (f) of the distinction of the 'I' and 'Not I,' of ourselves and outward objects. But when we attempt to gather up these elements in a single system, we discover that the links by which we combine them are apt to be mere words. We are in a country which has never been cleared or surveyed; here and there only does a gleam of light come through the darkness of the forest.

(2) These fragments, although they can never become science in the ordinary sense of the word, are a real part of knowledge and may be of great value in education. We may be able to add a good deal to them from our own experience, and we may verify them by it. Self-examination is one of those studies which a man can pursue alone, by attention to himself and the processes of his individual mind. He may learn much about his own character and about the character of others, if he will 'make his mind sit down' and look at itself in the glass. The great, if not the only use of such a study is a practical one,—to know, first, human nature, and, secondly, our own nature, as it truly is.

(3) Hence it is important that we should conceive of the mind in the noblest and simplest manner. While acknowledging that language has been the greatest factor in the formation of human thought, we must endeavour to get rid of the disguises, oppositions, contradictions, which arise out of it. We must disengage ourselves from the ideas which the customary use of words has implanted in us. To avoid error as much as possible when we are speaking of things unseen, the principal terms which we use should be few, and we should not allow ourselves to be enslaved by them. Instead of seeking to frame a technical language, we should vary our forms of speech, lest they should degenerate into formulas. A difficult philosophical problem is better understood when translated into the vernacular.

I.a. Psychology is inseparable from language, and early language contains the first impressions or the oldest experience of man respecting himself. These impressions are not accurate representations of the truth; they are the reflections of a rudimentary age of philosophy. The first and simplest forms of thought are rooted so deep in human nature that they can never be got rid of; but they have been perpetually enlarged and elevated, and the use of many words has been transferred from the body to the mind. The spiritual and intellectual have thus become separated from the material—there is a cleft between them; and the heart and the conscience of man rise above the dominion of the appetites and create a new language in which they too find expression. As the differences of actions begin to be perceived, more and more names are needed. This is the first analysis of the human mind; having a general foundation in popular experience, it is moulded to a certain extent by hierophants and philosophers. (See Introd. to Cratylus.)

b. This primitive psychology is continually receiving additions from the first thinkers, who in return take a colour from the popular language of the time. The mind is regarded from new points of view, and becomes adapted to new conditions of knowledge. It seeks to isolate itself from matter and sense, and to assert its independence in thought. It recognizes that it is independent of the external world. It has five or six natural states or stages:—(1) sensation, in which it is almost latent or quiescent: (2) feeling, or inner sense, when the mind is just awakening: (3) memory, which is decaying sense, and from time to time, as with a spark or flash, has the power of recollecting or reanimating the buried past: (4) thought, in which images pass into abstract notions or are intermingled with them: (5) action, in which the mind moves forward, of itself, or under the impulse of want or desire or pain, to attain or avoid some end or consequence: and (6) there is the composition of these or the admixture or assimilation of them in various degrees. We never see these processes of the mind, nor can we tell the causes of them. But we know them by their results, and learn from other men that so far as we can describe to them or they to us the workings of the mind, their experience is the same or nearly the same with our own.

c. But the knowledge of the mind is not to any great extent derived from the observation of the individual by himself. It is the growing consciousness of the human race, embodied in language, acknowledged by experience, and corrected from time to time by the influence of literature and philosophy. A great, perhaps the most important, part of it is to be found in early Greek thought. In the

Theætetus of Plato it has not yet become fixed: we are still stumbling on the threshold. In Aristotle the process is more nearly completed, and has gained innumerable abstractions, of which many have had to be thrown away because relative only to the controversies of the time. In the interval between Thales and Aristotle were realized the distinctions of mind and body, of universal and particular, of infinite and infinitesimal, of idea and phenomenon; the class conceptions of faculties and virtues, the antagonism of the appetites and the reason; and connected with this, at a higher stage of development, the opposition of moral and intellectual virtue; also the primitive conceptions of unity, being, rest, motion, and the like. These divisions were not really scientific, but rather based on popular experience. They were not held with the precision of modern thinkers, but taken all together they gave a new existence to the mind in thought, and greatly enlarged and more accurately defined man's knowledge of himself and of the world. The majority of them have been accepted by Christian and Western nations. Yet in modern times we have also drifted so far away from Aristotle, that if we were to frame a system on his lines we should be at war with ordinary language and untrue to our own consciousness. And there have been a few both in mediaeval times and since the Reformation who have rebelled against the Aristotelian point of view. Of these eccentric thinkers there have been various types, but they have all a family likeness. According to them, there has been too much analysis and too little synthesis, too much division of the mind into parts and too little conception of it as a whole or in its relation to God and the laws of the universe. They have thought that the elements of plurality and unity have not been duly adjusted. The tendency of such writers has been to allow the personality of man to be absorbed in the universal, or in the divine nature, and to deny the distinction between matter and mind, or to substitute one for the other. They have broken some of the idols of Psychology: they have challenged the received meaning of words: they have regarded the mind under many points of view. But though they may have shaken the old, they have not established the new; their views of philosophy, which seem like the echo of some voice from the East, have been alien to the mind of Europe.

d. The Psychology which is found in common language is in some degree verified by experience, but not in such a manner as to give it the character of an exact science. We cannot say that words always correspond to facts. Common language represents the mind from different and even opposite points of view, which cannot be all of them equally true (compare Cratylus). Yet from diversity of statements and opinions may be obtained a nearer approach to the truth than is to be gained from any one of them. It also tends to correct itself, because it is gradually brought nearer to the common sense of mankind. There are some leading categories or classifications of thought, which, though unverified, must always remain the elements from which the science or study of the mind proceeds. For example, we must assume ideas before we can analyze them, and also a continuing mind to which they belong; the resolution of it into successive moments, which would say, with Protagoras, that the man is not the same person which he was a minute ago, is, as Plato implies in the Theætetus, an absurdity.

e. The growth of the mind, which may be traced in the histories of religions and philosophies and in the thoughts of nations, is one of the deepest and noblest modes of studying it. Here we are dealing with the reality, with the greater and, as it may be termed, the most sacred part of history. We study the mind of man as it begins to be inspired by a human or divine reason, as it is modified by circumstances, as it is distributed in nations, as it is renovated by great movements, which go beyond the limits of nations and affect human society on a scale still greater, as it is created or renewed by great minds, who, looking down from above, have a wider and more comprehensive vision. This is an ambitious study, of which most of us rather 'entertain conjecture' than arrive at any detailed or accurate knowledge. Later arises the reflection how these great ideas or movements of the world have been appropriated by the multitude and found a way to the minds of individuals. The real Psychology is that which shows how the increasing knowledge of nature and the increasing experience of life have always been slowly transforming the mind, how religions too have been modified in the course of ages 'that God may be all and in all.' E pollaplasion, eoe, to ergon e os nun zeteitai prostatteis.

f. Lastly, though we speak of the study of mind in a special sense, it may also be said that there is no science which does not contribute to our knowledge of it. The methods of science and their analogies are new faculties, discovered by the few and imparted to the many. They are to the mind, what the senses are to the body; or better, they may be compared to instruments such as the telescope or microscope by which the discriminating power of the senses, or to other mechanical inventions, by which the strength and skill of the human body is so immeasurably increased.

II. The new Psychology, whatever may be its claim to the authority of a science, has called attention to many facts and corrected many errors, which without it would have been unexamined. Yet it is also itself very liable to illusion. The evidence on which it rests is vague and indefinite. The field of consciousness is never seen by us as a whole, but only at particular points, which are always changing. The veil of language intercepts facts. Hence it is desirable that in making an approach to the study we should consider at the outset what are the kinds of error which most easily affect it, and note the differences which separate it from other branches of knowledge.

a. First, we observe the mind by the mind. It would seem therefore that we are always in danger of leaving out the half of that which is the subject of our enquiry. We come at once upon the difficulty of what is the meaning of the word. Does it differ as subject and object in the same manner? Can we suppose one set of feelings or one part of the mind to interpret another? Is the introspecting thought the same with the thought which is introspected? Has the mind the power of surveying its whole domain at one and the same time?—No more than the eye can take in the whole human body at a glance. Yet there may be a glimpse round the corner, or a thought transferred in a moment from one point of view to another, which enables us to see nearly the whole, if not at once, at any rate in succession. Such glimpses will hardly enable us to contemplate from within the mind in its true proportions. Hence the firmer ground of Psychology is not the consciousness of inward feelings but the observation of external actions, being the actions not only of ourselves, but of the innumerable persons whom we come across in life.

b. The error of supposing partial or occasional explanation of mental phenomena to be the only or complete ones. For example, we are disinclined to admit of the spontaneity or discontinuity of the mind—it seems to us like an effect without a cause, and therefore we suppose the train of our thoughts to be always called up by association. Yet it is probable, or indeed certain, that of many mental phenomena there are no mental antecedents, but only bodily ones.

c. The false influence of language. We are apt to suppose that when there are two or more words describing faculties or processes of the mind, there are real differences corresponding to them. But this is not the case. Nor can we determine how far they do or do not exist, or by what degree or kind of difference they are distinguished. The same remark may be made about figures of speech. They fill up the vacancy of knowledge; they are to the mind what too much colour is to the eye; but the truth is rather concealed than revealed by them.

d. The uncertain meaning of terms, such as Consciousness, Conscience, Will, Law, Knowledge, Internal and External Sense; these, in the language of Plato, 'we shamelessly use, without ever having taken the pains to analyze them.'

e. A science such as Psychology is not merely an hypothesis, but an hypothesis which, unlike the hypotheses of Physics, can never be verified. It rests only on the general impressions of mankind, and there is little or no hope of adding in any considerable degree to our stock of mental facts.

f. The parallelism of the Physical Sciences, which leads us to analyze the mind on the analogy of the body, and so to reduce mental operations to the level of bodily ones, or to confound one with the other.

g. That the progress of Physiology may throw a new light on Psychology is a dream in which scientific men are always tempted to indulge. But however certain we may be of the connexion between mind and body, the explanation of the one by the other is a hidden place of nature which has hitherto been investigated with little or no success.

h. The impossibility of distinguishing between mind and body.

Neither in thought nor in experience can we separate them. They seem to act together; yet we feel that we are sometimes under the dominion of the one, sometimes of the other, and sometimes, both in the common use of language and in fact, they transform themselves, the one into the good principle, the other into the evil principle; and then again the 'I' comes in and mediates between them. It is also difficult to distinguish outward facts from the ideas of them in the mind, or to separate the external stimulus to a sensation from the activity of the organ, or this from the invisible agencies by which it reaches the mind, or any process of sense from its mental antecedent, or any mental energy from its nervous expression.

i. The fact that mental divisions tend to run into one another, and that in speaking of the mind we cannot always distinguish differences of kind from differences of degree; nor have we any measure of the strength and intensity of our ideas or feelings.

j. Although heredity has been always known to the ancients as well as ourselves to exercise a considerable influence on human character, yet we are unable to calculate what proportion this birth-influence bears to nurture and education. But this is the real question. We cannot pursue the mind into embryology: we can only trace how, after birth, it begins to grow. But how much is due to the soil, how much to the original latent seed, it is impossible to distinguish. And because we are certain that heredity exercises a considerable, but undefined influence, we must not increase the wonder by exaggerating it.

k. The love of system is always tending to prevail over the historical investigation of the mind, which is our chief means of knowing it. It equally tends to hinder the other great source of our knowledge of the mind, the observation of its workings and processes which we can make for ourselves.

l. The mind, when studied through the individual, is apt to be isolated—this is due to the very form of the enquiry; whereas, in truth, it is indistinguishable from circumstances, the very language which it uses being the result of the instincts of long-forgotten generations, and every word which a man utters being the answer to some other word spoken or suggested by somebody else.

III. The tendency of the preceding remarks has been to show that Psychology is necessarily a fragment, and is not and cannot be a connected system. We cannot define or limit the mind, but we can describe it. We can collect information about it; we can enumerate the principal subjects which are included in the study of it. Thus we are able to rehabilitate Psychology to some extent, not as a branch of science, but as a collection of facts bearing on human life, as a part of the history of philosophy, as an aspect of Metaphysic. It is a fragment of a science only, which in all probability can never make any great progress or attain to much clearness or exactness. It is however a kind of knowledge which has a great interest for us and is always present to us, and of which we carry about the materials in our own bosoms. We can observe our minds and we can experiment upon them, and the knowledge thus acquired is not easily forgotten, and is a help to us in study as well as in conduct.

The principal subjects of Psychology may be summed up as follows:—

a. The relation of man to the world around him,—in what sense and within what limits can he withdraw from its laws or assert himself against them (Freedom and Necessity), and what is that which we suppose to be thus independent and which we call ourselves? How does the inward differ from the outward and what is the relation between them, and where do we draw the line by which we separate mind from matter, the soul from the body? Is the mind active or passive, or partly both? Are its movements identical with those of the body, or only preconcerted and coincident with them, or is one simply an aspect of the other?

b. What are we to think of time and space? Time seems to have a nearer connexion with the mind, space with the body; yet time, as well as space, is necessary to our idea of either. We see also that they have an analogy with one another, and that in Mathematics they often interpenetrate. Space or place has been said by Kant to be the form of the outward, time of the inward sense. He regards them as parts or forms of the mind. But this is an unfortunate and inexpressive way of describing their relation to us. For of all the phenomena present to the human mind they seem to have most the character of objective existence. There is no use in asking what is beyond or behind them; we cannot get rid of them. And to throw the laws of external nature which to us are the type of the immutable into the subjective side of the antithesis seems to be equally inappropriate.

Theætetus

c. When in imagination we enter into the closet of the mind and withdraw ourselves from the external world, we seem to find there more or less distinct processes which may be described by the words, 'I perceive,' 'I feel,' 'I think,' 'I want,' 'I wish,' 'I like,' 'I dislike,' 'I fear,' 'I know,' 'I remember,' 'I imagine,' 'I dream,' 'I act,' 'I endeavour,' 'I hope.' These processes would seem to have the same notions attached to them in the minds of all educated persons. They are distinguished from one another in thought, but they intermingle. It is possible to reflect upon them or to become conscious of them in a greater or less degree, or with a greater or less continuity or attention, and thus arise the intermittent phenomena of consciousness or self-consciousness. The use of all of them is possible to us at all times; and therefore in any operation of the mind the whole are latent. But we are able to characterise them sufficiently by that part of the complex action which is the most prominent. We have no difficulty in distinguishing an act of sight or an act of will from an act of thought, although thought is present in both of them. Hence the conception of different faculties or different virtues is precarious, because each of them is passing into the other, and they are all one in the mind itself; they appear and reappear, and may all be regarded as the ever-varying phases or aspects or differences of the same mind or person.

d. Nearest the sense in the scale of the intellectual faculties is memory, which is a mode rather than a faculty of the mind, and accompanies all mental operations. There are two principal kinds of it, recollection and recognition,—recollection in which forgotten things are recalled or return to the mind, recognition in which the mind finds itself again among things once familiar. The simplest way in which we can represent the former to ourselves is by shutting our eyes and trying to recall in what we term the mind's eye the picture of the surrounding scene, or by laying down the book which we are reading and recapitulating what we can remember of it. But many times more powerful than recollection is recognition, perhaps because it is more assisted by association. We have known and forgotten, and after a long interval the thing which we have seen once is seen again by us, but with a different feeling, and comes back to us, not as new knowledge, but as a thing to which we ourselves impart a notion already present to us; in Plato's words, we set the stamp upon the wax. Every one is aware of the difference between the first and second sight of a place, between a scene clothed with associations or bare and divested of them. We say to ourselves on revisiting a spot after a long interval: How many things have happened since I last saw this! There is probably no impression ever received by us of which we can venture to say that the vestiges are altogether lost, or that we might not, under some circumstances, recover it. A long-forgotten knowledge may be easily renewed and therefore is very different from ignorance. Of the language learnt in childhood not a word may be remembered, and yet, when a new beginning is made, the old habit soon returns, the neglected organs come back into use, and the river of speech finds out the dried-up channel.

e. 'Consciousness' is the most treacherous word which is employed in the study of the mind, for it is used in many senses, and has rarely, if ever, been minutely analyzed. Like memory, it accompanies all mental operations, but not always continuously, and it exists in various degrees. It may be imperceptible or hardly perceptible: it may be the living sense that our thoughts, actions, sufferings, are our own. It is a kind of attention which we pay to ourselves, and is intermittent rather than continuous. Its sphere has been exaggerated. It is sometimes said to assure us of our freedom; but this is an illusion: as there may be a real freedom without consciousness of it, so there may be a consciousness of freedom without the reality. It may be regarded as a higher degree of knowledge when we not only know but know that we know. Consciousness is opposed to habit, inattention, sleep, death. It may be illustrated by its derivative conscience, which speaks to men, not only of right and wrong in the abstract, but of right and wrong actions in reference to themselves and their circumstances.

f. Association is another of the ever-present phenomena of the human mind. We speak of the laws of association, but this is an expression which is confusing, for the phenomenon itself is of the most capricious and uncertain sort. It may be briefly described as follows. The simplest case of association is that of sense. When we see or hear separately one of two things, which we have previously seen or heard together, the occurrence of the one has a tendency to suggest the other. So the sight or name of a house may recall to our minds the memory of those who once lived there. Like may recall like and everything its opposite. The parts of a whole, the terms of a series, objects lying near, words having a customary order stick together in the mind. A word may bring back a passage of poetry or a whole system of philosophy; from one end of the world or from one pole of knowledge we may travel to the other in an indivisible instant. The long train of association by which we pass from one point to the other, involving every sort of complex relation, so sudden, so accidental, is one of the greatest wonders of mind...This process however is not always continuous, but often intermittent: we can think of things in isolation as well as in association; we do not mean that they must all hang from one another. We can begin again after an interval of rest or vacancy, as a new train of thought suddenly arises, as, for example, when we wake of a morning or after violent exercise. Time, place, the same colour or sound or smell or taste, will often call up some thought or recollection either accidentally or naturally associated with them. But it is equally noticeable that the new thought may occur to us, we cannot tell how or why, by the spontaneous action of the mind itself or by the latent influence of the body. Both science and poetry are made up of associations or recollections, but we must observe also that the mind is not wholly dependent on them, having also the power of origination.

There are other processes of the mind which it is good for us to study when we are at home and by ourselves,—the manner in which thought passes into act, the conflict of passion and reason in many stages, the transition from sensuality to love or sentiment and from earthly love to heavenly, the slow and silent influence of habit, which little by little changes the nature of men, the sudden change of the old nature of man into a new one, wrought by shame or by some other overwhelming impulse. These are the greater phenomena of mind, and he who has thought of them for himself will live and move in a better-ordered world, and will himself be a better-ordered man.

At the other end of the 'globus intellectualis,' nearest, not to earth and sense, but to heaven and God, is the personality of man, by which he holds communion with the unseen world. Somehow, he knows not how, somewhere, he knows not where, under this higher aspect of his being he grasps the ideas of God, freedom and immortality; he sees the forms of truth, holiness and love, and is satisfied with them. No account of the mind can be complete which does not admit the reality or the possibility of another life. Whether regarded as an ideal or as a fact, the highest part of man's nature and that in which it seems most nearly to approach the divine, is a phenomenon which exists, and must therefore be included within the domain of Psychology.

IV. We admit that there is no perfect or ideal Psychology. It is not a whole in the same sense in which Chemistry, Physiology, or Mathematics are wholes: that is to say, it is not a connected unity of knowledge. Compared with the wealth of other sciences, it rests upon a small number of facts; and when we go beyond these, we fall into conjectures and verbal discussions. The facts themselves are disjointed; the causes of them run up into other sciences, and we have no means of tracing them from one to the other. Yet it may be true of this, as of other beginnings of knowledge, that the attempt to put them together has tested the truth of them, and given a stimulus to the enquiry into them.

Psychology should be natural, not technical. It should take the form which is the most intelligible to the common understanding, because it has to do with common things, which are familiar to us all. It should aim at no more than every reflecting man knows or can easily verify for himself. When simple and unpretentious, it is least obscured by words, least liable to fall under the influence of Physiology or Metaphysic. It should argue, not from exceptional, but from ordinary phenomena. It should be careful to distinguish the higher and the lower elements of human nature, and not allow one to be veiled in the disguise of the other, lest through the slippery nature of language we should pass imperceptibly from good to evil, from nature in the higher to nature in the neutral or lower sense. It should assert consistently the unity of the human faculties, the unity of knowledge, the unity of God and law. The difference between the will and the affections and between the reason and the passions should also be recognized by it.

Its sphere is supposed to be narrowed to the individual soul; but it cannot be thus separated in fact. It goes back to the beginnings of things, to the first growth of language and philosophy, and to the whole science of man. There can be no truth or completeness in any study of the mind which is confined to the individual. The nature of language, though not the whole, is perhaps at present the most important element in our knowledge of it. It is not impossible that some numerical laws may be found to have a place in the relations of mind and matter, as in the rest of nature. The old Pythagorean fancy that the soul 'is or has in it harmony' may in some degree be realized. But the indications of such numerical harmonies are faint; either the secret of them lies deeper than we can discover, or nature may have rebelled against the use of them in the composition of men and animals. It is with qualitative rather than with quantitative differences that we are concerned in Psychology. The facts relating to the mind which we obtain from Physiology are negative rather than positive. They show us, not the processes of mental action, but the conditions of which when deprived the mind ceases to act. It would seem as if the time had not yet arrived when we can hope to add anything of much importance to our knowledge of the mind from the investigations of the microscope. The elements of Psychology can still only be learnt from reflections on ourselves, which interpret and are also interpreted by our experience of others. The history of language, of philosophy, and religion, the great thoughts or inventions or discoveries which move mankind, furnish the larger moulds or outlines in which the human mind has been cast. From these the individual derives so much as he is able to comprehend or has the opportunity of learning.

THEÆTETUS

by

Plato

Translated by Benjamin Jowett

PERSONS OF THE DIALOGUE: Socrates, Theodorus, Theætetus.

Euclid and Terpsion meet in front of Euclid's house in Megara; they enter the house, and the dialogue is read to them by a servant.

EUCLID: Have you only just arrived from the country, Terpsion?

TERPSION: No, I came some time ago: and I have been in the Agora looking for you, and wondering that I could not find you.

EUCLID: But I was not in the city.

TERPSION: Where then?

EUCLID: As I was going down to the harbour, I met Theætetus—he was being carried up to Athens from the army at Corinth.

TERPSION: Was he alive or dead?

EUCLID: He was scarcely alive, for he has been badly wounded; but he was suffering even more from the sickness which has broken out in the army.

Theætetus

TERPSION: The dysentery, you mean?

EUCLID: Yes.

TERPSION: Alas! what a loss he will be!

EUCLID: Yes, Terpsion, he is a noble fellow; only to-day I heard some people highly praising his behaviour in this very battle.

TERPSION: No wonder; I should rather be surprised at hearing anything else of him. But why did he go on, instead of stopping at Megara?

EUCLID: He wanted to get home: although I entreated and advised him to remain, he would not listen to me; so I set him on his way, and turned back, and then I remembered what Socrates had said of him, and thought how remarkably this, like all his predictions, had been fulfilled. I believe that he had seen him a little before his own death, when Theætetus was a youth, and he had a memorable conversation with him, which he repeated to me when I came to Athens; he was full of admiration of his genius, and said that he would most certainly be a great man, if he lived.

TERPSION: The prophecy has certainly been fulfilled; but what was the conversation? can you tell me?

EUCLID: No, indeed, not offhand; but I took notes of it as soon as I got home; these I filled up from memory, writing them out at leisure; and whenever I went to Athens, I asked Socrates about any point which I had forgotten, and on my return I made corrections; thus I have nearly the whole conversation written down.

TERPSION: I remember—you told me; and I have always been intending to ask you to show me the writing, but have put off doing so; and now, why should we not read it through?—having just come from the country, I should greatly like to rest.

EUCLID: I too shall be very glad of a rest, for I went with Theætetus as far as Erineum. Let us go in, then, and, while we are reposing, the servant shall read to us.

TERPSION: Very good.

EUCLID: Here is the roll, Terpsion; I may observe that I have introduced Socrates, not as narrating to me, but as actually conversing with the persons whom he mentioned—these were, Theodorus the geometrician (of Cyrene), and Theætetus. I have omitted, for the sake of convenience, the interlocutory words 'I said,' 'I remarked,' which he used when he spoke of himself, and again, 'he agreed,' or 'disagreed,' in the answer, lest the repetition of them should be troublesome.

TERPSION: Quite right, Euclid.

EUCLID: And now, boy, you may take the roll and read.

EUCLID'S SERVANT READS.

SOCRATES: If I cared enough about the Cyrenians, Theodorus, I would ask you whether there are any rising geometricians or philosophers in that part of the world. But I am more interested in our own Athenian youth, and I would rather know who among them are likely to do well. I observe them as far as I can myself, and I enquire of any one whom they follow, and I see that a great many of them follow you, in which they are quite right, considering your eminence in geometry and in other ways. Tell me then, if you have met with any one who is good for anything.

THEODORUS: Yes, Socrates, I have become acquainted with one very remarkable Athenian youth, whom I commend to you as well worthy of your attention. If he had been a beauty I should have been afraid to praise him, lest you should suppose that I was in love with him; but he is no beauty, and you must not be offended if I say that he is very like you; for he has a snub nose and projecting eyes,

Theætetus

although these features are less marked in him than in you. Seeing, then, that he has no personal attractions, I may freely say, that in all my acquaintance, which is very large, I never knew any one who was his equal in natural gifts: for he has a quickness of apprehension which is almost unrivalled, and he is exceedingly gentle, and also the most courageous of men; there is a union of qualities in him such as I have never seen in any other, and should scarcely have thought possible; for those who, like him, have quick and ready and retentive wits, have generally also quick tempers; they are ships without ballast, and go darting about, and are mad rather than courageous; and the steadier sort, when they have to face study, prove stupid and cannot remember. Whereas he moves surely and smoothly and successfully in the path of knowledge and enquiry; and he is full of gentleness, flowing on silently like a river of oil; at his age, it is wonderful.

SOCRATES: That is good news; whose son is he?

THEODORUS: The name of his father I have forgotten, but the youth himself is the middle one of those who are approaching us; he and his companions have been anointing themselves in the outer court, and now they seem to have finished, and are coming towards us. Look and see whether you know him.

SOCRATES: I know the youth, but I do not know his name; he is the son of Euphronius the Sunian, who was himself an eminent man, and such another as his son is, according to your account of him; I believe that he left a considerable fortune.

THEODORUS: Theætetus, Socrates, is his name; but I rather think that the property disappeared in the hands of trustees; notwithstanding which he is wonderfully liberal.

SOCRATES: He must be a fine fellow; tell him to come and sit by me.

THEODORUS: I will. Come hither, Theætetus, and sit by Socrates.

SOCRATES: By all means, Theætetus, in order that I may see the reflection of myself in your face, for Theodorus says that we are alike; and yet if each of us held in his hands a lyre, and he said that they were tuned alike, should we at once take his word, or should we ask whether he who said so was or was not a musician?

THEÆTETUS: We should ask.

SOCRATES: And if we found that he was, we should take his word; and if not, not?

THEÆTETUS: True.

SOCRATES: And if this supposed likeness of our faces is a matter of any interest to us, we should enquire whether he who says that we are alike is a painter or not?

THEÆTETUS: Certainly we should.

SOCRATES: And is Theodorus a painter?

THEÆTETUS: I never heard that he was.

SOCRATES: Is he a geometrician?

THEÆTETUS: Of course he is, Socrates.

SOCRATES: And is he an astronomer and calculator and musician, and in general an educated man?

THEÆTETUS: I think so.

SOCRATES: If, then, he remarks on a similarity in our persons, either by way of praise or blame, there is no particular reason why we should attend to him.

THEÆTETUS: I should say not.

Theætetus

SOCRATES: But if he praises the virtue or wisdom which are the mental endowments of either of us, then he who hears the praises will naturally desire to examine him who is praised: and he again should be willing to exhibit himself.

THEÆTETUS: Very true, Socrates.

SOCRATES: Then now is the time, my dear Theætetus, for me to examine, and for you to exhibit; since although Theodorus has praised many a citizen and stranger in my hearing, never did I hear him praise any one as he has been praising you.

THEÆTETUS: I am glad to hear it, Socrates; but what if he was only in jest?

SOCRATES: Nay, Theodorus is not given to jesting; and I cannot allow you to retract your consent on any such pretence as that. If you do, he will have to swear to his words; and we are perfectly sure that no one will be found to impugn him. Do not be shy then, but stand to your word.

THEÆTETUS: I suppose I must, if you wish it.

SOCRATES: In the first place, I should like to ask what you learn of Theodorus: something of geometry, perhaps?

THEÆTETUS: Yes.

SOCRATES: And astronomy and harmony and calculation?

THEÆTETUS: I do my best.

SOCRATES: Yes, my boy, and so do I; and my desire is to learn of him, or of anybody who seems to understand these things. And I get on pretty well in general; but there is a little difficulty which I want you and the company to aid me in investigating. Will you answer me a question: 'Is not learning growing wiser about that which you learn?'

THEÆTETUS: Of course.

SOCRATES: And by wisdom the wise are wise?

THEÆTETUS: Yes.

SOCRATES: And is that different in any way from knowledge?

THEÆTETUS: What?

SOCRATES: Wisdom; are not men wise in that which they know?

THEÆTETUS: Certainly they are.

SOCRATES: Then wisdom and knowledge are the same?

THEÆTETUS: Yes.

SOCRATES: Herein lies the difficulty which I can never solve to my satisfaction—What is knowledge? Can we answer that question? What say you? which of us will speak first? whoever misses shall sit down, as at a game of ball, and shall be donkey, as the boys say; he who lasts out his competitors in the game without missing, shall be our king, and shall have the right of putting to us any questions which he pleases...Why is there no reply? I hope, Theodorus, that I am not betrayed into rudeness by my love of conversation? I only want to make us talk and be friendly and sociable.

THEODORUS: The reverse of rudeness, Socrates: but I would rather that you would ask one of the young fellows; for the truth is, that I am unused to your game of question and answer, and I am too old to learn; the young will be more suitable, and they will improve more than I shall, for youth is always able to improve. And so having made a beginning with Theætetus, I would advise you to go on with him and not let him off.

SOCRATES: Do you hear, Theætetus, what Theodorus says? The

Theætetus

philosopher, whom you would not like to disobey, and whose word ought to be a command to a young man, bids me interrogate you. Take courage, then, and nobly say what you think that knowledge is.

THEÆTETUS: Well, Socrates, I will answer as you and he bid me; and if I make a mistake, you will doubtless correct me.

SOCRATES: We will, if we can.

THEÆTETUS: Then, I think that the sciences which I learn from Theodorus—geometry, and those which you just now mentioned—are knowledge; and I would include the art of the cobbler and other craftsmen; these, each and all of, them, are knowledge.

SOCRATES: Too much, Theætetus, too much; the nobility and liberality of your nature make you give many and diverse things, when I am asking for one simple thing.

THEÆTETUS: What do you mean, Socrates?

SOCRATES: Perhaps nothing. I will endeavour, however, to explain what I believe to be my meaning: When you speak of cobbling, you mean the art or science of making shoes?

THEÆTETUS: Just so.

SOCRATES: And when you speak of carpentering, you mean the art of making wooden implements?

THEÆTETUS: I do.

SOCRATES: In both cases you define the subject matter of each of the two arts?

THEÆTETUS: True.

SOCRATES: But that, Theætetus, was not the point of my question: we wanted to know not the subjects, nor yet the number of the arts or sciences, for we were not going to count them, but we wanted to know the nature of knowledge in the abstract. Am I not right?

THEÆTETUS: Perfectly right.

SOCRATES: Let me offer an illustration: Suppose that a person were to ask about some very trivial and obvious thing—for example, What is clay? and we were to reply, that there is a clay of potters, there is a clay of oven-makers, there is a clay of brick-makers; would not the answer be ridiculous?

THEÆTETUS: Truly.

SOCRATES: In the first place, there would be an absurdity in assuming that he who asked the question would understand from our answer the nature of 'clay,' merely because we added 'of the image-makers,' or of any other workers. How can a man understand the name of anything, when he does not know the nature of it?

THEÆTETUS: He cannot.

SOCRATES: Then he who does not know what science or knowledge is, has no knowledge of the art or science of making shoes?

THEÆTETUS: None.

SOCRATES: Nor of any other science?

THEÆTETUS: No.

SOCRATES: And when a man is asked what science or knowledge is, to give in answer the name of some art or science is ridiculous; for the question is, 'What is knowledge?' and he replies, 'A knowledge of this or that.'

Theætetus

THEÆTETUS: True.

SOCRATES: Moreover, he might answer shortly and simply, but he makes an enormous circuit. For example, when asked about the clay, he might have said simply, that clay is moistened earth—what sort of clay is not to the point.

THEÆTETUS: Yes, Socrates, there is no difficulty as you put the question. You mean, if I am not mistaken, something like what occurred to me and to my friend here, your namesake Socrates, in a recent discussion.

SOCRATES: What was that, Theætetus?

THEÆTETUS: Theodorus was writing out for us something about roots, such as the roots of three or five, showing that they are incommensurable by the unit: he selected other examples up to seventeen—there he stopped. Now as there are innumerable roots, the notion occurred to us of attempting to include them all under one name or class.

SOCRATES: And did you find such a class?

THEÆTETUS: I think that we did; but I should like to have your opinion.

SOCRATES: Let me hear.

THEÆTETUS: We divided all numbers into two classes: those which are made up of equal factors multiplying into one another, which we compared to square figures and called square or equilateral numbers;—that was one class.

SOCRATES: Very good.

THEÆTETUS: The intermediate numbers, such as three and five, and every other number which is made up of unequal factors, either of a greater multiplied by a less, or of a less multiplied by a greater, and when regarded as a figure, is contained in unequal sides;—all these we compared to oblong figures, and called them oblong numbers.

SOCRATES: Capital; and what followed?

THEÆTETUS: The lines, or sides, which have for their squares the equilateral plane numbers, were called by us lengths or magnitudes; and the lines which are the roots of (or whose squares are equal to) the oblong numbers, were called powers or roots; the reason of this latter name being, that they are commensurable with the former [i.e., with the so-called lengths or magnitudes] not in linear measurement, but in the value of the superficial content of their squares; and the same about solids.

SOCRATES: Excellent, my boys; I think that you fully justify the praises of Theodorus, and that he will not be found guilty of false witness.

THEÆTETUS: But I am unable, Socrates, to give you a similar answer about knowledge, which is what you appear to want; and therefore Theodorus is a deceiver after all.

SOCRATES: Well, but if some one were to praise you for running, and to say that he never met your equal among boys, and afterwards you were beaten in a race by a grown-up man, who was a great runner—would the praise be any the less true?

THEÆTETUS: Certainly not.
SOCRATES: And is the discovery of the nature of knowledge so small a matter, as just now said? Is it not one which would task the powers of men perfect in every way?

THEÆTETUS: By heaven, they should be the top of all perfection!

SOCRATES: Well, then, be of good cheer; do not say that Theodorus was mistaken about you, but do your best to ascertain the true nature of knowledge, as well as of other things.

THEÆTETUS: I am eager enough, Socrates, if that would bring to light the truth.

SOCRATES: Come, you made a good beginning just now; let your own answer about roots be your model, and as you comprehended them all in one class, try and bring the many sorts of knowledge under one definition.

THEÆTETUS: I can assure you, Socrates, that I have tried very often, when the report of questions asked by you was brought to me; but I can neither persuade myself that I have a satisfactory answer to give, nor hear of any one who answers as you would have him; and I cannot shake off a feeling of anxiety.

SOCRATES: These are the pangs of labour, my dear Theætetus; you have something within you which you are bringing to the birth.

THEÆTETUS: I do not know, Socrates; I only say what I feel.

SOCRATES: And have you never heard, simpleton, that I am the son of a midwife, brave and burly, whose name was Phaenarete?

THEÆTETUS: Yes, I have.

SOCRATES: And that I myself practise midwifery?

THEÆTETUS: No, never.

SOCRATES: Let me tell you that I do though, my friend: but you must not reveal the secret, as the world in general have not found me out; and therefore they only say of me, that I am the strangest of mortals and drive men to their wits' end. Did you ever hear that too?

THEÆTETUS: Yes.

SOCRATES: Shall I tell you the reason?

THEÆTETUS: By all means.

SOCRATES: Bear in mind the whole business of the midwives, and then you will see my meaning better:—No woman, as you are probably aware, who is still able to conceive and bear, attends other women, but only those who are past bearing.

THEÆTETUS: Yes, I know.

SOCRATES: The reason of this is said to be that Artemis—the goddess of childbirth—is not a mother, and she honours those who are like herself; but she could not allow the barren to be midwives, because human nature cannot know the mystery of an art without experience; and therefore she assigned this office to those who are too old to bear.

THEÆTETUS: I dare say.

SOCRATES: And I dare say too, or rather I am absolutely certain, that the midwives know better than others who is pregnant and who is not?

THEÆTETUS: Very true.

SOCRATES: And by the use of potions and incantations they are able to arouse the pangs and to soothe them at will; they can make those bear who have a difficulty in bearing, and if they think fit they can smother the embryo in the womb.

THEÆTETUS: They can.

SOCRATES: Did you ever remark that they are also most cunning matchmakers, and have a thorough knowledge of what unions are likely to produce a brave brood?

THEÆTETUS: No, never.

SOCRATES: Then let me tell you that this is their greatest pride, more than cutting the umbilical cord. And if you reflect, you will see that the same art which cultivates and gathers in the fruits of the earth, will be most likely to know in what soils the several plants or seeds should be deposited.

THEÆTETUS: Yes, the same art.

SOCRATES: And do you suppose that with women the case is otherwise?

THEÆTETUS: I should think not.

SOCRATES: Certainly not; but midwives are respectable women who have a character to lose, and they avoid this department of their profession, because they are afraid of being called procuresses, which is a name given to those who join together man and woman in an unlawful and unscientific way; and yet the true midwife is also the true and only matchmaker.

THEÆTETUS: Clearly.

SOCRATES: Such are the midwives, whose task is a very important one, but not so important as mine; for women do not bring into the world at one time real children, and at another time counterfeits which are with difficulty distinguished from them; if they did, then the discernment of the true and false birth would be the crowning achievement of the art of midwifery—you would think so?

THEÆTETUS: Indeed I should.

SOCRATES: Well, my art of midwifery is in most respects like theirs; but differs, in that I attend men and not women; and look after their souls when they are in labour, and not after their bodies: and the triumph of my art is in thoroughly examining whether the thought which the mind of the young man brings forth is a false idol or a noble and true birth. And like the midwives, I am barren, and the reproach which is often made against me, that I ask questions of others and have not the wit to answer them myself, is very just—the reason is, that the god compels me to be a midwife, but does not allow me to bring forth. And therefore I am not myself at all wise, nor have I anything to show which is the invention or birth of my own soul, but those who converse with me profit. Some of them appear dull enough at first, but afterwards, as our acquaintance ripens, if the god is gracious to them, they all make astonishing progress; and this in the opinion of others as well as in their own. It is quite clear that they never learned anything from me; the many fine discoveries to which they cling are of their own making. But to me and the god they owe their delivery. And the proof of my words is, that many of them in their ignorance, either in their self-conceit despising me, or falling under the influence of others, have gone away too soon; and have not only lost the children of whom I had previously delivered them by an ill bringing up, but have stifled whatever else they had in them by evil communications, being fonder of lies and shams than of the truth; and they have at last ended by seeing themselves, as others see them, to be great fools. Aristeides, the son of Lysimachus, is one of them, and there are many others. The truants often return to me, and beg that I would consort with them again—they are ready to go to me on their knees—and then, if my familiar allows, which is not always the case, I receive them, and they begin to grow again. Dire are the pangs which my art is able to arouse and to allay in those who consort with me, just like the pangs of women in childbirth; night and day they are full of perplexity and travail which is even worse than that of the women. So much for them. And there are others, Theætetus, who come to me apparently having nothing in them; and as I know that they have no need of my art, I coax them into marrying some one, and by the grace of God I can generally tell who is likely to do them good. Many of them I have given away to Prodicus, and many to other inspired sages. I tell you this long story, friend Theætetus, because I suspect, as indeed you seem to think yourself, that you are in labour—great with some conception. Come then to me, who am a midwife's son and myself a midwife, and do your best to answer the questions which I will ask you. And if I abstract and expose your first-born, because I discover upon inspection that the conception which you have formed is a vain shadow, do not quarrel with me on that account, as the manner of women is when their first children are taken from them. For I have actually known some who were ready to bite me when I deprived them of a darling folly; they did not perceive that I acted from goodwill, not knowing that no god is the enemy of man—that was not within the range of their ideas; neither am I their enemy in all this, but it would be wrong for me to admit falsehood, or to stifle the truth. Once more, then, Theætetus, I repeat my old question, 'What is knowledge?'—and do not say that you cannot tell; but quit yourself like a man, and by the help of God you will be able to tell.

THEÆTETUS: At any rate, Socrates, after such an exhortation I should be ashamed of not trying to do my best. Now he who knows perceives what he knows, and, as far as I can see at present, knowledge is perception.

SOCRATES: Bravely said, boy; that is the way in which you should express your opinion. And now, let us examine together this conception of yours, and see whether it is a true birth or a mere wind-egg:—You say that knowledge is perception?

THEÆTETUS: Yes.

SOCRATES: Well, you have delivered yourself of a very important doctrine about knowledge; it is indeed the opinion of Protagoras, who has another way of expressing it. Man, he says, is the measure of all things, of the existence of things that are, and of the non-existence of things that are not:—You have read him?

THEÆTETUS: O yes, again and again.

SOCRATES: Does he not say that things are to you such as they appear to you, and to me such as they appear to me, and that you and I are men?

THEÆTETUS: Yes, he says so.

SOCRATES: A wise man is not likely to talk nonsense. Let us try to understand him: the same wind is blowing, and yet one of us may be cold and the other not, or one may be slightly and the other very cold?

THEÆTETUS: Quite true.

SOCRATES: Now is the wind, regarded not in relation to us but absolutely, cold or not; or are we to say, with Protagoras, that the wind is cold to him who is cold, and not to him who is not?

THEÆTETUS: I suppose the last.

SOCRATES: Then it must appear so to each of them?

THEÆTETUS: Yes.

SOCRATES: And 'appears to him' means the same as 'he perceives.'

THEÆTETUS: True.

SOCRATES: Then appearing and perceiving coincide in the case of hot and cold, and in similar instances; for things appear, or may be supposed to be, to each one such as he perceives them?

THEÆTETUS: Yes.

SOCRATES: Then perception is always of existence, and being the same as knowledge is unerring?

THEÆTETUS: Clearly.

Theætetus

SOCRATES: In the name of the Graces, what an almighty wise man Protagoras must have been! He spoke these things in a parable to the common herd, like you and me, but told the truth, 'his Truth,' (In allusion to a book of Protagoras' which bore this title.) in secret to his own disciples.

THEÆTETUS: What do you mean, Socrates?

SOCRATES: I am about to speak of a high argument, in which all things are said to be relative; you cannot rightly call anything by any name, such as great or small, heavy or light, for the great will be small and the heavy light—there is no single thing or quality, but out of motion and change and admixture all things are becoming relatively to one another, which 'becoming' is by us incorrectly called being, but is really becoming, for nothing ever is, but all things are becoming. Summon all philosophers—Protagoras, Heracleitus, Empedocles, and the rest of them, one after another, and with the exception of Parmenides they will agree with you in this. Summon the great masters of either kind of poetry—Epicharmus, the prince of Comedy, and Homer of Tragedy; when the latter sings of

> 'Ocean whence sprang the gods, and mother Tethys,'

does he not mean that all things are the offspring, of flux and motion?

THEÆTETUS: I think so.

SOCRATES: And who could take up arms against such a great army having Homer for its general, and not appear ridiculous? (Compare Cratylus.)

THEÆTETUS: Who indeed, Socrates?

SOCRATES: Yes, Theætetus; and there are plenty of other proofs which will show that motion is the source of what is called being and becoming, and inactivity of not-being and destruction; for fire and warmth, which are supposed to be the parent and guardian of all other things, are born of movement and of friction, which is a kind of motion;—is not this the origin of fire?

THEÆTETUS: It is.

SOCRATES: And the race of animals is generated in the same way?

THEÆTETUS: Certainly.

SOCRATES: And is not the bodily habit spoiled by rest and idleness, but preserved for a long time by motion and exercise?

THEÆTETUS: True.

SOCRATES: And what of the mental habit? Is not the soul informed, and improved, and preserved by study and attention, which are motions; but when at rest, which in the soul only means want of attention and study, is uninformed, and speedily forgets whatever she has learned?

THEÆTETUS: True.

SOCRATES: Then motion is a good, and rest an evil, to the soul as well as to the body?

THEÆTETUS: Clearly.

SOCRATES: I may add, that breathless calm, stillness and the like waste and impair, while wind and storm preserve; and the palmary argument of all, which I strongly urge, is the golden chain in Homer, by which he means the sun, thereby indicating that so long as the sun and the heavens go round in their orbits, all things human and divine are and are preserved, but if they were chained up and their motions ceased, then all things would be destroyed, and, as the saying is, turned upside down.

Theætetus

THEÆTETUS: I believe, Socrates, that you have truly explained his meaning.

SOCRATES: Then now apply his doctrine to perception, my good friend, and first of all to vision; that which you call white colour is not in your eyes, and is not a distinct thing which exists out of them. And you must not assign any place to it: for if it had position it would be, and be at rest, and there would be no process of becoming.

THEÆTETUS: Then what is colour?

SOCRATES: Let us carry the principle which has just been affirmed, that nothing is self-existent, and then we shall see that white, black, and every other colour, arises out of the eye meeting the appropriate motion, and that what we call a colour is in each case neither the active nor the passive element, but something which passes between them, and is peculiar to each percipient; are you quite certain that the several colours appear to a dog or to any animal whatever as they appear to you?

THEÆTETUS: Far from it.

SOCRATES: Or that anything appears the same to you as to another man? Are you so profoundly convinced of this? Rather would it not be true that it never appears exactly the same to you, because you are never exactly the same?

THEÆTETUS: The latter.

SOCRATES: And if that with which I compare myself in size, or which I apprehend by touch, were great or white or hot, it could not become different by mere contact with another unless it actually changed; nor again, if the comparing or apprehending subject were great or white or hot, could this, when unchanged from within, become changed by any approximation or affection of any other thing. The fact is that in our ordinary way of speaking we allow ourselves to be driven into most ridiculous and wonderful contradictions, as Protagoras and all who take his line of argument would remark.

THEÆTETUS: How? and of what sort do you mean?

SOCRATES: A little instance will sufficiently explain my meaning: Here are six dice, which are more by a half when compared with four, and fewer by a half than twelve—they are more and also fewer. How can you or any one maintain the contrary?

THEÆTETUS: Very true.

SOCRATES: Well, then, suppose that Protagoras or some one asks whether anything can become greater or more if not by increasing, how would you answer him, Theætetus?

THEÆTETUS: I should say 'No,' Socrates, if I were to speak my mind in reference to this last question, and if I were not afraid of contradicting my former answer.

SOCRATES: Capital! excellent! spoken like an oracle, my boy! And if you reply 'Yes,' there will be a case for Euripides; for our tongue will be unconvinced, but not our mind. (In allusion to the well-known line of Euripides, Hippol.: e gloss omomoch e de thren anomotos.)

THEÆTETUS: Very true.

SOCRATES: The thoroughbred Sophists, who know all that can be known about the mind, and argue only out of the superfluity of their wits, would have had a regular sparring-match over this, and would have knocked their arguments together finely. But you and I, who have no professional aims, only desire to see what is the mutual relation of these principles,—whether they are consistent with each or not.

Theætetus

THEÆTETUS: Yes, that would be my desire.

SOCRATES: And mine too. But since this is our feeling, and there is plenty of time, why should we not calmly and patiently review our own thoughts, and thoroughly examine and see what these appearances in us really are? If I am not mistaken, they will be described by us as follows:—first, that nothing can become greater or less, either in number or magnitude, while remaining equal to itself—you would agree?

THEÆTETUS: Yes.

SOCRATES: Secondly, that without addition or subtraction there is no increase or diminution of anything, but only equality.

THEÆTETUS: Quite true.

SOCRATES: Thirdly, that what was not before cannot be afterwards, without becoming and having become.

THEÆTETUS: Yes, truly.

SOCRATES: These three axioms, if I am not mistaken, are fighting with one another in our minds in the case of the dice, or, again, in such a case as this—if I were to say that I, who am of a certain height and taller than you, may within a year, without gaining or losing in height, be not so tall—not that I should have lost, but that you would have increased. In such a case, I am afterwards what I once was not, and yet I have not become; for I could not have become without becoming, neither could I have become less without losing somewhat of my height; and I could give you ten thousand examples of similar contradictions, if we admit them at all. I believe that you follow me, Theætetus; for I suspect that you have thought of these questions before now.

THEÆTETUS: Yes, Socrates, and I am amazed when I think of them; by the Gods I am! and I want to know what on earth they mean; and there are times when my head quite swims with the contemplation of them.

SOCRATES: I see, my dear Theætetus, that Theodorus had a true insight into your nature when he said that you were a philosopher, for wonder is the feeling of a philosopher, and philosophy begins in wonder. He was not a bad genealogist who said that Iris (the messenger of heaven) is the child of Thaumas (wonder). But do you begin to see what is the explanation of this perplexity on the hypothesis which we attribute to Protagoras?

THEÆTETUS: Not as yet.

SOCRATES: Then you will be obliged to me if I help you to unearth the hidden 'truth' of a famous man or school.

THEÆTETUS: To be sure, I shall be very much obliged.

SOCRATES: Take a look round, then, and see that none of the uninitiated are listening. Now by the uninitiated I mean the people who believe in nothing but what they can grasp in their hands, and who will not allow that action or generation or anything invisible can have real existence.

THEÆTETUS: Yes, indeed, Socrates, they are very hard and impenetrable mortals.

SOCRATES: Yes, my boy, outer barbarians. Far more ingenious are the brethren whose mysteries I am about to reveal to you. Their first principle is, that all is motion, and upon this all the affections of which we were just now speaking are supposed to depend: there is nothing but motion, which has two forms, one active and the other passive, both in endless number; and out of the union and friction of them there is generated a progeny endless in number, having two forms, sense and the object of sense, which are ever breaking forth and coming to the birth at the same moment. The senses are variously named hearing, seeing, smelling; there is the sense of heat, cold, pleasure, pain, desire, fear, and many more which have names, as well as innumerable others which are without them; each has its kindred object,—each variety of colour has a corresponding variety of sight, and so with sound and hearing, and with the rest of the senses and the objects akin to them. Do you see, Theætetus, the bearings of this tale on the preceding argument?

THEÆTETUS: Indeed I do not.

SOCRATES: Then attend, and I will try to finish the story. The purport is that all these things are in motion, as I was saying, and that this motion is of two kinds, a slower and a quicker; and the slower elements have their motions in the same place and with reference to things near them, and so they beget; but what is begotten is swifter, for it is carried to fro, and moves from place to place. Apply this to sense:—When the eye and the appropriate object meet together and give birth to whiteness and the sensation connatural with it, which could not have been given by either of them going elsewhere, then, while the sight is flowing from the eye, whiteness proceeds from the object which combines in producing the colour; and so the eye is fulfilled with sight, and really sees, and becomes, not sight, but a seeing eye; and the object which combined to form the colour is fulfilled with whiteness, and becomes not whiteness but a white thing, whether wood or stone or whatever the object may be which happens to be coloured white. And this is true of all sensible objects, hard, warm, and the like, which are similarly to be regarded, as I was saying before, not as having any absolute existence, but as being all of them of whatever kind generated by motion in their intercourse with one another; for of the agent and patient, as existing in separation, no trustworthy conception, as they say, can be formed, for the agent has no existence until united with the patient, and the patient has no existence until united with the agent; and that which by uniting with something becomes an agent, by meeting with some other thing is converted into a patient. And from all these considerations, as I said at first, there arises a general reflection, that there is no one self-existent thing, but everything is becoming and in relation; and being must be altogether abolished, although from habit and ignorance we are compelled even in this discussion to retain the use of the term. But great philosophers tell us that we are not to allow either the word 'something,' or 'belonging to something,' or 'to me,' or 'this,' or 'that,' or any other detaining name to be used, in the language of nature all things are being created and destroyed, coming into being and passing into new forms; nor can any name fix or detain them; he who attempts to fix them is easily refuted. And this should be the way of speaking, not only of particulars but of aggregates; such aggregates as are expressed in the word 'man,' or 'stone,' or any name of an animal or of a class. O Theætetus, are not these speculations sweet as honey? And do you not like the taste of them in the mouth?

THEÆTETUS: I do not know what to say, Socrates; for, indeed, I cannot make out whether you are giving your own opinion or only wanting to draw me out.

SOCRATES: You forget, my friend, that I neither know, nor profess to know, anything of these matters; you are the person who is in labour, I am the barren midwife; and this is why I soothe you, and offer you one good thing after another, that you may taste them. And I hope that I may at last help to bring your own opinion into the light of day: when this has been accomplished, then we will determine whether what you have brought forth is only a wind-egg or a real and genuine birth. Therefore, keep up your spirits, and answer like a man what you think.

THEÆTETUS: Ask me.

SOCRATES: Then once more: Is it your opinion that nothing is but what becomes?—the good and the noble, as well as all the other things which we were just now mentioning?

THEÆTETUS: When I hear you discoursing in this style, I think that there is a great deal in what you say, and I am very ready to assent.

Theætetus

SOCRATES: Let us not leave the argument unfinished, then; for there still remains to be considered an objection which may be raised about dreams and diseases, in particular about madness, and the various illusions of hearing and sight, or of other senses. For you know that in all these cases the esse-percipi theory appears to be unmistakably refuted, since in dreams and illusions we certainly have false perceptions; and far from saying that everything is which appears, we should rather say that nothing is which appears.

THEÆTETUS: Very true, Socrates.

SOCRATES: But then, my boy, how can any one contend that knowledge is perception, or that to every man what appears is?

THEÆTETUS: I am afraid to say, Socrates, that I have nothing to answer, because you rebuked me just now for making this excuse; but I certainly cannot undertake to argue that madmen or dreamers think truly, when they imagine, some of them that they are gods, and others that they can fly, and are flying in their sleep.

SOCRATES: Do you see another question which can be raised about these phenomena, notably about dreaming and waking?

THEÆTETUS: What question?

SOCRATES: A question which I think that you must often have heard persons ask:—How can you determine whether at this moment we are sleeping, and all our thoughts are a dream; or whether we are awake, and talking to one another in the waking state?

THEÆTETUS: Indeed, Socrates, I do not know how to prove the one any more than the other, for in both cases the facts precisely correspond;—and there is no difficulty in supposing that during all this discussion we have been talking to one another in a dream; and when in a dream we seem to be narrating dreams, the resemblance of the two states is quite astonishing.

SOCRATES: You see, then, that a doubt about the reality of sense is easily raised, since there may even be a doubt whether we are awake or in a dream. And as our time is equally divided between sleeping and waking, in either sphere of existence the soul contends that the thoughts which are present to our minds at the time are true; and during one half of our lives we affirm the truth of the one, and, during the other half, of the other; and are equally confident of both.

THEÆTETUS: Most true.

SOCRATES: And may not the same be said of madness and other disorders? the difference is only that the times are not equal.

THEÆTETUS: Certainly.

SOCRATES: And is truth or falsehood to be determined by duration of time?

THEÆTETUS: That would be in many ways ridiculous.

SOCRATES: But can you certainly determine by any other means which of these opinions is true?

THEÆTETUS: I do not think that I can.

SOCRATES: Listen, then, to a statement of the other side of the argument, which is made by the champions of appearance. They would say, as I imagine—Can that which is wholly other than something, have the same quality as that from which it differs? and observe, Theætetus, that the word 'other' means not 'partially,' but 'wholly other.'

THEÆTETUS: Certainly, putting the question as you do, that which is wholly other cannot either potentially or in any other way be the same.

SOCRATES: And must therefore be admitted to be unlike?

THEÆTETUS: True.

SOCRATES: If, then, anything happens to become like or unlike itself or another, when it becomes like we call it the same—when unlike, other?

THEÆTETUS: Certainly.

SOCRATES: Were we not saying that there are agents many and infinite, and patients many and infinite?

THEÆTETUS: Yes.

SOCRATES: And also that different combinations will produce results which are not the same, but different?

THEÆTETUS: Certainly.

SOCRATES: Let us take you and me, or anything as an example:—There is Socrates in health, and Socrates sick—Are they like or unlike?

THEÆTETUS: You mean to compare Socrates in health as a whole, and Socrates in sickness as a whole?

SOCRATES: Exactly; that is my meaning.

THEÆTETUS: I answer, they are unlike.

SOCRATES: And if unlike, they are other?

THEÆTETUS: Certainly.

SOCRATES: And would you not say the same of Socrates sleeping and waking, or in any of the states which we were mentioning?

THEÆTETUS: I should.

SOCRATES: All agents have a different patient in Socrates, accordingly as he is well or ill.

THEÆTETUS: Of course.

SOCRATES: And I who am the patient, and that which is the agent, will produce something different in each of the two cases?

THEÆTETUS: Certainly.

SOCRATES: The wine which I drink when I am in health, appears sweet and pleasant to me?

THEÆTETUS: True.

SOCRATES: For, as has been already acknowledged, the patient and agent meet together and produce sweetness and a perception of sweetness, which are in simultaneous motion, and the perception which comes from the patient makes the tongue percipient, and the quality of sweetness which arises out of and is moving about the wine, makes the wine both to be and to appear sweet to the healthy tongue.

THEÆTETUS: Certainly; that has been already acknowledged.

SOCRATES: But when I am sick, the wine really acts upon another and a different person?

THEÆTETUS: Yes.

SOCRATES: The combination of the draught of wine, and the Socrates who is sick, produces quite another result; which is the sensation of bitterness in the tongue, and the motion and creation of bitterness in and about the wine, which becomes not bitterness but something bitter; as I myself become not perception but percipient?

THEÆTETUS: True.

SOCRATES: There is no other object of which I shall ever have the same perception, for another object would give another perception, and would make the percipient other and different; nor can that object which affects me, meeting another subject, produce the same, or become similar, for that too would produce another result from another subject, and become different.

THEÆTETUS: True.

SOCRATES: Neither can I by myself, have this sensation, nor the object by itself, this quality.

THEÆTETUS: Certainly not.

SOCRATES: When I perceive I must become percipient of something—there can be no such thing as perceiving and perceiving nothing; the object, whether it become sweet, bitter, or of any other quality, must have relation to a percipient; nothing can become sweet which is sweet to no one.

THEÆTETUS: Certainly not.

SOCRATES: Then the inference is, that we (the agent and patient) are or become in relation to one another; there is a law which binds us one to the other, but not to any other existence, nor each of us to himself; and therefore we can only be bound to one another; so that whether a person says that a thing is or becomes, he must say that it is or becomes to or of or in relation to something else; but he must not say or allow any one else to say that anything is or becomes absolutely:—such is our conclusion.

THEÆTETUS: Very true, Socrates.

SOCRATES: Then, if that which acts upon me has relation to me and to no other, I and no other am the percipient of it?

THEÆTETUS: Of course.

SOCRATES: Then my perception is true to me, being inseparable from my own being; and, as Protagoras says, to myself I am judge of what is and what is not to me.

THEÆTETUS: I suppose so.

SOCRATES: How then, if I never err, and if my mind never trips in the conception of being or becoming, can I fail of knowing that which I perceive?

THEÆTETUS: You cannot.

SOCRATES: Then you were quite right in affirming that knowledge is only perception; and the meaning turns out to be the same, whether with Homer and Heracleitus, and all that company, you say that all is motion and flux, or with the great sage Protagoras, that man is the measure of all things; or with Theætetus, that, given these premises, perception is knowledge. Am I not right, Theætetus, and is not this your new-born child, of which I have delivered you? What say you?

THEÆTETUS: I cannot but agree, Socrates.

SOCRATES: Then this is the child, however he may turn out, which you and I have with difficulty brought into the world. And now that he is born, we must run round the hearth with him, and see whether he is worth rearing, or is only a wind-egg and a sham. Is he to be reared in any case, and not exposed? or will you bear to see him rejected, and not get into a passion if I take away your first-born?

THEODORUS: Theætetus will not be angry, for he is very good-natured. But tell me, Socrates, in heaven's name, is this, after all, not the truth?

Theætetus

SOCRATES: You, Theodorus, are a lover of theories, and now you innocently fancy that I am a bag full of them, and can easily pull one out which will overthrow its predecessor. But you do not see that in reality none of these theories come from me; they all come from him who talks with me. I only know just enough to extract them from the wisdom of another, and to receive them in a spirit of fairness. And now I shall say nothing myself, but shall endeavour to elicit something from our young friend.

THEODORUS: Do as you say, Socrates; you are quite right.

SOCRATES: Shall I tell you, Theodorus, what amazes me in your acquaintance Protagoras?

THEODORUS: What is it?

SOCRATES: I am charmed with his doctrine, that what appears is to each one, but I wonder that he did not begin his book on Truth with a declaration that a pig or a dog-faced baboon, or some other yet stranger monster which has sensation, is the measure of all things; then he might have shown a magnificent contempt for our opinion of him by informing us at the outset that while we were reverencing him like a God for his wisdom he was no better than a tadpole, not to speak of his fellow-men—would not this have produced an overpowering effect? For if truth is only sensation, and no man can discern another's feelings better than he, or has any superior right to determine whether his opinion is true or false, but each, as we have several times repeated, is to himself the sole judge, and everything that he judges is true and right, why, my friend, should Protagoras be preferred to the place of wisdom and instruction, and deserve to be well paid, and we poor ignoramuses have to go to him, if each one is the measure of his own wisdom? Must he not be talking 'ad captandum' in all this? I say nothing of the ridiculous predicament in which my own midwifery and the whole art of dialectic is placed; for the attempt to supervise or refute the notions or opinions of others would be a tedious and enormous piece of folly, if to each man his own are right; and this must be the case if Protagoras' Truth is the real truth, and the philosopher is not merely amusing himself by giving oracles out of the shrine of his book.

THEODORUS: He was a friend of mine, Socrates, as you were saying, and therefore I cannot have him refuted by my lips, nor can I oppose you when I agree with you; please, then, to take Theætetus again; he seemed to answer very nicely.

SOCRATES: If you were to go into a Lacedaemonian palestra, Theodorus, would you have a right to look on at the naked wrestlers, some of them making a poor figure, if you did not strip and give them an opportunity of judging of your own person?

THEODORUS: Why not, Socrates, if they would allow me, as I think you will, in consideration of my age and stiffness; let some more supple youth try a fall with you, and do not drag me into the gymnasium.

SOCRATES: Your will is my will, Theodorus, as the proverbial philosophers say, and therefore I will return to the sage Theætetus: Tell me, Theætetus, in reference to what I was saying, are you not lost in wonder, like myself, when you find that all of a sudden you are raised to the level of the wisest of men, or indeed of the gods?—for you would assume the measure of Protagoras to apply to the gods as well as men?

THEÆTETUS: Certainly I should, and I confess to you that I am lost in wonder. At first hearing, I was quite satisfied with the doctrine, that whatever appears is to each one, but now the face of things has changed.

SOCRATES: Why, my dear boy, you are young, and therefore your ear is quickly caught and your mind influenced by popular arguments. Protagoras, or some one speaking on his behalf, will doubtless say in reply,—Good people, young and old, you meet and harangue, and bring in the gods, whose existence or non-existence I banish from writing and speech, or you talk about the reason of

Theætetus

man being degraded to the level of the brutes, which is a telling argument with the multitude, but not one word of proof or demonstration do you offer. All is probability with you, and yet surely you and Theodorus had better reflect whether you are disposed to admit of probability and figures of speech in matters of such importance. He or any other mathematician who argued from probabilities and likelihoods in geometry, would not be worth an ace.

THEÆTETUS: But neither you nor we, Socrates, would be satisfied with such arguments.

SOCRATES: Then you and Theodorus mean to say that we must look at the matter in some other way?

THEÆTETUS: Yes, in quite another way.

SOCRATES: And the way will be to ask whether perception is or is not the same as knowledge; for this was the real point of our argument, and with a view to this we raised (did we not?) those many strange questions.

THEÆTETUS: Certainly.

SOCRATES: Shall we say that we know every thing which we see and hear? for example, shall we say that not having learned, we do not hear the language of foreigners when they speak to us? or shall we say that we not only hear, but know what they are saying? Or again, if we see letters which we do not understand, shall we say that we do not see them? or shall we aver that, seeing them, we must know them?

THEÆTETUS: We shall say, Socrates, that we know what we actually see and hear of them—that is to say, we see and know the figure and colour of the letters, and we hear and know the elevation or depression of the sound of them; but we do not perceive by sight and hearing, or know, that which grammarians and interpreters teach about them.

SOCRATES: Capital, Theætetus; and about this there shall be no dispute, because I want you to grow; but there is another difficulty coming, which you will also have to repulse.

THEÆTETUS: What is it?

SOCRATES: Some one will say, Can a man who has ever known anything, and still has and preserves a memory of that which he knows, not know that which he remembers at the time when he remembers? I have, I fear, a tedious way of putting a simple question, which is only, whether a man who has learned, and remembers, can fail to know?

THEÆTETUS: Impossible, Socrates; the supposition is monstrous.

SOCRATES: Am I talking nonsense, then? Think: is not seeing perceiving, and is not sight perception?

THEÆTETUS: True.

SOCRATES: And if our recent definition holds, every man knows that which he has seen?

THEÆTETUS: Yes.

SOCRATES: And you would admit that there is such a thing as memory?

THEÆTETUS: Yes.

SOCRATES: And is memory of something or of nothing?

THEÆTETUS: Of something, surely.

SOCRATES: Of things learned and perceived, that is?

THEÆTETUS: Certainly.

SOCRATES: Often a man remembers that which he has seen?

THEÆTETUS: True.

SOCRATES: And if he closed his eyes, would he forget?

THEÆTETUS: Who, Socrates, would dare to say so?

SOCRATES: But we must say so, if the previous argument is to be maintained.

THEÆTETUS: What do you mean? I am not quite sure that I understand you, though I have a strong suspicion that you are right.

SOCRATES: As thus: he who sees knows, as we say, that which he sees; for perception and sight and knowledge are admitted to be the same.

THEÆTETUS: Certainly.

SOCRATES: But he who saw, and has knowledge of that which he saw, remembers, when he closes his eyes, that which he no longer sees.

THEÆTETUS: True.

SOCRATES: And seeing is knowing, and therefore not-seeing is not-knowing?

THEÆTETUS: Very true.

SOCRATES: Then the inference is, that a man may have attained the knowledge of something, which he may remember and yet not know, because he does not see; and this has been affirmed by us to be a monstrous supposition.

THEÆTETUS: Most true.

SOCRATES: Thus, then, the assertion that knowledge and perception are one, involves a manifest impossibility?

THEÆTETUS: Yes.

SOCRATES: Then they must be distinguished?

THEÆTETUS: I suppose that they must.

SOCRATES: Once more we shall have to begin, and ask 'What is knowledge?' and yet, Theætetus, what are we going to do?

THEÆTETUS: About what?

SOCRATES: Like a good-for-nothing cock, without having won the victory, we walk away from the argument and crow.

THEÆTETUS: How do you mean?

SOCRATES: After the manner of disputers (Lys.; Phaedo; Republic), we were satisfied with mere verbal consistency, and were well pleased if in this way we could gain an advantage. Although professing not to be mere Eristics, but philosophers, I suspect that we have unconsciously fallen into the error of that ingenious class of persons.

THEÆTETUS: I do not as yet understand you.

SOCRATES: Then I will try to explain myself: just now we asked the question, whether a man who had learned and remembered could fail to know, and we showed that a person who had seen might remember when he had his eyes shut and could not see, and then he would at the same time remember and not know. But this was an impossibility. And so the Protagorean fable came to nought, and yours also, who maintained that knowledge is the same as perception.

THEÆTETUS: True.

SOCRATES: And yet, my friend, I rather suspect that the result would have been different if Protagoras, who was the father of the first of the two brats, had been alive; he would have had a great deal to say on their behalf. But he is dead, and we insult over his orphan child; and even the guardians whom he left, and of whom our friend Theodorus is one, are unwilling to give any help, and therefore I suppose that I must take up his cause myself, and see justice done?

THEODORUS: Not I, Socrates, but rather Callias, the son of Hipponicus, is guardian of his orphans. I was too soon diverted from the abstractions of dialectic to geometry. Nevertheless, I shall be grateful to you if you assist him.

SOCRATES: Very good, Theodorus; you shall see how I will come to the rescue. If a person does not attend to the meaning of terms as they are commonly used in argument, he may be involved even in greater paradoxes than these. Shall I explain this matter to you or to Theætetus?

THEODORUS: To both of us, and let the younger answer; he will incur less disgrace if he is discomfited.

SOCRATES: Then now let me ask the awful question, which is this:—Can a man know and also not know that which he knows?

THEODORUS: How shall we answer, Theætetus?

THEÆTETUS: He cannot, I should say.

SOCRATES: He can, if you maintain that seeing is knowing. When you are imprisoned in a well, as the saying is, and the self-assured adversary closes one of your eyes with his hand, and asks whether you can see his cloak with the eye which he has closed, how will you answer the inevitable man?

THEÆTETUS: I should answer, 'Not with that eye but with the other.'

SOCRATES: Then you see and do not see the same thing at the same time.

THEÆTETUS: Yes, in a certain sense.

SOCRATES: None of that, he will reply; I do not ask or bid you answer in what sense you know, but only whether you know that which you do not know. You have been proved to see that which you do not see; and you have already admitted that seeing is knowing, and that not-seeing is not-knowing: I leave you to draw the inference.

THEÆTETUS: Yes; the inference is the contradictory of my assertion.

SOCRATES: Yes, my marvel, and there might have been yet worse things in store for you, if an opponent had gone on to ask whether you can have a sharp and also a dull knowledge, and whether you can know near, but not at a distance, or know the same thing with more or less intensity, and so on without end. Such questions might have been put to you by a light-armed mercenary, who argued for pay. He would have lain in wait for you, and when you took up the position, that sense is knowledge, he would have made an assault upon hearing, smelling, and the other senses;—he would have shown you no mercy; and while you were lost in envy and admiration of his wisdom, he would have got you into his net, out of which you would not have escaped until you had come to an understanding about the sum to be paid for your release. Well, you ask, and how will Protagoras reinforce his position? Shall I answer for him?

THEÆTETUS: By all means.

SOCRATES: He will repeat all those things which we have been urging on his behalf, and then he will close with us in disdain, and say:—The worthy Socrates asked a little boy, whether the same man could remember and not know the same thing, and the boy said No, because he was frightened, and could not see what was coming, and then Socrates made fun of poor me. The truth is, O slatternly Socrates, that when you ask questions about any assertion of mine, and the person asked is found tripping, if he has answered as I should have answered, then I am refuted, but if he answers something else, then he is refuted and not I. For do you really suppose that any one would admit the memory which a man has of an impression which has passed away to be the same with that which he experienced at the time? Assuredly not. Or would he hesitate to acknowledge that the same man may know and not know the same thing? Or, if he is afraid of making this admission, would he ever grant that one who has become unlike is the same as before he became unlike? Or would he admit that a man is one at all, and not rather many and infinite as the changes which take place in him? I speak by the card in order to avoid entanglements of words. But, O my good sir, he will say, come to the argument in a more generous spirit; and either show, if you can, that our sensations are not relative and individual, or, if you admit them to be so, prove that this does not involve the consequence that the appearance becomes, or, if you will have the word, is, to the individual only. As to your talk about pigs and baboons, you are yourself behaving like a pig, and you teach your hearers to make sport of my writings in the same ignorant manner; but this is not to your credit. For I declare that the truth is as I have written, and that each of us is a measure of existence and of non-existence. Yet one man may be a thousand times better than another in proportion as different things are and appear to him. And I am far from saying that wisdom and the wise man have no existence; but I say that the wise man is he who makes the evils which appear and are to a man, into goods which are and appear to him. And I would beg you not to press my words in the letter, but to take the meaning of them as I will explain them. Remember what has been already said,—that to the sick man his food appears to be and is bitter, and to the man in health the opposite of bitter. Now I cannot conceive that one of these men can be or ought to be made wiser than the other: nor can you assert that the sick man because he has one impression is foolish, and the healthy man because he has another is wise; but the one state requires to be changed into the other, the worse into the better. As in education, a change of state has to be effected, and the sophist accomplishes by words the change which the physician works by the aid of drugs. Not that any one ever made another think truly, who previously thought falsely. For no one can think what is not, or, think anything different from that which he feels; and this is always true. But as the inferior habit of mind has thoughts of kindred nature, so I conceive that a good mind causes men to have good thoughts; and these which the inexperienced call true, I maintain to be only better, and not truer than others. And, O my dear Socrates, I do not call wise men tadpoles: far from it; I say that they are the physicians of the human body, and the husbandmen of plants—for the husbandmen also take away the evil and disordered sensations of plants, and infuse into them good and healthy sensations—aye and true ones; and the wise and good rhetoricians make the good instead of the evil to seem just to states; for whatever appears to a state to be just and fair, so long as it is regarded as such, is just and fair to it; but the teacher of wisdom causes the good to take the place of the evil, both in appearance and in reality. And in like manner the Sophist who is able to train his pupils in this spirit is a wise man, and deserves to be well paid by them. And so one man is wiser than another; and no one thinks falsely, and you, whether you will or not, must endure to be a measure. On these foundations the argument stands firm, which you, Socrates, may, if you please, overthrow by an opposite argument, or if you like you may put questions to me—a method to which no intelligent person will object, quite the reverse. But I must beg you to put fair questions: for there is great inconsistency in saying that you have a zeal for virtue, and then always behaving unfairly in argument. The unfairness of which I complain is that you do not distinguish between mere disputation and dialectic: the disputer may trip up his opponent as often as he likes, and make fun; but the dialectician will be in earnest, and only correct his adversary when necessary, telling him the errors into which he has fallen through his own fault, or that of the company which he has previously kept. If you do so, your adversary will lay the blame of his own confusion and perplexity on himself, and not on you. He will follow and love you, and will hate himself, and escape from himself into philosophy, in order that he may become different from what he was. But the other mode of arguing, which is practised by the many, will have just the opposite effect upon him; and as he grows older, instead of turning philosopher, he will come to hate philosophy. I would recommend you, therefore, as I said before, not to encourage yourself in this polemical and controversial temper, but to find out, in a friendly and congenial spirit, what we really mean when we say that all things are in motion, and that to every individual and state what appears, is. In this manner you will consider whether knowledge and sensation are the same or different, but you will not argue, as you were just now doing, from the customary use of names and words, which the vulgar pervert in all sorts of ways, causing infinite perplexity to one another. Such, Theodorus, is the very slight help which I am able to offer to your old friend; had he been living, he would have helped himself in a far more gloriose style.

THEODORUS: You are jesting, Socrates; indeed, your defence of him has been most valorous.

SOCRATES: Thank you, friend; and I hope that you observed Protagoras bidding us be serious, as the text, 'Man is the measure of all things,' was a solemn one; and he reproached us with making a boy the medium of discourse, and said that the boy's timidity was made to tell against his argument; he also declared that we made a joke of him.

THEODORUS: How could I fail to observe all that, Socrates?

SOCRATES: Well, and shall we do as he says?

THEODORUS: By all means.

SOCRATES: But if his wishes are to be regarded, you and I must take up the argument, and in all seriousness, and ask and answer one another, for you see that the rest of us are nothing but boys. In no other way can we escape the imputation, that in our fresh analysis of his thesis we are making fun with boys.

THEODORUS: Well, but is not Theætetus better able to follow a philosophical enquiry than a great many men who have long beards?

SOCRATES: Yes, Theodorus, but not better than you; and therefore please not to imagine that I am to defend by every means in my power your departed friend; and that you are to defend nothing and nobody. At any rate, my good man, do not sheer off until we know whether you are a true measure of diagrams, or whether all men are equally measures and sufficient for themselves in astronomy and geometry, and the other branches of knowledge in which you are supposed to excel them.

THEODORUS: He who is sitting by you, Socrates, will not easily avoid being drawn into an argument; and when I said just now that you would excuse me, and not, like the Lacedaemonians, compel me to strip and fight, I was talking nonsense—I should rather compare you to Scirrhon, who threw travellers from the rocks; for the Lacedaemonian rule is 'strip or depart,' but you seem to go about your work more after the fashion of Antaeus: you will not allow any one who approaches you to depart until you have stripped him, and he has been compelled to try a fall with you in argument.

SOCRATES: There, Theodorus, you have hit off precisely the nature of my complaint; but I am even more pugnacious than the giants of old, for I have met with no end of heroes; many a Heracles, many a Theseus, mighty in words, has broken my head; nevertheless I am always at this rough exercise, which inspires me like a passion. Please, then, to try a fall with me, whereby you will do yourself good as well as me.

THEODORUS: I consent; lead me whither you will, for I know that you are like destiny; no man can escape from any argument which you may weave for him. But I am not disposed to go further than you suggest.

Theætetus

SOCRATES: Once will be enough; and now take particular care that we do not again unwittingly expose ourselves to the reproach of talking childishly.

THEODORUS: I will do my best to avoid that error.

SOCRATES: In the first place, let us return to our old objection, and see whether we were right in blaming and taking offence at Protagoras on the ground that he assumed all to be equal and sufficient in wisdom; although he admitted that there was a better and worse, and that in respect of this, some who as he said were the wise excelled others.

THEODORUS: Very true.

SOCRATES: Had Protagoras been living and answered for himself, instead of our answering for him, there would have been no need of our reviewing or reinforcing the argument. But as he is not here, and some one may accuse us of speaking without authority on his behalf, had we not better come to a clearer agreement about his meaning, for a great deal may be at stake?

THEODORUS: True.

SOCRATES: Then let us obtain, not through any third person, but from his own statement and in the fewest words possible, the basis of agreement.

THEODORUS: In what way?

SOCRATES: In this way:—His words are, 'What seems to a man, is to him.'

THEODORUS: Yes, so he says.

SOCRATES: And are not we, Protagoras, uttering the opinion of man, or rather of all mankind, when we say that every one thinks himself wiser than other men in some things, and their inferior in others? In the hour of danger, when they are in perils of war, or of the sea, or of sickness, do they not look up to their commanders as if they were gods, and expect salvation from them, only because they excel them in knowledge? Is not the world full of men in their several employments, who are looking for teachers and rulers of themselves and of the animals? and there are plenty who think that they are able to teach and able to rule. Now, in all this is implied that ignorance and wisdom exist among them, at least in their own opinion.

THEODORUS: Certainly.

SOCRATES: And wisdom is assumed by them to be true thought, and ignorance to be false opinion.

THEODORUS: Exactly.

SOCRATES: How then, Protagoras, would you have us treat the argument? Shall we say that the opinions of men are always true, or sometimes true and sometimes false? In either case, the result is the same, and their opinions are not always true, but sometimes true and sometimes false. For tell me, Theodorus, do you suppose that you yourself, or any other follower of Protagoras, would contend that no one deems another ignorant or mistaken in his opinion?

THEODORUS: The thing is incredible, Socrates.

SOCRATES: And yet that absurdity is necessarily involved in the thesis which declares man to be the measure of all things.

THEODORUS: How so?

SOCRATES: Why, suppose that you determine in your own mind something to be true, and declare your opinion to me; let us assume, as he argues, that this is true to you. Now, if so, you must either say that the rest of us are not the judges of this opinion or judgment of yours, or that we judge you always to have a true opinion? But are there not thousands upon thousands who, whenever you form a judgment, take up arms against you and are of an opposite judgment and opinion, deeming that you judge falsely?

THEODORUS: Yes, indeed, Socrates, thousands and tens of thousands, as Homer says, who give me a world of trouble.

SOCRATES: Well, but are we to assert that what you think is true to you and false to the ten thousand others?

THEODORUS: No other inference seems to be possible.

SOCRATES: And how about Protagoras himself? If neither he nor the multitude thought, as indeed they do not think, that man is the measure of all things, must it not follow that the truth of which Protagoras wrote would be true to no one? But if you suppose that he himself thought this, and that the multitude does not agree with him, you must begin by allowing that in whatever proportion the many are more than one, in that proportion his truth is more untrue than true.

THEODORUS: That would follow if the truth is supposed to vary with individual opinion.

SOCRATES: And the best of the joke is, that he acknowledges the truth of their opinion who believe his own opinion to be false; for he admits that the opinions of all men are true.

THEODORUS: Certainly.

SOCRATES: And does he not allow that his own opinion is false, if he admits that the opinion of those who think him false is true?

THEODORUS: Of course.

SOCRATES: Whereas the other side do not admit that they speak falsely?

THEODORUS: They do not.

SOCRATES: And he, as may be inferred from his writings, agrees that this opinion is also true.

THEODORUS: Clearly.

SOCRATES: Then all mankind, beginning with Protagoras, will contend, or rather, I should say that he will allow, when he concedes that his adversary has a true opinion—Protagoras, I say, will himself allow that neither a dog nor any ordinary man is the measure of anything which he has not learned—am I not right?

THEODORUS: Yes.

SOCRATES: And the truth of Protagoras being doubted by all, will be true neither to himself to any one else?

THEODORUS: I think, Socrates, that we are running my old friend too hard.

SOCRATES: But I do not know that we are going beyond the truth. Doubtless, as he is older, he may be expected to be wiser than we are. And if he could only just get his head out of the world below, he would have overthrown both of us again and again, me for talking nonsense and you for assenting to me, and have been off and underground in a trice. But as he is not within call, we must make the best use of our own faculties, such as they are, and speak out what appears to us to be true. And one thing which no one will deny is, that there are great differences in the understandings of men.

THEODORUS: In that opinion I quite agree.

SOCRATES: And is there not most likely to be firm ground in the distinction which we were indicating on behalf of Protagoras, viz. that most things, and all immediate sensations, such as hot, dry, sweet, are only such as they appear; if however difference of opinion

Theætetus

is to be allowed at all, surely we must allow it in respect of health or disease? for every woman, child, or living creature has not such a knowledge of what conduces to health as to enable them to cure themselves.

THEODORUS: I quite agree.

SOCRATES: Or again, in politics, while affirming that just and unjust, honourable and disgraceful, holy and unholy, are in reality to each state such as the state thinks and makes lawful, and that in determining these matters no individual or state is wiser than another, still the followers of Protagoras will not deny that in determining what is or is not expedient for the community one state is wiser and one counsellor better than another—they will scarcely venture to maintain, that what a city enacts in the belief that it is expedient will always be really expedient. But in the other case, I mean when they speak of justice and injustice, piety and impiety, they are confident that in nature these have no existence or essence of their own—the truth is that which is agreed on at the time of the agreement, and as long as the agreement lasts; and this is the philosophy of many who do not altogether go along with Protagoras. Here arises a new question, Theodorus, which threatens to be more serious than the last.

THEODORUS: Well, Socrates, we have plenty of leisure.

SOCRATES: That is true, and your remark recalls to my mind an observation which I have often made, that those who have passed their days in the pursuit of philosophy are ridiculously at fault when they have to appear and speak in court. How natural is this!

THEODORUS: What do you mean?

SOCRATES: I mean to say, that those who have been trained in philosophy and liberal pursuits are as unlike those who from their youth upwards have been knocking about in the courts and such places, as a freeman is in breeding unlike a slave.

THEODORUS: In what is the difference seen?

SOCRATES: In the leisure spoken of by you, which a freeman can always command: he has his talk out in peace, and, like ourselves, he wanders at will from one subject to another, and from a second to a third,—if the fancy takes him, he begins again, as we are doing now, caring not whether his words are many or few; his only aim is to attain the truth. But the lawyer is always in a hurry; there is the water of the clepsydra driving him on, and not allowing him to expatiate at will: and there is his adversary standing over him, enforcing his rights; the indictment, which in their phraseology is termed the affidavit, is recited at the time: and from this he must not deviate. He is a servant, and is continually disputing about a fellow-servant before his master, who is seated, and has the cause in his hands; the trial is never about some indifferent matter, but always concerns himself; and often the race is for his life. The consequence has been, that he has become keen and shrewd; he has learned how to flatter his master in word and indulge him in deed; but his soul is small and unrighteous. His condition, which has been that of a slave from his youth upwards, has deprived him of growth and uprightness and independence; dangers and fears, which were too much for his truth and honesty, came upon him in early years, when the tenderness of youth was unequal to them, and he has been driven into crooked ways; from the first he has practised deception and retaliation, and has become stunted and warped. And so he has passed out of youth into manhood, having no soundness in him; and is now, as he thinks, a master in wisdom. Such is the lawyer, Theodorus. Will you have the companion picture of the philosopher, who is of our brotherhood; or shall we return to the argument? Do not let us abuse the freedom of digression which we claim.

THEODORUS: Nay, Socrates, not until we have finished what we are about; for you truly said that we belong to a brotherhood which is free, and are not the servants of the argument; but the argument is our servant, and must wait our leisure. Who is our judge? Or where is the spectator having any right to censure or control us, as he might the poets?

Theætetus

SOCRATES: Then, as this is your wish, I will describe the leaders; for there is no use in talking about the inferior sort. In the first place, the lords of philosophy have never, from their youth upwards, known their way to the Agora, or the dicastery, or the council, or any other political assembly; they neither see nor hear the laws or decrees, as they are called, of the state written or recited; the eagerness of political societies in the attainment of offices—clubs, and banquets, and revels, and singing-maidens,—do not enter even into their dreams. Whether any event has turned out well or ill in the city, what disgrace may have descended to any one from his ancestors, male or female, are matters of which the philosopher no more knows than he can tell, as they say, how many pints are contained in the ocean. Neither is he conscious of his ignorance. For he does not hold aloof in order that he may gain a reputation; but the truth is, that the outer form of him only is in the city: his mind, disdaining the littlenesses and nothingnesses of human things, is 'flying all abroad' as Pindar says, measuring earth and heaven and the things which are under and on the earth and above the heaven, interrogating the whole nature of each and all in their entirety, but not condescending to anything which is within reach.

THEODORUS: What do you mean, Socrates?

SOCRATES: I will illustrate my meaning, Theodorus, by the jest which the clever witty Thracian handmaid is said to have made about Thales, when he fell into a well as he was looking up at the stars. She said, that he was so eager to know what was going on in heaven, that he could not see what was before his feet. This is a jest which is equally applicable to all philosophers. For the philosopher is wholly unacquainted with his next-door neighbour; he is ignorant, not only of what he is doing, but he hardly knows whether he is a man or an animal; he is searching into the essence of man, and busy in enquiring what belongs to such a nature to do or suffer different from any other;—I think that you understand me, Theodorus?

THEODORUS: I do, and what you say is true.

SOCRATES: And thus, my friend, on every occasion, private as well as public, as I said at first, when he appears in a law-court, or in any place in which he has to speak of things which are at his feet and before his eyes, he is the jest, not only of Thracian handmaids but of the general herd, tumbling into wells and every sort of disaster through his inexperience. His awkwardness is fearful, and gives the impression of imbecility. When he is reviled, he has nothing personal to say in answer to the civilities of his adversaries, for he knows no scandals of any one, and they do not interest him; and therefore he is laughed at for his sheepishness; and when others are being praised and glorified, in the simplicity of his heart he cannot help going into fits of laughter, so that he seems to be a downright idiot. When he hears a tyrant or king eulogized, he fancies that he is listening to the praises of some keeper of cattle—a swineherd, or shepherd, or perhaps a cowherd, who is congratulated on the quantity of milk which he squeezes from them; and he remarks that the creature whom they tend, and out of whom they squeeze the wealth, is of a less tractable and more insidious nature. Then, again, he observes that the great man is of necessity as ill-mannered and uneducated as any shepherd—for he has no leisure, and he is surrounded by a wall, which is his mountain-pen. Hearing of enormous landed proprietors of ten thousand acres and more, our philosopher deems this to be a trifle, because he has been accustomed to think of the whole earth; and when they sing the praises of family, and say that some one is a gentleman because he can show seven generations of wealthy ancestors, he thinks that their sentiments only betray a dull and narrow vision in those who utter them, and who are not educated enough to look at the whole, nor to consider that every man has had thousands and ten thousands of progenitors, and among them have been rich and poor, kings and slaves, Hellenes and barbarians, innumerable. And when people pride themselves on having a pedigree of twenty-five ancestors, which goes back to Heracles, the son of Amphitryon, he cannot understand their poverty of ideas. Why are they unable to calculate that Amphitryon had a twenty-fifth ancestor, who might have been anybody, and was such as fortune made him, and he had a fiftieth, and so on? He amuses himself with the notion that they cannot count, and thinks that a little arithmetic would have got rid of their senseless vanity. Now, in all these cases our philosopher is derided by the vulgar, partly because he is thought to despise them, and also because he is ignorant of what is before him, and always at a loss.

THEODORUS: That is very true, Socrates.

SOCRATES: But, O my friend, when he draws the other into upper air, and gets him out of his pleas and rejoinders into the contemplation of justice and injustice in their own nature and in their difference from one another and from all other things; or from the commonplaces about the happiness of a king or of a rich man to the consideration of government, and of human happiness and misery in general—what they are, and how a man is to attain the one and avoid the other—when that narrow, keen, little legal mind is called to account about all this, he gives the philosopher his revenge; for dizzied by the height at which he is hanging, whence he looks down into space, which is a strange experience to him, he being dismayed, and lost, and stammering broken words, is laughed at, not by Thracian handmaidens or any other uneducated persons, for they have no eye for the situation, but by every man who has not been brought up a slave. Such are the two characters, Theodorus: the one of the freeman, who has been trained in liberty and leisure, whom you call the philosopher,—him we cannot blame because he appears simple and of no account when he has to perform some menial task, such as packing up bed-clothes, or flavouring a sauce or fawning speech; the other character is that of the man who is able to do all this kind of service smartly and neatly, but knows not how to wear his cloak like a gentleman; still less with the music of discourse can he hymn the true life aright which is lived by immortals or men blessed of heaven.

THEODORUS: If you could only persuade everybody, Socrates, as you do me, of the truth of your words, there would be more peace and fewer evils among men.

SOCRATES: Evils, Theodorus, can never pass away; for there must always remain something which is antagonistic to good. Having no place among the gods in heaven, of necessity they hover around the mortal nature, and this earthly sphere. Wherefore we ought to fly away from earth to heaven as quickly as we can; and to fly away is to become like God, as far as this is possible; and to become like him, is to become holy, just, and wise. But, O my friend, you cannot easily convince mankind that they should pursue virtue or avoid vice, not merely in order that a man may seem to be good, which is the reason given by the world, and in my judgment is only a repetition of an old wives' fable. Whereas, the truth is that God is never in any way unrighteous—he is perfect righteousness; and he of us who is the most righteous is most like him. Herein is seen the true cleverness of a man, and also his nothingness and want of manhood. For to know this is true wisdom and virtue, and ignorance of this is manifest folly and vice. All other kinds of wisdom or cleverness, which seem only, such as the wisdom of politicians, or the wisdom of the arts, are coarse and vulgar. The unrighteous man, or the sayer and doer of unholy things, had far better not be encouraged in the illusion that his roguery is clever; for men glory in their shame—they fancy that they hear others saying of them, 'These are not mere good-for-nothing persons, mere burdens of the earth, but such as men should be who mean to dwell safely in a state.' Let us tell them that they are all the more truly what they do not think they are because they do not know it; for they do not know the penalty of injustice, which above all things they ought to know—not stripes and death, as they suppose, which evil-doers often escape, but a penalty which cannot be escaped.

THEODORUS: What is that?

SOCRATES: There are two patterns eternally set before them; the one blessed and divine, the other godless and wretched: but they do not see them, or perceive that in their utter folly and infatuation they are growing like the one and unlike the other, by reason of their evil deeds; and the penalty is, that they lead a life answering to the pattern which they are growing like. And if we tell them, that unless they depart from their cunning, the place of innocence will not receive them after death; and that here on earth, they will live ever in the likeness of their own evil selves, and with evil friends—when they hear this they in their superior cunning will seem to be listening to the talk of idiots.

THEODORUS: Very true, Socrates.

SOCRATES: Too true, my friend, as I well know; there is, however, one peculiarity in their case: when they begin to reason in private about their dislike of philosophy, if they have the courage to hear the argument out, and do not run away, they grow at last strangely discontented with themselves; their rhetoric fades away, and they become helpless as children. These however are digressions from which we must now desist, or they will overflow, and drown the original argument; to which, if you please, we will now return.

THEODORUS: For my part, Socrates, I would rather have the digressions, for at my age I find them easier to follow; but if you wish, let us go back to the argument.

SOCRATES: Had we not reached the point at which the partisans of the perpetual flux, who say that things are as they seem to each one, were confidently maintaining that the ordinances which the state commanded and thought just, were just to the state which imposed them, while they were in force; this was especially asserted of justice; but as to the good, no one had any longer the hardihood to contend of any ordinances which the state thought and enacted to be good that these, while they were in force, were really good;—he who said so would be playing with the name 'good,' and would not touch the real question—it would be a mockery, would it not?

THEODORUS: Certainly it would.

SOCRATES: He ought not to speak of the name, but of the thing which is contemplated under the name.

THEODORUS: Right.

SOCRATES: Whatever be the term used, the good or expedient is the aim of legislation, and as far as she has an opinion, the state imposes all laws with a view to the greatest expediency; can legislation have any other aim?

THEODORUS: Certainly not.

SOCRATES: But is the aim attained always? do not mistakes often happen?

THEODORUS: Yes, I think that there are mistakes.

SOCRATES: The possibility of error will be more distinctly recognised, if we put the question in reference to the whole class under which the good or expedient falls. That whole class has to do with the future, and laws are passed under the idea that they will be useful in after-time; which, in other words, is the future.

THEODORUS: Very true.

SOCRATES: Suppose now, that we ask Protagoras, or one of his disciples, a question:—O, Protagoras, we will say to him, Man is, as you declare, the measure of all things—white, heavy, light: of all such things he is the judge; for he has the criterion of them in himself, and when he thinks that things are such as he experiences them to be, he thinks what is and is true to himself. Is it not so?

THEODORUS: Yes.

SOCRATES: And do you extend your doctrine, Protagoras (as we shall further say), to the future as well as to the present; and has he the criterion not only of what in his opinion is but of what will be, and do things always happen to him as he expected? For example, take the case of heat:—When an ordinary man thinks that he is going to have a fever, and that this kind of heat is coming on, and another person, who is a physician, thinks the contrary, whose opinion is likely to prove right? Or are they both right? —he will have a

Theætetus

heat and fever in his own judgment, and not have a fever in the physician's judgment?

THEODORUS: How ludicrous!

SOCRATES: And the vinegrower, if I am not mistaken, is a better judge of the sweetness or dryness of the vintage which is not yet gathered than the harp-player?

THEODORUS: Certainly.

SOCRATES: And in musical composition the musician will know better than the training master what the training master himself will hereafter think harmonious or the reverse?

THEODORUS: Of course.

SOCRATES: And the cook will be a better judge than the guest, who is not a cook, of the pleasure to be derived from the dinner which is in preparation; for of present or past pleasure we are not as yet arguing; but can we say that every one will be to himself the best judge of the pleasure which will seem to be and will be to him in the future?—nay, would not you, Protagoras, better guess which arguments in a court would convince any one of us than the ordinary man?

THEODORUS: Certainly, Socrates, he used to profess in the strongest manner that he was the superior of all men in this respect.

SOCRATES: To be sure, friend: who would have paid a large sum for the privilege of talking to him, if he had really persuaded his visitors that neither a prophet nor any other man was better able to judge what will be and seem to be in the future than every one could for himself?

THEODORUS: Who indeed?

SOCRATES: And legislation and expediency are all concerned with the future; and every one will admit that states, in passing laws, must often fail of their highest interests?

THEODORUS: Quite true.

SOCRATES: Then we may fairly argue against your master, that he must admit one man to be wiser than another, and that the wiser is a measure: but I, who know nothing, am not at all obliged to accept the honour which the advocate of Protagoras was just now forcing upon me, whether I would or not, of being a measure of anything.

THEODORUS: That is the best refutation of him, Socrates; although he is also caught when he ascribes truth to the opinions of others, who give the lie direct to his own opinion.

SOCRATES: There are many ways, Theodorus, in which the doctrine that every opinion of every man is true may be refuted; but there is more difficulty in proving that states of feeling, which are present to a man, and out of which arise sensations and opinions in accordance with them, are also untrue. And very likely I have been talking nonsense about them; for they may be unassailable, and those who say that there is clear evidence of them, and that they are matters of knowledge, may probably be right; in which case our friend Theætetus was not so far from the mark when he identified perception and knowledge. And therefore let us draw nearer, as the advocate of Protagoras desires; and give the truth of the universal flux a ring: is the theory sound or not? at any rate, no small war is raging about it, and there are combination not a few.

THEODORUS: No small, war, indeed, for in Ionia the sect makes rapid strides; the disciples of Heracleitus are most energetic upholders of the doctrine.

SOCRATES: Then we are the more bound, my dear Theodorus, to examine the question from the foundation as it is set forth by themselves.

Theætetus

THEODORUS: Certainly we are. About these speculations of Heracleitus, which, as you say, are as old as Homer, or even older still, the Ephesians themselves, who profess to know them, are downright mad, and you cannot talk with them on the subject. For, in accordance with their text-books, they are always in motion; but as for dwelling upon an argument or a question, and quietly asking and answering in turn, they can no more do so than they can fly; or rather, the determination of these fellows not to have a particle of rest in them is more than the utmost powers of negation can express. If you ask any of them a question, he will produce, as from a quiver, sayings brief and dark, and shoot them at you; and if you inquire the reason of what he has said, you will be hit by some other new-fangled word, and will make no way with any of them, nor they with one another; their great care is, not to allow of any settled principle either in their arguments or in their minds, conceiving, as I imagine, that any such principle would be stationary; for they are at war with the stationary, and do what they can to drive it out everywhere.

SOCRATES: I suppose, Theodorus, that you have only seen them when they were fighting, and have never stayed with them in time of peace, for they are no friends of yours; and their peace doctrines are only communicated by them at leisure, as I imagine, to those disciples of theirs whom they want to make like themselves.

THEODORUS: Disciples! my good sir, they have none; men of their sort are not one another's disciples, but they grow up at their own sweet will, and get their inspiration anywhere, each of them saying of his neighbour that he knows nothing. From these men, then, as I was going to remark, you will never get a reason, whether with their will or without their will; we must take the question out of their hands, and make the analysis ourselves, as if we were doing geometrical problem.

SOCRATES: Quite right too; but as touching the aforesaid problem, have we not heard from the ancients, who concealed their wisdom from the many in poetical figures, that Oceanus and Tethys, the origin of all things, are streams, and that nothing is at rest? And now the moderns, in their superior wisdom, have declared the same openly, that the cobbler too may hear and learn of them, and no longer foolishly imagine that some things are at rest and others in motion—having learned that all is motion, he will duly honour his teachers. I had almost forgotten the opposite doctrine, Theodorus,

'Alone Being remains unmoved, which is the name for the all.'

This is the language of Parmenides, Melissus, and their followers, who stoutly maintain that all being is one and self-contained, and has no place in which to move. What shall we do, friend, with all these people; for, advancing step by step, we have imperceptibly got between the combatants, and, unless we can protect our retreat, we shall pay the penalty of our rashness—like the players in the palaestra who are caught upon the line, and are dragged different ways by the two parties. Therefore I think that we had better begin by considering those whom we first accosted, 'the river-gods,' and, if we find any truth in them, we will help them to pull us over, and try to get away from the others. But if the partisans of 'the whole' appear to speak more truly, we will fly off from the party which would move the immovable, to them. And if I find that neither of them have anything reasonable to say, we shall be in a ridiculous position, having so great a conceit of our own poor opinion and rejecting that of ancient and famous men. O Theodorus, do you think that there is any use in proceeding when the danger is so great?

THEODORUS: Nay, Socrates, not to examine thoroughly what the two parties have to say would be quite intolerable.

SOCRATES: Then examine we must, since you, who were so reluctant to begin, are so eager to proceed. The nature of motion appears to be the question with which we begin. What do they mean when they say that all things are in motion? Is there only one kind of motion, or, as I rather incline to think, two? I should like to have your opinion upon this point in addition to my own, that I may err, if I must err, in your company; tell me, then, when a thing

Theætetus

changes from one place to another, or goes round in the same place, is not that what is called motion?

THEODORUS: Yes.

SOCRATES: Here then we have one kind of motion. But when a thing, remaining on the same spot, grows old, or becomes black from being white, or hard from being soft, or undergoes any other change, may not this be properly called motion of another kind?

THEODORUS: I think so.

SOCRATES: Say rather that it must be so. Of motion then there are these two kinds, 'change,' and 'motion in place.'

THEODORUS: You are right.

SOCRATES: And now, having made this distinction, let us address ourselves to those who say that all is motion, and ask them whether all things according to them have the two kinds of motion, and are changed as well as move in place, or is one thing moved in both ways, and another in one only?

THEODORUS: Indeed, I do not know what to answer; but I think they would say that all things are moved in both ways.

SOCRATES: Yes, comrade; for, if not, they would have to say that the same things are in motion and at rest, and there would be no more truth in saying that all things are in motion, than that all things are at rest.

THEODORUS: To be sure.

SOCRATES: And if they are to be in motion, and nothing is to be devoid of motion, all things must always have every sort of motion?

THEODORUS: Most true.

SOCRATES: Consider a further point: did we not understand them to explain the generation of heat, whiteness, or anything else, in some such manner as the following:—were they not saying that each of them is moving between the agent and the patient, together with a perception, and that the patient ceases to be a perceiving power and becomes a percipient, and the agent a quale instead of a quality? I suspect that quality may appear a strange and uncouth term to you, and that you do not understand the abstract expression. Then I will take concrete instances: I mean to say that the producing power or agent becomes neither heat nor whiteness but hot and white, and the like of other things. For I must repeat what I said before, that neither the agent nor patient have any absolute existence, but when they come together and generate sensations and their objects, the one becomes a thing of a certain quality, and the other a percipient. You remember?

THEODORUS: Of course.

SOCRATES: We may leave the details of their theory unexamined, but we must not forget to ask them the only question with which we are concerned: Are all things in motion and flux?

THEODORUS: Yes, they will reply.

SOCRATES: And they are moved in both those ways which we distinguished, that is to say, they move in place and are also changed?

THEODORUS: Of course, if the motion is to be perfect.

SOCRATES: If they only moved in place and were not changed, we should be able to say what is the nature of the things which are in motion and flux?

THEODORUS: Exactly.

SOCRATES: But now, since not even white continues to flow white, and whiteness itself is a flux or change which is passing into another

Theætetus

colour, and is never to be caught standing still, can the name of any colour be rightly used at all?

THEODORUS: How is that possible, Socrates, either in the case of this or of any other quality—if while we are using the word the object is escaping in the flux?

SOCRATES: And what would you say of perceptions, such as sight and hearing, or any other kind of perception? Is there any stopping in the act of seeing and hearing?

THEODORUS: Certainly not, if all things are in motion.

SOCRATES: Then we must not speak of seeing any more than of not-seeing, nor of any other perception more than of any non-perception, if all things partake of every kind of motion?

THEODORUS: Certainly not.

SOCRATES: Yet perception is knowledge: so at least Theætetus and I were saying.

THEODORUS: Very true.

SOCRATES: Then when we were asked what is knowledge, we no more answered what is knowledge than what is not knowledge?

THEODORUS: I suppose not.

SOCRATES: Here, then, is a fine result: we corrected our first answer in our eagerness to prove that nothing is at rest. But if nothing is at rest, every answer upon whatever subject is equally right: you may say that a thing is or is not thus; or, if you prefer, 'becomes' thus; and if we say 'becomes,' we shall not then hamper them with words expressive of rest.

THEODORUS: Quite true.

SOCRATES: Yes, Theodorus, except in saying 'thus' and 'not thus.' But you ought not to use the word 'thus,' for there is no motion in 'thus' or in 'not thus.' The maintainers of the doctrine have as yet no words in which to express themselves, and must get a new language. I know of no word that will suit them, except perhaps 'no how,' which is perfectly indefinite.

THEODORUS: Yes, that is a manner of speaking in which they will be quite at home.

SOCRATES: And so, Theodorus, we have got rid of your friend without assenting to his doctrine, that every man is the measure of all things—a wise man only is a measure; neither can we allow that knowledge is perception, certainly not on the hypothesis of a perpetual flux, unless perchance our friend Theætetus is able to convince us that it is.

THEODORUS: Very good, Socrates; and now that the argument about the doctrine of Protagoras has been completed, I am absolved from answering; for this was the agreement.

THEÆTETUS: Not, Theodorus, until you and Socrates have discussed the doctrine of those who say that all things are at rest, as you were proposing.

THEODORUS: You, Theætetus, who are a young rogue, must not instigate your elders to a breach of faith, but should prepare to answer Socrates in the remainder of the argument.

THEÆTETUS: Yes, if he wishes; but I would rather have heard about the doctrine of rest.

THEODORUS: Invite Socrates to an argument—invite horsemen to the open plain; do but ask him, and he will answer.

SOCRATES: Nevertheless, Theodorus, I am afraid that I shall not be able to comply with the request of Theætetus.

Theætetus

THEODORUS: Not comply! for what reason?

SOCRATES: My reason is that I have a kind of reverence; not so much for Melissus and the others, who say that 'All is one and at rest,' as for the great leader himself, Parmenides, venerable and awful, as in Homeric language he may be called;—him I should be ashamed to approach in a spirit unworthy of him. I met him when he was an old man, and I was a mere youth, and he appeared to me to have a glorious depth of mind. And I am afraid that we may not understand his words, and may be still further from understanding his meaning; above all I fear that the nature of knowledge, which is the main subject of our discussion, may be thrust out of sight by the unbidden guests who will come pouring in upon our feast of discourse, if we let them in—besides, the question which is now stirring is of immense extent, and will be treated unfairly if only considered by the way; or if treated adequately and at length, will put into the shade the other question of knowledge. Neither the one nor the other can be allowed; but I must try by my art of midwifery to deliver Theætetus of his conceptions about knowledge.

THEÆTETUS: Very well; do so if you will.

SOCRATES: Then now, Theætetus, take another view of the subject: you answered that knowledge is perception?

THEÆTETUS: I did.

SOCRATES: And if any one were to ask you: With what does a man see black and white colours? and with what does he hear high and low sounds?—you would say, if I am not mistaken, 'With the eyes and with the ears.'

THEÆTETUS: I should.

SOCRATES: The free use of words and phrases, rather than minute precision, is generally characteristic of a liberal education, and the opposite is pedantic; but sometimes precision is necessary, and I believe that the answer which you have just given is open to the charge of incorrectness; for which is more correct, to say that we see or hear with the eyes and with the ears, or through the eyes and through the ears.

THEÆTETUS: I should say 'through,' Socrates, rather than 'with.'

SOCRATES: Yes, my boy, for no one can suppose that in each of us, as in a sort of Trojan horse, there are perched a number of unconnected senses, which do not all meet in some one nature, the mind, or whatever we please to call it, of which they are the instruments, and with which through them we perceive objects of sense.

THEÆTETUS: I agree with you in that opinion.

SOCRATES: The reason why I am thus precise is, because I want to know whether, when we perceive black and white through the eyes, and again, other qualities through other organs, we do not perceive them with one and the same part of ourselves, and, if you were asked, you might refer all such perceptions to the body. Perhaps, however, I had better allow you to answer for yourself and not interfere. Tell me, then, are not the organs through which you perceive warm and hard and light and sweet, organs of the body?

THEÆTETUS: Of the body, certainly.

SOCRATES: And you would admit that what you perceive through one faculty you cannot perceive through another; the objects of hearing, for example, cannot be perceived through sight, or the objects of sight through hearing?

THEÆTETUS: Of course not.

SOCRATES: If you have any thought about both of them, this common perception cannot come to you, either through the one or the other organ?

Theætetus

THEÆTETUS: It cannot.

SOCRATES: How about sounds and colours: in the first place you would admit that they both exist?

THEÆTETUS: Yes.

SOCRATES: And that either of them is different from the other, and the same with itself?

THEÆTETUS: Certainly.

SOCRATES: And that both are two and each of them one?

THEÆTETUS: Yes.

SOCRATES: You can further observe whether they are like or unlike one another?

THEÆTETUS: I dare say.

SOCRATES: But through what do you perceive all this about them? for neither through hearing nor yet through seeing can you apprehend that which they have in common. Let me give you an illustration of the point at issue:—If there were any meaning in asking whether sounds and colours are saline or not, you would be able to tell me what faculty would consider the question. It would not be sight or hearing, but some other.

THEÆTETUS: Certainly; the faculty of taste.

SOCRATES: Very good; and now tell me what is the power which discerns, not only in sensible objects, but in all things, universal notions, such as those which are called being and not-being, and those others about which we were just asking—what organs will you assign for the perception of these notions?

THEÆTETUS: You are thinking of being and not being, likeness and unlikeness, sameness and difference, and also of unity and other numbers which are applied to objects of sense; and you mean to ask, through what bodily organ the soul perceives odd and even numbers and other arithmetical conceptions.

SOCRATES: You follow me excellently, Theætetus; that is precisely what I am asking.

THEÆTETUS: Indeed, Socrates, I cannot answer; my only notion is, that these, unlike objects of sense, have no separate organ, but that the mind, by a power of her own, contemplates the universals in all things.

SOCRATES: You are a beauty, Theætetus, and not ugly, as Theodorus was saying; for he who utters the beautiful is himself beautiful and good. And besides being beautiful, you have done me a kindness in releasing me from a very long discussion, if you are clear that the soul views some things by herself and others through the bodily organs. For that was my own opinion, and I wanted you to agree with me.

THEÆTETUS: I am quite clear.

SOCRATES: And to which class would you refer being or essence; for this, of all our notions, is the most universal?

THEÆTETUS: I should say, to that class which the soul aspires to know of herself.

SOCRATES: And would you say this also of like and unlike, same and other?

THEÆTETUS: Yes.

SOCRATES: And would you say the same of the noble and base, and of good and evil?

THEÆTETUS: These I conceive to be notions which are essentially relative, and which the soul also perceives by comparing in herself things past and present with the future.

SOCRATES: And does she not perceive the hardness of that which is hard by the touch, and the softness of that which is soft equally by the touch?

THEÆTETUS: Yes.

SOCRATES: But their essence and what they are, and their opposition to one another, and the essential nature of this opposition, the soul herself endeavours to decide for us by the review and comparison of them?

THEÆTETUS: Certainly.

SOCRATES: The simple sensations which reach the soul through the body are given at birth to men and animals by nature, but their reflections on the being and use of them are slowly and hardly gained, if they are ever gained, by education and long experience.

THEÆTETUS: Assuredly.

SOCRATES: And can a man attain truth who fails of attaining being?

THEÆTETUS: Impossible.

SOCRATES: And can he who misses the truth of anything, have a knowledge of that thing?

THEÆTETUS: He cannot.

SOCRATES: Then knowledge does not consist in impressions of sense, but in reasoning about them; in that only, and not in the mere impression, truth and being can be attained?

THEÆTETUS: Clearly.

SOCRATES: And would you call the two processes by the same name, when there is so great a difference between them?

THEÆTETUS: That would certainly not be right.

SOCRATES: And what name would you give to seeing, hearing, smelling, being cold and being hot?

THEÆTETUS: I should call all of them perceiving—what other name could be given to them?

SOCRATES: Perception would be the collective name of them?

THEÆTETUS: Certainly.

SOCRATES: Which, as we say, has no part in the attainment of truth any more than of being?

THEÆTETUS: Certainly not.

SOCRATES: And therefore not in science or knowledge?

THEÆTETUS: No.

SOCRATES: Then perception, Theætetus, can never be the same as knowledge or science?

THEÆTETUS: Clearly not, Socrates; and knowledge has now been most distinctly proved to be different from perception.

SOCRATES: But the original aim of our discussion was to find out rather what knowledge is than what it is not; at the same time we have made some progress, for we no longer seek for knowledge in perception at all, but in that other process, however called, in which the mind is alone and engaged with being.

Theætetus

THEÆTETUS: You mean, Socrates, if I am not mistaken, what is called thinking or opining.

SOCRATES: You conceive truly. And now, my friend, please to begin again at this point; and having wiped out of your memory all that has preceded, see if you have arrived at any clearer view, and once more say what is knowledge.

THEÆTETUS: I cannot say, Socrates, that all opinion is knowledge, because there may be a false opinion; but I will venture to assert, that knowledge is true opinion: let this then be my reply; and if this is hereafter disproved, I must try to find another.

SOCRATES: That is the way in which you ought to answer, Theætetus, and not in your former hesitating strain, for if we are bold we shall gain one of two advantages; either we shall find what we seek, or we shall be less likely to think that we know what we do not know—in either case we shall be richly rewarded. And now, what are you saying?—Are there two sorts of opinion, one true and the other false; and do you define knowledge to be the true?

THEÆTETUS: Yes, according to my present view.

SOCRATES: Is it still worth our while to resume the discussion touching opinion?

THEÆTETUS: To what are you alluding?

SOCRATES: There is a point which often troubles me, and is a great perplexity to me, both in regard to myself and others. I cannot make out the nature or origin of the mental experience to which I refer.

THEÆTETUS: Pray what is it?

SOCRATES: How there can be false opinion—that difficulty still troubles the eye of my mind; and I am uncertain whether I shall leave the question, or begin over again in a new way.

THEÆTETUS: Begin again, Socrates,—at least if you think that there is the slightest necessity for doing so. Were not you and Theodorus just now remarking very truly, that in discussions of this kind we may take our own time?

SOCRATES: You are quite right, and perhaps there will be no harm in retracing our steps and beginning again. Better a little which is well done, than a great deal imperfectly.

THEÆTETUS: Certainly.

SOCRATES: Well, and what is the difficulty? Do we not speak of false opinion, and say that one man holds a false and another a true opinion, as though there were some natural distinction between them?

THEÆTETUS: We certainly say so.

SOCRATES: All things and everything are either known or not known. I leave out of view the intermediate conceptions of learning and forgetting, because they have nothing to do with our present question.

THEÆTETUS: There can be no doubt, Socrates, if you exclude these, that there is no other alternative but knowing or not knowing a thing.

SOCRATES: That point being now determined, must we not say that he who has an opinion, must have an opinion about something which he knows or does not know?

THEÆTETUS: He must.

SOCRATES: He who knows, cannot but know; and he who does not know, cannot know?

THEÆTETUS: Of course.

Theætetus

SOCRATES: What shall we say then? When a man has a false opinion does he think that which he knows to be some other thing which he knows, and knowing both, is he at the same time ignorant of both?

THEÆTETUS: That, Socrates, is impossible.

SOCRATES: But perhaps he thinks of something which he does not know as some other thing which he does not know; for example, he knows neither Theætetus nor Socrates, and yet he fancies that Theætetus is Socrates, or Socrates Theætetus?

THEÆTETUS: How can he?

SOCRATES: But surely he cannot suppose what he knows to be what he does not know, or what he does not know to be what he knows?

THEÆTETUS: That would be monstrous.

SOCRATES: Where, then, is false opinion? For if all things are either known or unknown, there can be no opinion which is not comprehended under this alternative, and so false opinion is excluded.

THEÆTETUS: Most true.

SOCRATES: Suppose that we remove the question out of the sphere of knowing or not knowing, into that of being and not-being.

THEÆTETUS: What do you mean?

SOCRATES: May we not suspect the simple truth to be that he who thinks about anything, that which is not, will necessarily think what is false, whatever in other respects may be the state of his mind?

THEÆTETUS: That, again, is not unlikely, Socrates.

SOCRATES: Then suppose some one to say to us, Theætetus:—Is it possible for any man to think that which is not, either as a self-existent substance or as a predicate of something else? And suppose that we answer, 'Yes, he can, when he thinks what is not true.'—That will be our answer?

THEÆTETUS: Yes.

SOCRATES: But is there any parallel to this?

THEÆTETUS: What do you mean?

SOCRATES: Can a man see something and yet see nothing?

THEÆTETUS: Impossible.

SOCRATES: But if he sees any one thing, he sees something that exists. Do you suppose that what is one is ever to be found among non-existing things?

THEÆTETUS: I do not.

SOCRATES: He then who sees some one thing, sees something which is?

THEÆTETUS: Clearly.

SOCRATES: And he who hears anything, hears some one thing, and hears that which is?

THEÆTETUS: Yes.

SOCRATES: And he who touches anything, touches something which is one and therefore is?

THEÆTETUS: That again is true.

Theætetus

SOCRATES: And does not he who thinks, think some one thing?

THEÆTETUS: Certainly.

SOCRATES: And does not he who thinks some one thing, think something which is?

THEÆTETUS: I agree.

SOCRATES: Then he who thinks of that which is not, thinks of nothing?

THEÆTETUS: Clearly.

SOCRATES: And he who thinks of nothing, does not think at all?

THEÆTETUS: Obviously.

SOCRATES: Then no one can think that which is not, either as a self-existent substance or as a predicate of something else?

THEÆTETUS: Clearly not.

SOCRATES: Then to think falsely is different from thinking that which is not?

THEÆTETUS: It would seem so.

SOCRATES: Then false opinion has no existence in us, either in the sphere of being or of knowledge?

THEÆTETUS: Certainly not.

SOCRATES: But may not the following be the description of what we express by this name?

THEÆTETUS: What?

SOCRATES: May we not suppose that false opinion or thought is a sort of heterodoxy; a person may make an exchange in his mind, and say that one real object is another real object. For thus he always thinks that which is, but he puts one thing in place of another; and missing the aim of his thoughts, he may be truly said to have false opinion.

THEÆTETUS: Now you appear to me to have spoken the exact truth: when a man puts the base in the place of the noble, or the noble in the place of the base, then he has truly false opinion.

SOCRATES: I see, Theætetus, that your fear has disappeared, and that you are beginning to despise me.

THEÆTETUS: What makes you say so?

SOCRATES: You think, if I am not mistaken, that your 'truly false' is safe from censure, and that I shall never ask whether there can be a swift which is slow, or a heavy which is light, or any other self-contradictory thing, which works, not according to its own nature, but according to that of its opposite. But I will not insist upon this, for I do not wish needlessly to discourage you. And so you are satisfied that false opinion is heterodoxy, or the thought of something else?

THEÆTETUS: I am.

SOCRATES: It is possible then upon your view for the mind to conceive of one thing as another?

THEÆTETUS: True.

SOCRATES: But must not the mind, or thinking power, which misplaces them, have a conception either of both objects or of one of them?

THEÆTETUS: Certainly.

Theætetus

SOCRATES: Either together or in succession?

THEÆTETUS: Very good.

SOCRATES: And do you mean by conceiving, the same which I mean?

THEÆTETUS: What is that?

SOCRATES: I mean the conversation which the soul holds with herself in considering of anything. I speak of what I scarcely understand; but the soul when thinking appears to me to be just talking—asking questions of herself and answering them, affirming and denying. And when she has arrived at a decision, either gradually or by a sudden impulse, and has at last agreed, and does not doubt, this is called her opinion. I say, then, that to form an opinion is to speak, and opinion is a word spoken,—I mean, to oneself and in silence, not aloud or to another: What think you?

THEÆTETUS: I agree.

SOCRATES: Then when any one thinks of one thing as another, he is saying to himself that one thing is another?

THEÆTETUS: Yes.

SOCRATES: But do you ever remember saying to yourself that the noble is certainly base, or the unjust just; or, best of all—have you ever attempted to convince yourself that one thing is another? Nay, not even in sleep, did you ever venture to say to yourself that odd is even, or anything of the kind?

THEÆTETUS: Never.

SOCRATES: And do you suppose that any other man, either in his senses or out of them, ever seriously tried to persuade himself that an ox is a horse, or that two are one?

THEÆTETUS: Certainly not.

SOCRATES: But if thinking is talking to oneself, no one speaking and thinking of two objects, and apprehending them both in his soul, will say and think that the one is the other of them, and I must add, that even you, lover of dispute as you are, had better let the word 'other' alone (i.e. not insist that 'one' and 'other' are the same (Both words in Greek are called eteron: compare Parmen.; Euthyd.)). I mean to say, that no one thinks the noble to be base, or anything of the kind.

THEÆTETUS: I will give up the word 'other,' Socrates; and I agree to what you say.

SOCRATES: If a man has both of them in his thoughts, he cannot think that the one of them is the other?

THEÆTETUS: True.

SOCRATES: Neither, if he has one of them only in his mind and not the other, can he think that one is the other?

THEÆTETUS: True; for we should have to suppose that he apprehends that which is not in his thoughts at all.

SOCRATES: Then no one who has either both or only one of the two objects in his mind can think that the one is the other. And therefore, he who maintains that false opinion is heterodoxy is talking nonsense; for neither in this, any more than in the previous way, can false opinion exist in us.

THEÆTETUS: No.

SOCRATES: But if, Theætetus, this is not admitted, we shall be driven into many absurdities.

THEÆTETUS: What are they?

SOCRATES: I will not tell you until I have endeavoured to consider the matter from every point of view. For I should be ashamed of us if we were driven in our perplexity to admit the absurd consequences of which I speak. But if we find the solution, and get away from them, we may regard them only as the difficulties of others, and the ridicule will not attach to us. On the other hand, if we utterly fail, I suppose that we must be humble, and allow the argument to trample us under foot, as the sea-sick passenger is trampled upon by the sailor, and to do anything to us. Listen, then, while I tell you how I hope to find a way out of our difficulty.

THEÆTETUS: Let me hear.

SOCRATES: I think that we were wrong in denying that a man could think what he knew to be what he did not know; and that there is a way in which such a deception is possible.

THEÆTETUS: You mean to say, as I suspected at the time, that I may know Socrates, and at a distance see some one who is unknown to me, and whom I mistake for him—then the deception will occur?

SOCRATES: But has not that position been relinquished by us, because involving the absurdity that we should know and not know the things which we know?

THEÆTETUS: True.

SOCRATES: Let us make the assertion in another form, which may or may not have a favourable issue; but as we are in a great strait, every argument should be turned over and tested. Tell me, then, whether I am right in saying that you may learn a thing which at one time you did not know?

THEÆTETUS: Certainly you may.

SOCRATES: And another and another?

THEÆTETUS: Yes.

SOCRATES: I would have you imagine, then, that there exists in the mind of man a block of wax, which is of different sizes in different men; harder, moister, and having more or less of purity in one than another, and in some of an intermediate quality.

THEÆTETUS: I see.

SOCRATES: Let us say that this tablet is a gift of Memory, the mother of the Muses; and that when we wish to remember anything which we have seen, or heard, or thought in our own minds, we hold the wax to the perceptions and thoughts, and in that material receive the impression of them as from the seal of a ring; and that we remember and know what is imprinted as long as the image lasts; but when the image is effaced, or cannot be taken, then we forget and do not know.

THEÆTETUS: Very good.

SOCRATES: Now, when a person has this knowledge, and is considering something which he sees or hears, may not false opinion arise in the following manner?

THEÆTETUS: In what manner?

SOCRATES: When he thinks what he knows, sometimes to be what he knows, and sometimes to be what he does not know. We were wrong before in denying the possibility of this.

THEÆTETUS: And how would you amend the former statement?

SOCRATES: I should begin by making a list of the impossible cases which must be excluded. (1) No one can think one thing to be another when he does not perceive either of them, but has the memorial or seal of both of them in his mind; nor can any mistaking of one thing for another occur, when he only knows one, and does not

Theætetus

know, and has no impression of the other; nor can he think that one thing which he does not know is another thing which he does not know, or that what he does not know is what he knows; nor (2) that one thing which he perceives is another thing which he perceives, or that something which he perceives is something which he does not perceive; or that something which he does not perceive is something else which he does not perceive; or that something which he does not perceive is something which he perceives; nor again (3) can he think that something which he knows and perceives, and of which he has the impression coinciding with sense, is something else which he knows and perceives, and of which he has the impression coinciding with sense;—this last case, if possible, is still more inconceivable than the others; nor (4) can he think that something which he knows and perceives, and of which he has the memorial coinciding with sense, is something else which he knows; nor so long as these agree, can he think that a thing which he knows and perceives is another thing which he perceives; or that a thing which he does not know and does not perceive, is the same as another thing which he does not know and does not perceive;—nor again, can he suppose that a thing which he does not know and does not perceive is the same as another thing which he does not know; or that a thing which he does not know and does not perceive is another thing which he does not perceive:—All these utterly and absolutely exclude the possibility of false opinion. The only cases, if any, which remain, are the following.

THEÆTETUS: What are they? If you tell me, I may perhaps understand you better; but at present I am unable to follow you.

SOCRATES: A person may think that some things which he knows, or which he perceives and does not know, are some other things which he knows and perceives; or that some things which he knows and perceives, are other things which he knows and perceives.

THEÆTETUS: I understand you less than ever now.

SOCRATES: Hear me once more, then:—I, knowing Theodorus,

and remembering in my own mind what sort of person he is, and also what sort of person Theætetus is, at one time see them, and at another time do not see them, and sometimes I touch them, and at another time not, or at one time I may hear them or perceive them in some other way, and at another time not perceive them, but still I remember them, and know them in my own mind.

THEÆTETUS: Very true.

SOCRATES: Then, first of all, I want you to understand that a man may or may not perceive sensibly that which he knows.

THEÆTETUS: True.

SOCRATES: And that which he does not know will sometimes not be perceived by him and sometimes will be perceived and only perceived?

THEÆTETUS: That is also true.

SOCRATES: See whether you can follow me better now: Socrates can recognize Theodorus and Theætetus, but he sees neither of them, nor does he perceive them in any other way; he cannot then by any possibility imagine in his own mind that Theætetus is Theodorus. Am I not right?

THEÆTETUS: You are quite right.

SOCRATES: Then that was the first case of which I spoke.

THEÆTETUS: Yes.

SOCRATES: The second case was, that I, knowing one of you and not knowing the other, and perceiving neither, can never think him whom I know to be him whom I do not know.

THEÆTETUS: True.

Theætetus

SOCRATES: In the third case, not knowing and not perceiving either of you, I cannot think that one of you whom I do not know is the other whom I do not know. I need not again go over the catalogue of excluded cases, in which I cannot form a false opinion about you and Theodorus, either when I know both or when I am in ignorance of both, or when I know one and not the other. And the same of perceiving: do you understand me?

THEÆTETUS: I do.

SOCRATES: The only possibility of erroneous opinion is, when knowing you and Theodorus, and having on the waxen block the impression of both of you given as by a seal, but seeing you imperfectly and at a distance, I try to assign the right impression of memory to the right visual impression, and to fit this into its own print: if I succeed, recognition will take place; but if I fail and transpose them, putting the foot into the wrong shoe—that is to say, putting the vision of either of you on to the wrong impression, or if my mind, like the sight in a mirror, which is transferred from right to left, err by reason of some similar affection, then 'heterodoxy' and false opinion ensues.

THEÆTETUS: Yes, Socrates, you have described the nature of opinion with wonderful exactness.

SOCRATES: Or again, when I know both of you, and perceive as well as know one of you, but not the other, and my knowledge of him does not accord with perception—that was the case put by me just now which you did not understand.

THEÆTETUS: No, I did not.

SOCRATES: I meant to say, that when a person knows and perceives one of you, his knowledge coincides with his perception, he will never think him to be some other person, whom he knows and perceives, and the knowledge of whom coincides with his perception—for that also was a case supposed.

THEÆTETUS: True.

SOCRATES: But there was an omission of the further case, in which, as we now say, false opinion may arise, when knowing both, and seeing, or having some other sensible perception of both, I fail in holding the seal over against the corresponding sensation; like a bad archer, I miss and fall wide of the mark—and this is called falsehood.

THEÆTETUS: Yes; it is rightly so called.

SOCRATES: When, therefore, perception is present to one of the seals or impressions but not to the other, and the mind fits the seal of the absent perception on the one which is present, in any case of this sort the mind is deceived; in a word, if our view is sound, there can be no error or deception about things which a man does not know and has never perceived, but only in things which are known and perceived; in these alone opinion turns and twists about, and becomes alternately true and false;—true when the seals and impressions of sense meet straight and opposite—false when they go awry and crooked.

THEÆTETUS: And is not that, Socrates, nobly said?

SOCRATES: Nobly! yes; but wait a little and hear the explanation, and then you will say so with more reason; for to think truly is noble and to be deceived is base.

THEÆTETUS: Undoubtedly.

SOCRATES: And the origin of truth and error is as follows:—When the wax in the soul of any one is deep and abundant, and smooth and perfectly tempered, then the impressions which pass through the senses and sink into the heart of the soul, as Homer says in a parable, meaning to indicate the likeness of the soul to wax (Kerh Kerhos); these, I say, being pure and clear, and having a sufficient depth of wax, are also lasting, and minds, such as these, easily learn

Theætetus

and easily retain, and are not liable to confusion, but have true thoughts, for they have plenty of room, and having clear impressions of things, as we term them, quickly distribute them into their proper places on the block. And such men are called wise. Do you agree?

THEÆTETUS: Entirely.

SOCRATES: But when the heart of any one is shaggy—a quality which the all-wise poet commends, or muddy and of impure wax, or very soft, or very hard, then there is a corresponding defect in the mind—the soft are good at learning, but apt to forget; and the hard are the reverse; the shaggy and rugged and gritty, or those who have an admixture of earth or dung in their composition, have the impressions indistinct, as also the hard, for there is no depth in them; and the soft too are indistinct, for their impressions are easily confused and effaced. Yet greater is the indistinctness when they are all jostled together in a little soul, which has no room. These are the natures which have false opinion; for when they see or hear or think of anything, they are slow in assigning the right objects to the right impressions—in their stupidity they confuse them, and are apt to see and hear and think amiss—and such men are said to be deceived in their knowledge of objects, and ignorant.

THEÆTETUS: No man, Socrates, can say anything truer than that.

SOCRATES: Then now we may admit the existence of false opinion in us?

THEÆTETUS: Certainly.

SOCRATES: And of true opinion also?

THEÆTETUS: Yes.

SOCRATES: We have at length satisfactorily proven beyond a doubt there are these two sorts of opinion?

THEÆTETUS: Undoubtedly.

SOCRATES: Alas, Theætetus, what a tiresome creature is a man who is fond of talking!

THEÆTETUS: What makes you say so?

SOCRATES: Because I am disheartened at my own stupidity and tiresome garrulity; for what other term will describe the habit of a man who is always arguing on all sides of a question; whose dulness cannot be convinced, and who will never leave off?

THEÆTETUS: But what puts you out of heart?

SOCRATES: I am not only out of heart, but in positive despair; for I do not know what to answer if any one were to ask me:—O Socrates, have you indeed discovered that false opinion arises neither in the comparison of perceptions with one another nor yet in thought, but in union of thought and perception? Yes, I shall say, with the complacence of one who thinks that he has made a noble discovery.

THEÆTETUS: I see no reason why we should be ashamed of our demonstration, Socrates.

SOCRATES: He will say: You mean to argue that the man whom we only think of and do not see, cannot be confused with the horse which we do not see or touch, but only think of and do not perceive? That I believe to be my meaning, I shall reply.

THEÆTETUS: Quite right.

SOCRATES: Well, then, he will say, according to that argument, the number eleven, which is only thought, can never be mistaken for twelve, which is only thought: How would you answer him?

THEÆTETUS: I should say that a mistake may very likely arise

Theætetus

between the eleven or twelve which are seen or handled, but that no similar mistake can arise between the eleven and twelve which are in the mind.

SOCRATES: Well, but do you think that no one ever put before his own mind five and seven,—I do not mean five or seven men or horses, but five or seven in the abstract, which, as we say, are recorded on the waxen block, and in which false opinion is held to be impossible; did no man ever ask himself how many these numbers make when added together, and answer that they are eleven, while another thinks that they are twelve, or would all agree in thinking and saying that they are twelve?

THEÆTETUS: Certainly not; many would think that they are eleven, and in the higher numbers the chance of error is greater still; for I assume you to be speaking of numbers in general.

SOCRATES: Exactly; and I want you to consider whether this does not imply that the twelve in the waxen block are supposed to be eleven?

THEÆTETUS: Yes, that seems to be the case.

SOCRATES: Then do we not come back to the old difficulty? For he who makes such a mistake does think one thing which he knows to be another thing which he knows; but this, as we said, was impossible, and afforded an irresistible proof of the non-existence of false opinion, because otherwise the same person would inevitably know and not know the same thing at the same time.

THEÆTETUS: Most true.

SOCRATES: Then false opinion cannot be explained as a confusion of thought and sense, for in that case we could not have been mistaken about pure conceptions of thought; and thus we are obliged to say, either that false opinion does not exist, or that a man may not know that which he knows;—which alternative do you prefer?

THEÆTETUS: It is hard to determine, Socrates.

SOCRATES: And yet the argument will scarcely admit of both. But, as we are at our wits' end, suppose that we do a shameless thing?

THEÆTETUS: What is it?

SOCRATES: Let us attempt to explain the verb 'to know.'

THEÆTETUS: And why should that be shameless?

SOCRATES: You seem not to be aware that the whole of our discussion from the very beginning has been a search after knowledge, of which we are assumed not to know the nature.

THEÆTETUS: Nay, but I am well aware.

SOCRATES: And is it not shameless when we do not know what knowledge is, to be explaining the verb 'to know'? The truth is, Theætetus, that we have long been infected with logical impurity. Thousands of times have we repeated the words 'we know,' and 'do not know,' and 'we have or have not science or knowledge,' as if we could understand what we are saying to one another, so long as we remain ignorant about knowledge; and at this moment we are using the words 'we understand,' 'we are ignorant,' as though we could still employ them when deprived of knowledge or science.

THEÆTETUS: But if you avoid these expressions, Socrates, how will you ever argue at all?

SOCRATES: I could not, being the man I am. The case would be different if I were a true hero of dialectic: and O that such an one were present! for he would have told us to avoid the use of these terms; at the same time he would not have spared in you and me the faults which I have noted. But, seeing that we are no great wits, shall I venture to say what knowing is? for I think that the attempt may be worth making.

Theætetus

THEÆTETUS: Then by all means venture, and no one shall find fault with you for using the forbidden terms.

SOCRATES: You have heard the common explanation of the verb 'to know'?

THEÆTETUS: I think so, but I do not remember it at the moment.

SOCRATES: They explain the word 'to know' as meaning 'to have knowledge.'

THEÆTETUS: True.

SOCRATES: I should like to make a slight change, and say 'to possess' knowledge.

THEÆTETUS: How do the two expressions differ?

SOCRATES: Perhaps there may be no difference; but still I should like you to hear my view, that you may help me to test it.

THEÆTETUS: I will, if I can.

SOCRATES: I should distinguish 'having' from 'possessing': for example, a man may buy and keep under his control a garment which he does not wear; and then we should say, not that he has, but that he possesses the garment.

THEÆTETUS: It would be the correct expression.

SOCRATES: Well, may not a man 'possess' and yet not 'have' knowledge in the sense of which I am speaking? As you may suppose a man to have caught wild birds—doves or any other birds—and to be keeping them in an aviary which he has constructed at home; we might say of him in one sense, that he always has them because he possesses them, might we not?

THEÆTETUS: Yes.

SOCRATES: And yet, in another sense, he has none of them; but they are in his power, and he has got them under his hand in an enclosure of his own, and can take and have them whenever he likes;—he can catch any which he likes, and let the bird go again, and he may do so as often as he pleases.

THEÆTETUS: True.

SOCRATES: Once more, then, as in what preceded we made a sort of waxen figment in the mind, so let us now suppose that in the mind of each man there is an aviary of all sorts of birds—some flocking together apart from the rest, others in small groups, others solitary, flying anywhere and everywhere.

THEÆTETUS: Let us imagine such an aviary—and what is to follow?

SOCRATES: We may suppose that the birds are kinds of knowledge, and that when we were children, this receptacle was empty; whenever a man has gotten and detained in the enclosure a kind of knowledge, he may be said to have learned or discovered the thing which is the subject of the knowledge: and this is to know.

THEÆTETUS: Granted.

SOCRATES: And further, when any one wishes to catch any of these knowledges or sciences, and having taken, to hold it, and again to let them go, how will he express himself?—will he describe the 'catching' of them and the original 'possession' in the same words? I will make my meaning clearer by an example:—You admit that there is an art of arithmetic?

THEÆTETUS: To be sure.

SOCRATES: Conceive this under the form of a hunt after the science of odd and even in general.

THEÆTETUS: I follow.

SOCRATES: Having the use of the art, the arithmetician, if I am not mistaken, has the conceptions of number under his hand, and can transmit them to another.

THEÆTETUS: Yes.

SOCRATES: And when transmitting them he may be said to teach them, and when receiving to learn them, and when receiving to learn them, and when having them in possession in the aforesaid aviary he may be said to know them.

THEÆTETUS: Exactly.

SOCRATES: Attend to what follows: must not the perfect arithmetician know all numbers, for he has the science of all numbers in his mind?

THEÆTETUS: True.

SOCRATES: And he can reckon abstract numbers in his head, or things about him which are numerable?

THEÆTETUS: Of course he can.

SOCRATES: And to reckon is simply to consider how much such and such a number amounts to?

THEÆTETUS: Very true.

SOCRATES: And so he appears to be searching into something which he knows, as if he did not know it, for we have already admitted that he knows all numbers;—you have heard these perplexing questions raised?

THEÆTETUS: I have.

SOCRATES: May we not pursue the image of the doves, and say that the chase after knowledge is of two kinds? one kind is prior to possession and for the sake of possession, and the other for the sake of taking and holding in the hands that which is possessed already. And thus, when a man has learned and known something long ago, he may resume and get hold of the knowledge which he has long possessed, but has not at hand in his mind.

THEÆTETUS: True.

SOCRATES: That was my reason for asking how we ought to speak when an arithmetician sets about numbering, or a grammarian about reading? Shall we say, that although he knows, he comes back to himself to learn what he already knows?

THEÆTETUS: It would be too absurd, Socrates.

SOCRATES: Shall we say then that he is going to read or number what he does not know, although we have admitted that he knows all letters and all numbers?

THEÆTETUS: That, again, would be an absurdity.

SOCRATES: Then shall we say that about names we care nothing?—any one may twist and turn the words 'knowing' and 'learning' in any way which he likes, but since we have determined that the possession of knowledge is not the having or using it, we do assert that a man cannot not possess that which he possesses; and, therefore, in no case can a man not know that which he knows, but he may get a false opinion about it; for he may have the knowledge, not of this particular thing, but of some other;—when the various numbers and forms of knowledge are flying about in the aviary, and wishing to capture a certain sort of knowledge out of the general store, he takes the wrong one by mistake, that is to say, when he thought eleven to be twelve, he got hold of the ring-dove which he had in his mind, when he wanted the pigeon.

THEÆTETUS: A very rational explanation.

SOCRATES: But when he catches the one which he wants, then he is not deceived, and has an opinion of what is, and thus false and true opinion may exist, and the difficulties which were previously raised disappear. I dare say that you agree with me, do you not?

THEÆTETUS: Yes.

SOCRATES: And so we are rid of the difficulty of a man's not knowing what he knows, for we are not driven to the inference that he does not possess what he possesses, whether he be or be not deceived. And yet I fear that a greater difficulty is looking in at the window.

THEÆTETUS: What is it?

SOCRATES: How can the exchange of one knowledge for another ever become false opinion?

THEÆTETUS: What do you mean?

SOCRATES: In the first place, how can a man who has the knowledge of anything be ignorant of that which he knows, not by reason of ignorance, but by reason of his own knowledge? And, again, is it not an extreme absurdity that he should suppose another thing to be this, and this to be another thing;—that, having knowledge present with him in his mind, he should still know nothing and be ignorant of all things?—you might as well argue that ignorance may make a man know, and blindness make him see, as that knowledge can make him ignorant.

THEÆTETUS: Perhaps, Socrates, we may have been wrong in making only forms of knowledge our birds: whereas there ought to have been forms of ignorance as well, flying about together in the mind, and then he who sought to take one of them might sometimes catch a form of knowledge, and sometimes a form of ignorance; and thus he would have a false opinion from ignorance, but a true one from knowledge, about the same thing.

SOCRATES: I cannot help praising you, Theætetus, and yet I must beg you to reconsider your words. Let us grant what you say—then, according to you, he who takes ignorance will have a false opinion—am I right?

THEÆTETUS: Yes.

SOCRATES: He will certainly not think that he has a false opinion?

THEÆTETUS: Of course not.

SOCRATES: He will think that his opinion is true, and he will fancy that he knows the things about which he has been deceived?

THEÆTETUS: Certainly.

SOCRATES: Then he will think that he has captured knowledge and not ignorance?

THEÆTETUS: Clearly.

SOCRATES: And thus, after going a long way round, we are once more face to face with our original difficulty. The hero of dialectic will retort upon us:—'O my excellent friends, he will say, laughing, if a man knows the form of ignorance and the form of knowledge, can he think that one of them which he knows is the other which he knows? or, if he knows neither of them, can he think that the one which he knows not is another which he knows not? or, if he knows one and not the other, can he think the one which he knows to be the one which he does not know? or the one which he does not know to be the one which he knows? or will you tell me that there are other forms of knowledge which distinguish the right and wrong birds, and which the owner keeps in some other aviaries or graven on waxen blocks according to your foolish images, and which he may be said to know while he possesses them, even though he have them not at hand in his mind? And thus, in a perpetual circle, you will be compelled to go round and round, and you will make no progress.' What are we to say in reply, Theætetus?

THEÆTETUS: Indeed, Socrates, I do not know what we are to say.

SOCRATES: Are not his reproaches just, and does not the argument truly show that we are wrong in seeking for false opinion until we know what knowledge is; that must be first ascertained; then, the nature of false opinion?

THEÆTETUS: I cannot but agree with you, Socrates, so far as we have yet gone.

SOCRATES: Then, once more, what shall we say that knowledge is?—for we are not going to lose heart as yet.

THEÆTETUS: Certainly, I shall not lose heart, if you do not.

SOCRATES: What definition will be most consistent with our former views?

THEÆTETUS: I cannot think of any but our old one, Socrates.

SOCRATES: What was it?

THEÆTETUS: Knowledge was said by us to be true opinion; and true opinion is surely unerring, and the results which follow from it are all noble and good.

SOCRATES: He who led the way into the river, Theætetus, said 'The experiment will show;' and perhaps if we go forward in the search, we may stumble upon the thing which we are looking for; but if we stay where we are, nothing will come to light.

THEÆTETUS: Very true; let us go forward and try.

SOCRATES: The trail soon comes to an end, for a whole profession is against us.

THEÆTETUS: How is that, and what profession do you mean?

SOCRATES: The profession of the great wise ones who are called orators and lawyers; for these persuade men by their art and make them think whatever they like, but they do not teach them. Do you imagine that there are any teachers in the world so clever as to be able to convince others of the truth about acts of robbery or violence, of which they were not eye-witnesses, while a little water is flowing in the clepsydra?

THEÆTETUS: Certainly not, they can only persuade them.

SOCRATES: And would you not say that persuading them is making them have an opinion?

THEÆTETUS: To be sure.

SOCRATES: When, therefore, judges are justly persuaded about matters which you can know only by seeing them, and not in any other way, and when thus judging of them from report they attain a true opinion about them, they judge without knowledge, and yet are rightly persuaded, if they have judged well.

THEÆTETUS: Certainly.

SOCRATES: And yet, O my friend, if true opinion in law courts and knowledge are the same, the perfect judge could not have judged rightly without knowledge; and therefore I must infer that they are not the same.

THEÆTETUS: That is a distinction, Socrates, which I have heard made by some one else, but I had forgotten it. He said that true

Theætetus

opinion, combined with reason, was knowledge, but that the opinion which had no reason was out of the sphere of knowledge; and that things of which there is no rational account are not knowable—such was the singular expression which he used—and that things which have a reason or explanation are knowable.

SOCRATES: Excellent; but then, how did he distinguish between things which are and are not 'knowable'? I wish that you would repeat to me what he said, and then I shall know whether you and I have heard the same tale.

THEÆTETUS: I do not know whether I can recall it; but if another person would tell me, I think that I could follow him.

SOCRATES: Let me give you, then, a dream in return for a dream:— Methought that I too had a dream, and I heard in my dream that the primeval letters or elements out of which you and I and all other things are compounded, have no reason or explanation; you can only name them, but no predicate can be either affirmed or denied of them, for in the one case existence, in the other non-existence is already implied, neither of which must be added, if you mean to speak of this or that thing by itself alone. It should not be called itself, or that, or each, or alone, or this, or the like; for these go about everywhere and are applied to all things, but are distinct from them; whereas, if the first elements could be described, and had a definition of their own, they would be spoken of apart from all else. But none of these primeval elements can be defined; they can only be named, for they have nothing but a name, and the things which are compounded of them, as they are complex, are expressed by a combination of names, for the combination of names is the essence of a definition. Thus, then, the elements or letters are only objects of perception, and cannot be defined or known; but the syllables or combinations of them are known and expressed, and are apprehended by true opinion. When, therefore, any one forms the true opinion of anything without rational explanation, you may say that his mind is truly exercised, but has no knowledge; for he who cannot give and receive a reason for a thing, has no knowledge of that thing; but when he adds rational explanation, then, he is perfected in knowledge and may be all that I have been denying of him. Was that the form in which the dream appeared to you?

THEÆTETUS: Precisely.

SOCRATES: And you allow and maintain that true opinion, combined with definition or rational explanation, is knowledge?

THEÆTETUS: Exactly.

SOCRATES: Then may we assume, Theætetus, that to-day, and in this casual manner, we have found a truth which in former times many wise men have grown old and have not found?

THEÆTETUS: At any rate, Socrates, I am satisfied with the present statement.

SOCRATES: Which is probably correct—for how can there be knowledge apart from definition and true opinion? And yet there is one point in what has been said which does not quite satisfy me.

THEÆTETUS: What was it?

SOCRATES: What might seem to be the most ingenious notion of all:—That the elements or letters are unknown, but the combination or syllables known.

THEÆTETUS: And was that wrong?

SOCRATES: We shall soon know; for we have as hostages the instances which the author of the argument himself used.

THEÆTETUS: What hostages?

SOCRATES: The letters, which are the elements; and the syllables, which are the combinations;—he reasoned, did he not, from the

Theætetus

letters of the alphabet?

THEÆTETUS: Yes; he did.

SOCRATES: Let us take them and put them to the test, or rather, test ourselves:—What was the way in which we learned letters? and, first of all, are we right in saying that syllables have a definition, but that letters have no definition?

THEÆTETUS: I think so.

SOCRATES: I think so too; for, suppose that some one asks you to spell the first syllable of my name:— Theætetus, he says, what is *so*?

THEÆTETUS: I should reply S and O.

SOCRATES: That is the definition which you would give of the syllable?

THEÆTETUS: I should.

SOCRATES: I wish that you would give me a similar definition of the S.

THEÆTETUS: But how can any one, Socrates, tell the elements of an element? I can only reply, that S is a consonant, a mere noise, as of the tongue hissing; B, and most other letters, again, are neither vowel-sounds nor noises. Thus letters may be most truly said to be undefined; for even the most distinct of them, which are the seven vowels, have a sound only, but no definition at all.

SOCRATES: Then, I suppose, my friend, that we have been so far right in our idea about knowledge?

THEÆTETUS: Yes; I think that we have.

SOCRATES: Well, but have we been right in maintaining that the syllables can be known, but not the letters?

THEÆTETUS: I think so.

SOCRATES: And do we mean by a syllable two letters, or if there are more, all of them, or a single idea which arises out of the combination of them?

THEÆTETUS: I should say that we mean all the letters.

SOCRATES: Take the case of the two letters S and O, which form the first syllable of my own name; must not he who knows the syllable, know both of them?

THEÆTETUS: Certainly.

SOCRATES: He knows, that is, the S and O?

THEÆTETUS: Yes.

SOCRATES: But can he be ignorant of either singly and yet know both together?

THEÆTETUS: Such a supposition, Socrates, is monstrous and unmeaning.

SOCRATES: But if he cannot know both without knowing each, then if he is ever to know the syllable, he must know the letters first; and thus the fine theory has again taken wings and departed.

THEÆTETUS: Yes, with wonderful celerity.

SOCRATES: Yes, we did not keep watch properly. Perhaps we ought to have maintained that a syllable is not the letters, but rather one single idea framed out of them, having a separate form distinct from them.

THEÆTETUS: Very true; and a more likely notion than the other.

Theætetus

SOCRATES: Take care; let us not be cowards and betray a great and imposing theory.

THEÆTETUS: No, indeed.

SOCRATES: Let us assume then, as we now say, that the syllable is a simple form arising out of the several combinations of harmonious elements—of letters or of any other elements.

THEÆTETUS: Very good.

SOCRATES: And it must have no parts.

THEÆTETUS: Why?

SOCRATES: Because that which has parts must be a whole of all the parts. Or would you say that a whole, although formed out of the parts, is a single notion different from all the parts?

THEÆTETUS: I should.

SOCRATES: And would you say that all and the whole are the same, or different?

THEÆTETUS: I am not certain; but, as you like me to answer at once, I shall hazard the reply, that they are different.

SOCRATES: I approve of your readiness, Theætetus, but I must take time to think whether I equally approve of your answer.

THEÆTETUS: Yes; the answer is the point.

SOCRATES: According to this new view, the whole is supposed to differ from all?

THEÆTETUS: Yes.

SOCRATES: Well, but is there any difference between all (in the plural) and the all (in the singular)? Take the case of number:— When we say one, two, three, four, five, six; or when we say twice three, or three times two, or four and two, or three and two and one, are we speaking of the same or of different numbers?

THEÆTETUS: Of the same.

SOCRATES: That is of six?

THEÆTETUS: Yes.

SOCRATES: And in each form of expression we spoke of all the six?

THEÆTETUS: True.

SOCRATES: Again, in speaking of all (in the plural) is there not one thing which we express?

THEÆTETUS: Of course there is.

SOCRATES: And that is six?

THEÆTETUS: Yes.

SOCRATES: Then in predicating the word 'all' of things measured by number, we predicate at the same time a singular and a plural?

THEÆTETUS: Clearly we do.

SOCRATES: Again, the number of the acre and the acre are the same; are they not?

THEÆTETUS: Yes.

SOCRATES: And the number of the stadium in like manner is the stadium?

THEÆTETUS: Yes.

SOCRATES: And the army is the number of the army; and in all similar cases, the entire number of anything is the entire thing?

THEÆTETUS: True.

SOCRATES: And the number of each is the parts of each?

THEÆTETUS: Exactly.

SOCRATES: Then as many things as have parts are made up of parts?

THEÆTETUS: Clearly.

SOCRATES: But all the parts are admitted to be the all, if the entire number is the all?

THEÆTETUS: True.

SOCRATES: Then the whole is not made up of parts, for it would be the all, if consisting of all the parts?

THEÆTETUS: That is the inference.

SOCRATES: But is a part a part of anything but the whole?

THEÆTETUS: Yes, of the all.

SOCRATES: You make a valiant defence, Theætetus. And yet is not the all that of which nothing is wanting?

THEÆTETUS: Certainly.

SOCRATES: And is not a whole likewise that from which nothing is absent? but that from which anything is absent is neither a whole nor all;—if wanting in anything, both equally lose their entirety of nature.

THEÆTETUS: I now think that there is no difference between a whole and all.

SOCRATES: But were we not saying that when a thing has parts, all the parts will be a whole and all?

THEÆTETUS: Certainly.

SOCRATES: Then, as I was saying before, must not the alternative be that either the syllable is not the letters, and then the letters are not parts of the syllable, or that the syllable will be the same with the letters, and will therefore be equally known with them?

THEÆTETUS: You are right.

SOCRATES: And, in order to avoid this, we suppose it to be different from them?

THEÆTETUS: Yes.

SOCRATES: But if letters are not parts of syllables, can you tell me of any other parts of syllables, which are not letters?

THEÆTETUS: No, indeed, Socrates; for if I admit the existence of parts in a syllable, it would be ridiculous in me to give up letters and seek for other parts.

SOCRATES: Quite true, Theætetus, and therefore, according to our present view, a syllable must surely be some indivisible form?

THEÆTETUS: True.

SOCRATES: But do you remember, my friend, that only a little while ago we admitted and approved the statement, that of the first

Theætetus

elements out of which all other things are compounded there could be no definition, because each of them when taken by itself is uncompounded; nor can one rightly attribute to them the words 'being' or 'this,' because they are alien and inappropriate words, and for this reason the letters or elements were indefinable and unknown?

THEÆTETUS: I remember.

SOCRATES: And is not this also the reason why they are simple and indivisible? I can see no other.

THEÆTETUS: No other reason can be given.

SOCRATES: Then is not the syllable in the same case as the elements or letters, if it has no parts and is one form?

THEÆTETUS: To be sure.

SOCRATES: If, then, a syllable is a whole, and has many parts or letters, the letters as well as the syllable must be intelligible and expressible, since all the parts are acknowledged to be the same as the whole?

THEÆTETUS: True.

SOCRATES: But if it be one and indivisible, then the syllables and the letters are alike undefined and unknown, and for the same reason?

THEÆTETUS: I cannot deny that.

SOCRATES: We cannot, therefore, agree in the opinion of him who says that the syllable can be known and expressed, but not the letters.

THEÆTETUS: Certainly not; if we may trust the argument.

SOCRATES: Well, but will you not be equally inclined to disagree with him, when you remember your own experience in learning to read?

THEÆTETUS: What experience?

SOCRATES: Why, that in learning you were kept trying to distinguish the separate letters both by the eye and by the ear, in order that, when you heard them spoken or saw them written, you might not be confused by their position.

THEÆTETUS: Very true.

SOCRATES: And is the education of the harp-player complete unless he can tell what string answers to a particular note; the notes, as every one would allow, are the elements or letters of music?

THEÆTETUS: Exactly.

SOCRATES: Then, if we argue from the letters and syllables which we know to other simples and compounds, we shall say that the letters or simple elements as a class are much more certainly known than the syllables, and much more indispensable to a perfect knowledge of any subject; and if some one says that the syllable is known and the letter unknown, we shall consider that either intentionally or unintentionally he is talking nonsense?

THEÆTETUS: Exactly.

SOCRATES: And there might be given other proofs of this belief, if I am not mistaken. But do not let us in looking for them lose sight of the question before us, which is the meaning of the statement, that right opinion with rational definition or explanation is the most perfect form of knowledge.

THEÆTETUS: We must not.

Theætetus

SOCRATES: Well, and what is the meaning of the term 'explanation'? I think that we have a choice of three meanings.

THEÆTETUS: What are they?

SOCRATES: In the first place, the meaning may be, manifesting one's thought by the voice with verbs and nouns, imaging an opinion in the stream which flows from the lips, as in a mirror or water. Does not explanation appear to be of this nature?

THEÆTETUS: Certainly; he who so manifests his thought, is said to explain himself.

SOCRATES: And every one who is not born deaf or dumb is able sooner or later to manifest what he thinks of anything; and if so, all those who have a right opinion about anything will also have right explanation; nor will right opinion be anywhere found to exist apart from knowledge.

THEÆTETUS: True.

SOCRATES: Let us not, therefore, hastily charge him who gave this account of knowledge with uttering an unmeaning word; for perhaps he only intended to say, that when a person was asked what was the nature of anything, he should be able to answer his questioner by giving the elements of the thing.

THEÆTETUS: As for example, Socrates…?

SOCRATES: As, for example, when Hesiod says that a waggon is made up of a hundred planks. Now, neither you nor I could describe all of them individually; but if any one asked what is a waggon, we should be content to answer, that a waggon consists of wheels, axle, body, rims, yoke.

THEÆTETUS: Certainly.

SOCRATES: And our opponent will probably laugh at us, just as he would if we professed to be grammarians and to give a grammatical account of the name of Theætetus, and yet could only tell the syllables and not the letters of your name—that would be true opinion, and not knowledge; for knowledge, as has been already remarked, is not attained until, combined with true opinion, there is an enumeration of the elements out of which anything is composed.

THEÆTETUS: Yes.

SOCRATES: In the same general way, we might also have true opinion about a waggon; but he who can describe its essence by an enumeration of the hundred planks, adds rational explanation to true opinion, and instead of opinion has art and knowledge of the nature of a waggon, in that he attains to the whole through the elements.

THEÆTETUS: And do you not agree in that view, Socrates?

SOCRATES: If you do, my friend; but I want to know first, whether you admit the resolution of all things into their elements to be a rational explanation of them, and the consideration of them in syllables or larger combinations of them to be irrational—is this your view?

THEÆTETUS: Precisely.

SOCRATES: Well, and do you conceive that a man has knowledge of any element who at one time affirms and at another time denies that element of something, or thinks that the same thing is composed of different elements at different times?

THEÆTETUS: Assuredly not.

SOCRATES: And do you not remember that in your case and in that of others this often occurred in the process of learning to read?

Theætetus

THEÆTETUS: You mean that I mistook the letters and misspelt the syllables?

SOCRATES: Yes.

THEÆTETUS: To be sure; I perfectly remember, and I am very far from supposing that they who are in this condition have knowledge.

SOCRATES: When a person at the time of learning writes the name of Theætetus, and thinks that he ought to write and does write Th and e; but, again, meaning to write the name of Theododorus, thinks that he ought to write and does write T and e—can we suppose that he knows the first syllables of your two names?

THEÆTETUS: We have already admitted that such a one has not yet attained knowledge.

SOCRATES: And in like manner be may enumerate without knowing them the second and third and fourth syllables of your name?

THEÆTETUS: He may.

SOCRATES: And in that case, when he knows the order of the letters and can write them out correctly, he has right opinion?

THEÆTETUS: Clearly.

SOCRATES: But although we admit that he has right opinion, he will still be without knowledge?

THEÆTETUS: Yes.

SOCRATES: And yet he will have explanation, as well as right opinion, for he knew the order of the letters when he wrote; and this we admit to be explanation.

THEÆTETUS: True.

SOCRATES: Then, my friend, there is such a thing as right opinion united with definition or explanation, which does not as yet attain to the exactness of knowledge.

THEÆTETUS: It would seem so.

SOCRATES: And what we fancied to be a perfect definition of knowledge is a dream only. But perhaps we had better not say so as yet, for were there not three explanations of knowledge, one of which must, as we said, be adopted by him who maintains knowledge to be true opinion combined with rational explanation? And very likely there may be found some one who will not prefer this but the third.

THEÆTETUS: You are quite right; there is still one remaining. The first was the image or expression of the mind in speech; the second, which has just been mentioned, is a way of reaching the whole by an enumeration of the elements. But what is the third definition?

SOCRATES: There is, further, the popular notion of telling the mark or sign of difference which distinguishes the thing in question from all others.

THEÆTETUS: Can you give me any example of such a definition?

SOCRATES: As, for example, in the case of the sun, I think that you would be contented with the statement that the sun is the brightest of the heavenly bodies which revolve about the earth.

THEÆTETUS: Certainly.

SOCRATES: Understand why:—the reason is, as I was just now saying, that if you get at the difference and distinguishing characteristic of each thing, then, as many persons affirm, you will get at the definition or explanation of it; but while you lay hold only of the common

Theætetus

and not of the characteristic notion, you will only have the definition of those things to which this common quality belongs.

THEÆTETUS: I understand you, and your account of definition is in my judgment correct.

SOCRATES: But he, who having right opinion about anything, can find out the difference which distinguishes it from other things will know that of which before he had only an opinion.

THEÆTETUS: Yes; that is what we are maintaining.

SOCRATES: Nevertheless, Theætetus, on a nearer view, I find myself quite disappointed; the picture, which at a distance was not so bad, has now become altogether unintelligible.

THEÆTETUS: What do you mean?

SOCRATES: I will endeavour to explain: I will suppose myself to have true opinion of you, and if to this I add your definition, then I have knowledge, but if not, opinion only.

THEÆTETUS: Yes.

SOCRATES: The definition was assumed to be the interpretation of your difference.

THEÆTETUS: True.

SOCRATES: But when I had only opinion, I had no conception of your distinguishing characteristics.

THEÆTETUS: I suppose not.

SOCRATES: Then I must have conceived of some general or common nature which no more belonged to you than to another.

THEÆTETUS: True.

SOCRATES: Tell me, now—How in that case could I have formed a judgment of you any more than of any one else? Suppose that I imagine Theætetus to be a man who has nose, eyes, and mouth, and every other member complete; how would that enable me to distinguish Theætetus from Theodorus, or from some outer barbarian?

THEÆTETUS: How could it?

SOCRATES: Or if I had further conceived of you, not only as having nose and eyes, but as having a snub nose and prominent eyes, should I have any more notion of you than of myself and others who resemble me?

THEÆTETUS: Certainly not.

SOCRATES: Surely I can have no conception of Theætetus until your snub-nosedness has left an impression on my mind different from the snub-nosedness of all others whom I have ever seen, and until your other peculiarities have a like distinctness; and so when I meet you to-morrow the right opinion will be re-called?

THEÆTETUS: Most true.

SOCRATES: Then right opinion implies the perception of differences?

THEÆTETUS: Clearly.

SOCRATES: What, then, shall we say of adding reason or explanation to right opinion? If the meaning is, that we should form an opinion of the way in which something differs from another thing, the proposal is ridiculous.

THEÆTETUS: How so?

Theætetus

SOCRATES: We are supposed to acquire a right opinion of the differences which distinguish one thing from another when we have already a right opinion of them, and so we go round and round:— the revolution of the scytal, or pestle, or any other rotatory machine, in the same circles, is as nothing compared with such a requirement; and we may be truly described as the blind directing the blind; for to add those things which we already have, in order that we may learn what we already think, is like a soul utterly benighted.

THEÆTETUS: Tell me; what were you going to say just now, when you asked the question?

SOCRATES: If, my boy, the argument, in speaking of adding the definition, had used the word to 'know,' and not merely 'have an opinion' of the difference, this which is the most promising of all the definitions of knowledge would have come to a pretty end, for to know is surely to acquire knowledge.

THEÆTETUS: True.

SOCRATES: And so, when the question is asked, What is knowledge? this fair argument will answer 'Right opinion with knowledge,'—knowledge, that is, of difference, for this, as the said argument maintains, is adding the definition.

THEÆTETUS: That seems to be true.

SOCRATES: But how utterly foolish, when we are asking what is knowledge, that the reply should only be, right opinion with knowledge of difference or of anything! And so, Theætetus, knowledge is neither sensation nor true opinion, nor yet definition and explanation accompanying and added to true opinion?

THEÆTETUS: I suppose not.

SOCRATES: And are you still in labour and travail, my dear friend, or have you brought all that you have to say about knowledge to the birth?

THEÆTETUS: I am sure, Socrates, that you have elicited from me a good deal more than ever was in me.

SOCRATES: And does not my art show that you have brought forth wind, and that the offspring of your brain are not worth bringing up?

THEÆTETUS: Very true.

SOCRATES: But if, Theætetus, you should ever conceive afresh, you will be all the better for the present investigation, and if not, you will be soberer and humbler and gentler to other men, and will be too modest to fancy that you know what you do not know. These are the limits of my art; I can no further go, nor do I know aught of the things which great and famous men know or have known in this or former ages. The office of a midwife I, like my mother, have received from God; she delivered women, I deliver men; but they must be young and noble and fair.

And now I have to go to the porch of the King Archon, where I am to meet Meletus and his indictment. To-morrow morning, Theodorus, I shall hope to see you again at this place.

Parmenides

by

Plato

Translated by Benjamin Jowett

INTRODUCTION AND ANALYSIS

THE AWE WITH which Plato regarded the character of 'the great' Parmenides has extended to the dialogue which he calls by his name. None of the writings of Plato have been more copiously illustrated, both in ancient and modern times, and in none of them have the interpreters been more at variance with one another. Nor is this surprising. For the Parmenides is more fragmentary and isolated than any other dialogue, and the design of the writer is not expressly stated. The date is uncertain; the relation to the other writings of Plato is also uncertain; the connexion between the two parts is at first sight extremely obscure; and in the latter of the two we are left in doubt as to whether Plato is speaking his own sentiments by the lips of Parmenides, and overthrowing him out of his own mouth, or whether he is propounding consequences which would have been admitted by Zeno and Parmenides themselves. The contradictions which follow from the hypotheses of the one and many have been regarded by some as transcendental mysteries; by others as a mere illustration, taken at random, of a new method. They seem to have been inspired by a sort of dialectical frenzy, such as may be supposed to have prevailed in the Megarian School (compare Cratylus, etc.). The criticism on his own doctrine of Ideas has also been considered, not as a real criticism, but as an exuberance of the metaphysical imagination which enabled Plato to go beyond himself. To the latter part of the dialogue we may certainly apply the words in which he himself describes the earlier philosophers in the Sophist: 'They went on their way rather regardless of whether we understood them or not.'

The Parmenides in point of style is one of the best of the Platonic writings; the first portion of the dialogue is in no way defective in ease and grace and dramatic interest; nor in the second part, where there was no room for such qualities, is there any want of clearness or precision. The latter half is an exquisite mosaic, of which the small pieces are with the utmost fineness and regularity adapted to one another. Like the Protagoras, Phaedo, and others, the whole is a narrated dialogue, combining with the mere recital of the words spoken, the observations of the reciter on the effect produced by them. Thus we are informed by him that Zeno and Parmenides were not altogether pleased at the request of Socrates that they would examine into the nature of the one and many in the sphere of Ideas, although they received his suggestion with approving smiles. And we are glad to be told that Parmenides was 'aged but well-favoured,' and that Zeno was 'very good-looking'; also that Parmenides affected to decline the great argument, on which, as Zeno knew from experience, he was not unwilling to enter. The character of Antiphon, the half-brother of Plato, who had once been inclined to philosophy, but has now shown the hereditary disposition for horses, is very naturally described. He is the sole depositary of the famous dialogue; but, although he receives the strangers like a courteous gentleman, he is impatient of the trouble of reciting it. As they enter, he has been giving orders to a bridle-maker; by this slight touch Plato verifies the previous description of him. After a little persuasion he is induced to favour the Clazomenians, who come from a distance, with a rehearsal. Respecting the visit of Zeno and Parmenides to Athens, we may observe—first, that such a visit is consistent with dates, and may possibly have occurred; secondly, that Plato is very likely to have invented the meeting ('You, Socrates, can easily invent Egyptian tales or anything else,' Phaedrus); thirdly, that no reliance can be placed on the circumstance as determining the date of Parmenides and Zeno; fourthly, that the same occasion appears to be referred to by Plato in two other places (Theaet., Soph.).

Many interpreters have regarded the Parmenides as a 'reductio ad absurdum' of the Eleatic philosophy. But would Plato have been likely to place this in the mouth of the great Parmenides himself, who appeared to him, in Homeric language, to be 'venerable and awful,' and to have a 'glorious depth of mind'? (Theaet.). It may be admitted that he has ascribed to an Eleatic stranger in the Sophist opinions which went beyond the doctrines of the Eleatics. But the Eleatic stranger expressly criticises the doctrines in which he had been brought up; he admits that he is going to 'lay hands on his father Parmenides.' Nothing of this kind is said of Zeno and Parmenides. How then, without a word of explanation, could Plato assign to them the refutation of their own tenets?

The conclusion at which we must arrive is that the Parmenides is not a refutation of the Eleatic philosophy. Nor would such an explanation afford any satisfactory connexion of the first and second parts of the dialogue. And it is quite inconsistent with Plato's own relation to the Eleatics. For of all the pre-Socratic philosophers, he speaks of them with the greatest respect. But he could hardly have passed upon them a more unmeaning slight than to ascribe to their great master tenets the reverse of those which he actually held.

Two preliminary remarks may be made. First, that whatever latitude we may allow to Plato in bringing together by a 'tour de force,' as in the Phaedrus, dissimilar themes, yet he always in some way seeks to find a connexion for them. Many threads join together in one the love and dialectic of the Phaedrus. We cannot conceive that the great artist would place in juxtaposition two absolutely divided and incoherent subjects. And hence we are led to make a second remark: viz. that no explanation of the Parmenides can be satisfactory which does not indicate the connexion of the first and second parts. To suppose that Plato would first go out of his way to make Parmenides attack the Platonic Ideas, and then proceed to a similar but more fatal assault on his own doctrine of Being, appears to be the height of absurdity.

Perhaps there is no passage in Plato showing greater metaphysical power than that in which he assails his own theory of Ideas. The arguments are nearly, if not quite, those of Aristotle; they are the objections which naturally occur to a modern student of philosophy. Many persons will be surprised to find Plato criticizing the very conceptions which have been supposed in after ages to be peculiarly characteristic of him. How can he have placed himself so completely without them? How can he have ever persisted in them after seeing the fatal objections which might be urged against them? The consideration of this difficulty has led a recent critic (Ueberweg), who in general accepts the authorised canon of the Platonic writings, to condemn the Parmenides as spurious. The accidental want of external evidence, at first sight, seems to favour this opinion.

In answer, it might be sufficient to say, that no ancient writing of equal length and excellence is known to be spurious. Nor is the silence of Aristotle to be hastily assumed; there is at least a doubt whether his use of the same arguments does not involve the inference that he knew the work. And, if the Parmenides is spurious, like Ueberweg, we are led on further than we originally intended, to pass a similar condemnation on the Theaetetus and Sophist, and therefore on the Politicus (compare Theaet., Soph.). But the objection is in reality fanciful, and rests on the assumption that the doctrine of the Ideas was held by Plato throughout his life in the same form. For the truth is, that the Platonic Ideas were in constant process of growth and transmutation; sometimes veiled in poetry and mythology, then again emerging as fixed Ideas, in some passages regarded as absolute and eternal, and in others as relative to the human mind, existing in and derived from external objects as well as transcending them. The anamnesis of the Ideas is chiefly insisted upon in the mythical portions of the dialogues, and really occupies a very small space in the entire works of Plato. Their transcendental existence is not asserted, and is therefore implicitly denied in the Philebus; different forms are ascribed to them in the Republic, and they are mentioned in the Theaetetus, the Sophist, the Politicus, and the Laws, much as Universals would be spoken of in modern books. Indeed, there are very faint traces of the transcendental doctrine of Ideas, that is, of their existence apart from the mind, in any of Plato's writings, with the exception of the Meno, the Phaedrus, the Phaedo, and in portions of the Republic. The stereotyped form which Aristotle has given to them is not found in Plato (compare Essay on the Platonic Ideas in the Introduction to the Meno.)

The full discussion of this subject involves a comprehensive sur-

Parmenides

vey of the philosophy of Plato, which would be out of place here. But, without digressing further from the immediate subject of the Parmenides, we may remark that Plato is quite serious in his objections to his own doctrines: nor does Socrates attempt to offer any answer to them. The perplexities which surround the one and many in the sphere of the Ideas are also alluded to in the Philebus, and no answer is given to them. Nor have they ever been answered, nor can they be answered by any one else who separates the phenomenal from the real. To suppose that Plato, at a later period of his life, reached a point of view from which he was able to answer them, is a groundless assumption. The real progress of Plato's own mind has been partly concealed from us by the dogmatic statements of Aristotle, and also by the degeneracy of his own followers, with whom a doctrine of numbers quickly superseded Ideas.

As a preparation for answering some of the difficulties which have been suggested, we may begin by sketching the first portion of the dialogue:—

Cephalus, of Clazomenae in Ionia, the birthplace of Anaxagoras, a citizen of no mean city in the history of philosophy, who is the narrator of the dialogue, describes himself as meeting Adeimantus and Glaucon in the Agora at Athens. 'Welcome, Cephalus: can we do anything for you in Athens?' 'Why, yes: I came to ask a favour of you. First, tell me your half-brother's name, which I have forgotten—he was a mere child when I was last here;—I know his father's, which is Pyrilampes.' 'Yes, and the name of our brother is Antiphon. But why do you ask?' 'Let me introduce to you some countrymen of mine, who are lovers of philosophy; they have heard that Antiphon remembers a conversation of Socrates with Parmenides and Zeno, of which the report came to him from Pythodorus, Zeno's friend.' 'That is quite true.' 'And can they hear the dialogue?' 'Nothing easier; in the days of his youth he made a careful study of the piece; at present, his thoughts have another direction: he takes after his grandfather, and has given up philosophy for horses.'

'We went to look for him, and found him giving instructions to a worker in brass about a bridle. When he had done with him, and had learned from his brothers the purpose of our visit, he saluted me as an old acquaintance, and we asked him to repeat the dialogue. At first, he complained of the trouble, but he soon consented. He told us that Pythodorus had described to him the appearance of Parmenides and Zeno; they had come to Athens at the great Panathenaea, the former being at the time about sixty-five years old, aged but well-favoured—Zeno, who was said to have been beloved of Parmenides in the days of his youth, about forty, and very good-looking:—that they lodged with Pythodorus at the Ceramicus outside the wall, whither Socrates, then a very young man, came to see them: Zeno was reading one of his theses, which he had nearly finished, when Pythodorus entered with Parmenides and Aristoteles, who was afterwards one of the Thirty. When the recitation was completed, Socrates requested that the first thesis of the treatise might be read again.'

'You mean, Zeno,' said Socrates, 'to argue that being, if it is many, must be both like and unlike, which is a contradiction; and each division of your argument is intended to elicit a similar absurdity, which may be supposed to follow from the assumption that being is many.' 'Such is my meaning.' 'I see,' said Socrates, turning to Parmenides, 'that Zeno is your second self in his writings too; you prove admirably that the all is one: he gives proofs no less convincing that the many are nought. To deceive the world by saying the same thing in entirely different forms, is a strain of art beyond most of us.' 'Yes, Socrates,' said Zeno; 'but though you are as keen as a Spartan hound, you do not quite catch the motive of the piece, which was only intended to protect Parmenides against ridicule by showing that the hypothesis of the existence of the many involved greater absurdities than the hypothesis of the one. The book was a youthful composition of mine, which was stolen from me, and therefore I had no choice about the publication.' 'I quite believe you,' said Socrates; 'but will you answer me a question? I should like to know, whether you would assume an idea of likeness in the abstract, which is the contradictory of unlikeness in the abstract, by participation in either or both of which things are like or unlike or partly both. For the same things may very well partake of like and unlike in the concrete, though like and unlike in the abstract are irreconcilable. Nor does there appear to me to be any absurdity in maintaining that the same things may partake of the one and many,

Parmenides

though I should be indeed surprised to hear that the absolute one is also many. For example, I, being many, that is to say, having many parts or members, am yet also one, and partake of the one, being one of seven who are here present (compare Philebus). This is not an absurdity, but a truism. But I should be amazed if there were a similar entanglement in the nature of the ideas themselves, nor can I believe that one and many, like and unlike, rest and motion, in the abstract, are capable either of admixture or of separation.'

Pythodorus said that in his opinion Parmenides and Zeno were not very well pleased at the questions which were raised; nevertheless, they looked at one another and smiled in seeming delight and admiration of Socrates. 'Tell me,' said Parmenides, 'do you think that the abstract ideas of likeness, unity, and the rest, exist apart from individuals which partake of them? and is this your own distinction?' 'I think that there are such ideas.' 'And would you make abstract ideas of the just, the beautiful, the good?' 'Yes,' he said. 'And of human beings like ourselves, of water, fire, and the like?' 'I am not certain.' 'And would you be undecided also about ideas of which the mention will, perhaps, appear laughable: of hair, mud, filth, and other things which are base and vile?' 'No, Parmenides; visible things like these are, as I believe, only what they appear to be: though I am sometimes disposed to imagine that there is nothing without an idea; but I repress any such notion, from a fear of falling into an abyss of nonsense.' 'You are young, Socrates, and therefore naturally regard the opinions of men; the time will come when philosophy will have a firmer hold of you, and you will not despise even the meanest things. But tell me, is your meaning that things become like by partaking of likeness, great by partaking of greatness, just and beautiful by partaking of justice and beauty, and so of other ideas?' 'Yes, that is my meaning.' 'And do you suppose the individual to partake of the whole, or of the part?' 'Why not of the whole?' said Socrates. 'Because,' said Parmenides, 'in that case the whole, which is one, will become many.' 'Nay,' said Socrates, 'the whole may be like the day, which is one and in many places: in this way the ideas may be one and also many.' 'In the same sort of way,' said Parmenides, 'as a sail, which is one, may be a cover to many—that is your meaning?' 'Yes.' 'And would you say that each man is covered by the whole sail, or by a part only?' 'By a part.' 'Then the ideas have parts, and the objects partake of a part of them only?' 'That seems to follow.' 'And would you like to say that the ideas are really divisible and yet remain one?' 'Certainly not.' 'Would you venture to affirm that great objects have a portion only of greatness transferred to them; or that small or equal objects are small or equal because they are only portions of smallness or equality?' 'Impossible.' 'But how can individuals participate in ideas, except in the ways which I have mentioned?' 'That is not an easy question to answer.' 'I should imagine the conception of ideas to arise as follows: you see great objects pervaded by a common form or idea of greatness, which you abstract.' 'That is quite true.' 'And supposing you embrace in one view the idea of greatness thus gained and the individuals which it comprises, a further idea of greatness arises, which makes both great; and this may go on to infinity.' Socrates replies that the ideas may be thoughts in the mind only; in this case, the consequence would no longer follow. 'But must not the thought be of something which is the same in all and is the idea? And if the world partakes in the ideas, and the ideas are thoughts, must not all things think? Or can thought be without thought?' 'I acknowledge the unmeaningness of this,' says Socrates, 'and would rather have recourse to the explanation that the ideas are types in nature, and that other things partake of them by becoming like them.' 'But to become like them is to be comprehended in the same idea; and the likeness of the idea and the individuals implies another idea of likeness, and another without end.' 'Quite true.' 'The theory, then, of participation by likeness has to be given up. You have hardly yet, Socrates, found out the real difficulty of maintaining abstract ideas.' 'What difficulty?' 'The greatest of all perhaps is this: an opponent will argue that the ideas are not within the range of human knowledge; and you cannot disprove the assertion without a long and laborious demonstration, which he may be unable or unwilling to follow. In the first place, neither you nor any one who maintains the existence of absolute ideas will affirm that they are subjective.' 'That would be a contradiction.' 'True; and therefore any relation in these ideas is a relation which concerns themselves only; and the objects which are named after them, are relative to one another only, and have nothing to do with the ideas themselves.' 'How do you mean?' said Socrates. 'I may illustrate my meaning in this way: one of us has a slave; and the idea of a slave in the abstract is relative to the idea of a master in the abstract; this correspondence of ideas, however, has nothing to do with the particular relation of our slave to us.—Do you see my meaning?' 'Perfectly.' 'And absolute knowledge in the same way corresponds to absolute truth and being, and particular knowledge to particular truth and being.' 'Clearly.' 'And there is a subjective knowledge which is of subjective truth, having many kinds, general and particular. But the ideas themselves are not subjective, and therefore are not within our ken.' 'They are not.' 'Then the beautiful and the good in their own nature are unknown to us?' 'It would seem so.' 'There is a worse consequence yet.' 'What is that?' 'I think we must admit that absolute knowledge is the most exact knowledge, which we must therefore attribute to God. But then see what follows: God, having this exact knowledge, can have no knowledge of human things, as we have divided the two spheres, and forbidden any passing from one to the other:—the gods have knowledge and authority in their world only, as we have in ours.' 'Yet, surely, to deprive God of knowledge is monstrous.'—'These are some of the difficulties which are involved in the assumption of absolute ideas; the learner will find them nearly impossible to understand, and the teacher who has to impart them will require superhuman ability; there will always be a suspicion, either that they have no existence, or are beyond human knowledge.' 'There I agree with you,' said Socrates. 'Yet if these difficulties induce you to give up universal ideas, what becomes of the mind? and where are the reasoning and reflecting powers? philosophy is at an end.' 'I certainly do not see my way.' 'I think,' said Parmenides, 'that this arises out of your attempting to define abstractions, such as the good and the beautiful and the just, before you have had sufficient previous training; I noticed your deficiency when you were talking with Aristoteles, the day before yesterday. Your enthusiasm is a wonderful gift; but I fear that unless you discipline yourself by dialectic while you are young, truth will elude your grasp.' 'And what kind of discipline would you recommend?' 'The training which you heard Zeno practising; at the same time, I admire your saying to him that you did not care to consider the difficulty in reference to visible objects, but only in relation to ideas.' 'Yes; because I think that in visible objects you may easily show any number of inconsistent consequences.' 'Yes; and you should consider, not only the consequences which follow from a given hypothesis, but the consequences also which follow from the denial of the hypothesis. For example, what follows from the assumption of the existence of the many, and the counter-argument of what follows from the denial of the existence of the many: and similarly of likeness and unlikeness, motion, rest, generation, corruption, being and not being. And the consequences must include consequences to the things supposed and to other things, in themselves and in relation to one another, to individuals whom you select, to the many, and to the all; these must be drawn out both on the affirmative and on the negative hypothesis,—that is, if you are to train yourself perfectly to the intelligence of the truth.' 'What you are suggesting seems to be a tremendous process, and one of which I do not quite understand the nature,' said Socrates; 'will you give me an example?' 'You must not impose such a task on a man of my years,' said Parmenides. 'Then will you, Zeno?' 'Let us rather,' said Zeno, with a smile, 'ask Parmenides, for the undertaking is a serious one, as he truly says; nor could I urge him to make the attempt, except in a select audience of persons who will understand him.' The whole party joined in the request.

Here we have, first of all, an unmistakable attack made by the youthful Socrates on the paradoxes of Zeno. He perfectly understands their drift, and Zeno himself is supposed to admit this. But they appear to him, as he says in the Philebus also, to be rather truisms than paradoxes. For every one must acknowledge the obvious fact, that the body being one has many members, and that, in a thousand ways, the like partakes of the unlike, the many of the one. The real difficulty begins with the relations of ideas in themselves, whether of the one and many, or of any other ideas, to one another and to the mind. But this was a problem which the Eleatic philosophers had never considered; their thoughts had not gone beyond the contradictions of matter, motion, space, and the like.

It was no wonder that Parmenides and Zeno should hear the novel speculations of Socrates with mixed feelings of admiration and displeasure. He was going out of the received circle of disputation into a region in which they could hardly follow him. From the crude idea of Being in the abstract, he was about to proceed to universals or general notions. There is no contradiction in material things partaking of the ideas of one and many; neither is there any contradiction in the ideas of one and many, like and unlike, in themselves. But the contradiction arises when we attempt to conceive ideas in their connexion, or to ascertain their relation to phenomena. Still he affirms the existence of such ideas; and this is the position which is now in turn submitted to the criticisms of Parmenides.

To appreciate truly the character of these criticisms, we must remember the place held by Parmenides in the history of Greek philosophy. He is the founder of idealism, and also of dialectic, or, in modern phraseology, of metaphysics and logic (Theaet., Soph.). Like Plato, he is struggling after something wider and deeper than satisfied the contemporary Pythagoreans. And Plato with a true instinct recognizes him as his spiritual father, whom he 'revered and honoured more than all other philosophers together.' He may be supposed to have thought more than he said, or was able to express. And, although he could not, as a matter of fact, have criticized the ideas of Plato without an anachronism, the criticism is appropriately placed in the mouth of the founder of the ideal philosophy.

There was probably a time in the life of Plato when the ethical teaching of Socrates came into conflict with the metaphysical theories of the earlier philosophers, and he sought to supplement the one by the other. The older philosophers were great and awful; and they had the charm of antiquity. Something which found a response in his own mind seemed to have been lost as well as gained in the Socratic dialectic. He felt no incongruity in the veteran Parmenides correcting the youthful Socrates. Two points in his criticism are especially deserving of notice. First of all, Parmenides tries him by the test of consistency. Socrates is willing to assume ideas or principles of the just, the beautiful, the good, and to extend them to man (compare Phaedo); but he is reluctant to admit that there are general ideas of hair, mud, filth, etc. There is an ethical universal or idea, but is there also a universal of physics?—of the meanest things in the world as well as of the greatest? Parmenides rebukes this want of consistency in Socrates, which he attributes to his youth. As he grows older, philosophy will take a firmer hold of him, and then he will despise neither great things nor small, and he will think less of the opinions of mankind (compare Soph.). Here is lightly touched one of the most familiar principles of modern philosophy, that in the meanest operations of nature, as well as in the noblest, in mud and filth, as well as in the sun and stars, great truths are contained. At the same time, we may note also the transition in the mind of Plato, to which Aristotle alludes (Met.), when, as he says, he transferred the Socratic universal of ethics to the whole of nature.

The other criticism of Parmenides on Socrates attributes to him a want of practice in dialectic. He has observed this deficiency in him when talking to Aristoteles on a previous occasion. Plato seems to imply that there was something more in the dialectic of Zeno than in the mere interrogation of Socrates. Here, again, he may perhaps be describing the process which his own mind went through when he first became more intimately acquainted, whether at Megara or elsewhere, with the Eleatic and Megarian philosophers. Still, Parmenides does not deny to Socrates the credit of having gone beyond them in seeking to apply the paradoxes of Zeno to ideas; and this is the application which he himself makes of them in the latter part of the dialogue. He then proceeds to explain to him the sort of mental gymnastic which he should practise. He should consider not only what would follow from a given hypothesis, but what would follow from the denial of it, to that which is the subject of the hypothesis, and to all other things. There is no trace in the Memorabilia of Xenophon of any such method being attributed to Socrates; nor is the dialectic here spoken of that 'favourite method' of proceeding by regular divisions, which is described in the Phaedrus and Philebus, and of which examples are given in the Politicus and in the Sophist. It is expressly spoken of as the method which Socrates had heard Zeno practise in the days of his youth (compare Soph.).

The discussion of Socrates with Parmenides is one of the most remarkable passages in Plato. Few writers have ever been able to anticipate 'the criticism of the morrow' on their favourite notions. But Plato may here be said to anticipate the judgment not only of the morrow, but of all after- ages on the Platonic Ideas. For in some points he touches questions which have not yet received their solution in modern philosophy.

The first difficulty which Parmenides raises respecting the Platonic ideas relates to the manner in which individuals are connected with them. Do they participate in the ideas, or do they merely resemble them? Parmenides shows that objections may be urged against either of these modes of conceiving the connection. Things are little by partaking of littleness, great by partaking of greatness, and the like. But they cannot partake of a part of greatness, for that will not make them great, etc.; nor can each object monopolise the whole. The only answer to this is, that 'partaking' is a figure of speech, really corresponding to the processes which a later logic designates by the terms 'abstraction' and 'generalization.' When we have described accurately the methods or forms which the mind employs, we cannot further criticize them; at least we can only criticize them with reference to their fitness as instruments of thought to express facts.

Socrates attempts to support his view of the ideas by the parallel of the day, which is one and in many places; but he is easily driven from his position by a counter illustration of Parmenides, who compares the idea of greatness to a sail. He truly explains to Socrates that he has attained the conception of ideas by a process of generalization. At the same time, he points out a difficulty, which appears to be involved—viz. that the process of generalization will go on to infinity. Socrates meets the supposed difficulty by a flash of light, which is indeed the true answer 'that the ideas are in our minds only.' Neither realism is the truth, nor nominalism is the truth, but conceptualism; and conceptualism or any other psychological theory falls very far short of the infinite subtlety of language and thought.

But the realism of ancient philosophy will not admit of this answer, which is repelled by Parmenides with another truth or half-truth of later philosophy, 'Every subject or subjective must have an object.' Here is the great though unconscious truth (shall we say?) or error, which underlay the early Greek philosophy. 'Ideas must have a real existence;' they are not mere forms or opinions, which may be changed arbitrarily by individuals. But the early Greek philosopher never clearly saw that true ideas were only universal facts, and that there might be error in universals as well as in particulars.

Socrates makes one more attempt to defend the Platonic Ideas by representing them as paradigms; this is again answered by the 'argumentum ad infinitum.' We may remark, in passing, that the process which is thus described has no real existence. The mind, after having obtained a general idea, does not really go on to form another which includes that, and all the individuals contained under it, and another and another without end. The difficulty belongs in fact to the Megarian age of philosophy, and is due to their illogical logic, and to the general ignorance of the ancients respecting the part played by language in the process of thought. No such perplexity could ever trouble a modern metaphysician, any more than the fallacy of 'calvus' or 'acervus,' or of 'Achilles and the tortoise.' These 'surds' of metaphysics ought to occasion no more difficulty in speculation than a perpetually recurring fraction in arithmetic.

It is otherwise with the objection which follows: How are we to bridge the chasm between human truth and absolute truth, between gods and men? This is the difficulty of philosophy in all ages: How can we get beyond the circle of our own ideas, or how, remaining within them, can we have any criterion of a truth beyond and independent of them? Parmenides draws out this difficulty with great clearness. According to him, there are not only one but two chasms: the first, between individuals and the ideas which have a common name; the second, between the ideas in us and the ideas absolute. The first of these two difficulties mankind, as we may say, a little parodying the language of the Philebus, have long agreed to treat as obsolete; the second remains a difficulty for us as well as for the Greeks of the fourth century before Christ, and is the stumblingblock of Kant's Kritik, and of the Hamiltonian adaptation of Kant, as well as of the Platonic ideas. It has been said that 'you cannot criticize Revelation.' 'Then how do you know what is Revelation, or that there is one at all,' is the immediate rejoinder—'You know nothing of things in themselves.' 'Then how do you know that there are things in themselves?' In some respects, the difficulty pressed harder upon the Greek than upon ourselves. For conceiving of God more under the attribute of knowledge than we do, he was more under the necessity of separating the divine from the human, as two spheres which had no communication with one another.

Parmenides

It is remarkable that Plato, speaking by the mouth of Parmenides, does not treat even this second class of difficulties as hopeless or insoluble. He says only that they cannot be explained without a long and laborious demonstration: 'The teacher will require superhuman ability, and the learner will be hard of understanding.' But an attempt must be made to find an answer to them; for, as Socrates and Parmenides both admit, the denial of abstract ideas is the destruction of the mind. We can easily imagine that among the Greek schools of philosophy in the fourth century before Christ a panic might arise from the denial of universals, similar to that which arose in the last century from Hume's denial of our ideas of cause and effect. Men do not at first recognize that thought, like digestion, will go on much the same, notwithstanding any theories which may be entertained respecting the nature of the process. Parmenides attributes the difficulties in which Socrates is involved to a want of comprehensiveness in his mode of reasoning; he should consider every question on the negative as well as the positive hypothesis, with reference to the consequences which flow from the denial as well as from the assertion of a given statement.

The argument which follows is the most singular in Plato. It appears to be an imitation, or parody, of the Zenonian dialectic, just as the speeches in the Phaedrus are an imitation of the style of Lysias, or as the derivations in the Cratylus or the fallacies of the Euthydemus are a parody of some contemporary Sophist. The interlocutor is not supposed, as in most of the other Platonic dialogues, to take a living part in the argument; he is only required to say 'Yes' and 'No' in the right places. A hint has been already given that the paradoxes of Zeno admitted of a higher application. This hint is the thread by which Plato connects the two parts of the dialogue.

The paradoxes of Parmenides seem trivial to us, because the words to which they relate have become trivial; their true nature as abstract terms is perfectly understood by us, and we are inclined to regard the treatment of them in Plato as a mere straw-splitting, or legerdemain of words. Yet there was a power in them which fascinated the Neoplatonists for centuries afterwards. Something that they found in them, or brought to them—some echo or anticipation of a great truth or error, exercised a wonderful influence over

Plato

their minds. To do the Parmenides justice, we should imagine similar aporiai raised on themes as sacred to us, as the notions of One or Being were to an ancient Eleatic. 'If God is, what follows? If God is not, what follows?' Or again: If God is or is not the world; or if God is or is not many, or has or has not parts, or is or is not in the world, or in time; or is or is not finite or infinite. Or if the world is or is not; or has or has not a beginning or end; or is or is not infinite, or infinitely divisible. Or again: if God is or is not identical with his laws; or if man is or is not identical with the laws of nature. We can easily see that here are many subjects for thought, and that from these and similar hypotheses questions of great interest might arise. And we also remark, that the conclusions derived from either of the two alternative propositions might be equally impossible and contradictory.

When we ask what is the object of these paradoxes, some have answered that they are a mere logical puzzle, while others have seen in them an Hegelian propaedeutic of the doctrine of Ideas. The first of these views derives support from the manner in which Parmenides speaks of a similar method being applied to all Ideas. Yet it is hard to suppose that Plato would have furnished so elaborate an example, not of his own but of the Eleatic dialectic, had he intended only to give an illustration of method. The second view has been often overstated by those who, like Hegel himself, have tended to confuse ancient with modern philosophy. We need not deny that Plato, trained in the school of Cratylus and Heracleitus, may have seen that a contradiction in terms is sometimes the best expression of a truth higher than either (compare Soph.). But his ideal theory is not based on antinomies. The correlation of Ideas was the metaphysical difficulty of the age in which he lived; and the Megarian and Cynic philosophy was a 're-ductio ad absurdum' of their isolation. To restore them to their natural connexion and to detect the negative element in them is the aim of Plato in the Sophist. But his view of their connexion falls very far short of the Hegelian identity of Being and Not-being. The Being and Not-being of Plato never merge in each other, though he is aware that 'determination is only negation.'

After criticizing the hypotheses of others, it may appear presumptuous to add another guess to the many which have been already offered. May we say, in Platonic language, that we still seem to see vestiges of a track which has not yet been taken? It is quite possible that the obscurity of the Parmenides would not have existed to a contemporary student of philosophy, and, like the similar difficulty in the Philebus, is really due to our ignorance of the mind of the age. There is an obscure Megarian influence on Plato which cannot wholly be cleared up, and is not much illustrated by the doubtful tradition of his retirement to Megara after the death of Socrates. For Megara was within a walk of Athens (Phaedr.), and Plato might have learned the Megarian doctrines without settling there.

We may begin by remarking that the theses of Parmenides are expressly said to follow the method of Zeno, and that the complex dilemma, though declared to be capable of universal application, is applied in this instance to Zeno's familiar question of the 'one and many.' Here, then, is a double indication of the connexion of the Parmenides with the Eristic school. The old Eleatics had asserted the existence of Being, which they at first regarded as finite, then as infinite, then as neither finite nor infinite, to which some of them had given what Aristotle calls 'a form,' others had ascribed a material nature only. The tendency of their philosophy was to deny to Being all predicates. The Megarians, who succeeded them, like the Cynics, affirmed that no predicate could be asserted of any subject; they also converted the idea of Being into an abstraction of Good, perhaps with the view of preserving a sort of neutrality or indifference between the mind and things. As if they had said, in the language of modern philosophy: 'Being is not only neither finite nor infinite, neither at rest nor in motion, but neither subjective nor objective.'

This is the track along which Plato is leading us. Zeno had attempted to prove the existence of the one by disproving the existence of the many, and Parmenides seems to aim at proving the existence of the subject by showing the contradictions which follow from the assertion of any predicates. Take the simplest of all notions, 'unity'; you cannot even assert being or time of this without involving a contradiction. But is the contradiction also the final conclusion? Probably no more than of Zeno's denial of the many, or of Parmenides' assault upon the Ideas; no more than of the earlier dialogues 'of search.' To us there seems to be no residuum of this

Plato

long piece of dialectics. But to the mind of Parmenides and Plato, 'Gott-betrunkene Menschen,' there still remained the idea of 'being' or 'good,'which could not be conceived, defined, uttered, but could not be got rid of. Neither of them would have imagined that their disputation ever touched the Divine Being (compare Phil.). The same difficulties about Unity and Being are raised in the Sophist; but there only as preliminary to their final solution.

If this view is correct, the real aim of the hypotheses of Parmenides is to criticize the earlier Eleatic philosophy from the point of view of Zeno or the Megarians. It is the same kind of criticism which Plato has extended to his own doctrine of Ideas. Nor is there any want of poetical consistency in attributing to the 'father Parmenides' the last review of the Eleatic doctrines. The latest phases of all philosophies were fathered upon the founder of the school.

Other critics have regarded the final conclusion of the Parmenides either as sceptical or as Heracleitean. In the first case, they assume that Plato means to show the impossibility of any truth. But this is not the spirit of Plato, and could not with propriety be put into the mouth of Parmenides, who, in this very dialogue, is urging Socrates, not to doubt everything, but to discipline his mind with a view to the more precise attainment of truth. The same remark applies to the second of the two theories. Plato everywhere ridicules (perhaps unfairly) his Heracleitean contemporaries: and if he had intended to support an Heracleitean thesis, would hardly have chosen Parmenides, the condemner of the 'undiscerning tribe who say that things both are and are not,' to be the speaker. Nor, thirdly, can we easily persuade ourselves with Zeller that by the 'one' he means the Idea; and that he is seeking to prove indirectly the unity of the Idea in the multiplicity of phenomena.

We may now endeavour to thread the mazes of the labyrinth which Parmenides knew so well, and trembled at the thought of them.

The argument has two divisions: There is the hypothesis that

1. One is.
2. One is not.

If one is, it is nothing. If one is not, it is everything.

But is and is not may be taken in two senses: Either one is one, Or, one has being, from which opposite consequences are deduced,

> 1.a. If one is one, it is nothing.
> 1.b. If one has being, it is all things.

To which are appended two subordinate consequences:

> 1.aa. If one has being, all other things are.
> 1.bb. If one is one, all other things are not.

The same distinction is then applied to the negative hypothesis:

> 2.a. If one is not one, it is all things.
> 2.b. If one has not being, it is nothing.

Involving two parallel consequences respecting the other or remainder:

> 2.aa. If one is not one, other things are all.
> 2.bb. If one has not being, other things are not.

* * *

'I cannot refuse,' said Parmenides, 'since, as Zeno remarks, we are alone, though I may say with Ibycus, who in his old age fell in love, I, like the old racehorse, tremble at the prospect of the course which I am to run, and which I know so well. But as I must attempt this laborious game, what shall be the subject? Suppose I take my own hypothesis of the one.' 'By all means,' said Zeno. 'And who will answer me? Shall I propose the youngest? he will be the most likely to say what he thinks, and his answers will give me time to breathe.' 'I am the youngest,' said Aristoteles, 'and at your service; proceed with your questions.'—The result may be summed up as follows:—

1.a. One is not many, and therefore has no parts, and therefore is not a whole, which is a sum of parts, and therefore has neither beginning, middle, nor end, and is therefore unlimited, and therefore formless, being neither round nor straight, for neither round nor straight can be defined without assuming that they have parts; and therefore is not in place, whether in another which would encircle and touch the one at many points; or in itself, because that which is self-containing is also contained, and therefore not one but two. This being premised, let us consider whether one is capable either of motion or rest. For motion is either change of substance, or motion on an axis, or from one place to another. But the one is incapable of change of substance, which implies that it ceases to be itself, or of motion on an axis, because there would be parts around the axis; and any other motion involves change of place. But existence in place has been already shown to be impossible; and yet more impossible is coming into being in place, which implies partial existence in two places at once, or entire existence neither within nor without the same; and how can this be? And more impossible still is the coming into being either as a whole or parts of that which is neither a whole nor parts. The one, then, is incapable of motion. But neither can the one be in anything, and therefore not in the same, whether itself or some other, and is therefore incapable of rest. Neither is one the same with itself or any other, or other than itself or any other. For if other than itself, then other than one, and therefore not one; and, if the same with other, it would be other, and other than one. Neither can one while remaining one be other than other; for other, and not one, is the other than other. But if not other by virtue of being one, not by virtue of itself; and if not by virtue of itself, not itself other, and if not itself other, not other than anything. Neither will one be the same with itself. For the nature of the same is not that of the one, but a thing which becomes the same with anything does not become one; for example, that which becomes the same with the many becomes many and not one. And therefore if the one is the same with itself, the one is not one with itself; and therefore one and not one. And therefore one is neither other than other, nor the same with itself. Neither will the one be like or unlike itself or other; for likeness is sameness of affections, and the one and the same are different. And one having any affection which is other than being one would be more than one. The one, then, cannot have the same affection with and therefore cannot be like itself or other; nor can the one have any other affection than its own, that is, be unlike itself or any other, for this would imply that it was more than one. The one, then, is neither like nor unlike itself or other. This being the case, neither can the one be equal or unequal to itself or other. For equality implies sameness of measure, as inequality implies a greater or less number of measures. But the one, not having sameness, cannot have sameness of measure; nor a greater or less number of measures, for that would imply parts and multitude. Once more, can one be older or younger than itself or other? or of the same age with itself or other? That would imply likeness and unlikeness, equality and inequality. Therefore one cannot be in time, because that which is in time is ever becoming older and younger than itself, (for older and younger are relative terms, and he who becomes older becomes younger,) and is also of the same age with itself. None of which, or any other expressions of time, whether past, future, or present, can be affirmed of one. One neither is, has been, nor will be, nor becomes, nor has, nor will become. And, as these are the only modes of being, one is not, and is not one. But to that which is not, there is no attribute or relative, neither name nor word nor idea nor science nor perception nor opinion appertaining. One, then, is neither named, nor uttered, nor known, nor perceived, nor imagined. But can all this be true? 'I think not.'

1.b. Let us, however, commence the inquiry again. We have to work out all the consequences which follow on the assumption that the one is. If one is, one partakes of being, which is not the same with one; the words 'being' and 'one' have different meanings. Observe the consequence: In the one of being or the being of one are two parts, being and one, which form one whole. And each of the two parts is also a whole, and involves the other, and may be further subdivided into one and being, and is therefore not one but two; and thus one is never one, and in this way the one, if it is, becomes many and infinite. Again, let us conceive of a one which by an effort of abstraction we separate from being: will this abstract one be one or many? You say one only; let us see. In the first place, the being of one is other than one; and one and being, if different, are so because they both partake of the nature of other, which is therefore neither one nor being; and whether we take being and other, or being and one, or one and other, in any case we have two things which separately are called either, and together both. And both are two and either of two is severally one, and if one be added to any of the pairs, the sum is three; and two is an even number, three an odd; and two units exist twice, and therefore there are twice two; and three units exist thrice, and therefore there are thrice three, and taken together they give twice three and thrice two: we have even numbers multiplied into even, and odd into even, and even into odd numbers. But if one is, and both odd and even numbers are implied in one, must not every number exist? And number is infinite, and therefore existence must be infinite, for all and every number partakes of being; therefore being has the greatest number of parts, and every part, however great or however small, is equally one. But can one be in many places and yet be a whole? If not a whole it must be divided into parts and represented by a number corresponding to the number of the parts. And if so, we were wrong in saying that being has the greatest number of parts; for being is coequal and coextensive with one, and has no more parts than one; and so the abstract one broken up into parts by being is many and infinite. But the parts are parts of a whole, and the whole is their containing limit, and the one is therefore limited as well as infinite in number; and that which is a whole has beginning, middle, and end, and a middle is equidistant from the extremes; and one is therefore of a certain figure, round or straight, or a combination of the two, and being a whole includes all the parts which are the whole, and is therefore self-contained. But then, again, the whole is not in the parts, whether all or some. Not in all, because, if in all, also in one; for, if wanting in any one, how in all?—not in some, because the greater would then be contained in the less. But if not in all, nor in any, nor in some, either nowhere or in other. And if nowhere, nothing; therefore in other. The one as a whole, then, is in another, but regarded as a sum of parts is in itself; and is, therefore, both in itself and in another. This being the case, the one is at once both at rest and in motion: at rest, because resting in itself; in motion, because it is ever in other. And if there is truth in what has preceded, one is the same and not the same with itself and other. For everything in relation to every other thing is either the same with it or other; or if neither the same nor other, then in the relation of part to a whole or whole to a part. But one cannot be a part or whole in relation to one, nor other than one; and is therefore the same with one. Yet this sameness is again contradicted by one being in another place from itself which is in the same place; this follows from one being in itself and in another; one, therefore, is other than itself. But if anything is other than anything, will it not be other than other? And the not one is other than the one, and the one than the not one; therefore one is other than all others. But the same and the other exclude one another, and therefore the other can never be in the same; nor can the other be in anything for ever so short a time, as for that time the other will be in the same. And the other, if never in the same, cannot be either in the one or in the not one. And one is not other than not one, either by reason of other or of itself; and therefore they are not other than one another at all. Neither can the not one partake or be part of one, for in that case it would be one; nor can the not one be number, for that also involves one. And therefore, not being other than the one or related to the one as a whole to parts or parts to a whole, not one is the same as one. Wherefore the one is the same and also not the same with the others and also with itself; and is therefore like and unlike itself and the others, and just as different from the others as they are from the one, neither more nor less. But if neither more nor less, equally different; and therefore the one and the others have the same relations. This may be illustrated by the case of names: when you repeat the same name twice over, you mean the same thing; and when you say that the other is other than the one, or the one other than the other, this very word other (eteron), which is attributed to both, implies sameness. One, then, as being other than others, and other as being other than one, are alike in that they have the relation of otherness; and likeness is similarity of relations. And everything as being other of everything is also like everything. Again, same and other, like and unlike, are opposites: and since in virtue of being other than the others the one is like them, in virtue of being the same it must be unlike. Again, one, as having the same relations, has no difference of relation, and is therefore not unlike, and therefore like; or, as having different relations, is different and unlike. Thus, one, as being the same and not the same with itself and others—for both these reasons and for either of them—is also like and unlike itself and the others. Again, how far can one touch itself and the others? As existing in others, it touches the others; and as existing in itself, touches only itself. But from another point of view, that which touches another must be next in order of place; one, therefore, must be next in order of place to itself, and would therefore be two, and in two places. But one cannot be two, and therefore cannot be in contact with itself. Nor again can one touch the other. Two objects are required to make one contact; three objects make two contacts; and all the objects in the world, if placed in a series, would have as many contacts as there are objects, less one. But if one only exists, and not two, there is no contact. And the others, being other than one, have no part in one, and therefore none in number, and therefore two has no existence, and therefore there is no contact. For all which reasons, one has and has not contact with itself and the others.

Once more, Is one equal and unequal to itself and the others? Suppose one and the others to be greater or less than each other or equal to one another, they will be greater or less or equal by reason of equality or greatness or smallness inhering in them in addition to their own proper nature. Let us begin by assuming smallness to be inherent in one: in this case the inherence is either in the whole or in a part. If the first, smallness is either coextensive with the whole one, or contains the whole, and, if coextensive with the one, is equal to the one, or if containing the one will be greater than the one. But smallness thus performs the function of equality or of greatness, which is impossible. Again, if the inherence be in a part, the same contradiction follows: smallness will be equal to the part or greater than the part; therefore smallness will not inhere in anything, and except the idea of smallness there will be nothing small. Neither will greatness; for greatness will have a greater;—and there will be no small in relation to which it is great. And there will be no great or small in objects, but greatness and smallness will be relative only to each other; therefore the others cannot be greater or less than the one; also the one can neither exceed nor be exceeded by the others, and they are therefore equal to one another. And this will be true also of the one in relation to itself: one will be equal to itself as well as to the others (talla). Yet one, being in itself, must also be about itself, containing and contained, and is therefore greater and less than itself. Further, there is nothing beside the one and the others; and as these must be in something, they must therefore be in one another; and as that in which a thing is is greater than the thing, the inference is that they are both greater and less than one another, because containing and contained in one another. Therefore the one is equal to and greater and less than itself or other, having also measures or parts or numbers equal to or greater or less than itself or other.

But does one partake of time? This must be acknowledged, if the one partakes of being. For 'to be' is the participation of being in present time, 'to have been' in past, 'to be about to be' in future time. And as time is ever moving forward, the one becomes older than itself; and therefore younger than itself; and is older and also younger when in the process of becoming it arrives at the present; and it is always older and younger, for at any moment the one is, and therefore it becomes and is not older and younger than itself but during an equal time with itself, and is therefore contemporary with itself.

And what are the relations of the one to the others? Is it or does it become older or younger than they? At any rate the others are more than one, and one, being the least of all numbers, must be prior in time to greater numbers. But on the other hand, one must come into being in a manner accordant with its own nature. Now one has parts or others, and has therefore a beginning, middle, and end, of which the beginning is first and the end last. And the parts come into existence first; last of all the whole, contemporaneously with the end, being therefore younger, while the parts or others are older than the one. But, again, the one comes into being in each of the parts as much as in the whole, and must be of the same age with them. Therefore one is at once older and younger than the parts or others, and also contemporaneous with them, for no part can be a part which is not one. Is this true of becoming as well as being? Thus much may be affirmed, that the same things which are older or younger cannot become older or younger in a greater degree than they were at first by the addition of equal times. But, on the other hand, the one, if older than others, has come into being a longer time than they have. And when equal time is added to a longer and shorter, the relative difference between them is diminished. In this way that which was older becomes younger, and that which was younger becomes older, that is to say, younger and older than at first; and they ever become and never have become, for then they would be. Thus the one and others always are and are becoming and not becoming younger and also older than one another. And one, partaking of time and also partaking of becoming older and younger, admits of all time, present, past, and future—was, is, shall be—was becoming, is becoming, will become. And there is science of the one, and opinion and name and expression, as is already implied in the fact of our inquiry.

Yet once more, if one be one and many, and neither one nor many, and also participant of time, must there not be a time at which one as being one partakes of being, and a time when one as not being one is deprived of being? But these two contradictory states cannot be experienced by the one both together: there must be a time of transition. And the transition is a process of generation and destruction, into and from being and not-being, the one and the others. For the generation of the one is the destruction of the others, and the generation of the others is the destruction of the one. There is also separation and aggregation, assimilation and dissimilation, increase, diminution, equalization, a passage from motion to rest, and from rest to motion in the one and many. But when do all these changes take place? When does motion become rest, or rest motion? The answer to this question will throw a light upon all the others. Nothing can be in motion and at rest at the same time; and therefore the change takes place 'in a moment'—which is a strange expression, and seems to mean change in no time. Which is true also of all the other changes, which likewise take place in no time.

1.aa. But if one is, what happens to the others, which in the first place are not one, yet may partake of one in a certain way? The others are other than the one because they have parts, for if they had no parts they would be simply one, and parts imply a whole to which they belong; otherwise each part would be a part of many, and being itself one of them, of itself, and if a part of all, of each one of the other parts, which is absurd. For a part, if not a part of one, must be a part of all but this one, and if so not a part of each one;

and if not a part of each one, not a part of any one of many, and so not of one; and if of none, how of all? Therefore a part is neither a part of many nor of all, but of an absolute and perfect whole or one. And if the others have parts, they must partake of the whole, and must be the whole of which they are the parts. And each part, as the word 'each' implies, is also an absolute one. And both the whole and the parts partake of one, for the whole of which the parts are parts is one, and each part is one part of the whole; and whole and parts as participating in one are other than one, and as being other than one are many and infinite; and however small a fraction you separate from them is many and not one. Yet the fact of their being parts furnishes the others with a limit towards other parts and towards the whole; they are finite and also infinite: finite through participation in the one, infinite in their own nature. And as being finite, they are alike; and as being infinite, they are alike; but as being both finite and also infinite, they are in the highest degree unlike. And all other opposites might without difficulty be shown to unite in them.

1.bb. Once more, leaving all this: Is there not also an opposite series of consequences which is equally true of the others, and may be deduced from the existence of one? There is. One is distinct from the others, and the others from one; for one and the others are all things, and there is no third existence besides them. And the whole of one cannot be in others nor parts of it, for it is separated from others and has no parts, and therefore the others have no unity, nor plurality, nor duality, nor any other number, nor any opposition or distinction, such as likeness and unlikeness, some and other, generation and corruption, odd and even. For if they had these they would partake either of one opposite, and this would be a participation in one; or of two opposites, and this would be a participation in two. Thus if one exists, one is all things, and likewise nothing, in relation to one and to the others.

2.a. But, again, assume the opposite hypothesis, that the one is not, and what is the consequence? In the first place, the proposition, that one is not, is clearly opposed to the proposition, that not one is not. The subject of any negative proposition implies at once knowledge and difference. Thus 'one' in the proposition—'The one is not,' must be something known, or the words would be unintelligible; and again this 'one which is not' is something different from other things. Moreover, this and that, some and other, may be all attributed or related to the one which is not, and which though non-existent may and must have plurality, if the one only is non-existent and nothing else; but if all is not-being there is nothing which can be spoken of. Also the one which is not differs, and is different in kind from the others, and therefore unlike them; and they being other than the one, are unlike the one, which is therefore unlike them. But one, being unlike other, must be like itself; for the unlikeness of one to itself is the destruction of the hypothesis; and one cannot be equal to the others; for that would suppose being in the one, and the others would be equal to one and like one; both which are impossible, if one does not exist. The one which is not, then, if not equal is unequal to the others, and in equality implies great and small, and equality lies between great and small, and therefore the one which is not partakes of equality. Further, the one which is not has being; for that which is true is, and it is true that the one is not. And so the one which is not, if remitting aught of the being of non-existence, would become existent. For not being implies the being of not-being, and being the not-being of not-

being; or more truly being partakes of the being of being and not of the being of not-being, and not-being of the being of not-being and not of the not-being of not-being. And therefore the one which is not has being and also not-being. And the union of being and not-being involves change or motion. But how can not-being, which is nowhere, move or change, either from one place to another or in the same place? And whether it is or is not, it would cease to be one if experiencing a change of substance. The one which is not, then, is both in motion and at rest, is altered and unaltered, and becomes and is destroyed, and does not become and is not destroyed.

2.b. Once more, let us ask the question, If one is not, what happens in regard to one? The expression 'is not' implies negation of being:—do we mean by this to say that a thing, which is not, in a certain sense is? or do we mean absolutely to deny being of it? The latter. Then the one which is not can neither be nor become nor perish nor experience change of substance or place. Neither can rest, or motion, or greatness, or smallness, or equality, or unlike-

Parmenides

ness, or likeness either to itself or other, or attribute or relation, or now or hereafter or formerly, or knowledge or opinion or perception or name or anything else be asserted of that which is not.

2.aa. Once more, if one is not, what becomes of the others? If we speak of them they must be, and their very name implies difference, and difference implies relation, not to the one, which is not, but to one another. And they are others of each other not as units but as infinities, the least of which is also infinity, and capable of infinitesimal division. And they will have no unity or number, but only a semblance of unity and number; and the least of them will appear large and manifold in comparison with the infinitesimal fractions into which it may be divided. Further, each particle will have the appearance of being equal with the fractions. For in passing from the greater to the less it must reach an intermediate point, which is equality. Moreover, each particle although having a limit in relation to itself and to other particles, yet it has neither beginning, middle, nor end; for there is always a beginning before the beginning, and a middle within the middle, and an end beyond he end, because the infinitesimal division is never arrested by the one. Thus all being is one at a distance, and broken up when near, and like at a distance and unlike when near; and also the particles which compose being seem to be like and unlike, in rest and motion, in generation and corruption, in contact and separation, if one is not.

2.bb. Once more, let us inquire, If the one is not, and the others of the one are, what follows? In the first place, the others will not be the one, nor the many, for in that case the one would be contained in them; neither will they appear to be one or many; because they have no communion or participation in that which is not, nor semblance of that which is not. If one is not, the others neither are, nor appear to be one or many, like or unlike, in contact or separation. In short, if one is not, nothing is.

The result of all which is, that whether one is or is not, one and the others, in relation to themselves and to one another, are and are not, and appear to be and appear not to be, in all manner of ways.

I. On the first hypothesis we may remark: first, That one is one is an identical proposition, from which we might expect that no further consequences could be deduced. The train of consequences which follows, is inferred by altering the predicate into 'not many.' Yet, perhaps, if a strict Eristic had been present, oios aner ei kai nun paren, he might have affirmed that the not many presented a different aspect of the conception from the one, and was therefore not identical with it. Such a subtlety would be very much in character with the Zenonian dialectic. Secondly, We may note, that the conclusion is really involved in the premises. For one is conceived as one, in a sense which excludes all predicates. When the meaning of one has been reduced to a point, there is no use in saying that it has neither parts nor magnitude. Thirdly, The conception of the same is, first of all, identified with the one; and then by a further analysis distinguished from, and even opposed to it. Fourthly, We may detect notions, which have reappeared in modern philosophy, e.g. the bare abstraction of undefined unity, answering to the Hegelian 'Seyn,' or the identity of contradictions 'that which is older is also younger,' etc., or the Kantian conception of an a priori synthetical proposition 'one is.'

II. In the first series of propositions the word 'is' is really the copula; in the second, the verb of existence. As in the first series, the negative consequence followed from one being affirmed to be equivalent to the not many; so here the affirmative consequence is deduced from one being equivalent to the many.

In the former case, nothing could be predicated of the one, but now everything—multitude, relation, place, time, transition. One is regarded in all the aspects of one, and with a reference to all the consequences which flow, either from the combination or the separation of them. The notion of transition involves the singular extra-temporal conception of 'suddenness.' This idea of 'suddenness' is based upon the contradiction which is involved in supposing that anything can be in two places at once. It is a mere fiction; and we may observe that similar antinomies have led modern philosophers to deny the reality of time and space. It is not the infinitesimal of time, but the negative of time. By the help of this invention the conception of change, which sorely exercised the minds of early thinkers, seems to be, but is not really at all explained. The difficulty arises out of the imperfection of language, and should therefore be no longer regarded as a difficulty at all. The only way of meeting it, if it exists, is to acknowledge that this rather puzzling double conception is necessary to the expression of the phenomena of motion or change, and that this and similar double notions, instead of being anomalies, are among the higher and more potent instruments of human thought.

The processes by which Parmenides obtains his remarkable results may be summed up as follows: (1) Compound or correlative ideas which involve each other, such as, being and not-being, one and many, are conceived sometimes in a state of composition, and sometimes of division: (2) The division or distinction is sometimes heightened into total opposition, e.g. between one and same, one and other: or (3) The idea, which has been already divided, is regarded, like a number, as capable of further infinite subdivision: (4) The argument often proceeds '*a dicto secundum quid ad dictum simpliciter*' and conversely: (5) The analogy of opposites is misused by him; he argues indiscriminately sometimes from what is like, sometimes from what is unlike in them: (6) The idea of being or not-being is identified with existence or non-existence in place or time: (7) The same ideas are regarded sometimes as in process of transition, sometimes as alternatives or opposites: (8) There are no degrees or kinds of sameness, likeness, difference, nor any adequate conception of motion or change: (9) One, being, time, like space in Zeno's puzzle of Achilles and the tortoise, are regarded sometimes as continuous and sometimes as discrete: (10) In ome parts of the argument the abstraction is so rarefied as to become not only fallacious, but almost unintelligible, e.g. in the contradiction which is elicited out of the relative terms older and younger: (11) The relation between two terms is regarded under contradictory aspects, as for example when the existence of the one and the non-existence of the one are equally assumed to involve the existence of the many: (12) Words are used through long chains of argument, sometimes loosely, sometimes with the precision of numbers or of geometrical figures.

The argument is a very curious piece of work, unique in literature. It seems to be an exposition or rather a 'reductio ad absurdum' of the Megarian philosophy, but we are too imperfectly acquainted with this last to speak with confidence about it. It would be safer to say that it is an indication of the sceptical, hyperlogical fancies which prevailed among the contemporaries of Socrates. It throws an indistinct light upon Aristotle, and makes us aware of the debt which the world owes to him or his school. It also bears a resemblance to some modern speculations, in which an attempt is made to narrow language in such a manner that number and figure may be made a calculus of thought. It exaggerates one side of logic and forgets the rest. It has the appearance of a mathematical process; the inventor of it delights, as mathematicians do, in eliciting or discovering an unexpected result. It also helps to guard us against some fallacies by showing the consequences which flow from them.

In the Parmenides we seem to breathe the spirit of the Megarian philosophy, though we cannot compare the two in detail. But Plato also goes beyond his Megarian contemporaries; he has split their straws over again, and admitted more than they would have desired. He is indulging the analytical tendencies of his age, which can divide but not combine. And he does not stop to inquire whether the distinctions which he makes are shadowy and fallacious, but 'whither the argument blows' he follows.

III. The negative series of propositions contains the first conception of the negation of a negation. Two minus signs in arithmetic or algebra make a plus. Two negatives destroy each other. This abstruse notion is the foundation of the Hegelian logic. The mind must not only admit that determination is negation, but must get through negation into affirmation. Whether this process is real, or in any way an assistance to thought, or, like some other logical forms, a mere figure of speech transferred from the sphere of mathematics, may be doubted. That Plato and the most subtle philosopher of the nineteenth century should have lighted upon the same notion, is a singular coincidence of ancient and modern thought.

IV. The one and the many or others are reduced to their strictest arithmetical meaning. That one is three or three one, is a proposition which has, perhaps, given rise to more controversy in the world than any other. But no one has ever meant to say that three and one are to be taken in the same sense. Whereas the one and many of the Parmenides have precisely the same meaning; there is no notion of one personality or substance having many attributes or qualities. The truth seems to be rather the opposite of that which Socrates implies: There is no contradiction in the concrete, but in the abstract; and the more abstract the idea, the more palpable will be the contradiction. For just as nothing can persuade us that the number one is the number three, so neither can we be persuaded that any abstract idea is identical with its opposite, although they may both inhere together in some external object, or some more comprehensive conception. Ideas, persons, things may be one in one sense and many in another, and may have various degrees of unity and plurality. But in whatever sense and in whatever degree they are one they cease to be many; and in whatever degree or sense they are many they cease to be one.

Two points remain to be considered: 1st, the connexion between the first and second parts of the dialogue; 2ndly, the relation of the Parmenides to the other dialogues.

I. In both divisions of the dialogue the principal speaker is the same, and the method pursued by him is also the same, being a criticism on received opinions: first, on the doctrine of Ideas; secondly, of Being. From the Platonic Ideas we naturally proceed to the Eleatic One or Being which is the foundation of them. They are the same philosophy in two forms, and the simpler form is the truer and deeper. For the Platonic Ideas are mere numerical differences, and the moment we attempt to distinguish between them, their transcendental character is lost; ideas of justice, temperance, and good, are really distinguishable only with reference to their application in the world. If we once ask how they are related to individuals or to the ideas of the divine mind, they are again merged in the aboriginal notion of Being. No one can answer the questions which Parmenides asks of Socrates. And yet these questions are asked with the express acknowledgment that the denial of ideas will be the destruction of the human mind. The true answer to the difficulty here thrown out is the establishment of a rational psychology; and this is a work which is commenced in the Sophist. Plato, in urging the difficulty of his own doctrine of Ideas, is far from denying that some doctrine of Ideas is necessary, and for this he is paving the way.

In a similar spirit he criticizes the Eleatic doctrine of Being, not intending to deny Ontology, but showing that the old Eleatic notion, and the very name 'Being,' is unable to maintain itself against the subtleties of the Megarians. He did not mean to say that Being or Substance had no existence, but he is preparing for the development of his later view, that ideas were capable of relation. The fact that contradictory consequences follow from the existence or non-existence of one or many, does not prove that they have or have not existence, but rather that some different mode of conceiving them is required. Parmenides may still have thought that 'Being was,' just as Kant would have asserted the existence of 'things in themselves,' while denying the transcendental use of the Categories.

Several lesser links also connect the first and second parts of the dialogue: (1) The thesis is the same as that which Zeno has been already discussing: (2) Parmenides has intimated in the first part, that the method of Zeno should, as Socrates desired, be extended to Ideas: (3) The difficulty of participating in greatness, smallness, equality is urged against the Ideas as well as against the One.

II. The Parmenides is not only a criticism of the Eleatic notion of Being, but also of the methods of reasoning then in existence, and in this point of view, as well as in the other, may be regarded as an introduction to the Sophist. Long ago, in the Euthydemus, the vulgar application of the 'both and neither' Eristic had been subjected to a similar criticism, which there takes the form of banter and irony, here of illustration.

The attack upon the Ideas is resumed in the Philebus, and is followed by a return to a more rational philosophy. The perplexity of the One and Many is there confined to the region of Ideas, and replaced by a theory of classification; the Good arranged in classes is also contrasted with the barren abstraction of the Megarians. The war is carried on against the Eristics in all the later dialogues, sometimes with a playful irony, at other times with a sort of contempt. But there is no lengthened refutation of them. The Parmenides belongs to that stage of the dialogues of Plato in which he is partially under their influence, using them as a sort of 'critics or diviners' of the truth of his own, and of the Eleatic theories. In the Theaetetus a similar negative dialectic is employed in the attempt to define science, which after every effort remains undefined still. The same question is revived from the objective side in the Sophist: Being and Not-being are no longer exhibited in opposition, but are now reconciled; and the true nature of Not-being is discovered and made the basis of the correlation of ideas. Some links are probably missing which might have been supplied if we had trustworthy accounts of Plato's oral teaching.

To sum up: the Parmenides of Plato is a critique, first, of the Platonic Ideas, and secondly, of the Eleatic doctrine of Being. Neither are absolutely denied. But certain difficulties and consequences are shown in the assumption of either, which prove that the Platonic as well as the Eleatic doctrine must be remodelled. The negation and contradiction which are involved in the conception of the One and Many are preliminary to their final adjustment. The Platonic Ideas are tested by the interrogative method of Socrates; the Eleatic One or Being is tried by the severer and perhaps impossible method of hypothetical consequences, negative and affirmative. In the latter we have an example of the Zenonian or Megarian dialectic, which proceeded, not 'by assailing premises, but conclusions'; this is worked out and improved by Plato. When primary abstractions are used in every conceivable sense, any or every conclusion may be deduced from them. The words 'one,' 'other,' 'being,' 'like,' 'same,' 'whole,' and their opposites, have slightly different meanings, as they are applied to objects of thought or objects of sense—to number, time, place, and to the higher ideas of the reason;—and out of their different meanings this 'feast' of contradictions 'has been provided.'

*   *   *

THE PARMENIDES OF PLATO belongs to a stage of philosophy which has passed away. At first we read it with a purely antiquarian or historical interest; and with difficulty throw ourselves back into a state of the human mind in which Unity and Being occupied the attention of philosophers. We admire the precision of the language, in which, as in some curious puzzle, each word is exactly fitted into every other, and long trains of argument are carried out with a sort of geometrical accuracy. We doubt whether any abstract notion could stand the searching cross-examination of Parmenides; and may at last perhaps arrive at the conclusion that Plato has been using an imaginary method to work out an unmeaning conclusion. But the truth is, that he is carrying on a process which is not either useless or unnecessary in any age of philosophy. We fail to understand him, because we do not realize that the questions which he is discussing could have had any value or importance. We suppose them to be like the speculations of some of the Schoolmen, which end in nothing. But in truth he is trying to get rid of the stumblingblocks of thought which beset his contemporaries. Seeing that the Megarians and Cynics were making knowledge impossible, he takes their 'catchwords' and analyzes them from every conceivable point of view. He is criticizing the simplest and most general of our ideas, in which, as they are the most comprehensive, the danger of error is the most serious; for, if they remain unexamined, as in a mathematical demonstration, all that flows from them is affected, and the error pervades knowledge far and wide. In the beginning of philosophy this correction of human ideas was even more necessary than in our own times, because they were more bound up with words; and words when once presented to the mind exercised a greater power over thought. There is a natural realism which says, 'Can there be a word devoid of meaning, or an idea which is an idea of nothing?' In modern times mankind have often given too great importance to a word or idea. The philosophy of the ancients was still more in slavery to them, because they had not the experience of error, which would have placed them above the illusion.

The method of the Parmenides may be compared with the process of purgation, which Bacon sought to introduce into philosophy. Plato is warning us against two sorts of 'Idols of the Den': first, his own Ideas, which he himself having created is unable to connect in any way with the external world; secondly, against two idols in particular, 'Unity' and 'Being,' which had grown up in the pre-Socratic philosophy, and were still standing in the way of all progress and development of thought. He does not say with Bacon, 'Let us make truth by experiment,' or 'From these vague and inexact notions let us turn to facts.' The time has not yet arrived for a purely inductive philosophy. The instruments of thought must first be forged, that they may be used hereafter by modern inquirers. How, while mankind were disputing about universals, could they classify phenomena? How could they investigate causes, when they had not as yet learned to distinguish between a cause and an end? How could they make any progress in the sciences without first arranging them?

Parmenides

These are the deficiencies which Plato is seeking to supply in an age when knowledge was a shadow of a name only. In the earlier dialogues the Socratic conception of universals is illustrated by his genius; in the Phaedrus the nature of division is explained; in the Republic the law of contradiction and the unity of knowledge are asserted; in the later dialogues he is constantly engaged both with the theory and practice of classification. These were the 'new weapons,' as he terms them in the Philebus, which he was preparing for the use of some who, in after ages, would be found ready enough to disown their obligations to the great master, or rather, perhaps, would be incapable of understanding them.

Numberless fallacies, as we are often truly told, have originated in a confusion of the 'copula,' and the 'verb of existence.' Would not the distinction which Plato by the mouth of Parmenides makes between 'One is one' and 'One has being' have saved us from this and many similar confusions? We see again that a long period in the history of philosophy was a barren tract, not uncultivated, but unfruitful, because there was no inquiry into the relation of language and thought, and the metaphysical imagination was incapable of supplying the missing link between words and things. The famous dispute between Nominalists and Realists would never have been heard of, if, instead of transferring the Platonic Ideas into a crude Latin phraseology, the spirit of Plato had been truly understood and appreciated. Upon the term substance at least two celebrated theological controversies appear to hinge, which would not have existed, or at least not in their present form, if we had 'interrogated' the word substance, as Plato has the notions of Unity and Being. These weeds of philosophy have struck their roots deep into the soil, and are always tending to reappear, sometimes in new-fangled forms; while similar words, such as development, evolution, law, and the like, are constantly put in the place of facts, even by writers who profess to base truth entirely upon fact. In an unmetaphysical age there is probably more metaphysics in the common sense (i.e. more a priori assumption) than in any other, because there is more complete unconsciousness that we are resting on our own ideas, while we please ourselves with the conviction that we are resting on facts. We do not consider how much metaphysics are required to place us above metaphysics, or how difficult it is to prevent the forms of expression which are ready made for our use from outrunning actual observation and experiment.

In the last century the educated world were astonished to find that the whole fabric of their ideas was falling to pieces, because Hume amused himself by analyzing the word 'cause' into uniform sequence. Then arose a philosophy which, equally regardless of the history of the mind, sought to save mankind from scepticism by assigning to our notions of 'cause and effect,' 'substance and accident,' 'whole and part,' a necessary place in human thought. Without them we could have no experience, and therefore they were supposed to be prior to experience—to be incrusted on the 'I'; although in the phraseology of Kant there could be no transcendental use of them, or, in other words, they were only applicable within the range of our knowledge. But into the origin of these ideas, which he obtains partly by an analysis of the proposition, partly by development of the 'ego,' he never inquires—they seem to him to have a necessary existence; nor does he attempt to analyse the various senses in which the word 'cause' or 'substance' may be employed.

The philosophy of Berkeley could never have had any meaning, even to himself, if he had first analyzed from every point of view the conception of 'matter.' This poor forgotten word (which was 'a very good word' to describe the simplest generalization of external objects) is now superseded in the vocabulary of physical philosophers by 'force,' which seems to be accepted without any rigid examination of its meaning, as if the general idea of 'force' in our minds furnished an explanation of the infinite variety of forces which exist in the universe. A similar ambiguity occurs in the use of the favourite word 'law,' which is sometimes regarded as a mere abstraction, and then elevated into a real power or entity, almost taking the place of God. Theology, again, is full of undefined terms which have distracted the human mind for ages. Mankind have reasoned from them, but not to them; they have drawn out the conclusions without proving the premises; they have asserted the premises without examining the terms. The passions of religious parties have been roused to the utmost about words of which they could have given no explanation, and which had really no distinct meaning. One sort of them, faith, grace, justification, have been the symbols of one class of disputes; as the words substance, nature, person, of another, revelation, inspiration, and the like, of a third. All of them have been the subject of endless reasonings and inferences; but a spell has hung over the minds of theologians or philosophers which has prevented them from examining the words themselves. Either the effort to rise above and beyond their own first ideas was too great for them, or there might, perhaps, have seemed to be an irreverence in doing so. About the Divine Being Himself, in whom all true theological ideas live and move, men have spoken and reasoned much, and have fancied that they instinctively know Him. But they hardly suspect that under the name of God even Christians have included two characters or natures as much opposed as the good and evil principle of the Persians.

To have the true use of words we must compare them with things; in using them we acknowledge that they seldom give a perfect representation of our meaning. In like manner when we interrogate our ideas we find that we are not using them always in the sense which we supposed. And Plato, while he criticizes the inconsistency of his own doctrine of universals and draws out the endless consequences which flow from the assertion either that 'Being is' or that 'Being is not,' by no means intends to deny the existence of universals or the unity under which they are comprehended. There is nothing further from his thoughts than scepticism. But before proceeding he must examine the foundations which he and others have been laying; there is nothing true which is not from some point of view untrue, nothing absolute which is not also relative (compare Republic).

And so, in modern times, because we are called upon to analyze our ideas and to come to a distinct understanding about the meaning of words; because we know that the powers of language are very unequal to the subtlety of nature or of mind, we do not therefore renounce the use of them; but we replace them in their old connexion, having first tested their meaning and quality, and having corrected the error which is involved in them; or rather always remembering to make allowance for the adulteration or alloy which they contain. We cannot call a new metaphysical world into existence any more than we can frame a new universal language; in thought as in speech, we are dependent on the past. We know that the words 'cause' and 'effect' are very far from representing to us the continuity or the complexity of nature or the different modes or degrees in which phenomena are connected. Yet we accept them as the best expression which we have of the correlation of forces or objects. We see that the term 'law' is a mere abstraction, under which laws of matter and of mind, the law of nature and the law of the land are included, and some of these uses of the word are confusing, because they introduce into one sphere of thought associations which belong to another; for example, order or sequence is apt to be confounded with external compulsion and the internal workings of the mind with their material antecedents. Yet none of them can be dispensed with; we can only be on our guard against the error or confusion which arises out of them. Thus in the use of the word 'substance' we are far from supposing that there is any mysterious substratum apart from the objects which we see, and we acknowledge that the negative notion is very likely to become a positive one. Still we retain the word as a convenient generalization, though not without a double sense, substance, and essence, derived from the two-fold translation of the Greek *ousia*.

So the human mind makes the reflection that God is not a person like ourselves—is not a cause like the material causes in nature, nor even an intelligent cause like a human agent—nor an individual, for He is universal; and that every possible conception which we can form of Him is limited by the human faculties. We cannot by any effort of thought or exertion of faith be in and out of our own minds at the same instant. How can we conceive Him under the forms of time and space, who is out of time and space? How get rid of such forms and see Him as He is? How can we imagine His relation to the world or to ourselves? Innumerable contradictions follow from either of the two alternatives, that God is or that He is not. Yet we are far from saying that we know nothing of Him, because all that we know is subject to the conditions of human thought. To the old belief in Him we return, but with corrections. He is a person, but not like ourselves; a mind, but not a human mind; a cause, but not a material cause, nor yet a maker or artificer. The words which we use are imperfect expressions of His true nature;

but we do not therefore lose faith in what is best and highest in ourselves and in the world.

'A little philosophy takes us away from God; a great deal brings us back to Him.' When we begin to reflect, our first thoughts respecting Him and ourselves are apt to be sceptical. For we can analyze our religious as well as our other ideas; we can trace their history; we can criticize their perversion; we see that they are relative to the human mind and to one another. But when we have carried our criticism to the furthest point, they still remain, a necessity of our moral nature, better known and understood by us, and less liable to be shaken, because we are more aware of their necessary imperfection. They come to us with 'better opinion, better confirmation,' not merely as the inspirations either of ourselves or of another, but deeply rooted in history and in the human mind.

PARMENIDES

by

Plato

Translated by Benjamin Jowett

PERSONS OF THE DIALOGUE: Cephalus, Adeimantus, Glaucon, Antiphon, Pythodorus, Socrates, Zeno, Parmenides, Aristoteles.

CEPHALUS REHEARSES A DIALOGUE which is supposed to have been narrated in his presence by Antiphon, the half-brother of Adeimantus and Glaucon, to certain Clazomenians.

We had come from our home at Clazomenae to Athens, and met Adeimantus and Glaucon in the Agora. Welcome, Cephalus, said Adeimantus, taking me by the hand; is there anything which we can do for you in Athens?

Yes; that is why I am here; I wish to ask a favour of you.

What may that be? he said.

I want you to tell me the name of your half brother, which I have forgotten; he was a mere child when I last came hither from Clazomenae, but that was a long time ago; his father's name, if I remember rightly, was Pyrilampes?

Yes, he said, and the name of our brother, Antiphon; but why do you ask?

Let me introduce some countrymen of mine, I said; they are lovers of philosophy, and have heard that Antiphon was intimate with a certain Pythodorus, a friend of Zeno, and remembers a conversation which took place between Socrates, Zeno, and Parmenides many years ago, Pythodorus having often recited it to him.

Quite true.

And could we hear it? I asked.

Nothing easier, he replied; when he was a youth he made a careful study of the piece; at present his thoughts run in another direction; like his grandfather Antiphon he is devoted to horses. But, if that is what you want, let us go and look for him; he dwells at Melita, which is quite near, and he has only just left us to go home.

Accordingly we went to look for him; he was at home, and in the act of giving a bridle to a smith to be fitted. When he had done with the smith, his brothers told him the purpose of our visit; and he saluted me as an acquaintance whom he remembered from my former visit, and we asked him to repeat the dialogue. At first he was not very willing, and complained of the trouble, but at length he consented. He told us that Pythodorus had described to him the appearance of Parmenides and Zeno; they came to Athens, as he said, at the great Panathenaea; the former was, at the time of his visit, about 65 years old, very white with age, but well favoured. Zeno was nearly 40 years of age, tall and fair to look upon; in the days of his youth he was reported to have been beloved by Parmenides. He said that they lodged with Pythodorus in the Ceramicus, outside the wall, whither Socrates, then a very young man, came to see them, and many others with him; they wanted to hear the writings of Zeno, which had been brought to Athens for the first time on the occasion of their visit. These Zeno himself read to them in the absence of Parmenides, and had very nearly finished when Pythodorus entered, and with him Parmenides and Aristoteles who was afterwards one of the Thirty, and heard the little that remained of the dialogue. Pythodorus had heard Zeno repeat them before.

When the recitation was completed, Socrates requested that the first thesis of the first argument might be read over again, and this having been done, he said: What is your meaning, Zeno? Do you maintain that if being is many, it must be both like and unlike, and that this is impossible, for neither can the like be unlike, nor the unlike like—is that your position?

Just so, said Zeno.

And if the unlike cannot be like, or the like unlike, then according to you, being could not be many; for this would involve an impossibility. In all that you say have you any other purpose except to disprove the being of the many? and is not each division of your treatise intended to furnish a separate proof of this, there being in all as many proofs of the not-being of the many as you have composed arguments? Is that your meaning, or have I misunderstood you?

No, said Zeno; you have correctly understood my general purpose.

I see, Parmenides, said Socrates, that Zeno would like to be not only one with you in friendship but your second self in his writings too; he puts what you say in another way, and would fain make believe that he is telling us something which is new. For you, in your poems, say The All is one, and of this you adduce excellent proofs; and he on the other hand says There is no many; and on behalf of this he offers overwhelming evidence. You affirm unity, he denies plurality. And so you deceive the world into believing that you are saying different things when really you are saying much the same. This is a strain of art beyond the reach of most of us.

Yes, Socrates, said Zeno. But although you are as keen as a Spartan hound in pursuing the track, you do not fully apprehend the true motive of the composition, which is not really such an artificial work as you imagine; for what you speak of was an accident; there was no pretence of a great purpose; nor any serious intention of deceiving the world. The truth is, that these writings of mine were meant to protect the arguments of Parmenides against those who make fun of him and seek to show the many ridiculous and contradictory results which they suppose to follow from the affirmation of the one. My answer is addressed to the partisans of the many, whose attack I return with interest by retorting upon them that their hypothesis of the being of many, if carried out, appears to be still more ridiculous than the hypothesis of the being of one. Zeal for my master led me to write the book in the days of my youth, but some one stole the copy; and therefore I had no choice whether it should be published or not; the motive, however, of writing, was not the ambition of an elder man, but the pugnacity of a young one. This you do not seem to see, Socrates; though in other respects, as I was saying, your notion is a very just one.

I understand, said Socrates, and quite accept your account. But tell me, Zeno, do you not further think that there is an idea of likeness in itself, and another idea of unlikeness, which is the opposite of likeness, and that in these two, you and I and all other things to which we apply the term many, participate—things which participate in likeness become in that degree and manner like; and so far as they participate in unlikeness become in that degree unlike, or both like and unlike in the degree in which they participate in both? And may not all things partake of both opposites, and be both like and unlike, by reason of this participation?—Where is the wonder? Now if a person could prove the absolute like to become unlike, or the absolute unlike to become like, that, in my opinion, would indeed be a wonder; but there is nothing extraordinary, Zeno, in showing that the things which only partake of likeness and unlikeness experience both. Nor, again, if a person were to show that all is one by partaking of one, and at the same time many by partaking of many, would that be very astonishing. But if he were to show me that the absolute one was many, or the absolute many one, I should be truly amazed. And so of all the rest: I should be surprised to hear that the natures or ideas themselves had these opposite qualities; but not if a person wanted to prove of me that I was many and also one. When he wanted to show that I was many he would say that I have a right and a left side, and a front and a back, and an upper and a lower half, for I cannot deny that I partake of multitude; when, on the other hand, he wants to prove that I am one, he will say, that we who are here assembled are seven, and that I am one and partake of the one. In both instances he proves his case. So again, if a person shows that such things as wood, stones, and the like, being many are also one, we admit that he shows the coexistence of the one and many, but he does not show that the many are one or the one many; he is uttering not a paradox but a truism. If however, as I just now suggested, some one were to abstract simple notions of like, unlike, one, many, rest, motion, and similar ideas, and then to show that these admit of admixture and separation in themselves, I should be very much astonished. This part of the argument appears to be treated by you, Zeno, in a very spirited manner; but, as I was saying, I should be far more amazed if any one found in the ideas themselves which are apprehended by reason, the same puzzle and entanglement which you have shown to exist in visible objects.

While Socrates was speaking, Pythodorus thought that Parmenides and Zeno were not altogether pleased at the successive steps of the argument; but still they gave the closest attention, and often looked at one another, and smiled as if in admiration of him. When he had finished, Parmenides expressed their feelings in the following words:—

Socrates, he said, I admire the bent of your mind towards philosophy; tell me now, was this your own distinction between ideas in themselves and the things which partake of them? and do you think that there is an idea of likeness apart from the likeness which we possess, and of the one and many, and of the other things which Zeno mentioned?

I think that there are such ideas, said Socrates.

Parmenides proceeded: And would you also make absolute ideas of the just and the beautiful and the good, and of all that class?

Yes, he said, I should.

And would you make an idea of man apart from us and from all other human creatures, or of fire and water?

I am often undecided, Parmenides, as to whether I ought to include them or not.

And would you feel equally undecided, Socrates, about things of which the mention may provoke a smile?—I mean such things as hair, mud, dirt, or anything else which is vile and paltry; would you suppose that each of these has an idea distinct from the actual objects with which we come into contact, or not?

Certainly not, said Socrates; visible things like these are such as they appear to us, and I am afraid that there would be an absurdity in assuming any idea of them, although I sometimes get disturbed, and begin to think that there is nothing without an idea; but then again, when I have taken up this position, I run away, because I am afraid that I may fall into a bottomless pit of nonsense, and perish; and so I return to the ideas of which I was just now speaking, and occupy myself with them.

Yes, Socrates, said Parmenides; that is because you are still young; the time will come, if I am not mistaken, when philosophy will have a firmer grasp of you, and then you will not despise even the meanest things; at your age, you are too much disposed to regard the opinions of men. But I should like to know whether you mean that there are certain

Parmenides

ideas of which all other things partake, and from which they derive their names; that similars, for example, become similar, because they partake of similarity; and great things become great, because they partake of greatness; and that just and beautiful things become just and beautiful, because they partake of justice and beauty?

Yes, certainly, said Socrates that is my meaning.

Then each individual partakes either of the whole of the idea or else of a part of the idea? Can there be any other mode of participation?

There cannot be, he said.

Then do you think that the whole idea is one, and yet, being one, is in each one of the many?

Why not, Parmenides? said Socrates.

Because one and the same thing will exist as a whole at the same time in many separate individuals, and will therefore be in a state of separation from itself.

Nay, but the idea may be like the day which is one and the same in many places at once, and yet continuous with itself; in this way each idea may be one and the same in all at the same time.

I like your way, Socrates, of making one in many places at once. You mean to say, that if I were to spread out a sail and cover a number of men, there would be one whole including many—is not that your meaning?

I think so.

And would you say that the whole sail includes each man, or a part of it only, and different parts different men?

The latter.

Then, Socrates, the ideas themselves will be divisible, and things which participate in them will have a part of them only and not the whole idea existing in each of them?

That seems to follow.

Then would you like to say, Socrates, that the one idea is really divisible and yet remains one?

Certainly not, he said.

Suppose that you divide absolute greatness, and that of the many great things, each one is great in virtue of a portion of greatness less than absolute greatness—is that conceivable?

Plato

No.

Or will each equal thing, if possessing some small portion of equality less than absolute equality, be equal to some other thing by virtue of that portion only?

Impossible.

Or suppose one of us to have a portion of smallness; this is but a part of the small, and therefore the absolutely small is greater; if the absolutely small be greater, that to which the part of the small is added will be smaller and not greater than before.

How absurd!

Then in what way, Socrates, will all things participate in the ideas, if they are unable to participate in them either as parts or wholes?

Indeed, he said, you have asked a question which is not easily answered.

Well, said Parmenides, and what do you say of another question?

What question?

I imagine that the way in which you are led to assume one idea of each kind is as follows:—You see a number of great objects, and when you look at them there seems to you to be one and the same idea (or nature) in them all; hence you conceive of greatness as one.

Very true, said Socrates.

And if you go on and allow your mind in like manner to embrace in one view the idea of greatness and of great things which are not the idea, and to compare them, will not another greatness arise, which will appear to be the source of all these?

It would seem so.

Then another idea of greatness now comes into view over and above absolute greatness, and the individuals which partake of it; and then another, over and above all these, by virtue of which they will all be great, and so each idea instead of being one will be infinitely multiplied.

But may not the ideas, asked Socrates, be thoughts only, and have no proper existence except in our minds, Parmenides? For in that case each idea may still be one, and not experience this infinite multiplication.

And can there be individual thoughts which are thoughts of nothing?

Impossible, he said.

The thought must be of something?

Yes.

Of something which is or which is not?

Of something which is.

Must it not be of a single something, which the thought recognizes as attaching to all, being a single form or nature?

Yes.

And will not the something which is apprehended as one and the same in all, be an idea?

From that, again, there is no escape.

Then, said Parmenides, if you say that everything else participates in the ideas, must you not say either that everything is made up of thoughts, and that all things think; or that they are thoughts but have no thought?

The latter view, Parmenides, is no more rational than the previous one. In my opinion, the ideas are, as it were, patterns fixed in nature, and other things are like them, and resemblances of them—what is meant by the participation of other things in the ideas, is really assimilation to them.

But if, said he, the individual is like the idea, must not the idea also be like the individual, in so far as the individual is a resemblance of the idea? That which is like, cannot be conceived of as other than the like of like.

Impossible.

And when two things are alike, must they not partake of the same idea?

They must.

And will not that of which the two partake, and which makes them alike, be the idea itself?

Certainly.

Then the idea cannot be like the individual, or the individual like the idea; for if they are alike, some further idea of likeness will always be coming to light, and if that be like anything else, another; and new ideas will be always arising, if the idea resembles that which partakes of it?

Quite true.

The theory, then, that other things participate in the ideas by resemblance, has to be given up, and some other mode of participation devised?

It would seem so.

Do you see then, Socrates, how great is the difficulty of affirming the ideas to be absolute?

Yes, indeed.

And, further, let me say that as yet you only understand a small part of the difficulty which is involved if you make of each thing a single idea, parting it off from other things.

What difficulty? he said.

There are many, but the greatest of all is this:—If an opponent argues that these ideas, being such as we say they ought to be, must remain unknown, no one can prove to him that he is wrong, unless he who denies their existence be a man of great ability and knowledge, and is willing to follow a long and laborious demonstration; he will remain unconvinced, and still insist that they cannot be known.

What do you mean, Parmenides? said Socrates.

In the first place, I think, Socrates, that you, or any one who maintains the existence of absolute essences, will admit that they cannot exist in us.

No, said Socrates; for then they would be no longer absolute.

True, he said; and therefore when ideas are what they are in relation to one another, their essence is determined by a relation among themselves, and has nothing to do with the resemblances, or whatever they are to be termed, which are in our sphere, and from which we receive this or that name when we partake of them. And the things which are within our sphere and have the same names with them, are likewise only relative to one another, and not to the ideas which have the same names with them, but belong to themselves and not to them.

What do you mean? said Socrates.

I may illustrate my meaning in this way, said Parmenides:—A master has a slave; now there is nothing absolute in the relation between them, which is simply a relation of one man to another. But there is also an idea of mastership in the abstract, which is relative to the idea of slavery in the abstract. These natures have nothing to do with us, nor we with them; they are concerned with themselves only, and we with ourselves. Do you see my meaning?

Yes, said Socrates, I quite see your meaning.

And will not knowledge—I mean absolute knowledge—answer to absolute truth?

Certainly.

And each kind of absolute knowledge will answer to each kind of absolute being?

Yes.

But the knowledge which we have, will answer to the truth which we have; and again, each kind of knowledge which we have, will be a knowledge of each kind of being which we have?

Certainly.

But the ideas themselves, as you admit, we have not, and cannot have?

No, we cannot.

And the absolute natures or kinds are known severally by the absolute idea of knowledge?

Yes.

And we have not got the idea of knowledge?

No.

Then none of the ideas are known to us, because we have no share in absolute knowledge?

I suppose not.

Then the nature of the beautiful in itself, and of the good in itself, and all other ideas which we suppose to exist absolutely, are unknown to us?

It would seem so.

I think that there is a stranger consequence still.

What is it?

Would you, or would you not say, that absolute knowledge, if there is such a thing, must be a far more exact knowledge than our knowledge; and the same of beauty and of the rest?

Yes.

And if there be such a thing as participation in absolute knowledge, no one is more likely than God to have this most exact knowledge?

Certainly.

But then, will God, having absolute knowledge, have a knowledge of human things?

Why not?

Because, Socrates, said Parmenides, we have admitted that the ideas are not valid in relation to human things; nor human things in relation to them; the relations of either are limited to their respective spheres.

Yes, that has been admitted.

And if God has this perfect authority, and perfect knowledge, his authority cannot rule us, nor his knowledge know us, or any human thing; just as our authority does not extend to the gods, nor our knowledge know anything which is divine, so by parity of reason they, being gods, are not our masters, neither do they know the things of men.

Yet, surely, said Socrates, to deprive God of knowledge is monstrous.

These, Socrates, said Parmenides, are a few, and only a few of the difficulties in which we are involved if ideas really are and we determine each one of them to be an absolute unity. He who hears what may be said against them will deny the very existence of them—and even if they do exist, he will say that they must of necessity be unknown to man; and he will seem to have reason on his side, and as we were remarking just now, will be very difficult to convince; a man must be gifted with very considerable ability before he can learn that everything has a class and an absolute essence; and still more remarkable will he be who discovers all these things for himself, and having thoroughly investigated them is able to teach them to others.

I agree with you, Parmenides, said Socrates; and what you say is very much to my mind.

And yet, Socrates, said Parmenides, if a man, fixing his attention on these and the like difficulties, does away with ideas of things and will not
admit that every individual thing has its own determinate idea which is always one and the same, he will have nothing on which his mind can rest; and so he will utterly destroy the power of reasoning, as you seem to me to have particularly noted.

Parmenides

Very true, he said.

But, then, what is to become of philosophy? Whither shall we turn, if the ideas are unknown?

I certainly do not see my way at present.

Yes, said Parmenides; and I think that this arises, Socrates, out of your attempting to define the beautiful, the just, the good, and the ideas generally, without sufficient previous training. I noticed your deficiency, when I heard you talking here with your friend Aristoteles, the day before yesterday. The impulse that carries you towards philosophy is assuredly noble and divine; but there is an art which is called by the vulgar idle talking, and which is often imagined to be useless; in that you must train and exercise yourself, now that you are young, or truth will elude your grasp.

And what is the nature of this exercise, Parmenides, which you would recommend?

That which you heard Zeno practising; at the same time, I give you credit for saying to him that you did not care to examine the perplexity in reference to visible things, or to consider the question that way; but only in reference to objects of thought, and to what may be called ideas.

Why, yes, he said, there appears to me to be no difficulty in showing by this method that visible things are like and unlike and may experience anything.

Quite true, said Parmenides; but I think that you should go a step further, and consider not only the consequences which flow from a given hypothesis, but also the consequences which flow from denying the hypothesis; and that will be still better training for you.

What do you mean? he said.

I mean, for example, that in the case of this very hypothesis of Zeno's about the many, you should inquire not only what will be the consequences to the many in relation to themselves and to the one, and to the one in relation to itself and the many, on the hypothesis of the being of the many, but also what will be the consequences to the one and the many in their relation to themselves and to each other, on the opposite hypothesis. Or, again, if likeness is or is not, what will be the consequences in either of these cases to the subjects of the hypothesis, and to other things, in relation both to themselves and to one another, and so of unlikeness; and the same holds good of motion and rest, of generation and destruction, and even of being and not-being. In a word, when you suppose anything to be or not to be, or to be in any way affected, you must look at the consequences in relation to the thing itself, and to any other things which you choose,—to each of them singly, to more than one, and to all; and so of other things, you must look at them in relation to themselves and to anything else which you suppose either to be or not to be, if you would train yourself perfectly and see the real truth.

That, Parmenides, is a tremendous business of which you speak, and I do not quite understand you; will you take some hypothesis and go through the steps?—then I shall apprehend you better.

That, Socrates, is a serious task to impose on a man of my years.

Then will you, Zeno? said Socrates.

Zeno answered with a smile:—Let us make our petition to Parmenides himself, who is quite right in saying that you are hardly aware of the extent of the task which you are imposing on him; and if there were more of us I should not ask him, for these are not subjects which any one, especially at his age, can well speak of before a large audience; most people are not aware that this roundabout progress through all things is the only way in which the mind can attain truth and wisdom. And therefore, Parmenides, I join in the request of Socrates, that I may hear the process again which I have not heard for a long time.

When Zeno had thus spoken, Pythodorus, according to Antiphon's report of him, said, that he himself and Aristoteles and the whole company entreated Parmenides to give an example of the process. I cannot refuse, said Parmenides; and yet I feel rather like Ibycus, who, when in his old age, against his will, he fell in love, compared himself to an old racehorse, who was about to run in a chariot race, shaking with fear at the course he knew so well—this was his simile of himself. And I also experience a trembling when I remember through what an ocean of words I have to wade at my time of life. But I must indulge you, as Zeno says that I ought, and we are alone. Where shall I begin? And what shall be our first hypothesis, if I am to attempt this laborious pastime? Shall I begin with myself, and

Parmenides

take my own hypothesis the one? and consider the consequences which follow on the supposition either of the being or of the not-being of one?

By all means, said Zeno.

And who will answer me? he said. Shall I propose the youngest? He will not make difficulties and will be the most likely to say what he thinks; and his answers will give me time to breathe.

I am the one whom you mean, Parmenides, said Aristoteles; for I am the youngest and at your service. Ask, and I will answer.

Parmenides proceeded: 1.a. If one is, he said, the one cannot be many?

Impossible.

Then the one cannot have parts, and cannot be a whole?

Why not?

Because every part is part of a whole; is it not?

Yes.

And what is a whole? would not that of which no part is wanting be a whole?

Certainly.

Then, in either case, the one would be made up of parts; both as being a whole, and also as having parts?

To be sure.

And in either case, the one would be many, and not one?

True.

But, surely, it ought to be one and not many?

It ought.

Then, if the one is to remain one, it will not be a whole, and will not have parts?

No.

But if it has no parts, it will have neither beginning, middle, nor end; for these would of course be parts of it.

Right.

But then, again, a beginning and an end are the limits of everything?

Certainly.

Then the one, having neither beginning nor end, is unlimited?

Yes, unlimited.

And therefore formless; for it cannot partake either of round or straight.

But why?

Why, because the round is that of which all the extreme points are equidistant from the centre?

Yes.

And the straight is that of which the centre intercepts the view of the extremes?

True.

Then the one would have parts and would be many, if it partook either of a straight or of a circular form?

Assuredly.

But having no parts, it will be neither straight nor round?

Right.

And, being of such a nature, it cannot be in any place, for it cannot be either in another or in itself.

How so?

Because if it were in another, it would be encircled by that in which it was, and would touch it at many places and with many parts; but that which is one and indivisible, and does not partake of a circular nature, cannot be touched all round in many places.

Certainly not.

But if, on the other hand, one were in itself, it would also be contained by nothing else but itself; that is to say, if it were really in itself; for nothing can be in anything which does not contain it.

Impossible.

But then, that which contains must be other than that which is contained? for the same whole cannot do and suffer both at once; and if so, one will be no longer one, but two?

True.

Then one cannot be anywhere, either in itself or in another?

No.

Further consider, whether that which is of such a nature can have either rest or motion.

Why not?

Why, because the one, if it were moved, would be either moved in place or changed in nature; for these are the only kinds of motion.

Parmenides

Yes.

And the one, when it changes and ceases to be itself, cannot be any longer one.

It cannot.

It cannot therefore experience the sort of motion which is change of nature?

Clearly not.

Then can the motion of the one be in place?

Perhaps.

But if the one moved in place, must it not either move round and round in the same place, or from one place to another?

It must.

And that which moves in a circle must rest upon a centre; and that which goes round upon a centre must have parts which are different from the centre; but that which has no centre and no parts cannot possibly be carried round upon a centre?

Impossible.

But perhaps the motion of the one consists in change of place?

Perhaps so, if it moves at all.

And have we not already shown that it cannot be in anything?

Yes.

Then its coming into being in anything is still more impossible; is it not?

I do not see why.

Why, because anything which comes into being in anything, can neither as yet be in that other thing while still coming into being, nor be altogether out of it, if already coming into being in it.

Certainly not.

And therefore whatever comes into being in another must have parts, and then one part may be in, and another part out of that other; but that which has no parts can never be at one and the same time neither wholly within nor wholly without anything.

True.

And is there not a still greater impossibility in that which has no parts, and is not a whole, coming into being anywhere, since it cannot come into being either as a part or as a whole?

Clearly.

Then it does not change place by revolving in the same spot, nor by going somewhere and coming into being in something; nor again, by change in itself?

Very true.

Then in respect of any kind of motion the one is immoveable?

Immoveable.

But neither can the one be in anything, as we affirm?

Yes, we said so.

Then it is never in the same?

Why not?

Because if it were in the same it would be in something.

Certainly.

And we said that it could not be in itself, and could not be in other?

True.

Then one is never in the same place?

It would seem not.

But that which is never in the same place is never quiet or at rest?

Never.

One then, as would seem, is neither at rest nor in motion?

It certainly appears so.

Neither will it be the same with itself or other; nor again, other than itself or other.

How is that?

If other than itself it would be other than one, and would not be one.

True.

And if the same with other, it would be that other, and not itself; so that upon this supposition too, it would not have the nature of one, but would be other than one?

It would.

Then it will not be the same with other, or other than itself?

It will not.

Neither will it be other than other, while it remains one; for not one, but only other, can be other than other, and nothing else.

True.

Then not by virtue of being one will it be other?

Certainly not.

But if not by virtue of being one, not by virtue of itself; and if not by virtue of itself, not itself, and itself not being other at all, will not be other than anything?

Right.

Neither will one be the same with itself.

How not?

Surely the nature of the one is not the nature of the same.

Why not?

It is not when anything becomes the same with anything that it becomes one.

What of that?

Anything which becomes the same with the many, necessarily becomes many and not one.

True.

But, if there were no difference between the one and the same, when a thing became the same, it would always become one; and when it became one, the same?

Certainly.

And, therefore, if one be the same with itself, it is not one with itself, and will therefore be one and also not one.

Surely that is impossible.

And therefore the one can neither be other than other, nor the same with itself.

Impossible.

And thus the one can neither be the same, nor other, either in relation to itself or other?

No.

Neither will the one be like anything or unlike itself or other.

Why not?

Because likeness is sameness of affections.

Yes.

And sameness has been shown to be of a nature distinct from oneness?

That has been shown.

But if the one had any other affection than that of being one, it would be affected in such a way as to be more than one; which is impossible.

True.

Then the one can never be so affected as to be the same either with another or with itself?

Clearly not.

Then it cannot be like another, or like itself?

No.

Nor can it be affected so as to be other, for then it would be affected in such a way as to be more than one.

It would.

That which is affected otherwise than itself or another, will be unlike itself or another, for sameness of affections is likeness.

True.

But the one, as appears, never being affected otherwise, is never unlike itself or other?

Never.

Then the one will never be either like or unlike itself or other?

Plainly not.

Again, being of this nature, it can neither be equal nor unequal either to itself or to other.

How is that?

Why, because the one if equal must be of the same measures as that to which it is equal.

True.

And if greater or less than things which are commensurable with it, the one will have more measures than that which is less, and fewer than that which is greater?

Yes.

And so of things which are not commensurate with it, the one will have greater measures than that which is less and smaller than that which is greater.

Certainly.

But how can that which does not partake of sameness, have either the same measures or have anything else the same?

Impossible.

And not having the same measures, the one cannot be equal either with itself or with another?

Parmenides

It appears so.

But again, whether it have fewer or more measures, it will have as many parts as it has measures; and thus again the one will be no longer one but will have as many parts as measures.

Right.

And if it were of one measure, it would be equal to that measure; yet it has been shown to be incapable of equality.

It has.

Then it will neither partake of one measure, nor of many, nor of few, nor of the same at all, nor be equal to itself or another; nor be greater or less than itself, or other?

Certainly.

Well, and do we suppose that one can be older, or younger than anything, or of the same age with it?

Why not?

Why, because that which is of the same age with itself or other, must partake of equality or likeness of time; and we said that the one did not partake either of equality or of likeness?

We did say so.

And we also said, that it did not partake of inequality or unlikeness.

Very true.

How then can one, being of this nature, be either older or younger than anything, or have the same age with it?

In no way.

Then one cannot be older or younger, or of the same age, either with itself or with another?

Clearly not.

Then the one, being of this nature, cannot be in time at all; for must not that which is in time, be always growing older than itself?

Certainly.

And that which is older, must always be older than something which is younger?

True.

Then, that which becomes older than itself, also becomes at the same time younger than itself, if it is to have something to become older than.

What do you mean?

I mean this:—A thing does not need to become different from another thing which is already different; it *is* different, and if its different has become, it has become different; if its different will be, it will be different; but of that which is becoming different, there cannot have been, or be about to be, or yet be, a different—the only different possible is one which is becoming.

That is inevitable.

But, surely, the elder is a difference relative to the younger, and to nothing else.

True.

Then that which becomes older than itself must also, at the same time, become younger than itself?

Yes.

But again, it is true that it cannot become for a longer or for a shorter time than itself, but it must become, and be, and have become, and be about to be, for the same time with itself?

That again is inevitable.

Then things which are in time, and partake of time, must in every case, I suppose, be of the same age with themselves; and must also become at once older and younger than themselves?

Yes.

But the one did not partake of those affections?

Not at all.

Then it does not partake of time, and is not in any time?

So the argument shows.

Well, but do not the expressions 'was,' and 'has become,' and 'was becoming,' signify a participation of past time?

Certainly.

And do not 'will be,' 'will become,' 'will have become,' signify a participation of future time?

Yes.

And 'is,' or 'becomes,' signifies a participation of present time?

Certainly.

And if the one is absolutely without participation in time, it never had become, or was becoming, or was at any time, or is now become or is becoming, or is, or will become, or will have become, or will be, hereafter.

Parmenides

Most true.

But are there any modes of partaking of being other than these?

There are none.

Then the one cannot possibly partake of being?

That is the inference.

Then the one is not at all?

Clearly not.

Then the one does not exist in such way as to be one; for if it were and partook of being, it would already be; but if the argument is to be trusted, the one neither is nor is one?

True.

But that which is not admits of no attribute or relation?

Of course not.

Then there is no name, nor expression, nor perception, nor opinion, nor knowledge of it?

Clearly not.

Then it is neither named, nor expressed, nor opined, nor known, nor does anything that is perceive it.

So we must infer.

But can all this be true about the one?

I think not.

1.b. Suppose, now, that we return once more to the original hypothesis; let us see whether, on a further review, any new aspect of the question appears.

I shall be very happy to do so.

We say that we have to work out together all the consequences, whatever they may be, which follow, if the one is?

Yes.

Then we will begin at the beginning:—If one is, can one be, and not partake of being?

Impossible.

Then the one will have being, but its being will not be the same with the one; for if the same, it would not be the being of the one; nor would the one have participated in being, for the proposition that one is would have been identical with the proposition that one is one; but our hypothesis is not if one is one, what will follow, but if one is:—am I not right?

Quite right.

We mean to say, that being has not the same significance as one?

Of course.

And when we put them together shortly, and say 'One is,' that is equivalent to saying, 'partakes of being'?

Quite true.

Once more then let us ask, if one is what will follow. Does not this hypothesis necessarily imply that one is of such a nature as to have parts?

How so?

In this way:—If being is predicated of the one, if the one is, and one of being, if being is one; and if being and one are not the same; and since

the one, which we have assumed, is, must not the whole, if it is one, itself be, and have for its parts, one and being?

Certainly.

And is each of these parts—one and being—to be simply called a part, or must the word 'part' be relative to the word 'whole'?

The latter.

Then that which is one is both a whole and has a part?

Certainly.

Again, of the parts of the one, if it is—I mean being and one—does either fail to imply the other? is the one wanting to being, or being to the one?

Impossible.

Thus, each of the parts also has in turn both one and being, and is at the least made up of two parts; and the same principle goes on for ever, and every part whatever has always these two parts; for being always involves one, and one being; so that one is always disappearing, and becoming two.

Certainly.

And so the one, if it is, must be infinite in multiplicity?

Clearly.

Let us take another direction.

What direction?

We say that the one partakes of being and therefore it is?

Yes.

Parmenides

And in this way, the one, if it has being, has turned out to be many?

True.

But now, let us abstract the one which, as we say, partakes of being, and try to imagine it apart from that of which, as we say, it partakes—will this abstract one be one only or many?

One, I think.

Let us see:—Must not the being of one be other than one? for the one is not being, but, considered as one, only partook of being?

Certainly.

If being and the one be two different things, it is not because the one is one that it is other than being; nor because being is being that it is other than the one; but they differ from one another in virtue of otherness and difference.

Certainly.

So that the other is not the same—either with the one or with being?

Certainly not.

And therefore whether we take being and the other, or being and the one, or the one and the other, in every such case we take two things, which may be rightly called both.

How so.

In this way—you may speak of being?

Yes.

And also of one?

Yes.

Then now we have spoken of either of them?

Yes.

Well, and when I speak of being and one, I speak of them both?

Certainly.

And if I speak of being and the other, or of the one and the other,—in any such case do I not speak of both?

Yes.

And must not that which is correctly called both, be also two?

Undoubtedly.

And of two things how can either by any possibility not be one?

It cannot.

Then, if the individuals of the pair are together two, they must be severally one?

Clearly.

And if each of them is one, then by the addition of any one to any pair, the whole becomes three?

Yes.

And three are odd, and two are even?

Of course.

And if there are two there must also be twice, and if there are three there must be thrice; that is, if twice one makes two, and thrice one three?

Certainly.

There are two, and twice, and therefore there must be twice two; and there are three, and there is thrice, and therefore there must be thrice three?

Of course.

If there are three and twice, there is twice three; and if there are two and thrice, there is thrice two?

Undoubtedly.

Here, then, we have even taken even times, and odd taken odd times, and even taken odd times, and odd taken even times.

True.

And if this is so, does any number remain which has no necessity to be?

None whatever.

Then if one is, number must also be?

It must.

But if there is number, there must also be many, and infinite multiplicity of being; for number is infinite in multiplicity, and partakes also of being: am I not right?

Certainly.

And if all number participates in being, every part of number will also participate?

Yes.

Then being is distributed over the whole multitude of things, and nothing that is, however small or however great, is devoid of it? And, indeed, the very supposition of this is absurd, for how can that which is, be devoid of being?

Parmenides

In no way.

And it is divided into the greatest and into the smallest, and into being of all sizes, and is broken up more than all things; the divisions of it have no limit.

True.

Then it has the greatest number of parts?

Yes, the greatest number.

Is there any of these which is a part of being, and yet no part?

Impossible.

But if it is at all and so long as it is, it must be one, and cannot be none?

Certainly.

Then the one attaches to every single part of being, and does not fail in any part, whether great or small, or whatever may be the size of it?

True.

But reflect:—Can one, in its entirety, be in many places at the same time?

No; I see the impossibility of that.

And if not in its entirety, then it is divided; for it cannot be present with all the parts of being, unless divided.

True.

And that which has parts will be as many as the parts are?

Certainly.

Then we were wrong in saying just now, that being was distributed into the greatest number of parts. For it is not distributed into parts more than the one, into parts equal to the one; the one is never wanting to being, or being to the one, but being two they are co-equal and co-extensive.

Certainly that is true.

The one itself, then, having been broken up into parts by being, is many and infinite?

True.

Then not only the one which has being is many, but the one itself distributed by being, must also be many?

Certainly.

Further, inasmuch as the parts are parts of a whole, the one, as a whole, will be limited; for are not the parts contained by the whole?

Certainly.

And that which contains, is a limit?

Of course.

Then the one if it has being is one and many, whole and parts, having limits and yet unlimited in number?

Clearly.

And because having limits, also having extremes?

Certainly.

And if a whole, having beginning and middle and end. For can anything be a whole without these three? And if any one of them is wanting to anything, will that any longer be a whole?

No.

Then the one, as appears, will have beginning, middle, and end.

It will.

But, again, the middle will be equidistant from the extremes; or it would not be in the middle?

Yes.

Then the one will partake of figure, either rectilinear or round, or a union of the two?

True.

And if this is the case, it will be both in itself and in another too.

How?

Every part is in the whole, and none is outside the whole.

True.

And all the parts are contained by the whole?

Yes.

And the one is all its parts, and neither more nor less than all?

No.

And the one is the whole?

Of course.

But if all the parts are in the whole, and the one is all of them and the whole, and they are all contained by the whole, the one will be contained by the one; and thus the one will be in itself.

That is true.

But then, again, the whole is not in the parts—neither in all the parts, nor in some one of them. For if it is in all, it must be in one; for if there were any one in which it was not, it could not be in all the parts; for the part in which it is wanting is one of all, and if the whole is not in this, how can it be in them all?

It cannot.

Nor can the whole be in some of the parts; for if the whole were in some of the parts, the greater would be in the less, which is impossible.

Yes, impossible.

But if the whole is neither in one, nor in more than one, nor in all of the parts, it must be in something else, or cease to be anywhere at all?

Certainly.

If it were nowhere, it would be nothing; but being a whole, and not being in itself, it must be in another.

Very true.

The one then, regarded as a whole, is in another, but regarded as being all its parts, is in itself; and therefore the one must be itself in itself and also in another.

Certainly.

The one then, being of this nature, is of necessity both at rest and in motion?

How?

The one is at rest since it is in itself, for being in one, and not passing out of this, it is in the same, which is itself.

True.

And that which is ever in the same, must be ever at rest?

Certainly.

Well, and must not that, on the contrary, which is ever in other, never be in the same; and if never in the same, never at rest, and if not at rest, in motion?

True.

Then the one being always itself in itself and other, must always be both at rest and in motion?

Clearly.

And must be the same with itself, and other than itself; and also the same with the others, and other than the others; this follows from its previous affections.

How so?

Everything in relation to every other thing, is either the same or other; or if neither the same nor other, then in the relation of a part to a whole, or of a whole to a part.

Clearly.

And is the one a part of itself?

Certainly not.

Since it is not a part in relation to itself it cannot be related to itself as whole to part?

It cannot.

But is the one other than one?

No.

And therefore not other than itself?

Certainly not.

If then it be neither other, nor a whole, nor a part in relation to itself, must it not be the same with itself?

Certainly.

But then, again, a thing which is in another place from 'itself,' if this 'itself' remains in the same place with itself, must be other than 'itself,' for it will be in another place?

True.

Then the one has been shown to be at once in itself and in another?

Yes.

Thus, then, as appears, the one will be other than itself?

True.

Well, then, if anything be other than anything, will it not be other than that which is other?

Certainly.

And will not all things that are not one, be other than the one, and the one other than the not-one?

Of course.

Then the one will be other than the others?

True.

But, consider:—Are not the absolute same, and the absolute other, opposites to one another?

Of course.

Then will the same ever be in the other, or the other in the same?

593

They will not.

If then the other is never in the same, there is nothing in which the other is during any space of time; for during that space of time, however small, the other would be in the same. Is not that true?

Yes.

And since the other is never in the same, it can never be in anything that is.

True.

Then the other will never be either in the not-one, or in the one?

Certainly not.

Then not by reason of otherness is the one other than the not-one, or the not-one other than the one.

No.

Nor by reason of themselves will they be other than one another, if not partaking of the other.

How can they be?

But if they are not other, either by reason of themselves or of the other, will they not altogether escape being other than one another?

They will.

Again, the not-one cannot partake of the one; otherwise it would not have been not-one, but would have been in some way one.

True.

Nor can the not-one be number; for having number, it would not have been not-one at all.

It would not.

Again, is the not-one part of the one; or rather, would it not in that case partake of the one?

It would.

If then, in every point of view, the one and the not-one are distinct, then neither is the one part or whole of the not-one, nor is the not-one part or whole of the one?

No.

But we said that things which are neither parts nor wholes of one another, nor other than one another, will be the same with one another:—so we said?

Yes.

Then shall we say that the one, being in this relation to the not-one, is the same with it?

Let us say so.

Then it is the same with itself and the others, and also other than itself and the others.

That appears to be the inference.

And it will also be like and unlike itself and the others?

Perhaps.

Since the one was shown to be other than the others, the others will also be other than the one.

Yes.

And the one is other than the others in the same degree that the others are other than it, and neither more nor less?

True.

And if neither more nor less, then in a like degree?

Yes.

In virtue of the affection by which the one is other than others and others in like manner other than it, the one will be affected like the others and the others like the one.

How do you mean?

I may take as an illustration the case of names: You give a name to a thing?

Yes.

And you may say the name once or oftener?

Yes.

And when you say it once, you mention that of which it is the name? and when more than once, is it something else which you mention? or must it always be the same thing of which you speak, whether you utter the name once or more than once?

Of course it is the same.

And is not 'other' a name given to a thing?

Certainly.

Whenever, then, you use the word 'other,' whether once or oftener, you name that of which it is the name, and to no other do you give the name?

True.

Then when we say that the others are other than the one, and the one other than the others, in repeating the word 'other' we speak of that nature to which the name is applied, and of no other?

Quite true.

Then the one which is other than others, and the other which is other than the one, in that the word 'other' is applied to both, will be in the same condition; and that which is in the same condition is like?

Yes.

Then in virtue of the affection by which the one is other than the others, every thing will be like every thing, for every thing is other than every thing.

True.

Again, the like is opposed to the unlike?

Yes.

And the other to the same?

True again.

And the one was also shown to be the same with the others?

Yes.

And to be the same with the others is the opposite of being other than the others?

Certainly.

And in that it was other it was shown to be like?

Yes.

But in that it was the same it will be unlike by virtue of the opposite affection to that which made it like; and this was the affection of otherness.

Yes.

The same then will make it unlike; otherwise it will not be the opposite of the other.

True.

Then the one will be both like and unlike the others; like in so far as it is other, and unlike in so far as it is the same.

Yes, that argument may be used.

And there is another argument.

What?

In so far as it is affected in the same way it is not affected otherwise, and not being affected otherwise is not unlike, and not being unlike, is like; but in so far as it is affected by other it is otherwise, and being otherwise affected is unlike.

True.

Then because the one is the same with the others and other than the others, on either of these two grounds, or on both of them, it will be both like and unlike the others?

Certainly.

And in the same way as being other than itself and the same with itself, on either of these two grounds and on both of them, it will be like and unlike itself?

Of course.

Again, how far can the one touch or not touch itself and others?—consider.

I am considering.

The one was shown to be in itself which was a whole?

True.

And also in other things?

Yes.

In so far as it is in other things it would touch other things, but in so far as it is in itself it would be debarred from touching them, and would touch itself only.

Clearly.

Then the inference is that it would touch both?

It would.

But what do you say to a new point of view? Must not that which is to touch another be next to that which it is to touch, and occupy the place nearest to that in which what it touches is situated?

True.

Then the one, if it is to touch itself, ought to be situated next to itself, and occupy the place next to that in which itself is?

It ought.

And that would require that the one should be two, and be in two places at once, and this, while it is one, will never happen.

No.

Then the one cannot touch itself any more than it can be two?

It cannot.

Neither can it touch others.

Parmenides

Why not?

The reason is, that whatever is to touch another must be in separation from, and next to, that which it is to touch, and no third thing can be between them.

True.

Two things, then, at the least are necessary to make contact possible?

They are.

And if to the two a third be added in due order, the number of terms will be three, and the contacts two?

Yes.

And every additional term makes one additional contact, whence it follows that the contacts are one less in number than the terms; the first two terms exceeded the number of contacts by one, and the whole number of terms exceeds the whole number of contacts by one in like manner; and for every one which is afterwards added to the number of terms, one contact is added to the contacts.

True.

Whatever is the whole number of things, the contacts will be always one less.

True.

But if there be only one, and not two, there will be no contact?

How can there be?

And do we not say that the others being other than the one are not one and have no part in the one?

True.

Then they have no number, if they have no one in them?

Of course not.

Then the others are neither one nor two, nor are they called by the name of any number?

No.

One, then, alone is one, and two do not exist?

Clearly not.

And if there are not two, there is no contact?

There is not.

Then neither does the one touch the others, nor the others the one, if there is no contact?

Certainly not.

For all which reasons the one touches and does not touch itself and the others?

True.

Further—is the one equal and unequal to itself and others?

How do you mean?

If the one were greater or less than the others, or the others greater or less than the one, they would not be greater or less than each other in virtue of their being the one and the others; but, if in addition to their being what they are they had equality, they would be equal to one another, or if the one had smallness and the others greatness, or the one had greatness and the others smallness—whichever kind had greatness would be greater, and whichever had smallness would be smaller?

Certainly.

Then there are two such ideas as greatness and smallness; for if they were not they could not be opposed to each other and be present in that which is.

How could they?

If, then, smallness is present in the one it will be present either in the whole or in a part of the whole?

Certainly.

Suppose the first; it will be either co-equal and co-extensive with the whole one, or will contain the one?

Clearly.

If it be co-extensive with the one it will be co-equal with the one, or if containing the one it will be greater than the one?

Of course.

But can smallness be equal to anything or greater than anything, and have the functions of greatness and equality and not its own functions?

Impossible.

Then smallness cannot be in the whole of one, but, if at all, in a part only?

Yes.

And surely not in all of a part, for then the difficulty of the whole will recur; it will be equal to or greater than any part in which it is.

Certainly.

Then smallness will not be in anything, whether in a whole or in a part; nor will there be anything small but actual smallness.

True.

Neither will greatness be in the one, for if greatness be in anything there will be something greater other and besides greatness itself, namely, that in which greatness is; and this too when the small itself is not there, which the one, if it is great, must exceed; this, however, is impossible, seeing that smallness is wholly absent.

True.

But absolute greatness is only greater than absolute smallness, and smallness is only smaller than absolute greatness.

Very true.

Then other things not greater or less than the one, if they have neither greatness nor smallness; nor have greatness or smallness any power of exceeding or being exceeded in relation to the one, but only in relation to one another; nor will the one be greater or less than them or others, if it has neither greatness nor smallness.

Clearly not.

Then if the one is neither greater nor less than the others, it cannot either exceed or be exceeded by them?

Certainly not.

And that which neither exceeds nor is exceeded, must be on an equality; and being on an equality, must be equal.

Of course.

And this will be true also of the relation of the one to itself; having neither greatness nor smallness in itself, it will neither exceed nor be exceeded by itself, but will be on an equality with and equal to itself.

Certainly.

Then the one will be equal both to itself and the others?

Clearly so.

And yet the one, being itself in itself, will also surround and be without itself; and, as containing itself, will be greater than itself; and, as contained in itself, will be less; and will thus be greater and less than itself.

It will.

Now there cannot possibly be anything which is not included in the one and the others?

Of course not.

But, surely, that which is must always be somewhere?

Yes.

But that which is in anything will be less, and that in which it is will be greater; in no other way can one thing be in another.

True.

And since there is nothing other or besides the one and the others, and they must be in something, must they not be in one another, the one in the others and the others in the one, if they are to be anywhere?

That is clear.

But inasmuch as the one is in the others, the others will be greater than the one, because they contain the one, which will be less than the others, because it is contained in them; and inasmuch as the others are in the one, the one on the same principle will be greater than the others, and the others less than the one.

True.

The one, then, will be equal to and greater and less than itself and the others?

Clearly.

And if it be greater and less and equal, it will be of equal and more and less measures or divisions than itself and the others, and if of measures, also of parts?

Of course.

And if of equal and more and less measures or divisions, it will be in number more or less than itself and the others, and likewise equal in number to itself and to the others?

How is that?

It will be of more measures than those things which it exceeds, and of as many parts as measures; and so with that to which it is equal, and that than which it is less.

True.

And being greater and less than itself, and equal to itself, it will be of equal measures with itself and of more and fewer measures than itself; and if of measures then also of parts?

It will.

And being of equal parts with itself, it will be numerically equal to itself; and being of more parts, more, and being of less, less than itself?

Certainly.

And the same will hold of its relation to other things; inasmuch as it is greater than them, it will be more in number than them; and inasmuch as it is smaller, it will be less in number; and inasmuch as it is equal in size to other things, it will be equal to them in number.

Certainly.

Once more, then, as would appear, the one will be in number both equal to and more and less than both itself and all other things.

It will.

Does the one also partake of time? And is it and does it become older and younger than itself and others, and again, neither younger nor older than itself and others, by virtue of participation in time?

How do you mean?

If one is, being must be predicated of it?

Yes.

But to be (einai) is only participation of being in present time, and to have been is the participation of being at a past time, and to be about to be is the participation of being at a future time?

Very true.

Then the one, since it partakes of being, partakes of time?

Certainly.

And is not time always moving forward?

Yes.

Then the one is always becoming older than itself, since it moves forward in time?

Certainly.

And do you remember that the older becomes older than that which becomes younger?

I remember.

Then since the one becomes older than itself, it becomes younger at the same time?

Certainly.

Thus, then, the one becomes older as well as younger than itself?

Yes.

And it is older (is it not?) when in becoming, it gets to the point of time between 'was' and 'will be,' which is 'now': for surely in going from the past to the future, it cannot skip the present?

No.

And when it arrives at the present it stops from becoming older, and no longer becomes, but is older, for if it went on it would never be reached by the present, for it is the nature of that which goes on, to touch both the present and the future, letting go the present and seizing the future, while in process of becoming between them.

True.

But that which is becoming cannot skip the present; when it reaches the present it ceases to become, and is then whatever it may happen to be becoming.

Clearly.

And so the one, when in becoming older it reaches the present, ceases to become, and is then older.

Certainly.

And it is older than that than which it was becoming older, and it was becoming older than itself.

Yes.

And that which is older is older than that which is younger?

True.

Then the one is younger than itself, when in becoming older it reaches the present?

Certainly.

But the present is always present with the one during all its being; for whenever it is it is always now.

Certainly.

Then the one always both is and becomes older and younger than itself?

Truly.

And is it or does it become a longer time than itself or an equal time with itself?

An equal time.

But if it becomes or is for an equal time with itself, it is of the same age with itself?

Of course.
And that which is of the same age, is neither older nor younger?
No.
The one, then, becoming and being the same time with itself, neither is nor becomes older or younger than itself?
I should say not.
And what are its relations to other things? Is it or does it become older or younger than they?
I cannot tell you.
You can at least tell me that others than the one are more than the one—other would have been one, but the others have multitude, and are more than one?
They will have multitude.
And a multitude implies a number larger than one?
Of course.
And shall we say that the lesser or the greater is the first to come or to have come into existence?
The lesser.
Then the least is the first? And that is the one?
Yes.
Then the one of all things that have number is the first to come into being; but all other things have also number, being plural and not singular.
They have.
And since it came into being first it must be supposed to have come into being prior to the others, and the others later; and the things which came into being later, are younger than that which preceded them? And so the other things will be younger than the one, and the one older than other things?
True.
What would you say of another question? Can the one have come into being contrary to its own nature, or is that impossible?
Impossible.
And yet, surely, the one was shown to have parts; and if parts, then a beginning, middle and end?
Yes.
And a beginning, both of the one itself and of all other things,

comes into being first of all; and after the beginning, the others follow, until you reach the end?

Certainly.

And all these others we shall affirm to be parts of the whole and of the one, which, as soon as the end is reached, has become whole and one?

Yes; that is what we shall say.

But the end comes last, and the one is of such a nature as to come into being with the last; and, since the one cannot come into being except in accordance with its own nature, its nature will require that it should come into being after the others, simultaneously with the end.

Clearly.

Then the one is younger than the others and the others older than the one.

That also is clear in my judgment.

Well, and must not a beginning or any other part of the one or of anything, if it be a part and not parts, being a part, be also of necessity one?

Certainly.

And will not the one come into being together with each part—together with the first part when that comes into being, and together with the second part and with all the rest, and will not be wanting to any part, which is added to any other part until it has reached the last and become one whole; it will be wanting neither to the middle, nor to the first, nor to the last, nor to any of them, while the process of becoming is going on?

True.

Then the one is of the same age with all the others, so that if the one itself does not contradict its own nature, it will be neither prior nor posterior to the others, but simultaneous; and according to this argument the one will be neither older nor younger than the others, nor the others than the one, but according to the previous argument the one will be older and younger than the others and the others than the one.

Certainly.

After this manner then the one is and has become. But as to its becoming older and younger than the others, and the others than the one, and neither older nor younger, what shall we say? Shall we say as of being so also of becoming, or otherwise?

I cannot answer.

But I can venture to say, that even if one thing were older or younger than another, it could not become older or younger in a greater degree than it was at first; for equals added to unequals, whether to periods of time or to anything else, leave the difference between them the same as at first.

Of course.

Then that which is, cannot become older or younger than that which is, since the difference of age is always the same; the one is and has become older and the other younger; but they are no longer becoming so.

True.

And the one which is does not therefore become either older or younger than the others which are.

No.

But consider whether they may not become older and younger in another way.

In what way?

Just as the one was proven to be older than the others and the others than the one.

And what of that?

If the one is older than the others, has come into being a longer time than the others.

Yes.

But consider again; if we add equal time to a greater and a less time, will the greater differ from the less time by an equal or by a smaller portion than before?

By a smaller portion.

Then the difference between the age of the one and the age of the others will not be afterwards so great as at first, but if an equal time be added to both of them they will differ less and less in age?

Yes.

And that which differs in age from some other less than formerly, from being older will become younger in relation to that other than which it was older?

Yes, younger.

And if the one becomes younger the others aforesaid will become older than they were before, in relation to the one.

Certainly.

Then that which had become younger becomes older relatively to that which previously had become and was older; it never really is older, but is always becoming, for the one is always growing on the side of youth and the other on the side of age. And in like manner the older is always in process of becoming younger than the younger; for as they are always going in opposite directions they become in ways the opposite to one another, the younger older than the older, and the older younger than the younger. They cannot, however, have become; for if they had already become they would be and not merely become. But that is impossible; for they are always becoming both older and younger than one another: the one becomes younger than the others because it was seen to be older and prior, and the others become older than the one because they came into being later; and in the same way the others are in the same relation to the one, because they were seen to be older, and prior to the one.

That is clear.

Inasmuch then, one thing does not become older or younger than another, in that they always differ from each other by an equal number, the one cannot become older or younger than the others, nor the others than the one; but inasmuch as that which came into being earlier and that which came into being later must continually differ from each other by a different portion —in this point of view the others must become older and younger than the one, and the one than the others.

Certainly.

For all these reasons, then, the one is and becomes older and younger than itself and the others, and neither is nor becomes older or younger than itself or the others.

Certainly.

But since the one partakes of time, and partakes of becoming older and younger, must it not also partake of the past, the present, and the future?

Of course it must.

Parmenides

Then the one was and is and will be, and was becoming and is becoming and will become?

Certainly.

And there is and was and will be something which is in relation to it and belongs to it?

True.

And since we have at this moment opinion and knowledge and perception of the one, there is opinion and knowledge and perception of it?

Quite right.

Then there is name and expression for it, and it is named and expressed, and everything of this kind which appertains to other things appertains to the one.

Certainly, that is true.

Yet once more and for the third time, let us consider: If the one is both one and many, as we have described, and is neither one nor many, and participates in time, must it not, in as far as it is one, at times partake of being, and in as far as it is not one, at times not partake of being?

Certainly.

But can it partake of being when not partaking of being, or not partake of being when partaking of being?

Impossible.

Then the one partakes and does not partake of being at different times, for that is the only way in which it can partake and not partake of the same.

True.

And is there not also a time at which it assumes being and relinquishes being—for how can it have and not have the same thing unless it receives and also gives it up at some time?

Impossible.

And the assuming of being is what you would call becoming?

I should.

And the relinquishing of being you would call destruction?

I should.

The one then, as would appear, becomes and is destroyed by taking and giving up being.

Certainly.

And being one and many and in process of becoming and being destroyed, when it becomes one it ceases to be many, and when many, it ceases to be one?

Certainly.

And as it becomes one and many, must it not inevitably experience separation and aggregation?

Inevitably.

And whenever it becomes like and unlike it must be assimilated and dissimilated?

Yes.

And when it becomes greater or less or equal it must grow or diminish or be equalized?

True.

And when being in motion it rests, and when being at rest it changes to motion, it can surely be in no time at all?

How can it?

But that a thing which is previously at rest should be afterwards in motion, or previously in motion and afterwards at rest, without experiencing change, is impossible.

Impossible.

And surely there cannot be a time in which a thing can be at once neither in motion nor at rest?

There cannot.

But neither can it change without changing.

True.

When then does it change; for it cannot change either when at rest, or when in motion, or when in time?

It cannot.

And does this strange thing in which it is at the time of changing really exist?

What thing?

The moment. For the moment seems to imply a something out of which change takes place into either of two states; for the change is not from the state of rest as such, nor from the state of motion as such; but there is this curious nature which we call the moment lying between rest and motion, not being in any time; and into this and out of this what is in motion changes into rest, and what is at rest into motion.

So it appears.

And the one then, since it is at rest and also in motion, will change to either, for only in this way can it be in both. And in changing it changes in a moment, and when it is changing it will be in no time, and will not then be either in motion or at rest.

It will not.

And it will be in the same case in relation to the other changes, when it passes from being into cessation of being, or from not-being into becoming—then it passes between certain states of motion and rest, and neither is nor is not, nor becomes nor is destroyed.

Very true.

And on the same principle, in the passage from one to many and from many to one, the one is neither one nor many, neither separated nor aggregated; and in the passage from like to unlike, and from unlike to like, it is neither like nor unlike, neither in a state of assimilation nor of dissimilation; and in the passage from small to great and equal and back again, it will be neither small nor great, nor equal, nor in a state of increase, or diminution, or equalization.

True.

All these, then, are the affections of the one, if the one has being.

Of course.

1.aa. But if one is, what will happen to the others—is not that also to be considered?

Yes.

Let us show then, if one is, what will be the affections of the others than the one.

Let us do so.

Inasmuch as there are things other than the one, the others are not the one; for if they were they could not be other than the one.

Very true.

Nor are the others altogether without the one, but in a certain way they participate in the one.

In what way?

Because the others are other than the one inasmuch as they have parts; for if they had no parts they would be simply one.

Right.

And parts, as we affirm, have relation to a whole?

So we say.

And a whole must necessarily be one made up of many; and the parts will be parts of the one, for each of the parts is not a part of many, but of a whole.

How do you mean?

If anything were a part of many, being itself one of them, it will surely be a part of itself, which is impossible, and it will be a part of each one of the other parts, if of all; for if not a part of some one, it will be a part of all the others but this one, and thus will not be a part of each one; and if not a part of each, one it will not be a part of any one of the many; and not being a part of any one, it cannot be a part or anything else of all those things of none of which it is anything.

Clearly not.

Then the part is not a part of the many, nor of all, but is of a certain single form, which we call a whole, being one perfect unity framed out of all—of this the part will be a part.

Certainly.

If, then, the others have parts, they will participate in the whole and in the one.

True.

Then the others than the one must be one perfect whole, having parts.

Certainly.

And the same argument holds of each part, for the part must participate in the one; for if each of the parts is a part, this means, I suppose, that it is one separate from the rest and self-related; otherwise it is not each.

True.

But when we speak of the part participating in the one, it must clearly be other than one; for if not, it would not merely have participated, but would have been one; whereas only the itself can be one.

Very true.

Both the whole and the part must participate in the one; for the

Parmenides

whole will be one whole, of which the parts will be parts; and each part will be one part of the whole which is the whole of the part.

True.

And will not the things which participate in the one, be other than it?

Of course.

And the things which are other than the one will be many; for if the things which are other than the one were neither one nor more than one, they would be nothing.

True.

But, seeing that the things which participate in the one as a part, and in the one as a whole, are more than one, must not those very things which participate in the one be infinite in number?

How so?

Let us look at the matter thus:—Is it not a fact that in partaking of the one they are not one, and do not partake of the one at the very time when they are partaking of it?

Clearly.

They do so then as multitudes in which the one is not present?

Very true.

And if we were to abstract from them in idea the very smallest fraction, must not that least fraction, if it does not partake of the one, be a multitude and not one?

It must.

And if we continue to look at the other side of their nature, regarded simply, and in itself, will not they, as far as we see them, be unlimited in number?

Certainly.

And yet, when each several part becomes a part, then the parts have a limit in relation to the whole and to each other, and the whole in relation to the parts.

Just so.

The result to the others than the one is that the union of themselves and the one appears to create a new element in them which gives to them limitation in relation to one another; whereas in their own nature they have no limit.

That is clear.

612

Then the others than the one, both as whole and parts, are infinite, and also partake of limit.

Certainly.

Then they are both like and unlike one another and themselves.

How is that?

Inasmuch as they are unlimited in their own nature, they are all affected in the same way.

True.

And inasmuch as they all partake of limit, they are all affected in the same way.

Of course.

But inasmuch as their state is both limited and unlimited, they are affected in opposite ways.

Yes.

And opposites are the most unlike of things.

Certainly.

Considered, then, in regard to either one of their affections, they will be like themselves and one another; considered in reference to both of them together, most opposed and most unlike.

That appears to be true.

Then the others are both like and unlike themselves and one another?

True.

And they are the same and also different from one another, and in motion and at rest, and experience every sort of opposite affection, as may be proved without difficulty of them, since they have been shown to have experienced the affections aforesaid?

True.

1.bb. Suppose, now, that we leave the further discussion of these matters as evident, and consider again upon the hypothesis that the one is, whether opposite of all this is or is not equally true of the others.

By all means.

Then let us begin again, and ask, If one is, what must be the affections of the others?

Let us ask that question.

Must not the one be distinct from the others, and the others from the one?

Parmenides

Why so?

Why, because there is nothing else beside them which is distinct from both of them; for the expression 'one and the others' includes all things.

Yes, all things.

Then we cannot suppose that there is anything different from them in which both the one and the others might exist?

There is nothing.

Then the one and the others are never in the same?

True.

Then they are separated from each other?

Yes.

And we surely cannot say that what is truly one has parts?

Impossible.

Then the one will not be in the others as a whole, nor as part, if it be separated from the others, and has no parts?

Impossible.

Then there is no way in which the others can partake of the one, if they do not partake either in whole or in part?

It would seem not.

Then there is no way in which the others are one, or have in themselves any unity?

There is not.

Nor are the others many; for if they were many, each part of them would be a part of the whole; but now the others, not partaking in any way of the one, are neither one nor many, nor whole, nor part.

True.

Then the others neither are nor contain two or three, if entirely deprived of the one?

True.

Then the others are neither like nor unlike the one, nor is likeness and unlikeness in them; for if they were like and unlike, or had in them likeness and unlikeness, they would have two natures in them opposite to one another.

That is clear.

But for that which partakes of nothing to partake of two things was held by us to be impossible?

Impossible.

Then the others are neither like nor unlike nor both, for if they were like or unlike they would partake of one of those two natures, which would be one thing, and if they were both they would partake of opposites which would be two things, and this has been shown to be impossible.

True.

Therefore they are neither the same, nor other, nor in motion, nor at rest, nor in a state of becoming, nor of being destroyed, nor greater, nor less, nor equal, nor have they experienced anything else of the sort; for, if they are capable of experiencing any such affection, they will participate in one and two and three, and odd and even, and in these, as has been proved, they do not participate, seeing that they are altogether and in every way devoid of the one.

Very true.

Therefore if one is, the one is all things, and also nothing, both in relation to itself and to other things.

Certainly.

2.a. Well, and ought we not to consider next what will be the consequence if the one is not?

Yes; we ought.

What is the meaning of the hypothesis—If the one is not; is there any difference between this and the hypothesis—If the not one is not?

There is a difference, certainly.

Is there a difference only, or rather are not the two expressions—if the one is not, and if the not one is not, entirely opposed?

They are entirely opposed.

And suppose a person to say:—If greatness is not, if smallness is not, or anything of that sort, does he not mean, whenever he uses such an expression, that 'what is not' is other than other things?

To be sure.

And so when he says 'If one is not' he clearly means, that what 'is not' is other than all others; we know what he means—do we not?

Yes, we do.

When he says 'one,' he says something which is known; and secondly something which is other than all other things; it makes no

Parmenides

difference whether he predicate of one being or not-being, for that which is said 'not to be' is known to be something all the same, and is distinguished from other things.

Certainly.

Then I will begin again, and ask: If one is not, what are the consequences? In the first place, as would appear, there is a knowledge of it, or the very meaning of the words, 'if one is not,' would not be known.

True.

Secondly, the others differ from it, or it could not be described as different from the others?

Certainly.

Difference, then, belongs to it as well as knowledge; for in speaking of the one as different from the others, we do not speak of a difference in the others, but in the one.

Clearly so.

Moreover, the one that is not is something and partakes of relation to 'that,' and 'this,' and 'these,' and the like, and is an attribute of 'this'; for the one, or the others than the one, could not have been spoken of, nor could any attribute or relative of the one that is not have been or been spoken of, nor could it have been said to be anything, if it did not partake of 'some,' or of the other relations just now mentioned.

True.

Being, then, cannot be ascribed to the one, since it is not; but the one that is not may or rather must participate in many things, if it and nothing else is not; if, however, neither the one nor the one that is not is supposed not to be, and we are speaking of something of a different nature, we can predicate nothing of it. But supposing that the one that is not and nothing else is not, then it must participate in the predicate 'that,' and in many others.

Certainly.

And it will have unlikeness in relation to the others, for the others being different from the one will be of a different kind.

Certainly.

And are not things of a different kind also other in kind?

Of course.

And are not things other in kind unlike?

They are unlike.

And if they are unlike the one, that which they are unlike will clearly be unlike them?

Clearly so.

Then the one will have unlikeness in respect of which the others are unlike it?

That would seem to be true.

And if unlikeness to other things is attributed to it, it must have likeness to itself.

How so?

If the one have unlikeness to one, something else must be meant; nor will the hypothesis relate to one; but it will relate to something other than one?

Quite so.

But that cannot be.

No.

Then the one must have likeness to itself?

It must.

Again, it is not equal to the others; for if it were equal, then it would at once be and be like them in virtue of the equality; but if one has no being, then it can neither be nor be like?

It cannot.

But since it is not equal to the others, neither can the others be equal to it?

Certainly not.

And things that are not equal are unequal?

True.

And they are unequal to an unequal?

Of course.

Then the one partakes of inequality, and in respect of this the others are unequal to it?

Very true.

And inequality implies greatness and smallness?

Yes.

Then the one, if of such a nature, has greatness and smallness?

That appears to be true.

Parmenides

And greatness and smallness always stand apart?

True.

Then there is always something between them?

There is.

And can you think of anything else which is between them other than equality?

No, it is equality which lies between them.

Then that which has greatness and smallness also has equality, which lies between them?

That is clear.

Then the one, which is not, partakes, as would appear, of greatness and smallness and equality?

Clearly.

Further, it must surely in a sort partake of being?

How so?

It must be so, for if not, then we should not speak the truth in saying that the one is not. But if we speak the truth, clearly we must say what is. Am I not right?

Yes.

And since we affirm that we speak truly, we must also affirm that we say what is?

Certainly.

Then, as would appear, the one, when it is not, is; for if it were not to be when it is not, but (Or, 'to remit something of existence in relation to not-being.') were to relinquish something of being, so as to become not-being, it would at once be.

Quite true.

Then the one which is not, if it is to maintain itself, must have the being of not-being as the bond of not-being, just as being must have as a bond the not-being of not-being in order to perfect its own being; for the truest assertion of the being of being and of the not-being of not-being is when being partakes of the being of being, and not of the being of not-being—that is, the perfection of being; and when not-being does not partake of the not-being of not-being but of the being of not-being—that is the perfection of not-being.

Most true.

Since then what is partakes of not-being, and what is not of being, must not the one also partake of being in order not to be?

Certainly.

Then the one, if it is not, clearly has being?

Clearly.

And has not-being also, if it is not?

Of course.

But can anything which is in a certain state not be in that state without changing?

Impossible.

Then everything which is and is not in a certain state, implies change?

Certainly.

And change is motion—we may say that?

Yes, motion.

And the one has been proved both to be and not to be?

Yes.

And therefore is and is not in the same state?

Yes.

Thus the one that is not has been shown to have motion also, because it changes from being to not-being?

That appears to be true.

But surely if it is nowhere among what is, as is the fact, since it is not, it cannot change from one place to another?

Impossible.

Then it cannot move by changing place?

No.

Nor can it turn on the same spot, for it nowhere touches the same, for the same is, and that which is not cannot be reckoned among things that are?

It cannot.

Then the one, if it is not, cannot turn in that in which it is not?

No.

Neither can the one, whether it is or is not, be altered into other than itself, for if it altered and became different from itself, then we could not be still speaking of the one, but of something else?

True.

But if the one neither suffers alteration, nor turns round in the same place, nor changes place, can it still be capable of motion?

Impossible.

Now that which is unmoved must surely be at rest, and that which is at rest must stand still?

Certainly.

Then the one that is not, stands still, and is also in motion?

That seems to be true.

But if it be in motion it must necessarily undergo alteration, for anything which is moved, in so far as it is moved, is no longer in the same state, but in another?

Yes.

Then the one, being moved, is altered?

Yes.

And, further, if not moved in any way, it will not be altered in any way?

No.

Then, in so far as the one that is not is moved, it is altered, but in so far as it is not moved, it is not altered?

Right.

Then the one that is not is altered and is not altered?

That is clear.

And must not that which is altered become other than it previously was, and lose its former state and be destroyed; but that which is not altered can neither come into being nor be destroyed?

Very true.

And the one that is not, being altered, becomes and is destroyed; and not being altered, neither becomes nor is destroyed; and so the one that is not becomes and is destroyed, and neither becomes nor is destroyed?

True.

2.b. And now, let us go back once more to the beginning, and see whether these or some other consequences will follow.

Let us do as you say.

If one is not, we ask what will happen in respect of one? That is the question.

Yes.

Do not the words 'is not' signify absence of being in that to which we apply them?

Just so.

And when we say that a thing is not, do we mean that it is not in one way but is in another? or do we mean, absolutely, that what is not has in no sort or way or kind participation of being?

Quite absolutely.

Then, that which is not cannot be, or in any way participate in being?

It cannot.

And did we not mean by becoming, and being destroyed, the assumption of being and the loss of being?

Nothing else.

And can that which has no participation in being, either assume or lose being?

Impossible.

The one then, since it in no way is, cannot have or lose or assume being in any way?

True.

Then the one that is not, since it in no way partakes of being, neither perishes nor becomes?

No.

Then it is not altered at all; for if it were it would become and be destroyed?

True.

But if it be not altered it cannot be moved?

Certainly not.

Nor can we say that it stands, if it is nowhere; for that which stands must always be in one and the same spot?

Of course.

Then we must say that the one which is not never stands still and never moves?

Neither.

Nor is there any existing thing which can be attributed to it; for if there had been, it would partake of being?

That is clear.

And therefore neither smallness, nor greatness, nor equality, can be attributed to it?

No.

Nor yet likeness nor difference, either in relation to itself or to others?

Clearly not.

Well, and if nothing should be attributed to it, can other things be attributed to it?

Certainly not.

And therefore other things can neither be like or unlike, the same, or different in relation to it?

They cannot.

Nor can what is not, be anything, or be this thing, or be related to or the attribute of this or that or other, or be past, present, or future. Nor can knowledge, or opinion, or perception, or expression, or name, or any other thing that is, have any concern with it?

No.

Then the one that is not has no condition of any kind?

Such appears to be the conclusion.

2.aa. Yet once more; if one is not, what becomes of the others? Let us determine that.

Yes; let us determine that.

The others must surely be; for if they, like the one, were not, we could not be now speaking of them.

True.

But to speak of the others implies difference—the terms 'other' and 'different' are synonymous?

True.

Other means other than other, and different, different from the different?

Yes.

Then, if there are to be others, there is something than which they will be other?

Certainly.

And what can that be?—for if the one is not, they will not be other than the one.

They will not.

Then they will be other than each other; for the only remaining alternative is that they are other than nothing.

True.

And they are each other than one another, as being plural and not singular; for if one is not, they cannot be singular, but every particle of them is infinite in number; and even if a person takes that which appears to be the smallest fraction, this, which seemed one, in a moment evanesces into many, as in a dream, and from being the smallest becomes very great, in comparison with the fractions into which it is split up?

Very true.

And in such particles the others will be other than one another, if others are, and the one is not?

Exactly.

And will there not be many particles, each appearing to be one, but not being one, if one is not?

True.

And it would seem that number can be predicated of them if each of them appears to be one, though it is really many?

It can.

And there will seem to be odd and even among them, which will also have no reality, if one is not?

Yes.

And there will appear to be a least among them; and even this will seem large and manifold in comparison with the many small fractions which are contained in it?

Certainly.

And each particle will be imagined to be equal to the many and little; for it could not have appeared to pass from the greater to the less without having appeared to arrive at the middle; and thus would arise the appearance of equality.

Yes.

And having neither beginning, middle, nor end, each separate particle yet appears to have a limit in relation to itself and other.

How so?

Because, when a person conceives of any one of these as such, prior to the beginning another beginning appears, and there is another end, remaining after the end, and in the middle truer middles within but smaller, because no unity can be conceived of any of them, since the one is not.

Parmenides

Very true.

And so all being, whatever we think of, must be broken up into fractions, for a particle will have to be conceived of without unity?

Certainly.

And such being when seen indistinctly and at a distance, appears to be one; but when seen near and with keen intellect, every single thing appears to be infinite, since it is deprived of the one, which is not?

Nothing more certain.

Then each of the others must appear to be infinite and finite, and one and many, if others than the one exist and not the one.

They must.

Then will they not appear to be like and unlike?

In what way?

Just as in a picture things appear to be all one to a person standing at a distance, and to be in the same state and alike?

True.

But when you approach them, they appear to be many and different; and because of the appearance of the difference, different in kind from, and unlike, themselves?

True.

And so must the particles appear to be like and unlike themselves and each other.

Certainly.

And must they not be the same and yet different from one another, and in contact with themselves, although they are separated, and having every sort of motion, and every sort of rest, and becoming and being destroyed, and in neither state, and the like, all which things may be easily enumerated, if the one is not and the many are?

Most true.

2.bb. Once more, let us go back to the beginning, and ask if the one is not, and the others of the one are, what will follow.

Let us ask that question.

In the first place, the others will not be one?

Impossible.

Nor will they be many; for if they were many one would be contained in them. But if no one of them is one, all of them are nought, and therefore they will not be many.

True.

If there be no one in the others, the others are neither many nor one.

They are not.

Nor do they appear either as one or many.

Why not?

Because the others have no sort or manner or way of communion with any sort of not-being, nor can anything which is not, be connected with any of the others; for that which is not has no parts.

True.

Nor is there an opinion or any appearance of not-being in connexion with the others, nor is not-being ever in any way attributed to the others.

No.

Then if one is not, there is no conception of any of the others either as one or many; for you cannot conceive the many without the one.

You cannot.

Then if one is not, the others neither are, nor can be conceived to be either one or many?

It would seem not.

Nor as like or unlike?

No.

Nor as the same or different, nor in contact or separation, nor in any of those states which we enumerated as appearing to be;—the others neither are nor appear to be any of these, if one is not?

True.

Then may we not sum up the argument in a word and say truly: If one is not, then nothing is?

Certainly.

Let thus much be said; and further let us affirm what seems to be the truth, that, whether one is or is not, one and the others in relation to themselves and one another, all of them, in every way, are and are not, and appear to be and appear not to be.

Most true.